Microprocessor Hardware and Software Concepts

AMIN R. ISMAIL

University of Dayton

VICTOR M. ROONEY

University of Dayton

MICROPROCESSOR HARDWARE AND SOFTWARE CONCEPTS

Macmillan Publishing Company

New York

Collier Macmillan Publishers

London

To the "little ones,"
Melissa Ann Rooney, Rinan and Rivka Ismail.

Macmillan Publishing Company
866 Third Avenue, New York, New York 10022

Collier Macmillan Canada, Inc.

LIBRARY OF CONGRESS CATALOGING IN PUBLICATION DATA

Ismail, Amin R.
  Microprocessor Hardware and Software Concepts.

  Includes index.
    1. Microprocessors.   2. Microcomputers.   3. Computer software.   4. Intel 8085 (Microprocessor)   I. Rooney, Victor M.   II. Title.
  QA76.5.I832   1987   004.16   86-5261
  ISBN 0-02-403470-3

Printing: 1 2 3 4 5 6 7 8   Year: 6 7 8 9 0 1 2 3 4 5

ISBN 0-02-403470-3

PREFACE

With the rapid advances in microprocessors and related technology it is obvious that we must be in a continuous learning process. We believe that in this learning process it is essential for us to understand the concepts rather than only to memorize facts. This philosophy will be followed throughout the book, in the hope that memorization will not be required; it will, however, be minimized.

Following this philosophy, each topic covered in this book will begin by establishing its purpose. Once the purpose is understood, its conceptual implementation will be developed through the use of function-block diagrams for hardware-oriented discussions. It is these function blocks that will aid in understanding the specific chips used for actual system implementation. Once the hardware is understood, the software that controls and manipulates the hardware will be studied. Emphasis is placed on the use of proper techniques and the application of the appropriate tools in the development of microprocessor software. It is important to note that throughout the text we emphasize the relationships between hardware and software, and their integration into a system.

The ideal approach to studying microprocessors would be first to study a generic standard with the intent of understanding the abstract conceptual principles and then later to apply those principles to a specific microprocessor. This approach, although academically sound, is not time efficient, as the theoretical concepts and their applications would be treated as two separate subjects displaced in time. Hence we have chosen to discuss concepts using specific chips as models. Also, because there is no generic standard for a microprocessor, we have chosen a microprocessor whose operation encompasses most of the concepts utilized by other currently available microprocessors. We believe that this "pseudostandard" microprocessor is the 8085.

By studying the 8085 microprocessor and its support chips, the reader will learn those concepts necessary to understand the detailed workings of the microprocessor- and microcomputer-based systems. The advent of LSI and VLSI technology has led to the manufacture of new microprocessors that have several functions integrated on a single chip. The trend in the design of newer microprocessors is to simplify their use and require less understanding by the user. However, we believe that by learning microprocessors and their associated systems in detail, one can apply ingenuity to the design and utilization of such systems. An analogy can be seen with the advent of the electronic calculator. One need not understand the mechanics of arithmetic to get answers from an electronic calculator. However, to understand and interpret those answers, one needs an understanding of the solution—which requires that the concepts of arithmetic be understood. It is therefore important that the reader realize that the essence of studying microprocessors lies in the concepts rather than in the specifics. A specific chip may become obsolete, but the concepts will remain the same. The thesis of this text is that if the reader learns and understands the concepts presented, regardless of the chip used as the teaching vehicle, he or she will be able to apply these concepts to other chips and hence will be able to self-teach as technology advances. Of course, it is the reader who has the ultimate responsibility for staying technically current.

From the table of contents one can see that the text studies 8-bit microprocessors. The integration of a microprocessor into a system requires that the concepts of buses, control signals, memory, and I/O be understood. Thus, with a focus on the 8085 microprocessor, the text covers the architecture of the microprocessor, memory design and addressing, I/O addressing, interrupts and DMA, programmable chips, and the microprocessor's instruction set. But it is obvious that even a microprocessor system with sophisticated hardware is not worth much without the appropriate software. An understanding of the proper development tools and techniques is vital to the efficient design of a microprocessor system. Two of the most universally accepted tools, assemblers and compilers, are discussed in detail. In assembly language programming, the techniques of absolute and relocatable assembly and the applications of macros and conditional assembly give the reader a firm foundation for software development. The concept of assembly language programming is then extended to compiler-level programming in which the model used to illustrate compiler- and high-level programming concepts is the popular "C" compiler. In the final chapters of the book, two other 8-bit microprocessors are surveyed. The survey concentrates on the similarities and differences (with the 8085) rather than on an in-depth study of each microprocessor and illustrates that the same concepts can be applied to almost any commercially available microprocessor.

A.R.I.
V.M.R.

CONTENTS

7 PROGRAMMABLE CHIPS: PARALLEL AND SERIAL I/O 227

8 SOFTWARE DEVELOPMENT: TECHNIQUES AND TOOLS 273

9 INTRODUCTION TO ASSEMBLY LANGUAGE PROGRAMMING 289

CHAPTER 1

Introduction to Digital Computers

1-1

Introduction

Digital computers play a major role in today's society. For business applications they perform such tasks as keeping track of inventory, payroll, accounts receivable, accounts payable, and word processing. Industrial applications are of the control type; that is, the computer will govern such functions as chemical flow, assembly line operation, machine speed and position, and other such process controls. Medical applications include patient monitoring, body chemical analysis, blood-gas analysis, electrocardiograms—and the list goes on. Both industry and the home can use computers for energy management, security, as an appointments secretary, and for many other duties.

In each of the cases cited, the computer is given input data, which may be in the form of numbers given by the user or voltages from a machine. From these input data it can perform calculations and make decisions. For the world of commerce, calculations are often the only task required, whereas for industrial applications, such as process control, the computer may first perform calculations, then arrive at a decision based on those calculations, and, finally, regulate a machine in accordance with that decision. With this interrelationship of computer, person, and machine in mind, one might begin to form a general function-block diagram of a computerized system. That is, in addition to the computer, this system must have input and output devices with which the computer can communicate to person and/or machine. This basic concept is illustrated in Figure 1-1.

It is the goal of this text to teach the reader how to design and construct a microprocessor-based computer system. To accomplish this goal the reader must understand and be able to utilize both hardware—the actual electronics of the computer—and software—the intangible instructions that make the electronics work.

This chapter introduces the most fundamental concepts of a digital computer by categorizing computer operations into various functions. These functions will then be pictorially represented by a block and appropriately labeled. To demonstrate the interrelationships among each of these blocks, communicative links will be shown, represented by lines. The result will be a function-block diagram of a computer, illustrating the necessary building blocks and their interrelationships. An example of such a diagram is shown in Figure 1-6. The purpose of this approach is to help the reader visualize the required functions and their communicative links. By understanding these requirements, the study of specific chips, toward the goal of utilizing them in a computer design, will be a logical process, not a memorized one.

1-2

Development of a Computer System

One usually associates a computer with performing computations and making decisions. These computations and decisions are performed by the computer's *central processing unit* (CPU). Hence the computer's "mind" is the CPU, although it has no intelligence except the pseudointelligence "given" to it by its user. That is, the CPU is given explicit instructions by the user as to the operations to be performed. This set of instructions is known as a *program*, and

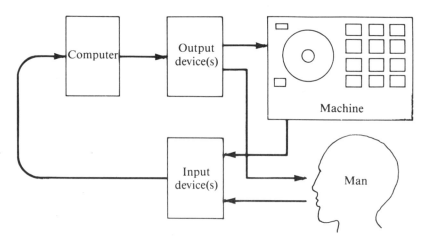

FIGURE 1-1. Computer interfacing with man and machine.

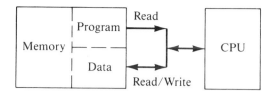

FIGURE 1-2. The CPU and memory.

the person who writes the program is known as the *programmer*. Just as a person records, in his or her memory, a set of instructions for doing a task, a computer is designed to do likewise. Thus a CPU requires a *memory* to store its program (the instructions). This memory not only stores the program but also stores data when so instructed. Because memory serves two purposes—to store programs and data—we shall imagine it as being divided into two parts: *program memory* and *data memory*.

Figure 1-2 is a block diagram of a CPU and its memory. Notice in Figure 1-2 that the CPU only ''reads'' from program memory (arrow goes to the CPU), whereas it both ''reads'' and ''writes'' from data memory; that is, it must store (*write*) and retrieve (*read*) data (indicated by a bidirectional arrow).

The CPU will also need to communicate with external *input* and *output* devices (I/O peripherals), such as teletypes, keyboards, printers, and displays. Often these I/O devices are not compatible (regarding voltage levels, timing, and the like) with the CPU and require interfacing. Hence an I/O interface block and I/O devices are added, as shown in Figure 1-3. As can be seen from the arrow directions of Figure 1-3, some I/O devices are shown as input devices (0 and N), whereas others are shown as output devices (1).

Notice in Figure 1-3 that all data exchanges between memory and an I/O device must pass through the CPU, which slows the exchange. In some data transfers, time is of paramount importance, and to meet this criterion, some computer systems allow the memory to be accessed directly by an I/O device.

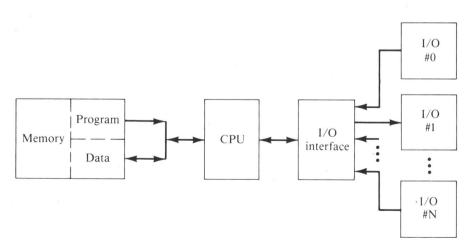

FIGURE 1-3. The CPU, memory, and I/O.

This feature is known as *direct memory access* (DMA). DMA is I/O initiated and is used by I/O devices to access memory directly, thereby circumventing the CPU. DMA is illustrated in Figure 1-4, in which I/O device 0 is shown as having direct access to memory via the data line (interfacing may be necessary).

In Figure 1-4, note the communication among I/O device 0, the DMA function block, and the CPU. The requesting I/O device must first request a DMA and does so via the DMA request line. Because the CPU is to be bypassed, it must be notified of the request so that it can isolate itself from the process. When the CPU isolates itself from the system, it will acknowledge its isolation by sending a signal over the DMA acknowledge line. Once I/O device 0 receives an acknowledgment of the CPU's isolation, it begins to access memory directly by way of the data line. It is important to notice the communication exchange: First the request and then an acknowledgment of the request, which signals the "ok" to proceed. This communication of request and acknowledge is termed *handshaking*. This specific example is DMA handshaking—others will follow. This example illustrates DMA for the purpose of writing to memory (device 0's arrow direction indicates that it is an input device); however, the same DMA concept is true for read operations.

The next function block to consider is interrupt request logic. Most computer systems have what is termed *interrupt capability*, which essentially means that an I/O device can interrupt the CPU during an operation. To understand why interrupt capability is desirable, it must be realized that (1) an I/O device needs the CPU's attention only when data is to be exchanged between the CPU and the I/O device and that (2) some I/O devices operate much more slowly than

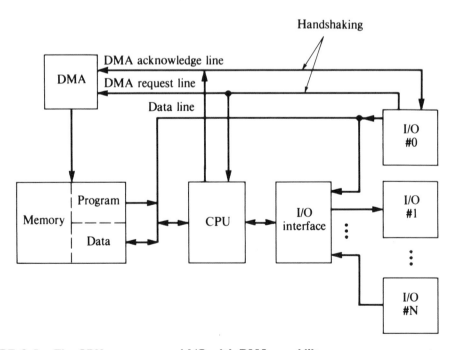

FIGURE 1-4. The CPU, memory, and I/O with DMA capability.

the CPU does, causing the CPU to have to wait for the I/O device during data exchanges. Considering these two points, it is more efficient for the CPU to be allowed to perform other tasks and be interrupted by an I/O device only when the I/O device needs the attention of the CPU and is ready for a data exchange. Interrupt capability is illustrated in Figure 1-5. Notice that the actual interrupt request is not made directly to the CPU but is applied to combinational logic (AND and OR gates, and the like, termed *interrupt request logic*), which establishes priority (when there is more than one interrupting device) and performs other "housekeeping" tasks.

There are two remaining blocks to be added to Figure 1-5, the controller and the clock. The *controller* is the "traffic cop"; that is, it correlates the activities of the various function blocks to see that there are no conflicts among them. To exercise this control, it must have a control line going to the other function blocks. The *clock* provides the system's timing. The timing of all activities is referenced to this basic clock. Figure 1-6 repeats Figure 1-5 with these two blocks added.

A synopsis of the microcomputer system of Figure 1-6 is that it has

1. *I/O* (input and output) capability to communicate with the user and machines.
2. *Interrupt* capability to create a more efficient system (that is, the CPU can be interrupted by I/O devices when needed).

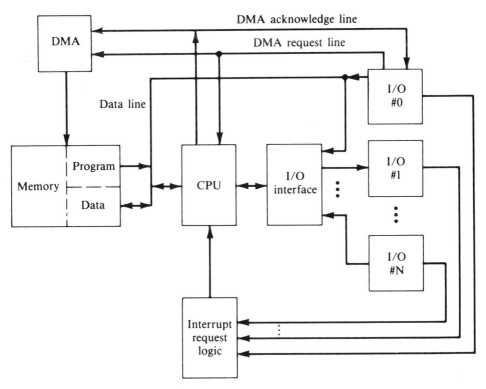

FIGURE 1-5. The CPU, memory, I/O, DMA with interrupt capability.

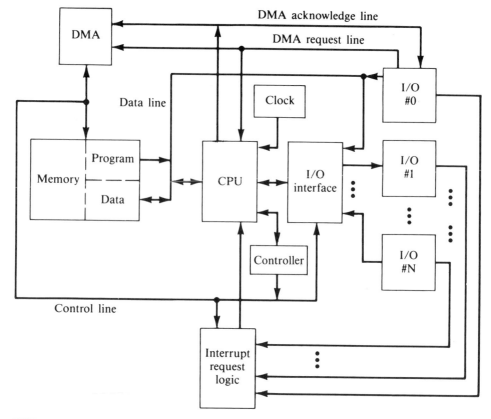

FIGURE 1-6. Microprocessor-based computer (microcomputer).

3. *DMA* (direct memory access) capability to allow an I/O device to have direct access to memory *without* the CPU's direct involvement.

The required function blocks of this system are

1. *CPU* (central processing unit), which is the system's "brain."
2. *Memory*, which is used to store programs and data.
3. *Controller*, which is the system's traffic cop in that it provides nonconflicting uses of communication links among the blocks.
4. *Interrupt request logic*, which receives interrupt requests from I/O devices to interrupt the CPU. This logic may establish priorities of the interrupt request.
5. I/O *interface*, which provides proper voltage levels, timing, and so on, between an I/O device and the computer system.
6. *Clock*, which provides the system's timing. Other blocks will, directly or indirectly, get their timing from this block.

The term *architecture* describes the conceptual configuration of Figure 1-6 because it shows the function blocks required to *construct* this system. Later references will be made to other architectures, such as CPU architecture and controller architecture. Architecture implies simply a function-block diagram showing the combination of function blocks and their system configuration.

Computer Bus Structures

Next, we shall modify Figure 1-6 slightly to illustrate the system's *bus structure*. A bus is an interconnecting pathway among the function blocks. It will still be an architectural drawing, but now it will show the buses, rather than lines, that connect the system's function blocks. By way of illustration, consider the simple architectural drawing of Figure 1-7(a). Figure 1-7(b) is considered the same architectural drawing as (a), but now showing the buses that connect the blocks, rather than the conceptual lines of (a). Notice that the bus interconnections of (b) are closer than (a) to being a wiring diagram. The bus representation of Figure 1-7(b) allows a better picture of the actual wiring without having to show a detailed wiring diagram, which for large complex drawings can become messy. However, when actual connections are to be made, a wiring schematic showing pin connections and other details, such as that of Figure 1-7(c), may become necessary. Also notice from Figure 1-7(c) that the wiring connections of the buses are in parallel.

Figure 1-6 will now be reconfigured and redrawn to show its bus structure. To develop this new drawing, let us begin with Figure 1-2, which shows the CPU communicating with memory. Recall that all program instructions and data are stored in memory. Each program instruction and piece of data is stored at a specific location in memory that is identifiable by a unique number called an *address*. The terminology address is derived from the concept of one's personal mailing address; that is, one's mailing address is used to identify a location (one's residence or business) so that a communication link can be established between the sender and receiver so as to exchange information. By comparison, the CPU and memory must establish similar communication links in order to exchange data. Hence, in the mailing address concept, the term *memory address* is used to describe the identification number of a specific memory location. Later, the term address will be expanded to include the identification numbers of I/O devices.

Because each location in memory has a unique address, when the CPU wishes to write or read to or from a specific memory location, it must first specify the memory address of that location. Because the CPU must have access to memory locations, it also must have a medium through which it can supply the memory addresses. This medium is a bus, and because of its function it is termed the *address bus*. The address bus concept is illustrated in Figure 1-8. Notice that Figure 1-8 still shows memory as being composed of program memory and data memory, both being addressed (in parallel) by the address bus. Also notice that addresses are *unidirectional*—from the CPU only.

Once the CPU addresses a memory location, the CPU will either write into that memory location or read from it. Thus there must also be a bidirectional bus between memory and the CPU over which these data may flow. In this case

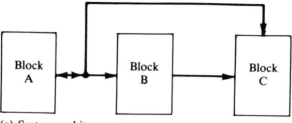

(a) System architecture

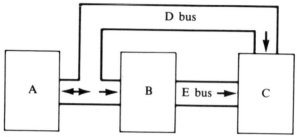

(b) System architecture emphasızıng
bus structure

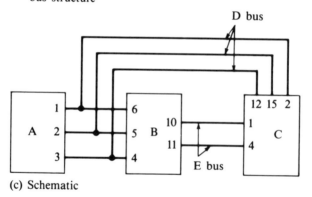

(c) Schematic

FIGURE 1-7. Various representations of communication paths between function blocks: (a) system architecture, (b) system architecture emphasizing bus structure, (c) system schematic.

the term *data* is meant in the broadest sense and includes program instructions. This bus will be termed the *data bus* and is represented in Figure 1-9. Hence the communication links of Figure 1-2 are now the address and data buses of Figure 1-9. Again note that bus connections are parallel connections. It is important to realize that only one memory location is putting data on the data bus at any given moment and that that is the location being addressed. If more than one memory location attempted to put data on the data bus at any given time, the CPU would not receive any intelligible data. When more than one device, memory location, and so on, compete for the control of a bus, this bus competition is termed a *bus contention* and must be avoided.

Next consider the I/O configuration of Figure 1-3. From Figure 1-3 observe

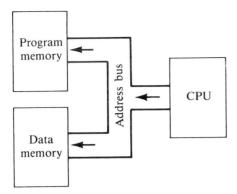

FIGURE 1-8.   Address bus.

that there is a *bidirectional* path between the CPU and I/O—considering the I/O interface to be transparent, where *transparent* means "as though it were not there." After some thought, one soon realizes that because the CPU will be reading (inputting data) and writing (outputting data) to the I/O devices, just as it did to memory, a bidirectional bus such as the data bus is needed. In fact, the same data bus may be used for I/O data, which is shown in Figure 1-10(a).

There must be a means to select, or address, which I/O device is to communicate with the CPU. To do this, the CPU will be required first to address (select) the desired I/O, just as it selected the desired memory location. The CPU will output this I/O address on the address bus just as for memory, but now the address will select an I/O device rather than a memory location. The I/O selection is made via the I/O select lines of Figure 1-10(b), which simply activate the selected I/O device.

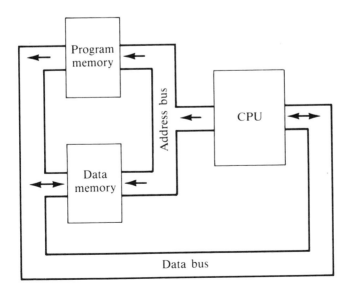

FIGURE 1-9.   Address and data bus.

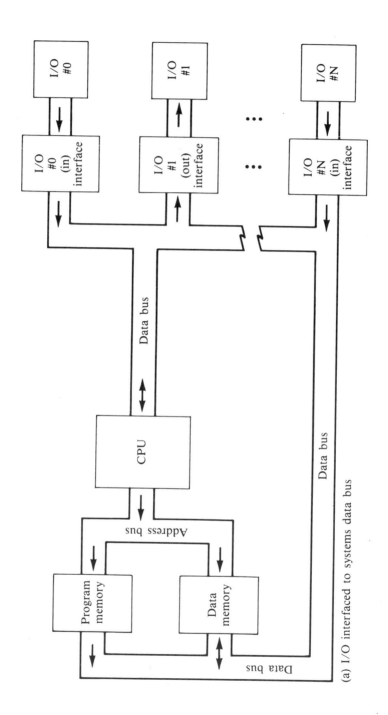

(a) I/O interfaced to systems data bus

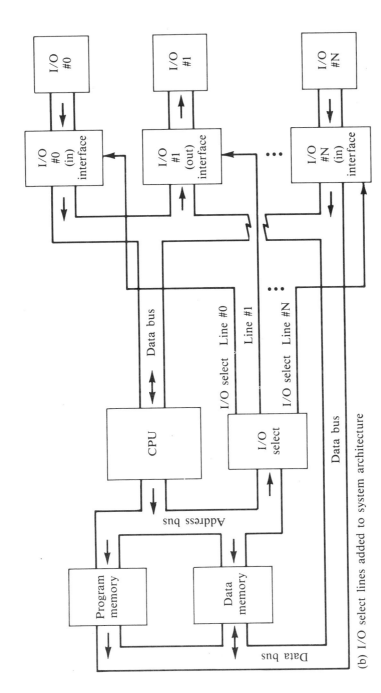

(b) I/O select lines added to system architecture

FIGURE 1-10. (a) I/O interfaced to the system data bus; (b) the addition of I/O select lines to the system architecture.

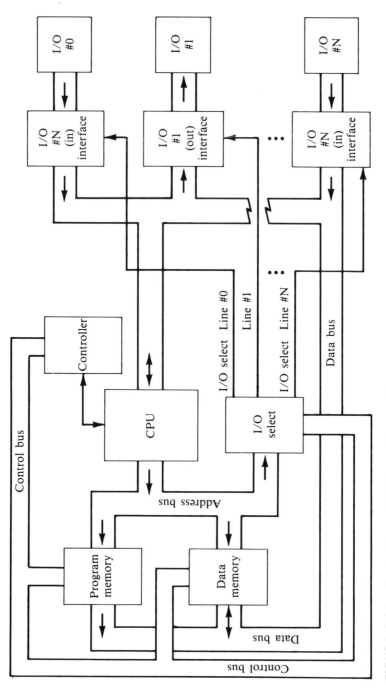

FIGURE 1-11. Control bus added to system architecture.

INTRODUCTION TO DIGITAL COMPUTERS

The remaining bus to consider is the *control bus*. The primary function of the control bus is to carry the control signals generated by the system controller of Figure 1-6. To understand the function of these control signals, and hence the control bus, recall that the controller is the system's traffic cop. Buses are often shared by more than one function block, which is known as *multiplexing*, making it necessary to regulate which function block will control the shared bus; otherwise, bus contention will ensue. Thus the controller will regulate which function block has control of the multiplexed bus at any given time. This concept requires that the control bus go to each function block that requires the use of a shared bus. As shown in Figure 1-10(b), the data bus is multiplexed, which requires that the following blocks be connected to the control bus: program memory, data memory, and the I/O interface. Controlling the I/O select function block will result in proper control of the I/O interfacing blocks, eliminating the need to connect the interface blocks directly to the control bus. The control bus is illustrated in Figure 1-11.

Figure 1-11 shows that the system illustrated has three buses: an address bus, a data bus, and a control bus; hence this figure represents a *three-bus architecture*.

Also note that there is bidirectional communication between the controller and the CPU, as indicated by the arrow directions. As will be shown later, the controller is really an interpreter for the CPU; that is, the controller will interpret commands from the CPU that instruct it regarding which control signal to generate.

1-4

DMA, Interrupt, and Clock

Because the remainder of the functions (DMA, interrupt, and clock) do not necessarily require buses, they will simply be added to Figure 1-11, as shown in Figure 1-12. Also, Figure 1-11 must be modified to allow an I/O device with DMA (0) capability to control the address bus and data bus during DMA operation. This is necessary because the CPU is to be isolated from the process and therefore cannot furnish the memory addresses of where the DMA is to occur within memory, nor is it or the controller involved in the data flow between the I/O device and memory. Then it becomes the responsibility of the DMA-requesting I/O device to furnish these required memory addresses and to take control of the control and data buses. Figure 1-12 illustrates I/O device 0 with DMA capability as having access to the address bus and control bus for DMA operations; that is, these buses are shown directly connected to I/O device 0. It must be emphasized that the I/O device issues memory addresses and control signals during DMA operations. As for control of the data bus, assume that somehow the I/O interface will "connect" the I/O device to the data bus and that the I/O device will take control of the control bus at the proper time for the DMA, the proper time being when a DMA acknowledge is received. This is indicated by a line from the DMA acknowledge to the I/O interface of device 0. The total computer architecture of Figure 1-6 is illustrated in Figure 1-12, which shows the various buses.

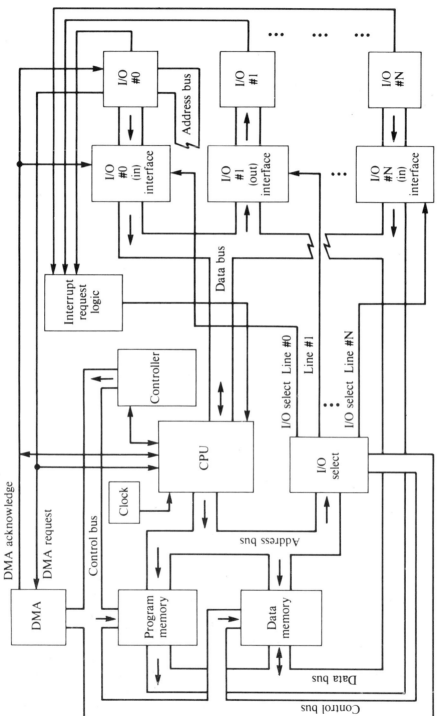

FIGURE 1-12. System architecture with I/O device 0 having **DMA capability.**

Summary

Our work in this chapter is summarized in Figure 1-12, which illustrates a system with a three-bus structure. I/O device 0 has the ability to issue a memory address over the address bus during a DMA and controls the control bus for the purpose of directly accessing memory. The data bus is bidirectional and serves as the medium for receiving and transmitting data between the CPU and the other function blocks. These data often result from an addressed memory location or selected I/O device. The control bus carries control signals that regulate the use of a multiplexed bus to eliminate bus contention.

In chapters to follow we shall study the specific chips that are to perform the functions required of each function block shown in Figure 1-12. It is important therefore that the reader understand the fundamental concepts of this computer architecture.

Review Questions and Problems

1. Even though the CPU provides the computer's computational functions, why is it not proper to refer to it as a computer?

2. Describe how a computer is instructed to do a task.

3. What two basic purposes are served by memory?

4. What is meant by each of the following statements?
   (a) The CPU is writing to memory or I/O.
   (b) The CPU is reading from memory or I/O.

5. Describe the purpose(s) of each bus.
   (a) Address bus.
   (b) Data bus.
   (c) Control bus.

6. Relative to the CPU, explain what is meant by interrupt and DMA capability, and the advantage of each.

7. Why is a controller necessary to a computer system?

8. When using the term *architecture* to describe a system, what is meant?

9. Briefly discuss bus contention and why it must be avoided.

10. Relative to Figure 1-12, what is the function of an I/O select line?

11. How are I/O select lines ''selected'' to become active?

12.   Why does Figure 1-12 show I/O device 0 connected to the address bus and control bus?

13.   Discuss the meaning of the term *handshaking* and indicate why it is necessary.

14.   State the purpose(s) of the I/O interface block of Figure 1-12.

15.   What function is served by the clock of Figure 1-12?

CHAPTER 2

8085 Microprocessor Architecture

Introduction

The architecture of a general-purpose microcomputer was discussed in Chapter 1 and illustrated in Figure 1-12. From that discussion the reader should have acquired an understanding of the various function blocks and buses and of their interrelationship, which will serve as the foundation for this chapter and others.

The CPU function block of Figure 1-12 is always implemented by a microprocessor unit (MPU), which may be a 4-, 8-, or 16-bit MPU (n-bit indicates the number of data bits it can process in parallel internally), whichever is suitable for the application. However, a MPU may implement other function blocks as well, such as the clock and controller. Hence, by proper selection of the MPU, the number of integrated circuits (ICs or chips) required to implement a design can be minimized (or as is often said, the *chip count* can be reduced). The 8085, an 8-bit MPU, does indeed include function blocks in addition to the CPU. Notice in Figure 2-12 that the 8085 MPU includes the clock, controller, and limited portions of function blocks: DMA, interrupt request logic, I/O interfacing, and data memory (the register array).

This chapter develops the architectural concepts of the MPU that are oriented to the 8085 MPU. The approach to MPU architectural development will be first

17

to "reason" a CPU architecture, which is to serve as our generic CPU standard. Once this is understood, we shall study Intel's 8085 MPU architecture and see how the 8085 microprocessor specifically implements those concepts, as well as others. To facilitate the study of the 8085 MPU we shall explain its architecture piece by piece. Because the 8085 MPU's architecture encompasses more than just the CPU, we shall divide its architectural function blocks into those that are essential and those that are not. The function blocks that are essential are required of a CPU and hence are common to all MPUs. Those that are not essential are not found within a CPU architecture and consequently may or may not be present in any specific MPU. In our studies of the 8085 we shall combine the essential and nonessential function blocks into an interrelated system.

To conclude our study of the 8085 we shall investigate the 8085's pin configuration (that is, the physical position of each pin on the 8085 chip, identified by function).

2-2

CPU Architectural Function Blocks

To reiterate, the essential function blocks of a MPU are those required in CPU architecture. Hence we shall begin the study of MPUs by rationalizing an architecture for a CPU. We must realize that the CPU is responsible for all arithmetic and logic operations, such as addition, subtraction, ANDing, and ORing. Thus the CPU's architecture must contain a function block that carries them out. As in combinational logic, such a function block is termed an *arithmetic logic unit* (ALU). Moreover, because the ALU performs arithmetic and logic operations, it must be able to store the results within the CPU. A set of flip-flops, which together form a *register,* provides this storage. This register's name indicates its function, which is to *accumulate* ALU results, and so it is called an *accumulator* (A). Figure 2-1 illustrates the ALU and accumulator, in which registers X and Y serve as the data input registers.

To illustrate the utilization of the function blocks in Figure 2-1, consider the addition of the contents of registers X and Y. As stated by the direction of the arrows, registers X and Y serve as inputs to the ALU; the output, the result, is deposited in register A. This operation is expressed mathematically as

$$X + Y \rightarrow A \qquad (2\text{-}1)$$

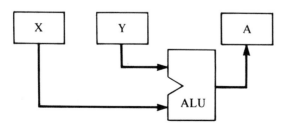

FIGURE 2-1. ALU with inputs X and Y and output A.

where + is used to indicate an arithmetic addition. Notice that the arrow indicates "deposited in register." If a logic OR operation is performed, the result is also deposited in register A and is mathematically expressed as

$$X \vee Y \rightarrow A \qquad (2\text{-}2)$$

The logic ANDing of X and Y is expressed as

$$X \wedge Y \rightarrow A \qquad (2\text{-}3)$$

which again indicates that the results of the operation X AND Y are deposited in register A. Finally, if the expression

$$X - Y \rightarrow A \qquad (2\text{-}4)$$

is implemented, then Equation (2-4) states that the difference between X and Y is deposited in register A. Some microprocessors provide register economy by combining registers X and A into a single register, called register A. Figure 2-2 illustrates such an architecture. Figure 2-2 simply illustrates that the result of an ALU operation between registers A and Y will be stored in register A. Note that the original data content of the register A is destroyed; that is, the ALU operation was a *destructive operation,* as it destroyed the original contents of A. The "load A" and "load Y" of Figure 2-2 are the input data paths used to load registers A and Y with the values with which the ALU operations are to work. At this time it is not necessary to understand the origin of the data that are being used.

As an application of the concept represented in Figure 2-2, suppose that two numbers are to be added, say 03 and 02, which are represented algebraically by Equation (2-5). The values 03 and 02 must first be loaded into A and Y, respectively, via the load A and load Y inputs. The addition is then performed in the ALU, resulting in an output of 05 by the ALU. The sum of 05 is then automatically deposited in register A, thus destroying the original contents of A (03). But destroying the original contents of A is of no consequence, because if it must be saved, another register will be provided for this purpose, as we shall see later. The mathematical expressions of Equations (2-1), (2-2), (2-3), and (2-4) implemented by the architecture of Figure 2-2 instead of Figure 2-1 are

$$A + Y \rightarrow A \qquad (2\text{-}5)$$

$$A \vee Y \rightarrow A \qquad (2\text{-}6)$$

$$A \wedge Y \rightarrow A \qquad (2\text{-}7)$$

$$A - Y \rightarrow A \qquad (2\text{-}8)$$

As can be seen, Equation (2-5) is equivalent to Equation (2-1) when implemented with the function blocks of Figure 2-2, where A is loaded with the value originally contained in register X of Equation (2-1). Equation (2-6) states that the contents of registers A and Y are ORed together and the result deposited in register A. Equations (2-7) and (2-8) should be self-explanatory.

Not all microprocessors combine registers X and A; what is essential is the concept that all MPUs have an ALU, as a CPU does. The details of ALU implementation, that is, how ALU inputs and outputs are achieved, are decided by the microprocessor designer. The 8085 MPU implements the ALU as illustrated by Figure 2-2.

To continue our explanation of CPU architecture function blocks, let us ask two questions: (1) How does the CPU receive the sequence of instructions that make up the program? and (2) Once the CPU receives an instruction, how does it "know" how to interpret and execute it? To answer the first question, recall that the procedure is for the CPU to fetch instructions from program memory, where each instruction is stored at a specific memory location identifiable by a unique address. From Figure 1-9, we see that the CPU will furnish the memory address of the instruction on the address bus, as indicated by the arrow direction. Once addressed, that memory location will "dump" a copy of its contents, the instruction, on the data bus from where it is received by the CPU; that is, the CPU *reads* that memory location. Thus, in order for the CPU to address memory, via the address bus, and to receive the instruction from memory, via the data bus, two more function blocks must be added to Figure 2-2. The function block that addresses memory for instructions is termed the *program counter* (PC), and the function block used to receive instructions from memory, via the data bus, is called the *data bus latch*. Here, a latch is a register whose primary function is latching data from a bus. Because the data bus latch is used to latch both instructions and data from the data bus, a distinction must be made between the two. Therefore, another function block (register) is needed to store just instructions. That register is called the *instruction register* (IR) and will be used to store instructions latched by the data bus latch, and data will be sent to other CPU registers. The data bus latch, PC, and IR function blocks are shown in Figure 2-3 and represent the answer to our first question.

The term *program counter* exemplifies how the CPU receives the sequence of instructions that make up the program. The PC is used exclusively to address memory for program instructions (never to address memory for data), which

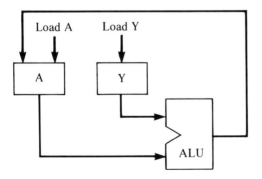

FIGURE 2-2. ALU with inputs A and Y and output A.

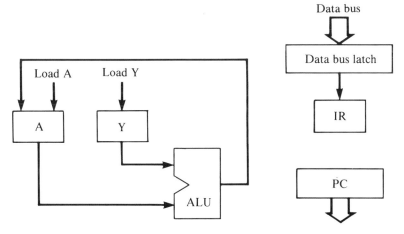

FIGURE 2-3. Development of 8085 architecture: The addition of data bus latch, IR, and PC.

explains the "program" portion of program counter. The "counter" portion of the term is derived from its counter action. That is, after the execution of an instruction, the CPU *automatically* increments the PC by one (PC = PC + 1), thus operating the PC as a sequential up-counter.

Requiring program instructions to be stored in memory in sequential order enables the PC to access properly each instruction in the order required. As an example, suppose that a program consists of five instructions that are stored in sequential memory locations, beginning at memory location 100. To fetch and execute this program, the PC must first contain address 100, which is loaded on the address bus. This causes the contents of memory location 100 (the first instruction), to be loaded on the data bus and the CPU then latches it, via the data bus latch. Once latched by the data bus latch, the instruction then is latched by the IR. The CPU then executes that instruction and increments the program counter by one (PC = 100 + 1 = 101), which is the address of the second instruction. The CPU then, again, loads the contents of its PC (PC = 101) on the address bus, which in turn causes memory location 101 to load its contents on the data bus from where it is latched by the data bus latch and then by the IR. Again, after executing the second instruction, the CPU increments its PC by one (PC = 101 + 1 = 102), which is the memory address of the third instruction. This cycle of instruction fetching, executing, and incrementing the PC continues until the entire program has been read from memory and executed. Note that it is this counter action of the PC that lets the CPU know where in memory the next instruction is to be found.

To answer the second question, "Once the CPU receives an instruction, how does it 'know' how to interpret and execute it?" let us recall that *all* program instructions are binary codes. For example, the binary code instructing the 8085 to perform an addition is the 8-bit code 10000000, and that to perform a logic AND is 10100111. That is, every MPU instruction has a unique binary code. Thus, to "identify" an instruction, the CPU can simply decode the binary code latched by the IR, using a decoder similar to those in digital electronics (for a review of decoders, the reader can refer to the 8205 of this text). And so to identify (decode) an instruction latched by the IR of Figure 2-3 let us add a decoder, which we shall call the *IR decoder*, as illustrated in Figure 2-4.

Once an instruction has been uniquely identified (decoded), it must be executed by the CPU. To execute the instruction, let us imagine another function block, called the *control unit* (CU). It is the CU that actually expedites the execution of an instruction within the CPU and that controls the instruction fetch operations, that is, loading the contents of the PC (the memory address) on the address bus, causing the data bus latch and IR to latch the addressed instruction, via the data bus, and incrementing the PC. As can be imagined, instruction fetching and executing require the total control of the CPU architecture. To provide that control, the CU's output is control lines that go to all of the function blocks, as seen in Figure 2-4. We shall have much more to say about the CU, but for now remember that it is this function block that actually controls the instruction fetches and execution, and for that reason all other function blocks are under its control, via the CU control lines.

To summarize, an instruction is latched by the data bus latch off the data bus, and from there it is latched by the IR under control of the CU. The instruction is then identified (decoded) by the IR decoder, and its identity is passed on to

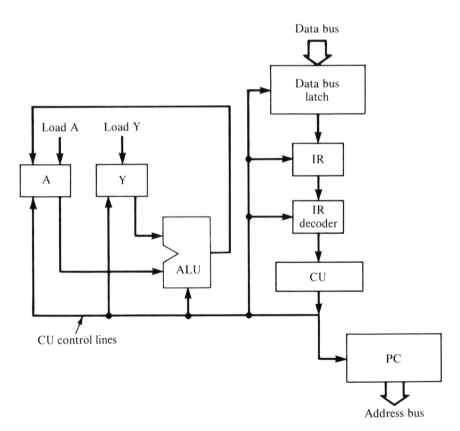

FIGURE 2-4. Development of CPU architecture: The addition of IR decoder and CU.

the CU. The CU then executes that instruction and will then increment the PC. Hence, the PC, IR, IR decoder, and CU are solutions to our questions and are illustrated in Figure 2-4.

The CPU architecture of Figure 2-4 provides the necessary function blocks to fetch an instruction from memory, but it does not provide for fetching data—recall that the PC is used only to address memory for instructions. Thus Figure 2-4 will require modification to allow memory addressing to fetch data. We shall therefore add another function block to Figure 2-4 which will be used to address memory for data and is called the *data counter* (DC), as shown in Figure 2-5. The data counter is used to "hold" a memory address on the address bus when the CPU is fetching data from memory. The DC is similar to the PC. Both address memory; however, the DC does not have the automatic counter action that the PC processes. For, unlike program instructions, data may not be in sequential memory locations. Hence, the content of the DC is under the

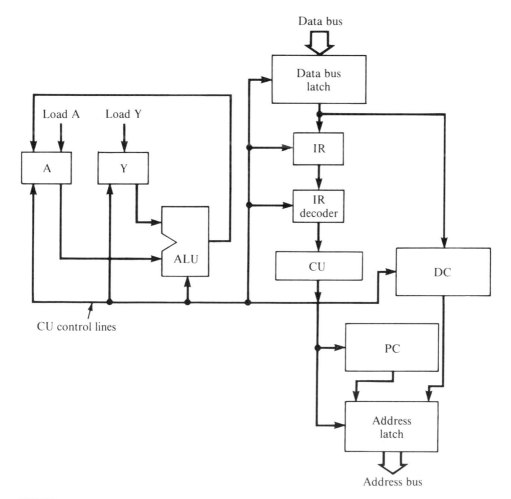

FIGURE 2-5. Development of CPU architecture: The addition of DC and address latch.

control of the user, via program instructions (the programmer knows where the data are stored, we hope). That is, the DC is under program control. Because the content of the DC is under program control, its content will be determined by instructions contained in program memory. These instructions will reference other memory locations for the address value (data) to be loaded in the DC. After this DC address value is fetched from program memory and latched by the data bus latch, it must then be latched by the DC. Figure 2-5 shows the output of the data bus latch going to both the IR and DC, with the CU determining which function block will latch the content of the data bus latch, the IR or DC.

There are now two function blocks that must have access to the address bus, the PC and DC, but only one is to have access at any given time, depending whether an instruction or data is being addressed. Thus we must provide a single function block that has access to the address bus, with the PC and DC acting as inputs to it. This function block will be termed the *address latch,* and as its name implies, it will latch a memory address from either the PC or DC, depending on whether an instruction or data is being fetched. The CU will determine whether the content of the PC or the DC is latched by the address latch, as it is the CU that controls instruction and data fetching; that is, the CU "knows" whether an instruction or data is being fetched from memory. Figure 2-4 is modified, as shown in Figure 2-5, to show a DC and PC acting as inputs to an address latch, where this latch interfaces with the address bus. Because the address latch is controlled by the CU, the CU's control lines go to the address latch as well as to the PC and DC.

At this point the reader may ask, "Once data is fetched from memory, where is it stored in the CPU until it is used?" If we assume that all data fetched from memory will be processed by the ALU, then the data fetched from memory must be latched by registers A and/or Y, as these two registers serve as inputs to the ALU. And because this data is fetched via the data bus and brought internally into the CPU, via the data bus latch, there must be a path between the data bus latch and registers A and Y. Figure 2-6 shows a path between the data bus latch and registers A and Y, by having the output of the data bus latch serve as an input to A and Y, as well as to the IR and DC. The CU decides whether register A or Y, the IR, or the DC will latch the content of the data bus latch. Also note that there is no longer a need for inputs load A and load Y of Figure 2-5, as the data bus latch can serve as the source of data for registers A and Y. Thus Figure 2-6 no longer shows these two inputs. Let us consider an example that utilizes the architecture of Figure 2-6.

EXAMPLE 2-1
Suppose for this example that we wished to add the data of memory locations 0200 and 0253.

Solution
The program to accomplish this task is shown in Table 2-1, in which, for this example, the five required program instructions are stored in sequential memory locations, beginning at 0100 and ending with 0104. We also see in Table 2-1 that memory locations 0200 and 0253 contain the values to be added, 03 and

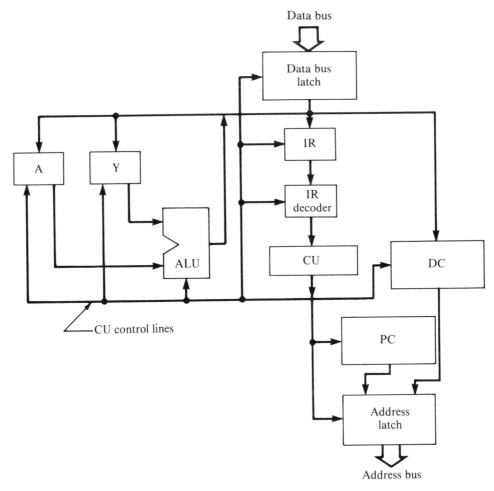

FIGURE 2-6. Development of CPU architecture: The removal of load A and Y inputs.

02, respectively. From our previous discussion we know that each instruction has a unique binary code that is stored at memory locations 0100 to 0104, rather than the symbolic representation of those instructions as shown (LXI DC, 0200, and so forth) in Table 2-1. It is to read Table 2-1 more easily that the symbolic representation was chosen over the actual binary coding. Also, as we shall see later, some instructions will require more than one memory location, but for simplicity, we shall assume that each instruction of Table 2-1 can be stored at a single memory location. Remember that the purpose of this example is to demonstrate how the architecture of Figure 2-6 is controlled by the user, via a program to add two numbers, and not to dwell on the details of instruction coding, and so forth, which will be covered later.

To begin relating the program of Table 2-1 and the architecture of Figure 2-6, let us assume that the PC is set to 0100 (PC = 0100). Because the CPU has not been told what to do, it must first fetch an instruction. The instruction

TABLE 2-1. A Program to Add the Contents of Memory Locations 0200 and 0253

Memory Location	Memory Location Content
0100	LXI DC,0200
0101	MOV A,DC
0102	LXI DC,0253
0103	MOV Y,DC
0104	ADD
.	.
.	.
.	.
0200	03
.	.
.	.
0253	02

fetch will be under the CU's control, as are all CPU operations. The CU will cause the address latch to latch the content of the PC, which is 0100, and then load that address on the address bus. The content of address 0100 is then loaded on the data bus, which is the instruction LXI DC,0200, as seen from Table 2-1, from where the CU, via its control lines, will cause the data bus latch to latch it. Then the CU will cause the IR to latch that instruction from the data bus latch. Next, the IR decoder will decode that unique binary code in the IR, which represents the instruction LXI DC,0200 and then send the appropriate signals for that instruction to the CU. The CU now knows that it is to execute the instruction LXI DC,0200, which will load the DC register with the immediate data, which is the numerical value 0200. The CU then executes this instruction, causing DC = 0200 and then increments the PC, which will result in PC = 0101. To fetch the next instruction (MOV A,DC), the same cyclical actions are repeated. That is, the CU causes the address latch to latch the PC's contents, which is now 0101, and load that value on the address bus. This accesses memory location 0101 and causes it to load its content, the instruction MOV A,DC, on the data bus. The CU then causes the data bus latch to latch that instruction off the data bus. Next the CU causes, via its control lines, the IR to latch the content of the data bus latch. The IR decoder then decodes the content of the IR (instruction MOV A,DC) and again sends the appropriate signals to the CU. The CU now knows that it is to execute the instruction MOV A,DC, which is to move (MOV) the data in the memory location addressed by the DC into the accumulator (A). For the CU to execute this instruction, it must cause the address latch to latch the content of the DC (DC = 0200 from the previous instruction) and then to load that address on the address bus, which will access memory location 0200. From Table 2-1 we see that accessing memory location 0200 will cause 03 to be loaded on the data bus. The CU will then cause the data bus latch to latch that data (03) off the data bus and next cause register A to latch it from the data bus latch. Hence, register A now contains the value 03. This concludes the execution of instruction MOV A,DC, and as a result, the CU increments the PC, which is then 0102 (PC = 0102). Again the CPU goes through the instruction fetch cycle, under control of the CU, causing the address latch to latch the PC's content (0102) and then loading that address on the address bus, thereby allowing the content of that memory location to be latched by the IR via the data bus latch. The instruction fetched from memory location 0102 is LXI DC,0253, which when executed by the CU will result in the DC = 0253 and the PC's being incremented (PC = 0103). The CPU again goes through the instruction fetch cycle, under control of the CU, which results in the binary code for instruction MOV Y,DC's being latched by the IR. Then the IR decoder decodes this instruction and sends the appropriate signals to the CU. For the CU to execute the MOV Y,DC instruction, it must fetch the data (02) from the memory location provided by the content of the DC (DC = 0253) and place that data in register Y. It does so by causing the address latch to latch the content of the DC and then loading that address on the address bus. The content of memory location 0253 is then loaded on the data bus from where the CU causes register Y to latch it via the data bus latch. This concludes the execution of the instruction MOV Y,DC, and the PC is incremented by the CU to 0104. Again the CPU goes through the instruction fetch cycle, resulting in the binary code for ADD being latched by the IR. To execute this instruction, the CU will cause the contents of registers A and Y to be input to the ALU and then added with the sum (05) being stored in register A. Hence, the original content of A (03) is replaced (destroyed) with the sum (05) of registers A and Y; that is, A + Y = A. After execution, the CU increments the PC (PC = 0105), and the next instruction (not shown) is fetched and executed. ∎

From Example 2-1 the reader should have noticed patterns in utilizing the architecture of Figure 2-6. That is,

1. The CU ''knows'' what steps must be taken to execute every instruction and to do so controls all other function blocks, via its output, which are control lines.
2. All memory addresses are provided via the address latch. If an instruction is being fetched from memory, the PC will be the source of the address, whereas if data is being fetched, the DC will be the source. The CU determines whether the content of the address latch comes from the PC or the DC.
3. The path of all instructions and data is from the data bus to the data bus latch and then to the IR for instructions and to register A or Y for data, where the CU controls whether the IR or register A or Y will latch the content of the data bus latch.

In studying the CPU patterns in Example 2-1, you may have observed that additional modifications of the CPU architecture are required. The third pattern implies that the path among the data bus latch output, the DC, registers A and Y, and the IR is really a data bus inside the CPU. This is because multiple bits (an instruction or data) must flow in parallel from the data bus to the DC, the IR, or register A or Y whenever the CPU reads memory. Figure 2-6 is modified in Figure 2-7 to make this path a bus, called an *internal data bus*. Notice that the data bus latch is an interface between the CPU's internal data bus and the

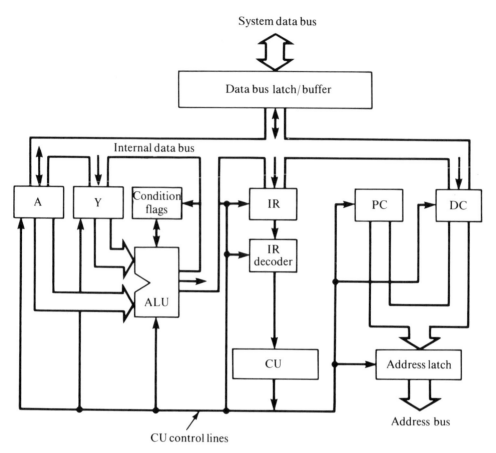

FIGURE 2-7. Development of CPU architecture: The internal data bus and its interface with the system data bus.

system's data bus. Also, because the output of the PC and the DC forms a common input to the address latch, with multiple parallel lines, the connection among the PC, DC, and address latch is represented as a bus in Figure 2-7. The CPU architecture of Figure 2-6 is structured so as to allow only the reading of memory, and no writing. But the user may wish to have the CPU *write* to memory, such as storing in memory the ALU result of A + Y of Example 2-1. Thus the interface between the CPU's internal data bus and the system's data bus—the data bus latch—must be made bidirectional. And for the data bus latch to be bidirectional (1) it must be a latch in order for the CPU to read what is on the system's data bus, and (2) it must provide a data path between the CPU's internal data bus and the system's data bus so as to allow CPU write operations, but the data bus latch must be able to isolate these two buses when the CPU is not writing to the system—otherwise bus contention would ensue. A *buffer* (*tristate logic*) provides the capability of interfacing these two buses for write operations. Hence, the data bus latch of Figure 2-6 is relabeled the *data bus latch/buffer* and is the interface between the system's data bus and the CPU's internal data bus and is under the control of the CU.

To understand how the data bus latch/buffer can be electronically implemented, consider Figure 2-8a, which has N + 1 positive edge-triggered flip-flops serving as latches and a pair of tristate logic gates per latch serving as buffers. From the timing diagram of Figure 2-8b, we see that when both CU control lines are low, the system's data bus is isolated from the CPU's internal data bus, as both tristate logic gates (W and R) are in the high-Z state (high impedance). This bus isolation allows the two buses to work independently. When the CU read control line goes high, causing a positive edge pulse to appear at input C of each flip-flop, the flip-flop latches the logic level at its input D. And when this control line remains high, it causes the tristate logic gates labeled R to become active, thus loading the contents of each flip-flop on the CPU's internal data bus. Notice during this read-time interval that the CU write control line is low, thereby putting all of the tristate logic gates labeled W in the high-Z state. When the CPU is to write to the system (memory), via the system data bus, the CU drives its write control line high, as illustrated in Figure 2-8b. The CU write control line's going high causes all tristate logic gates labeled W to be active, thereby logically connecting the system's data bus and the CPU's internal data bus. The reader should understand the concepts of latching and buffering, for they are often used when interfacing.

Let us now consider an example that utilizes the CPU architecture of Figure 2-7.

EXAMPLE 2-2

Suppose that Example 2-1 is to be modified so that the sum (05) stored in register A is to be stored at memory location 0300.

Solution

The program of Table 2-1 still applies. What is needed are additional instructions that will copy the contents of register A (the sum) into memory locaton 0300. Two more instructions (LX1 DC,0300 and MOV DC,A) will suffice. The instruction LXI DC,0300 is stored at memory location 0105, and MOV DC,A is stored at memory location 0106. This program is executed after the ADD instruction of Table 2-1 has been executed and the PC has been incremented by one (PC = 0104 + 1 = 105) under control of the CU. The CU then again goes into an instruction fetch cycle, by loading the contents of the PC (PC = 0105) on the address bus, which causes the contents of memory location 0105 (LX1 DC,0300) to be loaded on the system's data bus. The CU then drives high its read control line (see Figure 2-8b), which causes the CPU's data bus latch/buffer to latch the instruction from the system's data bus. The CU then loads the contents of the data bus latch/buffer on the CPU's internal data bus, via the tristate logic gates labeled R, from where the IR latches it. After the IR decoder decodes that instruction, the CU executes it, resulting in the contents of the DC being 0300 and the PC being incremented by one (PC = 0106). Again, the CPU executes an instruction fetch cycle, resulting in the instruction MOV DC,A being executed by the CU. MOV DC,A states that the contents of A is to be copied in the memory location as addressed by the DC: To execute this instruction, the CU causes register A to load its content (05) on the CPU's internal data bus and at the same time to drive high its write control line (see Figure

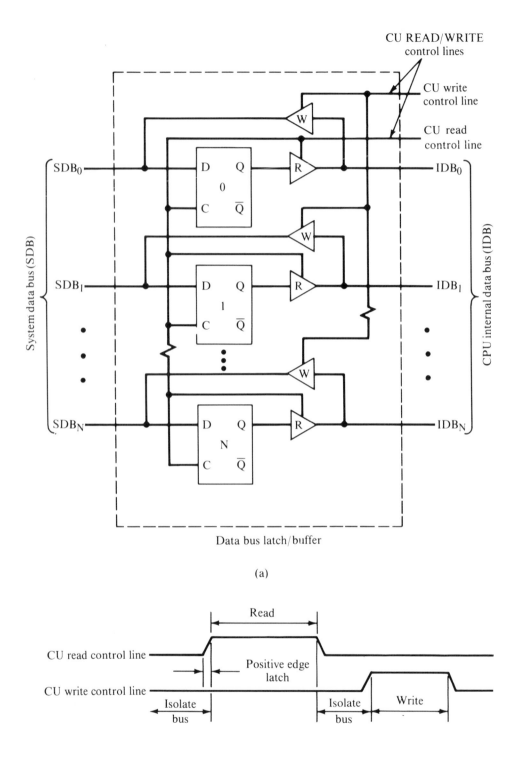

(a)

Data bus latch/buffer

CU timing

(b)

FIGURE 2-8. Data bus latch/buffer and CU timing.

2-8b), which will drive active all the W tristate logic gates, thereby connecting the CPU's internal data bus to the system's data bus. Connecting these buses writes the data from the CPU to the system's data bus. Also at this time, the CU causes the contents of the DC (DC = 0300) to be loaded on the address bus, causing memory location 0300 to store whatever is on the system's data bus, which is a copy of register A's contents (05). ■

The last function block we shall add to the CPU architecture of Figure 2-6, which is shown in Figure 2-7, is the condition flags. Condition flags are flip-flops whose logic state indicates the resultant "condition" of an arithmetic or logic operation performed by the ALU. The number of such flip-flops, or flags, varies from one MPU to another, although we shall consider just five, as follows:

1. *Sign flag* (S). If set (the 1-state), the result of the ALU arithmetic operation was such that the most significant bit was a logic 1. If reset (0 state), the most significant bit of the result was 0.
2. *Carry flag* (C). If a carry or a borrow results from an ALU arithmetic operation, then the C flag will be set; otherwise it will be reset.
3. *Parity flag* (P). If the result of an ALU operation has even parity, then the P flag will be set; otherwise, it will be reset.
4. *Auxiliary carry flag* (AC). If a carry results between the fourth and fifth bits after an ALU operation, the AC flag will be set; otherwise, it will be reset.
5. *Zero flag* (Z). If the result of an ALU operation is 0, then the Z flag will be set; otherwise, it will be reset.

These condition flags allow the CPU to make decisions. For instance, suppose that the task of a program was to identify all juniors in a university's student listing. The binary code representing juniors would be stored in register Y of Figure 2-7. Then the class level (freshman, sophomore, and so on) for each student would be loaded one at a time in register A, and a subtraction would be performed in the ALU between registers A and Y (A − Y). If the Z flag is set, the result will be 0 (A = Y), and hence the student is a junior, but if the Z flag is reset (A ≠ Y), the student is at a level other than a junior. Thus by examining the Z flag, a decision as to a students status can be made.

The condition flags' function block of Figure 2-7 is shown as bidirectional, relative to the ALU. This means that in addition to the ALU's determining the condition flags' logic state, a flag's logic state may serve as input data to the ALU.

We shall consider Figure 2-7 as a "standard" for CPU architecture.

2-3

8085 Architecture

Now we are ready to study the 8085 MPU. As we stated in the introduction to this chapter, we shall study the 8085 by categorizing its architecture into essential and nonessential function blocks, with the essential function blocks being basically the same as the CPU illustrated in Figure 2-7.

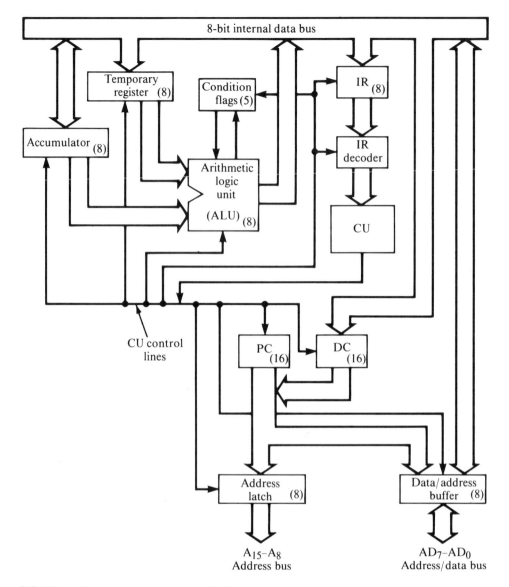

FIGURE 2-9. The portion of the 8085 architecture that represents a CPU.

8085 Essential Function Blocks

Figure 2-9 illustrates those essential 8085 architectural function blocks that comprise a CPU. Note the parenthesized number in each function block, which represents the register's bit size. We see that all data-handling registers (A and temporary register) are 8-bits, as is the internal data bus. For this reason, the 8085 is known as an *8-bit MPU*, or in "computer jargon," an *8-bit machine*. We also see that the PC is a 16-bit register and that therefore all memory addresses are 16 bits.

Comparing the CPU architecture of Figure 2-7 with the 8085 architecture of Figure 2-9, we see that the 8085 MPU architecture includes the CPU's function blocks but identifies register Y as a temporary register and implements the address latch and the data bus latch/buffer in a slightly different manner. There is no difference between register Y and the temporary register—just a difference in names. The address latch and the data bus latch/buffer are implemented in this manner in order to conserve the number of pins on the chip, by time sharing, known as *multiplexing,* the address and data pins. Under the CU's control, the AD_0–AD_7 pins are time shared between serving as address pins A_0–A_7 and data pins D_0–D_7. The timing diagram of Figure 2-10 illustrates the multiplexing of pins AD_0–AD_7.

Let us suppose that the timing diagram of Figure 2-10 represents the address pins A_8–A_{15} and the multiplexed address/data pins AD_0–AD_7 during an instruction fetch cycle. As we see from Figure 2-10, address pins A_8–A_{15} have the high-order address *byte* (8 bits are known as a byte) present during the entire addressing cycle, represented by time interval t_C. Pins AD_0–AD_7 are time shared by serving as address pins A_0–A_7 during time interval t_A (providing the PC's lower-order byte) and then as data pins D_0–D_7 during time interval t_D. During an instruction fetch cycle, the CU loads the PC's content on pins A_8–A_{15} and AD_0–AD_7 during time interval t_A, which provides the 16-bit memory address A_0–A_{15}. This address accesses the addressed memory location and causes it to load a copy of its content (the instruction) on pins AD_0–AD_7, which are now serving as data pins D_0–D_7 during time interval t_D. During time interval t_D the CU causes the data/address buffer to latch the instruction from pins AD_0–AD_7, from where the IR will then latch it. We can conclude that even though the 8085 accesses the address and data buses in a slightly different way from the CPU architecture of Figure 2-7, there is conceptually no difference. Also, notice that the data/address buffer is really a data/address buffer/latch and is so named in Figure 2-11.

Now we are ready to investigate those nonessential function blocks that tend to distinguish one MPU from another. An analogy is the essentials of an automobile: its wheels, power plant, drive train, and braking and steering mechanisms. Its nonessentials, which distinguish one automobile from another, are such items as engine size, transmission, front or rear drive, body styling, interior details, handling characteristics, and the like.

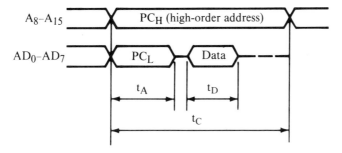

FIGURE 2-10. Timing diagram of multiplexed address/data pins AD_0–AD_7.

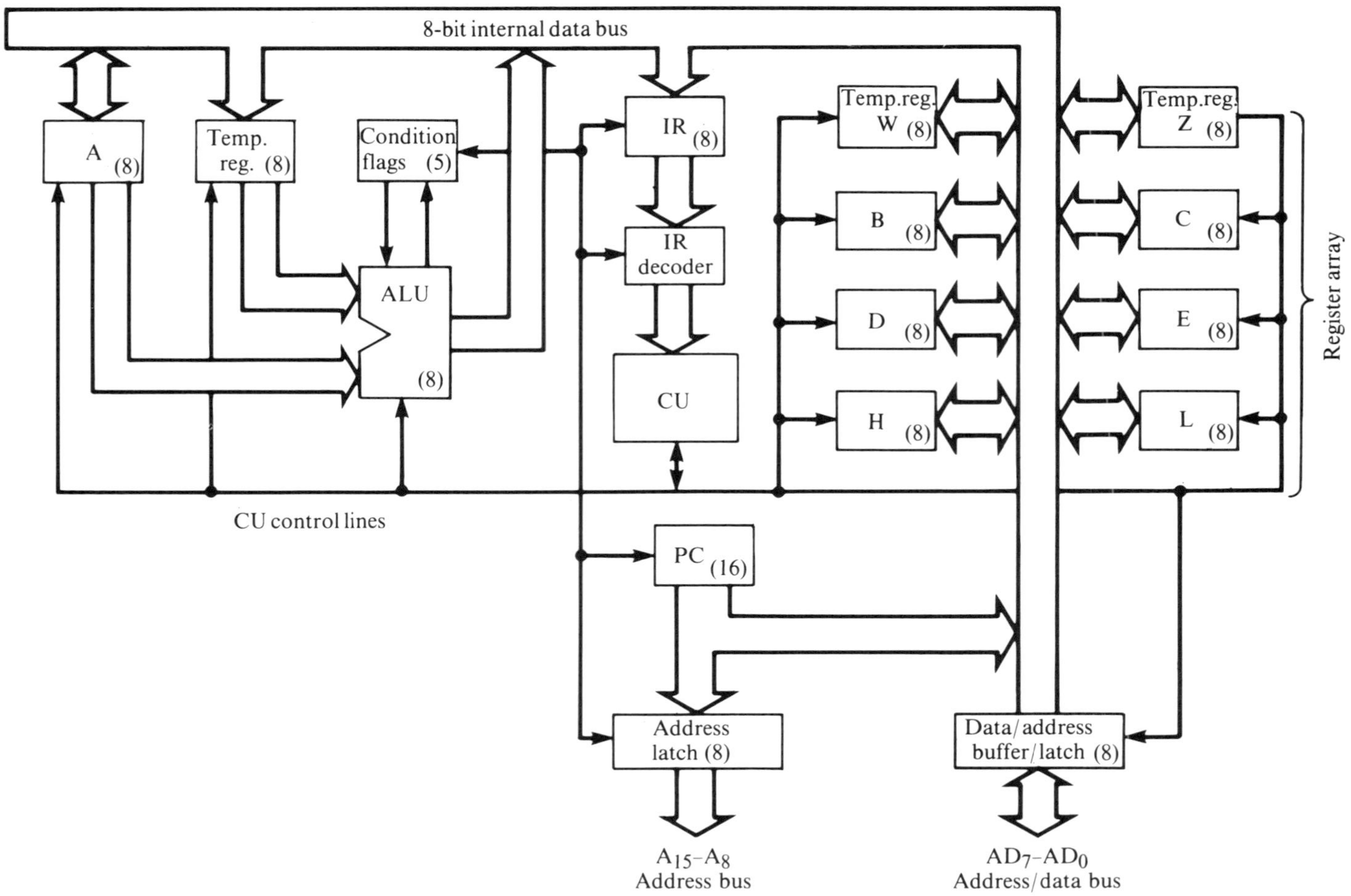

FIGURE 2-11. The CPU and register array of the 8085 MPU.

As stated in Section 2-1, the 8085's MPU architecture also includes function blocks (which are nonessential): clock, controller, and portions of the DMA, interrupt request logic, I/O interfacing, and data memory.

8085 Nonessential Function Blocks

It is convenient, but not necessary, to have some memory inside the MPU, acting as a place to store partial results of an ALU operation, or data that are to be used by the ALU. This internal memory is similar to that of many hand-held calculators.

Figure 2-11 is the architecture of Figure 2-9 with an array of registers added, which, except for W and Z, are to serve as internal memory. Note from Figure 2-11 that these registers (B, C, D, E, H, L, W, and Z) can be read or written to, via the 8-bit internal data bus. The CU electronically controls the accessing of the register array and does so in a way similar to controlling the data bus latch/buffer of Figure 2-8.

The term *internal memory* is seldom used to describe these internal memory registers, but rather, the terms *secondary accumulators* or, more often, *scratch-pad memory* are used. They are called secondary accumulators because they accumulate ALU results, which are secondary to the primary accumulating responsibilities of register A. When the term *scratch-pad memory* is used, it is to denote that when these registers are used to store data it is a temporary use, and so they are being used as one would use a scratch pad.

Also note that the architecture of Figure 2-11 does not have a DC function block, which is present in Figure 2-9. The reason for not specifying a specific DC function block in Figure 2-11 is that in the interest of register economy, the 8085 was designed so that those registers comprising the register array can be programmed to serve the dual purpose of functioning as a DC and/or as scratch-pad memory. That is, under program control, the user will determine whether registers within the register array will serve as a DC or scratch-pad memory. When functioning as a DC, two registers are paired in order to provide a 16-bit address. As an example of the programmable dual nature of the register array registers, let us rewrite the program of Examples 2-1 and 2-2 (see Table 2-1) for the 8085 architecture, as represented by Figure 2-11.

EXAMPLE 2-3

As we did in Examples 2-1 and 2-2, add the contents, which is in parentheses, of memory locations 0200H(03H) and 0253 (02H), and store the result (05H) at memory location 0300H, where the symbol H is used to indicate hexadecimal values. The program to achieve this task is given in Table 2-2, which is similar to the program of Table 2-1 but written with actual 8085 instructions.

Solution

The first instruction (LXI H,0200H) loads (symbolized by L) register pair H and L (X represents *register pair*) with the immediate (I) data 0200H. This instruction prepares register pair H and L to be used as a DC, by loading in the desired memory address (0200H). Note from Table 2-2 that this instruction is a three-byte instruction requiring memory locations 0100H, 0101H, and 0102H to store it (each memory location can store one byte, as dictated by the system's data bus size). The second instruction (MOV B,M) causes the MPU to read the content of memory location M, with register pair H and L used to supply the memory address (the symbol M indicates register pair H and L), and moves (MOV) that data byte into register B. The execution of this instruction loads the content (03H) of memory location M (0200H) into register B. This instruction uses register B as a scratch-pad memory register and register pair H and L as a DC. The third instruction (LXI H,0253H), which again is a three-byte instruction, changes the contents of H and L to 0253H. The fourth instruction (MOV A,M) uses H and L as a DC and loads the addressed memory location (0253H) content (02H) into register A. The fifth instruction (ADD adds the contents of register B and A and automatically stores the result (05H) in register A. The sixth instruction (LXI D, 0300H) loads register pair D and E with 0300H, which prepares register pair D and E to be used as a DC. The final instruction (STAX D) stores (ST) the content of register A (05H) at the memory location supplied by register pair (X) D and E (0300H). This instruction uses register pair D and E as a DC. ∎

Summarizing Example 2-3, the reader should understand that register pair H and L (M) served as a DC in the second and fourth instruction of Table 2-2 and that register pair D and E served as a DC in the seventh instruction. The second and fifth instructions used register B as a scratch-pad register.

TABLE 2-2. An 8085 Program to Add the Contents of Memory Locations 0200 and 0253 and Store the Result at Location 0300

Memory location (hex values)	Memory location content
0100H(Hex)	
0101H	LXI H, 0200H (Hex)
0102H	
0103H	MOV B, M
0104H	
0105H	LXI H, 0253H
0106H	
0107H	MOV A, M
0108H	ADD B
0109H	
010AH	LXI D, 0300H
010BH	
010CH	STAX D
.	.
.	.
.	.
0200H	03H
.	.
.	.
.	.
0253H	02H

Up to this point we have not discussed the accessing of I/O by a MPU, which is accomplished in much the same fashion as when a MPU is accessing memory, as we discussed in Chapter 1. That is, each I/O is assigned a unique address, and whenever the MPU wishes to access a specific I/O device, it does so by addressing it via the address bus and I/O selector of Figure 1-12.

There are two classifications of I/O addressing: *memory-mapped I/O* and *isolated I/O*. A memory-mapped I/O addressing technique has no *software* distinction between memory and I/O addresses; that is, every memory reference instruction can access either memory or I/O. In a memory-mapped system, only the hardware distinguishes memory from I/O. If in Example 2-3, a keyboard were assigned address 0200H, when the second instruction (MOV B,M) was executed, the address 0200H would be loaded on the address bus, thus accessing the keyboard for a data byte. The logic for the name *memory-mapped I/O* is that the user (programmer), when writing programs, must keep track (via a memory map) of those memory addresses assigned to memory and those assigned to I/O. The isolate I/O techniques of addressing I/O has separate instructions for addressing I/O and memory. The 8085 has many memory reference instructions (MOV A, M, STAX D, and so on) where there are only two I/O instructions. These two I/O instructions are IN ADDR and OUT ADDR, with ADDR used here to represent an 8-bit I/O address. As an example of an isolated I/O system, suppose that an input device, such as a keyboard, were assigned the I/O address of 06H. To access that keyboard for data input to the MPU, the instruction IN O6H would be used. In an isolated I/O system, a distinction between memory and I/O is made in both software and hardware.

The 8085 MPU can be used in either a memory-mapped I/O system or an isolated I/O system. When the 8085 is being used in an isolated I/O system, registers W and Z are used to contain the I/O address. Because the 8085 uses only 8-bit I/O addresses, but the address bus is 16-bits, registers W and Z are copies of each other. Thus, for an 8085 isolate I/O system, one would find the high-order byte of an I/O address (A_{15}–A_8) to be a duplicate of the lower-order byte (AD_7–AD_0), known as the *address mirror effect*.

One last note concerning Figure 2-11. The designation *temporary register* means that the register is not programmable by the user (no instruction accesses it directly) but is used by the 8085's CU in the instruction execution process. The temporary register of Figure 2-11, which implements the Y register of Figure 2-7, is used by the CU to execute all ALU instructions involving register A and other registers. As an example, when executing the instruction ADD B, which adds the content of registers B and A, the CU loads the content of register B into the temporary register and then instructs the ALU to add the contents of registers A and the temporary register.

To complete the 8085 architecture, we shall add the remaining nonessential function blocks (clock, controller, DMA, interrupt request logic and I/O interfacing) to Figure 2-11, which is illustrated in Figure 2-12. As we see from Figure 2-12, the clock has inputs X_1 and X_2 and output CLK OUT, X_1 and X_2 allowing the user to choose the primary source for clocking the MPU and the system—depending on the clock accuracy and expense desired by the user. X_1 and X_2 may be driven by oscillators such as a crystal or an RC network. The frequency of X_1 and X_2 is divided by two and waveshaped into pulses and made available to the system (external to the MPU) at output CLK OUT as well as to the CU, which gives internal timing to the CU for instruction execution.

The system controller of Figure 2-12 serves the same function as does the controller function block of Figure 1-12; that is, it controls usage of the system's multiplexed buses (namely, the data bus) in order to prevent bus contention. This requires the system controller to have control over all of the system's function blocks that share a multiplexed bus. The system's function block bus usage control is implemented by the system controller via control signals generated by it and transmitted to the various function blocks via the control bus. From Figure 2-12 we see three *primary control signals,* IO/$\overline{\text{M}}$, $\overline{\text{RD}}$, and $\overline{\text{WR}}$. The logic state of primary control signal IO/$\overline{\text{M}}$ indicates whether the MPU is accessing I/O or memory. As indicated by the nomenclature (a bar over the top, representing negation, indicates an active low), if output IO/$\overline{\text{M}}$ is a high, an I/O device is to have use of the data bus, and if output IO/$\overline{\text{M}}$ is low, then the data bus is being used by memory. The primary control signals $\overline{\text{RD}}$ and $\overline{\text{WR}}$ provide the timing for the MPU's read and write operations, respectively. The primary control signal $\overline{\text{RD}}$ is active (low) whenever the MPU is reading either an I/O device or memory. The primary control signal $\overline{\text{WR}}$ is low when the MPU is writing to either I/O or memory. These three primary control signals are used to generate control bus control signals. If a control bus control signal is needed that is an active low for an I/O read (indicated by the symbol $\overline{\text{I/O R}}$), the primary control signals IO/$\overline{\text{M}}$ and $\overline{\text{RD}}$ can be NANDed, as illustrated in Figure 2-13. We also see from Figure 2-13 that to generate a control bus control signal that is an active low for a memory read ($\overline{\text{MEM R}}$), the primary control signals IO/$\overline{\text{M}}$ and $\overline{\text{RD}}$ are NANDed. To generate a control bus control signal to control an I/O write ($\overline{\text{I/O W}}$), the primary control signals IO/$\overline{\text{M}}$ and $\overline{\text{WR}}$ are NANDed. To generate a memory write ($\overline{\text{MEM W}}$) control bus control signal, primary control signals IO/$\overline{\text{M}}$ and $\overline{\text{WR}}$ are NANDed. These control bus control signals ($\overline{\text{I/O R}}$, $\overline{\text{MEM R}}$, $\overline{\text{I/O W}}$, and $\overline{\text{MEM W}}$) differentiate memory from I/O in the hardware, as required by an isolated I/O system. A memory-mapped I/O system requires only control bus control signals $\overline{\text{RD}}$ and $\overline{\text{WR}}$, as I/O is not differentiated from memory.

Figure 2-15 illustrates how the combinational logic of Figure 2-13 is connected to the 8085 to form the control bus for an isolated I/O system. Figure 2-15 also shows how the other two buses are implemented, which we shall discuss shortly.

The READY input to the system controller function block of Figure 2-12 allows the 8085 MPU to interface with slow memory and I/O devices for read or write operations. The CU of the MPU checks the logic state of this input. When reading from the system's data bus, the CU checks the logic state of the READY input. If the READY input is high, then the CU "knows" that the addressed memory location, or I/O device, has its data on the system's data bus and that it can be latched by the data/bus buffer/latch of Figure 2-12. However, if the READY input is low, the CU knows that the addressed memory location, or I/O device, has not had time to put its data on the system's data bus and so the CU will wait. The CU waits by idling (entering a *wait state*) until the addressed memory, or I/O device, drives high the READY input before latching data from the system's data bus. In summary, if memory or I/O has too long

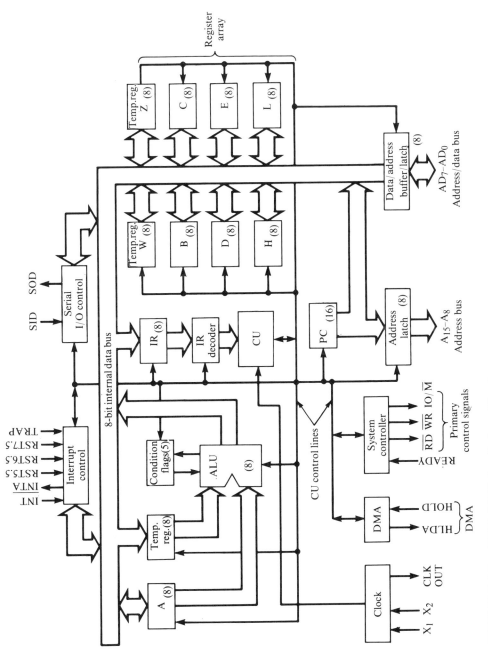

FIGURE 2-12. 8085 MPU detailed architecture.

39

Truth table for generating control signals

$\overline{\text{RD}}$	$\overline{\text{WR}}$	$\text{IO}/\overline{\text{M}}$	Operation required	Required control signal
0	0	0	None; illegal since	None
0	0	1	$\overline{\text{RD}} = \overline{\text{WR}} = 0$	
0	1	0	Read memory	$\overline{\text{MEM R}}$
0	1	1	Read I/O	$\overline{\text{I/O R}}$
1	0	0	Write to memory	$\overline{\text{MEM W}}$
1	0	1	Write to I/O	$\overline{\text{I/O W}}$
1	1	0	None since	None
1	1	1	$\overline{\text{RD}} = \overline{\text{WR}} = 1$	

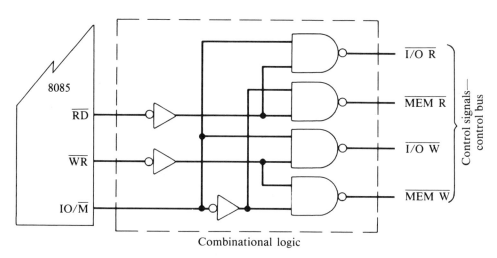

FIGURE 2-13. **Generation of control signals for an isolated I/O system.**

an *access time,* which is the time from when addressed to loading its data on the system's data bus, the slow memory or I/O must use the READY input to coordinate 8085 read operations. The same is true for 8085 write operations; that is, before the 8085 outputs data on the system's data bus to write to an addressed memory location or I/O device, it first checks the logic state of the READY input to see if the addressed memory location or I/O device is ready. Thus it is the responsibility of the addressed to determine the logic state of the READY input.

The DMA function block of Figure 2-12 allows an I/O device to access memory directly rather than via the MPU. An I/O device with DMA capability can request a DMA by driving high the HOLD input. When the MPU has finished executing the instruction in the IR at the time of the request, it acknowledges the DMA request by driving high the HLDA (HOLD acknowledge) output and at the same time isolating itself from the system's buses by putting all address, data, and control lines in the high-impedance state (high-Z). With the MPU isolated from the system's buses, the requesting I/O device can take control of those buses and access memory directly. This requires that the I/O device furnish the memory address of the locations to be accessed and the necessary control bus control signals ($\overline{\text{MEM R}}$ and $\overline{\text{MEM W}}$). The HLDA output is used by the MPU to signal the I/O device to begin accessing memory.

The next nonessential 8085 MPU function block of Figure 2-12 to be discussed is the interrupt control. The interrupt control function block has five inputs and one output. The five inputs (INT, RST 5.5, and so on) all are interrupt requests, and output $\overline{\text{INTA}}$ is an interrupt acknowledge. Interrupts are studied in depth in another chapter, and for that reason we shall not elaborate on them at this time.

The serial I/O control function block of Figure 2-12 allows the 8085 to interface directly with *serial I/O devices* (devices that read and write data one bit at a time). The SID input is for serial input data, and the SOD output is for serial output data. *Parallel I/O devices* are those that communicate in data bytes and so communicate over the system's data bus and are the type of I/O devices we have discussed thus far. Of course, a serial I/O device can also communicate over the system's data bus, but seven of the eight data bus lines would not be used—wasteful. As a point of interest, there are chips which interface serial I/O devices to an 8-bit parallel data bus. The 8251 is just such a chip and is presented in Chapter 7.

Since the introduction of the control unit in Figure 2-4, the reader has been given program examples that stated repeatedly that the CU

1. "Knew" how to execute every instruction once "told" the instruction to be executed, via the IR decoder.
2. Expedited instruction execution by controlling the other function blocks.

From this description of the CU's responsibilities in the MPU architecture and the program examples given, the reader must begin to feel that the CU is the brain of the MPU. Such an observation is correct. The control unit is a *special-purpose computer* within the MPU and has the sole function of executing instructions. As is the case for all computers, it requires a program to instruct it. The program required by the CU gives it the precise procedures to be followed in executing the instructions, such as the procedures of Example 2-3. This program is termed the *microprogram* and is manufactured as an intregal part of the CU and is not alterable or accessible to the user. For this reason there is little need to discuss it further, except to let the reader know that there is an exception for a type of microprocessor called a *bit-slice microprocessor*. For these microprocessors the user must create the microprogram, but because of their complexity and lack of common usage, we shall not study them in this textbook.

We have developed the 8085 MPU architecture as represented in Figure 2-12. The architecture of Figure 2-12 is more detailed than the illustrations furnished by Intel (the manufacturer) in its data sheets. A manufacturer must

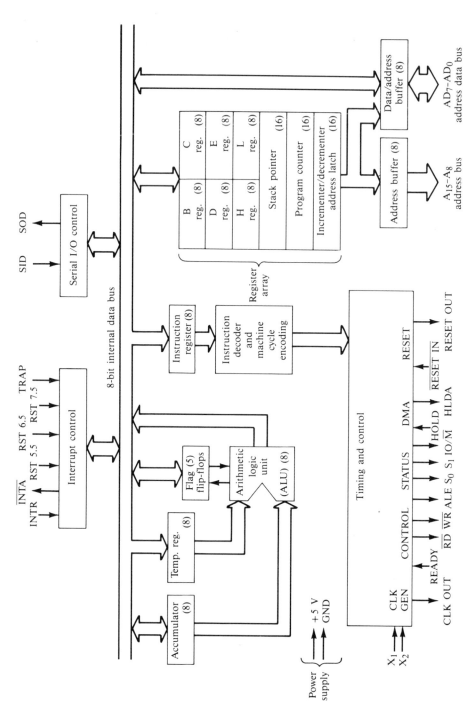

FIGURE 2-14. 8085 MPU architecture. (Courtesy of Intel.)

assume that a user has some background when using its product and therefore already has a basic understanding of how it works—even if that understanding is generic. Hence, in data sheets some of the details often are omitted in order to keep the illustration uncluttered. Figure 2-14 is the 8085 MPU architecture as copied from an Intel data sheet.

In viewing Figure 2-14 we see that the CU's control lines, registers W and Z, and that portion of the internal data bus servicing the register array have been omitted for simplicity's sake. Also, the function-block clock, DMA, and system controller have been combined into a single function block labeled *timing and control,* and there is a new 16-bit register (*stack pointer*). Lastly, there are four additional inputs and an output: ALE, S_0, S_1, RESET OUT, and $\overline{\text{RESET IN}}$.

$\overline{\text{RESET IN}}$ and RESET OUT are system controller signals and enable the system to be reset. If the user wishes to reset the system, the MPU included, the $\overline{\text{RESET IN}}$ input will be driven low. The MPU resets its PC to zero, returning to memory location zero to fetch an instruction and then driving high the RESET OUT, which is used by the system designer to reset the rest of the system. S_0 and S_1 are system controller signals, or data bus status signals, indicating the MPU's status of its usage of the system's data bus for each phase of an instruction fetch or execution. These outputs are not often used, but the type of device requiring data bus status, via S_0 and S_1, is one that must "know" when and how the MPU is using the system's data bus in order to carry out its function(s). Table 2-3 shows the logic state of S_0 and S_1. A device requiring MPU status often means that it wants to use the system's data bus when the MPU does not need it, or the device requires advance notice of read or write operations.

ALE (address latch enable) is an output used by an external latch as a strobe pulse to latch the address on the multiplexed lines AD_0–AD_7, which demultiplexes the address/data bus, as illustrated in Figure 2-15. ALE can also be used to latch the MPU status off status lines S_0 and S_1 if desired. ALE is generated by the MPU during period T_1 (see Figure 2-16) of each machine cycle (M_n), signaling the beginning of a new MPU read or write operation. The 8085 timing diagram of Figure 2-16, which should be compared with Figure 2-10, is for the two-byte I/O write instruction OUT ADDR. In the first machine cycle of Figure 2-16 (M_1), the *operation code* (*op code*) OUT is fetch from memory. During machine cycle M_2, the MPU fetches the I/O address (represented by ADDR) from memory and loads it in registers W and Z. During M_3, the MPU writes to the addressed I/O. As previously stated, machine cycles M_1 and M_2 are MPU memory read operations, and from Figure 2-16 we see that primary control signal IO/$\overline{\text{M}}$ is low for M_1 and M_2. Also from Figure 2-16 we see that $\overline{\text{RD}}$,

TABLE 2-3. Truth Table for MPU Status Signals S_0 and S_1

S_1	S_0	System data bus usage
0	0	Idled via HALT instruction
0	1	MPU write
1	0	MPU read
1	1	MPU read for instruction fetch

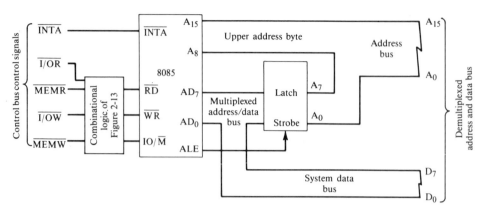

FIGURE 2-15. Demultiplexing of address/data bus by latching low-order byte of an address.

which provides proper timing for all MPU read operations, is pulsed low during M_1 and M_2 at the proper time. M_3 is the I/O write machine cycle, and we see that primary control signal $IO/\overline{M}$ is high during M_3. Also during M_3, primary control signal $\overline{WR}$, which provides timing for MPU write operations, is pulsed low when the MPU has written data on the multiplexed data bus. In each machine cycle we see that ALE is pulsed high during T_1, when the low-order

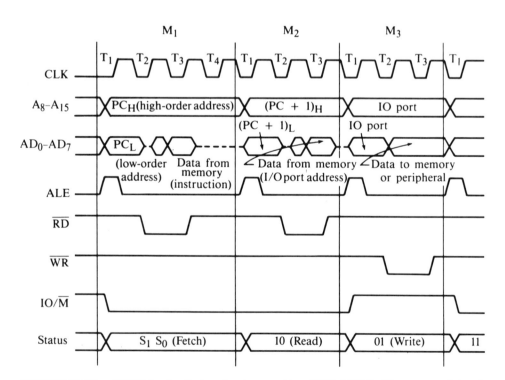

FIGURE 2-16. 8085 basic timing for instruction **OUT ADDR.** (Courtesy of Intel Corp.)

byte of a memory address (PC_L), or an I/O address, is on the multiplexed address/data bus (also refer to Figure 2-15). Recall that the upper address bus (A_8–A_{15}) also contains an I/O address, because of the address mirror effect.

To understand the purpose of the stack pointer (SP), let us first discuss the meaning of the term *stack*. The stack is an area of memory (read/write memory) so defined by the user. The stack enables the MPU not to lose permanently any MPU register data when interrupted by an I/O device and also to "know" where in memory to return to resume program execution after it completes servicing the interrupting I/O device. This is accomplished by the MPU's "pushing" its register's contents and the *program return address* (content of the PC) on the stack. When the MPU has finished servicing the interrupt requesting I/O device, it then "pops" the register's content from the stack and back into the appropriate register and, lastly, pops the return address from the stack and into the MPU's PC. The "pushing" and "popping" of the MPU's register's contents to and from the stack are under program control. As we shall see later, the user has instructions PUSH and POP for this purpose. Pushing the return address on the stack is automatic and is done by the MPU as the result of the MPU's acknowledging an interrupt request, whereas popping the return address is the result of a return (RET) instruction. The MPU also uses the stack in a similar manner when executing instructions that cause the MPU to "jump" to subroutines from which it must return. It is the SP, a 16-bit register, that addresses the stack; that is, it points to the last stack location accessed. We shall become more familiar with the stack in later chapters.

It is of interest to understand why the name *stack* was given to an area of memory serving the purpose just discussed. The reason the term *stack* is used to describe this user-defined portion of memory is that the microprocessor stacks the return address and the data of registers to be "saved" in this portion of memory, much like stacking plates. Using this analogy of stacking plates, we see that to retrieve the first plate stacked, all of the plates must be retrieved in exactly the reverse order. This type of stack is known as *first in, last out* (FILO). There is another type of stack that operates in a fashion similar to having the data stored on a unidirectional lazy susan. This means that the first data loaded onto the stack will be the first data retrieved from the stack, or *first in, first out* (FIFO). The 8085 utilizes the FILO stack operation.

This completes our development study of the 8085's MPU architecture. Next we shall view the 8085's pin configuration and summarize each pin function.

2-4

8085 Pin Configuration

Figure 2-17 is the pin configuration of the 8085, and a summary of each pin is as follows:

A_8–A_{15}.   These are address pins that furnish the eight most significant bits of a memory address or an 8-bit I/O address, whichever is being addressed by the MPU. These address pins are tristated and are put in the high-Z state during hold (DMA) or halt operations.

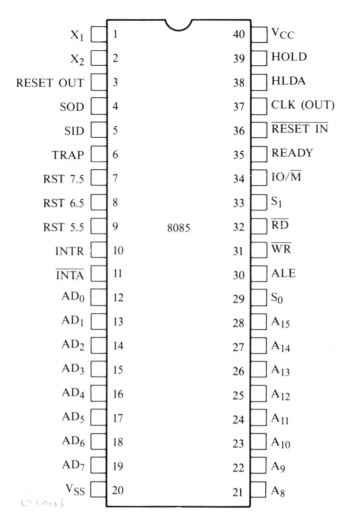

FIGURE 2-17. 8085 pin configuration. (Courtesy of Intel Corp.)

AD$_0$–AD$_7$. These eight pins function as multiplexed data/address pins and are also tristated. As previously stated, when used as address pins they have the lower-order byte of a 16-bit memory address or an 8-bit I/O address, whichever is being addressed. At other times, pins AD$_0$–AD$_7$ serve as data pins.

ALE (address latch enable). This is a tristated output used by the MPU to strobe the external latch being used to demultiplex the address/data pins AD$_0$–AD$_7$. It can also be used to latch the data bus status off pins S$_0$ and S$_1$. The strobe pulse output on pin ALE is generated by the MPU during T$_1$ of each machine cycle and therefore indicates the beginning of a machine cycle. During a hold or halt, this pin is put by the MPU in the high-Z state.

S$_0$, S$_1$ (data bus status). These outputs indicate the status of the data bus for the MPU's use for each machine cycle. S$_1$ can be used as an advance read/

write status by those devices requiring setup time when being accessed (addressed).

$\overline{\text{RD}}$ **(read).** This is a tristate output and provides primary timing for the MPU's read operation (memory or I/O). During the time interval while $\overline{\text{RD}}$ is low, the MPU latches the data byte present on the system's data bus, via pins AD_0–AD_7. $\overline{\text{RD}}$ is put in the high-Z state during hold (DMA) and halt operations.

$\overline{\text{WR}}$ **(write).** This is a tristate output that provides primary timing for the MPU's write operations. During the time that $\overline{\text{WR}}$ is low, the MPU writes data on the system's data bus via pins AD_0–AD_7. $\overline{\text{WR}}$ is put in the high-Z state during hold (DMA) and halt operations.

IO/$\overline{\text{M}}$ (IO/memory). The logic level of this tristate output indicates whether the MPU is addressing I/O or memory for each machine cycle. When addressing I/O, the logic level is high, and when addressing memory, it is low. IO/$\overline{\text{M}}$ is put in the high-Z state for hold and halt operations.

Interrupts. The 8085 has *multilevel interrupts* (more than one interrupt request pin), which are INTR, RST 5.5, RST 6.5, RST 7.5, and TRAP. All except TRAP are *maskable;* that is, they can be enabled or disabled via software. We shall study these pins and their uses in greater detail in the following chapters.

$\overline{\text{INTA}}$**.** This output provides an acknowledgement of an interrupt request via the INTR interrupt request pin. Its use will be explained later.

HOLD (DMA). A device requesting a DMA is required to drive this input pin high. Upon the MPU's acknowledgment of the DMA's request, the MPU puts pins A_8–A_{15}, AD_0–AD_7, $\overline{\text{RD}}$, $\overline{\text{WR}}$, IO/$\overline{\text{M}}$, and ALE in the high-Z state in order that the requesting device may take control of the system's buses.

HLDA. The output of this pin signals an acknowledgment of a DMA request. While HLDA is at a logic 1 level, the DMA's requesting device may take control of the system's buses; hence HLDA is used to enable the DMA's requesting device to begin the DMA process.

$\overline{\text{RESET IN}}$**.** A low on this pin requests the MPU and the system to be reset. When the MPU acknowledges the reset request, the PC is reset (PC = 0000H), as well the interrupt enable flip-flop (to be studied) and HLDA.

RESET OUT. This output is used by the MPU to acknowledge a reset request and to reset the rest of the system.

READY. A logic 1 applied at this input pin by an addressed memory or I/O device indicates that the addressed I/O device or memory is ready to receive or transmit data from or to the MPU.

SID (serial input data). This input pin is used by the MPU to read a bit of data from an I/O device, such as when the MPU is reading data from a serial I/O device. The logic level of a data bit at this input pin is loaded into the most significant bit of the accumulator (register A) when instruction RIM (to be studied) is executed.

SOD (serial output data). The most significant bit of the MPU's accumulator (A) is output at this output pin when the instruction SIM is executed (to be studied).

X_1, X_2. These inputs are used to connect a crystal, which is the source for generating the clock pulse CLK and to provide timing for the CU.

CLK. The signal of this output pin is a clock pulse that can be used by the system's components if needed.

V_{cc}. This is an input pin used to connect a $+5$-V power supply.

V_{ss}. Ground.

2-5

Comparative Study of the 8080's MPU

Because of the popularity of the 8085's predecessor, the 8080, we believe that it deserves a brief comparative investigation. Also, because the 8080 was one of the first 8-bit microprocessors to emerge in the industry, the architecture of many newer 8-bit microprocessors is based on the 8080. The 8080 architecture and system configuration are illustrated in Figure 2-18. As seen from Figure 2-18a, the 8080 has basically the same architecture as does the 8085. The greatest differences are that the 8080 does not have (1) an on-board system controller, (2) an on-board clock, (3) serial I/O capability, (4) multilevel interrupt capability, (5) a multiplexed address/data bus, and (6) a single power supply.

We see from the Figure 2-18b that the 8080 requires two support chips, the clock (8224) and the system controller (8228). The 8080 and the two support chips of Figure 2-18b are known as the *8080 Primary Standard System*. From Figure 2-18b we see that the system controller (8228) controls usage of the system's buses via control bus control signals $\overline{\text{MEM R}}$, $\overline{\text{MEM W}}$, and so on, which are the same control signals generated by the logic gates of Figure 2-13. We also note that in addition to generating control signals, the 8228 acts as a data bus driver. The 8080 has a limited drive capability, hence the need for the data bus driver.

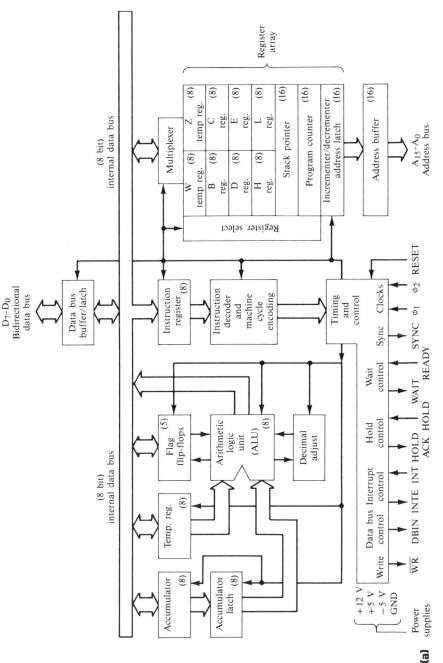

FIGURE 2-18. (a) The 8080 architecture. (Courtesy of Intel Corp.)

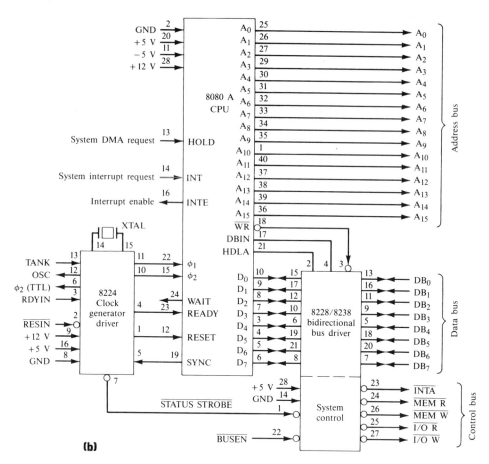

FIGURE 2-18 (cont'd). (b) Primary standard system. (Courtesy of Intel Corp.)

The primary timing signals $\overline{RD}$ and $\overline{WR}$ for the 8085 are DBIN (data bus input) and $\overline{WR}$ for the 8080. From Figure 2-18b the reader can see that the 8080 also has a HOLD pin, which means that it has DMA capability.

The reader should compare the bus architectures of the 8080 and the 8085 by comparing Figures 2-15 and 2-18b.

As for software, the 8080's instruction set is a subset of the 8085's. The 8085 can therefore execute all 8080 instructions and has two additional instructions (RIM and SIM) that deal with the 8085's serial I/O pins SID and SOD and its multilevel interrupt pins RST 5.5, RST 6.5, and RST 7.5. The jargon to describe the 8085's software compatibility with the 8080 is that the 8085 instruction set is *upward compatible* with the 8080's instruction set.

The object of Figure 2-18 is not to study the 8080 microprocessor and support chips but merely to illustrate the comparison between the 8080 and its successor, the 8085. The general similarities and differences are fairly obvious when one compares the architecture of the 8085 and the 8080, shown in Figures 2-14 and 2-18, respectively.

Summary

1. The 8085's MPU architecture contains a CPU, clock, system controller, DMA, interrupt control, serial I/O control, and data memory (scratch-pad memory).
2. The 8085's MPU architecture has three ways to address memory, each to address memory for a different kind of data, which are
   (a) a PC, which addresses memory for instructions.
   (b) a DC (register array), which addresses memory for general data.
   (c) an SP, which addresses a specific area of memory (the stack) for a specific kind of data—copies of the MPU's registers' contents and return addresses. Pushing and popping the MPU's registers contents on and off the stack are under program control via the instructions PUSH and POP. The MPU automatically pushes the return address on the stack as the result of an interrupt acknowledge, but popping it off requires the instruction RET.
3. When addressing I/O in an isolated I/O system, the 8085 provides a copy of the 8-bit address on pins AD_0–AD_7 and A_8–A_{15}.
4. The lower-order address pins are multiplexed with data lines AD_0–AD_7. The ALE enables the demultiplexing of these lines, as illustrated in Figure 2-15.
5. The 8085 has scratch-pad memory (register array).
6. Control bus control signals are generated from the primary control signals $IO/\overline{M}$, $\overline{WR}$, and $\overline{RD}$, as illustrated in Figure 2-13 and configured in the system as shown in Figure 2-15.
7. There are five condition flags.
8. The 8085's MPU is implemented with a 40-pin chip.
9. The 8085's MPU has an architecture similar to that of the 8080, and its instruction set is upward compatible with the 8080's instruction set.

REVIEW QUESTIONS AND PROBLEMS

1. Refer to data books that have architectural representations of the 6800 and Z-80 (also see the appropriate chapters of this textbook), and determine which function blocks of Figure 1-12 each contains.

2. What is the primary function of a CPU?

3. In regard to the architecture of a CPU, discuss those function blocks required, and briefly explain why they are necessary.

4. When one wishes a design to be able to isolate electrically its output, what is used to provide that isolation?

5. When the output of two or more registers is electrically connected to a common bus, why must each register have the ability to be electrically isolated from that bus?

6. Explain why the inputs of latches (registers) electrically connected to a bus do not require buffering.

7. What is the purpose of the data bus latch/buffer of Figure 2-7.

8. Using Figure 2-8, explain how the CU controls buffering of the system's data bus and the CPU's internal data bus.

9. In regard to Figure 2-7, discuss the events of an instruction fetch emphasizing the CU's role.

10. In regard to Figure 2-7, discuss the events of a data memory's read or write operations.

11. Using Example 2-1, determine the resultant logic state of the Z-flag.

12. For the following problems, determine the logic state of the Z-flag.:
    (a) $0011 + 0100$ (b) $0011 \wedge 0100$ (c) $0011 \vee 0100$

13. Using Figure 2-8 as a model, design the scratch-pad registers of Figure 2-11.

14. Using Figure 2-8(a) as a model, design the data/address buffer/latch of Figure 2-12.

15. What is the main difference between a memory-mapped and an isolated I/O system?

16. What is meant by an MPU register's being nonprogrammable?

17. Why must an addressed memory location or an I/O device determine the logic state of the READY pin?

18. The primary control signals of Figure 2-12 serve what function?

19. Discuss the MPU's wait state relative to the MPU's write operations.

20. What is the difference between a serial I/O and a parallel I/O, and how does the 8085's MPU architecture differentiate between them?

21. In regard to Figure 2-12, explain how DMA handshaking is accomplished.

22. Why is DMA handshaking necessary?

23. During a DMA, why must the I/O device control the system's buses, and how is it told that it can take control of those buses?

24. Using an oscilloscope, what is the simplest way to distinguish one MPU machine cycle from another?

25. How is the signal output at the ALE pin used by the system designer?

26. Explain why pins A_8–A_{15}, AD_0–AD_7, ALE, $\overline{RD}$, $\overline{WR}$, and $IO/\overline{M}$ are tristated and when are they put in the high-Z state.

27. Discuss the various means that the 8085's MPU has to address memory, emphasizing the difference in each method's purpose.

28. Using Figure 2-15 as a model, design the demultiplexing latch, using D-type flip-flops.

29. What registers in the 8085 are used for I/O addresses for
    (a) isolated I/O. (How many bits?)
    (b) memory-mapped I/O. (How many bits?)

30. Discuss the significance of primary timing signals $\overline{RD}$ and $\overline{WR}$ relative to the system's design use.

31. Compare the architectures of the 8080 and the 8085.

32. From Figure 2-18, compare the 8080 and 8085 bus configurations, and discuss your observations.

CHAPTER 3

Memory and I/O: Preliminary Concepts and Addressing

3-1

Introduction

In Chapter 2 we discussed the 8085 MPU architecture and the relationship of that architecture to the system's buses (address, data, and system control). The goal of this chapter is to integrate memory, I/O, and the buses into a system. We shall begin with some preliminary investigation of memory chips and I/O interface requirements and then study addressing techniques. The integration of these concepts will enable us to design a memory and an I/O system. In order to keep this chapter as straightforward and simple as possible, many important details, such as loading and timing, will be deferred to Chapter 4.

3-2

Memory

A system's memory is usually composed of two different types of memory chips, *read-only-memory* (ROM) and *read/write memory* (R/W). As implied by the name, a MPU cannot alter the contents of a ROM, because write operations are not to be performed; that is, the MPU performs only read operations on a ROM.

In contrast, the MPU may read or write to a R/W memory chip, thus requiring the MPU to be able to alter its contents. It is this ability, or inability, of the MPU to alter a memory chip's contents that determines its use in a system's memory. For instance, because a ROM's contents cannot be altered by the MPU, this enables ROM manufacturers to design ROMs so that their contents retention is independent of power. That is, once a ROM has been programmed, the power may be removed from the chip without losing its contents, which can be read when power is restored. Hence, the program that is the primary means of accessing the computer's hardware, known as the *monitor,* must be stored in ROM. This is necessary because on ''power-up'' the user must be able to communicate with the MPU, via its hardware (keyboard, disc, and so on), and because the monitor makes this possible, it must not be lost when the system is ''powered down.'' R/W memories are used in the system memory whenever the content of a memory location must be altered by either the MPU or an I/O device with write DMA capability.

Note the terminology used to describe a device (usually a memory chip) that does not lose its contents when power is removed. Such a device is described as being *nonvolatile.* All ROMs are nonvolatile, and some R/W memory chips are nonvolatile.

Read-Only Memory (ROM)

There are four types of ROMs: (1) mask ROM (MROM), (2) programmable ROM (PROM), (3) erasable programmable ROM (EPROM), and (4) electrically alterable ROM (EAPROM). Each has its own characteristic(s) that make one more suitable for an application than another, including cost and programming time constraints.

The mask ROM (MROM) derives the name from its manufacturing process. In manufacturing a semiconductor chip, a photomasking process is used, and in manufacturing an MROM, the manufacturer uses photomask to program its contents, thus making its contents an unalterable part of the chip. Manufacturers have a masking charge of approximately $2000, and in addition, a minimum quantity of chips must be ordered at approximately $5 to $20 each, depending on the quantity ordered. The buyer must supply the manufacturer with the data (program) to be stored in the MROM. Thus, if the buyer gives one bit of erroneous data to the manufacturer, the MROMs manufactured will be worthless, and a month of manufacturing time will have been wasted. Hence, MROMs are used for high-volume applications for which the MROM's contents are certain, which means MROMs are not suitable for the product design and development stage (programs are always being rewritten in these stages).

The programmable ROM (PROM) is manufactured so that it can be programmed by the user in the field, thus greatly reducing the turn-around time of programming a ROM, when compared with MROMs. This type of ROM is manufactured with a ''fuse'' in each memory cell, and the user can program a logic 1 or 0 by either blowing or not blowing the fuse. The fuses are in either the base or the emitter of the transistors forming a memory cell. The user inserts the PROM into a device known as a *PROM programmer* which ''burns'' the appropriate 1's and 0's into the PROM, as determined by the user, by forcing excessive current through those fuses to be blown. Like MROMs, once programmed their contents cannot be changed, but unlike MROMs, for small quantities they are much cheaper, and their programming time can be minutes rather than weeks. The expense of a PROM programmer relative to overall cost is minimal. PROMs are used for applications with low volume and when programming time must be short, such as in the design and development environment.

An erasable programmable ROM (EPROM) has the advantages of a PROM without the disadvantage of not being able to be reprogrammed. To erase the content of an EPROM, the user exposes the silicone chip to ultraviolet (UV) light for a few minutes via a quartz ''window'' that exposes the silicone wafer. Once the EPROM's contents are erased, it may be reprogrammed. An EPROM is programmed in much the same way as a PROM is, through devices known as *EPROM programmers* that program EPROMs according to the user's instructions. EPROMs are very popular, especially for low-volume, reusable applications, such as in development and design or for limited quantity production. This text will use mostly EPROMs in its design examples.

The electrically alterable ROM (EAPROM) is much like the EPROM except that it is altered electrically by the system rather than by ultraviolet light or an external device. However, unlike the EPROM, the EAPROM's write cycle is much longer (milliseconds) than its read cycle (microseconds). As a result, EAPROM's are used in applications in which data storage is infrequent and reading data from memory is the norm. Because of the infrequent data storage, some people call EAPROM's *read-mostly* memories.

In this chapter we shall approach ROMs from a generic point of view; that is, regardless of the type of ROM or its technology (TTL, MOS, and the like), they all appear basically the same in architecture, purpose, and method of accessing their contents. As previously stated, each memory location (ROM or R/W) is identifiable by a unique address, when memory addresses are supplied by the MPU's PC, SP, or DC, via the address bus (an exception is during a DMA, when the I/O device supplies the memory addresses). A memory chip must then have enough address pins to form the same number of unique addresses (binary combinations) as there are memory locations within the chip. For instance, if a memory chip has 8 memory locations, then 3 address pins are required ($2^3 = 8$), and if the memory chip has 1024 memory locations, then 10 address pins are required ($2^{10} = 1024$), as indicated by Equation (3-1).

$$2^n = \text{number of binary combinations} \qquad (3\text{-}1)$$

Figure 3-1 illustrates a 1K (1024 memory locations) memory by showing 10 address pins (A_0–A_9). There must also be output pins from which the contents of an addressed memory location can be accessed; that is, there must be a pin for each bit of a memory location. Figure 3-1 shows 8 such pins, labeled O_0 to O_7. Thus the ROM of Figure 3-1 has a capacity of 1024 memory locations, with each being able to store 8 bits of data. This is known as a 1K $\times$ 8 memory.

To complete the ROM chip of Figure 3-1, two more pins are required. One pin is needed to enable the chip ($\overline{CE}$) so that the address on the address pins is internally decoded, in order to select the addressed location. A second pin ($\overline{OE}$) is needed to enable the output buffers so that the addressed location can

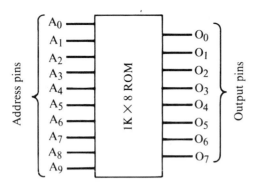

FIGURE 3-1. 1K × 8 ROM.

output its content at output pins O_0–O_7. These additional inputs are illustrated in Figure 3-2, from which we see that input $\overline{CE}$ enables not only the internal address decoder but also the output buffer's enable AND gate. The $\overline{OE}$ pin is needed because the ROM output pins are connected to the system's data bus, and to prevent bus contention they must be buffered with tristate logic. Some ROMs combine the $\overline{CE}$ and $\overline{OE}$ pin into a single pin, thereby enabling the internal address decoder and the output buffers at the same time. However, separating the functions of pins $\overline{CE}$ and $\overline{OE}$ allows the chip to operate more efficiently. That is, the internal address decoder of Figure 3-2 cannot decode an address instantly, and therefore there will be a delay time between the time when the address is applied to pins A_0–A_9 and when the addressed location is actually selected (accessed) by the internal decoder (known as *access time* t_{acc}). Once time t_{acc} has elapsed, the data is accessible and can be read from the addressed memory location by driving $\overline{OE}$ low, as indicated in the simplified timing diagram of Figure 3-2b. By separating the two functions, the internal decoder can be enabled before the output buffers are, thus fulfilling the chip's *address setup time* requirement. The chip also consumes less power, by enabling the output buffers only when needed. When just the internal address decoder is enabled, the chip consumes much less power than when the output buffers are also active.

Returning to Figure 2-16, we see in each machine cycle that the address is on the address bus approximately one clock period (T_1) before the MPU will read the data bus (the MPU reads the data bus when $\overline{RD}$ goes low). Then the memory chip's address decoder can be enabled before it enables its output buffers, by using the address to drive $\overline{CE}$ low at the beginning of the machine cycle and using $\overline{RD}$ (or $\overline{MEM\ R}$ of Figure 2-13) to enable $\overline{OE}$, which is approximately one clock period later.

R/W Memory (RAM)

We shall begin our discussion of R/W memories by explaining a misnomer that has become synonymous with the term *read/write*. The misnomer is *RAM*, which stands for *random access memory* and refers to the relatively constant access time of all memory locations within a memory chip. That is, if the access time is 500 nsec when addressing memory location 00H, then it will also be 500

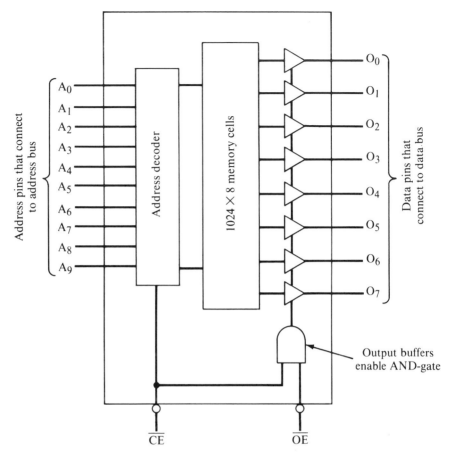

1K × 8 ROM architecture

(a)

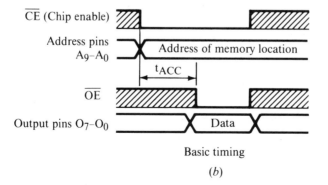

Basic timing

(b)

FIGURE 3-2.   1K × 8 ROM and basic timing.

nsec when addressing, say, location FFH. Hence, any location within the chip can be accessed *at random,* and the access time will remain the same. At this point the reader might be wondering what random access and read/write have to do with each other. For modern chip technology, the answer is nothing. Obviously ROMs are also RAMs, as their access time is the same for each memory location within the chip, even when the locations are selected at random. In contrast, storage media that have *serial addressing,* such as magnetic tape, do not have a constant access time for random addressing. If a tape is positioned at one end and then addressed for a location at its other end, the access time will be much longer than if the next address accessed is the next location on the tape. In earlier times, magnetic cores were used for the most common R/W memory. Magnetic core memories are random access read/write memories, and over the years the term *RAM* was mistakenly used as a synonym to describe its read/write characteristic. As a result, the term *RAM* has become synonymous with read/write (R/W), and in this textbook we shall follow this convention and use RAM to describe a R/W memory.

A typical RAM has the architecture represented in Figure 3-3, from which we see that there are eight address pins, and using Equation (3-1) we calculate there are 256 (2^8) memory locations. Also we see that there are eight data lines labeled IO_n. When input pin $\overline{CE}$ is driven to a logic zero, the address at address pins A_0–A_7 are decoded (selecting the addressed location), and AND gates R and W are enabled. Once the address has been internally decoded (t_{acc} has elapsed) and input $\overline{RD}$ is then driven low, the tristate buffers labeled O_n become active, and the content of the addressed location is loaded on the data bus via the IO pins. That is, the memory location is read. However, if input $\overline{WR}$ is driven low, then the tristate buffers labeled I_n will be activated, and the data on the IO pins will be written into the addressed memory location.

3-3

I/O Ports

As stated in Chapter 1, I/O devices are input and output devices used to communicate with the MPU, via the data bus, as illustrated in Figure 1-12. Let us broaden that definition by stating that an I/O device is any device that can be addressed by the MPU, via an address on the address bus, and is not a part of memory. Notice with this new and broader definition that for a device to be classified as an I/O, it simply must be addressable via the address bus and not be part of memory, but it need not be connected to the data bus, as are those I/O devices of Figure 1-12. An example of such an I/O device is an addressable flip-flop. The MPU can set or reset this flip-flop (to indicate some condition or status) by addressing the flip-flop's SET or RESET inputs via an address on the address bus. The output (Q) of this flip-flop is not tied to the system's data bus, as indicated in Figure 3-4. Also observe from Figure 3-4 that the flip-flop requires two I/O addresses, one for the SET input and the other for the RESET input.

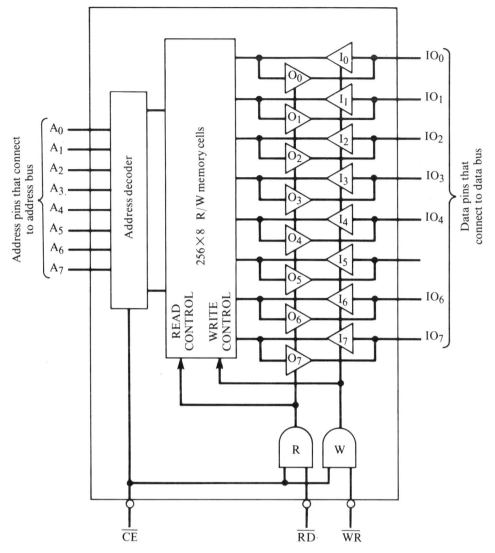

FIGURE 3-3.   1K × 8 R/W (RAM) memory.

Thus far we have discussed the I/O as a physical device. Let us now focus on the I/O's logical addressing aspect. In viewing Figures 1-12 and 3-4 we see that the I/O select lines simply do as their name implies: select the I/O device addressed by the MPU. When an MPU-based system is designed and manufactured for general use, such as a microcomputer, the manufacturer may not know every type of I/O device to be interfaced by the user with that system. But the manufacturer is aware that the user will want options for interfacing various I/O devices and so will make available to the user some I/O select lines. The user can use these lines to select those I/O devices needed to interface with the system. If the user is to interface I/O devices requiring the system's data bus,

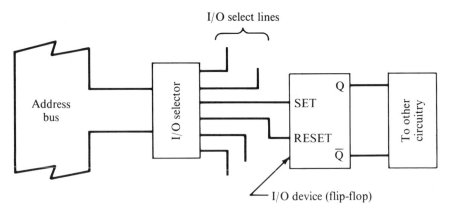

FIGURE 3-4. Example of an I/O device that is not connected to the data bus.

then the user must also supply the interface circuitry of Figure 1-12. The term that distinguishes between an I/O device and its logical address is *I/O port*. An I/O port describes an I/O address that is available for use. If an I/O port is used to activate the interface (buffer) of an input device to the system's data bus, it becomes an *input port*. But if the I/O port is used to activate the interface (latch) of an output device, it is termed an *output port*.

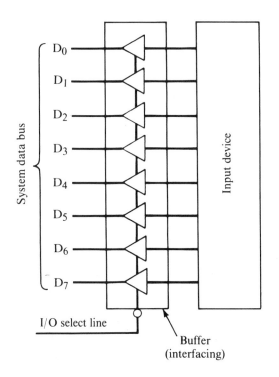

FIGURE 3-5. Interfacing an input device to the system.

Input Device Buffering

From Figure 1-12 and previous discussions of I/O devices, we know that some of the I/O ports available will be used as input ports when the input devices need the system's data bus. These input devices must be connected electrically to the data bus when being read by the MPU but must be otherwise isolated (buffered) from the data bus (in order to prevent bus contention). Their interfacing to the data bus will require tristate logic gates, as illustrated in Figure 3-5. When the MPU addresses an input port, its I/O select line goes low, thereby activating its tristate logic gates, which will electrically connect the input device to the data bus. When the MPU is not addressing an input port, its I/O select line is not active, and so the buffers are in a high-Z state and thereby isolate the input device from the data bus.

Output Device Latching

Return to Figure 2-16 and note that during M_3, beginning with the rising edge of T_2, the MPU has written data to the output port via the multiplexed pins AD_0–AD_7. Because this data is on the system's data bus for a short period of time, the output device must latch it. Figure 3-6 illustrates the concept that for

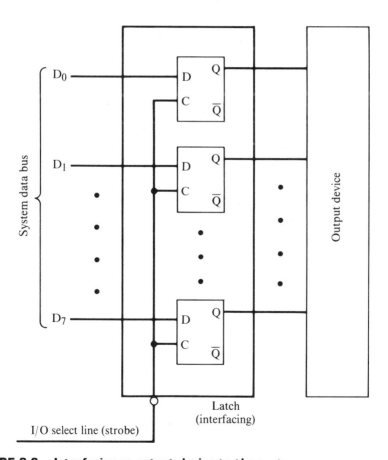

FIGURE 3-6. Interfacing an output device to the system.

a latch to latch a data byte off the data bus, the signal on its I/O select line is used as a strobe pulse to clock (at input C) the latch.

Addressing

To address either memory or I/O, both the address and the proper control signal (see Figure 2-16) must be present. The address selects the memory location or I/O port, whichever is being addressed, and the control signal provides the timing for the read or write operation.

We shall begin our study of addressing with the structure of the address bus. From our discussions of Figures 3-2 and 3-3, we know that every memory chip has an internal decoder that will decode the address on its address pins when $\overline{CE}$ is driven low and as a result will select the corresponding internal addressed memory location. Because there are many memory chips in a system and each is connected in parallel to the address bus, there are also many memory locations for the same *relative address* (the same address within each memory chip). That is, if there are five memory chips in the system, each with eight address pins (A_0–A_7) connected in parallel to the address bus, then there will be five memory locations (one per chip), corresponding to each of the 256 addresses. Thus, not only must the memory address select the location within the memory chip, but it must also select the chip with the desired memory location. Likewise, when addressing the I/O ports, the address on the address bus must select the addressed I/O port, which is similar to selecting a memory chip when addressing memory. We shall use the same technique in selecting I/O ports as when selecting memory chips.

There are basically two techniques to select (address) memory chips and I/O ports: (1) address decoding and (2) linear addressing.

Address Decoding

The address-decoding technique uses a decoder to decode an address on the address bus. The resulting active output is then used to select the addressed memory chip or I/O port. The I/O selector of Figure 1-12 illustrates the address-decoding technique, in which the I/O selector is implemented with a decoder and the outputs of the decoder are the I/O select lines. A decoder such as the one illustrated in Figure 3-7 can be used to decode an address on the address bus.

We see from the truth table of Figure 3-7 that if the input CE is high, the decoder will be enabled and will decode the logic levels at inputs A_0, A_1, and A_2. However, if CE is low, the decoder will be disabled, and regardless of the input's logic levels (X is a *don't care*), the outputs will be inactive (high).

Figure 3-8 illustrates the concept of decoding address bus address lines, in which the three address lines A_n, A_{n-1}, and A_{n-2} represent any three consecutive address lines. The blocks to be selected, which can be either I/O device interfaces or memory chips, are represented by blocks B_n. If A_n, and A_{n-1}, and A_{n-2} are at a logic low, then A_2, A_1, and A_0 will also be at a logic low, which makes output $\overline{O}_0$ low, as can be seen from the truth table of Figure 3-7. With

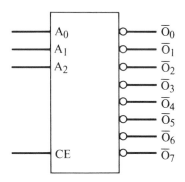

Truth Table

CE	A_2	A_1	A_0	$\overline{O}_0$	$\overline{O}_1$	$\overline{O}_2$	$\overline{O}_3$	$\overline{O}_4$	$\overline{O}_5$	$\overline{O}_6$	$\overline{O}_7$
1	0	0	0	0	1	1	1	1	1	1	1
1	0	0	1	1	0	1	1	1	1	1	1
1	0	1	0	1	1	0	1	1	1	1	1
1	0	1	1	1	1	1	0	1	1	1	1
1	1	0	0	1	1	1	1	0	1	1	1
1	1	0	1	1	1	1	1	1	0	1	1
1	1	1	0	1	1	1	1	1	1	0	1
1	1	1	1	1	1	1	1	1	1	1	0
0	X	X	X	1	1	1	1	1	1	1	1

FIGURE 3-7. Decoder.

$\overline{O}_0$ low (active) and the other outputs high (inactive), block B_0 is selected. If $A_n = 0$, $A_{n-1} = 1$, and $A_{n-2} = 0$, then $\overline{O}_2$ will be active and B_2 will be selected. Note that if CE were driven low, all outputs would be inactive (high), and none of the blocks of Figure 3-8 could be selected, regardless of the logic levels at inputs A_2, A_1, and A_0. Also note that because there are three inputs to the decoder (A_2, A_1, and A_0), there are 2^3 outputs, as indicated by Equation (3-1).

Figure 3-9 illustrates a memory system in which address decoding is used to select the addressed memory chip. Each memory chip has eight address pins (A_7–A_0), resulting in a memory capacity of 256 bytes for each chip. These address pins are connected in parallel to address bus address lines A_7–A_0, causing these address lines to select the same memory location within each chip, as indicated in Figure 3-9a. Address lines A_{10}, A_9, and A_8 are connected to the decoder inputs A_2, A_1, and A_0, respectively. Address lines A_{10}, A_9, and A_8 are decoded by the decoder and select the corresponding memory chip, as indicated

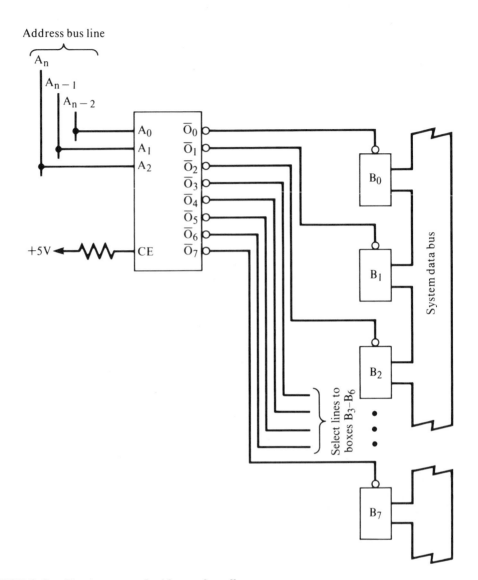

FIGURE 3-8. The concept of address decoding.

in Figure 3-9a. Address lines A_{15}–A_{11} are used to enable the decoder, via CE, and to prevent overlapping addresses, termed *foldback* (to be explained). NOR gate input IO/$\overline{M}$ will disable the page selector unless memory is being addressed (refer to Figure 2-16); that is, A_{15}–A_{11} and IO/$\overline{M}$ must be low in order to drive high the output of the NOR gate. When a memory address is on the address bus and if A_{15}–A_{11} all are logic lows, then the decoder will decode address lines A_{10}, A_9, and A_8 and so select the appropriate memory chip via the decoder output $\overline{O}_n$. That is, decoder output $\overline{O}_n$ will be driven low, as result of decoding the address, and thus enable the appropriate memory chip via its $\overline{CE}$ input. All memory addresses for Figure 3-9 are given in Table 3-1.

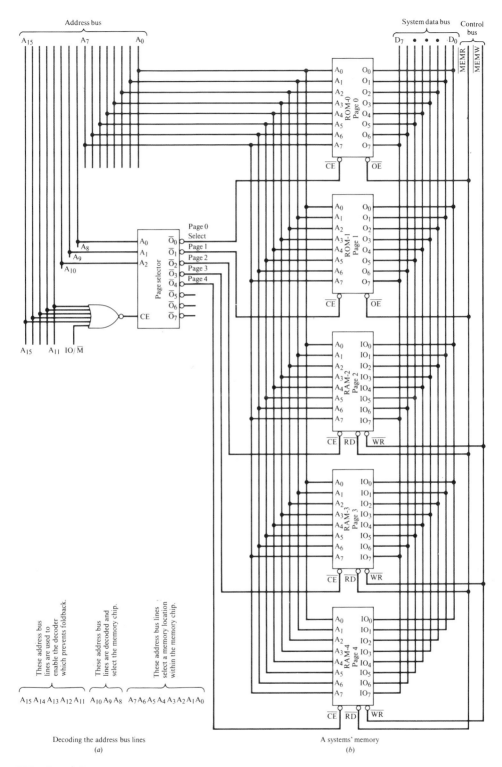

FIGURE 3-9. Absolute memory address decoding.

TABLE 3-1. Address Decoding for Figure 3-9.

Memory Address in hex	Page selected (A_{10}, A_9, A_8)	Prevents Foldback A_{15}	A_{14}	A_{13}	A_{12}	A_{11}	Page Select A_{10}	A_9	A_8	Memory Address Within Chip A_7	A_6	A_5	A_4	A_3	A_2	A_1	A_0
0 0 0 0	0	0	0	0	0	0	0	0	0	0	0	0	0	0	0	0	0
0 0 0 1		0	0	0	0	0	0	0	0	0	0	0	0	0	0	0	1
0 0 0 2		0	0	0	0	0	0	0	0	0	0	0	0	0	0	1	0
0 0 0 3		0	0	0	0	0	0	0	0	0	0	0	0	0	0	1	1
...				...				...				...					
0 0 F F		0	0	0	0	0	0	0	0	1	1	1	1	1	1	1	1
0 1 0 0	1	0	0	0	0	0	0	0	1	0	0	0	0	0	0	0	0
...				...				...				...					
0 1 F F		0	0	0	0	0	0	0	1	1	1	1	1	1	1	1	1
0 2 0 0	2	0	0	0	0	0	0	1	0	0	0	0	0	0	0	0	0
...				...				...				...					
0 2 F F		0	0	0	0	0	0	1	0	1	1	1	1	1	1	1	1
0 3 0 0	3	0	0	0	0	0	0	1	1	0	0	0	0	0	0	0	0
...				...				...				...					
0 3 F F		0	0	0	0	0	0	1	1	1	1	1	1	1	1	1	1
0 4 0 0	4	0	0	0	0	0	1	0	0	0	0	0	0	0	0	0	0
...				...				...				...					
0 4 F F		0	0	0	0	0	1	0	0	1	1	1	1	1	1	1	1

To understand Table 3-1, refer to Figure 3-9a. Table 3-1 shows that the memory addresses within each chip begin at 00H(hex) and end with FFH (256 locations), as illustrated in the A_7–A_0 columns. Address lines A_{10}, A_9, and A_8 select the *memory page*, as indicated by columns A_{10}–A_8 (the page select column). Address lines A_{15}–A_{11} must be low to prevent foldback. *Foldback* means that more than one address will address a memory location or I/O port; that is, addresses will fold back on one another. To understand foldback, imagine the NOR gate of Figure 3-9b removed and CE of the page selector is tied high, as in Figure 3-8. Under these conditions, address lines A_{15}–A_{11} are not used in addressing memory and therefore become "don't cares." With A_{15}–A_{11} acting as "don't care" address lines, then addresses 0000H, 0800H, 1800H, and F800H (as well as many others) will fold back on one another and address the same memory location, which for this example is memory location 00H of page 0. In fact, with address lines A_{15}–A_{11} acting as don't cares, there will be 2^5 (32) foldback addresses for each memory location within each chip, as can be verified by decoding all of the possible address combinations for address lines A_{15}–A_0 of Table 3-1.

Lastly, we see from Figure 3-9b that the control signal $\overline{\text{MEM R}}$ is used to enable the output for a memory read operation and that $\overline{\text{MEM W}}$ will latch the data byte on the data bus into memory for a memory write operation. Recalling the discussion on memory access time (t_{acc}) and the timing diagram of Figure 3-2b, we understand that the memory chip is enabled first and then the read or write operation is performed.

Address decoding for I/O ports is the same in concept as illustrated in Figure 3-8 and is similar to address decoding for memory as illustrated in Figure 3-9. The differences in address decoding for I/O ports, as compared with memory (Figure 3-9) are (1) the output of the decoder selects the I/O port, which then activates the I/O device interface, such as B_n of Figure 3-8 (note there are no address lines (A_7–A_0) connected to block B_n, as there are in Figure 3-9); and (2) as discussed in Chapter 2, I/O port addresses are 8 bits that are address mirrored on the 16-bit address bus via the 8085's registers W and Z.

Figure 3-10 illustrates the concept of I/O address decoding as implemented in Figure 3-8. The I/O port selector is a decoder that decodes an *I/O port number* (I/O address) on the address bus. In this system, only eight I/O devices are interfaced to the system; hence only three address lines ($2^3 = 8$) must be decoded (A_2–A_0). In order to prevent I/O address foldback, address lines A_7–A_3 are used (along with control signals) to enable the decoder via the NOR gate driving CE. The I/O read and write control bus control signals $\overline{\text{I/O R}}$ and $\overline{\text{I/O W}}$ are also used to enable the I/O port selector, as indicated in the timing diagram of Figure 3-11. This is allowable as there is no internal address decoder within the interface chips (buffers and latches), as there is in memory chips, and therefore there is not any access time to consider. This enables a read or write operation to occur at the same time that the address is decoded. As indicated in Figure 3-11 for I/O read operations, when $\overline{\text{I/O R}}$ goes active (see Figures 2-13 and 2-16), the addressed port select line of Figure 3-10 will also be driven low, thereby activating the addressed input buffer, which will then load a data byte from that input device on the data bus. For I/O write operations, when

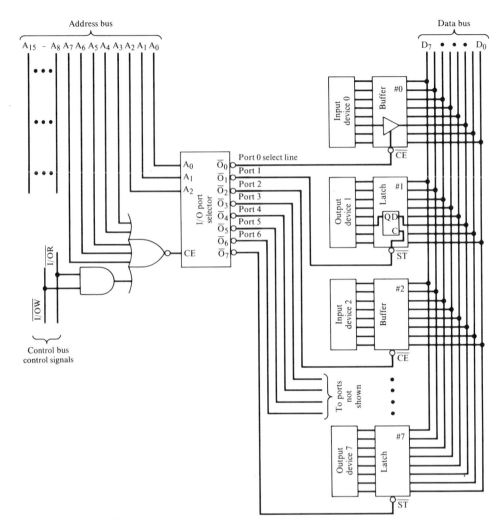

FIGURE 3-10. Absolute I/O address decoding.

$\overline{\text{I/O W}}$ goes low, the addressed port select line also goes low, which will cause the selected latch to latch the data byte that is on the data bus.

Figures 3-10 and 3-11 show only eight select lines, but if more are needed, a configuration such as Figure 3-12 can be implemented. Of course, a configuration similar to Figure 3-12 can be used to expand the page selector of Figure 3-9.

The decoders of Figure 3-12 are basically connected in the same way as the decoder of Figure 3-10 is, the difference being address line A_3. The logic level of A_3 selects decoder number 0 of Figure 3-12 when in the low state and decoder number 1 when in the high state.

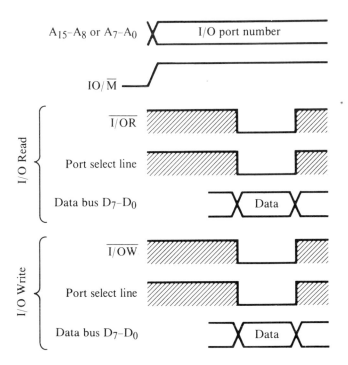

FIGURE 3-11. I/O timing diagram

Before concluding our discussion on address decoding, we shall integrate the memory system of Figure 3-9 and the I/O system of Figure 3-10, as shown in Figure 3-13. We believe Figure 3-13 to be basically self-explanatory, although we shall briefly discuss the I/O port selector's address lines A_8, A_9, and A_{10}. From Figure 3-10 we see that address lines A_0, A_1, and A_2 were used to select the addressed port. Recall that for I/O addressing in an isolated I/O system, address lines A_7–A_0 and A_{15}–A_8 are duplicates of each other. Therefore, address lines A_0 and A_8 have the same address bit, as do A_1 and A_9, A_2 and A_{10}, A_3 and A_{11}, and so forth. We have chosen to use A_8, A_9, and A_{10}, as in Figure 3-13, rather than A_0, A_1, and A_2, as in Figure 3-10, only for the convenience of drawing Figure 3-13.

Linear Addressing

Linear addressing is a technique that simplifies the hardware by eliminating the need for a decoder (the page selector for memory and the I/O selector for I/O). Rather than using a decoder to select the addressed device (either a memory chip or I/O interface), the address lines of the address bus are used. The concept of linear addressing is illustrated in Figure 3-14. The reader should compare Figures 3-8 and 3-14.

Figure 3-14 shows that if address line A_n is high, block B_0, which represents either a memory chip or an I/O device interface, will be selected, and if address line A_{n+1+M} is high, B_M will be selected.

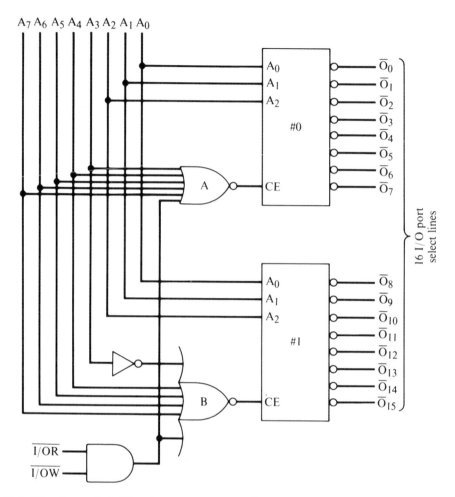

FIGURE 3-12. Expanded I/O selector.

Figure 3-15 is a specific example of linear addressing, in which address line A_8 ($A_8 = 0$) is used to select page 0. A_9 is used to select page 1, and so forth.

Linear addressing is convenient from a hardware standpoint, the cost being the loss of addresses. The reader should verify that linear addressing "wastes" addresses—be it memory or I/O.

We believe that now the reader can apply the concepts of linear addressing, as illustrated in Figure 3-8, to I/O. There will also be example applications of linear addressing in later chapters.

Memory-mapped I/O Addressing

Thus far, all addressing techniques discussed in this chapter have been of the isolated I/O variety, as can be verified by the control bus control signals of Figures 3-10 and 3-12. Recall from Chapter 2 that a memory-mapped I/O system

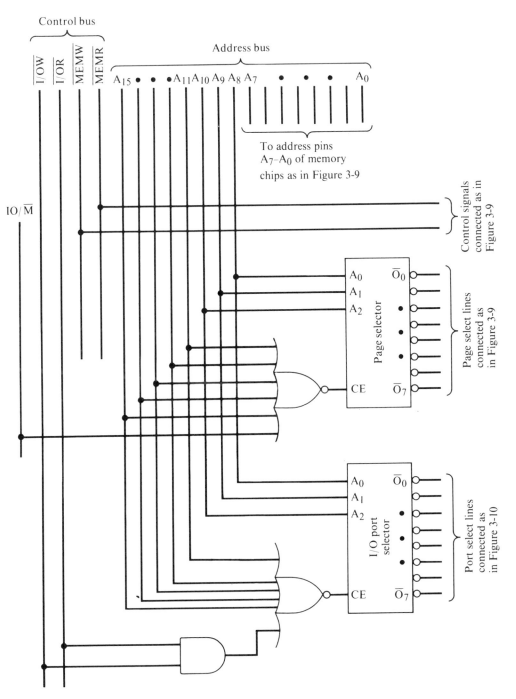

FIGURE 3-13.   Memory and I/O port addressing for an isolated I/O system with address decoding.

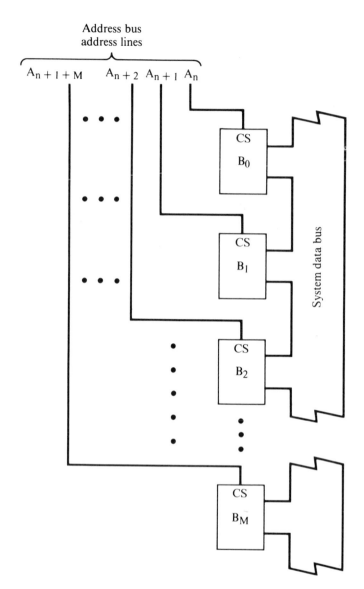

FIGURE 3-14. The concept of linear addressing.

was defined as a system that does not distinguish between memory and I/O in the software (there are I/O instructions such as IN or OUT, but they cannot be used). Because they cannot use I/O-related instructions, the control bus control signals $\overline{\text{I/O R}}$ and $\overline{\text{I/O W}}$ will not be generated, as can be seen in Figure 2-13 ($\text{IO}/\overline{\text{M}}$ will always be low when active). Because a memory-mapped I/O system does not differentiate between I/O and memory, the primary control signals $\overline{\text{RD}}$ and $\overline{\text{WR}}$ are sufficient control bus control signals. To change Figures 3-10 and 3-12 into memory-mapped I/O systems, one can replace the I/O control signals $\overline{\text{I/O R}}$ and $\overline{\text{I/O W}}$ with $\overline{\text{RD}}$ and $\overline{\text{WR}}$, respectively. The address bus ad-

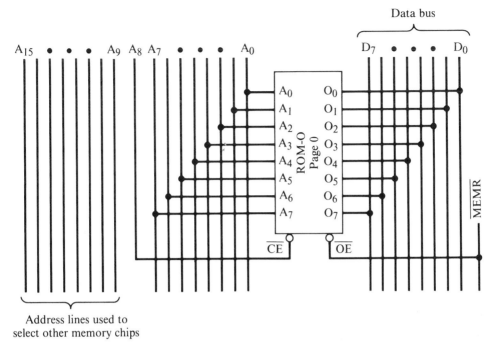

FIGURE 3-15. Linear addressing of page O.

dress lines must also be changed because (1) all sixteen address lines will now be used to address the I/O (recall that only 8 bits are used for I/O addresses in the isolated I/O system) and (2) I/O ports are treated as memory locations and therefore must be assigned memory addresses that are not assigned to memory.

For a concrete example of a memory-mapped system, let us redesign and integrate the isolate I/O memory system of Figure 3-9 and the isolated I/O system of Figure 3-10. We shall begin by constructing a memory map, which is shown in Figure 3-16. The memory map provides a quick visual reference of assigned memory addresses. The memory addresses for the memory map of Figure 3-16 are taken from Table 3-1. To determine the I/O port address, refer to Figure 3-17 and notice that address lines A_{12}, A_{13}, and A_{14} are used as inputs by the I/O selector. Hence these three address lines are decoded when addressing I/O ports. Address line A_{11} selects the selector by using linear addressing, a low for the page selector and a high for the I/O port selector. The page selector NOR gate prevents the memory addresses from folding back (overlapping) on the I/O port addresses (A_{14}, A_{13}, and A_{12}) or on any unused addresses (A_{15}). Note there is no need to input $\overline{IO/M}$ to this NOR gate (as in Figure 3-9), as all addresses are treated as memory addresses. The I/O NOR gate will, first, prevent address foldback on unused addresses (A_8, A_9, A_{10}, and A_{15}); second, prevent foldback on I/O addresses not assigned (A_7–A_0 are to address memory only) via the OR gate (3); and, third, enable the I/O port selector via the AND gate (2) when either $\overline{RD}$ or $\overline{WR}$ goes active and A_{11} is high. The reader should compare Figure 3-17 with Figure 3-13 and observe that the main difference between an

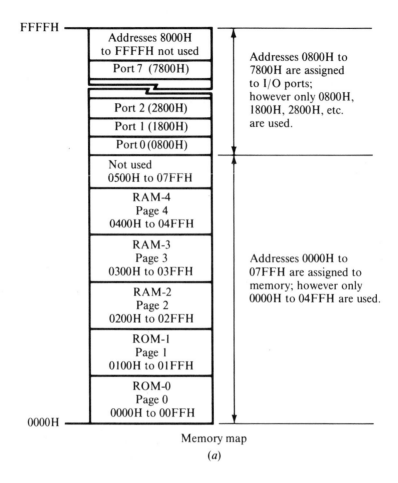

Memory map

(a)

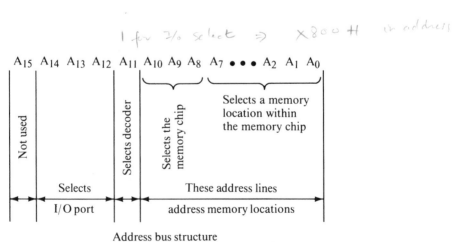

Address bus structure

(b)

FIGURE 3-16. Memory map and address bus structure for the redesign and integration of Figures 3-9 and 3-10 into a memory-mapped I/O system.

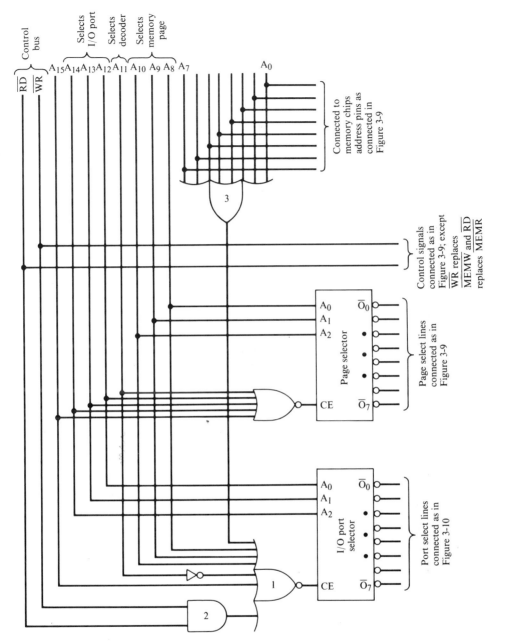

FIGURE 3-17. Memory-mapped I/O system corresponding to the memory map of Figure 3-16.

isolated I/O system and a memory-mapped I/O system is that a memory-mapped I/O system requires only primary control signals $\overline{RD}$ and $\overline{WR}$ to regulate usage of the system's data bus. Of course, memory mapping also requires a non-overlapping address assignment (between memory and I/O ports), and so A_{11} is used in the linear addressing mode.

The advantages of a memory-mapped I/O system are that the hardware requirements are reduced, thereby also reducing the system's chip count (eliminating the combinational logic of Figure 2-13). The memory-mapped I/O system also expands the instructions available for accessing I/O ports (recall that for the isolated I/O system, only two instructions are available: IN and OUT). The disadvantage is that physical memory locations are sacrificed for I/O port addresses. It is important that the reader fully understand this disadvantage, for if a system requires a large memory capacity, this can eliminate the use of a memory-mapped I/O design. We encourage the reader to verify the addresses that are lost, through the memory map of Figure 3-16.

3-5

Summary

This chapter has investigated memory chips and I/O interfacing. We categorized memory chips into ROM and R/W (RAM) and then studied how they are accessed. To access a memory chip, it must be chip enabled first, via an address on the Address Bus, and then either a read or write operation is performed, by activating either the $\overline{RD}$ or $\overline{WR}$ pin ($\overline{OE}$ for ROM). The proper timing for performing read and write operations is provided by control bus control signals $\overline{MEM\ R}$ and $\overline{MEM\ W}$ ($\overline{RD}$ and $\overline{WR}$ for memory-mapped I/O systems).

I/O devices require interfacing to the system's data bus. Interfacing is implemented using a buffer for input devices and latches for output devices. The appropriate interface (buffer or latch) is activated by a port select line.

There are two general addressing techniques, address decoding and linear addressing. Address decoding decodes an address on the address bus and then selects either a memory chip or an I/O port to use the system's data bus. Linear addressing uses the address bus's address lines to select either a memory chip or an I/O port, thereby eliminating the need for address decoders (page and I/O port selectors).

I/O port addresses use two system design techniques, isolated I/O or memory-mapped I/O. Isolated I/O systems separate memory from I/O in both software and hardware. The separation in the software is accomplished by the MPU's having instructions that address the I/O specifically (IN and OUT). The hardware separation is provided via separate control bus control signals ($\overline{I/O\ R}$ and $\overline{I/O\ W}$). Memory-mapped I/O systems do not differentiate between memory and I/O. The number of instructions that reference I/O are larger (than for an isolated I/O system) and more flexible; however, its address usage is not as efficient.

Memory maps are a visual method to refer to memory address assignments. Memory maps are valuable aids to both the system designer and the system user and should be provided for all system designs.

1. Discuss the advantages, disadvantages, and applications, of each type of ROM.

2. Define the term *nonvolatile*.

3. It was stated that there are nonvolatile RAMs. Describe the characteristics of a nonvolatile RAM and its application(s).

4. Why is it necessary to put the system's monitor in ROM rather than RAM?

5. Why is the term *RAM* a misnomer when used to describe a memory chip's read/write capability?

6. How does the number of address pins on a memory chip indicate that chip's memory capacity?

7. How can one determine the bit size of each memory location within a chip?

8. Define the term *access time* (t_{acc}), and explain what is responsible for it.

9. Why must the output or input/output of memory chips be buffered from the system's data bus?

10. Explain why a memory chip's chip enable pin is enabled before its output enable pin for ROM or its read/write pin(s) for RAM. Relate your answer to Problem 8.

11. What type of interfacing must be used to interface an input or output device to a system's data bus? Explain your answer.

12. Explain how the control bus control signals control memory and I/O.

13. Explain the difference between an I/O device and an I/O port.

14. In a general sense, what does the system controller control, and why is this control necessary?

15. Linear addressing and address decoding are two hardware-oriented classifications of addressing either memory or I/O ports. Discuss each technique, and describe the advantages and disadvantages of each.

16. Isolated I/O and memory-mapped I/O are two software-oriented classifications of addressing. Discuss each technique, and describe their advantages and disadvantages.

17. Explain why a system may be either an isolated I/O or a memory-mapped system using either linear or address-decoding techniques.

18. Design a 6K isolated I/O memory system with address decoding. The memory should have 2K of ROM and 4K of RAM, with both the ROM and RAM chips having eleven address pins. Assume each memory location is a byte in length and has the same architecture as shown in Figures 3-2 and 3-3. Provide a memory map for your design.

19. Answer Problem 18 using linear addressing.

20. Expand your design of Problem 18 to include five I/O ports.

21. Expand your design of Problem 19 to include five I/O ports.

22. Answer Problem 18 using a memory-mapped I/O system with five I/O ports.

23. Define the term *foldback* and show that it can exist in both memory and I/O, using your designs of Problems 18, 19, and 22.

24. Using the decoder of Figure 3-7, design an expanded selector (page or I/O) allowing sixty-four selections. Use a scheme similar to the one given in Figure 3-8, in which B_0, B_1, and B_3 are decoders.

25. Discuss the difference in timing between a scheme such as that given in Figure 3-12 and your design of Problem 24.

26. Redesign Figure 3-17 to be compatible with an 8080 MPU. Refer to Figure 2-18 for the 8080 MPU Primary Standard System.

CHAPTER 4

Memory and I/O Characteristics and an 8085 Primary Design

Introduction

Chapter 3 investigated memory and I/O addressing interfacing but not loading, interfacing of different technologies (TTL, MOS, and the like), or timing requirements. This chapter will study those topics. These details are essential because (1) the drive capability (the sinking and sourcing of current) of every chip is limited and must not be exceeded; (2) the voltage logic level of each chip within the system must be compatible; and (3) system timing is primarily derived from and established by the MPU, and so the system's components (memory, I/O interfacing, and so on) must be capable of operating properly within those time constraints.

8085 Electrical Characteristics

Figure 4-1 shows two blocks with connecting lines (1 and 2). The current I_1 is a representation of block B driving block A; that is, B is supplying the current requirement of A. For this current flow direction, block B is driving block A,

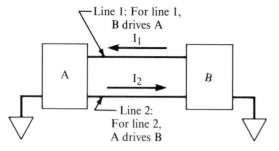

FIGURE 4-1. Current sinking and sourcing.

or block B is *sourcing* current I_1 (block B is the *source* of I_1), and block A is acting as a current *sink*. For line 2, block A is the source, and block B is acting as the sink (A is driving B). If the current flow direction of I_1 and/or I_2 were reversed, then the sink and sourcing roles of blocks A and B would also be reversed. Thus the current's direction determines whether a component is acting as the current's sink or source.

For components to be electrically compatible, their current requirements must be compatible for both direction and magnitude. That is, if blocks A and B have an electrical connection between them and both blocks are acting as current sources, as illustrated in Figure 4-2a, this type of connection will be incompatible and thus require an interface, as illustrated in Figure 4-2b. The interface of Figure 4-2b serves as a sink for the source currents of both A and B. In regard

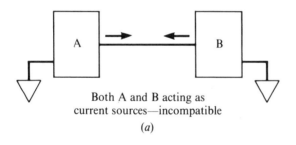

Both A and B acting as
current sources—incompatible

(*a*)

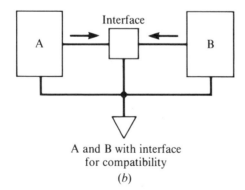

A and B with interface
for compatibility

(*b*)

FIGURE 4-2. The concept of sourcing and sinking incompatibility.

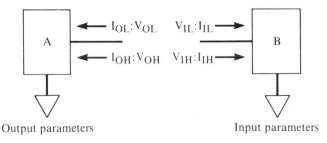

Output parameters   Input parameters

FIGURE 4-3. Voltage and current notation.

to magnitude and direction compatibility, whatever are the current requirements of one block the other must be capable of handling, otherwise interfacing is required.

Figure 4-3 illustrates the convention of labeling currents and their corresponding voltages. All currents are labeled I and voltages V, with subscripts that indicate whether they are input (I) or output (O), as well as their logic level (H or L). Hence, I_{OL} is an output (O) current for the logic low (L) state, and its corresponding voltage is V_{OL}. Notice from Figure 4-3 that all currents are represented as being sinked by the blocks, regardless of whether they are input or output. The data sheet for the device (block A or B) will indicate the specific magnitudes and directions of these currents. If the current direction agrees with the direction of Figure 4-3, it will be given as a positive value in the data sheet, otherwise it is a negative value. For instance, if $I_{OL} = -1$ mA then block A can source 1 mA of current when its ouput is in the logic low state.

Table 4-1 lists the 8085A's electrical characteristics. When an 8085 output pin is in a logic-low state (V_{OL}), its maximum voltage is 0.45 V, and that pin can sink (I_{OL} is positive) up to 2 mA of current. When an output pin is a logic high (V_{OH}), it has a guaranteed minimum of 2.4 V and will source (I_{OH} is negative) up to 400 μA. The corresponding currents (I_{IL} and I_{IH}) of the input voltages V_{IL} and V_{IH} are not listed. This is because the inputs are MOS, and so they ideally have zero input current, regardless of their logic level (MOS

TABLE 4-1. 8085A Electrical Specifications*

Symbol	Parameter	Min.	Max.	Units	Test Conditions
V_{IL}	Input Low Voltage	-0.5	$+0.8$	V	
V_{IH}	Input High Voltage	2.0	$V_{CC}+0.5$	V	
V_{OL}	Output Low Voltage		0.45	V	$I_{OL} = 2mA$
V_{OH}	Output High Voltage	2.4		V	$I_{OH} = -400\mu A$
I_{CC}	Power Supply Current		170	mA	
I_{IL}	Input Leakage		± 10	μA	$0 \leqslant V_{IN} \leqslant V_{CC}$
I_{LO}	Output Leakage		± 10	μA	$0.45V \leqslant V_{out} \leqslant V_{CC}$
V_{ILR}	Input Low Level, RESET	-0.5	$+0.8$	V	
V_{IHR}	Input High Level, RESET	2.4	$V_{CC}+0.5$	V	
V_{HY}	Hysteresis, RESET	0.25		V	

D.C. CHARACTERISTICS ($T_A = 0°C$ to $70°C$, $V_{CC} = 5V \pm 5\%$, $V_{SS} = 0V$; unless otherwise specified)
*Courtesy of Intel Corp.

devices should not require current to operate). Any existing current is due to leakage, which is labeled I_{IL} in Table 4-1, with the subscript IL representing input leakage. Because I_{IL} = + or − 10 μA, an 8085A input can sink (+) or source (−) 10 μA of leakage current. Table 4-1 also provides a leakage current value for output pins (I_{LO}). I_{LO} will be of little interest, however, as we are given I_{OL} and I_{OH}, and any additional leakage current is negligible. These electrical characteristics will be used when interfacing other components to the 8085, which we shall do later in this chapter.

4-3

8085 Timing Characteristics

As we stated, much of the system's timing is derived from the MPU's timing characteristics. The 8085 MPU receives its timing via input pins X_1 and X_2 (see Figures 2-14 and 2-17). Figure 4-4 illustrates the various methods used for driving input pins X_1 and X_2; however, this textbook will assume that a crystal is used, as it is the more stable.

The driving frequency of inputs X_1 and X_2 is determined by the MPU's operating speed. There is a minimum and maximum frequency (pulse repetition rate) on which the 8085 can operate, and it is the enhancement of operating

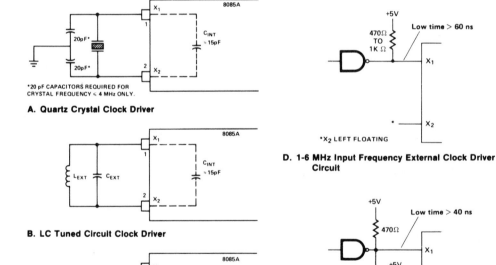

A. Quartz Crystal Clock Driver

B. LC Tuned Circuit Clock Driver

C. RC Circuit Clock Driver

D. 1-6 MHz Input Frequency External Clock Driver Circuit

E. 1-10 MHz Input Frequency External Clock Driver Circuit

FIGURE 4-4. Methods for driving the clock inputs X_1 and X_2. (Courtesy of Intel Corp.)

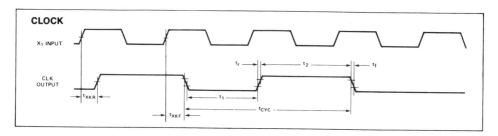

FIGURE 4-5. External driving frequency and resultant internal and output clock frequency. (Courtesy of Intel Corp.)

frequency that differentiates one type of 8085 from another. For instance, the 8085A operates at a maximum frequency of 3 MHz, and the 8085A-2 can operate at 5 MHz. All versions of the 8085 divide the input frequency of X_1 and X_2 by a factor of 2, which is illustrated in Figure 4-5. The clock signal of Figure 4-5 is output at pin 37 (CLK) of Figure 2-17 and is the same internal clock signal as those of Figures 2-16 and 4-5. From Figure 4-5 we see that a clock period is labeled t_{CYC}, and from Table 4-2 we find that the 8085A's operating range for t_{CYC} is from 320 nsec to 2000 nsec, which is a minimum of 0.5 MHz and a maximum of 3.125 MHz. To operate the 8085A at its max-

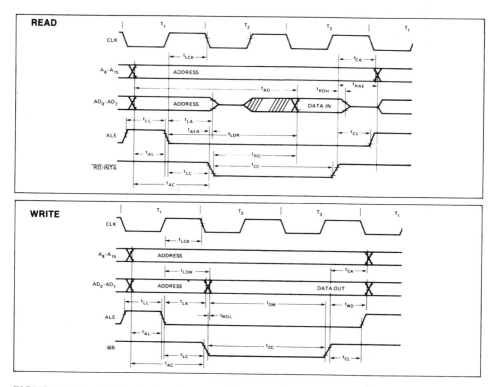

FIGURE 4-6. 8085 timing diagrams for read and write operations. (Courtesy of Intel Corp.)

TABLE 4-2. 8085 Timing Characteristics*

Symbol	Parameter	8085A Min.	8085A Max.	8085A·2 Min.	8085A·2 Max.	Units
t_{CYC}	CLK Cycle Period	320	2000	200	2000	ns
t_1	CLK Low Time (Standard CLK Loading)	80		40		ns
t_2	CLK High Time (Standard CLK Loading)	120		70		ns
t_r, t_f	CLK Rise and Fall Time		30		30	ns
t_{XKR}	X_1 Rising to CLK Rising	30	120	30	100	ns
t_{XKF}	X_1 Rising to CLK Falling	30	150	30	110	ns
t_{AC}	A_{8-15} Valid to Leading Edge of Control	270		115		ns
t_{ACL}	A_{0-7} Valid to Leading Edge of Control	240		115		ns
t_{AD}	A_{0-15} Valid to Valid Data In		575		350	ns
t_{AFR}	Address Float After Leading Edge of READ ($\overline{INTA}$)		0		0	ns
t_{AL}	A_{8-15} Valid Before Trailing Edge of ALE	115		50		ns
t_{ALL}	A_{0-7} Valid Before Trailing Edge of ALE	90		50		ns
t_{ARY}	READY Valid from Address Valid		220		100	ns
t_{CA}	Address (A_{8-15}) Valid After Control	120		60		ns
t_{CC}	Width of Control Low ($\overline{RD}$, $\overline{WR}$, $\overline{INTA}$) Edge of ALE	400		230		ns
t_{CL}	Trailing Edge of Control to Leading Edge of ALE	50		25		ns
t_{DW}	Data Valid to Trailing Edge of $\overline{WRITE}$	420		230		ns
t_{HABE}	HLDA to Bus Enable		210		150	ns
t_{HABF}	Bus Float After HLDA		210		150	ns
t_{HACK}	HLDA Valid to Trailing Edge of CLK	110		40		ns
t_{HDH}	HOLD Hold Time	0		0		ns

imum speed (3.125 MHz), a crystal frequency of 6.250 MHz (twice the internal clock frequency) is required.

Figure 4-6 presents timing diagrams for an 8085 read and write operation. Values for each type of 8085, such as the 8085A, 8085-2, and 8085AH-1, are found in a data table supplied by the manufacturer, and Table 4-2 is just such a table for the 8085A and 8085A-2. We shall not study all the timing parameters of Figure 4-6 but only those needed to ensure proper timing for most memory chips and I/O interfaces.

Before studying the timing details of Figure 4-6, let us take note of some of the conventions used. To sample these conventions, we can view just the address/data pins AD_0–AD_7 of the read timing diagram, for these conventions apply to all pins or bus lines. A crossover, which forms an ''X'', such as at the beginning of t_{AC}, is a *general* representation, which means that the logic level of each pin or line indicated may be in transition from one logic level to another. The lines at the top and bottom of the X means that the logic level of some pins or lines may remain the same during this transitional time. For instance, if AD_0–AD_7 were outputting 10110110 before time t_{AC} and then were changed to 10110001 at the beginning of t_{AC}, the X in the timing diagram would

TABLE 4-2.   Continued

Symbol	Parameter	8085A Min.	8085A Max.	8085A·2 Min.	8085A·2 Max.	Units
t_{HDS}	HOLD Setup Time to Trailing Edge of CLK	170		120		ns
t_{INH}	INTR Hold Time	0		0		ns
t_{INS}	INTR, RST, and TRAP Setup Time to Falling Edge of CLK	160		150		ns
t_{LA}	Address Hold Time After ALE	100		50		ns
t_{LC}	Trailing Edge of ALE to Leading Edge of Control	130		60		ns
t_{LCK}	ALE Low During CLK High	100		50		ns
t_{LDR}	ALE to Valid Data During Read		460		270	ns
t_{LDW}	ALE to Valid Data During Write		200		120	ns
t_{LL}	ALE Width	140		80		ns
t_{LRY}	ALE to READY Stable		110		30	ns
t_{RAE}	Trailing Edge of $\overline{READ}$ to Re-Enabling of Address	150		90		ns
t_{RD}	$\overline{READ}$ (or $\overline{INTA}$) to Valid Data		300		150	ns
t_{RV}	Control Trailing Edge to Leading Edge of Next Control	400		220		ns
t_{RDH}	Data Hold Time After $\overline{READ}$ $\overline{INTA}$	0		0		ns
t_{RYH}	READY Hold Time	0		0		ns
t_{RYS}	READY Setup Time to Leading Edge of CLK	110		100		ns
t_{WD}	Data Valid After Trailing Edge of $\overline{WRITE}$	100		60		ns
t_{WDL}	LEADING Edge of WRITE to Data Valid		40		20	ns

A.C. CHARACTERISTICS (T_A = 0°C to 70°C, V_{CC} = 5V ± 5%, V_{SS} = 0V)
*Courtesy of Intel Corp.

represent the logic-level transition of those bits that changed (the last 3 bits), and the lines above and below the X, would represent those bits that did not change (the first 5 bits). The horizontal straight line between the logic 1 and 0 level (indicating no logic level) represents when the pins are in the high-Z state, which is shown at the end of t_{LA}. The hatched lines just after the Hi-Z representation show the condition when unknown or unspecified logic levels are being output.

Timing Requirement for Demultiplexing Address/Data Pins AD_0–AD_7

From Figure 2-15 we know that a latch must be used to demultiplex pins AD_0–AD_7 and that the output of ALE will provide the latching pulse. What we must determine now is when the latching should occur relative to the timing of ALE and when the lower byte of the address will be on pins AD_0–AD_7. From Figure 4-6 we see that the lower byte of the address is not stable on pins AD_0–AD_7 until after the positive edge (0 to 1) of ALE; thus the negative edge (1 to 0) of ALE must be used as the latching signal. Later in this chapter when we choose a latch to demultiplex pins AD_0–AD_7 we will choose an octal latch with a negative edge trigger (see Figure 4-26).

Read Operation Timing. When an 8085 is performing a read operation, whether its memory or I/O, the MPU's timing is the same. First, the 8085 addresses the device, via the address bus, and then the addressed device must load its data byte on the data bus and hold it there over the time interval that the MPU will be latching (reading) data from the data bus, which occurs on the positive edge of T_3. From Chapter 3 we understand that the control bus control signals ($\overline{\text{MEM R}}$ and $\overline{\text{I/O R}}$ for isolated I/O or $\overline{\text{RD}}$ for memory-mapped I/O) provide proper timing for memory and I/O read operations (review the timing diagrams of Figures 3-2 and 3-11 and the control signals of Figure 3-17). Whereas the control signals provide the necessary timing, the primary control signal $\overline{\text{RD}}$ is the timing source for all read operations (refer to Figure 2-13).

According to the READ timing diagram of Figure 4-6, the first major event is the 8085 outputting an address via pins AD_0–AD_7 and A_8–A_{15}. All else is referenced to that event. Then, t_{AC} sec after an address is output, the 8085 drives its $\overline{\text{RD}}$ pin low, which either directly (memory-mapped I/O) or indirectly (isolated I/O) is used to enable the output buffer of the addressed device (refer to Figures 3-2, 3-3, and 3-5), thus loading a data byte on the data bus. The data byte must be on the data bus by t_{AD} sec (as indicated by the label DATA IN), which is approximately t_{RD} sec from the time $\overline{\text{RD}}$ was driven low. We can reason why the data byte must be on the data bus during the interval labeled DATA IN, by viewing the CLK timing during this interval. CLK provides internal timing for the MPU and the MPU's CU uses the positive edge (0 to 1) of T_3 to latch the data byte on the data bus into the data/address buffer/latch (see Figure 2-12). Therefore, the data byte must be on the data bus and be stable when the positive edge of T_3 occurs. The reader might wonder, "Does the data byte being read by the MPU have to be on the data bus exactly t_{RD} sec from the time $\overline{\text{RD}}$ went low (t_{AD} sec after the address was loaded on the address bus)?" The answer to this question is no, the data byte may be loaded on the data bus before t_{RD} sec have elapsed, as long as t_{AC} sec have elapsed since the address was output. This is permissible, as pins AD_0–AD_7 are not being used for any particular purpose in the time interval t_{AD}–t_{AC}, and therefore the data byte may be loaded on the data bus in this "idle" interval. However, note that the data byte will be unstable until t_{RD} has elapsed, as the 8085 is outputting some unknown (and meaningless) data for portions of this interval—thus there could be bus contention during this time. But this bus contention presents no problem, as there are no devices latching data from the data bus.

Figure 4-6 shows that the data byte may be loaded on the data bus t_{AC} sec from when the address is output on the address bus but must be present by the time t_{RD} sec have elapsed from when $\overline{\text{RD}}$ went low. The reader should understand that if erroneous data is on the data bus when the positive edge of T_3 appears, the MPU will latch it and treat it as if it were valid data. Therefore, the system designer must check the "speed" of all devices to be read by the MPU to make certain they are compatible with the 8085, by being fast enough to load their data on the data bus by t_{AD} sec, and if not, the designer must use the READY pin. We shall consider "slow" devices later in this chapter.

Write Operation Timing. A write operation by the MPU requires the 8085 to output a data byte on the data bus, via pins AD_0–AD_7, at some specified time, and during that time the addressed device (memory or I/O) must latch that data off the data bus. Figure 4-6 gives the WRITE timing parameters for the 8085.

As with read operations, a primary control signal will serve as the timing source for write operation control, and for a write operation, it is $\overline{WR}$. As seen from Figure 4-6, $\overline{WR}$ goes active t_{AC} sec from the time the 8085 outputs the device's address. At approximately the same time $\overline{WR}$ goes low, the 8085 outputs the data byte at pins AD_0–AD_7. The data byte is held on data pins AD_0–AD_7 for the duration of $\overline{WR}$'s being low (t_{CC} sec) plus approximately t_{WD} sec. Because the data is present and stable on the data bus when the positive edge (0 to 1) of $\overline{WR}$ occurs (data is not stable on the negative edge), the positive edge of $\overline{WR}$ can serve (directly or indirectly) as a strobe for the latch of the addressed device (review Figures 3-3, 3-6, 3-9, 3-10, and 3-17). If the device being strobed by the positive edge of $\overline{WR}$ has a delay time from when strobed until when latching actually occurs, the write delay time (t_{WD}) will provide a timing margin.

In conclusion, the primary timing signal $\overline{WR}$ will either directly (memory-mapped I/O) or indirectly (isolated I/O) provide the timing for all 8085 write operations. The positive edge of $\overline{WR}$ will serve as a latch strobe pulse. When time delays (propagation delays) are involved, there is a safety margin, as the data is held on the data bus by the 8085 for t_{WD} sec after the positive edge of $\overline{WR}$. If the device being written to by the 8085 is too "slow," even with timing margin t_{WD}, then the 8085's READY pin can be utilized.

4-4

ROM Electrical and Timing Characteristics

When integrating a ROM (or any other device) into a microprocessor-based system, we must (1) be certain that the voltage levels are compatible for both logic levels, (2) ensure that the ROM currents are compatible with the system, (3) buffer the outputs if not done so by the ROM (to prevent bus contention), and (4) determine the access time so that if the ROM is too slow, the 8085s READY pin can be utilized. Items 1 and 2 will be determined by the electrical characteristics, and item 4 from the timing characteristics. Item 3 is determined from the data sheets (most, if not all, memories have on-board buffers).

Figure 4-7 is a general description of Intel's 2716, as reproduced from an Intel data catalog. From Figure 4-7 we see that the 2716 has 16K bits arranged in a 2K × 8 (2K bytes) fashion. We also see there are various versions of the 2716 (2716-1, 2716-2, and the like), which have different access times. The power dissipation when active is 525 mW ($\overline{OE}$ and $\overline{CE}$ are low; refer to Section 3-2 and Figure 3-2) and 132 mW in the standby mode ($\overline{CE}$ = H and $\overline{OE}$ = X). From the pin configuration it is seen that the 2716 and 2732A are pin compatible, but notice that a system design change is necessary, as pin 21 of the 2732A is an address pin. Pins 20 and 18 of the 2716 have a dual function.

2716*
16K (2K x 8) UV ERASABLE PROM

- **Fast Access Time**
  - **2716-1: 350 ns Max.**
  - **2716-2: 390 ns Max.**
  - **2716: 450 ns Max.**
  - **2716-5: 490 ns Max.**
  - **2716-6: 650 ns Max.**
- **Single +5V Power Supply**
- **Low Power Dissipation**
  - **Active Power: 525 mW Max.**
  - **Standby Power: 132 mW Max.**

- **Pin Compatible to Intel 2732A EPROM**
- **Simple Programming Requirements**
  - **Single Location Programming**
  - **Programs with One 50 ms Pulse**
- **Inputs and Outputs TTL Compatible During Read and Program**
- **Completely Static**

The Intel® 2716 is a 16,384-bit ultraviolet erasable and electrically programmable read-only memory (EPROM). The 2716 operates from a single 5-volt power supply, has a static standby mode, and features fast single-address location programming. It makes designing with EPROMs faster, easier and more economical.

The 2716, with its single 5-volt supply and with an access time up to 350 ns, is ideal for use with the newer high-performance +5V microprocessors such as Intel's 8085 and 8086. A selected 2716-5 and a 2716-6 are available for slower speed applications. The 2716 is also the first EPROM with a static standby mode which reduces the power dissipation without increasing access time. The maximum active power dissipation is 525 mW while the maximum standby power dissipation is only 132 mW, a 75% savings.

The 2716 has the simplest and fastest method yet devised for programming EPROMs—single-pulse, TTL-level programming. No need for high voltage pulsing because all programming controls are handled by TTL signals. Program any location at any time—either individually, sequentially or at random, with the 2716's single-address location programming. Total programming time for all 16,384 bits is only 100 seconds.

*Part(s) also available in extended temperature range for Military and Industrial grade applications.

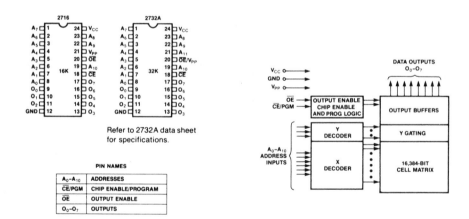

Figure 1. Pin Configuration   Figure 2. Block Diagram

FIGURE 4-7. General description of Intel's 2716 EPROM. (Courtesy of Intel Corp.)

As seen from Table 4-3, when the 2716 is being programmed ($V_{PP} = 25$ V), pin $\overline{OE}$ is driven to V_{IH} (high), and $\overline{CE}$ is pulsed. This and other mode selections are given in Table 4-3. The block diagram (architecture) of Figure 4-7 states that the 2716's outputs are buffered (tristate logic gates).

TABLE 4-3. 2716 Mode Selection*

Mode	Pins CE/PGM (18)	OE (20)	V_{PP} (21)	V_{CC} (24)	Outputs (9-11, 13-17)
Read	V_{IL}	V_{IL}	$+5$	$+5$	D_{OUT}
Standby	V_{IH}	Don't Care	$+5$	$+5$	High Z
Program	Pulsed V_{IL} to V_{IH}	V_{IH}	$+25$	$+5$	D_{IN}
Program Verify	V_{IL}	V_{IL}	$+25$	$+5$	D_{OUT}
Program Inhibit	V_{IL}	V_{IH}	$+25$	$+5$	High Z

*Courtesy of Intel Corp.

2716 Electrical Specifications

Table 4-4 gives the electrical specifications for the 2716. From an interfacing point of view, we are concerned with two general specifications: the input and output voltage levels and the sinking and sourcing of current. We must also determine which pins of the 2716 are connected to the pins of which device and then determine whether they are electrically compatible. Using Figure 3-9 as a model, let us form a simple block diagram that illustrates the pin connections of the various chips interfaced with the 2716. Figure 4-8 is a block-diagram representation of Figure 3-9 for a single 2716. A diagonal line with a number at the top indicates the number of wiring connections being represented.

Figure 4-8 illustrates that for the 2716, (1) address pins A_0–A_7 are driven by the address/data demultiplexer (the latch), (2) address pins A_8–A_{10} are being driven by pins A_8–A_{10} of the 8085, (3) the $\overline{CS}$ pin is driven by a page select line of the page selector, (4) $\overline{OE}$ is driven by $\overline{MEM\ R}$ (see Figures 2-13 and 3-9) for an isolated I/O system (or by $\overline{RD}$ for a memory-mapped I/O system), and (5) output data pins O_0–O_7 must drive pins AD_0–AD_7 of the 8085. Thus pins A_0–A_{10}, $\overline{CS}$, and $\overline{OE}$ are 2716 inputs that must be driven by the component indicated. We shall refer to Table 4-4 and determine the 2716 input electrical requirements to be met by these drivers. From Table 4-4 we find that 2716 driver must (1) supply a minimum of 2.0 V when an input is to be driven high

TABLE 4-4. 2716 Electrical Specifications*

Symbol	Parameter	Limits Min.	Typ.	Max.	Units	Test Conditions
I_{LI}	Input Load Current			10	μA	$V_{IN} = 5.25V$
I_{LO}	Output Leakage Current			10	μA	$V_{OUT} = 5.25V$
I_{PP1}	V_{PP} Current			5	mA	$V_{PP} = 5.25V$
I_{CC1}	V_{CC} Current (Standby)		10	25	mA	$\overline{CE} = V_{IH}, \overline{OE} = V_{IL}$
I_{CC2}	V_{CC} Current (Active)		57	100	mA	$\overline{OE} = \overline{CE} = V_{IL}$
V_{IL}	Input Low Voltage	-0.1		0.8	V	
V_{IH}	Input High Voltage	2.0		$V_{CC}+1$	V	
V_{OL}	Output Low Voltage			0.45	V	$I_{OL} = 2.1$ mA
V_{OH}	Output High Voltage	2.4			V	$I_{OH} = -400\ \mu A$

*Courtesy of Intel Corp.

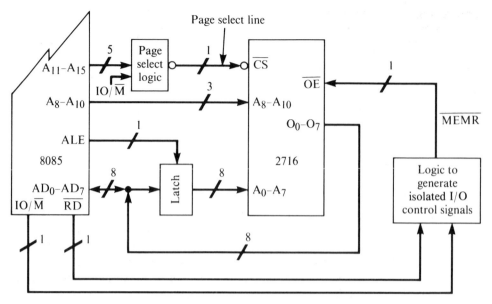

FIGURE 4-8. Block diagram of a 2716 interfaced to a system.

($V_{IH} = 2.0$ $_{Min}$), (2) supply a maximum of 0.8 V when an input is to be driven low ($V_{IL} = 0.8$ V_{Max}), and (3) require no more than 10 μA of current for an input, regardless of the logic level ($I_{LI} = 10$ μA). When the 2716 is the driver, the specifications from Table 4-4 state that the component being driven must (1) not require less than 0.45 V to represent a logic low at its inputs ($V_{OL} = 0.45$ V_{Max}) nor require more than 2.1 mA of sink current ($I_{OL} = 2.1$ mA) and (2) be able to interpret an input voltage level of 2.4 V, or greater, as a logic high ($V_{OH} = 2.4$ $_{Min}$ V) and require no more than 400 μA of source current from the 2716 ($I_{OH} = -400$ μA).

Because specific components have not been selected to implement the latch and page selector of Figure 4-8, we do not know their electrical characteristics, and therefore we can not check their compatibility with the 2716. However, we can compare the electrical characteristics of the 8085 and 2716 for compatibility.

Example 4-1

Compare the electrical characteristics of the 2716 and 8085 for compatibility when configured as represented in Figure 4-8.

Solution

We must compare the 8085's output parameters with the 2716's input parameters (the 8085 is driving the 2716) for address pins A_8-A_{10}. (*Note:* For a memory-mapped I/O system, $\overline{RD}$ would be driving $\overline{OE}$.) We must also compare the 2716's output characteristics with the 8085's input characteristics (the 2716 is driving the 8085) for pins O_0-O_7 and AD_0-AD_7. To compare the 8085's electrical output parameters with the 2716's input electrical parameters, we refer to Table 4-1 for the 8085 and Table 4-4 for the 2716.

8085 (Driver)	2716 (Driven)
$V_{OL} = 0.45\ V_{Max}$ $V_{OH} = 2.4\ V_{Min}$	$V_{IL} = 0.8\ V_{Max}$ $V_{IH} = 2.0\ V_{Min}$
$I_{OL} = 2mA$ $I_{OH} = -400\ \mu A$	$I_{LI} = 10\ \mu A\ max$

As we see from the two specifications, the 8085 will output 0.45 V maximum when outputting a logic 0, and the 2716 will interpret any input voltage equal to or below 0.8 V as a logic 0; hence, the two are voltage compatible for V_{OL} and V_{IL}. Next these same pins must be compared for the logic 1 state. The 8085 will output a minimum of 2.4 V for a logic 1, and the 2716 will interput any voltage equal to or greater than 2.0 V as a logic 1; hence, the two are compatible for the logic high level (V_{OH} and V_{IH}). Because they are voltage compatible for both logic levels, the voltage requirements have been met.

Now we shall compare the 8085 (driver) and 2716 (driven) for current compatibility. The 2716 has a maximum of 10 μA of input load current I_{LI}, and because an 8085 output is capable of sourcing up to 400 μA ($I_{OH} = -400\ \mu A$) they are current compatible for the logic 1 state. In the logic low state the 8085 is capable of sinking up to 2 mA ($I_{OL} = 2$ mA), and the 2716 can source a maximum of 10 μA (I_{LI}); hence they are also current compatible for the logic 0 state. Note that the 2716's inputs are MOS and therefore are voltage controlled (ideally requiring no current), but as all devices deviate from the ideal, there will be a small amount of leakage. I_{LI} represents that input leakage current and may flow in either direction (sink or source), depending on the input potential. In conclusion, the 8085 and 2716 are directly compatible. ∎

2716 Timing Specifications

The timing diagram for the 2716 is provided in Figure 4-9, and Table 4-5 gives the values for the parameters of Figure 4-9. From Figure 4-9 we see that the time required by the 2716 to decode internally an address applied at pins A_0–A_{10} and to have the contents of that location output at pins O_0–O_7 is labeled access time t_{ACC}. The access time of a memory chip must be faster than the read time t_{AD} of the MPU. Table 4-5 indicates that the maximum access time for the 2716 is 450 nsec, and from Table 4-2 we find t_{AD} to be a maximum of 575 nsec for the 8085, which indicates that the 2716 is fast enough to be interfaced with an 8085. From Figure 4-9 we find that in order to achieve the fastest access time, $\overline{CE}$ must be low for least t_{CE} sec before t_{ACC} sec have elapsed. To show that this condition was met for previous designs, recall the addressing schemes of Chapter 3. When a memory chip is selected (using either address decoding or linear addressing), input $\overline{CE}$ is driven low at approximately the same time the address appears on the address bus (see Figures 3-9 and 3-15). There is a slight delay (approximately 15 nsec) in address decoding because of the propagation delay of the page selector, which is usually negligible. Table 4-5 states that t_{CE} is a maximum of 450 nsec, which means that if $\overline{CE}$ is driven low at its maximum allowed time (450 nsec), its going low will coincide with the address being

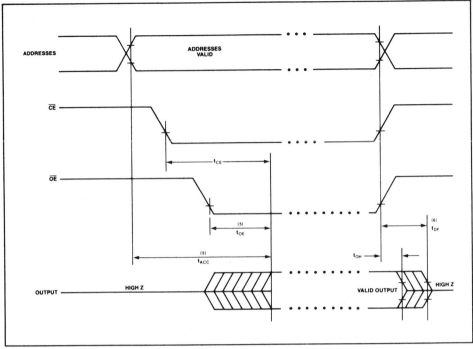

NOTES:
1. V$_{CC}$ must be applied simultaneously or before V$_{PP}$ and removed simultaneously or after V$_{PP}$.
2. V$_{PP}$ may be connected to V$_{CC}$ except during programming. The supply current would then be the sum of I$_{CC}$ and I$_{PP1}$.
3. Typical values are for T$_A$ = 25°C and nominal supply voltages.
4. This parameter is only sampled and is not 100% tested.
5. $\overline{OE}$ may be delayed up to t$_{ACC}$–t$_{OE}$ after the falling edge of $\overline{CE}$ without impact on t$_{ACC}$.
6. t$_{DF}$ is specified from $\overline{OE}$ or $\overline{CE}$, whichever occurs first.

FIGURE 4-9. 2716 timing diagram. (Courtesy of Intel Corp.)

applied to the address pins and hence equal the access time t$_{ACC}$. This is also the case for a linear addressed system and approaches that of address decoding. Thus for both addressing schemes, $\overline{CE}$ will be driven low at approximately its maximum allowable time, thereby allowing the fastest possible access time.

Turning our attention to the relationship between $\overline{OE}$ and t$_{ACC}$ of Figure 4-9, we see that when $\overline{OE}$ is driven low, there is a delay of t$_{OE}$ sec before the data is output at pins O$_0$–O$_7$. If t$_{OE}$ is greater than the 120 nsec specified in Table 4-5, the data will still be output at pins O$_0$–O$_7$ by the time t$_{ACC}$ sec have elapsed; however, power will have been dissipated needlessly. Recall from Chapter 3 and Figure 4-7 that the power dissipation jumps from 132 mW to 525 mW when $\overline{OE}$ becomes active. Therefore, in the interest of conserving power, but still achieving the fastest access time, $\overline{OE}$ should be driven low, as near t$_{OE}$ sec as possible (see note 5 of Figure 4-9). If $\overline{OE}$ is driven low t$_{DLY}$ sec later than that shown in Figure 4-9, as illustrated in Figure 4-10, there will be an increase in the overall effective access time (t$_{EFF}$). The same is true if driving $\overline{CE}$ low is delayed from that indicated in Figure 4-9; there would be a corresponding increase in the overall effective access time.

In conclusion, for the 2716 to be time compatible with the 8085, the access

TABLE 4-5. 2716 Timing Specifications*

Symbol	Parameter	Limits (ns)										Test Conditions
		2716		2716-1		2716-2		2716-5		2716-6		
		Min.	Max.	Min.	Max.	Min.	Max.	Min.	Max.	Min.	Max.	
t_{ACC}	Address to Output Delay		450		350		390		450		450	$\overline{CE} = \overline{OE} = V_{IL}$
t_{CE}	$\overline{CE}$ to Output Delay		450		350		390		490		650	$\overline{OE} = V_{IL}$
t_{OE}	Output Enable to Output Delay		120		120		120		160		200	$\overline{CE} = V_{IL}$
t_{DF}	Output Enable High to Output Float	0	100	0	100	0	100	0	100	0	100	$\overline{CE} = V_{IL}$
t_{OH}	Output Hold from Addresses, $\overline{CE}$ or $\overline{OE}$ Whichever Occurred First	0		0		0		0		0		$\overline{CE} = \overline{OE} = V_{IL}$

*Courtesy of Intel Corp.

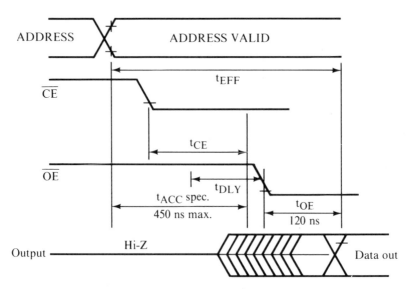

FIGURE 4-10. Demonstrating the effects of $\overline{OE}$ and t_{OE} on the effective access time t_{EFF}.

time (t_{ACC}) of the 2716 must be equal to or less than that of the 8085's read time (t_{AD}), which is expressed mathematically in Equation (4-1):

$$\left(ROM \right) \qquad t_{ACC} < t_{AD} \qquad \xrightarrow{8085's \ read} \qquad (4\text{-}1)$$

From Table 4-2 we see that t_{AD} = 575 nsec, and from Table 4-5 we find that the access time t_{ACC} for the 2716 is a maximum of 450 nsec. Applying these values to Equation (4-1), we find that the overall timing of the 2716 is compatible with that of the 8085A.

The details of complying with Equation (4-1) center on the timing of the 8085's $\overline{RD}$ signal and the 2716's input $\overline{OE}$. Using $\overline{RD}$ to directly or indirectly drive $\overline{OE}$, $\overline{OE}$ will be driven low approximately t_{AC} sec (see Figure 4-6) from when the 8085 outputs an address (neglecting any propagation delays), and the 2716 will then output data at pins O_0–O_7 after a delay of t_{OE} sec (see Figure 4-9). Then from the time the 8085 outputs an address to when the 2716 outputs data, which is the *effective access time t_{EFF}*, t_{AC} + t_{OE} sec will have elapsed. Figure 4-6 states that the data must be on the data bus by the time t_{AD} sec have elapsed. Then the relationship between t_{AC} + t_{OE} and t_{AD} can be expressed mathematically, as given in Equation (4-2):

$$t_{EFF} = t_{AC} + t_{OE} < t_{AD} \qquad (4\text{-}2)$$

Applying Equation (4-2), we know that t_{AC} is a minimum of 270 nsec and that t_{OE} is a maximum of 120 nsec; thus

$$t_{EFF} = t_{AC} + t_{OE} = 270 \text{ nsec} + 120 \text{ nsec} = 390 \text{ nsec}$$

which satisfies Equation (4-2). However, because t_{EFF} (390 nsec) is less than t_{ACC} (450 nsec), where t_{ACC} is the fastest guaranteed access time for a 2716, then the actual access time will default to t_{ACC} sec. Thus to Equation (4-2) let us add: If the effective access time is less than t_{ACC}

$$t_{EFF} < t_{ACC} \qquad (4\text{-}2a)$$

then the effective access time will default to t_{ACC}

$$t_{EFF} = t_{ACC} \qquad (4\text{-}2b)$$

As we previously determined from Equation (4-1), the actual access time of the 2716 (450 nsec) is less than t_{AD} of the 8085A (575 nsec); therefore a 2716 is time compatible with an 8085A.

The values given for the 8085A's timing parameters are for maximum operating speed. Hence, if a slower crystal is used to drive X_1 and X_2, the parameters of Table 4-2 will slow down proportionally. Table 4-6 provides equations stating

TABLE 4-6. 8085 Bus Timing Parameters Expressed as Functions of t_{CYC} and Wait States

t_{AL}	—	$(1/2)\ T - 50$	MIN
t_{LA}	—	$(1/2)\ T - 60$	MIN
t_{LL}	—	$(1/2)\ T - 40$	MIN
t_{LCK}	—	$(1/2)\ T - 60$	MIN
t_{LC}	—	$(1/2)\ T - 30$	MIN
t_{AD}	—	$(5/2 + N)\ T - 225$	MAX
t_{RD}	—	$(3/2 + N)\ T - 200$	MAX
t_{RAE}	—	$(1/2)\ T - 60$	MIN
t_{CA}	—	$(1/2)\ T - 40$	MIN
t_{DW}	—	$(3/2 + N)\ T - 60$	MIN
t_{WD}	—	$(1/2)\ T - 80$	MIN
t_{CC}	—	$(3/2 + N)\ T - 80$	MIN
t_{CL}	—	$(1/2)\ T - 110$	MIN
t_{ARY}	—	$(3/2)\ T - 260$	MAX
t_{HACK}	—	$(1/2)\ T - 50$	MIN
t_{HABF}	—	$(1/2)\ T + 30$	MAX
t_{HABE}	—	$(1/2)\ T + 30$	MAX
t_{AC}	—	$(2/2)\ T - 50$	MIN
t_1	—	$(1/2)\ T - 80$	MIN
t_2	—	$(1/2)\ T - 40$	MIN
t_{RV}	—	$(3/2)\ T - 80$	MIN
t_{INS}	—	$(1/2)\ T + 200$	MIN
	—		

NOTE: N is equal to the total WAIT states.

T = t_{CYC}.

Courtesy of Intel Corp.

the relationship between the timing parameters and t_{CYC} ($T = t_{CYC}$) and the relationship of the timing parameters and wait states (N) that result from interfacing slow I/O and/or memory (by slow we mean that their access time is too long). We shall deal with slow devices later. Let us consider some examples using Table 4-6.

Example 4-2
Using the equations of Table 4-6, determine the values for timing parameters t_{AD}, t_{AC}, and t_{CC} for the allowable operating range of t_{CYC}, and then compare those values with those of Table 4-2. Wait states should not be considered; therefore N = 0. The values of t_{CYC} are (a) 320 nsec and (b) 2000 nsec.

Solution
(a) t_{CYC} = 320 nsec is for the maximum operating frequency (3.125 MHz) of the 8085. Comparing the calculated values with those of Table 4-2 will check the validity of Table 4-6's equations.

$$t_{AD} = [(5/2 + N) T - 225] \text{ nsec} = [5/2 (320) - 225] \text{ nsec}$$

$$t_{AD} = 575 \text{ nsec}$$

$$t_{AC} = (T - 50) \text{ nsec} = 320 - 50 \text{ nsec} = 270 \text{ nsec}$$

$$t_{CC} = [(3/2) T - 80] \text{ nsec} = [3/2 (320) - 80] \text{ nsec} = 400 \text{ nsec}$$

All of these parameters values agree with the values of Table 4-2.

(b) t_{CYC} = 2000 nsec, which is the 8085A's slowest operating frequency.

$$t_{AD} = [(5/2) 2,000 - 225] \text{ nsec} = 4775 \text{ nsec}$$

$$t_{AC} = (2,000 - 50) \text{ nsec} = 1950 \text{ nsec}$$

$$t_{CC} [(3/2) 2,000 - 80] \text{ nsec} = 2920 \text{ nsec}$$

From the values of Example 4-2 we can conclude that the operating ranges of these parameters are

$$575 \text{ nsec} < t_{AD} < 4,775 \text{ nsec} \qquad (4\text{-}3)$$

$$270 \text{ nsec} < t_{AC} < 1,950 \text{ nsec} \qquad (4\text{-}4)$$

$$400 \text{ nsec} < t_{CC} < 2,920 \text{ nsec} \qquad (4\text{-}5)$$

∎

Example 4-3
Let us verify that Equations (4-1) and (4-2) are satisfied for a 2716 when the 8085A is operating at its slowest speed.

Solution

Using the right-hand values of Equation (4-3) and (4-4) for the 8085A's timing parameters and applying those values to the 2716, as represented by Equations (4-1) and (4-2), we find

(a) For $t_{ACC} < t_{AD}$ that
$\quad$ 450 nsec < 4775 nsec
(b) For $t_{EFF} = t_{AC} + t_{OE} < t_{AD}$ that
$\quad t_{EFF} = (1,950 + 120)$ nsec $= 1870$ nsec < 4775 nsec

As expected, the 2716 is also compatible with the 8085A when operated at its minimum operating speed.

Notice in part (b) of Example 4-3 that t_{EFF} is greater than t_{ACC}. As a result, the 2716 will actually load its data on the data bus 1,870 nsec after the address was output on the address bus; that is, for this example the actual access time of the 2716 is t_{EFF} and not t_{ACC}. ∎

4-5

RAM Electrical and Timing Characteristics

There are many R/W memory chips that could be studied, but we believe that a thorough study of just one is sufficient for the reader to learn the concepts necessary to integrate any RAM into a memory system. The RAM we shall study is the 2114A, which is a 1024 × 4-bit RAM. The reason for choosing the 2114A is that its memory locations are only a nibble wide (4-bit storage), which will require the pairing of 2114As. Also, the number of address pins is different from that of the 2716 EPROM, which allows the reader to investigate and understand the hardware or software cost of not having a like number of address pins for all memory chips. This approach requires a little more inter-facing design effort but will broaden the reader's design ability.

From Figure 4-11 we see that the 2114A is a 4096-bit static RAM, with those bits arranged as 1024 memory locations and with each location having a 4-bit storage capacity (a 1024 × 4-bit memory). The term *static* means that a memory cell will remain in the last logic state written into it as long as power (V_{CC}) remains applied to the chip, as opposed to dynamic memory cells that must have their data refreshed continuously. As shown and stated, data lines I/O_1–I/O_4 are buffered with tristate logic gates. From the block diagram we see that when $\overline{CS}$ (pin 8) is low, both AND gates (which control the tristate buffers) are enabled, and so input $\overline{WE}$ will determine whether the write buffers are active (those on the left) or the read buffers (those on the right) are active. If $\overline{CS}$ and $\overline{WE}$ are low (a write), the top AND gate will output a logic 1, which activates the write buffers, and the bottom AND gate will output a logic 0, thereby driving the read buffers into the high-Z state. Thus a low on $\overline{WE}$ causes a write operation to occur, and a high causes a read operation to be performed. In the description of Figure 4-11 note that this chip does not require an address setup time. There-

2114A
1024 X 4 BIT STATIC RAM

	2114AL-1	2114AL-2	2114AL-3	2114AL-4	2114A-4	2114A-5
Max. Access Time (ns)	100	120	150	200	200	250
Max. Current (mA)	40	40	40	40	70	70

- **HMOS Technology**

- **Low Power, High Speed**

- **Identical Cycle and Access Times**

- **Single +5V Supply ±10%**

- **High Density 18 Pin Package**

- **Completely Static Memory - No Clock or Timing Strobe Required**

- **Directly TTL Compatible: All Inputs and Outputs**

- **Common Data Input and Output Using Three-State Outputs**

- **2114 Upgrade**

The Intel® 2114A is a 4096-bit static Random Access Memory organized as 1024 words by 4-bits using HMOS, a high performance MOS technology. It uses fully DC stable (static) circuitry throughout, in both the array and the decoding, therefore it requires no clocks or refreshing to operate. Data access is particularly simple since address setup times are not required. The data is read out nondestructively and has the same polarity as the input data. Common input/output pins are provided.

The 2114A is designed for memory applications where the high performance and high reliability of HMOS, low cost, large bit storage, and simple interfacing are important design objectives. The 2114A is placed in an 18-pin package for the highest possible density.

It is directly TTL compatible in all respects: inputs, outputs, and a single +5V supply. A separate Chip Select ($\overline{CS}$) lead allows easy selection of an individual package when outputs are or-tied.

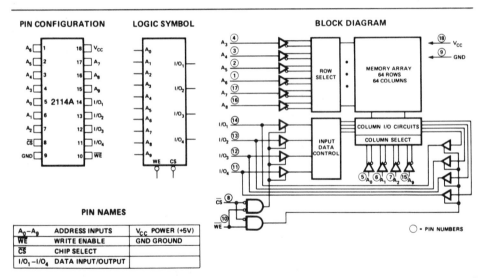

PIN NAMES

A_0–A_9	ADDRESS INPUTS	V_{CC}	POWER (+5V)
$\overline{WE}$	WRITE ENABLE	GND	GROUND
$\overline{CS}$	CHIP SELECT		
I/O_1–I/O_4	DATA INPUT/OUTPUT		

FIGURE 4-11. General description of Intel's 2114A Static RAM. (Courtesy of Intel.)

fore, $\overline{CS}$ does not have to be low before address decoding begins, which can be verified, as the block diagram does not show $\overline{CS}$ controlling the internal address decoders. Remember this when studying 2114A timing.

We use a bar above a symbol to indicate an active low signal. For continuity, the symbols used to identify pin function will be the same symbol used in all other illustrations, such as the pin configuration, logic symbol, and block dia-

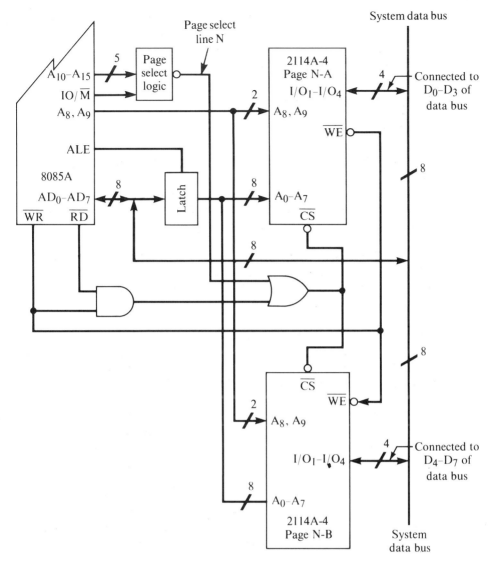

FIGURE 4-12. Block diagram of a 2114A pair interfaced to a memory mapped I/O system with address decoding.

gram. However, not all use this convention. For instance, the logic symbol of Figure 4-11, as furnished by Intel Corp., did not have bars (negation signs) at the top of WE and CS. The reasoning for not negating WE and CS in the logic symbol illustration is that because a circle (inverter) is used to indicate an active low input (or output) and those symbols (WE and CS) are diagrammatically located "inside" the logic symbol (the rectangle), then those symbolic representation should be different from that used to represent the external pin. We believe that because the user does not have access "inside" the chip of an integrated circuit, all signal symbolic representations should be the same as those used to represent pin functions, which are external and accessible, regardless of where that symbol is drawn on the logic symbol or block diagram. And so we have added the negation signs above $\overline{WE}$ and $\overline{CS}$.

Figure 4-12 is a block diagram of a pair of 2114As interfaced to a memory-mapped I/O system with address decoding (a memory-mapped I/O system is used for variety in the example systems). Because the 2114A has 4-bit storage for each memory location, to be interfaced to an 8-bit data bus structure, two 2114As must be paralleled. The data pins (I/O_1–I/O_4) of page N-A are connected to the lower-order nibble of the system's data bus (D_0–D_3), and page N-B's data pins are connected to the higher-order nibble (D_4–D_7). The address pins of each 2114A (A_0–A_9) are connected in parallel to the corresponding address bus lines (A_0–A_9). The chip select ($\overline{CS}$) pin of each chip is also parallel, so that they are selected as a pair, thus forming an 8-bit memory (1,024 × 8). To select this pair of 2114As, which make up page N, two events must occur simultaneously: (1) Either $\overline{WR}$ or $\overline{RD}$ must be low, thus driving the output of the AND-gate low; and (2) Page select line N must be low. If both inputs to the OR gate are low (page N has been addressed *and* the 8085 wants to perform either a read or a write operation with page N), the $\overline{CS}$ pins of both 2114As will be driven low, and the chips will be enabled. The $\overline{WE}$ input will control whether a read or write operation is performed.

2114A Electrical Specifications

Table 4-7 gives the electrical specifications of Intel's 2114 family of memory chips. The difference between the 2114AL (low power) and the 2114A is power consumption. The 2114AL draws a maximum of 40 mA, and the 2114A draws 70 mA.

Let us consider the input parameters of the 211A-4. V_{IL} is a maximum of 0.8 V; therefore any input voltage less than 0.8 V (down to a minimum of -3 V) will be interpreted as a logic 0 by a 2114A-4. V_{IH} is a minimum of 2.0 V (up to a maximum of 6.0 V); therefore any input voltage within the range of 2.0 V to 6.0 V will be interpreted by the 2114A-4 as a logic 1.

The output voltage parameters of the 2114A-4 state that when a 2114A-4 outputs a logic 0, the maximum voltage level will be 0.4 V (or less) and that while in the logic 0 state it will act as a current sink able to sink a minimum of 2.1 mA (I_{OL} = 2.1 mA Min). When a 2114A-4 output is in the logic 1 state, the (maximum) voltage output is 2.4 V (V_{OH} = 2.4 V), and when in that logic state, the output acts as a current source able to source a minimum of 1 mA (I_{OH} = -1.0 mA).

As an example of utilizing the data of Table 4-7, determine whether the 2114A-4 and 8085 are electrically compatible.

Example 4-4

From the electrical parameter specifications of Table 4-1 and 4-7, determine whether the 8085A and 2114A are electrically compatible.

Solution

From Figure 4-12 we see that 8085 pins AD_0–AD_7, A_8, A_9, and $\overline{WR}$ must drive 2114A-4 pins I/O_1–I/O_4, A_8, A_9, and $\overline{WE}$, respectively, for a write operation. The 8085 must drive two 2114A-4 $\overline{WE}$ pins and two A_8 and A_9 pins. Because

TABLE 4-7. 2114A Electrical Specifications*

Symbol	Parameter	2114AL-1/L-2/L-3/L-4			2114A-4/-5			Unit	Conditions
		Min.	Typ.[1]	Max.	Min.	Typ.[1]	Max.		
$|I_{LI}|$	Input Load Current (All Input Pins)			10			10	μA	$V_{IN} = 0$ to 5.5V
$|I_{LO}|$	I/O Leakage Current			10			10	μA	$\overline{CS} = V_{IH}$, $V_{I/O} = $ GND to VCC
I_{CC}	Power Supply Current		25	40		50	70	mA	$V_{CC} = $ max, $I_{I/O} = 0$ mA, $T_A = 0°C$
V_{IL}	Input Low Voltage	-3.0		0.8	-3.0		0.8	V	
V_{IH}	Input High Voltage	2.0		6.0	2.0		6.0	V	
I_{OL}	Output Low Current	2.1	9.0		2.1	9.0		mA	$V_{OL} = 0.4V$
I_{OH}	Output High Current	-1.0	-2.5		-1.0	-2.5		mA	$V_{OH} = 2.4V$
I_{OS}	Output Short Circuit Current			40			40	mA	

*Courtesy of Intel Corp.

for a write operation the 8085 drives the 2114A-4, the 8085 output electrical parameters V_{OH}, V_{OL}, I_{OL}, and I_{OH} will be compared with the corresponding 2114A-4 input parameters.

8085A (Driver)	2114A (Driven)
$V_{OL} = 0.45\ V_{MAX}$ $V_{OH} = 2.4\ V_{MIN}$	$V_{IL} = 0.8\ V_{MAX}$ $V_{IH} = 2.0\ V_{MIN}$
$I_{OL} = 2mA$ $I_{OH} = -400\ \mu A$	$I_{LI} = 10\ \mu A$

The 8085A has a guaranteed maximum voltage of 0.45 V for a logic 0 output voltage (V_{OL}), and the 2114A-4 will interpret an input voltage (V_{IL}), which is equal to or less than 0.8 V, as a logic 0; thus, the two are compatible for the logic 0 condition. When an 8085A outputs a logic 1, its voltage (V_{OH}) is guaranteed to be a minimum of 2.4 V. Because the 2114A-4 will interpret as a logic 1 an input voltage that is equal to or greater than 2.0 (V_{IH}), the 8085A and 2114A-4 are also voltage compatible for the logic 1 condition.

Let us now determine whether the 2114A-4 and 8085A are current compatible. When the 8085A is driving another device, a 2114A pair in this case, an 8085A output in the logic 0 state acts as a current sink and can sink 2 mA ($I_{OL} = 2$ mA). When an 8085A output is in the logic 1 state, it acts as a current source capable of sourcing up to 400 μA ($I_{OH} = -400\ \mu A$). Because the 2114A does not require an input current to operate but may have a leakage of 10 μA (I_{LI}), of which the 8085A is more than capable of handling, the two chips are current compatible. For those cases when the 8085A is driving two 2114A inputs, we reason that because one 2114A has only 10 μA of input current, then for an 8085A to drive a pair of 2114A inputs, the effective input current is 20 μA. Even for this condition the 8085A fan-out (how many inputs, or pairs of inputs, can be driven by the 8085A) for driving a pair of 2114As is

$$\text{low state } 2 \times 10^{-3} / 10 \times 10^{-6} = 200$$
$$\text{high state } 400 \times 10^{-6} / 10 \times 10^{-6} = 40$$

Because the "worst case" determines the maximum fan-out, for an 8085A output to drive two 2114As in parallel, the 8085A's fan-out will be 40. Thus the 8085A and 2114A are current compatible when the 8085A is driving a 2114A pair.

It should be understood that a 2114A's input currents are leakage, as the 2114A is a MOS device. Also these input currents can be either sink or source, as indicated by the absolute value symbol used with I_{LI}.

Next we shall determine whether the 2114A can drive the 8085A, which is the case for read operations. Returning to Figure 4-12 we see that for a read operation, the output pins I/O_1–I/O_4 of the 2114A pair must drive pins AD_0–AD_7 of the 8085A. From Table 4-1 and 4-7,

2114A (Driver)	8085A (Driven)
$V_{OL} = 0.4 V_{MAX}$ $V_{OH} = 2.4 V_{MIN}$	$V_{IL} = 0.8 V_{MAX}$ $V_{IH} = 2.0 V_{MIN}$
$I_{LO} = +$ or $- 10$ μA (leakage)	$I_{IL} = +$ or $- 10$ μA (leakage)

An output voltage of a 2114A is a maximum of 0.4 V for a logic 0 and a minimum of 2.4 V for a logic 1. An 8085A input will interpret as a logic 0 an input voltage equal to or less than 0.8 V and as a logic 1 an input voltage equal to or greater than 2.0 V. The two are also voltage compatible when a 2114A is driving the 8085A.

The current specifications for both the 8085A and the 2114A are the same; that is, there is a maximum of 10 μA of leakage current which may be acting as either sink or source—it does not matter, as leakage current is not required for proper operation.

In conclusion, the 8085A and 2114A are electrically compatible whether acting as the driver or the driven. ∎

2114A Timing Specifications

The timing parameters and timing diagrams for the 2114A are provided in Figure 4-13, which is a reproduction from an Intel data catalog. We shall study the read cycle first.

The read cycle timing diagram states that the data of the memory location being addressed will be available at output pins I/O_1–I/O_4 (D_{OUT}) after t_A seconds have elapsed from when the address was applied to address pins A_0–A_9 *if* pin $\overline{CS}$ has been low for at least t_{CO} sec. Note that the 2114A does not have a read pin; however, the $\overline{WE}$ pin of the 2114A must be high, as stated in note 3 (also see note 5) of Figure 4-13. Using the 8085A primary control signal $\overline{RD}$ indirectly to drive $\overline{CS}$ of the 2114A, as indicated in Figure 4-12, will provide proper timing for a 2114A read operation.

From Figure 4-6, we know that the access time (t_A) of the 2114A must be less than the read time (t_{AD}) of the 8085A, or

$$t_A < t_{AD} \tag{4-6}$$

Substituting values from Table 4-2 and the read cycle table of Figure 4-13 (2114A-4) in Equation (4-6):

$$t_A = 200 \text{ nsec} < 575 \text{ nsec} = t_{AD}$$

This inequality is true (with a 375-nsec margin) and states that a 2114A-4 can have the content (data) of an addressed memory location available to output pins I/O_1–I/O_4 faster than the fastest 8085A read time can with a 375-nsec safety margin. Hence, the 8085A and 2114A-4 are time compatible for read operations.

The details and exact timing of a read operation can be determined from Figures 4-6 and 4-13 with reference to the system of Figure 4-12. Figure 4-12

A.C. CHARACTERISTICS T_A = 0°C to 70°C, V_{CC} = 5V ± 10%, unless otherwise noted.

READ CYCLE [1]

SYMBOL	PARAMETER	2114AL-1		2114AL-2		2114AL-3		2114A-4/L-4		2114A-5		UNIT
		Min.	Max.	Min.	Max.	Min.	Max.	Min.	Max.	Min.	Max.	
t_{RC}	Read Cycle Time	100		120		150		200		250		ns
t_A	Access Time		100		120		150		200		250	ns
t_{CO}	Chip Selection to Output Valid		70		70		70		70		85	ns
t_{CX}	Chip Selection to Output Active	10		10		10		10		10		ns
t_{OTD}	Output 3-state from Deselection		30		35		40		50		60	ns
t_{OHA}	Output Hold from Address Change	15		15		15		15		15		ns

WRITE CYCLE [2]

SYMBOL	PARAMETER	2114AL-1		2114AL-2		2114AL-3		2114A-4/L-4		2114A-5		UNIT
		Min.	Max.	Min.	Max.	Min.	Max.	Min.	Max.	Min.	Max.	
t_{WC}	Write Cycle Time	100		120		150		200		250		ns
t_W	Write Time	75		75		90		120		135		ns
t_{WR}	Write Release Time	0		0		0		0		0		ns
t_{OTW}	Output 3-state from Write		30		35		40		50		60	ns
t_{DW}	Data to Write Time Overlap	70		70		90		120		135		ns
t_{DH}	Data Hold from Write Time	0		0		0		0		0		ns

NOTES:
1. A Read occurs during the overlap of a low $\overline{CS}$ and a high $\overline{WE}$.
2. A Write occurs during the overlap of a low $\overline{CS}$ and a low $\overline{WE}$. t_W is measured from the latter of $\overline{CS}$ or $\overline{WE}$ going low to the earlier of $\overline{CS}$ or $\overline{WE}$ going high.

WAVEFORMS

READ CYCLE ③

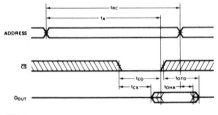

NOTES:
3. $\overline{WE}$ is high for a Read Cycle.
4. If the $\overline{CS}$ low transition occurs simultaneously with the $\overline{WE}$ low transition, the output buffers remain in a high impedance state.
5. $\overline{WE}$ must be high during all address transitions.

WRITE CYCLE

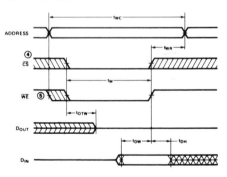

FIGURE 4-13. 2114A timing parameters and timing diagrams. (Courtesy of Intel Corp.)

gives us the logical relationship between $\overline{RD}$ and $\overline{CS}$, and a composite of Figures 4-6 and 4-13 illustrates the resultant effective timing.

From Figure 4-12 we see that if page N is addressed (page select line N is low) and $\overline{RD}$ is also active (low), then the OR gate output will be low, thus

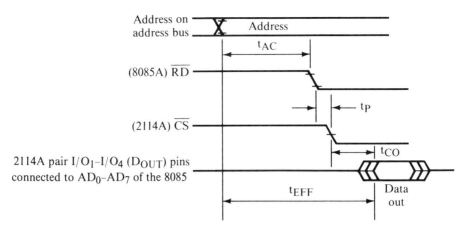

FIGURE 4-14. Effect access time t_{EFF} for the design of Figure 4-12.

driving low the $\overline{CS}$ of both 2114As. Because all timing is referenced to when the 8085A outputs an address on the address bus, we shall likewise construct a timing diagram using this as a reference. This timing diagram will illustrate the time relationship between $\overline{RD}$ and $\overline{CS}$. To construct it, we must begin with the 8085A timing of $\overline{RD}$ (t_{AC}), as given in Figure 4-6, and then refer to the 2114A for timing of $\overline{CS}$ (Figure 4-13) in order to determine when data is output by the 2114As (t_{CO}). Figure 4-14 illustrates the relationship between t_{AC} and t_{CO} for the design of Figure 4-12, using address timing as the reference point.

From Figure 4-14 we see that the effective access time (t_{EFF}) can be mathematically expressed as

$$t_{EFF} = t_{AC} + t_P + t_{CO} \qquad (4\text{-}7)$$

where t_P = the combined propagation time of the AND and OR gates, which is often negligible. We know that t_{EFF} is the actual access time for the 2114A-4 pair of Figure 4-12 and that access time t_A represents the fastest access time possible for a 2114A-4. Hence, the minimum possible time for t_{EFF} is t_A or, expressed mathematically,

$$t_{EFF} = t_{AC} + t_P + t_{CO} > t_A \qquad (4\text{-}8)$$

If t_{EFF} is less than t_A, the effective access time t_{EFF} will default to access time t_A. That is, if

$$t_{EFF} < t_A \qquad (4\text{-}8a)$$

then

$$t_{EFF} = t_A \qquad (4\text{-}8b)$$

Equations (4-8a) and (4-8b) are similar to the default condition expressed by Equations (4-2a) and (4-2b). For Figure 4-12 we find that

$$t_{EFF} = (270 + t_P + 70) \text{ nsec} \sim 340 \text{ nsec}$$

if t_P is neglected. Then for the design of Figure 4-12, even though a 2114A-4 can be accessed in 200 nsec, the effective access time for this design will take 340 nsec.

Example 4-5

Determine the effective access time t_{EFF} for the design of Figure 4-12 if a 1 MHz crystal is used to drive the 8085A internal clock.

Solution

If a 1-MHz crystal is used to drive the 8085A, the internal clock will be running at half that speed, which means

$$t_{CYC} = 1/0.5 \times 10^6 = 2000 \text{ nsec}$$

From Table 4-6

$$t_{AC} = (T - 50) \text{ nsec} = 1950 \text{ nsec}$$

Substituting this value in Equation (4-7),

$$t_{EFF} = (1950 + t_P + 70) \text{ nsec} \sim 2020 \text{ nsec},$$

if t_P is neglected. Thus to access a data byte from the system of Figure 4-12, with the 8085A running at its slowest speed, takes 1950 nsec. With an access time (t_A) of 200 nsec, a 2114A-4 obviously exceeds the 8085A's access time requirements for the conditions stated. ∎

The write cycle timing diagram of Figure 4-13 states that the data at data pins I/O_1–I/O_4 (D_{IN}) will be latched (written into) by the 2114A on the positive edge (0 to 1) of $\overline{WE}$ or $\overline{CS}$, whichever occurs first (see note 2 of Figure 4-13). If the 8085A is writing data to a 2114A, or a 2114A pair, it must have the data on the data bus at this time. As a result, the write timing will be oriented to the positive edge of $\overline{WE}$ or $\overline{CS}$. Also note from Figure 4-13 that a write cycle can occur in a minimum of t_{WC} sec, whereas t_{WC} ends t_{WR} sec after the positive edge of $\overline{WE}$. Thus time t_{WC} is a variable that is dependent on the positive edge of $\overline{WE}$ or $\overline{CS}$. Hence, it is the positive edge of $\overline{WE}$ or $\overline{CS}$ that determines the write cycle time t_{WC}. The minimum time that a write cycle can be performed by a 2114A-4 is 120 nsec, according to the table of Figure 4-13.

When correlating the timing between an 8085A and a 2114A, we see from Figure 4-6 that an 8085 will write a data byte to the data bus approximately t_{AC} sec after it outputs an address, which corresponds to when the 8085 drives $\overline{WR}$ low. The addressed 2114A must latch that data byte off the data bus using the positive edge of $\overline{WR}$ as a strobe pulse. From Figure 4-12 we see that $\overline{WE}$

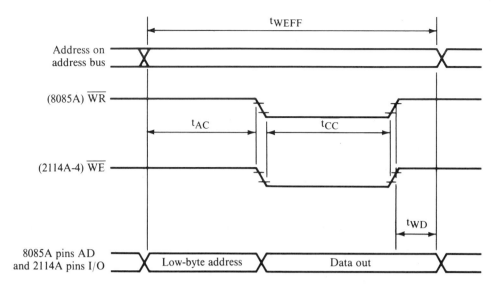

FIGURE 4-15. Effective write time t_WEFF for the design of Figure 4-12.

is driven by $\overline{WR}$ of the 8085A; therefore, the positive edge of $\overline{WE}$ will be that of $\overline{WR}$. Requiring that the positive edge of $\overline{WR}$ not occur until after t_{WC} sec (recall that t_{WC} is the minimum time the 2114A can perform a write cycle), then

WRITE (RAM) $\qquad$ $t_{AC} + t_{CC} > t_{WC}$ $\qquad$ (4-9)

From the appropriate tables for the 2114A-4 and the 8085A, Equation (4-9) becomes

$$(270 + 400)\ nsec = 670\ nsec > 200\ nsec$$

This inequality states that for an 8085A operating at maximum speed, approximately 670 nsec will elapse before the positive edge of $\overline{WR}$ and $\overline{WE}$ occurs. As long as this time is greater than the minimum write cycle time of 200 nsec (t_{WC}), the 2114A-4 and 8085A will be compatible for a write operation.

Figure 4-15 illustrates the detailed relationship between $\overline{WR}$ and $\overline{WE}$ timing and the effective write time, t_{WEFF}. Note that using $\overline{WR}$'s positive edge as a strobe for the 2114A, via $\overline{WE}$, is possible, as the 8085A will hold the data byte on the data bus t_{WD} sec after the positive edge of $\overline{WR}$. Therefore, a more accurate expression for the effective write cycle for the system of Figure 4-12 is

$$t_{WEFF} = t_{AC} + t_{CC} + t_{WD} \qquad (4\text{-}10)$$

Because Equation (4-10) is more comprehensive than Equation (4-9), Equation 4-9 should be replaced with Equation (4-11).

$$t_{WEFF} > t_{WC} \qquad (4\text{-}11)$$

Equation 4-11 is the criterion that must be met for the 2114A to respond quickly enough to an 8085A write operation.

Example 4-6

Determine the effective write cycle time t_{WEFF} and timing compatibility for the design of Figure 4-12 if the crystal frequency is 6.25 MHz (maximum). Also determine when the 2114A pair actually latches the data byte off the data bus.

Solution

For a crystal of 6.25 MHz the internal clock period is $t_{CYC} = 320$ nsec. From Table 4-2, $t_{AC} = 270$ nsec, $t_{CC} = 400$ nsec, and $t_{WD} = 100$ nsec. Substituting these values into Equation (4-10) yields $t_{WEFF} = (270 + 400 + 100)$ nsec $= 770$ nsec. From the write cycle table of Figure 4-13 we find that $t_{WC} = 200$ nsec minimum (the fastest 2114A-4 write cycle possible). From Equation (4-11), 770 nsec $>$ 200 nsec, which is true (by a large margin); therefore the 2114A pair and the 8085A of Figure 4-12 are compatible. To determine the time that latching actually occurs, refer to Figure 4-15. Because latching occurs on the positive edge of $\overline{WE}$ (and/or $\overline{CE}$), $t_{AC} + t_{CC}$ sec will have elapsed, or 270 + 400 nsec $= 670$ nsec. ∎

4-6

I/O Interface Design

The basic design concepts of I/O interfacing were covered in Section 3-3. Figures 3-5 and 3-6 illustrate the components used for interfacing I/O devices, and Figure 3-10 illustrates these components integrated into a system. This section will identify those chips that can be used to implement the interfacing components and will check the loading and timing characteristics of these components for compatibility with the 8085A.

Input I/O Interfacing

From Figure 3-5 we recall that tristate logic devices (buffers) are used to interface input devices to the system's data bus and that the logic state of these buffers are controlled by the I/O select line in an address-decoding system. From Figure 3-10 we see that these buffers must be capable of driving the data bus (pins AD_0–AD_7 of the 8085). We have chosen a 74LS244 to implement the buffers of Chapter 3. From Figure 4-16 and Table 4-1 we find that the

74LS244 (Driver)	8085A (Driven)
$V_{OL} = 0.5$ V	$V_{IL} = 0.8$ V
$V_{OH} = 2.0$ V	$V_{IH} = 2.0$ V
$I_{OL} = 24$ mA	$I_{IL} = +$ or $- 10$ μA
$I_{OH} = - 15$ mA	

74LS244 will output compatible voltage levels to the 8085A's inputs; therefore the two are voltage compatible. The output of a 74LS244 can sink 24 mA in the low state and source up to 15 mA in the high state (if needed). An input of an 8085A can sink or source 10 μA; hence the 74LS244's output is more than capable of driving an 8085A input.

Using a 74LS244 octal buffer to implement an input device interface, such as that shown in Figure 3-10, the 74LS244 can be configured as shown in Figure

BUFFERS

54/74LS244, S244

FUNCTION TABLE

Octal Buffers (3-State)

INPUTS				OUTPUTS	
$\overline{OE}_a$	I_a	$\overline{OE}_b$	I_b	Y_a	Y_b
L	L	L	L	L	L
L	H	L	H	H	H
H	X	H	X	(Z)	(Z)

H = HIGH voltage level   X = Don't care
L = LOW voltage level   (Z) = HIGH impedance (off) state

TYPE	TYPICAL PROPAGATION DELAY	TYPICAL SUPPLY CURRENT (Total)
74LS244	12ns	25mA
74S244	6ns	112mA

PIN CONFIGURATION

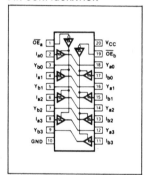

LOGIC SYMBOL

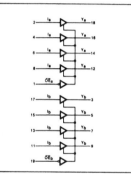

LOGIC SYMBOL (IEEE/IEC)

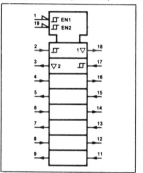

RECOMMENDED OPERATING CONDITIONS

PARAMETER			54/74LS			54/74S			UNIT
			Min	Nom	Max	Min	Nom	Max	
V_{CC}	Supply voltage	Mil	4.5	5.0	5.5	4.5	5.0	5.5	V
		Com'l	4.75	5.0	5.25	4.75	5.0	5.25	V
V_{IH}	HIGH-level input voltage		2.0			2.0			V
V_{IL}	LOW-level input voltage	Mil			+ 0.7			+ 0.8	V
		Com'l			+ 0.8			+ 0.8	V
I_{IK}	Input clamp current				− 18			− 18	mA
I_{OH}	HIGH-level output current	Mil			− 12			− 12	mA
		Com'l			− 15			− 15	mA
I_{OL}	LOW-level output current	Mil			12			48	mA
		Com'l			24			64	mA
T_A	Operating free-air temperature	Mil	− 55		+ 125	− 55		+ 125	°C
		Com'l	0		70	0		70	°C

NOTE
V_{IL} = + 0.7V MAX for 54S at T_A = + 125°C only.

FIGURE 4-16. Specifications for Signetics 74LS244. (Courtesy of Signetics.)

DC ELECTRICAL CHARACTERISTICS (Over recommended operating free-air temperature range unless otherwise noted.)

PARAMETER		TEST CONDITIONS[1]			54/74LS244			54/74S244			UNIT
					Min	Typ[2]	Max	Min	Typ[2]	Max	
ΔV_T Hysteresis ($V_{T+} - V_{T-}$)		$V_{CC} = $ MIN			0.2	0.4		0.2	0.4		V
V_{OH} HIGH-level output voltage		$V_{CC} = $ MIN, $V_{IH} = $ MIN, $V_{IL} = 0.5V$, $I_{OH} = $ MAX			2.0			2.0			V
		$V_{CC} = $ MIN, $V_{IH} = $ MIN, $V_{IL} = $ MAX, $I_{OH} = -3mA$			2.4	3.4		2.4			V
V_{OL} LOW-level output voltage	$V_{CC} = $ MIN, $V_{IH} = $ MIN, $V_{IL} = $ MAX	$I_{OL} = $ MAX	Mil			0.4			0.55	V
			Com'l			0.5			0.55	V
		$I_{OL} = 12mA$	74LS			0.4				V
V_{IK} Input clamp voltage		$V_{CC} = $ MIN, $I_I = I_{IK}$					-1.5			-1.2	V
I_{OZH} Off-state output current, HIGH-level voltage applied	$V_{CC} = $ MAX, $V_{IH} = $ MIN, $V_{IL} = $ MAX	$V_O = 2.7V$					20				μA
		$V_O = 2.4V$								50	μA
I_{OZL} Off-state output current, LOW-level voltage applied	$V_{CC} = $ MAX, $V_{IH} = $ MIN, $V_{IL} = $ MAX	$V_O = 0.4V$					-20				μA
		$V_O = 0.5V$								-50	μA
I_I Input current at maximum input voltage	$V_{CC} = $ MAX	$V_I = 5.5V$								1.0	mA
		$V_I = 7.0V$					0.1				mA
I_{IH} HIGH-level input current		$V_{CC} = $ MAX, $V_I = 2.7V$					20			50	μA
I_{IL} LOW-level input current	$V_{CC} = $ MAX	$V_I = 0.4V$								-0.2	mA
		$V_I = 0.5V$	$\overline{OE}$ inputs							-2.0	mA
			Other inputs							-0.4	mA

FIGURE 4-16. (continued)

4-17. As before, we use the negated notation ($\overline{OE}_a$ and $\overline{OE}_b$) to represent the pin notation.

The timing between the buffer of Figure 3-10 (implemented with a 74LS244) and a 8085A can be determined by referring to the read timing diagram of Figure 4-6. Because $\overline{RD}$ is used to drive the 74LS244 output enable pins $\overline{OE}_a$

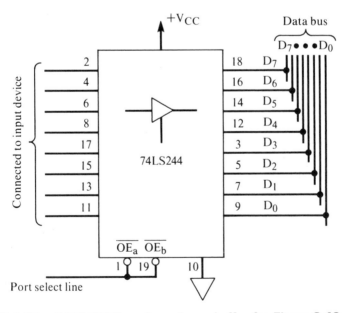

FIGURE 4-17. A 74LS244 configured as a buffer for Figure 3-10.

and $\overline{OE}_b$ (either directly or indirectly), the 74LS244 will be enabled on the negative edge of $\overline{RD}$ and will remain enabled until the positive edge of $\overline{RD}$. As a result, the 74LS244 buffer will be active t_{AC} sec from when the 8085A outputs an address and remain active for t_{CC} sec (neglecting any propagation delays). This will result in the addressed input device's loading its data byte on the data bus (8085A pins AD_0–AD_7) during time interval t_{CC}. Recalling that the 8085A uses the positive edge of the internal clock (CLK) period T_3 to latch data off the data bus, the data byte will be on the data bus at the proper time.

Output Device Interfacing

Referring again to Figures 3-6 and 3-10, we recall that output devices are interfaced to the system's data bus using a latch. From the write timing diagram of Figure 4-6 and our previous analysis of timing, we know that the 8085A will load the data byte on the data bus on the negative edge of $\overline{WR}$ and will hold that data on the data bus until the positive edge of $\overline{WR}$ plus t_{WD} sec. Because the 8085A holds the data byte on the data bus t_{WD} sec after the positive edge of $\overline{WR}$, the positive edge of $\overline{WR}$ can be used to latch data off the data bus. We shall use a positive edge latch to interface an output device to the system's data bus. The latch chosen is the 74LS374. Data for the Signetics 74LS374 are

LATCHES/FLIP-FLOPS	54/74LS373, 54/74LS374, S373, S374

- 8-bit transparent latch — '373
- 8-bit positive, edge-triggered register — '374
- 3-State output buffers
- Common 3-State Output Enable
- Independent register and 3-State buffer operation

'373 Octal Transparent Latch With 3-State Outputs
'374 Octal D Flip-Flop With 3-State Outputs

TYPE	TYPICAL PROPAGATION DELAY	TYPICAL SUPPLY CURRENT (Total)
74LS373	19ns	24mA
74S373	10ns	105mA
74LS374	19ns	27mA
74S374	8ns	116mA

PIN CONFIGURATION

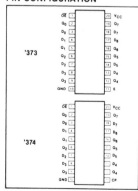

LOGIC SYMBOL

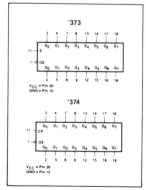

LOGIC SYMBOL (IEEE/IEC)

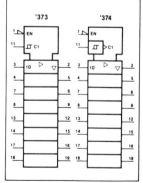

FIGURE 4-18. Specifications for Signetics 74LS374 latch. (Courtesy of Signetics.)

LOGIC DIAGRAM, '374

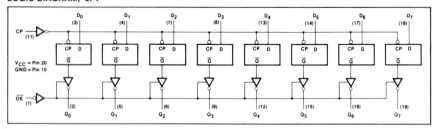

RECOMMENDED OPERATING CONDITIONS

PARAMETER			54/74LS			54/74S			UNIT
			Min	Nom	Max	Min	Nom	Max	
V_{CC}	Supply voltage	Mil	4.5	5.0	5.5	4.5	5.0	5.5	V
		Com'l	4.75	5.0	5.25	4.75	5.0	5.25	V
V_{IH}	HIGH-level input voltage		2.0			2.0			V
V_{IL}	LOW-level input voltage	Mil			+ 0.7			+ 0.8	V
		Com'l			+ 0.8			+ 0.8	V
I_{IK}	Input clamp current				− 18			− 18	mA
I_{OH}	HIGH-level output current	Mil			− 1.0			− 2.0	mA
		Com'l			− 2.6			− 6.5	mA
I_{OL}	LOW-level output current	Mil			12			20	mA
		Com'l			24			20	mA

PARAMETER		TEST CONDITIONS[1]		54/74LS373, 374			54/74S373, 374			UNIT
				Min	Typ[2]	Max	Min	Typ[2]	Max	
V_{OH}	HIGH-level output voltage	V_{CC} = MIN, V_{IH} = MIN, V_{IL} = MAX, I_{OH} = MAX	Mil	2.4	3.4		2.4	3.0		V
			Com'l	2.4	3.1		2.4	3.1		V
V_{OL}	LOW-level output voltage	V_{CC} = MIN, V_{IH} = MIN, V_{IL} = MAX	I_{OL} = MAX, Mil		0.25	0.4			0.5[4]	V
			I_{OL} = MAX, Com'l		0.35	0.5			0.5	V
			I_{OL} ≈ 12mA, 74LS		0.25	0.4				V
I_{IH}	HIGH-level input current	V_{CC} = MAX, V_i = 2.7V				20			50	µA
I_{IL}	LOW-level input current	V_{CC} = MAX	V_i = 0.4V			− 0.4				mA
			V_i = 0.5V						− 0.25	mA

FIGURE 4-18. (continued)

provided in Figure 4-18, which contains excerpts from a Signetics TLL logic data manual.

Because the 74LS374 will be driving the data bus, we must determine the electrical compatibility for the 74LS374 output (Q_0–Q_7) and the 8085A inputs (AD_0–AD_7).

74LS374 (Driver)	8085A (Driven)
V_{OL} = 0.4 V	V_{IL} = 0.8 V
V_{OH} = 2.4 V	V_{IH} = 2.0 V
I_{OL} = 24 mA	I_{IL} = + or − 10 µA
I_{OH} = − 2.6 mA	

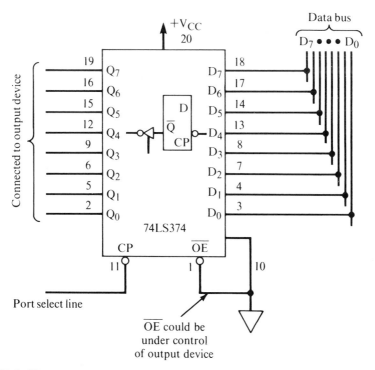

FIGURE 4-19. A 74LS374 configured as a latch for the design of Figure 3-10.

For those pins of the 8085A ($\overline{\text{WR}}$ if memory mapped) that must drive 74LS374 pins (CP), we find

8085A (Driver)	74LS374 (Driven)
$V_{OL} = 0.45$ V	$V_{IL} = 0.8$ V
$V_{OH} = 2.4$ V	$V_{IH} = 2.0$ V
$I_{OL} = 2$ mA	$I_{IL} = -0.4$ mA
$I_{OH} = -400$ μA	$I_{IH} = 20$ μA

When the 74LS374 is the driver, the voltage and currents are compatible. When the 8085A must drive a 74LS374 input, the voltages and currents are also compatible.

Because the 74LS374 is TTL technology, its input will source current in the low state ($I_{IL} = -0.4$ mA), and for the device to work properly, the driver must be able to sink that source current (TTL is a current-controlled logic family, thus requiring an input current). The 8085A can sink 2 mA ($I_{OL} = 2$ mA); therefore five such loads can be connected to an 8085A output; that is, it has a fan-out of five. If more than five such devices are required, then drivers must be incorporated in the design. (Drivers are discussed in Section 4-10.)

Address Decoder

The remaining component to be discussed is an address decoder, which can be used to implement the page selector and I/O port selector of Figure 3-13. Intel's 8205 was chosen as the chip to implement address decoders. Specifications for the 8205 are provided in Figure 4-20. Other decoders could have been used,

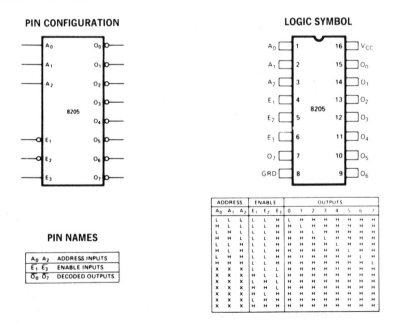

8205
HIGH SPEED 1 OUT OF 8 BINARY DECODER

- I/O Port or Memory Selector
- Simple Expansion — Enable Inputs
- High Speed Schottky Bipolar Technology — 18ns Max. Delay
- Directly Compatible with TTL Logic Circuits

- Low Input Load Current — .25 mA max., 1/6 Standard TTL Input Load
- Minimum Line Reflection — Low Voltage Diode Input Clamp
- Outputs Sink 10 mA min.
- 16-Pin Dual-In-Line Ceramic or Plastic Package

The Intel® 8205 decoder can be used for expansion of systems which utilize input ports, output ports, and memory components with active low chip select input. When the 8205 is enabled, one of its 8 outputs goes "low," thus a single row of a memory system is selected. The 3-chip enable inputs on the 8205 allow easy system expansion. For very large systems, 8205 decoders can be cascaded such that each decoder can drive 8 other decoders for arbitrary memory expansions.

The 8205 is packaged in a standard 16-pin dual in-line package, and its performance is specified over the temperature range of 0°C to +75°C, ambient. The use of Schottky barrier diode clamped transistors to obtain fast switching speeds results in higher performance than equivalent devices made with a gold diffussion process.

PIN CONFIGURATION

LOGIC SYMBOL

PIN NAMES

A_0 A_2	ADDRESS INPUTS
$\bar{E}_1$ $\bar{E}_3$	ENABLE INPUTS
$\bar{O}_0$ $\bar{O}_7$	DECODED OUTPUTS

ADDRESS			ENABLE			OUTPUTS							
A_0	A_1	A_2	E_1	E_2	E_3	0	1	2	3	4	5	6	7
L	L	L	L	L	H	L	H	H	H	H	H	H	H
H	L	L	L	L	H	H	L	H	H	H	H	H	H
L	H	L	L	L	H	H	H	L	H	H	H	H	H
H	H	L	L	L	H	H	H	H	L	H	H	H	H
L	L	H	L	L	H	H	H	H	H	L	H	H	H
H	L	H	L	L	H	H	H	H	H	H	L	H	H
L	H	H	L	L	H	H	H	H	H	H	H	L	H
H	H	H	L	L	H	H	H	H	H	H	H	H	L
X	X	X	L	L	L	H	H	H	H	H	H	H	H
X	X	X	H	L	L	H	H	H	H	H	H	H	H
X	X	X	L	H	L	H	H	H	H	H	H	H	H
X	X	X	H	H	L	H	H	H	H	H	H	H	H
X	X	X	L	H	H	H	H	H	H	H	H	H	H
X	X	X	H	L	H	H	H	H	H	H	H	H	H
X	X	X	H	H	H	H	H	H	H	H	H	H	H

FIGURE 4-20. Specifications for Intel's 8205 1 of 8 decoder. (Courtesy of Intel Corp.)

Symbol	Parameter	Limit		Unit	Test Conditions
		Min.	Max.		
I_F	INPUT LOAD CURRENT		−0.25	mA	$V_{CC} = 5.25V, V_F = 0.45V$
I_R	INPUT LEAKAGE CURRENT		10	µA	$V_{CC} = 5.25V, V_R = 5.25V$
V_C	INPUT FORWARD CLAMP VOLTAGE		−1.0	V	$V_{CC} = 4.75V, I_C = −5.0\,mA$
V_{OL}	OUTPUT "LOW" VOLTAGE		0.45	V	$V_{CC} = 4.75V, I_{OL} = 10.0\,mA$
V_{OH}	OUTPUT HIGH VOLTAGE	2.4		V	$V_{CC} = 4.75V, I_{OH} = −1.5\,mA$
V_{IL}	INPUT "LOW" VOLTAGE		0.85	V	$V_{CC} = 5.0V$
V_{IH}	INPUT "HIGH" VOLTAGE	2.0		V	$V_{CC} = 5.0V$
I_{SC}	OUTPUT HIGH SHORT CIRCUIT CURRENT	−40	−120	mA	$V_{CC} = 5.0V, V_{OUT} = 0V$
V_{OX}	OUTPUT "LOW" VOLTAGE @ HIGH CURRENT		0.8	V	$V_{CC} = 5.0V, I_{OX} = 40\,mA$
I_{CC}	POWER SUPPLY CURRENT		70	mA	$V_{CC} = 5.25V$

FIGURE 4-20.   (continued)

and the reader is encouraged also to check out the 74LS138. As in all cases, we shall use symbols that represent inputs and outputs indicative of the active logic level. Thus the logic symbol used in this textbook to represent an 8205 is that shown in Figure 4-21. Symbols $\overline{E}_1$ and $\overline{O}_0$ are shown "inside" and "outside" the chip to emphasize that we make no distinction as to where the symbol is placed physically in the drawing. To reiterate, the reason for this lack of distinction is that the user has only external access to a signal (represented by a symbol) via the chips pins, no internal access.

From Figure 4-20 we see that the propagation delay is a maximum of 18 nsec, which is small enough that it is often negligible, as in the examples of this chapter. The truth table states that to enable the 8205, the inputs $\overline{E}_1$ and $\overline{E}_2$ must be low and E_3 must be high. When the chip is enabled, inputs A_0, A_1, and A_2 are decoded, and the appropriate output $\overline{O}_n$ is driven low. The 8205 is much like the decoder of Figure 3-7, in which CE is E_3, and pins $\overline{E}_1$ and $\overline{E}_2$ do not exist.

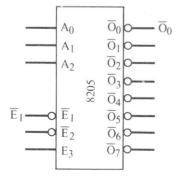

FIGURE 4-21.   Logic symbol for the 8205 as defined in this textbook.

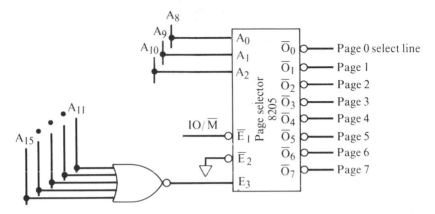

FIGURE 4-22. An 8205 implementing the page selector of Figure 3-9.

Example 4-7
Implement the page selector of Figure 3-9 using an 8205.

Solution
Everything is the same as illustrated in Figure 3-9 except that we must account for inputs $\overline{E}_1$ and $\overline{E}_2$. We shall utilize the 8085A signal IO/$\overline{M}$ to enable the page selector for memory operations and disable it for I/O operations. IO/$\overline{M}$ will also enable the page selector in the minimum allowable time. The 8205 will be enabled when IO/$\overline{M}$ goes low, which is at the same time a memory address is loaded on the address bus. This will result in the fastest access time, as the addressed page select line also becomes active when a memory address is output (recall our investigation of the 2716). IO/$\overline{M}$ can serve as an input to either $\overline{E}_1$ or $\overline{E}_2$. Figure 4-22 shows the design. ■

4-8

Memory and I/O Devices with Long Access Times

There are some devices (memory and I/O) that have access times (for read or write operations) exceeding that required to be directly compatible with the 8085A. When the 8085A is addressing one of these devices, the 8085 must somehow be "slowed" down." The method used to slow down the 8085A is to utilize the 8085A's READY pin. Using the READY pin does not actually slow down the 8085A (slowing the 8085A requires a "slower" crystal and this is undesirable) but, rather, causes the 8085A to wait some integral number of clock pulses before accessing the device. Figure 4-23 illustrates the 8085A's timing when wait states are required for either a read or a write operation.

The reader may wish to analyze Figure 4-23 by comparing it with the timing illustrated in Figure 4-6. Note that the timing difference between Figure 4-23

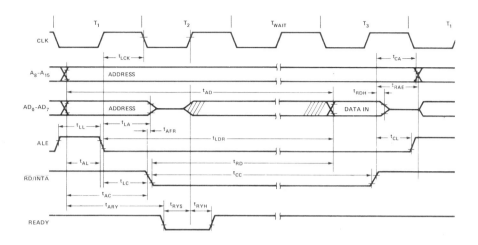

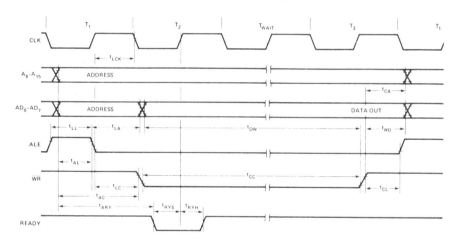

FIGURE 4-23. 8085 Timing for WAIT states. (Courtesy of Intel Corp.)

and those of Figure 4-6 center on an ''extra'' clock cycle labeled T_{WAIT}. Figure 4-23 illustrates that on the positive edge of T_2 the logic level of the READY pin is checked by the MPU's CU. If the logic level of the READY pin is high, then the timing of Figure 4-6 will apply, but if the READY pin is low and has been low for at least t_{RYS} sec, then the timing of Figure 4-23 will apply. As illustrated in Figure 4-23, when the READY pin is low, the 8085A idles by not using the next clock period (labeled T_{WAIT}) for internal operations and will continue to idle until the READY pin is high. At the positive edge of each t_{WAIT} clock pulse, the READY pin is checked, and when found high, the 8085A terminates the wait state and uses the next clock pulse (T_3) to continue internal

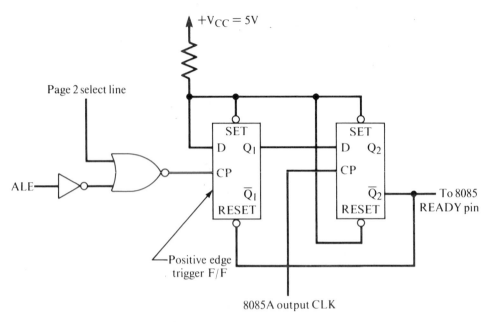

FIGURE 4-24. Logic to insert one **WAIT** state.

operations. Although this procedure does not slow down the 8085A, it does extend the read and write times t_{AD} and t_{DW}. The equations of Table 4-6 enable us to determine the number of required wait states (N), as well as to calculate their effects on other timing parameters.

Example 4-8
Suppose that page 2 of Figure 4-27 has an access time of 700 nsec. How many wait states are required for an 8085A-based system that is running at maximum speed?

Solution
From Table 4-6 we find that

$$t_{AD} = [(5/2 + N) T - 225] \text{ nsec}$$
$$= 700 \text{ nsec } (t_{AD} \text{ must not be faster than 700 nsec)}$$

Solving for N we find

$$N = (t_{AD} + 225) / T - 5/2$$
$$N = (700 + 225) / 320 - 5/2 = 2.89 - 2.5$$
$$N = 0.39$$

Because N must be an integer, $N = 1$ is required. One wait state will extend t_{CC} to

$$t_{CC} = [(3/2 + N) T - 80] \text{ nsec} = (2.5) 320 - 80 \text{ nsec}$$
$$t_{CC} = 720 \text{ nsec}$$

and extend t_{AD} to

$$t_{AD} = [(5/2 + 1) 320 - 225] \text{ nsec} = 895 \text{ nsec} \qquad \blacksquare$$

The circuit of Figure 4-24 can be used to insert one wait state.

The circuit of Figure 4-24 allows the page select line to determine whether or not a wait state is created. With this design, only those pages of memory requiring a wait state will generate one, via the page select line. The timing for the circuit of Figure 4-24 is given in Figure 4-25. As seen from Figure 4-25, the output of the NOR gate generates the positive edge needed to latch the high input (D) at flip-flop 1, causing $Q_1 = 1$. The positive edge of T_1 will then cause flip-flop 2 to latch the output of Q_1; thus output Q_2 will be high and $\overline{Q_2}$ will be low. The low output of $\overline{Q_2}$ drives the READY pin low and also resets flip-flop 1. On the positive edge of T_2, the READY pin is checked by the 8085A and

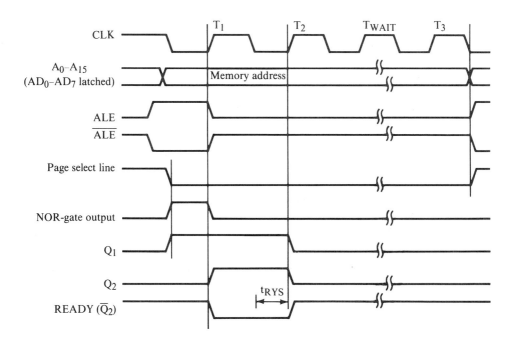

FIGURE 4-25. Timing for the logic of Figure 4-24.

found to be in a logic-low state, thus putting the 8085 in a wait state. Also, on the positive edge of T_2, flip-flop 2 latches the logic state of Q_1 (a low) which puts both flip-flops in the 0 state and the READY pin high. This condition will remain until that memory page is again addressed.

The above concepts also apply to I/O devices with a long access time.

An 8085 Primary Design

If one were to apply those concepts and practices previously learned to designing an 8085-based system, the end result might be like that shown in Figure 4-27, which represents a basic 8085-based design and will serve as the primary system for applications of the material covered in Chapters 5 and 6. Because Figure 4-27 will be used in studying other material, the reader should be sure not only to understand the concepts represented but also to be familiar with the system.

Figure 4-27 is an isolated I/O system using address decoding and having three pages of memory and two I/O devices. One of the pages of memory (page 2) has a long access time, as indicated by the wait state generator connected to its page select line. The 8085 primary system is composed of the 8085A, demultiplexer, and control signal generator (see Figure 2-15). It is from the 8085 primary system that the system's buses originate. The outputs of the control signal generator and the 8085A output $\overline{INTA}$ form the control bus. The address and data buses are formed by 8085A address pins A_{15}–A_8 and multiplexed address/data pins AD_7–AD_0.

Because the interrupt request pins (INTR, RST 5.5, and so on) and the hold pin (DMA) are grounded, the system does not have interrupt or DMA capability. Note that all input pins must have an appropriate logic level applied—never leave an input disconnected. Many inputs float high when not connected, and all unconnected inputs are susceptible to noise. In later chapters the system of Figure 4-27 will be modified to allow interrupts and DMA.

The circuitry attached to input $\overline{RESIN}$ of the 8085A will give an automatic reset request when the system is powered up. A reset request can be made thereafter by closing the reset switch. The automatic power-on reset is necessary so that the MPU's first action is always the same, to fetch and execute the instruction at the reset address (PC = 0000H). Thus, the first instruction of the system's program is stored at address 0000H so that on power-up the MPU will begin program execution with that instruction. If a power-on reset capability is not provided, then at power-on the PC will be some random number, which will result in an unpredictable data byte being fetched from memory.

The automatic power-on reset circuitry functions in the following manner: Upon power-up, V_{CC} becomes $+5$ V, which causes the capacitor to begin charging to a value of V_{CC}, according to the circuit's RC-time constant equation

$$V_C = V_{CC} (1 - e^{-t/RC}) \qquad (4-11)$$

8212
8-BIT INPUT/OUTPUT PORT

- Fully Parallel 8-Bit Data Register and Buffer
- Service Request Flip-Flop for Interrupt Generation
- Low Input Load Current — .25mA Max.
- Three State Outputs
- Outputs Sink 15mA
- 3.65V Output High Voltage for Direct Interface to 8008, 8080A, or 8085A CPU
- Asynchronous Register Clear
- Replaces Buffers, Latches and Multiplexers in Microcomputer Systems
- Reduces System Package Count

The 8212 input/output port consists of an 8-bit latch with 3-state output buffers along with control and device selection logic. Also included is a service request flip-flop for the generation and control of interrupts to the microprocessor.

The device is multimode in nature. It can be used to implement latches, gated buffers or multiplexers. Thus, all of the principal peripheral and input/output functions of a microcomputer system can be implemented with this device.

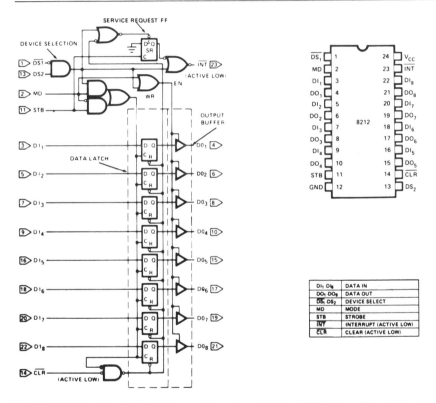

FIGURE 4-26. An 8212 being used to demultiplex 8085 pins AD_0–AD_7. (Courtesy of Intel Corp.)

The RC-time constant is designed so that $\overline{RESIN}$ is held active (low) for at least three clock periods, which is the minimum requirement for the 8085A to be

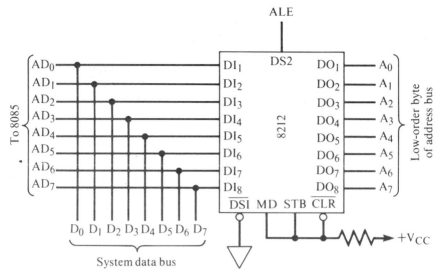

FIGURE 4-26. (continued)

reset. Under this condition Equation (4-11) becomes

$$V_C = V_{IL} < V_{CC} (1 - e^{-3T/RC}) \qquad (4\text{-}12)$$

where $T = t_{CYC}$. Equation (4-12) states that V_C—(Equation 4-11)—must be less than V_{IL} for 3T sec (three clock periods).

Solving Equation (4-12) for the minimum RC-time constant, we find

$$RC_{Min} > 3T/\ln [V_{CC}/(V_{CC} - V_{IL})] \qquad (4\text{-}13)$$

Once the capacitor becomes charged ($V_C > V_{IH}$), the input $\overline{RESIN}$ is inactive and will remain so until either the capacitor is short-circuited, via the reset switch, or the system is powered down and then again powered up at some later time.

Because there are two unknowns in Equation (4-13), another equation is needed. The second equation can be arrived at by realizing that the resistor R serves as a current-limiting component and that at $t = 0$ the capacitor appears as an equivalent short-circuit—substitute $t = 0$ into Equation (4-11). Then at $t = 0$,

$$I = V_{CC} / R \qquad (4\text{-}14)$$

Limiting the current to 0.1 mA at $t = 0$ requires

$$R = V_{CC} / I = 5 / 0.1 \times 10^{-3} = 50K$$

Then Equation (4-13) becomes

$$C > 3T / R \ln [V_{CC} / (V_{CC} - V_{IL})] \qquad (4\text{-}15)$$

or

$$C > 3T / 50 \times 10^3 \ln [V_{CC} / (V_{CC} - V_{IL})] \qquad (4\text{-}16)$$

Usually a large margin of safety is provided, and C is made to be in the micro-farad range.

To implement the 8085 primary system demultiplexer, a latch is required, of which there are many choices. The one we chose is the 8212 (a negative edge trigger is required), which is illustrated in Figure 4-26. The MD (mode) input enables either the device selects ($\overline{DS1}$ and DS2) or the STB as the latch strobe (C) signal. We shall use one of the device select inputs ($\overline{DS1}$) as the strobe pulse input, thus requiring MD to be held high. From the logic diagram we see that forcing MD high will also activate the 8212's output buffers. Intel's data sheet on the 8212 states, "The output Q of the flip-flop will follow the data input (D) while the clock input (C) is high. Latching will occur when the clock (C) returns low." Using ALE to drive $\overline{DS1}$ with MD $= 1$ will cause the 8212 to latch the data byte (the low-order byte of the address—see Figure 2-16) on the negative edge of ALE, and that latched byte will be output via pins DO_1–DO_8. We believe the reader can reason the remaining pin logic and resulting operation of the 8212 configured as in Figure 4-26.

The memory map for the design of Figure 4-27 will have some unused addresses. This is caused by dedicating address pins A_0–A_{10} for addressing locations within a chip and A_{11}–A_{13} for selecting the chip, as illustrated in Figure 4-28a. The reader should verify the memory map of Figure 4-28 and understand that the wasted (unused) memory locations are the result of an inconsistent number of address pins among the various memory chips. Pages 0 and 2 occupy 2K (2^{11}) each of the map, and page 1 occupies 1K (2^{10}). This results in page 1's having 1K of memory addresses for which there are no memory locations (one more address pin on the 2114 is required to address 2K memory locations). Having unavailable addresses puts a burden on the programmer, as he or she must be certain not to use those addresses. But there is a hardware solution and that is to divide all memory pages into 1K blocks. This requires the 2716 to have two page select lines dedicated to it, as illustrated in Figure 4-28b. The reader should develop a memory map for this type of design.

Page 2 of Figure 4-27 is imagined to have too long an access time, thus requiring a wait-state generator. See Example 4-8.

The interrupts (RST 5.5, RST 6.5, and so on) are not presently used (they will be shortly) and so are tied low. The same is true of the HOLD pin (DMA). To reiterate, all input pins must have an appropriate logic level applied—never leave an input disconnected. Many inputs float high when not connected, and all unconnected inputs are susceptible to noise.

We believe that the system of Figure 4-27 is straightforward but will require the reader to study it thoroughly.

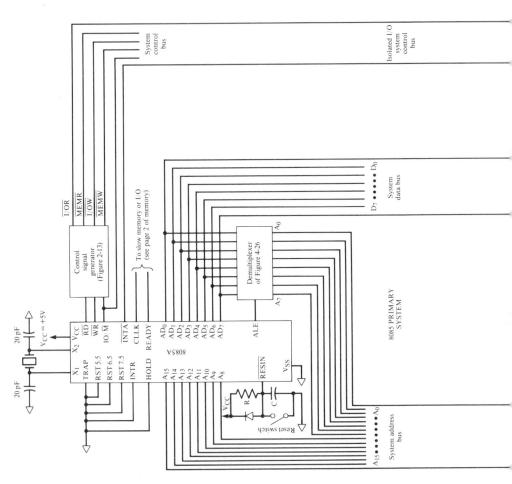

FIGURE 4-27. A basic 8085 system.

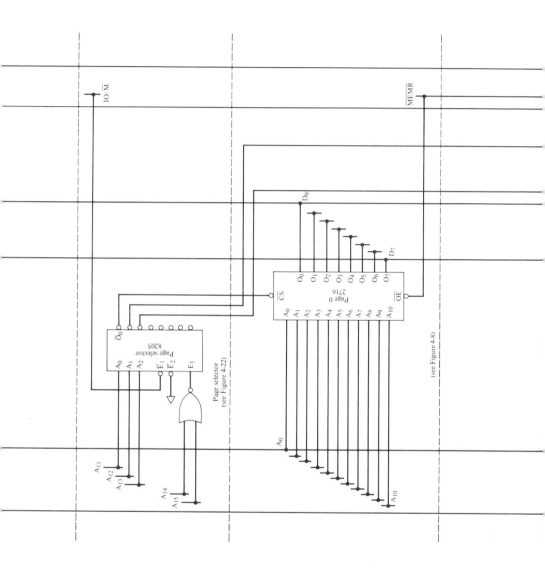

Page selector
(see Figure 4-22)

(see Figure 4-8)

127

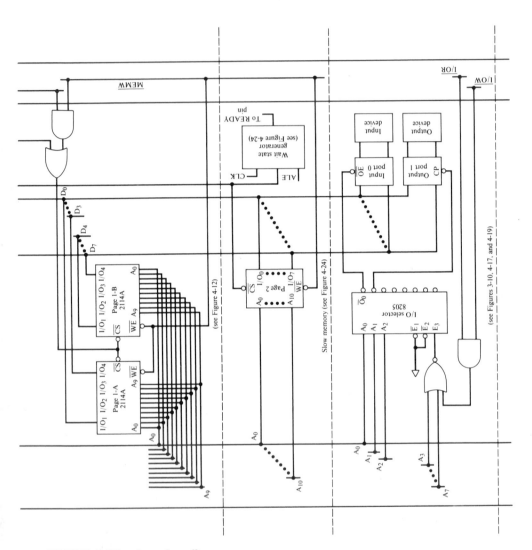

FIGURE 4-27. (continued)

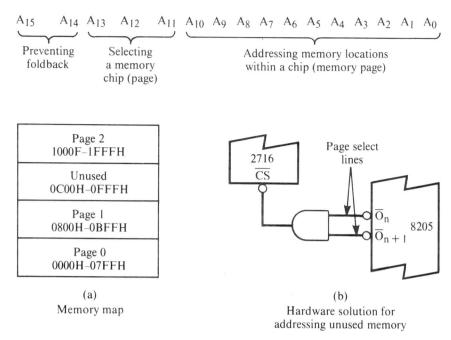

A_{15}	A_{14}	A_{13}	A_{12}	A_{11}	A_{10} A_9 A_8 A_7 A_6 A_5 A_4 A_3 A_2 A_1 A_0

Preventing foldback | Selecting a memory chip (page) | Addressing memory locations within a chip (memory page)

Page 2
1000F–1FFFH

Unused
0C00H–0FFFH

Page 1
0800H–0BFFH

Page 0
0000H–07FFH

(a)
Memory map

2716
$\overline{CS}$

Page select lines

$\overline{O}_n$
$\overline{O}_{n+1}$

8205

(b)
Hardware solution for addressing unused memory

FIGURE 4-28. **Decoding the address bus of Figure 4-27 and the resulting memory map.**

4-10

Adding Drivers to a Bus

Sometimes the driver component cannot handle the current requirements of the component(s) it is to drive. For example, recall that the 8085A cannot drive more than five 74LS374 latches. Whenever a driver's current capabilities are exceeded, a component with more current capability must be interfaced between the driver and the driven component(s). This type of interface is known as a *driver*, and the logic symbol used for drivers is shown in Figure 4-29.

The drivers of Figure 4-29 are tristate logic, which has been used as buffers thus far. Some use the term *buffer* and *driver* synonymously. The main criterion for a driver is that it be able to handle the required currents without altering the logic at its input, and therefore they need not be tristate. The configuration of Figure 4-29b shows that they can serve as bidirectional drivers (read or write) operations). It is usually buses that require drivers but it can also be a single line. Also, drivers are often required when a MOS device (8085A) must drive TTL loads (TTL requires current). It is recommended that the reader look up Intel's 8216 and, for comparison, a 74LS244.

In conclusion, when designing a system, if the current capabilities of any driver component is exceeded, then a driver, such as that illustrated in Figure 4-29, is required to be interfaced between the driver and the driven component. To determine whether a driver's current capabilities have been exceeded, simply

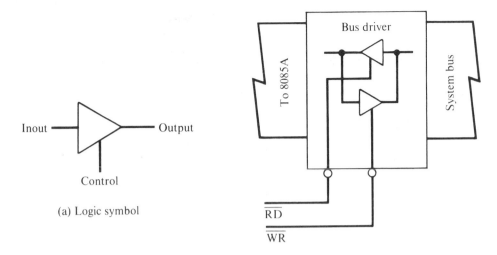

Inout ———▷——— Output

Control

(a) Logic symbol

Bus driver

To 8085A

System bus

$\overline{\text{RD}}$

$\overline{\text{WR}}$

(b) Logic configuration of driver

FIGURE 4-29. Logic symbol and logic configuration of a bus driver.

add (under worst-case conditions) those currents it must sink and source (I_{IL} and I_{IH}), and if these values are greater than I_{OL} or I_{OH}, then a driver is necessary.

4-11

Summary

When designing a MPU-bases system, both the electrical and timing character-istics of each component must be examined for compatibility. For the electrical characteristics the driver must fulfill the needs of the driven; that is, the electrical characteristics of the driver's output must be compatible with the input electrical characteristics of the driven. Both the voltage and the current characteristics (V_{OL} and V_{IL}, V_{OH} and V_{IH}, I_{OL} and I_{IL}, and I_{OH} and I_{IH}) must be compatible. If the driver's output current component is exceeded by the requirements of the driven component's input current, a driver interface is required.

Timing considerations are oriented to the MPU's timing. For the 8085A this requires that for read operations the access time of the device being read be less than t_{AD} (see Figure 4-6); otherwise a wait state (N) must be generated, via a wait-state generator and the 8085A's READY pin. We found that for read operations the negative edge of $\overline{\text{RD}}$ could be used to load the data byte of an addressed device on the data bus, as the 8085A uses the positive edge of T_3 to latch data off the data bus. For write operations the addressed device can use the positive edge of $\overline{\text{WR}}$ as a strobe to latch data off the data bus. If the addressed device cannot respond quickly enough for an 8085A write operation, it must generate the appropriate number (N) of wait states.

The 2716 is 2K $\times$ 8 EPROM with buffered outputs. The 2716 has a standby power feature that greatly reduces power consumption until the outputs are enabled. The 2114A is a 1K $\times$ 4 RAM with buffered outputs. Because the

2114A has ten address pins, there is one 1K of wasted memory (unused addresses) when it is used with a 2716, which has eleven address pins, unless the hardware solution of Figure 4-28b is used. The 2114A also requires pairing in an 8-bit system.

Input I/O devices require buffering when interfaced to the system's data bus, in order to prevent bus contention. These buffers are usually activated directly or indirectly by using signal $\overline{RD}$. Output I/O devices require latches as interfaces to the system's data bus, and the 8085A output signal $\overline{WR}$ is used directly or indirectly to strobe these latches.

There are two types of systems for addressing, address decoding and linear addressing. Address decoding uses decoders to select an addressed device, and linear addressing uses an address line to select a device. Address decoding utilizes all possible addresses, whereas linear addressing does not. And address decoding requires more hardware (a decoder) than does linear addressing.

REVIEW QUESTIONS AND PROBLEMS

1. Explain why the 8085A's electrical characteristics (see Table 4-1) do not show logic-level input currents I_{IL} and I_{IH} (the current I_{IL} of Table 4-1 is a leakage current—they unfortunately have the same nomenclature).

2. Why is it that input currents for MOS technology are not required for operation but that TTL technology does require input current (I_{IL})?

3. What electrical characteristics of the driver component are compared with which electrical characteristics of the driven?

4. In general, what is required for two components to be electrically compatible?

5. Demultiplex pins AD_0–AD_7 using a 74LS374.

6. In reference to the timing diagram of Figure 4-6
   (a) During what time interval is the 8085A using pins AD_0–AD_7 as address pins?
   (b) During what time interval are pins AD_0–AD_7 serving as data pins?
   (c) Why is it that the positive edge of ALE cannot be used as a strobe for the demultiplexer?

7. For write operations, Figure 4-6 shows that the 8085A holds the data byte at pins AD_0–AD_7 for t_{WD} sec after the positive edge of $\overline{WR}$. Why is the "extra" hold time t_{WD} necessary?

8. When comparing the timing parameters of memory and I/O with those of the 8085A, which 8085A parameters establish the timing criterion?

9. With reference to the timing diagram of Figure 4-6, explain why $\overline{RD}$ can serve as the read signal for memory or I/O.

10. It was stated that the positive edge of T_3 is used by the 8085A for reading (latching) data from the data bus. Using the timing diagram of Figure 4-6, explain why this appears to be a logical statement.

11. Compare the timing diagrams of Figures 4-6 and 4-23 and explain
    (a) How are wait states "inserted" for read and write operations? In your explanation, describe the timing.
    (b) How is the 8085A taken out of a wait state? Again, describe the timing.

12. For an 8085A system running at full speed, determine the actual read time t_{AD} for the number of wait states required for a device that has a read access time of
    (a) 1000 nsec
    (b) 1500 nsec
    (c) 2.5 msec
    (d) 10 msec

13. Repeat Problem 12 for 8085A write operations.

14. Design a wait-state generator for $N = 2$.

15. Redesign the I/O selector of Figure 4-27 to incorporate the timing needs of slow I/O, in which the selector is to decode the address as soon as possible (refer to the page selector design).

16. Explain the relationship among t_{ACC}, t_{CE}, and t_{OE} for the timing of a 2716, using Figure 4-9 as a reference.

17. In regard to the timing diagram of Figure 4-13, explain the relationship between t_A and t_{CO}.

18. Repeat Problem 17, but explain the relationship among t_{WC}, t_{WR}, and t_W.

19. Modify the timing diagram of Figure 4-13 for when $\overline{WE}$ goes low t_1 sec after the negative edge of $\overline{CS}$.

20. Explain the difference between
    (a) A memory-mapped I/O system and an isolated I/O system.
    (b) An address-decoded system and a linear-addressed system.

21. Change Figure 4-27 into a memory-mapped I/O system using linear addressing. Provide a memory map.

22. Modify the system of Figure 4-27 to incorporate slow output and input devices (devices 2 and 3).

23. Modify the system of Figure 4-27 to incorporate two additional memory chips and to make all addresses usable. These additional chips are to be 2732 memory

chips. Determine whether any of the buses will require current drivers with these additional chips.

24. Add drivers to the address and data buses of Figure 4-27.

25. Modify Figure 4-27 so that all memory locations are addressable. Explain your solution.

CHAPTER 5

Introduction to Programming with the 8085 Instruction Set

Introduction

This chapter begins by presenting the binary coding scheme of the 8085 instruction set, as well as Intel's symbolic representation of instructions (mnemonics). As the reader studies these topics, he or she should also get a feel for the instruction set and how those instructions can be used to instruct the MPU to achieve a task; that is, the reader should begin to develop programming skills. The reader should also understand the correlation between hardware and software and that software controls hardware. In our study we shall refer to schematics and timing diagrams such as those in Chapter 4.

8085 Instruction Set Coding Scheme

In this section we shall develop the binary coding scheme of the 8085 instruction set. Remember that the only instruction the MPU can "understand" (decode and execute) is a binary code. However, all those 1's and 0's would make it very confusing when being read by the user. For that reason the manufacturer's list of MPU instructions is given in two forms, of which one is intended for the user and the other for the MPU. The instruction set listing for the user is a *symbolic abbreviation* of the instruction and indicates the resultant MPU operation when executed. The instruction set listing for the MPU is the binary code for each instruction.

The term used to describe the symbolic representation of an instruction is *mnemonic,* which means "memory-aiding symbol."

Remember that the MPU must have a binary code in its IR before the CU can execute an instruction and that mnemonics are only a tool to aid the user in writing and reading program instructions. That is, programs are written in mnemonics so that the user and others reading a program can more easily interpret how the MPU is to accomplish a task. However, before the MPU can execute a program, it must first be translated into binary code and stored in memory (program memory). Hence it can be said that mnemonics is *human-oriented language,* whereas binary code is a *machine-oriented language* (microprocessors are often referred to as *machines*). In fact, some people use the terms *binary code* and *machine code* synonymously.

The process of translating an instruction from its mnemonic form to its machine code is termed *assembling.* If the user performs the assembling, the translating process is known as *hand-assembling.* But there are computer programs that assemble programs, which are called *assemblers* and are discussed in later chapters. This chapter will use hand assembly to introduce concepts that are common to assemblers.

If you, the reader, were the designer of a microprocessor such as the 8085, an integral part of your design would be the binary codes that instruct CPU operations via the IR, IR decoder, and CU. These binary codes are termed *op codes.* The collection, or repertoire, of op codes comprises the microprocessor's instruction set. For ease of coding instructions and minimizing decoding requirements in the CPU's IR decoder, you would like the op codes to have a logical pattern. In developing these binary codes you might begin by categorizing all MPU operations into groups and then assigning binary codes for each group. The 8085 microprocessor manufacturer categorizes MPU operations into four basic groups:

1. Data transfer.
2. Arithmetic and logic.
3. Branch control.
4. I/O and machine control.

TABLE 5-1. Coding for MPU Operations

OP_7	OP_6	MPU Operations
0	0	Manipulation of register contents
0	1	Data transfer among registers
1	0	Arithmetic and logic
1	1	Branch control and I/O

TABLE 5-2. Register Coding

Binary Code			Register
0	0	0	B
0	0	1	C
0	1	0	D
0	1	1	E
1	0	0	H
1	0	1	L
1	1	0	M (pseudo-register)
1	1	1	A

TABLE 5-3. RP Coding

Binary Code		Register Pair	
0	0	B	(B and C)
0	1	D	(D and E)
1	0	H	(H and L)
1	1	SP	

For coding purposes these groupings were slightly modified but still held to a group of four. Because basically any 8085 MPU operation is one of four groups, a 2-bit code will suffice for coding purposes. The two most significant bits (MSBs) of the op code are reserved to indicate MPU operation. When these two bits are decoded by the IR decoder, the CU knows which of the MPU internal circuits must be enabled to execute this category of instruction. Of course, the CU's microprogram instructs the CU how to execute the instruction. The coding for MPU operations according to group is approximately as shown in Table 5-1. The op-code bit positions are designated OP_0, OP_1, . . . , OP_7; hence OP_7 and OP_6 are the two MSBs.

From Table 5-1 we see that many operations will involve MPU internal registers A, B, C, and so on. Then in addition to coding MPU operations, a binary coding system is needed to specify those registers involved. A binary code will be required to specify not only individual registers but register pairs (RPs) as well (recall a data counter is formed from an RP). Intel's coding schemes for individual registers and register pairs are shown in Tables 5-2 and 5-3.

In Tables 5-2 and 5-3 we see two variations from a strict interpretation of the coding scheme. Table 5-2 contains a nonexistent M register and Table 5-3 contains the stack pointer (SP), which is a single 16-bit register and not a 16-bit register pair. These are just coding variations.

As a note, the symbol M is used in Intel's mnemonics to indicate register pair H and L. Whenever the symbol M is used in an instruction, it refers to a memory location where the address is the contents of RP H (H and L).

As an example of utilizing Tables 5-2 and 5-3 for determining machine code,

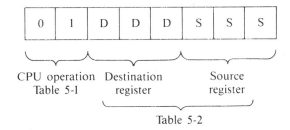

FIGURE 5-1. Machine code format for MOV r1,r2.

TABLE 5-4. Examples of Machine Code for MOV r1,r2

Mnemonic	Machine Code			Comments
MOV C,D	01	001	010	Move data from D to C
MOV D,C	01	010	001	Move data from C to D
MOV M,A	01	110	111	Move data from A to memory location M (RP H furnishes the address)
MOV A,M	01	111	110	Move data from M to A
MOV E,B	01	011	000	Move data from B to E

let us focus on the group "data transfer among registers" of Table 5-1. This group of instructions causes the CU to transfer data from one MPU register to another or to transfer data from memory to an MPU register (or vice versa). Intel's mnemonic code is MOV r1,r2 for this group, where MOV is the mnemonic for MOVE and r1,r2 represents the registers involved in the data transfer. Register r1 is the destination register of the data transfer, and r2 is the origin register of the data transfer. Specifically, if the content of register B is to be moved to register A, the mnemonic for that instruction will be MOV A,B, where r1 = A and r2 = B. To determine the machine code for MOV A,B, refer to the format of Figure 5-1, which is Intel's coding scheme for the MOV r1,r2 instruction. As shown in Figure 5-1, the binary code for a MOV r1,r2 operation is 01, which agrees with Table 5-1. The destination register, which is A, is to be coded according to Table 5-2 and that code placed in bit positions DDD of Figure 5-1. The source register, which is B, is also to be coded from Table 5-2 and its coding placed in bit positions SSS of Figure 5-1. Then the machine code for MOV A, B is 01111000. Other examples of coding the MOV r1,r2 instruction are shown in Table 5-4.

To continue with the deciphering of Intel's 8085 instruction set binary coding, return to Table 5-1. Now let us consider the coding of arithmetic and logic operations. This group of operations will use the MPU's ALU. The MPU architecture of Figure 2-12 shows the ALU with two inputs: register A and the temporary register. Hence all ALU operations must occur between the data of

TABLE 5-5. Binary and Mnemonic Coding ALU Operations

Binary Code	Arithmetic or Logic Operation	Mnemonics	
		Two Letters	Three Letters
0 0 0	Addition	AD	ADD
0 0 1	Add with carry	AC	ADC
0 1 0	Subtraction	SU	SUB
0 1 1	Subtract with borrow	SB	SBB
1 0 0	AND	AN	AND
1 0 1	Exclusive-OR	XR	XRA
1 1 0	OR	OR	ORA
1 1 1	Compare	CP	CMP

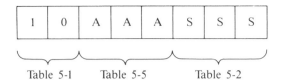

FIGURE 5-2. Machine code format for arithmetic and logic operations.

register A and the temporary register. The temporary register will be loaded by the CU with the contents of either a source register (scratch-pad memory) or external memory, depending on the specific instruction. With some thought it becomes obvious that the instructions of the arithmetic and logic groups must have a coding that will determine the ALU operation to be performed (add, subtract, OR, and so on) and also will indicate which register content is to be loaded into the temporary register. Because all ALU operations involve register A, it need not be specified in the instruction. Table 5-5 gives the coding scheme for arithmetic and logic operations.

The machine code format for arithmetic and logic operations is shown in Figure 5-2. As in Figure 5-1, SSS represents the source register, which is determined from Table 5-2. AAA is the 3-bit code of Table 5-5, representing the arithmetic or logic operation to be executed.

As an example of coding an arithmetic or logic instruction, consider ADD D. ADD D instructs the CU to add the content of register D to the accumulator A and the result to be placed in A (notice that from the mnemonic form, register A is understood). For machine coding we refer to the tables indicated in Figure 5-2, which results in a binary code of 10000010 for the instruction. Examples of other machine codes for various arithmetic or logic instructions are shown in Table 5-6.

TABLE 5-6. Examples of Arithmetic and Logic Instructions Machine Codes*

Machine Code	Mnemonic	Arithmetic or Logic Operation
10011110	SBB M	The content of the memory location whose address is contained in H and L is subtracted from the content of A. The result is placed in A.
10111000	CMP B	The content of B is compared (subtracted) with the content of A, and the result is indicated by appropriately altering the C and Z flags. The values being compared remain unchanged.
10101001	XRA C	The content of C is exclusive-ORed with the content of A. The result is placed in A.

*See Tables 5-1, 5-2, and 5-5.

TABLE 5-7. Machine Code for Branch Operations

Machine Code	Branch Operation
000	Return: Used to return the MPU to the execution of an interrupted program.
010	Jump: Used to jump from one memory location to another, with no intention of returning to the memory location where the jump instruction was given.
100	Call: Used to "call up" (jump to) a subroutine (another program) for execution, with the intention of returning after execution of the subroutine. As a result, a call instruction must store (in the stack) the return address.

The last category of MPU operations that we shall investigate is the coding scheme for the branch control and I/O groups of Table 5-1. In fact, we shall discuss only conditional branch operations, which should provide adequate understanding of the coding concepts for this group.

There are three types of branch operations. The branch operations and their binary codes are shown in Table 5-7. At this point the reader need not be concerned with every detail of branch operations, only with the overall concepts. Notice that a jump and a call both allow the MPU to transfer program execution from one memory location to another. However, the call stores on the stack the content of PC + 1 (next memory location), which is the return address, so that it may be recalled by the MPU when a return instruction is given.

As stated, we are coding conditional branch operations, which essentially means that the CU will check a condition flag for a proper logic state to determine whether the branch instruction is to be executed. Then the programmer (you) must be able to determine the machine code, which indicates (1) the branch operation to be executed, (2) the condition flag to be checked, and (3) the logic

TABLE 5-8. Machine Code for Condition Flag and Logic State

Machine Code	Condition Flag	Logic State of Flag	Mnemonic Code	Result of the MPU's ALU Operation
000	Zero	0	NZ	Is not zero
001	(Z flag)	1	Z	Is zero
010	Carry	0	NC	There is no carry
011	(C flag)	1	C	There is a carry
100	Parity	0	PO	Has odd parity
101	(P flag)	1	PE	Has even parity
110	Sign	0	P	Is positive
111	(S flag)	1	M	Is negative

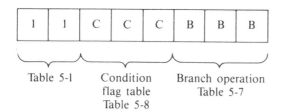

Table 5-1   Condition   Branch operation
               flag table   Table 5-7
               Table 5-8

FIGURE 5-3.   Machine code format for conditional branch instructions.

state required of the condition flag in order that the instruction execution be implemented. The coding requirement of 1 is satisfied by the binary codes of Table 5-7. For the requirements of 2 and 3, see Table 5-8. The machine code format is shown in Figure 5-3.

As an example of machine's coding a conditional branch instruction, let us consider the instruction JNZ ADR. The mnemonic JNZ represents "jump on nonzero," and ADR is symbolic of the operand, which is a memory address. When JNZ ADR is executed, the CU will check the logic state of the Z flag. If the Z flag is in a 0 state (see NZ of Table 5-8), program execution will be transferred (jump) to the memory location specified by the 16-bit binary number symbolically represented by ADR. However, if the Z flag is in a 1 state, the CU will not transfer program execution to the memory location specified by ADR but, rather, continue executing the program by fetching the next sequential instruction after JNZ ADR. To determine the machine code, refer first to Figure 5-3 for the format and then to Tables 5-8 and 5-7, as specified in Figure 5-3. Hence the mnemonic JNZ will be assembled into machine code 11 000 010. Of

TABLE 5-9.   Examples of Conditional Branch Instruction Machine Codes*

Machine Code			Mnemonic	MPU Operation
11	001	010	JZ ADR	Jump to the memory location specified by ADR if $Z = 1$; otherwise, continue program execution.
11	100	010	JPO ADR	Jump to the memory location specified by ADR if $P = 0$; otherwise, continue program execution.
11	001	100	CZ ADR	Jump to the memory location specified by ADR if $Z = 1$, and store (PUSH) the *address* of the next instruction on the stack; otherwise, continue program execution.
11	111	000	RM	If $S = 1$, retrieve (POP) two 8-bit codes from the stack and place them in the PC. Then return to the address specified by the PC and begin program execution. If $S = 0$, continue program execution.

*See Tables 5-1, 5-7, and 5-8.

TABLE 5-10. 8085A Instruction Set

Code	Instruction	Code	Instruction	Code	Instruction	Code	Instruction	Code	Instruction	Code	Instruction
00	NOP	2B	DCX H	56	MOV D,M	81	ADD C	AC	XRA H	D7	RST 2
01	LXI B,dble	2C	INR L	57	MOV D,A	82	ADD D	AD	XRA L	D8	RC
02	STAX B	2D	DCR L	58	MOV E,B	83	ADD E	AE	XRA M	D9	- - -
03	INX B	2E	MVI L,byte	59	MOV E,C	84	ADD H	AF	XRA A	DA	JC adr
04	INR B	2F	CMA	5A	MOV E,D	85	ADD L	B0	ORA B	DB	IN byte
05	DCR B	30	SIM	5B	MOV E,E	86	ADD M	B1	ORA C	DC	CC adr
06	MVI B,byte	31	LXI SP,dble	5C	MOV E,H	87	ADD A	B2	ORA D	DD	- - -
07	RLC	32	STA adr	5D	MOV E,L	88	ADC B	B3	ORA E	DE	SBI byte
08	- - -	33	INX SP	5E	MOV E,M	89	ADC C	B4	ORA H	DF	RST 3
09	DAD B	34	INR M	5F	MOV E,A	8A	ADC D	B5	ORA L	E0	RPO
0A	LDAX B	35	DCR M	60	MOV H,B	8B	ADC E	B6	ORA M	E1	POP H
0B	DCX B	36	MVI M,byte	61	MOV H,C	8C	ADC H	B7	ORA A	E2	JPO adr
0C	INR C	37	STC	62	MOV H,D	8D	ADC L	B8	CMP B	E3	XTHL
0D	DCR C	38	- - -	63	MOV H,E	8E	ADC M	B9	CMP C	E4	CPO adr
0E	MVI C,byte	39	DAD SP	64	MOV H,H	8F	ADC A	BA	CMP D	E5	PUSH H
0F	RRC	3A	LDA adr	65	MOV H,L	90	SUB B	BB	CMP E	E6	ANI byte
10	- - -	3B	DCX SP	66	MOV H,M	91	SUB C	BC	CMP H	E7	RST 4
11	LXI D,dble	3C	INR A	67	MOV H,A	92	SUB D	BD	CMP L	E8	RPE
12	STAX D	3D	DCR A	68	MOV L,B	93	SUB E	BE	CMP M	E9	PCHL
13	INX D	3E	MVI A,byte	69	MOV L,C	94	SUB H	BF	CMP A	EA	JPE adr
14	INR D	3F	CMC	6A	MOV L,D	95	SUB L	C0	RNZ	EB	XCHG
15	DCR D	40	MOV B,B	6B	MOV L,E	96	SUB M	C1	POP B	EC	CPE adr
16	MVI D,byte	41	MOV B,C	6C	MOV L,H	97	SUB A	C2	JNZ adr	ED	- - -

Code	Instruction	Code	Instruction	Code	Instruction	Code	Instruction	Code	Instruction	Code	Instruction
17	RAL	42	MOV B,D	6D	MOV L,L	98	SBB B	C3	JMP adr	EE	XRI byte
18	- -	43	MOV B,E	6E	MOV L,M	99	SBB C	C4	CNZ adr	EF	RST 5
19	DAD D	44	MOV B,H	6F	MOV L,A	9A	SBB D	C5	PUSH B	F0	RP
1A	LDAX D	45	MOV B,L	70	MOV M,B	9B	SBB E	C6	ADI byte	F1	POP PSW
1B	DCX D	46	MOV B,M	71	MOV M,C	9C	SBB H	C7	RST 0	F2	JP adr
1C	INR E	47	MOV B,A	72	MOV M,D	9D	SBB L	C8	RZ	F3	DI
1D	DCR E	48	MOV C,B	73	MOV M,E	9E	SBB M	C9	RET	F4	CP adr
1E	MVI E,byte	49	MOV C,C	74	MOV M,H	9F	SBB A	CA	JZ adr	F5	PUSH PSW
1F	RAR	4A	MOV C,D	75	MOV M,L	A0	ANA B	CB	- - -	F6	ORI byte
20	RIM	4B	MOV C,E	76	HLT	A1	ANA C	CC	CZ adr	F7	RST 6
21	LXI H,dble adr	4C	MOV C,H	77	MOV M,A	A2	ANA D	CD	CALL adr	F8	RM
22	SHLD adr	4D	MOV C,L	78	MOV A,B	A3	ANA E	CE	ACI byte	F9	SPHL
23	INX H	4E	MOV C,M	79	MOV A,C	A4	ANA H	CF	RST 1	FA	JM adr
24	INR H	4F	MOV C,A	7A	MOV A,D	A5	ANA L	D0	RNC	FB	EI
25	DCR H	50	MOV D,B	7B	MOV A,E	A6	ANA M	D1	POP D	FC	CM adr
26	MVI H,byte	51	MOV D,C	7C	MOV A,H	A7	ANA A	D2	JNC ADR	FD	- -
27	DAA	52	MOV D,D	7D	MOV A,L	A8	XRA B	D3	OUT byte	FE	CPI byte
28	- - -	53	MOV D,E	7E	MOV A,M	A9	XRA C	D4	CNC adr	FF	RST 7
29	DAD H	54	MOV D,H	7F	MOV A,A	AA	XRA D	D5	PUSH D		
2A	LHLD adr	55	MOV D,L	80	ADD B	AB	XRA E	D6	SUI byte		

D8 = constant, or logical/arithmetic expression that evalutes to an 8-bit data quantity.

Adr = 16-bit address.

D16 = constant, or logical/arithmetic expression that evaluates to a 16-bit data quantity.

(Courtesy of Intel Corp.)

143

course because an address is required, two more 8-bit binary numbers must follow 11 000 010. Then the JNZ instruction will require three 8-bit codes; the first represents the op code (11000010), and the next two codes specify the address. These three 8-bit codes will be stored in successive memory locations.

Other machine codes for various conditional branch instructions are shown in Table 5-9. Refer to Figure 5-3 for the binary formatting. To reiterate, the mechanics of instruction execution are not of primary importance at this time but, rather, the concepts of coding instructions.

This concludes our deciphering of Intel's machine coding of the 8085 instruction set. Even though only relatively few instructions were coded, we believe that enough examples were given that the concepts of instruction coding should be well understood. Also, from previous discussions the roles of the IR and IR decoder should be quite clear. Fortunately, it is not necessary to memorize an instruction-coding format, for Intel has already done most of the assembly for the user and provides the machine code in table form. Such a table is shown in Table 5-10 and in Appendix A. For brevity, machine codes are given in their hexadecimal equivalent rather than in binary form. This presentation will be used primarily throughout the remainder of this book.

Also notice in Table 5-10 that the term *byte* is used in instructions, such as OUT byte (machine code D3) and IN byte (machine code DB). Byte is defined to be any 8-bit binary number. Thus OUT byte is a two-byte instruction; the first byte for the op code and the second byte for the address of the output device. We shall henceforth use "byte" to describe any 8-bit word. That terminology probably arose by imagining that an 8-bit MPU would "bite" (latch) data from the data bus 8 bits at a time; hence, for the MPU, 8 bits comprise one byte. With this reasoning, half a byte (4 bits) is a *nibble*.

In viewing Table 5-10, you will note a number of unfamiliar instructions, but the next section will explain each.

5-3

8085 Instruction Set

Before writing a program for a microprocessor, the programmer must know the microprocessor's vocabulary, the microprocessor's instruction set. The instruction sets of microprocessors vary from type to type, and for that reason the designer/manufacturer of each type must make the instruction set available to the user. The instruction set and an explanation of MPU operations resulting from execution of an instruction are supplied by the manufacturer in a programming manual and/or user's manual. This section includes a reproduction of Intel's instruction set as taken from Intel's *MCS-80/85 User's Manual*. We encourage the reader to obtain an Intel manual containing the instruction set—there is no substitute for the real thing.

Do not attempt to memorize the instruction set and explanations; rather, concentrate on understanding the explanation of each instruction. This is the only reasonable approach, as there is just too much to memorize. As one uses the instructions, less and less reference to the manual will be required. Also, as one learns the instruction set for one type of microprocessor, the foundation is laid for understanding the principles of all microprocessor instruction sets.

To study this section:

1. Confirm the topics and concepts that we have already discussed. This includes
   a. Instruction categories (data transfer, and the like.).
   b. Condition flags and their meaning.
   c. Symbols, abbreviations, and register coding.
   d. Number of machine cycles required and control signals generated.
2. Read the explanation of each instruction and attempt to gain a feeling for MPU operations resulting from execution of that instruction.
3. Study the machine code format of each instruction and attempt to assemble some machine codes for various sample instructions. Verify your assembly of mnemonic code into machine code using Table 5-10. Also confirm the machine code of those examples given in Tables 5-4, 5-5, and 5-9.
4. Study and understand the various addressing modes used in programming the 8085. Some brief explanations and examples of addressing modes will be offered to supplement Intel's explanations. For concreteness of addressing modes, read Intel's explanation of each example instruction.
   a. *Direct addressing.* These are three-byte instructions in which the first byte is the op code, and the remaining two bytes furnish the memory address of the data operation (read or write). Examples are STA ADR, SHLD ADR, and LDA ADR.
   b. *Register addressing.* These are single-byte instructions that manipulate the MPU's register's contents. The instruction identifies (addresses) the register(s) to be involved in the manipulation. Examples are DCR B, DAD B, INX D, MOV B, E, and ANA D.
   c. *Register indirect addressing.* This type of instruction requires data from memory. However, being a single-byte instruction, the memory address cannot be coded as part of the instruction. To "extend" the addressing capability of these instructions the instruction specifies a register pair to serve as the DC. Examples are LDAX B, MOV B, M, ADD M, INR M, and STAX D.
   d. *Immediate addressing.* The data to be manipulated by the instruction is part of that instruction's machine code. As a result, this type of instruction is either two or three bytes. The first byte is the op code, and the next byte(s) is the data. Examples are LXI B, 253CH (H identifies 253C as being a hexadecimal value), MVI A, 3DH, and ADI 61H. Notice that the mnemonics identify immediate addressing with the symbol I.

Notice from the instruction set that when an instruction involves a register pair, Intel chose to use the symbol X in the mnemonic.

The following is a reproduction of the 8085 instruction set as reprinted from Intel's MCS-80/85 *User's Manual.** The term *cycle* refers to machine cycle (M_1, M_2, and so on), and the term *state* refers to a period (T_1, T_2, and so on), as indicated in Figure 2-16. Also note that some in the industry use the terms *CPU* and *MPU* synonymously, whereas others differentiate between them. From the following reprint we see that Intel uses the term *CPU* instead of *MPU*. Hence, from this point forward the terms *CPU* and *MPU* will have the same meaning in this textbook.

WHAT THE INSTRUCTION SET IS

A computer, no matter how sophisticated, can do only what it is instructed to do. A program is a sequence of instructions, each of which is recognized by the computer and causes it to perform an operation. Once a program is placed in memory space that is accessible to your CPU, you may run that same sequence of instructions as often as you wish to solve the same problem or to do the same function. The set of instructions to which the 8085A CPU will respond is permanently fixed in the design of the chip.

Each computer instruction allows you to initiate the performance of a specific operation. The 8085A implements a group of instructions that move data between registers, between a register and memory, and between a register and an I/O port. It also has arithmetic and logic instructions, conditional and unconditional branch instructions, and machine control instructions. The CPU recognizes these instructions only when they are coded in binary form.

SYMBOLS AND ABBREVIATIONS:

The following symbols and abbreviations are used in the subsequent description of the 8085A instructions:

SYMBOLS	MEANING
accumulator	Register A
addr	16-bit address quantity
data	8-bit quantity
data 16	16-bit data quantity
byte 2	The second byte of the instruction
byte 3	The third byte of the instruction
port	8-bit address of an I/O device
r,r1,r2	One of the registers A,B,C, D,E,H,L

*All mnemonics copyrighted © Intel Corporation 1976.

DDD,SSS — The bit pattern designating one of the registers A,B,C,D, E,H,L (DDD = destination, SSS = source):

DDD or SSS	REGISTER NAME
111	A
000	B
001	C
010	D
011	E
100	H
101	L

rp — One of the register pairs:

B represents the B,C pair with B as the high-order register and C as the low-order register;

D represents the D,E pair with D as the high-order register and E as the low-order register;

H represents the H,L pair with H as the high-order register and L as the low-order register;

SP represents the 16-bit stack pointer register.

RP — The bit pattern designating one of the register pairs B,D,H,SP:

RP	REGISTER PAIR
00	B-C
01	D-E
10	H-L
11	SP

rh — The first (high-order) register of a designated register pair.

rl — The second (low-order) register of a designated register pair.

5-1

PC	16-bit program counter register (PCH and PCL are used to refer to the high-order and low-order 8 bits respectively).
SP	16-bit stack pointer register (SPH and SPL are used to refer to the high-order and low-order 8 bits respectively).
r_m	Bit m of the register r (bits are number 7 through 0 from left to right).
LABEL	16-bit address of subroutine.

The condition flags:

Z	Zero
S	Sign
P	Parity
CY	Carry
AC	Auxiliary Carry
( )	The contents of the memory location or registers enclosed in the parentheses.
←	"Is transferred to"
∧	Logical AND
⩒	Exclusive OR
∨	Inclusive OR
+	Addition
−	Two's complement subtraction
•	Multiplication
↔	"Is exchanged with"
‾‾	The one's complement (e.g., $\overline{(A)}$)
n	The restart number 0 through 7
NNN	The binary representation 000 through 111 for restart number 0 through 7 respectively.

The instruction set encyclopedia is a detailed description of the 8085A instruction set. Each instruction is described in the following manner:

1. The MCS-85 macro assembler format, consisting of the instruction mnemonic and operand fields, is printed in **BOLDFACE** on the first line.

2. The name of the instruction is enclosed in parentheses following the mnemonic.

3. The next lines contain a symbolic description of what the instruction does.

4. This is followed by a narrative description of the operation of the instruction.

*All mnemonics copyrighted © Intel Corporation 1976.   5-2

5. The boxes describe the binary codes that comprise the machine instruction.

6. The last four lines contain information about the execution of the instruction. The number of machine cycles and states required to execute the instruction are listed first. If the instruction has two possible execution times, as in a conditional jump, both times are listed, separated by a slash. Next, data addressing modes are listed if applicable. The last line lists any of the five flags that are affected by the execution of the instruction.

5.3 INSTRUCTION AND DATA FORMATS

Memory used in the MCS-85 system is organized in 8-bit bytes. Each byte has a unique location in physical memory. That location is described by one of a sequence of 16-bit binary addresses. The 8085A can address up to 64K (K = 1024, or 2^{10}; hence, 64K represents the decimal number 65,536) bytes of memory, which may consist of both random-access, read-write memory (RAM) and read-only memory (ROM), which is also random-access.

Data in the 8085A is stored in the form of 8-bit binary integers:

DATA WORD

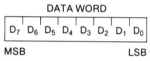

MSB   LSB

When a register or data word contains a binary number, it is necessary to establish the order in which the bits of the number are written. In the Intel 8085A, BIT 0 is referred to as the **Least Significant Bit (LSB)**, and BIT 7 (of an 8-bit number) is referred to as the **Most Significant Bit (MSB)**.

An 8085A program instruction may be one, two or three bytes in length. Multiple-byte instructions must be stored in successive memory locations; the address of the first byte is always used as the address of the instruction. The exact instruction format will depend on the particular operation to be executed.

Single Byte Instructions

Two-Byte Instructions

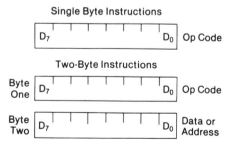

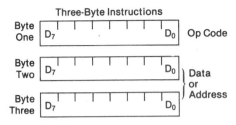

Three-Byte Instructions

Byte One — D_7 ... D_0 — Op Code

Byte Two — D_7 ... D_0 — Data or Address

Byte Three — D_7 ... D_0

5.4 ADDRESSING MODES:

Often the data that is to be operated on is stored in memory. When multi-byte numeric data is used, the data, like instructions, is stored in successive memory locations, with the least significant byte first, followed by increasingly significant bytes. The 8085A has four different modes for addressing data stored in memory or in registers:

- Direct — Bytes 2 and 3 of the instruction contain the exact memory address of the data item (the low-order bits of the address are in byte 2, the high-order bits in byte 3).

- Register — The instruction specifies the register or register pair in which the data is located.

- Register Indirect — The instruction specifies a register pair which contains the memory address where the data is located (the high-order bits of the address are in the first register of the pair the low-order bits in the second).

- Immediate — The instruction contains the data itself. This is either an 8-bit quantity or a 16-bit quantity (least significant byte first, most significant byte second).

Unless directed by an interrupt or branch institution, the execution of instructions proceeds through consecutively increasing memory locations. A branch instruction can specify the address of the next instruction to be executed in one of two ways:

- Direct — The branch instruction contains the address of the next instruction to be executed. (Except for the 'RST' instruction, byte 2 contains the low-order address and byte 3 the high-order address.)

- Register Indirect — The branch instruction indicates a register-pair which contains the address of the next instruction to be executed. (The high-order bits of the address are in the first register of the pair, the low-order bits in the second.)

The RST instruction is a special one-byte call instruction (usually used during interrupt sequences). RST includes a three-bit field; program control is transferred to the instruction whose address is eight times the contents of this three-bit field.

5.5 CONDITION FLAGS:

There are five condition flags associated with the execution of instructions on the 8085A. They are Zero, Sign, Parity, Carry, and Auxiliary Carry. Each is represented by a 1-bit register (or flip-flop) in the CPU. A flag is set by forcing the bit to 1; it is reset by forcing the bit to 0.

Unless indicated otherwise, when an instruction affects a flag, it affects it in the following manner:

Zero: If the result of an instruction has the value 0, this flag is set; otherwise it is reset.

Sign: If the most significant bit of the result of the operation has the value 1, this flag is set; otherwise it is reset.

Parity: If the modulo 2 sum of the bits of the result of the operation is 0, (i.e., if the result has even parity), this flag is set; otherwise it is reset (i.e., if the result has odd parity).

Carry: If the instruction resulted in a carry (from addition), or a borrow (from subtraction or a comparison) out of the high-order bit, this flag is set; otherwise it is reset.

Auxiliary Carry: If the instruction caused a carry out of bit 3 and into bit 4 of the resulting value, the auxiliary carry is set; otherwise it is reset. This flag is affected by single-precision additions, subtractions, increments, decrements, comparisons, and logical operations, but is principally used with additions and increments preceding a DAA (Decimal Adjust Accumulator) instruction.

*All mnemonics copyrighted©Intel Corporation 1976.   5-3

148   PROGRAMMING WITH THE 8085 INSTRUCTION SET

5.6 INSTRUCTION SET ENCYCLOPEDIA

In the ensuing dozen pages, the complete 8085A instruction set is described, grouped in order under five different functional headings, as follows:

1. **Data Transfer Group** — Moves data between registers or between memory locations and registers. Includes moves, loads, stores, and exchanges. (See below.)

2. **Arithmetic Group** — Adds, subtracts, increments, or decrements data in registers or memory.

3. **Logic Group** — ANDs, ORs, XORs, compares, rotates, or complements data in registers or between memory and a register.

4. **Branch Group** — Initiates conditional or unconditional jumps, calls, returns, and restarts.

5. **Stack, I/O, and Machine Control Group** — Includes instructions for maintaining the stack, reading from input ports, writing to output ports, setting and reading interrupt masks, and setting and clearing flags.

The formats described in the encyclopedia reflect the assembly language processed by Intel-supplied assembler, used with the Intellec® development systems.

5.6.1 Data Transfer Group

This group of instructions transfers data to and from registers and memory. **Condition flags are not affected by any instruction in this group.**

MOV r1, r2   (Move Register)

(r1) ← (r2)

The content of register r2 is moved to register r1.

		Cycles:	1
		States:	4 (8085), 5 (8080)
		Addressing:	register
		Flags:	none

MOV r, M   (Move from memory)

(r) ← ((H) (L))

The content of the memory location, whose address is in registers H and L, is moved to register r.

		Cycles:	2
		States:	7
		Addressing:	reg. indirect
		Flags:	none

MOV M, r   (Move to memory)

((H)) (L)) ← (r)

The content of register r is moved to the memory location whose address is in registers H and L.

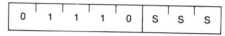

		Cycles:	2
		States:	7
		Addressing:	reg. indirect
		Flags:	none

MVI r, data   (Move Immediate)

(r) ← (byte 2)

The content of byte 2 of the instruction is moved to register r.

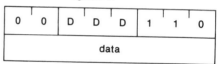

		Cycles:	2
		States:	7
		Addressing:	immediate
		Flags:	none

MVI M, data   (Move to memory immediate)

((H) (L)) ← (byte 2)

The content of byte 2 of the instruction is moved to the memory location whose address is in registers H and L.

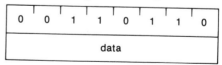

		Cycles:	3
		States:	10
		Addressing:	immed./reg. indirect
		Flags:	none

*All mnemonics copyrighted © Intel Corporation 1976.   5-4

LXI rp, data 16 (Load register pair immediate)
(rh) ← (byte 3),
(rl) ← (byte 2)
Byte 3 of the instruction is moved into the high-order register (rh) of the register pair rp. Byte 2 of the instruction is moved into the low-order register (rl) of the register pair rp.

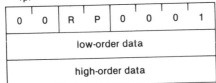

0	0	R	P	0	0	0	1
low-order data							
high-order data							

Cycles: 3
States: 10
Addressing: immediate
Flags: none

LDA addr (Load Accumulator direct)
(A) ← ((byte 3)(byte 2))
The content of the memory location, whose address is specified in byte 2 and byte 3 of the instruction, is moved to register A.

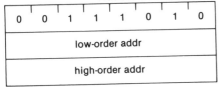

0	0	1	1	1	0	1	0
low-order addr							
high-order addr							

Cycles: 4
States: 13
Addressing: direct
Flags: none

STA addr (Store Accumulator direct)
((byte 3)(byte 2)) ← (A)
The content of the accumulator is moved to the memory location whose address is specified in byte 2 and byte 3 of the instruction.

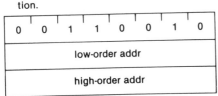

0	0	1	1	0	0	1	0
low-order addr							
high-order addr							

Cycles: 4
States: 13
Addressing: direct
Flags: none

LHLD addr (Load H and L direct)
(L) ← ((byte 3)(byte 2))
(H) ← ((byte 3)(byte 2) + 1)
The content of the memory location, whose address is specified in byte 2 and byte 3 of the instruction, is moved to register L. The content of the memory location at the succeeding address is moved to register H.

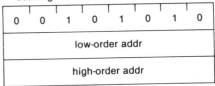

0	0	1	0	1	0	1	0
low-order addr							
high-order addr							

Cycles: 5
States: 16
Addressing: direct
Flags: none

SHLD addr (Store H and L direct)
((byte 3)(byte 2)) ← (L)
((byte 3)(byte 2) + 1) ← (H)
The content of register L is moved to the memory location whose address is specified in byte 2 and byte 3. The content of register H is moved to the succeeding memory location.

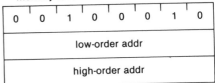

0	0	1	0	0	0	1	0
low-order addr							
high-order addr							

Cycles: 5
States: 16
Addressing: direct
Flags: none

LDAX rp (Load accumulator indirect)
(A) ← ((rp))
The content of the memory location, whose address is in the register pair rp, is moved to register A. Note: only register pairs rp = B (registers B and C) or rp = D (registers D and E) may be specified.

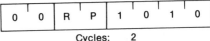

0	0	R	P	1	0	1	0

Cycles: 2
States: 7
Addressing: reg. indirect
Flags: none

*All mnemonics copyrighted © Intel Corporation 1976.   5-5

STAX rp (Store accumulator indirect)
((rp)) ← (A)
The content of register A is moved to the memory location whose address is in the register pair rp. Note: only register pairs rp = B (registers B and C) or rp = D (registers D and E) may be specified.

| 0 | 0 | R | P | 0 | 0 | 1 | 0 |

Cycles: 2
States: 7
Addressing: reg. indirect
Flags: none

XCHG (Exchange H and L with D and E)
(H) ↔ (D)
(L) ↔ (E)
The contents of registers H and L are exchanged with the contents of registers D and E.

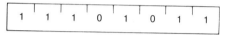

| 1 | 1 | 1 | 0 | 1 | 0 | 1 | 1 |

Cycles: 1
States: 4
Addressing: register
Flags: none

5.6.2 Arithmetic Group

This group of instructions performs arithmetic operations on data in registers and memory.

Unless indicated otherwise, all instructions in this group affect the Zero, Sign, Parity, Carry, and Auxiliary Carry flags according to the standard rules.

All subtraction operations are performed via two's complement arithmetic and set the carry flag to one to indicate a borrow and clear it to indicate no borrow.

ADD r (Add Register)
(A) ← (A) + (r)
The content of register r is added to the content of the accumulator. The result is placed in the accumulator.

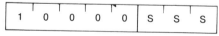

| 1 | 0 | 0 | 0 | 0 | S | S | S |

Cycles: 1
States: 4
Addressing: register
Flags: Z,S,P,CY,AC

5-6

ADD M (Add memory)
(A) ← (A) + ((H) (L))
The content of the memory location whose address is contained in the H and L registers is added to the content of the accumulator. The result is placed in the accumulator.

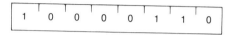

| 1 | 0 | 0 | 0 | 0 | 1 | 1 | 0 |

Cycles: 2
States: 7
Addressing: reg. indirect
Flags: Z,S,P,CY,AC

ADI data (Add immediate)
(A) ← (A) + (byte 2)
The content of the second byte of the instruction is added to the content of the accumulator. The result is placed in the accumulator.

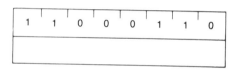

| 1 | 1 | 0 | 0 | 0 | 1 | 1 | 0 |

Cycles: 2
States: 7
Addressing: immediate
Flags: Z,S,P,CY,AC

ADC r (Add Register with carry)
(A) ← (A) + (r) + (CY)
The content of register r and the content of the carry bit are added to the content of the accumulator. The result is placed in the accumulator.

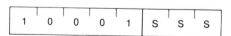

| 1 | 0 | 0 | 0 | 1 | S | S | S |

Cycles: 1
States: 4
Addressing: register
Flags: Z,S,P,CY,AC

ADC M   (Add memory with carry)

(A) ← (A) + ((H) (L)) + (CY)

The content of the memory location whose address is contained in the H and L registers and the content of the CY flag are added to the accumulator. The result is placed in the accumulator.

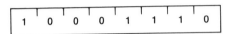

        Cycles: 2
        States: 7
 Addressing: reg. indirect
        Flags: Z,S,P,CY,AC

SUB M   (Subtract memory)

(A) ← (A) − ((H) (L))

The content of the memory location whose address is contained in the H and L registers is subtracted from the content of the accumulator. The result is placed in the accumulator.

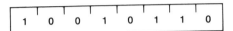

        Cycles: 2
        States: 7
 Addressing: reg. indirect
        Flags: Z,S,P,CY,AC

ACI data   (Add immediate with carry)

(A) ← (A) + (byte 2) + (CY)

The content of the second byte of the instruction and the content of the CY flag are added to the contents of the accumulator. The result is placed in the accumulator.

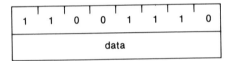

        Cycles: 2
        States: 7
 Addressing: immediate
        Flags: Z,S,P,CY,AC

SUI data   (Subtract immediate)

(A) ← (A) − (byte 2)

The content of the second byte of the instruction is subtracted from the content of the accumulator. The result is placed in the accumulator.

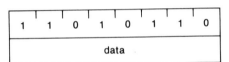

        Cycles: 2
        States: 7
 Addressing: immediate
        Flags: Z,S,P,CY,AC

SUB r   (Subtract Register)

(A) ← (A) − (r)

The content of register r is subtracted from the content of the accumulator. The result is placed in the accumulator.

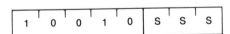

        Cycles: 1
        States: 4
 Addressing: register
        Flags: Z,S,P,CY,AC

SBB r   (Subtract Register with borrow)

(A) ← (A) − (r) − (CY)

The content of register r and the content of the CY flag are both subtracted from the accumulator. The result is placed in the accumulator.

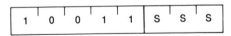

        Cycles: 1
        States: 4
 Addressing: register
        Flags: Z,S,P,CY,AC

*All mnemonics copyrighted ©Intel Corporation 1976.   5-7

152   **PROGRAMMING WITH THE 8085 INSTRUCTION SET**

SBB M (Subtract memory with borrow)
(A) ← (A) − ((H) (L)) − (CY)
The content of the memory location whose address is contained in the H and L registers and the content of the CY flag are both subtracted from the accumulator. The result is placed in the accumulator.

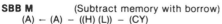

| 1 | 0 | 0 | 1 | 1 | 1 | 1 | 0 |

Cycles: 2
States: 7
Addressing: reg. indirect
Flags: Z,S,P,CY,AC

SBI data (Subtract immediate with borrow)
(A) ← (A) − (byte 2) − (CY)
The contents of the second byte of the instruction and the contents of the CY flag are both subtracted from the accumulator. The result is placed in the accumulator.

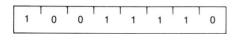

| 1 | 1 | 0 | 1 | 1 | 1 | 1 | 0 |
| data |

Cycles: 2
States: 7
Addressing: immediate
Flags: Z,S,P,CY,AC

INR r (Increment Register)
(r) ← (r) + 1
The content of register r is incremented by one. Note: All condition flags **except CY** are affected.

| 0 | 0 | D | D | D | 1 | 0 | 0 |

Cycles: 1
States: 4 (8085), 5 (8080)
Addressing: register
Flags: Z,S,P,AC

INR M (Increment memory)
((H) (L) ← ((H) (L)) + 1
The content of the memory location whose address is contained in the H and L registers is incremented by one. Note: All condition flags **except CY** are affected.

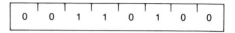

| 0 | 0 | 1 | 1 | 0 | 1 | 0 | 0 |

Cycles: 3
States: 10
Addressing: reg. indirect
Flags: Z,S,P,AC

DCR r (Decrement Register)
(r) ← (r) − 1
The content of register r is decremented by one. Note: All condition flags **except CY** are affected.

| 0 | 0 | D | D | D | 1 | 0 | 1 |

Cycles: 1
States: 4 (8085), 5 (8080)
Addressing: register
Flags: Z,S,P,AC

DCR M (Decrement memory)
((H) (L)) ← ((H) (L)) − 1
The content of the memory location whose address is contained in the H and L registers is decremented by one. Note: All condition flags **except CY** are affected.

| 0 | 0 | 1 | 1 | 0 | 1 | 0 | 1 |

Cycles: 3
States: 10
Addressing: reg. indirect
Flags: Z,S,P,AC

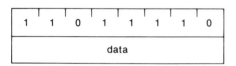

*All mnemonics copyrighted ©Intel Corporation 1976.   5-8

INX rp   (Increment register pair)

(rh) (rl) ← (rh) (rl) + 1

The content of the register pair rp is incremented by one. Note: **No condition flags are affected.**

Cycles:	1
States:	6 (8085), 5 (8080)
Addressing:	register
Flags:	none

DCX rp   (Decrement register pair)

(rh) (rl) ← (rh) (rl) − 1

The content of the register pair rp is decremented by one. Note: **No condition flags are affected.**

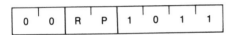

Cycles:	1
States:	6 (8085), 5 (8080)
Addressing:	register
Flags:	none

DAD rp   (Add register pair to H and L)

(H) (L) ← (H) (L) + (rh) (rl)

The content of the register pair rp is added to the content of the register pair H and L. The result is placed in the register pair H and L. Note: **Only the CY flag is affected.** It is set if there is a carry out of the double precision add; otherwise it is reset.

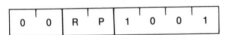

Cycles:	3
States:	10
Addressing:	register
Flags:	CY

DAA   (Decimal Adjust Accumulator)

The eight-bit number in the accumulator is adjusted to form two four-bit Binary-Coded-Decimal digits by the following process:

1. If the value of the lease significant 4 bits of the accumulator is greater than 9 **or** if the AC flag is set, 6 is added to the accumulator.

2. If the value of the most significant 4 bits of the accumulator is now greater than 9, **or** if the CY flag is set, 6 is added to the most significant 4 bits of the accumulator.

NOTE: All flags are affected.

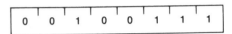

Cycles:	1
States:	4
Flags:	Z,S,P,CY,AC

5.6.3 Logical Group

This group of instructions performs logical (Boolean) operations on data in registers and memory and on condition flags.

Unless indicated otherwise, all instructions in this group affect the Zero, Sign, Parity, Auxiliary Carry, and Carry flags according to the standard rules.

ANA r   (AND Register)

(A) ← (A) ∧ (r)

The content of register r is logically ANDed with the content of the accumulator. The result is placed in the accumulator. **The CY flag is cleared and AC is set (8085). The CY flag is cleared and AC is set to the OR'ing of bits 3 of the operands (8080).**

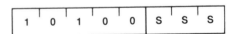

Cycles:	1
States:	4
Addressing:	register
Flags:	Z,S,P,CY,AC

ANA M   (AND memory)

(A) ← (A) ∧ ((H) (L))

The contents of the memory location whose address is contained in the H and L registers is logically ANDed with the content of the accumulator. The result is placed in the accumulator. **The CY flag is cleared and AC is set (8085). The CY flag is cleared and AC is set to the OR'ing of bits 3 of the operands (8080).**

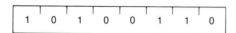

1	0	1	0	0	1	1	0

     Cycles: 2
     States: 7
 Addressing: reg. indirect
      Flags: Z,S,P,CY,AC

ANI data   (AND immediate)

(A) ← (A) ∧ (byte 2)

The content of the second byte of the instruction is logically ANDed with the contents of the accumulator. The result is placed in the accumulator. **The CY flag is cleared and AC is set (8085). The CY flag is cleared and AC is set to the OR'ing of bits 3 of the operands (8080).**

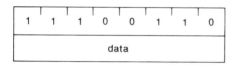

1	1	1	0	0	1	1	0
data							

     Cycles: 2
     States: 7
 Addressing: immediate
      Flags: Z,S,P,CY,AC

XRA r   (Exclusive OR Register)

(A) ← (A) ⊻ (r)

The content of register r is exclusive-OR'd with the content of the accumulator. The result is placed in the accumulator. **The CY and AC flags are cleared.**

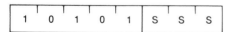

1	0	1	0	1	S	S	S

     Cycles: 1
     States: 4
 Addressing: register
      Flags: Z,S,P,CY,AC

XRA M   (Exclusive OR Memory)

(A) ← (A) ⊻ ((H) (L))

The content of the memory location whose address is contained in the H and L registers is exclusive-OR'd with the content of the accumulator. The result is placed in the accumulator. **The CY and AC flags are cleared.**

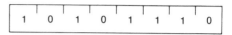

1	0	1	0	1	1	1	0

     Cycles: 2
     States: 7
 Addressing: reg. indirect
      Flags: Z,S,P,CY,AC

XRI data   (Exclusive OR immediate)

(A) ← (A) ⊻ (byte 2)

The content of the second byte of the instruction is exclusive-OR'd with the content of the accumulator. The result is placed in the accumulator. **The CY and AC flags are cleared.**

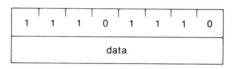

1	1	1	0	1	1	1	0
data							

     Cycles: 2
     States: 7
 Addressing: immediate
      Flags: Z,S,P,CY,AC

ORA r   (OR Register)

(A) ← (A) V (r)

The content of register r is inclusive-OR'd with the content of the accumulator. The result is placed in the accumulator. **The CY and AC flags are cleared.**

1	0	1	1	0	S	S	S

     Cycles: 1
     States: 4
 Addressing: register
      Flags: Z,S,P,CY,AC

    5-10

ORA M   (OR memory)
(A) ← (A) V ((H) (L))
The content of the memory location whose address is contained in the H and L registers is inclusive-OR'd with the content of the accumulator. The result is placed in the accumulator. **The CY and AC flags are cleared.**

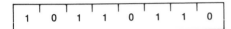

1	0	1	1	0	1	1	0

Cycles: 2
States: 7
Addressing: reg. indirect
Flags: Z,S,P,CY,AC

ORI data   (OR Immediate)
(A) ← (A) V (byte 2)
The content of the second byte of the instruction is inclusive-OR'd with the content of the accumulator. The result is placed in the accumulator. **The CY and AC flags are cleared.**

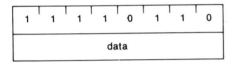

1	1	1	1	0	1	1	0
data							

Cycles: 2
States: 7
Addressing: immediate
Flags: Z,S,P,CY,AC

CMP r   (Compare Register)
(A) − (r)
The content of register r is subtracted from the accumulator. The accumulator remains unchanged. The condition flags are set as a result of the subtraction. **The Z flag is set to 1 if (A) = (r). The CY flag is set to 1 if (A) < (r).**

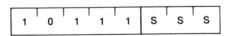

1	0	1	1	1	S	S	S

Cycles: 1
States: 4
Addressing: register
Flags: Z,S,P,CY,AC

*All mnemonics copyrighted © Intel Corporation 1976.   5-11

CMP M   (Compare memory)
(A) − ((H) (L))
The content of the memory location whose address is contained in the H and L registers is subtracted from the accumulator. The accumulator remains unchanged. The condition flags are set as a result of the subtraction. **The Z flag is set to 1 if (A) = ((H) (L)). The CY flag is set to 1 if (A) < ((H) (L)).**

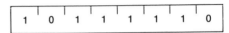

1	0	1	1	1	1	1	0

Cycles: 2
States: 7
Addressing: reg. indirect
Flags: Z,S,P,CY,AC

CPI data   (Compare immediate)
(A) − (byte 2)
The content of the second byte of the instruction is subtracted from the accumulator. The condition flags are set by the result of the subtraction. **The Z flag is set to 1 if (A) = (byte 2). The CY flag is set to 1 if (A) < (byte 2).**

1	1	1	1	1	1	1	0
data							

Cycles: 2
States: 7
Addressing: immediate
Flags: Z,S,P,CY,AC

RLC   (Rotate left)
$(A_{n+1}) ← (A_n)$; $(A_0) ← (A_7)$
(CY) ← (A_7)
The content of the accumulator is rotated left one position. The low order bit and the CY flag are both set to the value shifted out of the high order bit position. **Only the CY flag is affected.**

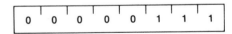

0	0	0	0	0	1	1	1

Cycles: 1
States: 4
Flags: CY

RRC   (Rotate right)
$(A_n) \leftarrow (A_{n+1}); (A_7) \leftarrow (A_0)$
$(CY) \leftarrow (A_0)$
The content of the accumulator is rotated right one position. The high order bit and the CY flag are both set to the value shifted out of the low order bit position. **Only the CY flag is affected.**

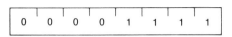

0	0	0	0	1	1	1	1

Cycles: 1
States: 4
Flags: CY

RAL   (Rotate left through carry)
$(A_{n+1}) \leftarrow (A_n); (CY) \leftarrow (A_7)$
$(A_0) \leftarrow (CY)$
The content of the accumulator is rotated left one position through the CY flag. The low order bit is set equal to the CY flag and the CY flag is set to the value shifted out of the high order bit. **Only the CY flag is affected.**

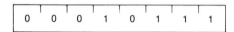

0	0	0	1	0	1	1	1

Cycles: 1
States: 4
Flags: CY

RAR   (Rotate right through carry)
$(A_n) \leftarrow (A_{n+1}); (CY) \leftarrow (A_0)$
$(A_7) \leftarrow (CY)$
The content of the accumulator is rotated right one position through the CY flag. The high order bit is set to the CY flag and the CY flag is set to the value shifted out of the low order bit. **Only the CY flag is affected.**

0	0	0	1	1	1	1	1

Cycles: 1
States: 4
Flags: CY

CMA   (Complement accumulator)
$(A) \leftarrow (\overline{A})$
The contents of the accumulator are complemented (zero bits become 1, one bits become 0). **No flags are affected.**

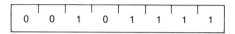

0	0	1	0	1	1	1	1

Cycles: 1
States: 4
Flags: none

CMC   (Complement carry)
$(CY) \leftarrow (\overline{CY})$
The CY flag is complemented. **No other flags are affected.**

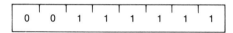

0	0	1	1	1	1	1	1

Cycles: 1
States: 4
Flags: CY

STC   (Set carry)
$(CY) \leftarrow 1$
The CY flag is set to 1. **No other flags are affected.**

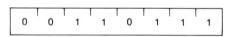

0	0	1	1	0	1	1	1

Cycles: 1
States: 4
Flags: CY

5.6.4 Branch Group

This group of instructions alter normal sequential program flow.

Condition flags are not affected by any instruction in this group.

The two types of branch instructions are unconditional and conditional. Unconditional transfers simply perform the specified operation on register PC (the program counter). Conditional transfers examine the status of one of the four processor flags to determine if the specified branch is to be executed. The conditions that may be specified are as follows:

CONDITION	CCC
NZ — not zero ($Z = 0$)	000
Z — zero ($Z = 1$)	001
NC — no carry ($CY = 0$)	010
C — carry ($CY = 1$)	011
PO — parity odd ($P = 0$)	100
PE — parity even ($P = 1$)	101
P — plus ($S = 0$)	110
M — minus ($S = 1$)	111

JMP addr   (Jump)

(PC) ← (byte 3) (byte 2)

Control is transferred to the instruction whose address is specified in byte 3 and byte 2 of the current instruction.

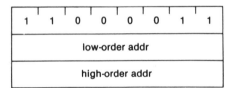

Cycles: 3
States: 10
Addressing: immediate
Flags: none

Jcondition addr (Conditional jump)

If (CCC),

(PC) ← (byte 3) (byte 2)

If the specified condition is true, control is transferred to the instruction whose address is specified in byte 3 and byte 2 of the current instruciton; otherwise, control continues sequentially.

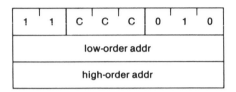

Cycles: 2/3 (8085), 3 (8080)
States: 7/10 (8085), 10 (8080)
Addressing: immediate
Flags: none

CALL addr   (Call)

((SP) − 1) ← (PCH)
((SP) − 2) ← (PCL)
(SP) ← (SP) − 2
(PC) ← (byte 3) (byte 2)

The high-order eight bits of the next instruction address are moved to the memory location whose address is one less than the content of register SP. The low-order eight bits of the next instruction address are moved to the memory location whose address is two less than the content of register SP. The content of register SP is decremented by 2. Control is transferred to the instruciton whose address is specified in byte 3 and byte 2 of the current instruction.

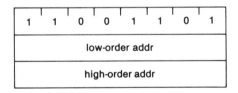

Cycles: 5
States: 18 (8085), 17 (8080)
Addressing: immediate/
             reg. indirect
Flags: none

Ccondition addr (Condition call)
If (CCC),
((SP) − 1) ← (PCH)
((SP) − 2) ← (PCL)
(SP) ← (SP) − 2
(PC) ← (byte 3) (byte 2)
If the specified condition is true, the actions specified in the CALL instruction (see above) are performed; otherwise, control continues sequentially.

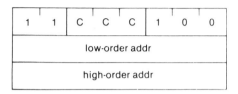

1	1	C	C	C	1	0	0

low-order addr

high-order addr

Cycles: 2/5 (8085), 3/5 (8080)
States: 9/18 (8085), 11/17 (8080)
Addressing: immediate/ reg. indirect
Flags: none

RET (Return)
(PCL) ← ((SP));
(PCH) ← ((SP) + 1);
(SP) ← (SP) + 2;
The content of the memory location whose address is specified in register SP is moved to the low-order eight bits of register PC. The content of the memory location whose address is one more than the content of register SP is moved to the high-order eight bits of register PC. The content of register SP is incremented by 2.

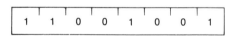

1	1	0	0	1	0	0	1

Cycles: 3
States: 10
Addressing: reg. indirect
Flags: none

Rcondition (Conditional return)
If (CCC),
(PCL) ← ((SP))
(PCH) ← ((SP) + 1)
(SP) ← (SP) + 2
If the specified condition is true, the actions specified in the RET instruction (see above) are performed; otherwise, control continues sequentially.

1	1	C	C	C	0	0	0

Cycles: 1/3
States: 6/12 (8085), 5/11 (8080)
Addressing: reg. indirect
Flags: none

RST n (Restart)
((SP) − 1) ← (PCH)
((SP) − 2) ← (PCL)
(SP) ← (SP) − 2
(PC) ← 8 * (NNN)
The high-order eight bits of the next instruction address are moved to the memory location whose address is one less than the content of register SP. The low-order eight bits of the next instruction address are moved to the memory location whose address is two less than the content of register SP. The content of register SP is decremented by two. Control is transferred to the instruction whose address is eight times the content of NNN.

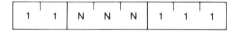

1	1	N	N	N	1	1	1

Cycles: 3
States: 12 (8085), 11 (8080)
Addressing: reg. indirect
Flags: none

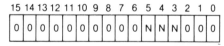

15	14	13	12	11	10	9	8	7	6	5	4	3	2	1	0
0	0	0	0	0	0	0	0	0	0	0	N	N	N	0	0

Program Counter After Restart

5-14

PCHL   (Jump H and L indirect —
               move H and L to PC)
(PCH) ← (H)
(PCL) ← (L)
The content of register H is moved to the
high-order eight bits of register PC. The
content of register L is moved to the low-
order eight bits of register PC.

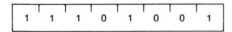

Cycles: 1
States: 6 (8085), 5 (8080)
Addressing: register
Flags: none

5.6.5 Stack, I/O, and Machine Control Group

This group of instructions performs I/O, manipulates the Stack, and alters internal control
flags.

Unless otherwise specified, **condition flags are
not affected by any instructions in this group.**

PUSH rp   (Push)
((SP) − 1) ← (rh)
((SP) − 2) ← (rl)
((SP) ← (SP) − 2

The content of the high-order register of
register pair rp is moved to the memory
location whose address is one less than
the content of register SP. The content of
the low-order register of register pair rp is
moved to the memory location whose address is two less than the content of
register SP. The content of register SP is
decremented by 2. **Note: Register pair rp =
SP may not be specified.**

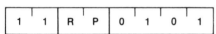

Cycles: 3
States: 12 (8085), 11 (8080)
Addressing: reg. indirect
Flags: none

PUSH PSW   (Push processor status word)
((SP) − 1) ← (A)
((SP) − 2)$_0$ ← (CY) , ((SP) − 2)$_1$ ← X
((SP) − 2)$_2$ ← (P) , ((SP) − 2)$_3$ ← X
((SP) − 2)$_4$ ← (AC) , ((SP) − 2)$_5$ ← X
((SP) − 2)$_6$ ← (Z) , ((SP) − 2)$_7$ ← (S)
(SP) ← (SP) − 2   X: Undefined.

The content of register A is moved to the
memory location whose address is one
less than register SP. The contents of the
condition flags are assembled into a processor status word and the word is moved
to the memory location whose address is
two less than the content of register SP.
The content of register SP is decremented
by two.

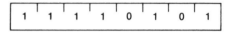

Cycles: 3
States: 12 (8085), 11 (8080)
Addressing: reg. indirect
Flags: none

FLAG WORD

D$_7$	D$_6$	D$_5$	D$_4$	D$_3$	D$_2$	D$_1$	D$_0$
S	Z	X	AC	X	P	X	CY

X: undefined

POP rp   (Pop)
(rl) ← ((SP))
(rh) ← ((SP) + 1)
(SP) ← (SP) + 2

The content of the memory location, whose
address is specified by the content of
register SP, is moved to the low-order
register of register pair rp. The content of
the memory location, whose address is one
more than the content of register SP, is
moved to the high-order register of register
rp. The content of register SP is incremented by 2. **Note: Register pair rp =
SP may not be specified.**

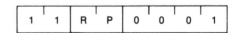

Cycles: 3
States: 10
Addressing: reg.indirect
Flags: none

POP PSW   (Pop processor status word)

$(CY) \leftarrow ((SP))_0$
$(P) \leftarrow ((SP))_2$
$(AC) \leftarrow ((SP))_4$
$(Z) \leftarrow ((SP))_6$
$(S) \leftarrow ((SP))_7$
$(A) \leftarrow ((SP) + 1)$
$(SP) \leftarrow (SP) + 2$

The content of the memory location whose address is specified by the content of register SP is used to restore the condition flags. The content of the memory location whose address is one more than the content of register SP is moved to register A. The content of register SP is incremented by 2.

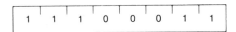

1	1	1	1	0	0	0	1

Cycles: 3
States: 10
Addressing: reg. indirect
Flags: Z,S,P,CY,AC

XTHL   (Exchange stack top with H and L)

$(L) \leftrightarrow ((SP))$
$(H) \leftrightarrow ((SP) + 1)$

The content of the L register is exchanged with the content of the memory location whose address is specified by the content of register SP. The content of the H register is exchanged with the content of the memory location whose address is one more than the content of register SP.

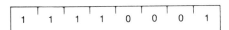

1	1	1	0	0	0	1	1

Cycles: 5
States: 16 (8085), 18 (8080)
Addressing: reg. indirect
Flags: none

SPHL   (Move HL to SP)

$(SP) \leftarrow (H) (L)$

The contents of registers H and L (16 bits) are moved to register SP.

1	1	1	1	1	0	0	1

Cycles: 1
States: 6 (8085), 5 (8080)
Addressing: register
Flags: none

IN port   (Input)

$(A) \leftarrow (data)$

The data placed on the eight bit bi-directional data bus by the specified port is moved to register A.

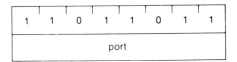

1	1	0	1	1	0	1	1
port							

Cycles: 3
States: 10
Addressing: direct
Flags: none

OUT port   (Output)

$(data) \leftarrow (A)$

The content of register A is placed on the eight bit bi-directional data bus for transmission to the specified port.

1	1	0	1	0	0	1	1
port							

Cycles: 3
States: 10
Addressing: direct
Flags: none

5-16

EI (Enable interrupts)

The interrupt system is enabled **following the execution of the next instruction. Interrupts are not recognized during the EI instruction.**

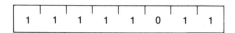

1	1	1	1	1	0	1	1

Cycles: 1
States: 4
Flags: none

NOTE: Placing an EI instruction on the bus in response to INTA during an INA cycle is prohibited. (8085)

DI (Disable interrupts)

The interrupt system is disabled **immediately following the execution of the DI instruction. Interrupts are not recognized during the DI instruction.**

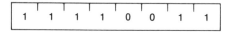

1	1	1	1	0	0	1	1

Cycles: 1
States: 4
Flags: none

NOTE: Placing a DI instruction on the bus in response to INTA during an INA cycle is prohibited. (8085)

HLT (Halt)

The processor is stopped. The registers and flags are unaffected. (8080) A second ALE is generated during the execution of HLT to strobe out the Halt cycle status information. (8085)

0	1	1	1	0	1	1	0

Cycles: 1+ (8085), 1 (8080)
States: 5 (8085), 7 (8080)
Flags: none

NOP (No op)

No operation is performed. The registers and flags are unaffected.

5-17

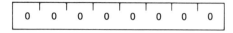

0	0	0	0	0	0	0	0

Cycles: 1
States: 4
Flags: none

RIM (Read Interrupt Masks) (8085 only)

The RIM instruction loads data into the accumulator relating to interrupts and the serial input. This data contains the following information:

- Current interrupt mask status for the RST 5.5, 6.5, and 7.5 hardware interrupts (1 = mask disabled)
- Current interrupt enable flag status (1 = interrupts enabled) except immediately following a TRAP interrupt. (See below.)
- Hardware interrupts pending (i.e., signal received but not yet serviced), on the RST 5.5, 6.5, and 7.5 lines.
- Serial input data.

Immediately following a TRAP interrupt, the RIM instruction must be executed as a part of the service routine if you need to retrieve current interrupt status later. Bit 3 of the accumulator is (in this special case only) loaded with the interrupt enable (IE) flag status that existed prior to the TRAP interrupt. Following an RST 5.5, 6.5, 7.5, or INTR interrupt, the interrupt flag flip-flop reflects the current interrupt enable status. Bit 6 of the accumulator (I7.5) is loaded with the status of the RST 7.5 flip-flop, which is always set (edge-triggered) by an input on the RST 7.5 input line, even when that interrupt has been previously masked. (See SIM Instruction.)

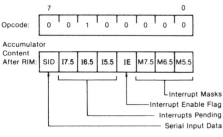

Cycles: 1
States: 4
Flags: none

SIM   (Set Interrupt Masks) (8085 only)

The execution of the SIM instruction uses the contents of the accumulator (which must be previously loaded) to perform the following functions:

- Program the interrupt mask for the RST 5.5, 6.5, and 7.5 hardware interrupts.
- Reset the edge-triggered RST 7.5 input latch.
- Load the SOD output latch.

To program the interrupt masks, first set accumulator bit 3 to 1 and set to 1 any bits 0, 1, and 2, which disable interrupts RST 5.5, 6.5, and 7.5, respectively. Then do a SIM instruction. If accumulator bit 3 is 0 when the SIM instruction is executed, the interrupt mask register will not change. If accumulator bit 4 is 1 when the SIM instruction is executed, the RST 7.5 latch is then reset. RST 7.5 is distinguished by the fact that its latch is always set by a rising edge on the RST 7.5 input pin, even if the jump to service routine is inhibited by masking. This latch remains high until cleared by a RESET IN, by a SIM Instruction with accumulator bit 4 high, or by an internal processor acknowledge to an RST 7.5 interrupt subsequent to the removal of the mask (by a SIM instruction). The RESET IN signal always sets all three RST mask bits.

If accumulator bit 6 is at the 1 level when the SIM instruction is executed, the state of accumulator bit 7 is loaded into the SOD latch and thus becomes available for interface to an external device. The SOD latch is unaffected by the SIM instruction if bit 6 is 0. SOD is always reset by the RESET IN signal.

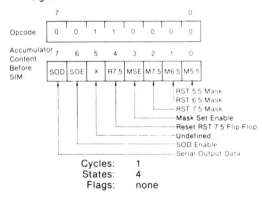

Cycles: 1
States: 4
Flags: none

*Intel Corporation, October 1979, pp. 5-1–5-18. Reprinted by permission.

Introduction to Flowcharts and Programming

This section will introduce programming; later chapters will provide depth and sophistication. When a program is to be written, the programmer must choose the language to be used. The choices are machine language, assembler language, or compiler language. *Machine language* is machine code and is the *only* language the microprocessor "understands." However, for human convenience the programmer may use other languages and then *translate* that language into machine code. Again, the act of translating instruction-set mnemonics into machine code is known as *assembly*. When assembly is performed by a computer, the computer program responsible for the translation is known as an *assembler*. Because an assembler "recognizes" instructions (in mnemonic form) from the instruction set and translates (assembles) them into machine code, the instruction set is referred to as an *assembler-level language*. Similarly, there are also programs that translate higher-level languages, such as FORTRAN and PL/1, into machine language. For these higher-level languages the translating program is known as a *compiler*; therefore FORTRAN and PL/1 are known as *compiler-level languages*. Two of the main differences between an assembler language and a compiler language are

1. Assembler languages are machine oriented; that is, the "words" (instructions) of the language refer to the MPU architecture (for example, registers), which requires knowledge of the microprocessor's workings. Compiler languages are task oriented; that is, the "words" of the language (program statements) refer to the program's objective (add, multiply, print, and so on) and not microprocessor architecture.

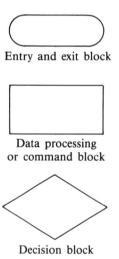

Entry and exit block

Data processing or command block

Decision block

FIGURE 5-4. Symbols used for flowcharts.

2. Compiler languages are more easily read by human beings, as their instructions appear closer to statements in English. It is the closeness to the English language that establishes a programming language level. Compiler languages, being the most like the English language, are the highest-level language; machine language is the least like English and therefore is the lowest-level language.

This chapter introduces programming at the assembler level.

Whenever one programs (at all language levels) it is desirable to begin by modularizing the program's task into steps, which is known as an *algorithm*. Once the algorithm is determined, it can be presented in graphical fashion (flowchart) and will then provide a "road map" with which the programmer can visualize each step and the role that that step plays in accomplishing the task. This allows the programmer to simplify programming by focusing on programming modules rather than attempting to program the entire task. Figure 5-4 illustrates the symbols to be used when determining a flowchart. An example will best illustrate flowchart concepts.

EXAMPLE 5-1

For a microprocessor-based system, such as that shown in Figure 4-27, develop a flowchart for a program that will collect a single byte of data from input port 0 and store that byte at memory location 0800H.

Solution

This programming task can be modularized by dividing the task into two steps:

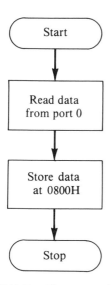

FIGURE 5-5. Flowchart for collecting a single data byte.

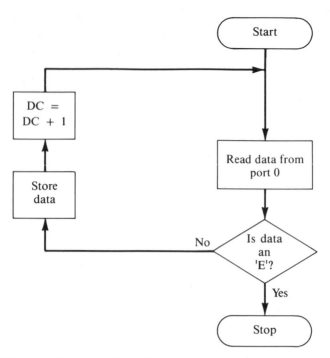

FIGURE 5-6. Flowchart for collecting multiple data bytes.

1. Read the data byte from input port 0.
2. Store the data at memory location 0800H.

The flowchart for this task is shown in Figure 5-5. ■

EXAMPLE 5-2

As in Example 5-1, collect data (decimal values) from input port 0. However, now the data are to be continuously collected and stored in successive memory locations, beginning with location 0800H, until an end command is given via port 0. The end command is the ASCII (pronounced "ask-key") character E, which is 45H (see Appendix B).

Solution
The algorithm is

1. Input data from port 0.
2. Determine whether the data collected from port 0 is an end command 'E', where ' ' indicates an ASCII character.
3. a. If yes
      (1) Terminate data collection.

b. If no
   (1) Store data at location given by DC (data counter).
   (2) Increment DC (DC + 1).
   (3) Return to port 0 for next byte of data.
The flowchart is presented in Figure 5-6. ■

EXAMPLE 5-3

Suppose that a program is required to accomplish the task of Example 5-2 with an additional requirement that a tally be kept of the number of data bytes stored. Store the number that is indicative of the data bytes stored (TALLY) at memory location 0FF0H.

Solution

To accomplish this additional programming task, we must modify steps 3a and 3b. Step 3b will now read

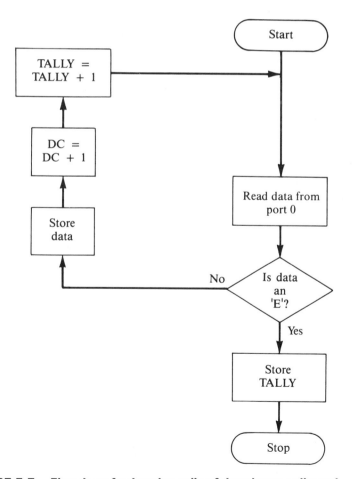

FIGURE 5-7.   Flowchart for keeping tally of data bytes collected.

3. b. If no
(1) Store data at location given by DC.
(2) Increment DC in preparation for storage of next data byte collected from port 0.
(3) Increment TALLY to account for data byte stored.

Step 3a will be modified to read

3. a. If yes
(1) Store TALLY at location 0FF0H.
(2) Terminate data collection.

The flowchart for Example 5-3 is Figure 5-7, which is essentially the flowchart of Figure 5-6 but modified to accommodate steps 3a and 3b.

∎

Now that we have constructed a few simple flowcharts, let us return to those flowcharts as aids to programming. Remember that a flowchart is a programming "road map."

EXAMPLE 5-4

Utilizing the flowchart of Figure 5-5, write a program that will accomplish the task stated in Example 5-1. It can be assumed that input port 0 has the data byte ready. The program is to be stored in ROM, beginning at memory location 0100H.

Solution

Because the program we are about to write is to originate at memory location 0100H, there must be an instruction to the assembler directing it to begin assembly at memory location 0100H. Instructions (directives) to the assembler are known as directives. The assembler directive that instructs the assembler as to the beginning address of assembly is the *origin (ORG) directive*. There are other directives (SET, EQU, and so on) which are explained and used in Chapter 9. To direct the assembler to begin assembly at memory location 0100H, the programmer simply writes ORG 0100H at the start of the program. Then for the start block of Figure 5-5, we write

```
ORG     0100H
```

Notice that ORG looks like an 8085 instruction in form, but because it does not appear in Table 5-10, it is not an 8085 instruction. Directives have meaning only to the assembler (not the microprocessor) and are not assembled. Because directives look like microprocessor instructions but in fact are not, they are also known as *pseudo-ops* (pseudo–op codes).

After the start block of Figure 5-5 is the command "Read data from port 0." Looking through the instruction set as given in Section 5-3, we find that the instruction IN PORT will carry out that command block. Notice that the byte

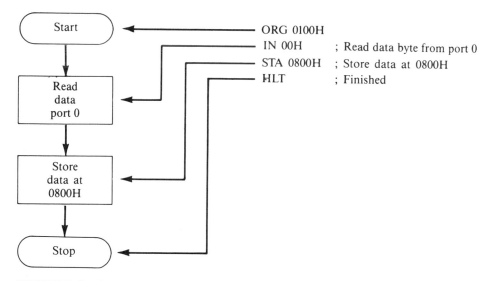

FIGURE 5-8. Program documented with flowchart and comments.

input from port 0 will reside in the accumulator (A) after the execution of IN 00H. At this point our program appears as

```
ORG    0100H
IN     00H
```

The next command block states that the data byte (in register A) is to be stored at memory location 0800H. From the instruction set we find three instructions that will accomplish the task: MOV M,r, where r is A; STA addr, where addr is 0800H; and STAX rp, where rp is either B or D. We notice that STAX H is the same instruction as MOV M,A. Of the three, STA 0800H is best, for the other two require that some register pair be initialized with address 0800H. Hence the program now appears as

```
ORG    0100H
IN     00H
STA    0800H
```

The last command block can be accomplished in two or three ways, but we shall use the most obvious, HLT. Thus the completed program is

```
ORG    0100H
IN     00H
STA    0800H
HLT
```

For complex programs the programmer will want to offer as much insight as possible into the purpose of each program instruction. And so, in addition to a flowchart, the program instructions will be further documented with *comments*.

Comments can be written to the right of an instruction, following a semicolon. The assembler will *not* assemble the semicolon (no such instruction) or anything to the right of the semicolon. Thus to document the program better, let us add comments:

```
ORG    0100H
IN     00H     ; Read data byte from port 0
STA    0800H   ; Store data at 0800H
HLT            ; Finished
```

A well-documented program is considered to be one having (1) a flowchart and (2) adequate comments. A fully documented program to accomplish the task of Example 5-1 is shown in Figure 5-8. ■

EXAMPLE 5-5

Write a program to accomplish the tasks prescribed in Example 5-2. The flowchart of Figure 5-6 is to be utilized in writing this program and also considered as part of program documentation.

Solution

The command block "Read data from port 0" of Figure 5-6 can be implemented with IN 00H. The decision block of Figure 5-6, "Is data an 'E'?" requires that the data byte received from port 0 be tested to determine whether an end command has been given.

Decisions in programming are based on the logic state of a condition flag. To alter the condition flag's logic state appropriately, we shall use the instruction CPI 'E'. From Section 5-3 we find that executing CPI 'E' will cause the ASCII value for E (45H) to be subtracted from the content of A, where A's content is the data byte from port 0, and the condition flags are appropriately affected by the subtraction.

Of most importance in writing this program is the Z flag, for if the result of the subtraction is zero, meaning that the data byte from port 0 equals 45H, then the Z flag will be set; otherwise, the Z flag will be reset. Thus Z = 1 is the Yes path of the flowchart and Z = 0 is the No path. We shall write this program so as to make "jump" the Yes path and allow the No path to be the consequence of not "jumping." Hence, if Z = 1, the program should jump to an instruction that will stop execution of the program. This calls for a conditional jump instruction. In Section 5-3 under "Branch Group" we find Jcondition addr. The J represents "jump," and "condition" refers to the condition flag/logic state of Table 5-8 (confirm the machine code format of Figure 5-3 with the format given in Section 5-3). The condition flag is Z; hence JZ is the mnemonic for the op code. From Section 5-3 we find that the instruction requires the address (two bytes) to which program execution is to be transferred. Until the program is written and assembled, that address is unknown. For unknown addresses we can use a symbolic address, just as algebraic symbols are used for unknowns in algebra. Let us use FIN as the symbolic address, or JZ FIN. We must identify the stop command (HLT instruction) of Figure 5-6 with an identifier; that is, we must label HLT as FIN. This is accomplished as FIN: HLT. Thus far, our program appears as follows:

```
     ORG 0100H
        IN 00H            ; Read data byte from port 0
        CPI 'E'           ; Compare data byte with 'E'
        JZ FIN            ; Stop if Z = 1 by transferring
           (program still ; program execution to memory
            to be written ; location FIN: otherwise,
            for No path)  ; continue
FIN:    HLT               ; Stop
```

We must now complete the program by undertaking the No branch of Figure 5-6. Following the No branch we must store the data byte compared with 'E' if $Z \neq 1$. From the instruction set of Section 5-3, we find that STA addr, STAX RP, or MOV M,A will suffice. The best of the three can be determined by realizing that the next command block requires that the memory storage location be incremented by one in preparation for storage of the next data byte. For this reason STA addr is a poor choice, as the address of STA addr cannot be incremented. Either STAX rp or MOV M,A is a good choice. Let us use STAX D. To increment the data counter, registers D and E, we may use INX D. Then to "STORE data" and "DC + 1" of Figure 5-6, we add to our program

```
     STAX D ; Store data byte
     INX  D ; DC = DC + 1
```

These additions, as well as others, are shown in Figure 5-9. Notice that RP D must be preloaded with the beginning memory location where the collected data bytes are to be stored (0800H). To initialize RP D we may use LXI rp, data, which for our case is LXI D, 0800 H. This instruction will be grouped with the Start of Figure 5-6, together with ORG 0100H, as shown in Figure 5-9.

The last function of Figure 5-6 is that after DC + 1, program execution must jump "back" to "Read data from port 0" in order to input the next data byte. To accomplish this jump we shall use JMP addr. The address to which program execution is to jump is IN 00H, which is not known until after assembly. Hence

```
         ORG 0100H
            LXI D,0800H   ; Initialize RP D
RETURN:     IN 00H        ; Read data byte from Port 0
            CPI 'E'       ; Compare data byte with 'E'
            JZ FIN        ; Stop if Z = 1 by transferring
                          ; program execution to memory
                          ; location FIN; otherwise,
                          ; continue
            STAX D        ; Store data byte
            INX D         ; DC = DC + 1
            JMP RETURN    ; Return for next data byte
FIN:        HLT           ; Stop
```

FIGURE 5-9. Example program using labels.

we shall assign a symbolic address (a label) to IN 00H and then refer to that symbolic address. The label assigned is RETURN, as shown in Figure 5-9.

The reader should be aware that for complete documentation, Figure 5-6 must be included with Figure 5-9. ■

Before undertaking more programming examples, let us return to Figures 5-8 and 5-9 and hand-assemble both programs. To gain the greatest benefits from this exercise, we shall assemble the instructions just as if we were an assembler. An assembler assigns memory addresses to assembled instructions via its location counter, and the ORG directive sets the location counter to the value specified. Hence ORG 0100H initializes the location counter to a value of 0100H.

All assembled numbers are in hexadecimal, and the H, specifying hexadecimal, often is omitted.

EXAMPLE 5-6

Hand-assemble the program of Figure 5-8.

Solution

The directive ORG 0100H sets the location counter to 0100H. The assembler (you in this case) next "sees" the IN 00H instruction and assembles that instruction into the machine code DB 00 (refer to Table 5-10). DB is to be stored at the address assigned by the location counter, which is 0100H. The assembler then increments its location counter and assigns the next assembled byte, 00, to memory location 0101H. The assembler then increments its location counter (LC = 0102H) and assembles the next instruction, which is STA 0800H. The assembled op code is 32, and 0800H is assembled into two hexadecimal values, 00 and 08. The low-order byte of the address is assembled first; refer to Section 5-3. Thus STA 0800H is a three-byte instruction with an assembled machine code of 32, 00, and 08; 32 is assigned memory location 0102H by the location counter; 00 is assigned to memory location 0103H; and 08 is assigned to memory location 0104 by the location counter. Again the location counter is incremented, and the assembled mnemonic code HLT (76) is assigned to memory location 0105H.

TABLE 5-11. Assembled Program of Figure 5-8

Instruction	Memory Location Assigned by Location Counter (Hex)	Machine Code of Assembled Instruction (Hex)
IN 00H	0100	DB
	0101	00
STA 0800H	0102	32
	0103	00
	0104	08
HLT	0105	76

The complete assembly of the program of Figure 5-8 is shown in Table 5-11. The assembled program of Table 5-11 would be programmed into memory for execution by the MPU. ∎

EXAMPLE 5-7

Assemble the program of Figure 5-9.

Solution

Notice that before this program can be assembled, addresses must be determined for the labels. Performing as most assemblers, we will need to make two passes of the program in order to complete its assembly. The function of each pass is (1) to assign values (memory addresses) to labels and, (2) once the values are assigned, to assemble the program. To accomplish the first pass of the assembler, we shall count the number of bytes of the program and from this information assign values to the labels. Table 5-12 shows the data byte count for the program of Figure 5-9.

From the data byte count of Table 5-12, and knowing that the program is to originate at memory location 0100H, we may determine the memory addresses to be assigned to labels RETURN and FIN simply by totaling the data bytes from the origin to the label. From Table 5-12 we find that RETURN is to be assigned the fourth memory location after memory address 0100H, which is 0103H (0100H is the first address). A convenient equation to use in determining addresses is

$$\text{memory address} = \text{address of origin} + (\text{data bytes} - 1) \qquad (5\text{-}1)$$

Using Equation (5-1) to determine the address of FIN, we have

memory address to be assigned to FIN

$$= 0100H + (10H - 1H) = 0100H + FH$$

$$= 010FH$$

Now that addresses have been determined for RETURN and FIN, we shall create

TABLE 5-12. First Pass of Assembly

Byte Count	Label	Instruction
3		LXI D,0800H
2	RETURN:	IN 00H
2		CPI 'E'
3		JZ FIN
1		STAX D
1		INX D
3		JMP RETURN
1	FIN:	HLT

TABLE 5-13. Symbol Table

Symbol	Memory Address Assigned by the Assembler (Hex)
RETURN	0103
FIN	010F

a table (Table 5-13) that readily gives this information to the programmer. This table is called a *symbol table* and completes the first pass of assembly.

We may now begin the second pass of assembly. The assembled machine code for the program of Figure 5-9 is shown in Table 5-14. ■

A summary of some important points of this example is as follows:

1. Most assemblers are two-pass assemblers, in which the first pass assigns the values to the labels and the second pass performs the actual assembly.
2. The assembler provides a symbol table for the programmer. This table identifies the labels (symbols) and the values assigned to them by the assembler's location counter.
3. The assembler will translate mnemonic code into bytes of machine code and assign these bytes to memory locations, as given by the location counter.

Thus the process of assembly includes the translation of mnemonics into machine

TABLE 5-14. Assembled Program of Figure 5-9

Program (exclude directives and comments)	Assembled Program	
	Memory Locations Assigned by Location Counter (Hex)	Machine Code (Hex)
LXI D,0800H	0100	11
	0101	00
	0102	08
RETURN: IN 00H	0103	DB
	0104	00
CPI 'E'	0105	FE
	0106	45
JZ FIN	0107	CA
	0108	0F
	0109	01
STAX D	010A	12
INX D	010B	13
JMP RETURN	010C	C3
	010D	03
	010E	01
FIN: HLT	010F	76

code and the assignment of memory addresses for the assembled mnemonic code. Thus the assembled program of Table 5-14 is actually just the two right-hand columns. That is, the computer system that is serving as host to the assembler is storing (probably on disk) the assembled program and assigned addresses of Figure 5-9, which is the two right-hand columns of Table 5-14. The assembled program and assigned addresses are stored by the assembler in the storage medium (disk) of the host computer, by the assembler, in such a fashion that when a ROM is programmed from this assembled program, it will cause a data byte to be programmed (stored) at its assigned memory location. Then the assembled program of Table 5-14 will be programmed in ROM so that data byte "11" will be stored at ROM address 0100. At ROM address 0101 the data byte "00" will be programmed (burned). This programming of the ROM will continue according to the assembled program of Table 5-14. Once the ROM is programmed, it is removed from the ROM programmer (a "box" that programs ROMs) and inserted in the prototype (the microprocessor-based system being designed), at which time the program can be executed by the microprocessor. Of course, the assembled program of Table 5-14 can be "down-loaded" (transferred from the host computer to the prototype) to the prototype's RAM and then executed. Either way the assembled bytes of Table 5-14 are stored at the assigned memory location.

EXAMPLE 5-8

Write a program to accomplish the task of Example 5-3 as documented in the flowchart of Figure 5-7. Just for a change, assemble this program beginning at memory location 0056H. Assemble the program giving the machine code and assigned memory address as well as a symbol table.

Solution
The program is similar to that of Figure 5-9 except for two additions:

1. Incrementing the TALLY in the No branch of Figure 5-7.
2. Storing the TALLY value in the Yes branch of Figure 5-7.

To assemble the program of Figure 5-10, we count the data bytes on the first pass in order to assign values (addresses) to symbols. This is shown in Table 5-15. Knowing that the assembler was directed to begin assembly at 0056H, the addresses for RETURN and FIN can be determined from Equation (5-1).

$$\text{address for label RETURN} = 0056 + (9 - 1) = 5E$$

$$\text{address of label FIN} = 0056 + (16 - 1) = 6B$$

Now that the assembler has made its first pass and has assigned values to symbols, that is, created a symbol table (Table 5-16), it is ready to make its second pass and actually assemble the mnemonics. The assembled program is shown in Table 5-17. As was the case for the assembled program of Table 5-14, the two columns comprising the assembled program of Table 5-17 are placed in the memory of the host computer and later programmed in ROM or RAM of the prototype at the memory locations indicated. The host

```
                    ORG 0056H

              ; Initialization Of Registers

                    LXI D,0800H      ; Initialize RP D
                    LXI H,0FF0H      ; Initialize M to store TALLY
                    MVI B,00H        ; Clear TALLY

              ; Program Begins

RETURN:             IN 00H           ; Read data from Port 0
                    CPI 'E'          ; Compare data byte with 'E'
                    JZ FIN           ; Stop if Z = 1
                    STAX D           ; Store data byte
                    INX D            ; DC = DC + 1
                    INR B            ; TALLY = TALLY + 1
                    JMP RETURN       ; Return for next data byte
FIN:                MOV M,B          ; Store TALLY
                    HLT              ; Stop
```

FIGURE 5-10. Program that implements the flowchart of Figure 5-7.

TABLE 5-15. First Pass of Assembler

Byte Count	Label	Instruction
3		LXI D,0800H
3		LXI H,0FF0H
2		MVI B,00H
2	RETURN:	IN 00H
2		CPI 'E'
3		JZ FIN
1		STAX D
1		INX D
1		INR B
3		JMP RETURN
1	FIN:	MOV M,B
1		HLT

TABLE 5-16. Symbol Table

Symbol	Memory Address Assigned by the Assembler (Hex)
RETURN	005E
FIN	006B

TABLE 5-17. Assembled Program of Figure 5-10

Program (exclude directives and comments)	Assembled Program	
	Memory Locations Assigned by Location Counter (Hex)	Machine Code (Hex)
LXI D,0800H	0056	11
	0057	00
	0058	80 08
LXI H,0FF0H	0059	21
	005A	F0
	005B	0F
MVI B,00H	005C	06
	005D	00
RETURN: IN 00H	005E	DB
	005F	00
CPI 'E'	0060	FE
	0061	45
JZ FIN	0062	CA
	0063	6B
	0064	00
STAX D	0065	12
INX D	0066	13
INR B	0067	04
JMP RETURN	0068	C3
	0069	5E
	006A	00
FIN: MOV M,B	006B	70
HLT	006C	76

computer will interface with a PROM programmer, which will actually program the assembled program in the PROM. ∎

EXAMPLE 5-9

Write a program that will add the content of memory location 0400H to the data collected from input port 0 of Figure 4-27. The sums are to be stored in memory, beginning at memory location 0C00H. The program is to be programmed in the system's ROM beginning at the first address of page 1. Once the program is written, assemble the program showing a symbol table.

Solution

We begin by developing a flowchart, which is shown in Figure 5-11.

In writing a program from Figure 5-11, let us first program the command block "read data from port 0." The reason for skipping the "Initialization of the system" is that we do not know what is required for initialization and will not know until we have programmed the other command blocks. As we program the other command blocks, we will keep a record of the initialization require-

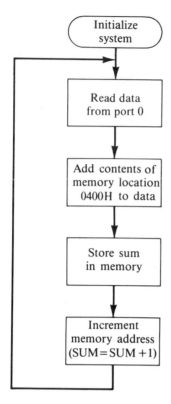

FIGURE 5-11. Flowchart for addition of two data bytes.

ments, and when finished we will return to the initialization command block and program it.

```
IN 00H          ; Read data from port 0
ADD M           ; Add data from memory (0400H)
                ; to accumulator (port 0)
```

(We must initialize H and L with 0400H.)

```
STAX B          ; Store sum in memory at
                ; memory location given by RP B
```

(We must initialize RP B with 0C00H.)

```
INX B           ; Increment sum storage
                ; location by one
JMP RETURN      ; Jump to IN 00H to
                ; read next data byte
```

(We must add the symbolic address RETURN, which is a label, to IN 00H.)
To initialize the system, we must include in the program

```
                    ORG 0800H

              ; Initialization

         LXI H,0400H      ; Initialize RP H (M)
         LXI B,0C00H      ; Initialize RP B

              ; Program

RETURN:   IN 00H          ; Read data from port 0
          ADD M           ; Add data from memory (0400H)
                          ; to A
          STAX B          ; Store sum in memory location
                          ; given by RP B
          INX B           ; Increment M
          JMP RETURN      ; Jump to RETURN
                          ; to read next data byte.
```

FIGURE 5-12.   Program to implement flowchart of Figure 5-11.

```
              LXI H,0400H
              LXI B,0C00H
```

Also, we must insert the directive ORG 0800H (beginning of page 1) in order to direct the assembler to begin assembly of this program at memory location 0800H. The completed program is shown in Figure 5-12. Notice from the program that we have no way of exiting from it except by a reset or, as we shall see, an interrupt, which is not a good practice. But for now we shall not be concerned with this problem.

Next we produce the symbol table of Table 5-18 and then assemble the program, as shown in Table 5-19.   ■

EXAMPLE 5-10

Write a program that will compare the data bytes from input port 0 of Figure 4-27 and the content of memory location 0800H until input port 0 inputs the end command 'E', at which time the system will enter an idle state. Data bytes from port 0 that are larger in value than the content of memory location 0800H are to be stored in memory, beginning at memory location 0801H. There are 20H memory ·locations allocated for storage of these data bytes, and if this storage capacity is exceeded, isolate input port 0 from the system and give an alarm error code by outputting 6H to output port 1, which is a light-emitting diode (LED) display. When the system is in a 6H error alarm state, the system

TABLE 5-18.   Symbol Table for Program of Figure 5-12

Symbol	Memory Address Assigned by the Assembler (Hex)
RETURN	0806

TABLE 5-19. Assembled Program of Figure 5-12

Program	Assembled Program Memory Locations Assigned by Location Counter	Machine Code
LXI H,0400H	0800	21
	0801	00
	0802	04
LXI B,0C00H	0803	01
	0804	00
	0805	0C
RETURN: IN 00H	0806	DB
	0807	00
ADD M	0808	86
STAX B	0809	02
INX B	080A	03
JMP RETURN	080B	C3
	080C	06
	080D	08

is to be put in an idle condition until the system is reset. For "bookkeeping" purposes, keep a tally of the number of data bytes that are not greater than the content of memory location 0800H. Load the assembled program in the system ROM beginning at location 0400H.

Solution

To flowchart this programming task, we shall modularize the requirements. These modules are

1. Initialize the system.
2. Input data from input port 0 and determine whether the data byte is an end command 'E'.
   a. If the data byte is not an 'E', compare it with the content of memory location 0800H (indicated by [0800H]), where [ ] indicates "content of. . . ."
      (1) If the data byte is greater than [0800H], then store the data byte. Keep a tally of data bytes stored and do not exceed the storage of 20H such data bytes.
         (a) If storage allotment is not exceeded, return to input port 0 for the next data byte.
         (b) If storage of the present data byte equals 20H memory locations used, isolate input port 0 from the system and idle the system. Also, output error code 06H to output port 1.
      (2) If the data byte is less than [0800H], ignore it. Keep a tally of the data bytes that are in this category. Return to input port 0 to collect the next data byte.
   b. If the data byte is an 'E', store the tally that recorded the number of data

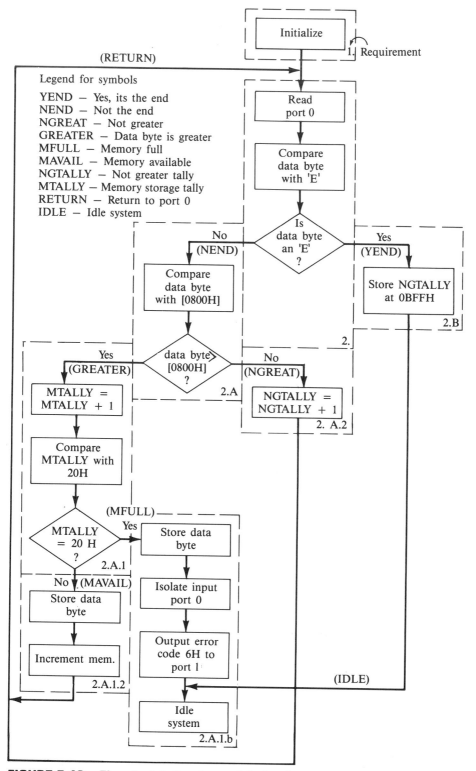

FIGURE 5-13. Flowchart indicating modularization of Example 5-10.

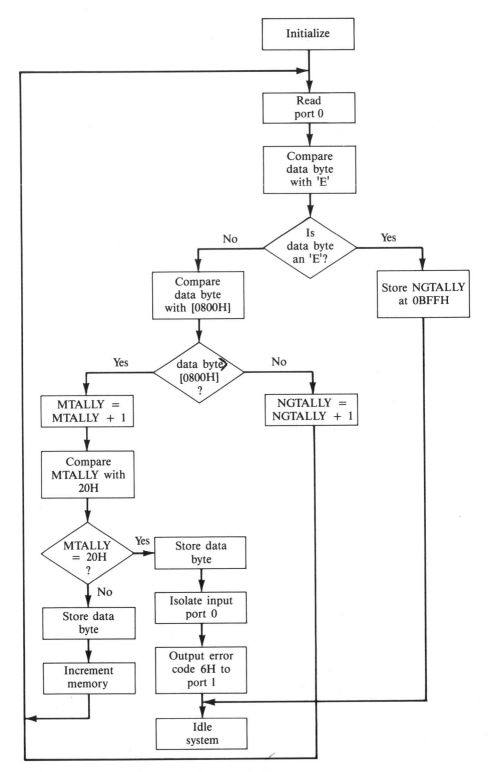

FIGURE 5-14. Flowchart for Example 5-10.

bytes that were not greater than [0800H] at memory location 0BFFH and idle the system.

Now that we have modularized the requirements, we can construct flowcharts for each module. These flowcharts will then be combined into one, as shown in Figure 5-13. Each dashed rectangle of Figure 5-13 is the modularization of the requirements. The number in the lower right corner identifies a requirement and the command blocks that implement it.

When writing the program from Figure 5-13 we find that symbolic addresses (labels) will be needed for jumps, both conditional and unconditional. Knowing that every branch (Yes/No leg) of a decision block implies the possible use of a label, we will assign labels to each conditional branch, as shown in parentheses in Figure 5-13. Figure 5-13 also shows two additional labels in parentheses for the unconditional jumps RETURN and IDLE. To present Figure 5-13 in a more conventional manner, the parenthesized labels and dashed modules have been removed, resulting in Figure 5-14.

A program to accomplish the task of Example 5-10 is shown in Figure 5-15. Even though Figure 5-14 will accompany the program as part of its documentation, Figure 5-13 was the one actually used to aid in writing the program. Notice that to implement the comparison stated by requirement 2.A, which is illustrated in Figure 5-13, a SUB instruction rather than CMP was used. This is because of the C flag's indicating quantities equal to or greater than the content of the accumulator, where we want only the greater-than indication; hence CMP would not work. Also, we see from Figure 5-15 that requirement 2.A.1.b uses output port 02H to isolate input port 0. It does so by addressing output port 02H, via the out I/O select 8205 of Figure 5-16, which results in a logic 1 being output by the isolation OR gate. This logic 1 is latched by the flip-flop shown, which holds $\overline{CE}$ of input port 0's buffer high, thereby driving its output into high-Z. The "bypass" OR gate allows the latch or the isolation OR gate to isolate input port 0, as can be seen from the truth tables for both OR gates provided in Figure 5-16. ∎

The math requirements of a task can eliminate MOS-technology microprocessors from some applications, especially when a rather lengthy mathematical program must be executed in a short period of time (a few hundred microseconds), as in a feedback-control application for a high-performance jet fighter aircraft. A means to "speed up" the determination of a mathematical answer is to use a look-up-table approach rather than actually performing the mathematical calculation. The next example will demonstrate that approach.

EXAMPLE 5-11

Using a look-up table, write a program that will square the integer decimal value input from input port 6. The result is to be output to output port 7. Use 'F' from port 6 to indicate when finished.

Solution

To use a look-up table, an addressing scheme known as *indexing* will be employed. In indexing, a register's content (the index register) serves as a point

```
                              ORG 0400H

                         ; Initialize System

Requirement         LXI H, 0801H              ; First storage location
number 1. of
Figure 5-12         MVI C,00H                 ; Clear C (NGTALLY)
                    MVI D,00H                 ; Clear D (MTALLY)

                         ; Initialization Complete

                    RETURN:   IN 00H          ; Read data byte 0
Requirement                   CPI 'E'         ; Compare data byte with 'E'
number 2
                              JZ YEND         ; Data byte is 'E' idle system
                              MOV B,A         ; Save data byte in B
Requirement
2.A                           LDA 0800H       ; Get data from 0800H
                              SUB B           ; Determine if data byte is larger
                              JC GREATER      ; Data byte is larger
2.A.2                         INR C           ; NGTALLY = NGTALLY + 1
                              JMP RETURN      ; Get next data byte

                    GREATER:  INR D           ; MTALLY = MTALLY + 1
                              MOV A,D         ; Move MTALLY into A
2.A.1                         CPI 20H         ; Compare MTALLY with 20H
                              JZ MFULL        ; If Z = 1 memory is full
                              MOV A,B         ; Restore A with data byte
2.A.1.a                       MOV M,A         ; Store data byte
                              INX H           ; Increment memory location
                              JMP RETURN      ; Get next data byte

                    YEND:     MOV A,C         ; Move NGTALLY to A
2.B                           STA 0BFFH       ; Store NGTALLY
                              JMP IDLE        ; Idle system

                    MFULL:    MOV A,B         ; Restore A with data byte
                              MOV M,A         ; Store data byte
                              OUT 02H         ; Isolate input port 0
                                              ; just by addressing port 02
2.A.1.b
                              MVI A, 06H      ; Move error code to A
                              OUT 01H         ; Output error code

                    IDLE:     JMP IDLE        ; Idle system
```

FIGURE 5-15. Program implementing flowchart of Figure 5-13 or 5-14.

of reference for addressing memory. That is, the content of the index register
is added to the content of another register, and it is this sum that is the *effective*
memory address. Specifically, we shall program in a PROM with values of 0
to 9 squared, which is the table that will be referenced; then as port 6 inputs
decimal values to be squared, these values will be indexed (added to) the index
register, which will result in the effective address desired. The content of this
memory location will then be accessed and output to port 7.

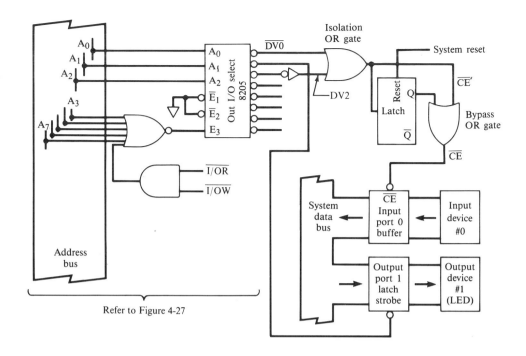

Truth table for isolation OR gate

$\overline{\text{DV0}}$	DV2	Output $\overline{\text{CE}}'$	Comment
0	0	0	Out port 2 not addr., buffer active
0	1	1	Buffer tri-state; therefore, input port 0 is isolated
1	0	1	
1	1	1	

Truth table for bypass OR gate

Q	$\overline{\text{CE}}'$	$\overline{\text{CE}}$	Comment
0	0	0	Port 0 addr. but not port 2; therefore, active buffer
0	1	1	Either port 0 is not addr. or port 2 is addr.; therefore, tri-state buffer
1	0	1	
1	1	1	

FIGURE 5-16.   Hardware to implement the program of Figure 5-15.

Assuming that the system to be programmed is that of Figure 4-27, with the additions of ports 6 and 7, we will somewhat arbitrarily store the program and look-up table in page 0. Let the program be stored in memory beginning at location 0100H and the table beginning with address 0200H. The flowchart and program are shown in Figure 5-17.

The program of Figure 5-17 is straightforward and needs little comment. The comments needed are those concerning the DB directive. DB directs the assembler to store the specified data bytes, that is, the operands, which in this case are 0D, 1D, . . . , 64D, and 81D, in *consecutive* memory locations, starting with the current setting of the location counter (D of the operands indicates to the assembler that the quantity is decimal). The location counter will be set to 0200H because of the ORG 0200H directive.   ∎

Our final example will emphasize the role of timing states in some types of programs.

; Initialization

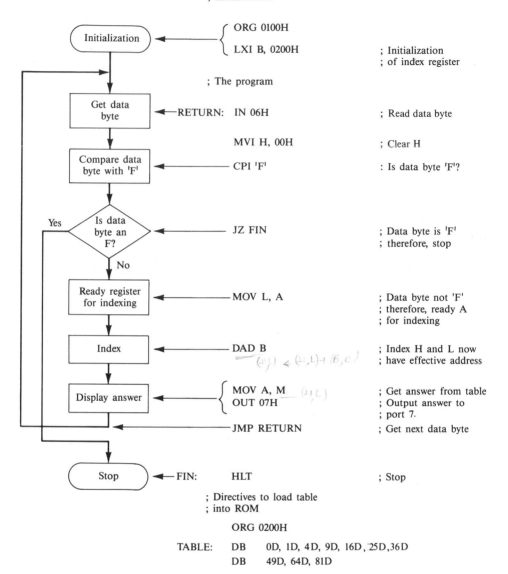

; Initialization

; ORG 0100H

; LXI B, 0200H   ; Initialization
                  ; of index register

; The program

RETURN: IN 06H   ; Read data byte

         MVI H, 00H   ; Clear H

         CPI 'F'   : Is data byte 'F'?

         JZ FIN   ; Data byte is 'F'
                   ; therefore, stop

         MOV L, A   ; Data byte not 'F'
                     ; therefore, ready A
                     ; for indexing

         DAD B   ; Index H and L now
                  ; have effective address

         MOV A, M   ; Get answer from table
         OUT 07H   ; Output answer to
                     ; port 7.

         JMP RETURN   ; Get next data byte

FIN: HLT   ; Stop

; Directives to load table
; into ROM

         ORG 0200H

TABLE: DB   0D, 1D, 4D, 9D, 16D, 25D, 36D
         DB   49D, 64D, 81D

FIGURE 5-17. Flowchart and program using index addressing.

EXAMPLE 5-12

The circuit of Figure 5-18 is to serve as a *programmable one-shot*. That is, the pulse duration is to be under control of the microprocessor and therefore can be varied according to a parameter (<B2>) of the program.

Solution

The flip-flop output Q is set and reset to create the proper pulse duration. SET and RESET of the flip-flop are treated as output ports by the micro-

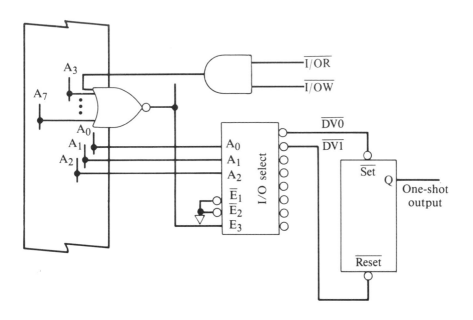

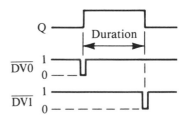

FIGURE 5-18. Programmable one-shot.

processor, output port 0 for set and port 1 for reset. The flowchart and program are given in Figure 5-19.

The program of Figure 5-19 will require a value $<B2>$, for it is this value that determines the pulse duration. Therefore, an equation is needed to determine the value of $<B2>$:

$$\text{pulse duration states} = \text{number loops} \times <B2> + \text{reset} \qquad (5\text{-}2)$$
$$= 14 \times <B2> + 10$$

$$\text{state period} = \frac{1}{\text{clock frequency}} = \frac{1}{f} \qquad (5\text{-}3)$$

$$\text{pulse duration time} = T_D = \text{pulse duration states} \times \text{state period} \qquad (5\text{-}4)$$

$$T_D = (14 \times <B2> + 10)\frac{1}{f} \qquad (5\text{-}5)$$

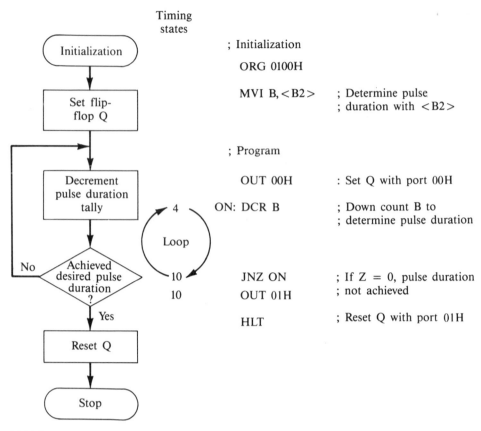

FIGURE 5-19. Flowchart and program for determining pulse duration of programmable one-shot.

Solving for <B2>, we have

$$<B2> = \frac{T_D f - 10}{14} \tag{5-6}$$

Suppose that a pulse duration of 0.5 ms is desired when the frequency is 2 MHz (crystal of 14 MHz). Then from Equation (5-6),

$$<B2> = \frac{(0.5 \times 10^{-3})(2 \times 10^{6}) - 10}{14}$$

$$= 70.7 \quad \text{decimal}$$

Because register B must have the hexidecimal equivalent of 70.7_{10} and $71_{10} = 47_{16}$; hence <B2> = 47H, which results in a small error. Thus for this case, MVI B,<B2> specifically becomes MVI B,47H. ∎

8085A Timing Diagram and the Instruction Set

As we know, in order for an 8085 to execute a program, it follows a cyclical process. This process can easily be seen in Figure 2-16, which is reproduced in Figure 5-20 for the reader's convenience. The essence of this cyclical process is that the 8085 will

1. Output the address of the device to be read or written to the address bus.
2. Output a strobe pulse (ALE) which can be used for latching (demultiplexing) the lower-order byte of the address.
3. Output a read or write signal ($\overline{RD}$ or $\overline{WR}$) which provides timing for the read or write operation.

The reader should verify that these three events always occur in each machine cycle (M_1, M_2, and M_3 of Figure 5-20).

To understand the necessity of the cyclical nature of the 8085, as illustrated in Figure 5-20, we must realize that an MPU must repeat the same process over and over: Fetch an instruction and then execute it. Because the MPU must always begin by fetching an instruction (otherwise it would not know what to do), it logically follows that to start the process it must supply the address of the memory location from where the instruction is to be fetched (the content of the

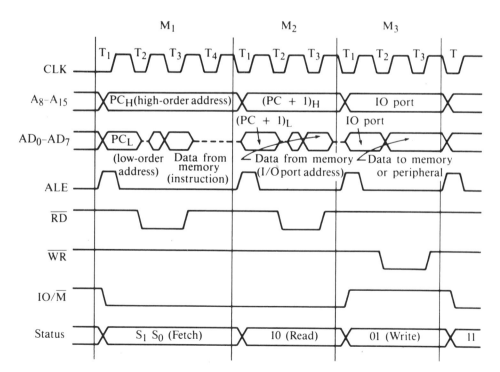

FIGURE 5-20.   A Reproduction of Figure 2-16. (Courtesy of Intel Corp.)

PC supplies the address). And because pins AD_0–AD_7 are multiplexed, the 8085 must also provide a strobe pulse with which the lower-order address byte can be latched (demultiplexed). Once memory has been addressed, the 8085 must then provide a read signal ($\overline{RD}$) that can be used to gate the content of the addressed memory location (the instruction) on the data bus. From our previous studies of timing diagrams in Chapter 4, this should be logical to the reader.

The cycle of events just described for reading memory are also true for reading an I/O port and for write operations (memory or I/O). Thus we can conclude that any time the 8085 is to perform a read or write operation, it will execute the previously listed three events. To confirm this statement, again review Figures 5-20, 4-6, and 4-23. We see from Figure 5-20 that Intel has subdivided the instruction fetch-and-execute timing diagram into machine cycles, each of which includes the three previously listed events. Specifically, Figure 5-20 is the fetch-and-execute timing diagram for the OUT instruction. Three machine cycles (M_1, M_2, and M_3) are required, and each machine cycle outputs (1) an address, (2) the strobe pulse ALE, and (3) a read or write timing signal $\overline{RD}$ or $\overline{WR}$. Figure 5-20 also shows that the positive edge of ALE can be used to define a machine cycle.

For an example of a fetch-and-execute timing diagram, we shall apply these concepts to the system of Figure 4-27.

EXAMPLE 5-13

Develop a fetch-and-execute timing diagram for the OUT instruction as it applies to the system of Figure 4-27. The op code for OUT is stored at memory location 0050H.

Solution

As seen from Figure 4-27, port 1 is the output port; hence, the instruction is OUT 01H. Looking up the OUT instruction in Section 5-3, we find that it requires three machine cycles and ten states (timing states T_1, T_2, and so on), which agrees with the timing diagram of Figure 5-20. To develop the fetch-and-execute timing diagram for the instruction OUT 01H, as it applies to the system of Figure 4-27, we shall simply modify the timing diagram of Figure 5-20. We shall add to the timing of Figure 5-20 the demultiplexed address and data buses, control signals $\overline{MEM\ R}$ and $\overline{I/O\ W}$, page 0 select line, and the select line for output port 1. This modified version of Figure 5-20 is illustrated in Figure 5-21.

Figure 5-21 is an overlay of Figures 5-20 and 4-6. The reader should correlate the information of Chapter 4 with Figure 5-21. At t_0 of Figure 5-21, the 8085 outputs the address 0050H (PC = 0050H) via pins AD_0–AD_7 and A_8–A_{15}. At t_1 the negative edge of ALE strobes the demultiplexer, and then address/data pins AD_0–AD_7 are demultiplexed, which results in the address bus's (A_0–A_{15}) making the 16-bit address 0050H available to the system. Because $IO/\overline{M}$ is low, the page selector is enabled, and address 0050H is decoded. As a result of decoding 0050H, page 0 select line ($\overline{O}_0$) goes low, which selects page 0. At t_2 the 8085 drives $\overline{RD}$ low and it remains low until t_4. $\overline{RD}$ is gated with $IO/\overline{M}$ (see Figure 2-13) to generate control bus control signal $\overline{MEM\ R}$, which enables the output enable pin ($\overline{OE}$) of page 0. Enabling $\overline{OE}$ of page 0 causes the data

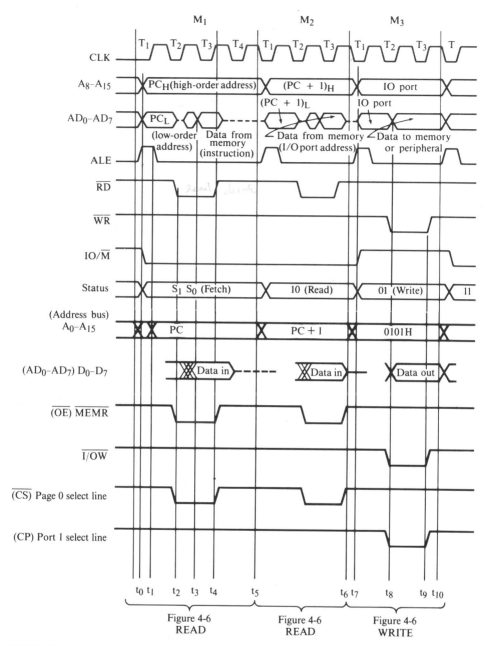

FIGURE 5-21. The Fetch-and-execute Timing-diagram for Instruction OUT 01H as it applies to Figure 4-27.

byte (op code) of location 0050H to be output on the data bus D_0-D_7 (labeled as *data in*). The op code D3H is latched off the data bus by the 8085 at t_4 (which is the positive edge of T_3), and it also loads that op code in the IR. The 8085 performs internal operations during clock period T_4 via the CU, and on the negative of T_4 (which is t_5), machine cycle M_1 ends and M_2 begins. The second machine cycle is another memory read operation that fetches the second byte (01H) of the OUT instruction. The address on the address bus during this cycle is 0051H. As in M_1, on the positive edge of T_3, the 8085 latches the data byte (operand 01H) off the data bus, but for this machine cycle that data byte is loaded into 8085 registers W and Z. Recall from Chapter 2 that registers W and Z are used as a pair when addressing I/O, resulting in a 16-bit address of 0101H. At t_6 the third machine cycle begins. At t_7 the 8085 outputs the address of port 1, which is 0101H. The 8085 drives $\overline{WR}$ low at t_8, thereby driving $\overline{I/O\ W}$ low. Also at t_8 the 8085 writes the content of its accumulator (A) on the data bus, which is labeled *data out*. When $\overline{I/O\ W}$ goes low, it enables the I/O selector of Figure 4-27, and address lines A_0–A_7 are decoded. Decoding address lines A_0–A_7 (01H) results in output $\overline{O}_1$ of the I/O selector going low, which is the port 1 select line. The positive edge of the port 1 select signal is used to strobe the CP of the latch attached to the port 1 select line. This completes the write operation. At t_{10}, another fetch-and-execute cycle begins; hence, t_{10} is the beginning of M_1 for another instruction fetch cycle. ■

When comparing Figure 5-21 with Figure 4-6 the reader should realize that

$$t_0 \text{ to } t_2 \text{ is } t_{AC}$$
$$t_0 \text{ to } t_3 \text{ is } t_{AD}$$
$$t_2 \text{ to } t_4 \text{ is } t_{CC}$$
$$t_7 \text{ to } t_8 \text{ is } t_{AC}$$
$$t_8 \text{ to } t_9 \text{ is } t_{CC}$$

Also notice that a machine cycle is required for every 8085 read or write operation.

5-6

SUMMARY

As one would expect, all MPU instructions are the result of a logical binary coding scheme. The binary coding scheme of these instructions is to divide the binary code into bit combinations that indicate the MPU operations (data transfer, and the like) and the MPU register(s) involved. The binary code that represents an instruction is read from memory by the MPU and loaded into its instruction register (IR), where it is then decoded by the MPU's IR decoder. Output signals from the IR decoder are input to the MPU's control unit (CU), which actually executes the instruction. The CU contains a program, which is stored within the CU at the time of manufacture, that instructs the CU on the details for instruction execution. This program is known as the MPU's microprogram.

Each microprocessor has an instruction set from which the program's instructions must be chosen. When programs are being written, the programmer avoids binary coding (machine code) but, rather, uses mnemonic coding. Before a program can be executed by the microprocessor, it must be translated from mnemonic code into machine code. To translate from mnemonic code into machine code, a computer program known as an assembler is used.

To aid in writing programs and in interpreting those already written, flowcharts are provided. These flowcharts are visual indicators of how program instructions are used to accomplish a given task. That is, flowcharts document how the programmer modularizes a programming task.

Note that all program decision branches are determined by the logic state of a condition flag.

From this chapter and previous chapters, the reader should now

1. Understand generally how machine code controls microprocessor operations via the IR decoder and CU.
2. Understand how the software controls the system hardware via the microprocessor and support chips.
3. Understand the concept of binary and mnemonic coding of instructions.
4. Be able to determine the timing diagram for a program, or at least the essential portions.
5. Be able to develop a flowchart for a relatively simple task.
6. Be able to write programs from flowcharts.
7. Be able to hand-assemble a program.
8. Understand the function of an assembler and generally how it performs that function.

REVIEW QUESTIONS AND PROBLEMS

1. Using Tables 5-1, 5-2, 5-3, 5-5, 5-7, and 5-8, determine the machine code for the instructions given. Confirm your coding with Table 5-10 or Appendix A.
(a) MOV A,M   (b) ADD E
(c) SUB C   (d) CMP C
(e) ADC H   (f) CNZ 1000H

2. Determine which binary codes are not officially part of the 8085 instruction set.

3. With reference to Section 5-3, Intel's instruction explanations state the number of machine cycles (listed as "cycles") required to fetch and execute each instruction. For the instructions given, justify each machine cycle required, and state and justify the control signal generated for each machine cycle.
(a) MOV r1,r2   (b) LXI rp,data 16
(c) STA addr   (d) LHLD addr
(e) STAX rp   (f) ADD r
(g) ADD M   (h) CALL addr
(i) RET   (j) RST N

4. Write a properly documented program (flowchart and comments) that will input data bytes from input device 0 of Figure 4-27. These data bytes are to be classified into two groups:
Group A: those less than 010H.
Group B: those equal to or greater than 010H.

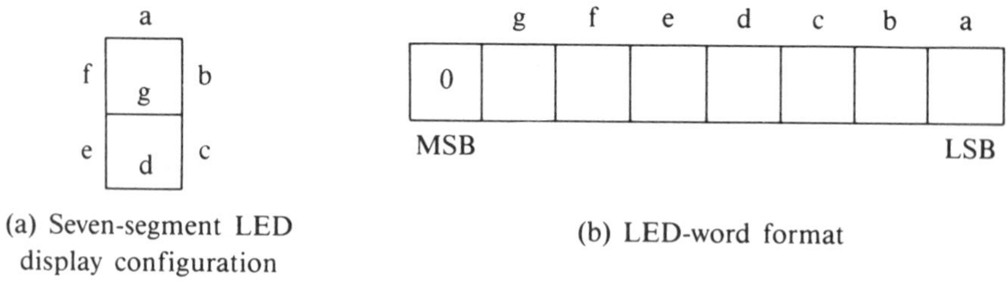

(a) Seven-segment LED
display configuration

(b) LED-word format

FIGURE 5-22. Seven-segment LED display and word format.

There is to be a tally for the number of data bytes falling in groups A and B (tally A and tally B). Data collection is to terminate when device 0 inputs an 'E'. Begin your program at 0050H.

5. Suppose that output device 3 is a seven-segment LED hex display. Modify the program of Problem 4 to include echoing (by device 3) of each input data byte. Assume that the input data bytes are in proper form to be written directly to device 3.

6. A seven-segment LED display has the format shown in Figure 5-22(a). Using the 8-bit format of Figure 5-20(b) to turn the LED segments of Figure 5-20(a) on and off (a "1" turns a segment on), write a program that will echo hexadecimal values input by device 0 via the seven-segment display represented by device 1 of Figure 4-27. Use a look-up-table approach. Be certain to document your program.

7. Most keyboard outputs are in ASCII binary code. Refer to Appendix B for the ASCII code and then write a program that will differentiate between alphabetic characters and decimal numeric values. Echo the numeric characters to device 5 in ASCII code. Begin this program at memory location 0150H.

8. Suppose that device 5 is a seven-segment LED display. Write a program that will convert a decimal ASCII character input by device 0 to an LED seven-segment display character and then echo that character via device 5. This program is to be located at beginning address 0050H. Document this program.

9. Hand-assemble the programs of Problems 4 to 7. On the first pass, create a symbol table.

10. For each instruction of Problem 4, discuss how the instruction controls the hardware of Figure 4-27.

11. Using Figure 5-21 as a model, construct a timing diagram for the IN instruction. Let the IN op code be stored at address 0080H.

CHAPTER 6

8085 Interrupts, Serial I/O Ports, and DMA

6-1

Introduction

The microprocessor-based system of Figure 4-27 was not given interrupt or DMA capability, as the interrupt pins and HOLD of the 8085 are permanently inactive (tied low). This chapter will develop the necessary concepts of hardware and software for the utilization of these features. Also, serial ports SID and SOD will be investigated.

6-2

Interrupts

Interrupts allow the MPU to be more productive, by permitting an I/O device (most often an input device) to interrupt the MPU only when that device needs servicing by the MPU, therefore freeing the MPU to perform other tasks. An analogy to the interrupt concept is the classroom, where the professor serves as the MPU and the students as I/O devices. Each student possesses two I/O device: an input device (speech mechanism for data transmission to the professor) and an output device (listening mechanism for receiving data from the professor).

The classroom scenario for this interrupt analogy is that the professor "lectures to the blackboard" (doing a productive task—lecturing and writing on the blackboard) and faces the class only when interrupted by an input device (a student requesting a service, perhaps to ask a question). The means of requesting an interrupt is that each student is given a string, all of which are tied to the professor's left index finger (assuming that the professor is writing with his or her right hand). When a student wishes to request service, he or she simply pulls the string. Once the string has been pulled, the professor acknowledges the request and interrupts the lecture. The professor then turns from the blackboard to face the class. The professor now wishes to service the interrupting student but is unable to do so because the identity of the requesting student is unknown. Thus the professor must *poll* the class to determine who requested the interrupt.

To implement this interrupting scheme, each student is given a flag mounted on his or her desk (much like a mailbox flag). They are to raise this flag (to identify themselves) in the up position upon requesting an interrupt; otherwise, it is to be in the down position. To poll the class the professor need only check the state (up or down) of each student's interrupt request flag.

Once the professor has identified the student who requested an interrupt, the professor can then begin servicing by "reading" data from the student (the student will ask the question). Then the professor "writes" the answer to the student's output device, and the student listens to the answer—we hope. This concludes the interrupt, at which time the professor returns to lecturing, continuing at that point of the lecture where interrupted.

From this example several analogies can be drawn:

1. The professor had just one finger to devote to interrupts, and all student interrupt requests were made via that single finger.
2. Because all interrupt requests were made over a single finger, rather than allocating individual fingers to particular students, the professor had to poll the class to identify the requesting student.
3. The order of events was as follows:
   a. The request was initiated by the student, and at the same time the student raised an interrupt request flag.
   b. The professor acknowledged the interrupt request.
   c. The professor polled the class to identify the requesting student by checking the status of *all* interrupt request flags (up or down).
   d. After student identification and service, the professor returned to the task being performed (lecturing) at the time of the interrupt.

From the first analogy the professor is said to have *single-level interrupt* capability. For a microprocessor this means that all interrupt requests are made via a single input pin of the MPU. As in the case of the second analogy, the MPU must poll the I/O devices to identify the requesting device. Polling occurs after the handshake (request and acknowledgment of the request constitute a handshake) and is a software routine that checks the logic state of each device's interrupt request flag, which is simply a flip-flop. This flip-flop is set high by the I/O device at the time the I/O device requests the interrupt. Once the interrupting I/O device is identified, the MPU will service it and then return to the task it was performing before the interrupt. Notice that polling takes time.

Now suppose that the professor decides to use all five fingers (thumb included) of his or her left hand in order to facilitate the interrupts. The professor could allocate four fingers to those students to whom he or she gives the highest priority. Each of these students would attach his or her string to the finger uniquely assigned to him or her, whereas the remainder of the class would still be collectively attached to the index finger. Whenever one of the four high-priority students wishes to request an interrupt, he or she would follow the same procedures as before, that is, pull the string and at the same time set the interrupt request flag high. Now the professor need not poll the class for the requesting student's identity. The student identity is immediately known, as there is a one-to-one correspondence between each of these high-priority students and a specific finger. For this analogy the professor is said to have *multilevel interrupt* capability.

Similar to the classroom analogy, any microprocessor with more than one interrupt pin has multilevel interrupt capability. Any I/O device that is singularly tied to one of these interrupt pins can be immediately identified by the MPU upon receiving an interrupt request from it. This allows the MPU to go directly to that I/O device and service it without having to poll first. This obviously will save time in processing interrupts. The term used to describe the MPU being "pointed" where to go is *vectoring*. Hence in this example the MPU was vectored to the I/O device requesting the interrupt (actually, the MPU will be vectored to the service routine of the I/O port).

As a result of a cursory examination of a microprocessor's pin configuration, one may reasonably assume that if the microprocessor has multilevel interrupt capability it also has vector capability. Vectoring, of course, means a reduction in program length and speed of servicing of those vectored I/O ports, as polling is not required.

In summary, a single-level interrupt capability (one interrupt pin) often requires polling for I/O interrupt request identification (no vectoring). Multilevel interrupt capability (more than one interrupt pin) usually provides vectoring, thereby reducing or eliminating polling routines.

6-3

Single-Level Interrupts and Polling

Because for single-level interrupt capability, there is a single pin (INTR) for interrupt request, each I/O device with interrupt capability will have its interrupt request flag ORed to the interrupt request pin of the microprocessor, as illustrated in Figure 6-1.

Knowing that for a single-level interrupt system the interrupt request flags must be polled, a scheme is needed that allows polling via software. Somehow the logic states of these interrupt request flags must be read by the MPU, and the circuit of Figure 6-2 will accomplish this task.

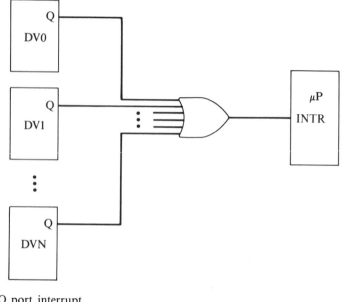

I/O port interrupt
request flags

FIGURE 6-1. Single-level interrupt capability.

Inspecting Figure 6-2, we see that when one or more interrupt request flags are raised, this request(s) will be ORed to the INTR pin of the MPU. Also, the output of the interrupt request OR gate will cause the IREQ latch to latch the logic states of these flags; that is, IREQ will latch their status. At the completion of the handshake (interrupt request and acknowledge), the MPU will vector to memory location 0038H. Vectoring to address 0038H is accomplished by tying the $\overline{\text{INTA}}$ (interrupt acknowledge) pin high via a 1-kΩ resistor, which is shown in Figure 6-2. Tying $\overline{\text{INTA}}$ high causes the MPU to execute an RST 7 instruction upon the acknowledgment of an interrupt request.

As seen from the instruction set of Section 5-3, RST 7 (n = 7) will cause the MPU to vector to memory location 0038H and then save the address of the next memory location (PC + 1), which is the address of the next instruction to have been executed *before* the interrupt, on the stack. Therefore, upon completion of servicing the interrupt, the MPU will "know" where to return in its program execution, by retrieving this saved address from the stack. Once the return address is saved on the stack, the PC content is changed to 0038H (NNN = 111), which is the cause for the MPU to vector to 0038H, as the PC content is gated on the address bus in implementing the RST 7 instruction.

Address 0038H is the beginning of the polling routine. The polling routine flowchart is given in Figure 6-3 and the routine in Figure 6-4. For simplicity the routine of Figure 6-4 assumes that only two, rather than eight, I/O devices have interrupt capability.

The program of Figure 6-4 is fairly simple. Notice from Figure 6-2 that the tristate buffers are addressed as 09; hence the instruction IN 09H will load the

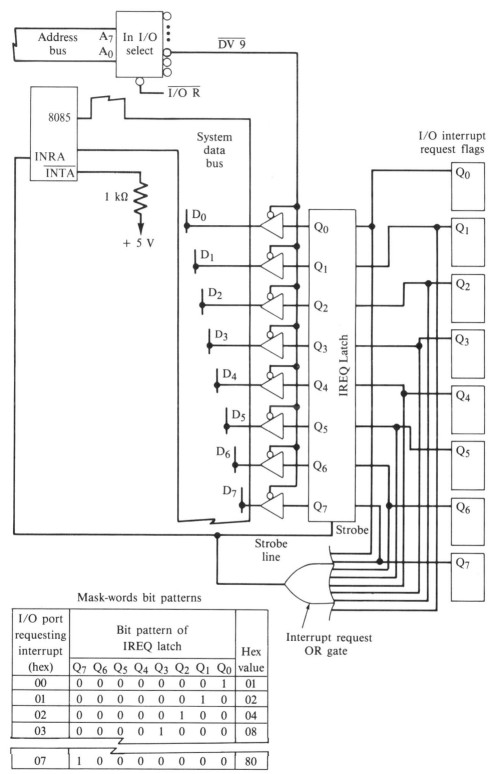

FIGURE 6-2. Logic circuit for polling.

Mask-words bit patterns

I/O port requesting interrupt (hex)	Bit pattern of IREQ latch								Hex value
	Q_7	Q_6	Q_5	Q_4	Q_3	Q_2	Q_1	Q_0	
00	0	0	0	0	0	0	0	1	01
01	0	0	0	0	0	0	1	0	02
02	0	0	0	0	0	1	0	0	04
03	0	0	0	0	1	0	0	0	08
07	1	0	0	0	0	0	0	0	80

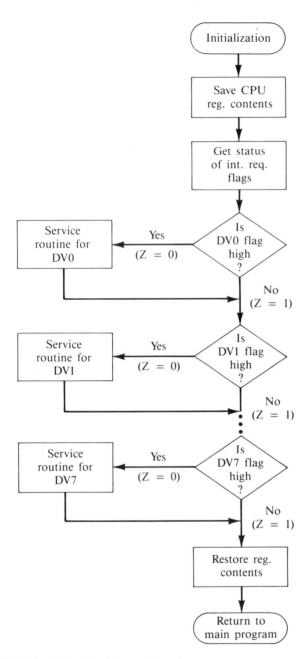

FIGURE 6-3. Flowchart for polling.

content of IREQ, which is the interrupt request flag's status, into the MPU's accumulator. Because a program's AND operation destroys the content of the accumulator, a copy must be made; hence the instruction MOV B,A. The second byte of the ANI instructions is referred to as a *mask word*, for it masks out all bits except those of interest. Their values can be reasoned by referring to Figure 6-2 and determining the bit pattern of IREQ for various interrupt requests. It

EXAMPLE 6-1

```
    ORG 0038H

; Initialization

    DI              ; Disable interrupt capability

; Save register contents

    PUSH PSW
    PUSH B
    PUSH D
    PUSH H

; Begin polling

    IN 09H          ; Get Interrupt request status flags
    MOV B,A         ; Copy status in B
    ANI 01H         ; Poll DV0
    CNZ SR0         ; If Z = 0 jump to service routine for DV0
    MOV A,B         ; Copy status in A
    ANI 02H         ; Poll DV1 with mask word 02H
    CNZ SR1         ; If Z = 0 jump to service routine for DV1

; Restore reg. contents

    POP H
    POP D
    POP B
    POP PSW
    EI              ; Enable interrupt capability
    RET             ; Return to main prog.
```

Figure 6-4. Polling routine for the hardware of Figure 6-2.

can be seen from the table of Figure 6-2 that if I/O device 00H alone had its interrupt request flag high, the bit pattern of register A would be 01H; similarly, mask word 02H for I/O device 1, 04H for I/O device 02, and so on. Thus, if any I/O device except I/O device 00 requested an interrupt, the instruction ANI 01H would result in A = 0, and the Z flag would be set (Z = 1). Under this condition, CNZ SR0 would not be executed. However, if I/O device 00H had requested an interrupt, and after the execution of ANI 01H, the accumulator contents would not be zero, resulting in Z = 0. In this case CNZ SR0 would be executed, which would cause the MPU to jump to the address represented by the symbol SR0, which is the beginning address of the service routine for I/O device 0.

6-4

Single-Level Interrupts and Vectoring

Thus far we have stated that if a microprocessor has single-level interrupt capability (single interrupt request pin), polling is often a necessary consequence.

However, this is not true for the 8080 (see Figure 2-18), nor is it true for the 8085's single interrupt request pin INTR. As will be shown, both of these pins can be used in a vectoring or polling interrupt mode.

To understand how the 8085's INTR interrupt request pin (and the 8080's INT) implements vectoring, the reader must be familiar with the RST N instruction and the read timing diagram of Figure 4-6, to which $\overline{\text{INTA}}$ is applicable for the dual timing of $\overline{\text{RD}}/\overline{\text{INTA}}$.

Referring to Section 5-3 and comparing instruction RST N with CALL ADDR, we realize that RST and CALL are similar instructions, though with two differences. First, the CALL instruction alters all 16 bits of the PC, and RST alters only 3 bits (3, 4, and 5) after the PC has been reset to 0000H. Obviously a CALL can point to any location within memory, whereas RST is limited to eight ($2^3 = 8$), and these eight vector addresses are indicated in Figure 6-5. The reader should verify them by substituting all possible binary combinations for NNN in the PC. The second difference between RST and CALL is that RST is a single-byte instruction, whereas CALL is a three-byte instruction.

Reviewing the timing diagram of Figure 4-6 for a read operation, we see that the timing for an interrupt acknowledge ($\overline{\text{INTA}}$) is the same as any other 8085 read operation. The difference is that an interrupt acknowledge read cycle processes the data byte read as an instruction. Thus, the data byte read from the data bus by the 8085 is treated as an op code and is therefore loaded into the IR for execution.

Summarizing the events for an interrupt request and the acknowledgment (handshaking):

1. The device requesting the interrupt does so by raising its interrupt request flag.
2. The 8085 will complete the execution of the instruction that it was executing at the time of the interrupt request, and when the execution is completed, it will enter an instruction fetch cycle. However, rather than using primary control signal $\overline{\text{RD}}$ for timing the read operation, the 8085 uses $\overline{\text{INTA}}$, because this instruction fetch cycle is the result of an interrupt acknowledge.
3. At the proper time, the 8085 drives $\overline{\text{INTA}}$ low, which will gate (as we shall see) the op code RST N on the data bus. On the positive edge of T_3 the 8085 will latch the RST N op code off the data bus and then load it in its IR.
4. The RST N op code is then decoded by the IR decoder and executed by the CU. In executing RST N, the 8085 will write the return address on the stack and then modify its PC according to the RST N instruction. Once the PC has been modified, the CU will gate the content of the PC on the address bus, which vectors the 8085 to the appropriate address. The 8085 will then fetch and execute the op code at that address, which is the first instruction of the service routine for the interrupt requesting device.

The control signal $\overline{\text{INTA}}$ is used to gate (jam) the desired instruction (RST N) on the data bus at the proper time. As shown for two RST instructions in Figure 6-5, when $\overline{\text{INTA}}$ becomes active, the tristate logic removes the buffer from its high-Z state, thus gating the binary bit pattern for an

RST N on the data bus. The IR then receives this machine code, and the CU executes it. Figure 6-5(c) gives the corresponding vector address for each RST N.

The 8085 (8228 for an 8080 system) has the feature that when $\overline{\text{INTA}}$ is tied high via a 1-kΩ resistor, as shown in Figure 6-2, the 8085 will automatically jam RST 7 in the IR. This feature saves hardware, of course.

With the circuits of Figure 6-5, only one RST N vector location can be utilized by the system, as the control signal $\overline{\text{INTA}}$ is dedicated to jamming a specific RST N instruction (RST 6) on the data bus. If more than one RST N is to be used, such as when dedicating an RST vector address to a specific I/O service routine, an encoder can be used to supply the bit pattern for bits NNN. This scheme is shown in Figure 6-6(a). Of course, with the scheme of Figure 6-6,

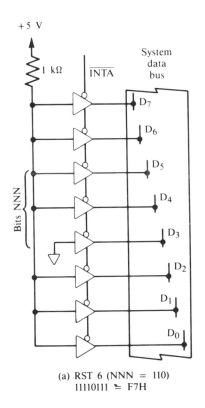

(a) RST 6 (NNN = 110)
11110111 ≃ F7H

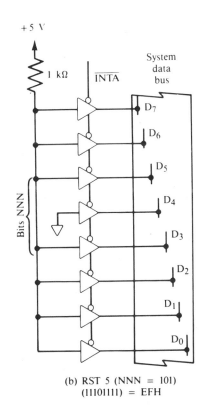

(b) RST 5 (NNN = 101)
(11101111) = EFH

Machine code (hex)	Mnemonic code	Vector address
C7	RST 0	0000H
CF	RST 1	0008H
D7	RST 2	0010H
DF	RST 3	0018H
E7	RST 4	0020H
EF	RST 5	0028H
F7	RST 6	0030H
FF	RST 7	0038H

memory location

FIGURE 6-5. Gating of RST 6 and RST 5 on the data bus.

only one interrupt request at a time can be received, as indicated from the encoder's truth table. Then a priority system such as that shown in Figure 6-6(b) is required. Priority is established since if a higher-priority I/O requests an interrupt, the $\overline{Q}$ output of its interrupt request flag will inhibit all lesser-priority AND gates.

An addition to the vectoring circuits of Figures 6-5 and 6-6 is the interrupt request OR gate of Figure 6-2. Also, with priority interrupts, as shown in Figure 6-6(b), there must be a means to "remember" interrupt requests that were ignored by the MPU while it was servicing other I/O devices (remember that all interrupt requests are made via a single interrupt pin). That is, if two or more I/O devices request an interrupt at the same time, or while the MPU is servicing another I/O device, the INTR pin will become active (via the OR gate) but will not indicate whether one or more I/O ports are requesting the interrupt. A combination of hardware and software will be used to resolve this problem. Figure 6-7 gives the hardware and Figure 6-8 gives the software. For simplicity, three I/O devices are shown, all of which are input devices.

To understand the operations of Figure 6-7, remember that

1. The interrupt request flags are flip-flops that are set by the requesting input device, via the interrupt request line. These flags are numbered to correspond to the input device that they serve. Notice that these flip-flops are treated as output devices and can be reset by addressing them as such.
2. AND gates 1 and 2 establish priority and also ensure that only one input to the encoder will be high and that "high" will be determined by the highest priority. These AND gates function similarly to those of Figure 6-6(b).
3. The interrupt request OR gate ORs the interrupt requests of all input devices, just as it did in Figures 6-1 and 6-2.

We shall arbitrarily assign input device 0's service routine to begin at memory location 0008H, which requires an RST 1 be jammed on the data bus (see Figure 6-5c) so that the MPU will vector to memory location 0008H as the result of an interrupt acknowledge ($\overline{\text{INTA}}$). The service routine for input device 1 will begin at memory location 0010H, which requires an RST 2. Finally, memory location 0018H will be assigned the service routine for input device 2, which requires RST 3. Note that RST 0 is not used (the encoder's low-order pin is held low), as this is the same vector address as for a system reset.

For simplicity the service routines of Figure 6-8 assume that input devices 0, 1, and 2 are of the simplest type and require just an IN instruction to acquire their data byte. It also assumed that the data byte is to be stored in memory. To understand the multiple ORG directives for each service routine, the reader must realize that there are eight storage locations between each RST location (RST 1 = 0008H and RST 2 = 0010H) and that eight memory locations are insufficient to store most service routines. Hence a JMP instruction is used to make more memory locations available for the service routines.

As an example of the priority interrupt system of Figure 6-7, let us suppose that input devices 0 and 2 requested interrupts at the same time. Of course, each of these input devices made the request by setting its respective interrupt request flag in the high state. The $\overline{Q}$ output of the interrupt request flag of input device

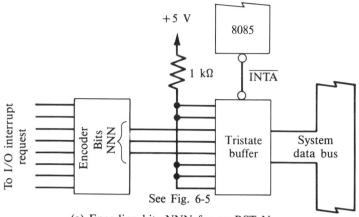

(a) Encoding bits NNN for an RST N
    instruction

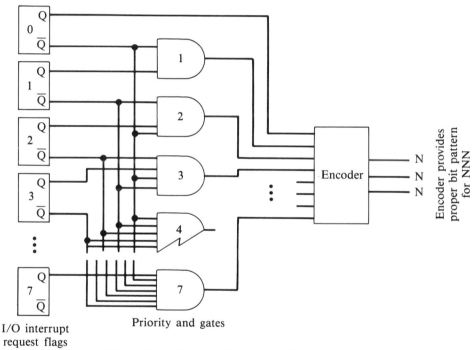

I/O interrupt
request flags

Priority and gates

(b) Implementing priority for encoder

Truth table for encoder

Input	Output (NNN)
00000001	000
00000010	001
00000100	010
00001000	011
00010000	100
00100000	101
01000000	110
10000000	111

FIGURE 6-6.   The development of vectored interrupts with priority.

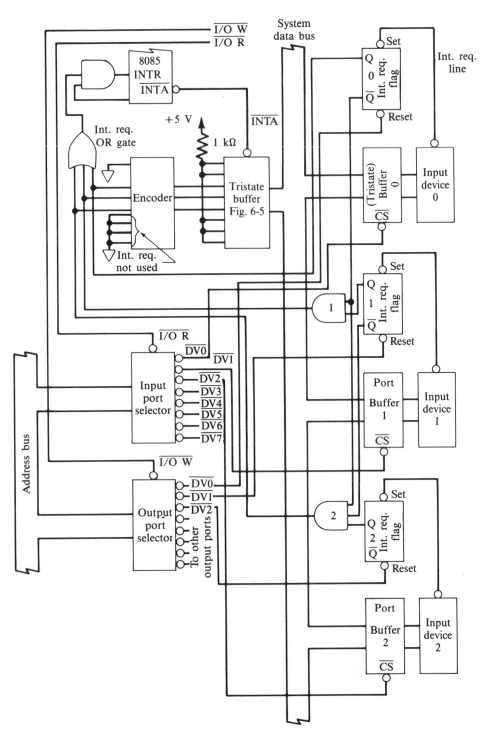

FIGURE 6-7. Logic circuit for priority interrupts with vectoring.

EXAMPLE 6-2

```
; Service routine for input device 0

    ORG 0008H
    JMP 0050H          ; Jump to more memory.
    ORG 0050H
    DI                 ; Disable INT.
    OUT 00H            ; Reset 0 interrupt request flag.

; Initialize MPU

; Save register contents

    PUSH PSW
    PUSH B
    PUSH D
    PUSH H
    LXI H,2100H        ; Initialize DC

; Service input device 0

    IN 00H             ; Get data byte.
    MOV M,A            ; Store data byte.

; Restore register contents

    POP H
    POP D
    POP B
    POP PSW

; Enable interrupts

    EI                 ; INTR enabled and INTE set.
    RET                ; Finished return to
                       ; Main prog.

; Service routine for input device 1

    ORG 0010H
    JMP 0060H          ; Jump to more memory.
    ORG 0060H
    DI                 ; Disable INTR.
    OUT 01H            ; Reset 1 interrupt request flag.

; Initialize MPU

; Save register contents

    PUSH PSW
    PUSH B
    PUSH D
    PUSH H
    LXI H,2200H        ; Initialize DC
```

FIGURE 6-8. Service routine for servicing I/O devices of Figure 6-7.

; Service input device 1

```
    IN 01H              ; Get data byte.
    MOV M,A             ; Store data byte.
```

; Restore register contents

```
    POP H
    POP D
    POP B
    POP PSW
```

; Enable interrupts

```
    EI                  ; INT enabled.
    RET                 ; Finished return to
                        ; Main prog.
```

; Service routine for input device 2

```
    ORG 0018H
    JMP 0070H           ; Jump to more memory.
    ORG 0070H
    DI                  ; Disable INTR.
    OUT 02H             ; Reset 2 interrupt request flag.
```

; Initialize MPU

; Save register contents

```
    PUSH PSW
    PUSH B
    PUSH D
    PUSH H

    LXI H,2300H         ; DC = 2300H.
```

; Service input device 02
```
    IN 02H              ; Get data byte.
    MOV M,A             ; Store data byte.
```

; Restore register contents

```
    POP H
    POP D
    POP B
    POP PSW
```

; Enable interrupts

```
    EI                  ; INTR enabled.
    RET                 ; Finished return to ·
                        ; Main prog.
```

FIGURE 6-8. (Continued)

0 is in the low state, thereby inhibiting AND gates 1 and 2. The output of these AND gates is zero, resulting in a bit pattern of 00000010 appearing at the encoder's input (notice that the LSB of the encoder is grounded). The output of the encoder is 001, as shown in the truth table of Figure 6-6(c). Because the Q output of flip-flop 0 is in the 1 state, this results in a high output for the interrupt request OR gate, resulting in the interrupt request of input device 0 being applied to pin INTR of the MPU. Before acknowledging the interrupt, the MPU completes execution of its present instruction. Upon completion of that instruction, the MPU acknowledges the interrupt request by generating the control signal INTA. INTA will enable the tristate buffer of Figure 6-7, thus gating RST 1 on the data bus, which vectors the MPU to memory location 0008H. From the program of Figure 6-8 it is seen that the service routine for input device 0 is at memory location 0008H. Because of a lack of available memory locations, the program jumps to 0050H. The DI instruction of this program is not necessary, as the interrupts were automatically disabled by the MPU upon interrupt acknowledge, but are included here as a reminder of the interrupts being disabled. When instruction OUT 00H is executed, the interrupt request flag 0 is reset, which enables AND gate 2. Because the interrupt request flag 2 is also high, AND gate 2 outputs a logic 1. The binary pattern that is now input to the encoder is 00001000, resulting in an output of 011, as seen from Figure 6-6(c). However, because the MPU's interrupts are disabled the interrupt request is not acknowledged and INTA is not activated, thereby, not jamming RST 3 in the IR. The PUSH instructions save the registers contents on the stack and LXI X initializes the DC. The next two instructions following (IN 00H and MOV M,A) actually service input device 0. The POP instructions restore the register contents. When EI is executed, it enables the interrupt capability, thus requesting another interrupt, as the interrupt request OR-gate output is high. The actual implementation of EI is delayed by the MPU until the execution of the next instruction, which is RET. When RET is executed, the MPU returns to the main program to resume program execution where it was before the interrupt. However, before it can resume program execution, it receives the interrupt request from input device 2. Of course, this was accomplished once EI was actually executed. As before, the interrupt request is acknowledged, INTA becomes low, and RST 3 is jammed on the data bus, causing the MPU to vector to memory location 0018H. The remainder of events is a repeat of those stated for servicing input device 0.

If one does not wish to design a priority interrupt request logic circuit, manufactured circuits may be purchased. The reader is referred to the 8214.

6-5

Multilevel Interrupts and Vectoring

Some microprocessors have more than one interrupt request pin, such as the 8085, which classifies them as having multilevel interrupt capability. When an interrupt request is made via RST 5.5, RST 6.5, RST 7.5, or TRAP, the MPU will be automatically vectored to a specific memory location. The vectoring is done automatically within the MPU, with no additional hardware required.

There are five levels of interrupts available on the 8085:

INTR: As we have seen, its use could result in software polling or vectoring via an RST instruction. This interrupt request input is exactly the same as the INT line of the 8080.

RST interrupt request: There are three of these interrupts (RST 5.5, RST 6.5, and RST 7.5). Whenever a request is made via one of these inputs, upon acknowledgment, the MPU will be automatically vectored to a specific location in memory and will also disable the INTR and RST interrupts. These interrupts can be enabled using the EI instruction. These locations are four addresses above the locations vectored to using RST 5, RST 6, and RST 7, which is the reason for the ".5" notation. These interrupt requests require no additional hardware, such as is the case when the MPU is vectored to a memory location resulting from RST 0, 1, 2, 3, 4, 5, 6, and 7. RST 5.5, 6.5, and 7.5 are priority interrupts; their priority and vector addresses are as follows:

- *RST 5.5:* Lowest priority. Vectors to memory location 2CH. It is voltage-level sensitive, requiring a high to be activated.
- *RST 6.5:* Second lowest priority. Vectors to memory location 34H. It also is voltage-level sensitive, requiring a high.
- *RST 7.5:* Highest priority. Vectors to memory location 3CH. It is edge sensitive and is activated on the rising edge (0 to 1) of the input signal, which would be a pulse. The rising edge of the interrupt request sets an internal flip-flop and therefore maintains the request. The flip-flop is automatically reset upon acknowledging the request. It also can be reset using a reset to the MPU or by the instruction SIM, as we shall see. RST 7.5 is the only interrupt with such an internal flip-flop; the others require the I/O device to maintain the request. Notice that this internal flip-flop serves as an interrupt request flag, such as illustrated in Figure 6-7.

TRAP: This is a nonmaskable interrupt and has the highest priority of all interrupts. When an interrupt is requested over this input, the MPU will vector to memory location 24H.

$\overline{INTA}$ is not affected by RST 5.5, RST 6.5, RST 7.5, or TRAP, as vectoring is accomplished automatically within the 8085.

6-6

8085 Serial Ports SID and SOD

As was stated in Chapter 2, the 8085 has two serial ports, SID and SOD. To read the single bit of data at input SID requires that the MPU execute the RIM instruction. Execution of RIM will result in the data bit at input SID being loaded into the most significant bit (MSB) of the accumulator (AC_7). To output a single bit of data, the MPU must execute instruction SIM. The execution of SIM results in the MPU's outputting the MSB of the accumulator (AC_7) to output SOD.

Serial Input Port SID and the RIM Instruction

From Section 5.3 we find that RIM loads into the accumulator (AC_7) the serial data bit as well as 7 other bits of information, as follows:

Interrupt masks (accumulator bits AC_0, AC_1, and AC_2): These 3 bits give the status of the maskable interrupts RST 5.5, 6.5, and 7.5. For instance, if after the execution of a RIM the accumulator bits are such that $AC_0 = 1$, $AC_1 = 0$, and $AC_2 = 1$, then RST 5.5 and 7.5 will be disabled or masked ($AC_0 = 1$, $AC_2 = 1$) and will not acknowledge any interrupt request, but RST 6.5 will be enabled and therefore can receive and will acknowledge interrupt request ($AC_1 = 0$). As we shall see, the RST interrupt inputs are masked by executing the SIM instruction.

Interrupt enable flag (AC_3): A logic 1 for AC_3 indicates that the entire interrupt system is enabled, whereas a 0 indicates that it is disabled. However, the TRAP interrupt request input is excluded—it cannot be disabled.

Pending interrupts (AC_4, AC_5, and AC_6): These 3 bits indicate whether an interrupt request is being made, via RST 5.5, RST 6.5, or RST 7.5, but for one reason or another is not being acknowledged by the MPU, such as when the interrupts are disabled using instruction DI. When the MPU "has time" to acknowledge the interrupt request, it can check the status of the RST interrupts, via the RIM instruction, and determine which inputs (RST 5.5, 6.5, or 7.5) are sending an interrupt request.

Serial input data bit (AC_7): As stated previously, this is the accumulator bit that receives the serial data bit from input port SID.

Serial Output Port SOD and the SIM Instruction

From reading the explanation of the SIM instruction in Section 5-3 we see that in addition to outputting the logic state of accumulator bit AC_7, via SOD, it also enables or disables (masks) the RST interrupt inputs (recall that the RIM instruction allows the status of those interrupts to be determined). In an example using the serial ports, we shall need RST 7.5. Recall that RST 7.5 has the latching interrupt request feature. Therefore, if an I/O device does not have an interrupt request flag (flip-flop) but instead produces a pulse when needing service from the MPU, that pulse can be used to set the RST 7.5 flip-flop. The RST 7.5 will remain high (making an interrupt request) until the RST 7.5 is "turned off" (reset). The RST 7.5 flip-flop is reset by executing the SIM instruction, by a system reset, or by acknowledging the request at the time of the request. The accumulator must be preloaded with the desired bit pattern (using instruction MVI A—or its equivalent) before SIM is executed.

Do not confuse the masking of an interrupt input with its logic state for making a request. Rather, masking simply means that the interrupt input is available for an interrupt request or that it has been masked "out" and is not available.

An 8085 Serial Port Application

To exemplify some of the uniqueness of the 8085 we must seek out an application that is unique to the 8085. This will require using the serial I/O and/or use of one or more of the RST interrupt request inputs. Let us suppose that we are using the 8085-based system of Figure 6-9 to collect data from a remote serial input device. The 8085 system is to assemble the serially collected data bits into a byte (using the MPU accumulator). Each byte is to be stored in memory and also printed out (echoed). Also suppose that the input device is relatively slow and therefore it is to interrupt the MPU only when it has a data bit. It is also reasonable to expect the printer to be slow; hence, when the printer's input buffer is empty (IBE = 1, which means that it is ready for another data byte from the MPU), it requests another data byte from the MPU. The request for another data byte is made via an interrupt request to the MPU via the printer's output IBE. Because IBE will be high until the request is acknowledged, a level-sensitive RST will be used (RST 5.5). The request generated by the serial input device will be a pulse, thus requiring RST 7.5 be used, as shown in Figure 6-9. The acknowledgment of the serial input device request will be issued using SOD. The serial input device will use the output of SOD to shift its buffer to the right one bit in preparation for the next data bit transmission.

The program that services the serial input device of Figure 6-9 is given in Figure 6-10. In order to focus on the essentials of this application it is assumed that the reader knows that PUSH and POP instructions probably (depending on the specific system) should be added to the program of Figure 6-10. It is also assumed that another program will be required to provide the current memory address as required for the MOV M,A instruction.

To explain the program of Figure 6-10, we shall refer to the hardware of Figure 6-9. The reader should also follow the flowchart of Figure 6-10. To begin, the serial input device fills its buffer and then generates an interrupt request by activating its interrupt request output, that is, by generating a pulse. This pulse is sensed by RST 7.5 of the 8085, which sets the internal flip-flop of RST 7.5. When the 8085 completes execution of its present instruction, it advances its PC by one and acknowledges the interrupt request. In acknowledging the request, the MPU resets the RST 7.5 flip-flop, automatically pushes the content of the PC on the stack, disables the interrupts, and then vectors to memory location 003CH. From the program of Figure 6-10 the reader sees that at address 003CH the MPU will fetch instruction MVI A,18H. This instruction loads register A with the proper byte (18H) according to the instruction format of SIM, which will mask out all the RST N.5 interrupts. This is done so that these interrupt inputs cannot acknowledge any interrupt request. Also, byte 18H will disable the SOD output, which is necessary, as we do not wish to acknowledge a data bit transmission at this time. After the execution of MVI A,18H the SIM instruction is fetched and executed. The next instruction fetched and executed is DI, which disables the remaining interrupt request input INTR. Instruction MVI C,00H clears register C of any previous data. MVI B,0F8H will

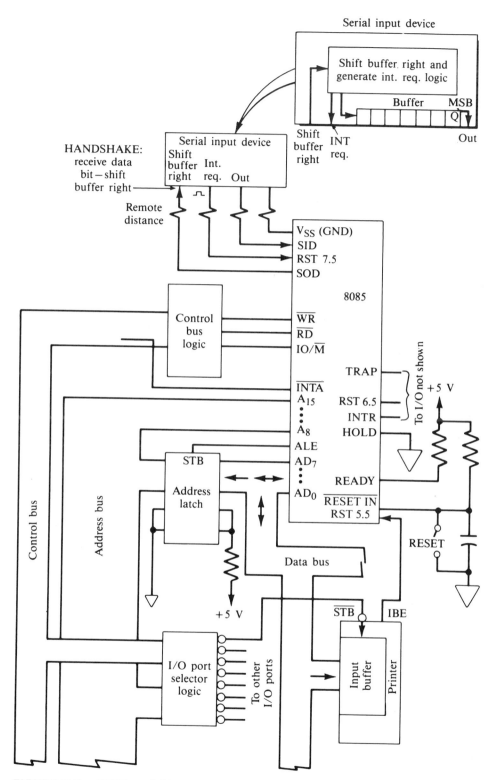

FIGURE 6-9. **8085 serial input port interface.**

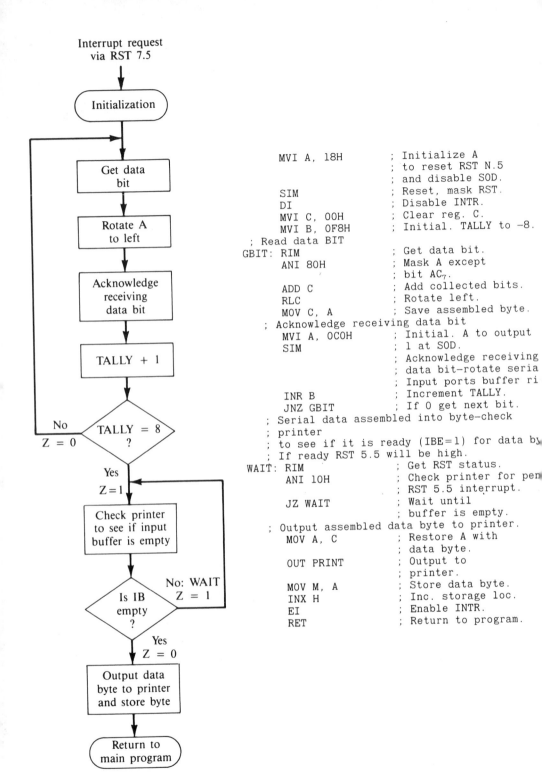

FIGURE 6-10. Program for the serial input device of Figure 6-9.

initialize the TALLY (register B) with -8 (two's complement). TALLY will be used to keep track of accumulator rotations as serial bits are input to the MPU and rotated in order to form a byte.

After the execution of MVI B,0F8H the MPU is initialized and ready to service the interrupt request of the serial input port. For all input ports thus far, the IN instruction has been used to read data from those ports. For this application the RIM instruction must be used. The execution of instruction RIM will cause the most significant bit (MSB) of the serial input device buffer (see upper right corner of Figure 6-9) to be loaded into the most significant bit (MSB) of the MPU's accumulator via input SID. We now have the first bit of a total of eight data bits that are to be read from the serial input port. As stated, the collected serial data bit is in the MSB of the accumulator, but because of the nature of the RIM instruction, the other seven bits of the accumulator contain information unrelated to the data byte of the serial input device that is being transmitted serially to the MPU's. To "rid" the accumulator of this unrelated information, bits AC_6–AC_0 of the accumulator are masked using the instruction ANI 80H. If the reader looks four instructions ahead (MVI A,0C0H), he or she will see that the accumulator must serve other functions, and hence the collected serial data bits will be destroyed.

As each serial data bit is collected, it must be properly positioned and then saved in a register other than A. The register chosen to save the collected data bits (content of A) is C (see instruction MOV C,A). Thus, after the mask instruction ANI 80H, the content of C is added to A using instruction ADD C. ADD C assembles those previously collected serial data bits, which were stored in C, to the most recently collected bit; however, the bit just collected is not in the proper bit position. The instruction RLC properly positions the most recently collected data bit. Instruction MOV C,A saves the content of A in register C, which is the partially assembled data byte. The MVI A,0C0H (the assembler requires that the 0 precede an alphanumeric value—A, B, C, D, E, and F) loads the accumulator with the proper bit pattern in order to output a 1 at output SOD when the SIM instruction is executed, in which SOD is used as an acknowledgment. That is, the execution of the SIM instruction following MVI A,0C0H will result in a high being output at SOD, which is input to the serial input device via its shift buffer right input—the output at SOD is an acknowledgment by the MPU that it received the last bit transmitted and is ready for another. The high input at shift buffer right will cause the serial input device to shift the content of its buffer one bit to the right in preparation for the next serial transmission. After execution of SIM, the MPU then executes INR B, in which B is the TALLY that keeps track of the number of shifts (there are to be eight). Next the TALLY must be checked to determine whether all data bits have been collected. Then after execution of INR B, the JNZ GBIT instruction is fetched. If the Z flag is a zero (meaning that TALLY $\neq$ 0), the MPU will execute the instruction, causing it to jump to address GBIT, which will collect the next data bit. If Z = 1, which means that all eight serial bits have been collected and assembled into a byte (and JNZ will not be executed), the MPU must store this byte in memory and transmit it to the printer to be printed.

Let us suppose that Z = 0 and jump to address GBIT. Upon jumping to address GBIT, the CPU again fetches and executes instruction RIM. Instruction

ANI 80H masks out nonrelated information in A. ADD C assembles the previously collected bits with the most recently collected bit. Instruction RLC causes MPU to rotate the accumulator left one bit, which properly positions the most recently collected bit. MOV C,A saves the content of A in register C just as before. Let us advance to instruction JNZ GBIT and this time assume that Z = 1, which means that the instruction will not be executed and the instruction at address (label) WAIT will be fetched and executed. When the MPU executes this RIM instruction, the accumulator is loaded with the byte, as indicated by the format of the RIM instruction. This time we are not reading in a serial data bit but, rather, obtaining the status of *pending* RST interrupts, specifically RST 5.5. For if RST 5.5 has a pending interrupt request (recall that a pending interrupt is all that can happen, as the interrupts are masked, the printer's input buffer is empty (IBE = 1), and the printer is ready to receive the assembled data byte. To check the accumulator for an RST 5.5 pending interrupt, ANI 10H is executed. If after the execution of ANI 10H, the Z flag is high (Z = 1) (the result of the AND operation was 00H), RST 5.5 will have no pending interrupts, and the MPU should wait for the printer to empty its buffer. It waits by staying in a loop, via JZ WAIT, and continuously checks for an RST 5.5 pending interrupt request via the RIM instruction in that loop. When IBE = 1 the execution of RIM and ANI 10H will result in Z = 0, meaning that the printer is ready to receive the data byte. When Z = 0 the MPU next executes MOV A,C. The MOV A,C instruction is required to restore the assembled data byte in the accumulator (recall that the assembled data byte was stored in C earlier). The data byte is then output on the data bus by the instruction OUT PRINT (OUT 00H), which also causes the printer to latch that byte from the data bus via the I/O port selector logic of Figure 6-9. The instructions MOV M,A and INX H simply store the data byte and increment the DC (H and L). Thus instruction EI enables the interrupt system. RET will cause the MPU to return to the return address.

6-10

Hex Keypad with Interrupt Capability

Most microcomputer systems need some sort of keyboard input port to serve as the primary communication between the user and the microcomputer. To develop the concept of how a microcomputer might determine which keyboard character was "typed" as a result of a key closure and also how the proper binary code is generated, the *hex keypad* (16 keys representing hex values 0–F) will be studied. Studying a hex keypad rather than a keyboard reduces the number of characters from 127 to just 16; however, even though simplified, the concept is still the same. We should mention that our study will rely on software to identify a key closure and then generate a corresponding binary code. There is hardware available to simplify the task.

We shall use the hex keypad of Figure 6-11, which is a 4 × 4 matrix. Basically, the manner in which the hex keypad of Figure 6-11 works is similar to an x-y coordinate system. That is, by knowing the row and column of the depressed key, one can easily identify the key. For instance, if the key closure

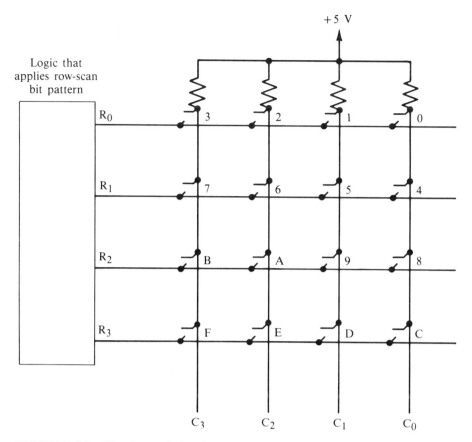

FIGURE 6-11. Hex-keypad circuit.

occurred in row 1 (R_1) and column 2 (C_2), which is noted as (R_1, C_2), key 6 would be depressed.

To determine the row and column of a depressed key, each row will be scanned. A row scan is made by pulling each row to a low, one at a time, and then checking the resulting logic state of each column. We see from Figure 6-11 that all columns are high, regardless of any row logic state, if no keys are closed. However, if R_1 is forced low with R_0, R_2, and R_3 all high (a row pattern of 1101) and key 6 is depressed, the column output will be $C_3 = 1$, $C_2 = 0$, $C_1 = 1$, and $C_0 = 1$ (1011). By forcing a row pattern of 1101 and receiving a column pattern of 1011, key 6 is identified as the depressed key. Table 6-1 illustrates for each row scan the resulting column pattern for each key closure.

Let us begin by determining how a key closure requests an interrupt of the MPU. The MPU of Figure 6-12 has previously written an OH to the row-scan latch; thus all rows are low. Without a key closure, each column is high, which is input to the interrupt request NAND gate, resulting in a low output. The logic 0 output of this NAND gate is input to the interrupt request input (INTR) of the 8085, thereby not requesting an interrupt. When a key is depressed, the corre-

TABLE 6-1. Row-Scan and Column Patterns for Key Closures

Row Scanned	Row Pattern for Each Row Scan				Resulting Column Patterns for Each Key Closure				Key Closure	Eight-Bit Hex Code to Be Generated
	R_3	R_2	R_1	R_0	C_3	C_2	C_1	C_0		
0	1	1	1	0	1	1	1	0	0	0 0 0 0 0 0 0 0
					1	1	0	1	1	0 0 0 0 0 0 0 1
					1	0	1	1	2	0 0 0 0 0 0 1 0
					0	1	1	1	3	0 0 0 0 0 0 1 1
1	1	1	0	1	1	1	1	0	4	0 0 0 0 0 1 0 0
					1	1	0	1	5	0 0 0 0 0 1 0 1
					1	0	1	1	6	0 0 0 0 0 1 1 0
					0	1	1	1	7	0 0 0 0 0 1 1 1
2	1	0	1	1	1	1	1	0	8	0 0 0 0 1 0 0 0
					1	1	0	1	9	0 0 0 0 1 0 0 1
					1	0	1	1	A	0 0 0 0 1 0 1 0
					0	1	1	1	B	0 0 0 0 1 0 1 1
3	0	1	1	1	1	1	1	0	C	0 0 0 0 1 1 0 0
					1	1	0	1	D	0 0 0 0 1 1 0 1
					1	0	1	1	E	0 0 0 0 1 1 1 0
					0	1	1	1	F	0 0 0 0 1 1 1 1

$$3 \quad 2 \quad 1 \quad 0$$

y-coordinate

sponding column line is driven low, thus causing the output of the interrupt request NAND gate to go high. This makes the keypad request an interrupt of the MPU.

Suppose that as a result of this interrupt request RST 5 is jammed on the data bus when $\overline{INTA}$ goes active. Then the MPU vectors to memory location 0028H (see Figure 6-5). The first instruction of the subroutine for servicing the hex keypad is at address 0028H (see Figure 6-14). That subroutine outputs the bit pattern of Table 6-1 to scan row 0 using the OUT 00H instruction. The bit pattern output on the data bus by instruction OUT 00H is 1110. The OUT 00H instruction also causes that bit pattern to be latched in the Row-Scan Latch when the I/O select output $\overline{DV0}$ goes active. As a result the rows will take on the logic states written into the Row-Scan Latch (1110 for row 0). If the key closure is not in row 0 (let us suppose that key 6 is closed), the resulting column logic levels will all be highs. The MPU will latch these highs via the column latch by having an IN 01H instruction following the OUT 00H instruction as seen in Figure 6-14. The IN 01H instruction will activate $\overline{DS}$ of the column latch, which will latch the logic states of the columns and also load these logic states (1111 for this case) into the MPU's accumulator. The MPU can then examine this bit pattern and determine that the key closed is not in that row. The MPU will then output the bit pattern to scan row 1 (1101). Since key 6 is in row 1, which now has a low applied to it, its closure causes column C_2 to be low, resulting in a

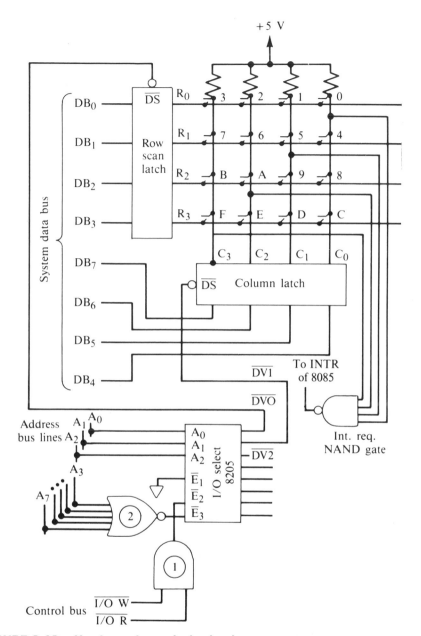

FIGURE 6-12. Hex-keypad scan logic circuit.

column bit pattern of 1011 (see Table 6-1). As stated, the IN 01H instruction following the OUT 00H instruction causes the column latch to latch that bit pattern and also to load that bit pattern into the accumulator of the MPU. The MPU can then examine its accumulator and from the bit pattern determine that key 6 is closed. Once the MPU knows that key 6 is depressed it returns to the program it was executing before the interrupt. The MPU will continue to execute instructions until the next interrupt request, at which time it will again vector to the keypad service routine at 0028H.

From the explanation above and Figure 6-12, let us generalize and summarize the events in chronological order.

1. All rows are held low via the Row Scan Latch. All rows being held low will cause an interrupt request to be generated when a key is closed since a key closure will force a column low, which is input to the Int. Req. NAND gate input, resulting in a high output.
2. The output of the Interrupt Request NAND-gate is applied to the interrupt request (INTR) of the 8085.
3. As was stated in 2, when the Interrupt Request NAND gate goes high it requests an interrupt of the MPU. Upon acknowledgment of the interrupt request ($\overline{\text{INTA}}$ goes active), the MPU will be vectored (if the RST jamming circuit of Figure 6-7 is used) to a specified memory address (RST 5—address 0028H was used above). Of course, the polling hardware and software of Figures 6-2 and 6-4 could be used to identify the keypad as the interrupting device. Once the MPU is vectored to the specified RST vector address, the MPU will begin the process of identifying the depressed key. The identifying process will begin by outputting each of four row-scan bit patterns according to the row-scan patterns shown in Table 6-1. To output the row-scan patterns, the instructions MOV A,D (row pattern) and OUT (port number) are used.
4. When a row-scan bit pattern is output by the MPU, that pattern is latched by the row-scan latch and also applied to the rows. If the depressed key is in the row that contains the logic 0 of the row-scan bit pattern (again refer to Table 6-1), the column of the depressed key will also be forced low, with the remaining rows being high. The resulting column bit pattern is latched by the column latch when the MPU executes the IN instruction, following the OUT instruction, as mentioned in item 3. The column latch has a tristate output, and so it not only latches the column bit pattern but also applies that bit pattern to lines DB_4–DB_7 of the system's data bus. Because of the input port instruction, the MPU latches the column bit pattern into its accumulator. The MPU then determines whether any of these 4 bits is low and, if so, which one of the four is low. Once the low column bit is identified for the corresponding low row bit (refer to Table 6-1), the key closure is identified and the MPU can issue (echo) the proper hex code.
5. The MPU then writes OH to the row-scan latch and returns to executing that program before being interrupted by the hex keypad—returning to service another interrupt of the keypad only when interrupted again.

From these six chronological steps, the flowchart of Figure 6-13 was developed.

A program to implement the flowchart of Figure 6-13 is given in Figure 6-14.

To understand the routine of Figure 6-14, the reader should refer to Table 6-1 for the row-scan bit patterns and resultant column bit patterns for any given key closure. The logic of the routine is indicated in the flowchart of Figure 6-13.

The program of Figure 6-14 was named KEYPAD, so that if the user of the system wishes to access it in any other routine, he or she may do so by a CALL instruction (or conditional jump, jump, and the like). The PUSH instructions

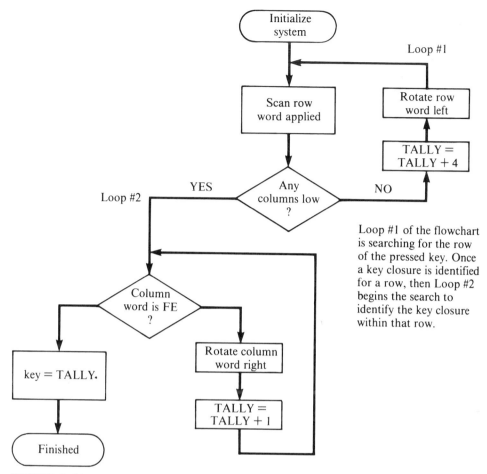

FIGURE 6-13. Flowchart for determining a key closure for the hardware of Figure 6-12.

save register contents on the stack. The MVI C, 00H clears register C, and MVI D, 0FEH loads register D with row 0's scan word. MOV A,D loads A with row 0's scan word. The OUT 00H instruction causes the row-scan latch to latch the bit pattern for row 0 and apply it to the keypad rows. Instruction IN 01H loads the resulting column bit pattern into the accumulator. From Figure 6-12 we see that only the uppermost 4 bits of the accumulator are used to retain the column bit pattern. The ORI 0FH instruction forces the lower 4 bits of the accumulator to all 1's (only the upper 4 bits of A contain column information). MOV B,A is used to save the resulting bit pattern of the accumulator. The content of A is copied in B, as the CMA instruction destroys the content of A, and we will need that data later during the column test. The CMA and ANI instructions are used to determine whether any columns of row 0 are low, which indicates a key closure. If any column is low, then after executing CMA, the accumulator bit representing it will be high. If all columns are high (no key closure) then after executing CMA, the accumulator will be zero. Thus ANI 0FFH being executed after CMA will result in $Z = 0$ if a column is low (a key

```
      ORG 0028H
; Keypad service routine

; Save register contents
         KEYPAD:  PUSH PSW
                  PUSH B
                  PUSH D
                  PUSH H
; Initialize registers D and C

                  MVI C, 00H    ; Clear C.
                  MVI D, 0FEH   ; Row 0 scan word.

; Begin row scan-loop #1
                  MOV A,D       ; Load scan word in A.
         AGAIN:   OUT 00H       ; Scan row.
                  IN 01H        ; Get resulting column bits.
                  ORI 0FH       ; Force lower nibble high.
                  MOV B,A       ; Save column word.

; Any columns low?

                  CMA           ; Complement accumulator.
                  ANI 0FFH      ; If yes, then Z = 0.
                  JNZ KEY       ; If Z = 0, key is in this
                                ; row, so jump to loop #2
                                ; and identify key.

; Z = 0 therefore remain in loop #1 and update the
; TALLY by four keys (TALLY = TALLY + 4)

                  MOV A,C       ; Move TALLY to A.
                  ADI 04H       ; TALLY + 4.
                  MOV C,A       ; Move TALLY to C.

; Get the next row scan word

                  MOV A, D      ; Restore A with row scan.
                  RLC           ; Rotate row scan left
                                ; to prepare for next scan.
                  MOV D, A      ; Save a copy in D.

; Scan next row
                  JMP AGAIN     ; Try again.

; Test columns of row (loop #2)

         KEY:     MOV A,B       ; Restore A with column
                                ; bit pattern.
         NEXT:    RAL           ; Rotate left into carry.
                  JNC DISPLAY   ; If C = 0 key is identified.
                  INR C         ; Update TALLY.
                  JMP NEXT      ; Try the next key.
         DISPLAY: MOV A,C       ; Get key hex value.
                  OUT LED       ; Output hex value to LED.
```

FIGURE 6-14. Hex-keypad service routine.

; Restore MPU registers

                POP H
                POP D
                POP B
                POP PSW

; Return to program being executed when
; interrupted

                EI   ; Enable interrupts.
                RET   ; Return.

FIGURE 6-14. (Continued)

closure) and Z = 1 if no columns are low. If Z = 0, then row 0 will have a column that is low, meaning that a key is depressed in row 0, and the instruction JNZ KEY jumps to the column test routine, which determines the specific key to be depressed. Referring to that routine under Test Columns of Row, we see that the first instruction, MOV A,B, restores the column bit pattern into A (recall that the contents of register A was destroyed with the CMA instruction). The column test routine then rotates the accumulator's most significant bit (MSB) into the carry and jumps (JNC) when a low is rotated into it. When a low is rotated into the carry, the key closure is identified and the MPU then jumps (JNC DISPLAY) to the routine that actually echoes the hex value to an LED. The remainder of the program is a repeat. It is recommended that the reader simulate a key closure and then trace through the hardware and software to verify its operation.

6-11

Direct Memory Access

Direct memory access (DMA) operations are quite simple to explain. The burden of design lies with the I/O device's having DMA capability. But because this textbook is not concerned with the design of peripheral devices, we shall discuss only their basic concepts, represented by the architecture of Figure 6-15. When an I/O device wishes direct memory access, it simply inputs a high on the HOLD pin of the MPU. When the MPU finishes executing its present instruction, it enters a state of limbo (the hold state) and does nothing but put its address, data, and control bus–related pins in the high-Z state. At this time the MPU acknowledges the hold request by outputing a high at its HLDA pin. The HLDA signal is used by the I/O device to enable its curcuitry to furnish memory addresses, via the address bus, the proper control signal ($\overline{\text{MEM R}}$ or $\overline{\text{MEM W}}$), via the control bus, and data, via the data bus. To summarize, the I/O device must supply the memory addresses and provide proper timing. Of course, for multidata bytes the I/O device must increment the memory address, much like a program counter, and then access the next data byte for the read or write operation. To provide timing the I/O port must supply the proper $\overline{\text{MEM R}}$ or $\overline{\text{MEM W}}$ control signal, whichever is appropriate.

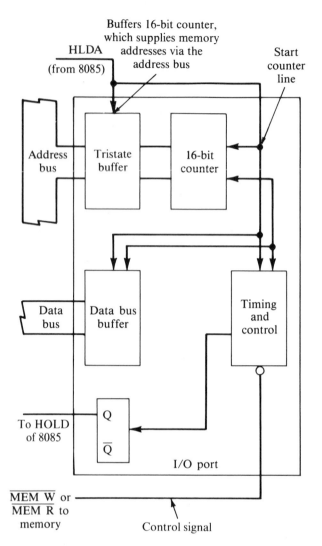

FIGURE 6-15. Architecture of DMA.

Summary

The 8085 is a multilevel interrupt microprocessor with five levels: RST 5.5, RST 6.5, RST 7.5, TRAP, and INTR. The three RST N.5 interrupts and TRAP provide automatic vectoring, and INTR is vectored by jamming the appropriate RST N op code on the data bus when the control bus control signal INTA goes low. INTA is an instruction fetch memory read timing signal that is the acknowledgment of an interrupt request. Therefore, the RST N op code jammed on the data bus is latched by the 8085 and then loaded in the 8085's IR, which it then executes. Executing RST N results in the MPU's vectoring to the specified address and storing the return address on the stack.

The 8085 has two serial ports, SID and SOD. SID is an input port that can be read with the RIM instruction, and SOD is an output port that writes out a bit of data via the SIM instruction. The SIM instruction allows interrupt pins RST 5.5, RST 6.5, and RST 7.5 to be masked (TRAP cannot be masked). In addition to reading in a data bit, via pin SID, the RIM instruction also provides the status of the interrupt pins RST 5.5, RST 6.5, and RST 7.5. The status information is composed of maskings and pending interrupts.

Keypads and keyboards are input devices common to microprocessor-based systems that enable the user to input to the system. There are hardware-encoded keypads and keyboards that can generate the appropriate code for a key closure, but we used software to identify the key closure and then to generate the appropriate code (hex in our example).

DMA is an I/O-initiated and -controlled operation. The I/O device requests a DMA by driving high the HOLD pin of the MPU. The 8085 MPU acknowledges the DMA request by outputting a high on its HLDA pin and also isolating itself from the system's buses by putting its address-, data-, and control-related pins in the high-Z state. The HLDA signal output by the MPU is used to enable the DMA circuitry of the I/O device, which generates memory addresses and appropriate read or write control signals.

REVIEW QUESTIONS AND PROBLEMS

1. Explain what is meant by the terms *single-level interrupt* and *multilevel interrupt*.

2. Of the two types of interrupts, single level and multilevel, which is more likely to require polling, and why?

3. In regard to servicing an interrupt request, explain the terms *polling* and *vectoring*.

4. Suppose that an interrupt request was made via I/O device 4 of the system represented by Figure 6-2. Modify the program of Figure 6-4 so that I/O device 4 is polled.

5. Make a timing diagram for Problem 4, beginning with interrupt request flag 4 being set high and ending with the first poll (instruction ANI 01H of Figure 6-4). To simplify the timing diagram as much as possible, omit showing the timing for all the PUSH instructions. Your timing diagram should show CLK, ALE, the address bus, the data bus, MEM R, I/O R, the output of interrupt request flag 0, and the output of the interrupt request OR gate of Figure 6-2. Explain the relationship among your timing diagram, the program instructions, and the hardware of Figure 6-2.

6. Using tristate logic as shown in Figure 6-5, design suitable circuits for jamming RST 2 and RST 4.

7. Construct a timing diagram for Figure 6-5(b), showing the events that occur, so that the MPU will be vectored to address 0028H. In your timing diagram, show the required control signals, address bus, and the data bus—stating the data (address, instruction, and so on) present on each bus.

8. Design a circuit to implement buffer 2 of Figure 6-7.

9. Explain the hardware of Figure 6-7 if input device 2 requested an interrupt. Refer to the program of Figure 6-8 in your explanations.

10. Explain the differences among the 8085 interrupts.

11. For what special application can TRAP serve?

12. Suppose that every second an 8085 were to monitor the "danger flag" of a chemical processor, and if raised, the processor were to be shut off. Design the 8085 system using serial port SID to test the danger flag and SOD to turn off the chemical processor. A real-time clock is to use TRAP for the 1-sec interrupt.

13. Explain the essence of the hex keypad's hardware and software.

14. For a key closure of 8, execute the program of Figure 6-14.

15. Suppose that the I/O device of Figure 6-15 were an input device with DMA capability. Show it interfaced to the system of Figure 4-27. Describe your interfacing.

CHAPTER 7

Programmable Chips: Parallel and Serial I/O

7·1

Introduction

For greater versatility a manufacturer will often design a chip that is multifunc-
tional, whose function can be selected by the user. This allows the chip to fulfill
various design application needs. The mechanism to select which function is to
be utilized is varied. However, when the function is selected by applying a
binary code to the chip, that is, by programming it, the chip is known as a
programmable chip. An example of such a chip is a *programmable priority
interrupt controller*. The versatility of this chip lies in its ability to be programmed to function as a polled interrupt, thereby implementing the logic of
Figure 6-2, or programmed to function as the priority vector interrupt logic,
such as the circuitry of Figure 6-7. Another example of a programmable chip
is a programmable timer, which provides various timing modes and intervals,
depending on the programmed binary code applied to the chip for decoding.

The binary code that programs the chip is often referred to as its *control word*.
The control word must be latched by an internal register of the programmable
chip for decoding purposes. This register will often be referred to as the control
register. Once the control word is programmed into the programmable chip
(latched by the chip), it is decoded and the chip will then implement the desired
function.

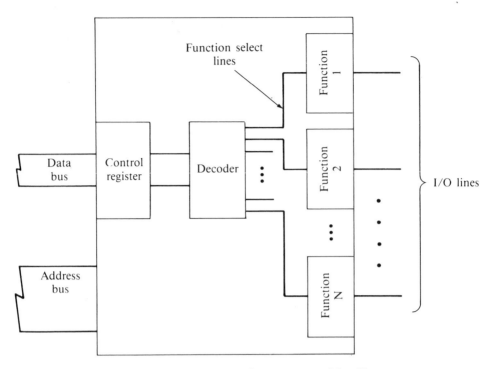

FIGURE 7-1. Conceptual architecture of a programmable chip.

In a microprocessor-based system, a programmable chip is programmed via the MPU; that is, the programmable chip is treated as an output port for the purpose of programming it. Hence the control word is first loaded into the MPU's accumulator, and then a write operation is executed to that output port. A generic architectural drawing of a programmable chip is offered in Figure 7-1.

Referring to Figure 7-1, to program the chip it must first be addressed to receive the control word. The OUT instruction is used to address the chip and to write the control word to the chip's control register. The control word is decoded, which activates one of the function select lines. This in turn selects the logic to implement the selected function. There are many specific programmable chips available; however, only the programmable peripheral interface (8255) and the programmable communication interface (8251) will be studied in this chapter.

7-2

Programmable Peripheral Interface (8255)

The 8255's programmable peripheral interface (PPI) has twenty-four programmable I/O pins. These twenty-four I/O pins are subdivided into three groups, each group consisting of eight pins. The three groupings are labeled as group A, group B, and group C. The 8255 may be programmed so that port A, B, or C can have access to the system's data bus as either input or output ports, as indicated by the simplified architectural drawing of Figure 7-2.

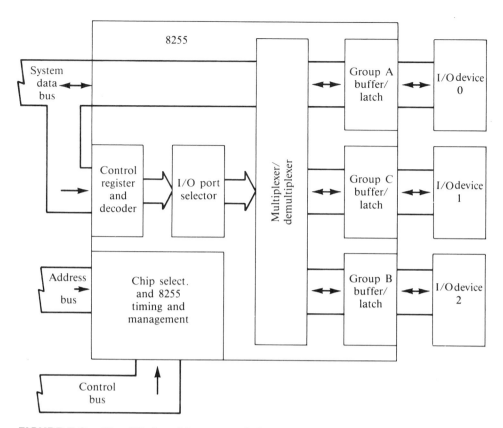

FIGURE 7-2. Simplified architecture of the PPI (8255).

Figure 7-2 shows that the 8255 is addressed for use via the address bus. When the address is decoded by the 8255, the port selected (A, B, C, or the control register) will have access to the system data bus. The multiplexer/demultiplexer implements the accessing of the system data bus by the selected port. The MPU programs the 8255 by writing a *control word* (an 8-bit code) to the control register, which will configure the I/O ports. The reader should notice that ports A, B, and C are shown as a buffer/latch. This dual function is required, as some ports require latching of the data byte and others require buffering between the 8255 and the port. Also shown as input to the 8255 is the control bus. This is necessary to provide system control and timing to the 8255 for read and write operations ($\overline{\text{I/O R}}$, $\overline{\text{I/O W}}$).

From what is known about the 8255 at this point, we can conclude that its programmability resides in the fact that its I/O pins can be programmed to serve as either input or output ports. Although this is true, other function variations are also programmable for this PPI. To investigate all programmable aspects of the 8255, refer to Intel's architectural drawing of the 8255 shown in Figure 7-3.

In viewing Figure 7-3 the reader should notice that group C of Figure 7-3 is actually divided into two 4-bit I/O ports. The upper 4 bits (PC_7–PC_4) are labeled as group A port C upper, and the lower 4 bits (PC_3–PC_0) are labeled as group

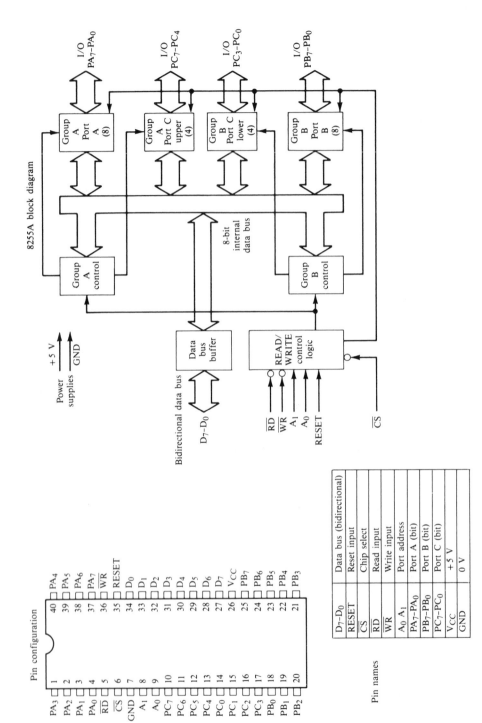

FIGURE 7-3. 8255 architecture. (Courtesy of Intel Corp.)

B port C lower. The reason for this division of port C is versatility. For some applications the user may wish to program groups A and B as I/O ports with handshaking (request and acknowledge) capability. Using the 8255 in this mode of operation, port C upper provides the necessary communication to implement handshaking for port A, and port C lower provides handshaking for port B. Group C upper and lower can also be programmed to function as an 8-bit port, as indicated in Figure 7-3—it is just a matter of the control word programmed into the 8255.

Because the specific control word programmed to the 8255 determines its functional configuration, or mode of operation, let our detailed investigation of this chip begin there. First we shall investigate the bit patterns for various control words and then the means by which they are programmed into the 8255.

7-3

8255 Operation Modes

There are three modes of operation, which are given in Table 7-1.

Mode 0

As stated in Table 7-1, when the 8255 is programmed for a mode 0 operation, groups A, B, and C function as I/O ports without handshaking. Each port (A, B, and C) must be programmed to be either an input or output port via the control word. Those ports defined to be output ports will latch the data byte that is being written to the external output device attached to that port, whereas those ports defined to serve as input ports do not latch the data byte they receive from their external input device.

Port C is unique in that its upper and lower groupings can be programmed separately. That is, the upper 4 bits can be programmed to serve as an input port, and the lower 4 bits are programmed to function as an output port, or vice versa. Or the upper and lower 4 bits can be combined to function as either an 8-bit input or an output port.

There are 16 different port configuration combinations that can be programmed from groups A, B, and C for a mode 0 operation. To determine the binary bit pattern of the control word required to program the 8255 for one of

TABLE 7-1. Modes of I/O Port Operations for the 8255

Mode	Comments
0	Basic I/O ports. Output ports are latched, while input ports are not latched. Ports A and B are 8-bit, while port C is divided into two 4-bit ports. Handshaking is not available.
1	I/O ports with handshaking. Ports A and B may be *either* input or output, where both are latched. Port C provides handshaking.
2	Port A becomes a bidirectional port with port C providing handshaking and control signals. Port B may function in mode 0 or 1.

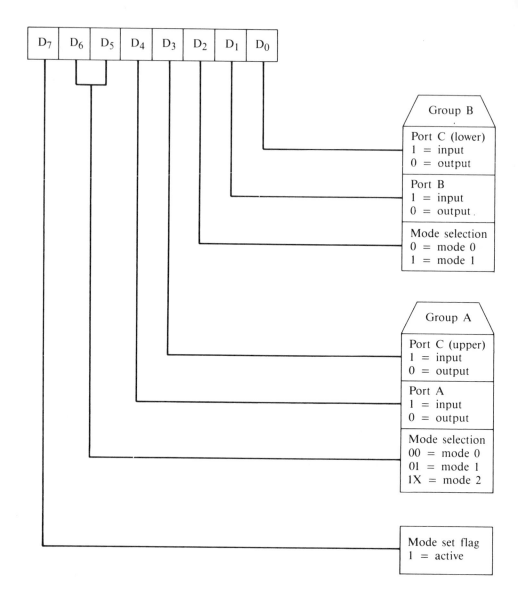

FIGURE 7-4. Control-word format for mode definition. (Courtesy of Intel Corp.)

these mode 0 port configuration combinations, refer to the control-word format of Figure 7-4. From Figure 7-4 it is seen that bits D_5 and D_6 determine the mode of operation for group A (00 for mode 0) and D_2 (0) for group B. D_7 must be high any time the 8255 is being programmed for a mode of operation. Bits D_4, D_3, D_1, and D_0 determine port configuration combinations.

Table 7-2 is essentially a truth table for bits D_4, D_3, D_1, and D_0, showing the possible 16-port configurations. Using Table 7-2 and the control-word format of Figure 7-4, let us determine the required binary bit pattern in order to program the 8255 so that all groups serve as output ports. From Table 7-2 we see that this requires bits D_4, D_3, D_1, and D_0 all to be logic 0's. Because this is to be

TABLE 7-2.   Mode 0 Port Definition Chart

D_4	D_3	D_1	D_0	Port A	Port C (upper)	Control Word #	Port B	Port C (lower)
0	0	0	0	Output	Output	0	Output	Output
0	0	0	1	Output	Output	1	Output	Input
0	0	1	0	Output	Output	2	Input	Output
0	0	1	1	Output	Output	3	Input	Input
0	1	0	0	Output	Input	4	Output	Output
0	1	0	1	Output	Input	5	Output	Input
0	1	1	0	Output	Input	6	Input	Output
0	1	1	1	Output	Input	7	Input	Input
1	0	0	0	Input	Output	8	Output	Output
1	0	0	1	Input	Output	9	Output	Input
1	0	1	0	Input	Output	10	Input	Output
1	0	1	1	Input	Output	11	Input	Input
1	1	0	0	Input	Input	12	Output	Output
1	1	0	1	Input	Input	13	Output	Input
1	1	1	0	Input	Input	14	Input	Output
1	1	1	1	Input	Input	15	Input	Input

a mode 0 operation, bits D_6, D_5, and D_2 are also to be logic 0's, as indicated in Figure 7-4. Also from Figure 7-4, bit D_7 must be a logic 1. This results in the control-word bit pattern shown in Figure 7-5. As seen from Figure 7-5(a), the control word is 80H; however, Intel refers to it as control word 0. As another example, let us program the 8255 so that port A is an output port, and ports B and C are input ports. This requires the control-word bit pattern of Figure 7-5(b). The hexadecimal value of the required bit pattern is 8BH and Intel refers to it as 7.

Although we have not studied all the details for programming a control word into an 8255, we do have sufficient knowledge to grasp the conceptual essence of the software required. The reader has been told that to program the 8255, it is treated as an output port, which means that an address is required. Because at this time the details of the required bit pattern of the address are unknown, let us use the symbolic address PPI0 (PPI mode 0). The program to program control word 0 [Figure 7-5(a)] is given in Figure 7-6.

Once we have the details of addressing and have finished studying the other modes of operations, we shall implement some example designs of both hardware and software.

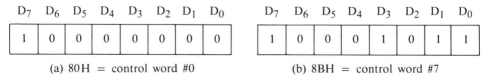

(a) 80H = control word #0   (b) 8BH = control word #7

FIGURE 7-5.   Example mode control-word patterns.

```
;These instructions program control-word 0
;into the 8225

    MVI A,80H       ; Initialize A with control-word
    OUT PPIO        ; The 8255 is programmed
```

FIGURE 7-6.   Example of software for programming an 8255.

Mode 1

Referring to Table 7-1, we see that a mode 1 operation is used when I/O ports require handshaking. Under this condition group C, upper and lower, functions as the inputs and outputs to provide handshaking capability. To repeat, an earlier discussion of Figure 7-3, groups A and C upper form one I/O port with handshaking capability, and groups B and C lower form another. The 8225 may be programmed so that groups A and B may be either an input or an output port. As an example, the 8255 architecture for a mode 1 operation with group A functioning as an input port and group B as an output port is illustrated in Figure 7-7(a). Notice that PC_7 and PC_6 are programmed to function as a 2-bit output port. These pins will be discussed in Section 7-5.

Focusing first on input port A of Figure 7-7, we see that bits PC_4 and PC_5 function as the handshaking medium between port A and the I/O device and that PC_3 will provide an interrupt request from port A to the 8085 flip-flop if INTE A is set. If input device 0 is ready to send a byte of data to the MPU, via port A of the 8255, it will strobe port A via $\overline{STB}_A$ (strobes PC_4), which causes port A to latch that data byte. Referring to the timing diagram of Figure 7-7(b), we see that once the data byte is latched, the 8255 activates IBF (PC_5), which indicates that port A's input buffer is full. When IBF goes high, and if flip-flop INTE A (interrupt enable for port A) is set, a logic 1 will result at the output of the INT REQ AND gate when $\overline{STB}_A$ goes inactive (high). This high is output at PC_3 ($INTR_A$) and will request an interrupt to the 8085. $INTR_A$ will remain high until port A is read by the MPU. As a result, $INTR_A$ can serve as an interrupt request flag for port A. If polling is used to service I/O, the logic circuit of Figure 6-2 will be used; however, if vectoring is to be used, the logic circuit of Figure 6-7 will be used. A more detailed example of hardware will be given later.

In order for the MPU to read data from input port A, an IN instruction is used. When the IN instruction is executed, control signal $\overline{I/O\ R}$ will be activated. Recall from Chapter 2 that the control signals $\overline{I/OR}$ and $\overline{I/OW}$ are produced by combining the 8085, $IO/\overline{M}$, $\overline{RD}$, and $\overline{WR}$ control signals. $\overline{I/O\ R}$ will be used (directly or indirectly) to activate $\overline{RD}$ of Figure 7-7. With the proper address on the address bus, as furnished by the operand of the IN instruction, the activation of $\overline{RD}$ will cause the data byte of input port A to be gated onto the system data bus and then latched by the MPU (register A). Because addressing the 8255 will be studied in Section 7-4, for now let us use the symbolic address RPA (read port A). IN RPA will result in the data byte of port A being gated on the system data bus and then latched by the accumulator of the MPU.

Let us now turn our attention to output port B of Figure 7-7 and the timing diagram of Figure 7-8. Handshaking between the 8255 and output port 0, for a mode 1, is accomplished via $\overline{OBF}_B$ (PC_1) and $\overline{ACK}_B$ (PC_2). When the MPU is

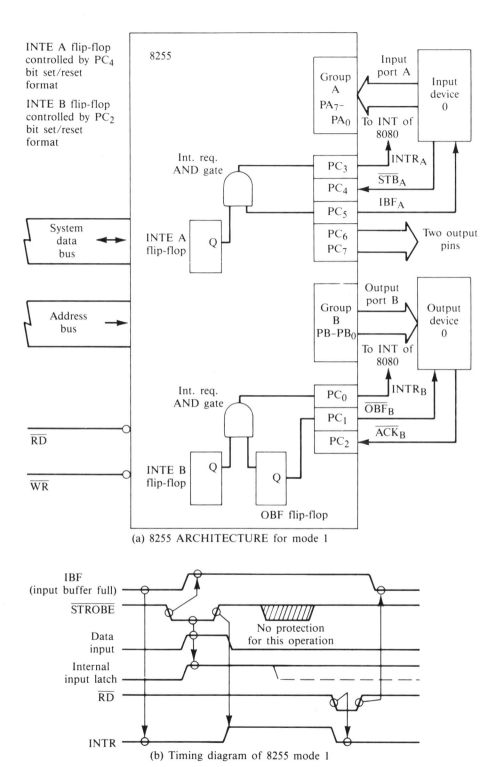

(a) 8255 ARCHITECTURE for mode 1

(b) Timing diagram of 8255 mode 1

FIGURE 7-7. The 8255 programmed in a mode 1 configuration. (Courtesy of Intel Corp.)

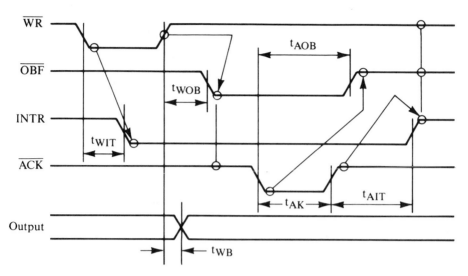

FIGURE 7-8. Timing diagram for mode 1 configuration. (Courtesy of Intel Corp.)

writing a data byte to an output device (output device 0 in this case), via an 8255, it uses the OUT instruction. The OUT instruction addresses the 8255 and also activates its control line $\overline{WR}$ (Write) via $\overline{I/OW}$. When $\overline{WR}$ goes active, it causes port B to latch the data byte off the system data bus. Port B then indicates that it has latched that data byte and that its output buffer is full; that is, it has a data byte for output device 0, by activating $\overline{OBF}_B$ on the rising edge of $\overline{WR}$. $\overline{OBF}_B$ is used by output device 0 to latch the data byte of output port B. When output device 0 has latched the data byte of port B, it acknowledges this action by driving $\overline{ACK}_B$ low. $\overline{ACK}_B$ going low causes $\overline{OBF}_B$ to become inactive (high), which states that port B's output buffer is now empty and therefore can receive another data byte from the MPU. Using interrupts to service output device 0 requires that (in order for the MPU to write another data byte to port B) an interrupt request ($INTR_B$) be generated by port B. $INTR_B$ interrupts the MPU and requests that the next data byte be transmitted. The generation of $INTR_B$ occurs mainly when $\overline{ACK}_B$ goes inactive. $\overline{ACK}_B$ going high sets the OBF flip-flop. When the OBF flip-flop and INTE B are set, output $INTR_B$ goes high, via the INT REQ AND gate for port B, thereby requesting an interrupt of the MPU. To acknowledge and service port B, either the polling logic circuit of Figure 6-2 or the vector circuit of Figure 6-7 can be used.

Next, let us examine the software required to implement the hardware of Figure 7-7. As before, we shall use a symbolic address (PPI1) to address the 8255 to load the proper control word into the control register of the 8255. For a mode 1 operation, two control words are required, one to determine port configuration (input or output) and the second to set or reset the interrupt enable flip-flops INTE A and INTE B. Figure 7-4 provides the format for the control word, which determines port configuration, and Figure 7-9 determines the logic state of INTE A and B. Both control words are written to the 8255's control register using the same address (PPI1 in this case). The 8255 is able to distinguish between the two by the logic state of bit D_7.

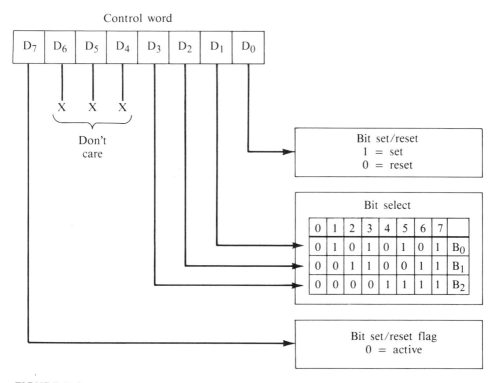

Control word

FIGURE 7-9. Bit set/reset control-word format. (Courtesy of Intel Corp.)

The bit pattern for the control word that determines the port configuration of Figure 7-7(a) is shown in Figure 7-10(a). The control word to set flip-flops INTE A and B is shown in Figure 7-10(b) and (c). Bit D_3 of Figure 7-10(a) defines PC_6 and PC_7 as output pins. D_0 of Figure 7-10(a) has no meaning, as all available group C pins associated with group B for a mode 1 operation are used for

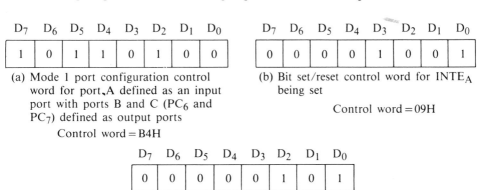

(a) Mode 1 port configuration control word for port A defined as an input port with ports B and C (PC_6 and PC_7) defined as output ports
Control word = B4H

(b) Bit set/reset control word for $INTE_A$ being set
Control word = 09H

(c) Bit set/reset control word for $INTE_B$ being set
Control word = 05H

FIGURE 7-10. Control words for programming an 8255 to function as the configuration shown in Figure 7-7.

handshaking—hence an "X" can be used to represent that we "don't care" which logic state is used. We shall show a 0 for bit D_0. As for the bit pattern of Figure 7-10(b) and (c), we are told (by the manufacturer) that PC_4 and PC_2 in Figure 7-7 set or reset INTE A and B. To set INTE A requires the binary combination indicated in column 4 (PC_4) of the table given in Figure 7-9, which is $B_2 = 1$, $B_1 = 0$, and $B_0 = 0$. Then as shown in Figure 7-10(b), $D_3 = 1$ (B_2), $D_2 = 0$ (B_1), and $D_1 = 0$ (B_0). To set INTE A, D_0 of Figure 7-10(b) is a 1. Also from Figure 7-9 we see that D_6, D_5, and D_4 are "don't care" logic states—we shall use 0's. To set INTE B requires another bit set/reset control word and is shown in Figure 7-10(c).

The program that configures the 8255, as shown in Figure 7-7, is given in Figure 7-11 of Example 7-1.

The program of Figure 7-11 is one that initializes the 8255 (programs it) and therefore would probably be executed on "power-up" of the microprocessor-based system. To read a data byte from port A or B requires software in addition to that given in Figure 7-11, mainly the IN instruction. Accessing ports A and B will be the next topic.

To write a program that accesses ports A and B, we must understand the various addresses that apply to an 8255. Because we still have not studied addressing the 8255, let us assign the symbolic address "PORTA" to port A and "PORTB" to port B. As an example program that services ports A and B, let us suppose that input port A is a terminal and output port B is a printer. A data byte input by port A is to be displayed (printed) at port B (displaying input data is known as *echoing*). Also, the input data byte is to be stored in memory at location STORE. The program of Figure 7-12, Example 7-2, will accomplish this task.

In the program of Example 7-2 imagine that vectored interrupts are used, port A's service routine is at location 0008H (RST 1), and port B's service routine begins at location 0010H (RST 2). Both service routines are simplified but are sufficient for presenting the concepts of reading and writing to the 8255. Remember that the program of Figure 7-11 must be executed before the program of Figure 7-12, so that the 8255 is properly programmed.

EXAMPLE 7-1

```
; This program will program the 8255
; of Figure 7-7 to perform the functions as shown

    MVI A,B4H      ; Initialize A with port
                   ; Configuration control-word
    OUT PPI1       ; Program PPI for mode 1
    MVI A,09H      ; Initialize A with bit Set/Reset
                   ; control-word for INTE A
    OUT PPI1       ; Set INTE A
    MVI A,05H      ; Initialize A with bit Set/Reset
                   ; control-word for INTE B
    OUT PPI1       ; Set INTE B

; The PPI of Figure 7-7 is now programmed
```

FIGURE 7-11. Instructions to program 8255 as configured in Figure 7-7.

EXAMPLE 7-2

```
; Service routine for port A

    ORG 0008H
    IN  PORTA      ; Get data byte from port A
                   ; This resets IBF to zero
                   ; hence INTR A goes low
    STA STORE      ; Store data byte at location STORE
    RET            ; Return to main program

; End of service routine
; Service routine for port B

    ORG 0010H
    LDA MEM        ; Load A with
                   ; data byte from memory
    OUT PORTB      ; Send data byte to port B
                   ; and active OBF.
    RET            ; Return to main program

; End of service routine
```

FIGURE 7-12.   Program for servicing ports A and B of Figure 7-7.

As seen from Figure 7-4, configurations other than that of Figure 7-7 are possible for a mode 1 operation. The hardware and software examples of Figures 7-7, 7-11, and 7-12 should be sufficient to grasp the concepts of a mode 1 operation for both input and output ports of an 8255.

Mode 2

Mode 2 configures the 8255 as shown in Figure 7-13. Group A functions as a bidirectional I/O port (input and output port) with handshaking. Port B may be programmed to function as either an input or output port in either a mode 0 or mode 1 operation. Both input and output data are latched by port A. There are three bits of group C (PC_2, PC_1, and PC_0) not used for mode 2 handshaking; they can be programmed to be either output or input pins; that is, these three pins can have access to 3 bits of the data bus for MPU read or write operations. However, if port B is programmed to function in a mode 1 operation, PC_2, PC_1, and PC_0 will function either as $\overline{ACK}$, $\overline{OBF}$, INTR (if programmed to an output port) or as $\overline{STB}$, $\overline{IBF}$, INTR (for input port) in order to provide handshaking for port B. Port C will be discussed in greater detail in Section 7-5.

As seen from Figure 7-13, handshaking for port A is provided by $\overline{OBF}_A$, $\overline{ACK}_A$, IBF_A, and $\overline{STB}_A$. $\overline{OBF}_A$ and $\overline{ACK}_A$ provide handshaking for port A functioning in write operations (MPU writing to the I/O device) and the pair IBF_A and $\overline{STB}_A$ provide handshaking for read operations. The handshaking of port A is identical to that previously explained for a mode 1 operation, with the exception of the common interrupt request, which is essentially an ORing of mode 1 read- or write-generated interrupts, as previously explained. Then in reality a mode 2 operation for port A is the combination of both a mode 1 input and output port with handshaking and the sharing of a common interrupt request.

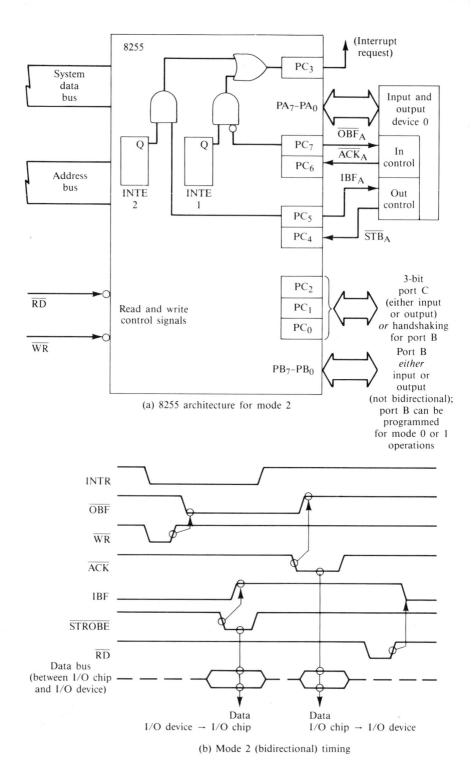

(a) 8255 architecture for mode 2

(b) Mode 2 (bidirectional) timing

FIGURE 7-13. The 8255 programmed in a mode 2 configuration. (Courtesy of Intel Corp.)

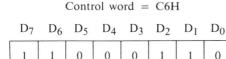

FIGURE 7-14. Control words for mode 2 operation.

The mode 2 control word will configure ports A, B, and C. Once configured, the MPU reads (IN) or writes (OUT) to the 8255 via the system data bus with input control signals read ($\overline{RD}$) and write ($\overline{WR}$) providing timing. The control signal $\overline{I/O\ R}$ will activate (directly or indirectly, just as any other I/O chip) $\overline{RD}$, and $\overline{I/O\ W}$ will activate $\overline{WR}$, as we shall see in detail when we study addressing of the 8255 in Section 7-4.

The control word for programming the 8255 to operate in mode 2 with port B functioning as a mode 1 input port with handshaking (PC_2, PC_1, and PC_0 provide handshaking) can be determined from Figure 7-4 and is illustrated in Figure 7-14(a). Notice that D_0 of Figure 7-14(a) is a "don't care," as PC_2–PC_0 provide handshaking and do not function as I/O pins. The bit set/reset control word for port B (PC_2 as stated in Figure 7-7) is given in Figure 7-14(b). All "don't cares" (X's) were arbitrarily assigned as lows.

The program that will program the 8255 for a mode 2 operation with group B configured as a mode 1 input port and group C (PC_2, PC_1, and PC_0) providing handshaking for port B is given in Figure 7-15 of Example 7-3. As before, a symbolic address (PPI2) is used to address the 8255 to load the mode and bit set/reset control words into the 8255 control register.

Once the program of Figure 7-15 is executed, then to write a data byte to port A, the instruction OUT PORTA will suffice, in which PORTA is a symbolic address, as used previously. To read a data byte from port A requires the instruction IN PORTA, in which PORTA is again the same symbolic address.

EXAMPLE 7-3

```
; This program programs an 8255 to
; operate in a mode 2 configuration with
; input port B operating in mode 1

    MVI A,0C6H    ; Initialize A with mode 2 control word
    OUT PPI2      ; Program 8255 for mode 2
    MVI A,05H     ; Initialize A with Set/Reset
                  ; control word for port B
    OUT PPI2      ; Set INTE B

; The 8255 is now programmed
```

FIGURE 7-15. Instructions to program an 8255 for mode 2.

To read a data byte from input port B requires the instruction IN PORTB, and instruction OUT PORTC writes to output port C (when available). A more specific and detailed example will be given later.

Addressing the 8255

To determine the appropriate address for the 8255, refer to Table 7-3. From Table 7-3 it is seen that A_1 and A_0 address the ports and control register for *all* modes of operation. That is, $A_1 = A_0 = 0$ addresses port A and $A_1 = 0$, $A_0 = 1$ addresses port B for either read or write operations. Control signals $\overline{RD}$ and $\overline{WR}$ determine the data direction (read or write). As an example of a read operation, Table 7-3 shows that when chip select ($\overline{CS}$) is low, $\overline{RD}$ is low (a read is being performed) and $\overline{WR} = 1$ with address $A_1 = A_0 = 0$, then port A gates its data byte on the system data bus. In this instance port A would have been previously programmed as an input port. In contrast, for a write operation, when address $A_1 = A_0 = 0$, $\overline{CS} = 0$, and $\overline{WR} = 0$ ($\overline{RD} = 1$), the data byte on the system data bus is latched by port A. $\overline{WR} = 0$, in conjunction with $A_1 = A_0 = 0$, requires port A to have previously been programmed as an output port. From Table 7-3 we see that to load a control word into the control register requires address $A_1 = A_0 = 1$ as well as control signals $\overline{RD} = 1$, $\overline{WR} = 0$, and $\overline{CS} = 0$.

EXAMPLE 7-4
As an example of integrating the 8255 into a microprocessor-based system, such a system as Figure 4-7, consider Figure 7-16.

TABLE 7-3. 8255 Addressing

A_1	A_0	$\overline{RD}$	$\overline{WR}$	$\overline{CS}$	Input Operation (read)
0	0	0	1	0	Port A $\Rightarrow$ data bus
0	1	0	1	0	Port B $\Rightarrow$ data bus
1	0	0	1	0	Port C $\Rightarrow$ data bus
					Output Operation (write)
0	0	1	0	0	Data bus $\Rightarrow$ port A
0	1	1	0	0	Data bus $\Rightarrow$ port B
1	0	1	0	0	Data bus $\Rightarrow$ port C
1	1	1	0	0	Data bus $\Rightarrow$ control
					Disable Function
X	X	X	X	1	Data bus $\Rightarrow$ tri-state
1	1	0	1	0	Illegal condition
X	X	1	1	0	Data bus $\Rightarrow$ tri-state

Courtesy Intel Corp.

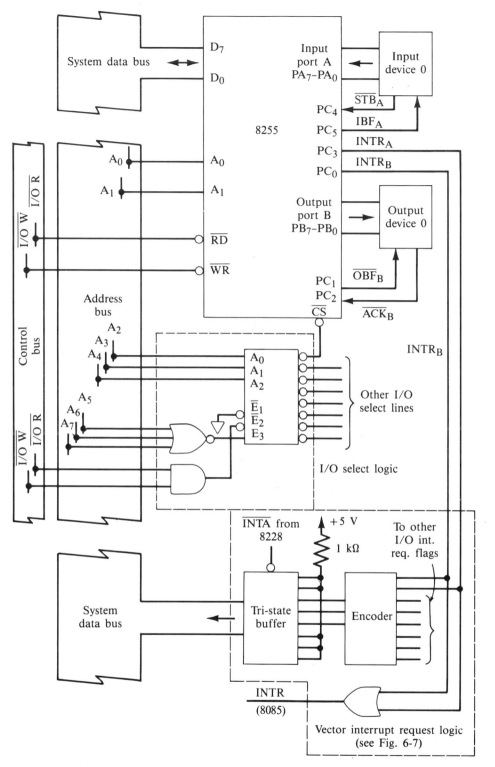

FIGURE 7-16. Hardware for an 8255 programmed to function in a mode 1 configuration.

Solution

As seen in Figure 7-16, the 8255 is addressed with A_0 and A_1 lines of the address bus. Address lines A_2–A_7 enable ($\overline{CS}$) the 8255 via the I/O select. The I/O select is an 8205 and operates in the same way as those discussed in Chapter 4. We see for this example that when address lines $A_2 = A_3 = A_4 = 0$, then select line 0 becomes active and is used to activate $\overline{CS}$ of the 8255. Control signals $\overline{I/O\ R}$ and $\overline{I/O\ W}$ activate $\overline{RD}$ and $\overline{WR}$, respectively.

To address the 8255 of Figure 7-16 requires A_7–A_2 to be as shown in Table 7-4. As stated previously, address lines A_7–A_2 of Figure 7-16 enable the 8255, and address lines A_0–A_1 address the port. The instruction IN or OUT determines whether the addressed port is being read or written to.

Returning to the program of Figure 7-6 and using it to program the mode control word to the 8255 of Figure 7-16, we see from Table 7-4 that the address for PPI0 is 03H. Similarly, the address for PPI1 and PPI2 of Figures 7-11 and 7-15 is also 03H, when applied to the hardware of Figure 7-16, as in each case the control register of the 8255 is being addressed. To reiterate, from Table 7-4 we see that any time port A of Figure 7-16 is addressed, the hexadecimal number 00H is to be used. Similarly, port B's address is 01H and port C's is 02H. The data byte direction, data bus to port or port to data bus, is determined by the op code IN or OUT (via $\overline{RD}$ or $\overline{WR}$).

To program the 8255 to function as indicated in Figure 7-16 and also to write service routines for ports A and B, we simply need to determine the proper address values from Table 7-4 and furnish them for the symbolic addresses of Examples 7-1 and 7-2. These modifications are shown in Figure 7-17 of Example 7-5.

As another example of hardware, let us apply an 8255 in a mode 2 operation with port B functioning in a mode 1 configuration (refer to Figure 7-13). The hardware is shown in Figure 7-18, which is the hardware of Figures 7-16 appropriately modified for a mode 2 as stated.

Because the hardware of Figure 7-18 is a combination of circuits discussed previously (Figures 6-7, 7-13, and 7-14), its operation needs little discussion. We see that input/output device 0 is a bidirectional I/O device and therefore is to be connected to port A, which is functioning in a mode 2 operation. The interrupt request from port A ($INTR_A$) generates an RST vectored interrupt. Port B is operating in a mode 1 operation. An interrupt request from port B also

TABLE 7-4. Addresses for the 8255 of Figure 7-16

Hex Addr.	8255 Chip Select						Port Addr.		Function Addressed
	A_7	A_6	A_5	A_4	A_3	A_2	A_1	A_0	
00	0	0	0	0	0	0	0	0	Port A
01	0	0	0	0	0	0	0	1	Port B
02	0	0	0	0	0	0	1	0	Port C
03	0	0	0	0	0	0	1	1	Control reg

Refer to Table 7-3

EXAMPLE 7-5

```
; Programming the 8255 to be configured
; as shown in Figure 7-14

    ORG 0100H
    MVI A,0BH ; Initialize A with mode
              ;   control-word
    OUT 03H   ; Program PPI for mode 1
    MVI A,09H ; Initialize A with bit Set/Reset for INTE A
    OUT 03H   ; Set INTE A
    MVI A,05H ; Initialize A with bit Set/Reset for INTE B
    OUT 03H   ; Set INTE B

; Service Routine for input port A

    ORG 0008H
    IN  00H   ; Get data byte from port A
    STA STORE ; Store data byte at location STORE
    RET       ; Return to main program

; Service Routine for output port B

    ORG 0010H
    LDA MEM   ; Load A with data byte stored at memory location MEM
    OUT 01H   ; Output data byte to port B
    RET       ; Return
```

FIGURE 7-17.   A routine for programming the 8255 of Figure 7-14.

causes a vectored interrupt. It might be pointed out that the input/output device 0 could be a combined terminal (input) and printer (output).

The software to service the 8255 for a mode 2 operation requires knowledge of the 8255's status word, which is explained in the next section.

7-5

8255 Status Word

The 8255 status word indicates the logic state of INTE, $\overline{OBF}$, IBF, and INTR$_A$ for both ports A and B for modes 1 and 2, as indicated in Figure 7-19. The 8255 status word is obtained by reading port C, which requires IN 02H (see Table 7-4) for the 8255 of Figure 7-16. To understand why port C is used for reading the 8255's status word, refer to the status word format of Figure 7-19 and also port C of Figures 7-7(a), 7-13, and 7-18, taking note of port C's limited number (three or fewer) of I/O pins. Reading port C (using IN 02H) will result in 8 bits from port C being latched by the MPU's accumulator (refer to instruction IN). But because port C has three or fewer I/O (INPUT) pins, the 5 or more bits not used to input data, via port C, must represent something else. The "something else" is the status (the present logic state) of those functions, as indicated in Figure 7-19.

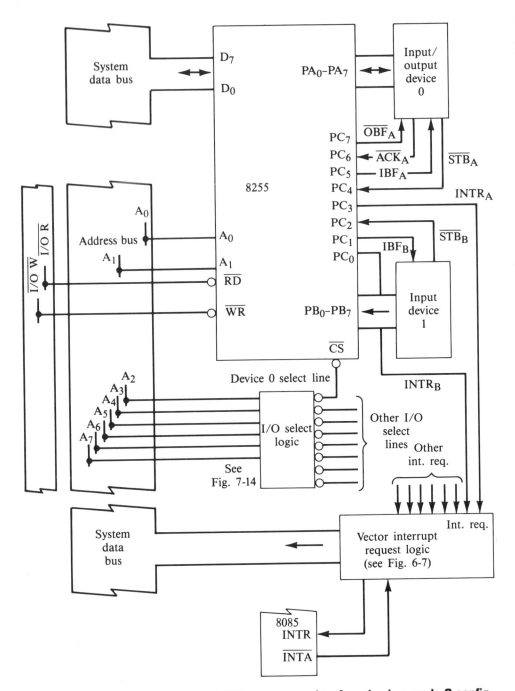

FIGURE 7-18. Hardware for an 8255 programmed to function in a mode 2 configuration.

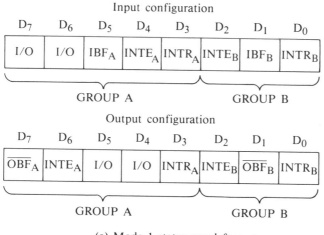

Input configuration

D₇	D₆	D₅	D₄	D₃	D₂	D₁	D₀

$$D_7 \quad D_6 \quad D_5 \quad D_4 \quad D_3 \quad D_2 \quad D_1 \quad D_0$$

| I/O | I/O | IBF_A | $INTE_A$ | $INTR_A$ | $INTE_B$ | IBF_B | $INTR_B$ |

GROUP A   GROUP B

Output configuration

$$D_7 \quad D_6 \quad D_5 \quad D_4 \quad D_3 \quad D_2 \quad D_1 \quad D_0$$

| $\overline{OBF}_A$ | $INTE_A$ | I/O | I/O | $INTR_A$ | $INTE_B$ | $\overline{OBF}_B$ | $INTR_B$ |

GROUP A   GROUP B

(a) Mode 1 status word format

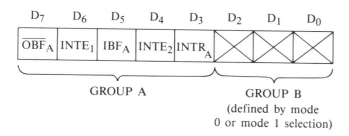

$$D_7 \quad D_6 \quad D_5 \quad D_4 \quad D_3 \quad D_2 \quad D_1 \quad D_0$$

| $\overline{OBF}_A$ | $INTE_1$ | IBF_A | $INTE_2$ | $INTR_A$ | | | |

GROUP A   GROUP B
(defined by mode
0 or mode 1 selection)

(b) Mode 2 status word format

FIGURE 7-19.   8255 status word format. (Courtesy of Intel Corp.)

To utilize an 8255 status word, review Figures 7-13 and 7-18. From Figure 7-18 we realize that if either the input or output of input/output device 0 requested an interrupt, a single interrupt request line ($INTR_A$) would be activated. In order for the MPU to determine which, or both, requested the interrupt, the MPU must poll both ports. It performs the poll by reading the 8255 status word from port C, obtaining the data of Figure 7-19(b), and then specifically determining the logic state of $\overline{OBF}$ and IBF using a *mask word*, as was done in Example 6-1. As seen from the timing diagram of Figure 7-13(b), when the 8255 is writing to I/O device 0, via port A, $\overline{OBF}$ goes low and remains in that logic state until the data byte of port A is latched by I/O device 0 and acknowledgment is given ($\overline{ACK}$ goes low). Also, we notice from Figure 7-13(b) that INTR is high when $\overline{OBF}$ becomes active. Thus to determine whether the input or output port requested the interrupt, a software poll of the mode 2 status word of Figure 7-19(b) can be made. Such a routine is given in Example 7-6, with Save Register Contents, and so on, omitted.

EXAMPLE 7-6

```
; This routine reads port C for a
; mode 2 operation and then determines
; whether input or output requested
; an interrupt. Assume that an interrupt
; request from port A of Figure 7-16 resulted
; in the CPU being vectored to 0038H
; (RST 7)

    ORG 0038H
    IN  02H          ; Read port C and obtain the
                     ; mode 2 status word of
                     ; Figure 7-17(b)
    MOV B,A          ; Copy the status word in B
    ANI 80H          ; Poll D₇ for OBF
    CZ  SROUT        ; If Z = 1, then OBFₐ = 0; jump
                     ; to service routine SR OUT
    MOV A,B          ; Restore status in A
    ANI 20H          ; Poll D₅ for high
    CNZ SRIN         ; If Z = 0, then IBFₐ = 1
                     ; and needs service
    RET              ; Return to main program
```

The reader should also be aware that the mode 2 status word of Figure 7-19(b) is needed when polling ports to determine which port requested an interrupt. This is an application of Example 6-1. That is, two of the interrupt request flag outputs (Q) of Figure 6-2 are replaced with $INTR_A$ and $INTR_B$ of Figure 7-18. Then when an interrupt request is made, a polling routine similar to that of Figure 6-4 is executed, which begins polling, just as in Example 6-1.

7-6

Summary of the 8255

The 8255 is a versatile programmable peripheral interface (PPI) chip. It can be programmed for a variety of I/O port configurations, and the port configurations possible can be classified into one of three operations:

1. *Mode 0:* This mode of operation provides elementary I/O interfacing requiring no handshaking.
2. *Mode 1:* This mode provides two 8-bit ports for I/O interfacing, requiring handshaking. Either of the two 8-bit ports may be either input or output. Both inputs and outputs are latched.
3. *Mode 2:* This mode of operation provides one 8-bit bidirectional port (port A) and another 8-bit port (port B), which may be programmed to function as either a mode 0 or 1 input or output port.

Table 7-5 is a reprint from Intel summarizing the 8255 port configurations according to mode.

TABLE 7-5. Mode Definition Summary Table

	Mode 0		Mode 1		Mode 2
	In	Out	In	Out	Group A Only
PA_0	IN	OUT	IN	OUT	↔
PA_1	IN	OUT	IN	OUT	↔
PA_2	IN	OUT	IN	OUT	↔
PA_3	IN	OUT	IN	OUT	↔
PA_4	IN	OUT	IN	OUT	↔
PA_5	IN	OUT	IN	OUT	↔
PA_6	IN	OUT	IN	OUT	↔
PA_7	IN	OUT	IN	OUT	↔
PB_0	IN	OUT	IN	OUT	—
PB_1	IN	OUT	IN	OUT	—
PB_2	IN	OUT	IN	OUT	—
PB_3	IN	OUT	IN	OUT	— Mode 0
PB_4	IN	OUT	IN	OUT	— or Mode 1
PB_5	IN	OUT	IN	OUT	— Only
PB_6	IN	OUT	IN	OUT	—
PB_7	IN	OUT	IN	OUT	—
PC_0	IN	OUT	$INTR_B$	$INTR_B$	I/O
PC_1	IN	OUT	IBF_B	$\overline{OBF}_B$	I/O
PC_2	IN	OUT	$\overline{STB}_B$	$\overline{ACK}_B$	I/O
PC_3	IN	OUT	$INTR_A$	$INTR_A$	$INTR_A$
PC_4	IN	OUT	$\overline{STB}_A$	I/O	$\overline{STB}_A$
PC_5	IN	OUT	IBF_A	I/O	IBF_A
PC_6	IN	OUT	I/O	$\overline{ACK}_A$	$\overline{ACK}_A$
PC_7	IN	OUT	I/O	$\overline{OBF}_A$	$\overline{OBF}_A$

Courtesy of Intel Corp.

Port C provides handshaking for ports A and B. Explanations of the handshaking functions provided by port C (for mode 1 or 2 operations, see Table 7-5) are as follows:

1. *Handshaking for input port (A or B):* Also refer to the timing diagram of Figure 7-7(b).
    a. $\overline{STB}$. This is an input to the 8255. It provides a strobe by driving $\overline{STB}$ low. This strobe pulse is used by the 8255 to latch the data byte from the peripheral device.
    b. IBF. When an input port of the 8255 has latched a data byte from the inputting peripheral, the 8255 acknowledges receiving the data byte transmission by driving IBF high, which states that that port's input buffer is full.
    c. INTR. When an input buffer is full (IBF = 1) the 8255 requires servicing by the MPU; that is, the MPU must read the port. To get the attention of the MPU, the 8255 generates an interrupt request via INTR. Before INTR can become active, INTE must be set, using the bit set/reset control word of Figure 7-9.

2. *Handshaking for output port (A or B):* In addition to Table 7-5, refer to the timing diagram, Figure 7-8.
   a. $\overline{OBF}$. When the MPU writes to an 8255 output port, the receiving port latches the data byte and then indicates that its output buffer is full by outputting a low on $\overline{OBF}$.
   b. $\overline{ACK}$. $\overline{OBF}$ going low is used by the peripheral device to latch the data byte from the 8255 output port. When the peripheral device has latched the data byte, it acknowledges the transaction by pulling $\overline{ACK}$ low. When $\overline{ACK}$ goes low, the 8255 is ready to receive another data byte from the MPU and as a result activates INTR.
   c. INTR. INTR is used to interrupt the MPU for the next data byte to be written to the peripheral.

To program the 8255 for any port configuration of Table 7-5 requires that a control word be written to the control register of the 8255. The control word format is given in Figure 7-4. In order to write a control word to the control register of an 8255, the appropriate address must be supplied. From Table 7-4 and specific hardware configuration of the address bus lines A_0–A_7, such as shown in Figure 7-16, the appropriate address can be determined. From Table 7-4 we see that A_0 and A_1 of the 8255 must be high in order to write a control word to the control register. Also from Table 7-4 we see that A_0 and A_1 of the 8255 select the port (A, B, or C) that is being read or written to.

Finally, when the MPU reads port C, it will read not only the I/O pins of port C (if any) but also the status of the 8255. The status word format for the 8255 is shown in Figure 7-19.

A system's wiring of an 8255 for each mode of operation is shown in Figure 7-20. Figure 7-21 shows some 8255 applications as suggested by Intel.

7·7

Serial Data Communications

In previous sections, applications of the 8255 illustrated the manner in which the chip could be used to allow the MPU to communicate with an external I/O device. That form of data communications is known as *parallel data communications*, as at a given instant, information was transmitted as groups of bits rather than a single bit at a time. For example, in Figure 7-14, input device 0 and output device 0 are connected to the 8255 chip by means of sixteen data lines (PA_0–PA_7 for input device 0, and PB_0–PB_7 for output device 0). The 8255 then receives and transmits data from and to these external I/O devices in the form of bytes (8 bits). In a serial data interface, an external device is connected to the port by means of a single data line. A byte of data is then transferred by shifting each bit (of the byte) over the interconnecting line, until all 8 bits are transferred.

The advantages of serial data transfers are obvious. Assuming that the MPU communicates with an external I/O device by using 8 bits of information, a parallel port would require a minimum of eight data lines connected to the external I/O device to accomplish the interface. A serial port, on the other hand,

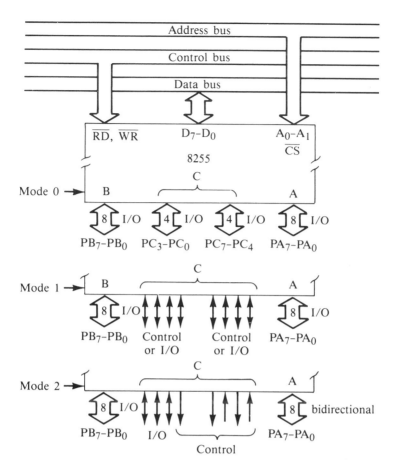

FIGURE 7-20. 8255 bus interfaces for various modes of operation. (Courtesy of Intel Corp.)

would require a minimum of one data line connected to the external I/O device to transmit and receive serial data. Note that both types of ports would have to have an additional line (ground) to provide a common reference for the logic voltages appearing on the data lines.

Eight data lines on a parallel interface or one data line on a serial interface would restrict communications to "one-way traffic" at a given instant. In other words, neither type of I/O port would be able to transmit and receive data to and from the external I/O device at the same time. When data communication is limited to either transmission or reception at any given instant, it is known as *half-duplex communication*. To overcome this limitation, a parallel port having sixteen data lines (eight to receive data, and eight to transmit data) would have the capability to transmit and receive data at the same time. The ability to receive and transmit data at the same time is known as *full-duplex communication*. Similarly, a serial port having two serial data lines (one to transmit serial data and one to receive serial data) would have the capability to operate in full duplex.

One of the main disadvantages of serial data communications is in the speed

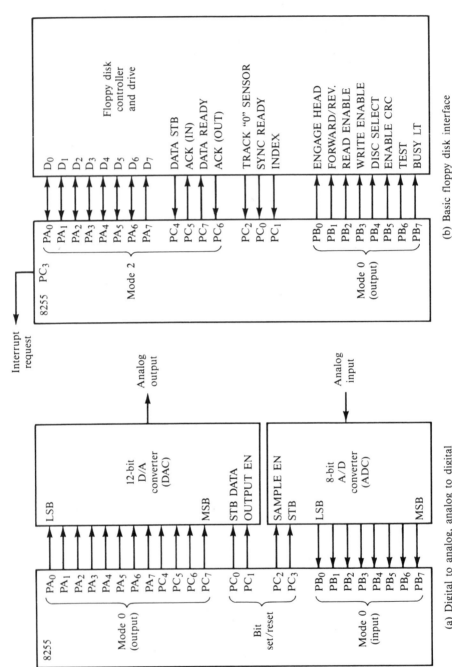

(a) Digital to analog, analog to digital

(b) Basic floppy disk interface

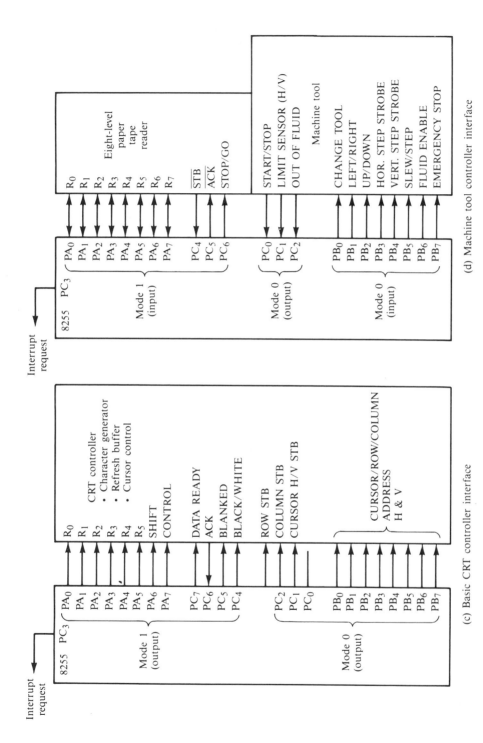

(c) Basic CRT controller interface

(d) Machine tool controller interface

FIGURE 7-21. Some example applications. (Courtesy of Intel Corp.)

with which data is transferred to and from the external I/O device. Because the serial port must shift out parallel data one bit at a time over a single line, and shift in serial data one bit at a time to construct a byte, the time required to do this limits the rate of data transmission. This overhead does not exist in a parallel data communications link.

7·8

Serial Data Interface

In previous sections it was shown that an external I/O device that communicated in parallel data could be connected to the MPU via a parallel I/O port (8255). Similarly, an external I/O device that communicates by using a serial data format can be connected to the MPU via a serial I/O port. Figure 7-22 illustrates a typical full-duplex data link between a serial data port and an external I/O device. In most cases, this external I/O device is a computer terminal (console) with a keyboard and a screen (or printer). The circuit in Figure 7-22 allows the MPU and external I/O device to communicate via a serial I/O port. The serial data link consists of three lines: a *transmit data line* (TxD) to transfer data from the serial port to the I/O device, a *receive data line* (RxD) to transfer data from the I/O device to the serial port, and a *signal ground* (GND) to reference the voltages appearing on the serial data lines. Note that the terms *transmit* and *receive* pertain to the serial port and not to the I/O device.

The interface between the MPU and the serial I/O port consists of a connection to the data bus (D_0–D_7) to enable data transfers to and from the MPU, a read line ($\overline{RD}$) to enable the MPU to read data from the serial port, a write line ($\overline{WR}$) to enable the MPU to write data to the serial port, and a chip select ($\overline{CS}$) line to select the chip for I/O operations when the appropriate I/O address appears on the address bus.

Notice that the circuit in Figure 7-22 uses linear addressing. Recall from Chapter 3 that this addressing technique uses an address line (A_0–A_{15}) to select a device. This simplifies the hardware by eliminating the I/O selector (decoder). However, the disadvantage in this addressing scheme is that the number of addressable I/O devices is limited to eight.

Referring to Figure 7-22, if the MPU executes an "OUT 2" instruction,

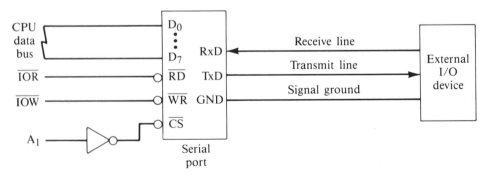

FIGURE 7-22.   Basic serial data link.

address line A_1 is set to a logic 1; the logic 1 on address line A_1 is inverted and used to select (via the $\overline{CS}$ line) the serial port for an output operation. The "OUT 2" instruction also activates the $\overline{I/O\ W}$ control line (connected to $\overline{WR}$ of the serial port) and thus allows the contents of the data bus (contents of register A) to be loaded into the serial port. On receiving the byte of data, the serial port then shifts the data one bit at a time over the TxD line to the external I/O device.

Similarly, if the external I/O device transmitted serial data over the RxD line of the serial port, the serial port would then shift each bit into an internal register and construct an 8-bit data byte. The MPU could then activate the $\overline{I/O\ R}$ ($\overline{RD}$ line of the serial port) and A_1 lines ($\overline{CS}$ of the serial port) by means of an IN 2 instruction to read the data received by the serial port (and stored in an internal register) from the external I/O device.

The serial port thus operates in a manner similar to a serial-to-parallel, parallel-to-serial shift register. Parallel data from the MPU is shifted out serially over the TxD line to the external I/O device. Serial data from the external I/O device is serially shifted into the serial port and assembled into a parallel byte for input to the MPU.

Notice in the circuit of Figure 7-22 that no provisions have been made for status readback. Because the rate at which serial data is transferred is often much slower than the operating speed of the MPU, the serial port must provide some sort of signal to the MPU, indicating that the serial data transfer has been completed. For example, if the MPU were to transmit a group of data bytes to the serial port, one byte at a time, without checking to see if the previous byte sent was completely shifted out on the TxD line, the serial port would not be able to "keep up" with the MPU, and this could lead to the transmission of erroneous data. Similarly, if the MPU attempted to read data received by the serial port (from the RxD line) without checking to see if the entire data byte was completely shifted in, the MPU could obtain erroneous data. *Status readback* is a process by which the MPU reads *status information* put out by the serial port. From this status information, the MPU determines whether the transmitting circuit of the serial port (transmitter) has completely transmitted the previous byte sent and is ready to accept another byte for transmission. Status information also allows the MPU to determine whether the receiving circuit (receiver) of the serial port has received and completely assembled a character from the external I/O device. Many serial ports provide the MPU with other types of status information, as will be seen later in this chapter. To accommodate this status readback facility for the serial data link in Figure 7-22, another line has been added to the serial port—the control/data ($C/\overline{D}$) line, shown in Figure 7-23.

The $C/\overline{D}$ line of the serial port allows the MPU to select between data transfers (previously discussed) or status information. With the $C/\overline{D}$ line set to a logic 0 (data mode), the circuit in Figure 7-23 operates in a manner similar to the circuit discussed in Figure 7-22; that is, an OUT 2 instruction causes data from register A to be transmitted over the TxD line and an IN 2 instruction reads data received over the RxD line.

When the $C/\overline{D}$ line is set to a logic 1, the serial port operates in the control mode, and allows the MPU to read status information. Notice that the $C/\overline{D}$ line

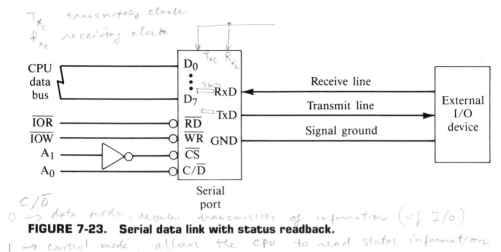

FIGURE 7-23. Serial data link with status readback.

of the serial port is tied to address line A_0 of the MPU. Now whenever the MPU executes an "IN 3" instruction, address line A_1 is set high and the $\overline{CS}$ line of the serial port is enabled; however, address line A_0 is also set high and the $C/\overline{D}$ line is held at a logic 1 level. (Note that for IN 2 and OUT 2 instructions, address line $A_0 = 0$, and the serial port is in the data mode.) The execution of the IN 3 instruction now provides the MPU with status information in the form of an 8-bit status word. A typical status word sent to the MPU is shown in Figure 7-24.

Note that the status word shown in Figure 7-24 appears in the MPU's accumulator as the result of the IN 3 instruction. In the status word of Figure 7-24, bit position 0 represents the least significant bit, and bit position 7 represents the most significant bit. Bit positions 0 and 1 represent the transmitter and receiver status, respectively. If the transmitter is ready to accept another byte for transmission, transmitter ready (TxRDY) will be set to a logic 1 by the serial port; otherwise, it will be reset to a logic 0. Similarly, if the receiver has received a serial data byte over the RxD line (receiver ready, RxRDY), bit position 1 will be set to a logic 1; otherwise, it will be reset to a logic 0. Note that if the RxRDY bit is set, the MPU must read the data received by the serial port. Otherwise, if another character is received over the RxD line, the original character received will be overwritten and hence lost (*overrun error*). At this stage it is assumed that bits 2, 3, 4, 5, 6, and 7 do not provide any status information and will not be used by the MPU.

Transmitting data to the external I/O device via the serial port is thus a two-step process. In order to transmit data to the external I/O device, the MPU must first check the $T \times RDY$ bit of the status word (transmitter ready status), wait for the transmitter to indicate a ready condition, and then send the data to the serial port for transmission over the TxD line. The software implementation of this process is shown in Figure 7-25. The code shown in Figure 7-25 is called the *console output* (CONOUT) subroutine, as it is used to transmit a single data byte (character) to the external I/O device (console) via the serial port. The CONOUT subroutine assumes that the character to be transmitted to the console is stored in register C *before* the subroutine is called.

The first instruction in the CONOUT subroutine is an IN 3 instruction that is used to input the serial port's status word into the MPU's accumulator. As mentioned before, bit position 0 of the status word will be set or reset depending

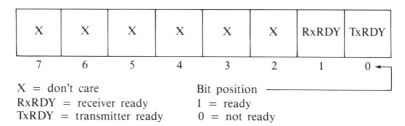

X	X	X	X	X	X	RxRDY	TxRDY
7	6	5	4	3	2	1	0

X = don't care   Bit position
RxRDY = receiver ready   1 = ready
TxRDY = transmitter ready   0 = not ready

FIGURE 7-24.   Format of serial port status word.

on the state of the serial port's transmitter. The next instruction, ANI 01H, is used to mask out bit position 0 of the status word; this is done by ANDing the contents of the accumulator (status word) with a 01H (00000001 binary). Now if the transmitter is ready (bit position 0 of status word = 1), the result of the ANI instruction will yield a 01H (nonzero) result. If the transmitter is not ready (bit position 0 of status word = 0), the result of the ANI instruction will yield a 00H (zero) result. The third instruction, JZ, is used to check the result of the ANI instruction. If the result is a zero (transmitter not ready), control will transfer to the address CONOUT, and the three-instruction sequence will be repeated, continuing until the transmitter is ready. If the result of the ANI instruction is a nonzero (transmitter is ready), control will transfer to the next instruction in sequence (MOV A,C), which gets the character to be transmitted into the accumulator. Finally, the OUT 2 instruction sends the character to the serial port for transmission over the TxD line to the console.

Just as transmitting data to the console is a two-step process, receiving data from the console is also a two-step process. The MPU must first determine whether a character has been received by the serial port from the console, by checking the state of the RxRDY bit. On detecting a receiver ready condition, the MPU can then input the data received into the accumulator. The implementation of this process is similar to the CONOUT subroutine and is shown in Figure 7-26. The subroutine shown in Figure 7-26 is called the *console input* (CONIN) subroutine, as its function is to input a character from the console. The character received from the console is returned to the calling program in the accumulator.

The CONIN subroutine works in a manner similar to the CONOUT subroutine. The first three instructions initiate a loop that causes the CPU to wait until the receiver of the serial port has completely shifted in a character over the RxD line. Notice that the ANI 02H instruction now masks out bit position 1 (RxRDY)

```
CONOUT:   IN    03H       ; Get status word
          ANI   01H       ; See if transmitter ready
          JZ    CONOUT    ; Wait till ready
          MOV   A,C       ; Else get data to be transmitted
          OUT   02H       ; Send to serial port
          RET
```

FIGURE 7-25.   Console output subroutine.

```
                                    Rx Ready Bit
        CONIN:   IN    03H           ; Get status word
                 ANI   02H           ; See if receiver ready
                 JZ    CONIN         ; Wait till ready
                 IN    02H           ; Else get char from serial port
                 RET
```

FIGURE 7-26. Console input subroutine.

of the status word. Once a receiver ready (RxRDY) condition is detected by the MPU, it executes the IN 02H instruction, which results in the latching of the "received data" into the accumulator.

Notice in the CONIN subroutine of Figure 7-26 that if the console did not transmit a character, the MPU would be in an infinite loop with no means of exit. Thus the only way the MPU could exit the loop created by the first three instructions would be through the detection of a character received by the serial port. In some cases it would be useful to have a subroutine that simply sampled the receiver status and returned a flag that indicated the state of the receiver (ready or not ready). This type of subroutine is known as a *console status* (CONSTS) subroutine and is shown in Figure 7-27.

The CONSTS subroutine in Figure 7-27 will set the accumulator to 00H if the receiver is not ready (the console has not transmitted a character) and to FFH if the receiver is ready (the console has transmitted a character). The calling program can then check the contents of the accumulator to determine whether a character was or was not received by the serial port. This eliminates the possibility of the MPU's remaining in a continuous loop in the event that no data was transmitted by the console. Thus if a character had to be transmitted to the console, the following instructions could be used:

(Set register C to the character
to be transmitted to the console)

CALL CONOUT

Similarly, to input a received character:

CALL CONIN
(Register A contains the character
received from the console)

To determine whether a character was received from the console:

CALL CONSTS
(Register A contains 00 if no character
received, FF if received

The three subroutines discussed in this section—CONOUT, CONIN, and CONSTS—are known as *utility subroutines,* and their applications will be demonstrated in later chapters.

```
CONSTS:  IN   03H      ; Get status word
         ANI  02H      ; See if receiver ready
         RZ            ; Reg A = 00 if not ready
         MVI  A,0FFH   ; Else Reg A = FF if ready
         RET
```

FIGURE 7-27. Console status subroutine.

7-9

Serial Data Transmission Format

In the preceding section it was seen that the serial port operates in a manner similar to a shift register. The serial port will usually have two shift registers: one to shift data from the RxD line into the serial port *(receiver shift register)* and one to shift data out of the serial port onto the TxD line *(transmitter shift register)*. Both the receiver and transmitter shift registers must therefore have a clock that will cause each bit of a character to be shifted into or out of the serial port at a predetermined transition of the clock pulse. The frequency of the clock will also determine the rate at which serial data is transmitted and received over the TxD and RxD lines of the serial port. Figure 7-28 shows the serial interface of Figure 7-23 with the *transmitter clock* ($\overline{\text{TxC}}$) and *receiver clock* ($\overline{\text{RxC}}$) added to the serial port.

The transmitter clock ($\overline{\text{TxC}}$) shown in Figure 7-28 is used to shift data out of the serial port; each bit is shifted over the TxD line on the *falling edge* of the clock. The frequency of the signal on $\overline{\text{TxC}}$ will also determine the rate (speed) at which data is transmitted over the TxD line. Similarly, the receiver clock ($\overline{\text{RxC}}$) is used to shift data into the serial port from the RxD line; each bit is sampled on the RxD line on the *rising edge* of the clock. The frequency of the receiver clock will determine the rate at which data is shifted into the serial port. Notice in Figure 7-28 that the $\overline{\text{TxC}}$ and $\overline{\text{RxC}}$ lines are tied together and connected to a common clock. In most cases the serial port transmits and receives data at the same rate, and so a common clock is provided for the trans-

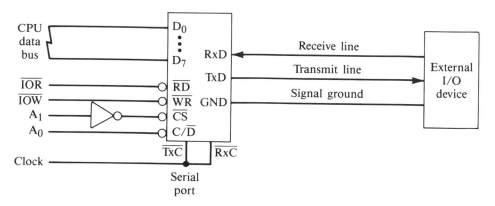

FIGURE 7-28.   Serial data link with transmitter and receiver clocks.

mitter and receiver shift registers. To illustrate the manner in which a serial bit stream is transmitted and received by the serial port, assume that the TxD and RxD lines of the serial port are connected together; now whatever data is transmitted over TxD is also received over RxD. Figure 7-29 shows the transmission of an 8-bit character (10101010) over the TxD line and its reception over the RxD line.

Referring to Figure 7-29, notice that the TxD line is held high until the falling edge of $\overline{\text{TxC}}$ causes a transition of the TxD line from a high to a low state. This transition is called the *start bit*, which when detected by the receiver causes the RxD line to be sampled at the rising edge of RxC. As each bit is transmitted over the TxD line on the falling edge of TxC, it is sampled over the RxD line on the rising edge of $\overline{\text{RxC}}$. This causes the receiver to sample data at approximately the midpoint of each bit transmitted. When all 8 bits have been transmitted, the TxD line returns to the high state, indicating the end of data transmission (the *stop bit*).

Because data is shifted in and out of the serial port at a particular edge of a clock pulse (rising or falling), the frequency of the clock attached to $\overline{\text{RxC}}$ and $\overline{\text{TxC}}$ will be equal to the rate at which each bit is shifted in or out of the serial port. This rate of serial data transfer therefore has the units of bits per second and is called the *baud rate*. For example, if the frequency of the clock attached to $\overline{\text{TxC}}$ and $\overline{\text{RxC}}$ were 9600 Hz, data would be transmitted and received at a rate of 9600 bits per second, or 9600 baud.

At this point it is important to note that if the serial port is transmitting data to the external I/O device at a particular baud rate, the external I/O device must receive that data at the same rate to avoid any sampling errors. Similarly, if the external I/O device transmitted data at a particular baud rate, the serial port must receive the data at the same rate. Because data is sampled by the receive line (of both the serial port and the external I/O device) at the midpoint of each bit transmitted, a slight variation (about 2 percent maximum) between the I/O device's clock and the serial port's clock would not pose a serious problem.

The type of serial data transmission discussed in this section is known as *asynchronous data transmission*, as both the serial port and the external I/O device have separate clocks (synchronized only by the detection of the start and

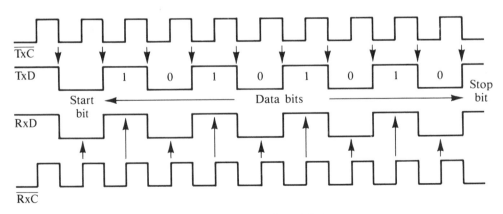

FIGURE 7-29. Transmission and reception of serial data.

stop bits) for transferring data; no synchronizing clock is transmitted with the serial data (as in synchronous data transmission).

Just as the serial port and the external I/O device must operate at the same baud rate, they must also be conditioned to operate with a certain protocol. A *protocol* is a formal set of conventions governing the format of message exchange between two communicating processes. In this case, the protocol identifies the "formalities" of data communications:

1. Number of data bits transferred.
2. Type of parity used during transmission.
3. Number of stop bits used at the end of transmission.
4. Definition of logic voltage levels.

Most serial ports and external I/O devices have the capability to transmit data in groups of 5, 6, 7, or 8 data bits. The number of data bits transferred depends on the type of data being transferred. For example, if a serial port and an external I/O device communicated with each other using the ASCII code, the number of data bits transferred would be seven, as ASCII is a 7-bit code. Similarly, communications using the EBCDIC code would require 8 data bits. Again, it is important that both devices communicate in the same code (and consequently with the same number of data bits) to avoid errors.

When data bits are transferred from one serial device to another, it is sometimes useful to have a mechanism to check to see that all data bits have been transmitted properly. Most serial devices use an automatic *parity check* on the data bits being transferred. These serial devices can be programmed to check for even parity, odd parity, or no parity check. For example, assume that two serial devices communicate with each other using the 7-bit ASCII code (refer to Appendix B) with even parity. Now if the ASCII character 'V' (1010110,56H) were to be transmitted by a serial port, it would be shifted over a serial line one bit at a time, starting with the least significant bit. After transmission of the most significant bit, the serial port would transmit one more bit, the *parity bit*. Because the ASCII character 'V' has even parity (that is, the number of 1 bits is even, 4), the parity bit transmitted will be zero to keep the total number of 1's transmitted to an even number. The device receiving the serial 8-bit character would automatically count the number of 1 bits transmitted. If the number of 1 bits counted were even, the transmission would be considered successful. If during transmission a 1 bit were gained or lost, the count would yield an odd number that would indicate a transmission error (*parity error*). As before, it is important that both serial devices conduct the same parity checks. If the transmitting device transmits data with even parity, the receiving device must check for even parity. Similarly, if odd parity is checked by the receiving device, the transmitting device must transmit data with odd parity.

As mentioned before, the stop bit indicates the end of data transmission. The stop bit is simply used to "space" out multiple transmissions of data and to allow the receiver to detect the start of the next character transmitted. The number of stop bits transmitted can be 1, $1\frac{1}{2}$, or 2. The receiver also expects one stop bit in most serial ports. However, some of the other peripheral devices are designed to detect two stop bits. It is all right for the transmitter to send two stop bits when the receiver is expecting only one. But if the receiver expects two stop bits, the transmitter cannot send only one.

Because serial data is often transmitted over fairly long distances, TTL logic levels are rarely used to represent a logic 1 and a logic 0, because of the low-noise-margin characteristic of TTL signals. To overcome this problem and to provide a higher noise immunity during the transfer of serial data, the RS232C logic voltage levels are used to represent bits of information. In the RS232C specification, data signals are considered as *marking* (logic 1) when they are at a negative voltage, and *spacing* (logic 0) when positive. A negative voltage in the range −3.0 to −15 V indicates a mark condition, and a positive voltage in the range +3.0 to +15 V indicates a space condition. A signal in the range +3.0 to −3.0 V is said to be in the *transition region* in which the logic level is undefined. Thus there usually is a hardware interface between two serial communicating devices that converts TTL logic levels to RS232C, and vice versa, in order to maintain standardization between serial communicating devices.

The number of data bits and stop bits, and the type of parity checking done in serial data transmissions set up the protocol of data transfer. Figure 7-30 illustrates the transmission of serial data for the following protocol: 7 data bits, even parity, 2 stop bits. Figure 7-30 shows the ASCII character 'V' transmitted by an external I/O device with the protocol previously specified. The character is received by the serial port by sampling the RxD line at the midpoint of each bit transmitted.

The high-to-low transition of the RxD line triggers the beginning of the start bit and causes the receiver clock to begin sampling data on the RxD line. The receiver checks the validity of the start bit by sampling its value at its midpoint. If it is still zero, it is a valid start bit. Once a valid start bit is detected, the receiver then starts a *bit counter* to count the number of data bits that follow. Each data bit is sampled at its approximate midpoint and shifted into the receiver. After 8 bits have been shifted in (7 data bits, 1 parity bit) the receiver then checks the parity of the data received. If the parity is even, it assumes that the data was transmitted successfully. If the parity is odd, the receiver signals an error condition (to be seen later). After 8 bits have been shifted in, the RxD line stays high for two clock periods (2 stop bits). The receiver samples the RxD line for stop-bit detection. If the line is low, an invalid stop bit is detected, indicating an error in the serial data transmission (a *framing error*). Notice that

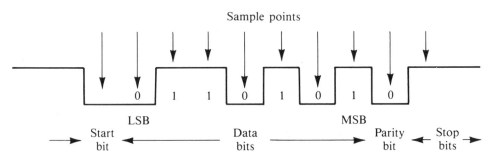

FIGURE 7-30. Transmission of the ASCII character 'V'.

the receiver will sample the stop bits only once, regardless of the number of stop bits transmitted. After the stop bits are detected, the RxD line returns to the high state in preparation for the next data transmission.

Observe that both serial communicating devices must conform to the same protocol and baud rate. If both devices did not operate at exactly the same baud rate and with the same serial protocol, data transfers would be completely unsynchronized and consequently would lead to transmission errors. Both serial devices, the serial port and the external I/O device, must therefore be set at the same baud rate and be "programmed" to operate with the same protocol. The same baud rate for both devices can easily be set by providing the same clock frequency at the $\overline{\text{TxC}}$ and $\overline{\text{RxC}}$ inputs of the serial port and the external I/O device. Most external I/O devices such as video terminals and printers have a set of switches to set the baud rate and transmission protocol. The serial port usually can be programmed to operate at a predefined protocol.

Recall from Figure 7-23 that the $C/\overline{D}$ line of the serial port was used to input status information to the MPU. This was done by setting the $C/\overline{D}$ line to a logic high by executing an IN 03H instruction (so that the $\overline{\text{RD}}$ line is activated). What if the $C/\overline{D}$ line were set to a logic high, by the execution of an OUT instruction? The OUT instruction (OUT 03H in this case) would cause the $C/\overline{D}$ line to stay high and the $\overline{\text{WR}}$ line and $\overline{\text{CS}}$ line to stay low (activated) and thus cause the contents of the accumulator to be sent to the serial port. Because the $C/\overline{D}$ line is high, the data sent to the serial port would not be transmitted over the TxD line but would be interpreted by the serial port as an instruction. This instruction could now be used by the MPU to dictate the protocol of data transmission to the serial port. This instruction is called the *mode instruction* and will be discussed in the next section.

7-10

The 8251 USART

The serial port discussed in Sections 7-8 and 7-9 is a commercially available chip known as the 8251 *universal synchronous/asynchronous receiver/ transmitter* (USART or UART). The 8251 is capable of both synchronous and asynchronous serial data transmission; however, this section will deal only with the asynchronous operation of the 8251. All the information pertaining to the serial port discussed in previous sections is applicable to the 8251. The 8251 is capable of sophisticated forms of serial data communications; however, this section will discuss only the elementary concepts needed for a simple serial interface.

Figure 7-31 shows the pin configuration and architectural block diagram of the 8251 USART. In the figure, notice that two sections of the 8251, the data bus buffer and the read/write control logic section, will provide the interface between the MPU and the 8251. The data bus buffer has eight data lines (D_0–D_7) that connect to the MPU's data bus and contains an 8-bit "holding" register for received data, status information, data to be transmitted, and control information (to be seen later). The read/write control logic section controls the flow of data within the 8251. The reset input to this section is used to reset all the

Pin configuration

Block diagram

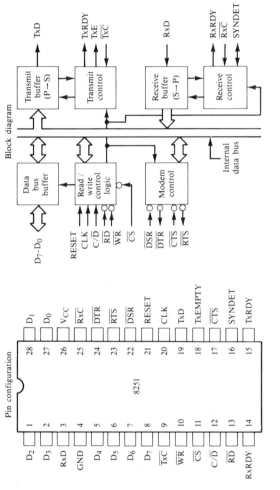

Pin name	Pin function
D_7–D_0	Data bus (8 bits)
$C/\overline{D}$	Control or data is to be written or read
$\overline{RD}$	Read data command
$\overline{WR}$	Write data or control command
$\overline{CS}$	Chip enable
CLK	Clock pulse (TTL)
RESET	Reset
$\overline{TxC}$	Transmitter clock
TxD	Transmitter data
$\overline{RxC}$	Receiver clock
RxD	Receiver data
RxRDY	Receiver ready (has character for 8080)
TxRDY	Transmitter ready (ready for character from 8080)

Pin name	Pin function
$\overline{DSR}$	Data set ready
$\overline{DTR}$	Data terminal ready
SYNDET	Sync detect
$\overline{RTS}$	Request to send data
$\overline{CTS}$	Clear to send data
TxE	Transmitter empty
V_{CC}	+5-V supply
GND	Ground

FIGURE 7-31. 8251 pin configuration and block diagram. (Courtesy of Intel Corp.)

TABLE 7-6. Basic Operations of the 8251

C/D̄	R̄D̄	W̄R̄	C̄S̄	Function	Operation
0	0	1	0	RxD data loaded on data bus	1
0	1	0	0	Data bus data to TxD line	2
1	0	1	0	Status word loaded on data bus	3
1	1	0	0	Control instruction to 8251	4
X	1	1	0	No operation	
X	X	X	1	No operation	

registers and flags within the 8251 and is normally connected to the reset signal of the MPU. The CLK input to this section is used to generate the internal timing of the 8251 and is normally connected to the 8085 CLK output. The C/D̄, R̄D̄, W̄R̄, and C̄S̄ inputs to this section provide the same functions as described in Sections 7-8 and 7-9. Table 7-6 illustrates the logic functions of these four inputs and will be used to describe the internal operation of the 8251. With reference to Table 7-6, notice that the 8251 is capable of four basic read/write operations; these operations are numbered in order after the description of each operation. Each operation of the 8251 will be discussed with reference to the block diagram shown in Figure 7-31.

Operation 1. Assuming that an external I/O device has transmitted serial data over the 8251's RxD line, the serial data is then assembled into a parallel word in the receive buffer. The receive control then causes the RxRDY bit of the status word to be set and also sets the RxRDY line to a logic 1. If the four control lines shown in Table 7-6 are conditioned for the first operation, this received data will be transferred from the receive buffer to the data bus buffer and onto the MPU's data bus.

Operation 2. With the four R/W control pins conditioned for operation 2, the contents of the MPU's data bus is loaded into the data bus buffer and transferred to the transmit buffer. The transmit buffer shifts the data out over the TxD line to the externally connected I/O device. When the entire character has been serially transmitted, the transmit control unit sets the TxRDY bit of the STATUS WORD and also sets the TxRDY output of the 8251 to a logic 1.

Note that the TxRDY and RxRDY output pins of the 8251 signal the same condition as do the TxRDY and RxRDY bits of the status word. The TxRDY and RxRDY output pins are provided for interrupt-driven applications. As discussed before, the R̄xC̄ and T̄xC̄ inputs to the receive and transmit control units, respectively, provide the baud rate for serial data transmission.

Operation 3. In this mode of operation, 8251 status information is loaded from the data bus buffer onto the MPU's data bus. As discussed before, the status word is an 8-bit word that supplies the status of the 8251's transmitter and receiver. The 8251 status word also provides other information, as shown in Figure 7-32. Notice in Figure 7-32 that the status word can provide more than receiver and transmitter status. It also provides status on error conditions

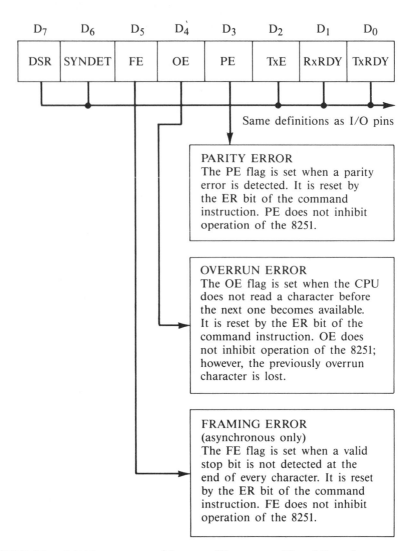

D$_7$	D$_6$	D$_5$	D$_4$	D$_3$	D$_2$	D$_1$	D$_0$
DSR	SYNDET	FE	OE	PE	TxE	RxRDY	TxRDY

Same definitions as I/O pins

PARITY ERROR
The PE flag is set when a parity error is detected. It is reset by the ER bit of the command instruction. PE does not inhibit operation of the 8251.

OVERRUN ERROR
The OE flag is set when the CPU does not read a character before the next one becomes available. It is reset by the ER bit of the command instruction. OE does not inhibit operation of the 8251; however, the previously overrun character is lost.

FRAMING ERROR
(asynchronous only)
The FE flag is set when a valid stop bit is not detected at the end of every character. It is reset by the ER bit of the command instruction. FE does not inhibit operation of the 8251.

FIGURE 7-32.   8251 status read format. (Courtesy of Intel Corp.)

that may have occurred during the transmission or reception of serial data, as well as status information on synchronous transmissions. The status word provided by the 8251 can be used with the CONOUT, CONIN, and CONSTS subroutines (Section 7-8) to check transmitter and receiver status before data is sent or received via the 8251.

Operation 4.   In this mode of operation, the 8251 can be programmed to operate at different protocols of serial data transmission. In this mode, the MPU must send two instructions to the 8251, the mode instruction and the command instruction. The format for the mode instruction is shown in Figure 7-33.

The MPU must send the mode instruction to the 8251 whenever the MPU (and consequently the 8251) is reset. The mode instruction specifies at which

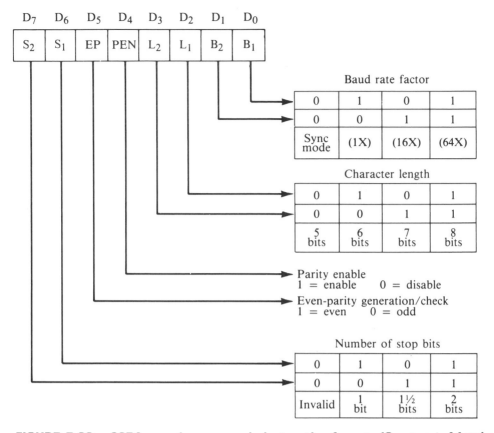

FIGURE 7-33. 8251 asynchronous mode instruction format. (Courtesy of Intel Corp.)

mode of operation the 8251 is to operate, synchronous or asynchronous, and if asynchronous, the format of serial data transmission (protocol). Thus with reference to Figure 7-33, if it were required to program the 8251 as follows,

Asynchronous mode
Seven data bits
Even-parity check
Two stop bits

the mode instruction 11111001 (F9H) would accomplish the task. Once the mode instruction is sent to the 8251 by the MPU via an OUT instruction, the 8251 maintains the same specified protocol until it is reset.

Notice that the first 2 bits of the mode instruction specify a baud-rate factor. This baud-rate factor sets up an internal divider to divide the $\overline{RxC}$ and $\overline{TxC}$ frequencies by the specified factor: $\times 1$, $\times 16$, or $\times 64$. For example, if a baud-rate factor of $\times 1$ were specified, the frequency required at the $\overline{TxC}$ and $\overline{RxC}$ inputs of the 8251 would have to be 9600 Hz, for a baud rate of 9600 baud. If a baud-rate factor of ×16 were specified, the frequency at $\overline{\text{TxC}}$ and $\overline{\text{RxC}}$ for 9600-baud operation would have to be 9600 × 16 = 153.6 kHz. Similarly, for a specified baud rate factor of ×64, the frequency at $\overline{\text{TxC}}$ and $\overline{\text{RxC}}$ for 9600-baud operation would have to be 9600 × 64 = 614.4 kHz. One of the reasons for providing this facility in the 8251 is that in many cases the $\overline{\text{TxC}}$ and $\overline{\text{RxC}}$ clock frequencies are obtained from the 8085 CLK output. Because this frequency has to be divided many times to obtain the desired baud rate, the 8251 has an internal divider that is capable of dividing the input frequency of $\overline{\text{TxC}}$ and $\overline{\text{RxC}}$ by a maximum of 64. This helps eliminate a lot of external circuitry that would otherwise be required. A baud-rate factor of ×1 can be used only with a common clock between the serial port and the external I/O device. In general, ×16 is used to ensure that the receiver samples the data near the center of each bit cell.

After the mode instruction is received by the 8251, the MPU can issue another instruction, the *command instruction*. Unlike the mode instruction, the command instruction can be issued to the 8251 any time during its operation. The command instruction provides other facilities for controlling the operation of the 8251, and its format is shown in Figure 7-34.

With reference to Figure 7-34, bit positions 0 (TxEN) and 2 (RxE) enable the transmitter and receiver sections of the 8251, respectively. These bits must be set to a logic 1 in the command instruction if the 8251 is to receive and transmit serial data. Bit position 4 (ER) can be used to reset the error flags of the status word if an error condition occurred during serial data transmission. Bit position 3 (SBRK) is used to interrupt data transmission over the TxD line by forcing it to a logic 0. Finally, bit position 6 (IR) is used to generate an internal reset to the 8251. This allows the 8251 to accept another mode instruction without having to provide a physical hardware reset to the MPU. The other bits in the command instruction are used in the synchronous mode and for more sophisticated handshaking techniques. Thus the basic command instruction required for normal operation of the 8251 is 00010101 (15H).

Assuming that the 8251 is connected to the MPU as shown in Figure 7-28, the following sequence of instructions can be used to program the 8251 for subsequent serial data transmissions:

```
MVI    A,0F9H    ; Mode instruction
OUT    03H       ; To 8251 control port
MVI    A,15H     ; Command instruction
OUT    03H       ; To 8251 control port
```

Assuming that the 8251 has been reset (externally or internally), the first two instructions supply the mode instruction to the 8251, and the next two instructions supply the command instruction to the 8251.

Figure 7-35 illustrates the complete interface among the 8251, the MPU, and an external serial I/O device. The circuit in Figure 7-35 is basically an extension of Figure 7-28 and includes the support circuitry for a basic serial interface. Notice in Figure 7-35 that a baud-rate generator has been added to supply the clocks for the $\overline{\text{TxC}}$ and $\overline{\text{RxC}}$ inputs to the 8251. This baud-rate generator can be a simple arrangement of dividers to divide the 8085 CLK frequency down

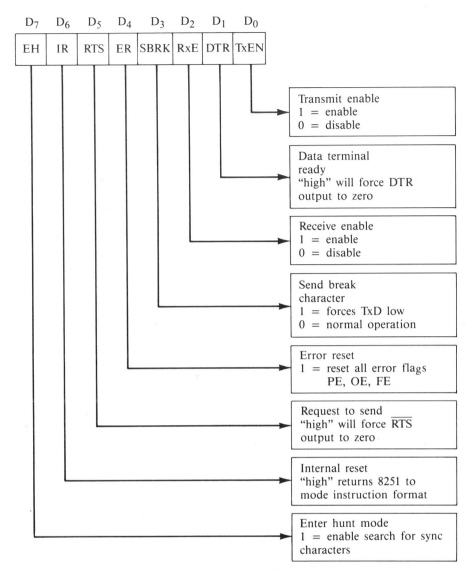

FIGURE 7-34. 8251 command instruction format. (Courtesy of Intel Corp.)

to the appropriate value, or it can be a separate square-wave oscillator. Also, the TxD and RxD lines to the 8251 require an interface to convert the TTL logic levels of the TxD and RxD lines to an RS232C voltage level.

The preceding four sections have discussed a basic serial asynchronous interface between the MPU and an external I/O device via the 8251 serial port. As mentioned before, the 8251 is a device capable of more sophisticated serial data communications in the synchronous mode and also of being connected to other I/O devices that require extensive handshaking. Even though these topics are beyond the scope of this chapter, a basic understanding of the concepts of serial data communications should allow the reader to experiment with other types of serial data interfaces.

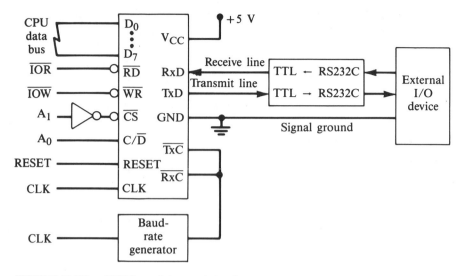

FIGURE 7-35. 8251 serial port interface.

Summary

Programmable chips have become common in microprocessor applications. The two programmable I/O chips discussed in this chapter illustrated some of these applications. The main advantage of having programmable chips in a system is in their ability to free the MPU from performing trivial tasks. Programmable chips also simplify the software and the hardware interface between the MPU and an external I/O device. These programmable chips are often thought of as "dedicated processors" designed to perform a particular task without elaborate intervention from the main processor.

This chapter dealt with the concepts of operation and applications of two programmable I/O chips, the 8251 and the 8255. There is a variety of other programmable chips dedicated to perform other functions for disk controlling, arithmetic processing, DMA/interrupt controlling, and so on. The concepts developed in this chapter can be applied to almost any type of programmable chip.

REVIEW QUESTIONS AND PROBLEMS

1. Using the architecture of Figure 7-1, explain generally how programmable chips function.

2. Briefly describe each pin (or pin grouping) listed in the table of Figure 7-3.

3. Determine the control word for

(a) Port A to be mode 0 input port with port B serving as a mode 1 output port. Port C is to be an input port.

(b) Port A to operate in a mode 2 fashion with ports B and C as mode 0 output ports.

4. Explain the various functions of pins PC_7–PC_0 for each mode of operation.

5. In detail explain handshaking relative to an 8255 port. Give examples of the pins involved for both input and output.

6. Describe the timing diagram of Figure 7-7(b).

7. For a mode 1 operation there are two control words that must be programmed into the 8255. Explain the purpose of each control word.

8. Use an 8255 to replace the row-scan latch and column latch of Figure 6-6. Explain your design.

9. Modify the program of Figure 6-18 to accommodate the hardware modification of Problem 8.

10. Using an 8255, add three I/O ports to the system of Figure 4-7. Ports A and B are to be output ports, and port C is to function as an input port (mode 0). Write appropriate instructions to program the 8255 and programs to service the ports.

11. Discuss the advantages and disadvantages of serial versus parallel data communications.

12. What is the difference between half-duplex and full-duplex data communications?

13. What is the main reason for having a status readback feature in a serial port? How does the $C/\overline{D}$ line accomplish this?

14. A serial port has the RxRDY bit at position 6 and the TxRDY bit at position 2 (refer to Figure 7-23). A logic 1 indicates a not-ready condition, and a logic 0 indicates a ready condition. Develop the CONIN, CONOUT, and CONSTS subroutines for the port. Assume that the data port is 10H and that the status port is 11H.

15. What is the baud rate? What is the purpose of the baud-rate factor provided by the 8251? Why must two serial devices communicate at the same baud rate?

16. What factors set up a serial data protocol? Discuss each factor. Why must two serial devices communicate with the same protocol?

17. Draw a timing diagram of the transmission of the ASCII character 'W', with odd parity and 2 stop bits. Repeat with even parity.

18. Describe the four operations of the 8251 USART.

19. Program the 8251 USART for the following protocol: 7 data bits, odd parity, 1 stop bit, ×1 baud-rate factor.

CHAPTER 8

Software Development: Techniques and Tools

Introduction

In almost every application of computers, whether they be micros, minis, or mainframes, the role of software development and related techniques is becoming exceedingly important. The objective of a computer's software is to make the hardware perform specified tasks. These tasks range from simple events such as monitoring lights and switches to more sophisticated tasks such as time sharing and data processing. As the tasks to be performed by the computer increase in complexity, so does the software, which leads to an insatiable demand for software development "tools" that can be used as an aid in program design.

Software development tools cannot be used efficiently without an understanding of the proper techniques. Just as one finds it difficult to tune the engine of an automobile without understanding how the electrical system works, in software development it is difficult to design efficient programs without having a good idea of the various techniques available. By using the proper techniques in designing a computer program, it is often easier to choose the appropriate software development tool that will lead to the generation of memory and speed-efficient program code.

The software development process can be broken down into five steps, from a definition of the problem to the final implementation of the computer program.

In many cases these steps can be combined or further broken down to suit the problem at hand. The following steps should, however, serve as a guide to the development of typical application programs.

1. *Problem recognition:* Before a solution can be found to a problem, the programmer must determine whether the problem can best be solved by means of a computer program. All problems cannot be solved by a computer, and in many cases a computer ''solution'' to a problem may even complicate matters further. This phase is thus a screening process used to recognize the existence of a problem, define the problem, and then determine whether the problem is best solved by a computer.

2. *Determining a method:* Once the problem has been screened and it has been deemed suitable for solution by a computer, the next phase is a search for the best method of solution (algorithm) to the problem. At this stage, the programmer must examine all the alternatives and select the method that is most efficient and economical. This stage selects not only the best algorithm to solve the problem but also the best programming language to fit the algorithm.

3. *Implementing the method:* The method of solution to the problem is usually broken down into one or more flowcharts or flow diagrams. These diagrams describe each stage in the implementation of the solution and consider the logic used in the method of solution. Flowcharts also allow the programmer to structure the solution in a logical manner, thus making it much easier to follow during program development and testing. Thus flowcharts make the solution to the problem more ''computer oriented'' than ''human oriented.''

4. *Coding from the flowchart:* The flowchart often provides a clear picture of the solution to the problem from the programming viewpoint. The process of translating a flowchart to a program is therefore much easier than if the program were to be constructed without a flowchart. The coding phase simply uses a sequence of instructions to the computer to satisfy the logic of the flow diagram. This phase is the actual implementation of the solution to the problem—the development of the program.

5. *Testing and debugging:* After the program has been completely implemented, it must be checked for correctness. During this phase, existing flaws as well as potential flaws in the program may be revealed. These flaws can exist in the algorithms that make up the program or can be caused by logical errors in the flowchart or possibly syntax errors made during the program implementation phase. The testing of a program thus involves exercising the program, exposing hidden flaws, and correcting these flaws. The process of finding hidden flaws in a program is known as *debugging* and often a programmer uses various tools to aid in the debugging process.

In the five phases of software development, the programmer must develop the right techniques for efficient program design and must have the right tools available for efficient implementation, testing, and debugging of the program.

8-2

Algorithms and Flowcharts

An *algorithm* is a term used to describe a set of procedures by which a given result is obtained; it is therefore a method of solution. A *flowchart* is a graphical representation for the definition, analysis, or solution of a problem, in which symbols are used to represent various operations, such as processing, I/O, decisions, and interrupts. Both algorithms and flowcharts allow programmers to work their way through the solution of a problem in an organized manner and to visualize the potential and existing flaws in the solution. Creation of an algorithm and/or flowchart is usually the first step in the development of a computer program.

Consider the task of designing a program to move a block of data from one area of memory to another. The block move would have to be conducted on a byte-to-byte basis; in other words, a byte would have to be moved from the source block to the destination block repeatedly until the entire process were completed. A general-purpose algorithm for this example would be as follows:

Step 1. Get a data byte from the source block.
Step 2. Put the byte into the destination block.
Step 3. See if all bytes have been moved. If so, stop. Otherwise, go to step 1.

A more specific version of the same algorithm would be

Step 1. Initialize a pointer to the starting address of the source block.
Step 2. Initialize a pointer to the starting address of the destination block.
Step 3. Initialize a count for the number of bytes to be moved.
Step 4. Get a byte from the source block.
Step 5. Put the byte into the destination block.
Step 6. Set the source pointer to the next byte.
Step 7. Set the destination pointer to the next byte.
Step 8. Subtract one from the count (decrement).
Step 9. Check the count. If the count is zero, stop. Otherwise, go to step 4.

Notice that in its first form, the algorithm could be implemented on almost any computer's instruction set. In other words, it was so generalized that it did not give specific details on how the move was to be performed. The second form was much more specific and implied the use of index registers. Thus the second form of the algorithm could be implemented only on a computer that had indexing capabilities. A third and final form of the same algorithm would narrow down the solution to the specific computer being used, as follows:

Step 1. Initialize RP H&L to the starting address of the source block.
Step 2. Initialize RP D&E to the starting address of the destination block.
Step 3. Initialize register B to the number of bytes to be moved.
Step 4. Move the data from the address specified by H&L to register A.
Step 5. Exchange the contents of RP H&L with D&E.
Step 6. Move the data from register A to the address specified by RP H&L.
Step 7. Exchange the contents of RP H&L with D&E.
Step 8. Increment the value of H&L.
Step 7. Increment the value of D&E.
Step 8. Decrement the value of register B.
Step 9. Check register B. If register B is zero, stop. Otherwise, go to step 4.

The final version of the algorithm is now so specific that it can be implemented only on an 8080/8085 (or compatible) microprocessor-based microcomputer. Also notice the relative ease of constructing a program once the algorithm has been written. The program to implement the following algorithm would be as follows:

```
        LXI  H,SOURCE      ; Source address to H&L
        LXI  D,DEST        ; Destination address to D&E
        MVI  B,COUNT       ; Reg B = Count
LOOP:   MOV  A,M           ; Get a source byte
        XCHG               ; Exchange pointers
        MOV  M,A           ; Put byte into destination
        XCHG               ; Exchange pointers
        INX  H             ; Point to next source byte
        INX  D             ; Point to next dest byte
        DCR  B             ; Count down
        JNZ  LOOP          ; Continue if not done
        HLT                ; Else, stop
```

A flowchart is a graphical technique of representing an algorithm. The first method used statements as steps in developing the solution to the problem; the flowchart uses symbols to describe the various steps to the solution. A list of the standard flowchart symbols is presented in Appendix C.

There are basically three types of flowcharts used to represent an algorithm. The first type is called a *general flowchart* (shown in Figure 8-1) and is used to describe the solution in a general form. The second type is the *algorithmic-*

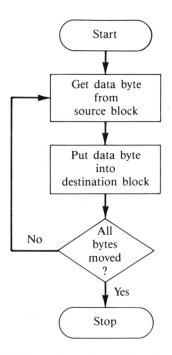

FIGURE 8-1. General flowchart for a block-move algorithm.

level flowchart (Figure 8-2), which describes the solution in specific steps but is still generalized in terms of the actual instructions to be used. The third type is the *instruction-level flowchart* (Figure 8-3), which expands on each step of the solution process by including specific instructions. Obviously, it is easiest to construct a program from the instruction-level flowchart. At this stage it

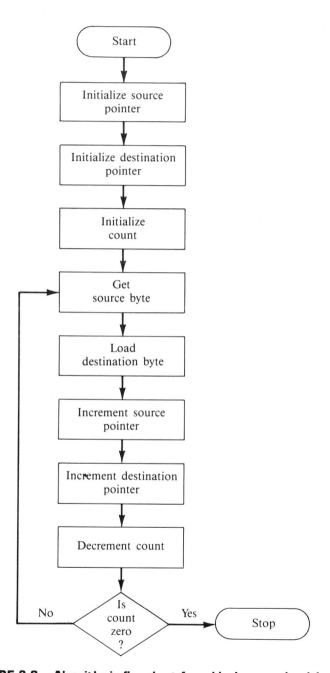

FIGURE 8-2. Algorithmic flowchart for a block-move algorithm.

should be noted that even though the instruction-level flowchart greatly simplifies the implementation of a program, because it is so specific, it can become fairly complex when representing rather large programs. For this reason, instruction-level flowcharts are often eliminated during the development of fairly complex programs.

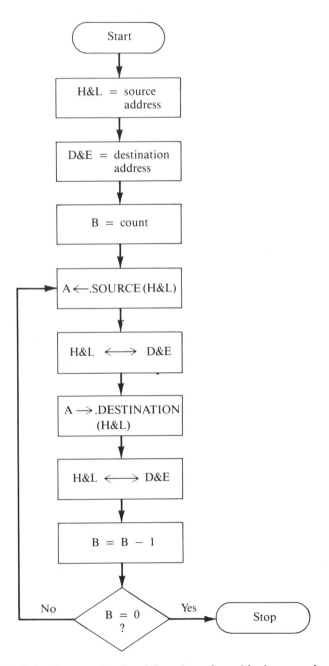

FIGURE 8-3. Instruction-level flowchart for a block-move algorithm.

Notice that the flowcharts shown in Figures 8-1 through 8-3 correspond closely to the three algorithms described before. The difference lies in the graphic representation of the algorithmic steps and decisions that are apparent in the flowcharts. This graphic representation makes it easier for the programmer to view the flow of the program.

In developing algorithms before the program is constructed, one can see existing and potential flaws in the solution process, as the steps in the algorithms are in plain English rather than in computer instructions. The logical process in developing a method of solution to a particular problem is to start with a general-purpose algorithm, expand that to individual steps (algorithmic level), include specifics in each step (instructional level), and then write the program. Depending on the experience of the programmer, he or she may wish to skip one or more steps in the process. It should be remembered, however, that algorithms aid the programmer not only in designing a solution to a problem but also in documenting the programmer's work. It is much easier for an observing person to read through algorithms before looking at the final program than to try to interpret the program directly. Also note that the comments in the final program correspond closely to the algorithms, thereby allowing one to understand easily how the program works.

The preceding example illustrated the use of algorithms for a typical assembly language program. It should be noted, however, that algorithms are not limited to assembly language programs. As will be seen later, algorithms can also be used to develop higher-level programs and in many cases aid the programmer in deciding which programming language to use.

8-3

Structure

In the approach to good program design known as *structured programming,* programs are designed hierarchically from the top down, that is, from the main program to the lowest-level subprograms. When done properly, the resulting algorithm structures are easy to understand, debug, and modify.

When a program is designed in a ''top-down'' manner, it is developed in a series of successive stages. The first stage, usually called the *main program,* implements the logic of the program at the top (highest) level. In this stage the details of program are usually ignored, and only the flow of the program at the highest level is considered. Subsequent stages in the program are used to refine the description of the flow at the main program level by including the actual details. These stages may also reference lower-level stages for further refinement of the details. The hierarchical stages in the program are usually implemented as *subroutines,* each dedicated to performing a single task or series of tasks. The main program is thus simply a series of CALLS to lower-level subprograms.

For example, consider a program that is to read a list of data bytes from an input port, sort the data bytes in a predetermined order, and output the sorted data bytes one at a time to an output port. The main program to implement this specification can simply be a sequence of three CALL instructions:

```
CALL GET
CALL SORT
CALL PUT
```

Notice that the main program calls three lower-level subroutines, GET, SORT, and PUT, in the right sequence. Also notice that the details of getting the data (GET), sorting the data (SORT), and outputting the data (PUT) are left out of the main program. The three subroutines refine the specifications by including the actual code to perform the task.

The GET subroutine reads the data from the input port into a sequence of memory locations. The GET subroutine can call another lower-level subroutine to do the actual input from the hardware device. The SORT subroutine then sorts the data in the previously filled memory locations. Finally, the PUT subroutine is called to output the sorted contents of the memory locations to the output device; as before, the actual output to the hardware device can be done by a calling a lower-level subroutine. The actual implementation of this specification will be presented in a subsequent chapter.

Notice that when a program is structured in a top-down hierarchical design, it is easier to view the flow of the program and easier to debug. Each level in the program can be tested and debugged independently, allowing for quicker diagnostic and development time. The lower-level subroutines can also be used over and over again in other application programs and often become utility subroutines. When an application program is designed using this structure, and the application program uses previously developed and tested utility subprograms, the application program is much easier to debug, as problems usually lie at the top level, where the code is in its simplest form. The advantages of designing structured programs will be seen in examples in later chapters.

Another case of a structured program is a *menu-driven application*. For example, consider an application program that constantly monitors the data from a keyboard. Upon receiving the key value, a certain action is performed depending on the key value; the keyboard is then monitored again for another key. The following table illustrates the functions performed, depending on certain key values.

Key	Function
A	Turn on assembly line
B	Turn off assembly line
C	Turn on oven
D	Turn off oven
E	Turn on alarm
F	Turn off alarm
G	Display oven temperature
H	Display parts count

The program is said to be menu driven because, depending on the selection of one key in the list of key values (menu), the program will perform an operation based on that selection. The general flowchart shown in Figure 8-4 represents the solution to the problem.

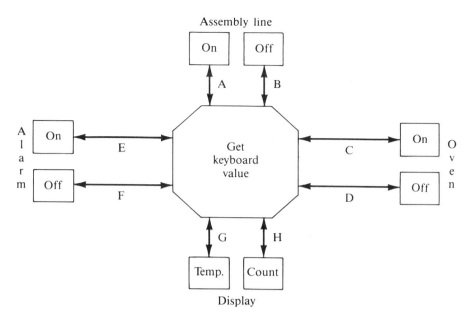

FIGURE 8-4. Menu-driven application program.

When actually implementing the algorithm, the program can be structured into one main program that monitors the value obtained from the keyboard and lower-level subroutines that implement the action to be performed when a particular command is received. On completion of each subroutine, control is returned to the main program. In Figure 8-4, the central octagon represents the main program, and each arrow emanating from the octagon represents a subroutine that will implement a certain action, depending on the key value obtained from the keyboard. If, for example, one of the specified functions does not work as intended, the problem is immediately narrowed down to the subroutine that implements that function. This eliminates the possibility of errors in other parts of the program.

Clarity of program structure offers many benefits to the programmer. When the structure of the program reflects the structure of the underlying algorithm, the program immediately becomes easier to write, debug, modify, and understand. Note that a nicely designed algorithm may be completely obscured if the programmer forces it into an unnatural mold.

8-4

Assemblers

An *assembler* is one of the most powerful tools used in developing microcomputer instruction code. An assembler is a program that translates instruction mnemonics and symbols into machine code for execution by the microcomputer. Note that an assembler is a program and not a piece of hardware.

The input to the assembler can be a sequence of program instructions written in mnemonic form: for example, the block-move program discussed previously. The output of the assembler is the sequence of bytes in binary machine code (represented in decimal, hexadecimal, or octal), which represents the operation codes and operands of each instruction in the correct sequence, as well as the address at which each group of bytes resides.

The input to the assembler is referred to as the *source code,* and the output of the assembler is referred to as the *object code*. The process by which the source code is translated into object code is called *assembly*. The software development tool that does the assembly is the assembler.

In previous examples, many programs were hand assembled. In other words, the program was written in mnemonics, and then the machine code for each mnemonic was derived from a list supplied by the microprocessor manufacturer and assembled into a sequence of machine instructions for execution by the processor. The obvious reason for using mnemonics in writing a program is that they are much easier to remember (hence the term *mnemonic*) than is the actual binary or hexadecimal representation of the machine code. For example, the instruction MOV A,M tells the programmer much more than does "01111110" or "7E."

Hand assembly is best suited for application programs that are fairly small and contain few program transfer instructions, such as JMPs and CALLs. However, when the size of the program is relatively large, hand assembly can become rather tedious and time-consuming. Also, if any changes have to be made in the hand-assembled program, all the program transfer instructions must be adjusted to reflect those changes. With an assembler, the process is automatic. The disadvantage of hand assembly was observed during the construction of the various example programs illustrated in previous chapters.

When using an assembler, changes in the program are made much more easily. All one has to do is make the appropriate modifications in the source code (the program written in mnemonics) and reassemble the program by using the assembler. More will be said about this in Chapter 9.

Currently, there is a variety of assemblers being supported for microcomputers. The two basic types of assemblers are the resident and cross assemblers. *Resident assemblers* are programs that reside on the microcomputer being used (the "target" microcomputer). In other words, an 8085-based microcomputer system can have a resident assembler that assembles programs for execution by the machine. A *cross assembler,* on the other hand, does not reside on the target microcomputer, but on another host computer system. The machine code generated by the cross assembler cannot be executed by the host computer. For example, a large mainframe Univac computer can have an 8085 assembler as part of its library. The assembler is capable of assembling 8085 programs, but the code generated by the assembler cannot be executed by the Univac (remember that each computer has a unique instruction set) as the Univac does not "recognize" 8085 machine code. The Univac can also have a resident assembler that takes programs written in Univac instructions, assembles them, and then submits the code to the computer for execution. Thus the principal difference between resident and cross assemblers is in the execution of the machine code generated.

Two other types of assemblers, absolute assemblers and relocatable assemblers, will be discussed in Chapter 9 and 10. In brief, an *absolute assembler* creates an object file that has *absolute* address references; that is, once the object file is created, it is ready to be loaded into the computer for execution at the address at which it was assembled. *Relocatable assemblers,* on the other hand, create object files that have *relative* addresses that are made absolute by a special program called a locator (discussed in a later section). The advantages of using such an assembler will be seen in following sections and chapters. Many of the assemblers discussed in this section have macro capabilities, which greatly aid in program development. *Macros* are relatively small segments of code that superficially allow the programmer to expand the instruction set of the microcomputer. These are called *macro assemblers* and will be discussed in great detail in Chapter 11. Many of the new assemblers currently available integrate absolute and relative assembly and macro capabilities into one package, thus allowing the user enormous flexibility in program design.

8-5

Compilers

Compilers are similar to assemblers in the function they perform. Both assemblers and compilers are translators. That is, they accept as input source code in the form of program instructions and translate it into object code in the form a machine can recognize. The object code generated by the compiler and assembler are for all practical purposes identical and indistinguishable. The significant difference between assemblers and compilers lies in the source code.

As mentioned in the preceding section, the source code of an assembler is primarily in the form of mnemonic program instructions. The assembly language programmer must have a fairly proficient knowledge of the processor to write such a program. Such a program is usually referred to as a *low-level program,* as the programmer has to construct intricate code to instruct the microprocessor at its lowest level. When programmers write programs in an upper-level language, they usually do not have to know the minute details of the microcomputer's hardware, such as registers, memory map, I/O map, and so on. The program is constructed by using "English-like" instructions called *statements,* which are passed on to the compiler as input. The compiler then translates these statements into machine code.

Assembly-level programs are machine oriented, whereas compiler-level languages are task oriented. Only a person who is experienced with the 8085 microprocessor would have an idea of what the assembly language program does. On the other hand, for the compiler version even a nonprogrammer could get a general idea of the program's function simply by looking at the overall program structure. Thus it can be concluded that compiler-level languages or, more specifically, upper- or higher-level languages are easier to write and easier to understand and therefore easier to debug.

The main disadvantage of using an upper-level language is that the programmer has absolutely no control over the object code generated by the compiler.

The code generation phase of the compiler is usually "built in" and cannot be influenced by program statements. This often leads to the generation of bulky code that is inefficient in terms of memory requirements as well as execution speed. This fact is understandable considering the tremendous task the compiler has to perform during the recognition phase. More will be said about compiler operation in Chapter 12.

Like assemblers, there are two basic types of compilers: *resident compilers* and *cross compilers*. The differences between the two are similar to the differences between resident and cross assemblers. With the advent of more sophisticated algorithms and new programming techniques, we now have efficient compilers called *optimizing compilers* that produce object code comparable to that of an assembly language program. The addition of new upper-level languages has also made it easier to write complex programs and to implement complex algorithms. Some of the newer compilers allow the user to integrate assembly language routines in the main sequence of program statements, thus allowing speed-critical program segments to operate more efficiently. Finally, the use of assembler–compiler–interpreter (to be shown later) combinations in software design has made the task of program development much easier than it had previously been.

8-6

Linkers and Locators

As mentioned previously, many resident compilers and assemblers create object code without any absolute addresses. The addresses within the code are all referenced to one memory location (usually zero) and are therefore termed *relative*. Because of this feature, the object code now becomes *relocatable*. In other words, if specific addresses are inserted into the relative object code, it can be moved to any memory location for execution. For absolute object code, it is not possible to execute a program at a memory location other than that specified during assembly. To do so would mean reassembling the source code at another specified memory location and obtaining new object code referenced to the new memory location. This could be quite time-consuming!

The function of the *locator* is to accept the relocatable object code as input, insert absolute address references (at a program base address specified by the user), and create absolute object code ready for execution. The advantage of using a scheme such as this can be illustrated by an example. A software manufacturer wants to sell an assembly language program to users of different types of computer systems (that is, the same microprocessors but different memory arrangement schemes). The manufacturer does not want to release the source code for the program, as some of the algorithms are considered to be proprietary information, but customizing the object file for each customer's memory map would be expensive. The solution to this problem is to supply the program in relocatable object code, so that each user could use a locator to relocate the program at a desired memory location.

To illustrate the utility of a *linker,* consider the following example. Assume that a programmer finds that an application program design is best accomplished by using a compiled, high-level language. However, certain parts of the design are speed critical and are most efficiently implemented in assembly language. Using a special tool called a linker, the programmer can write the application program in both an upper-level language and assembly language, obtain relocatable object code from the output of the assembler and compiler, and "link" the modules into one relocatable object code. The locator can then be used to locate the program referenced to a specified memory location.

Linking is also done with code generated by assembly language subprograms or modules. In many instances, a programmer uses various utility routines during program development. These utility routines (as the name suggests) are useful algorithms that can be used for a variety of applications. When using the conventional scheme in assembly language programming, whenever a utility is used in an application program, it must be included in the program as part of the source code. Using a relocatable assembler and a linker, the programmer references these utilities as they are needed without being concerned about including them in the source code. A *utility library* containing the utility routines in relocatable form is then constructed. Finally, the linker is used to link the application program to the utility library and to include the required utility modules in the final object code. Once the utility library has been constructed, it can be used repeatedly for different application programs.

Thus the primary function of the linker is to combine or link various modules of relocatable object code (usually subroutines) into a single program. Using a scheme such as this, a programmer can use a combination of many types of languages in developing a program. In many cases the linking and locating process is combined. Such a program is called a *linkage editor*.

8-7

Interpreters

Like compilers, *interpreters* are used with upper-level programming languages. The main difference between compilers and interpreters is that in interpreters, no object code is generated. An interpreter is usually coresident with the user's program. Each statement in the user's program is interpreted into machine code and then executed immediately by the computer. This means that the interpreter is part of any program the user writes. In contrast, a program that is compiled can run independently of the compiler; once the object code is created by the compiler, its function is over and it is no longer needed during the execution of the user's program. An interpreter works together with the user's program and provides the necessary translation and execution for the user's program statements. Because the user's program always has to be coresident with the interpreter, the combination requires a lot of memory space and is considerably slower than a compiled program. The primary advantage of using an interpreter is that no compilation is necessary. The program can be written, executed, tested, and debugged "on the spot." A compiled program, on the other hand, must be recompiled every time the source code is modified. Thus the important features to remember about interpreters are extremely fast development time, very slow execution time, and very large memory requirements.

Often the software development process requires testing and debugging the program using an interpreter. Once the bugs have been removed, the program is compiled into object code, which allows the final program to contain less development overhead, faster execution speed, and lower memory requirements.

8-8

Simulators and Dynamic Debuggers

Often when a programmer develops a program on a computer system other than the computer system for which the program is being developed, he or she faces the problem of testing and debugging the program. In such cases the program's object code is usually derived from the output of a cross assembler or cross compiler and thus cannot be executed on the host machine. In such cases a development tool called a *simulator* is used.

A simulator simulates the operation of the target computer system by tracing the contents of the microprocessor registers after each instruction is executed. Additional facilities provided by the simulator sometimes include the ability to alter the CPU's registers, the interrogation of I/O ports and memory locations, the calculation of instruction cycles, the breakpoints for stopping the program at critical locations, and the simulation of interrupts. Thus using the simulator, the programmer can detect the existing and/or potential flaws in the program before it is actually implemented on the target processor.

The main problem with simulators is that they do not execute a program in "real time." Because the simulator is usually resident on a different computer system, the instruction trace is conducted in conjunction with this computer's characteristics. As a result, precise simulation of interrupts and other speed-critical programs is practically impossible using a simulator. To conduct such testing, a tool is needed that is resident on a computer system with a microprocessor that is the same as the microprocessor on the target computer.

A *dynamic debugger* or dynamic debugging tool (DDT) is similar to a simulator. That is, it provides the programmer with the means to test and diagnose a program before it is actually implemented on the target microprocessor. A dynamic debugger resides on a computer system that contains the same microprocessor as the target system. This allows a real-time trace of each instruction being executed, and therefore a DDT can be used to test programs containing interrupt service routines and speed-critical segments. Program diagnostics is done with the maximum amount of accuracy when using a dynamic debugger, as the program is actually being executed by the development microcomputer.

8-9

Operating Systems

An *operating system* is the primary means of accessing the computer's hardware and software resources. As the name suggests, an operating system allows the user to "operate" the computer system. Operating systems are usually a combination of various software modules that give the user an extended repertoire of commands and facilities to use the computer system. The facilities of an operating system range from the most primitive, such as in a monitor, to the sophisticated facilities provided by disk operating systems (DOSs).

A *monitor* is an operating system in its most elementary form. The size of the monitor is relatively small (1 to 2 kilobytes), and therefore usually resides in ROM. Monitors are most commonly found on microcomputer development systems and development kits with limited resources. A typical monitor allows the user to load a program into memory (usually RAM), display and modify selected memory locations, display and modify the CPU registers, set program breakpoints, query I/O ports, and execute programs at a specified location. These facilities allow the user to develop relatively simple programs as well as to access the (rather limited) resources of the computer.

Some computer systems (particularly the expensive ones) have mass-storage hardware such as disks. This allows for the implementation of advanced software facilities. In such systems, the main piece of software that controls the entire hardware and software resources of the computer is called the *disk operating system*. The disk operating system is responsible for managing the files stored on disk, bringing various programs from disk into main memory (RAM), executing the programs, and giving the user a "transparent" interface to the hardware. When the user communicates through a transparent interface such as a disk operating system, he or she usually does not need to know much about the hardware environment, which allows the system to be used by people who do not know much about the specifics of the hardware.

There is a fine line between the exact definition of a monitor and a disk operating system. Many disk operating systems are called monitors, and many monitors provide some of the sophisticated facilities of a disk operating system. There are many types of operating systems. Disk operating systems usually provide assemblers, compilers, interpreters, dynamic debuggers, and text editors to create and edit program source code. Monitors are much more limited in the facilities they offer, although all operating systems enable the user(s) to access the computer's resources through software. Operating systems are divided into two types: single user and multiuser. As the names suggest, *single-user* operating systems allow only one user to use the processor at a time; *multiuser* operating systems use sophisticated hardware and software schemes for the simultaneous processing of multiple users. Many single- and multiuser operating systems provide *multitasking* facilities, which allow the processor to process simultaneously many programs (tasks). Multitasking facilities in an operating system often take maximum advantage of the CPU's processing speed and minimize the amount of "idle time" by having the CPU perform other tasks.

8-10

Summary

This chapter introduced the programming techniques used in software development and the various software development tools available to the user. Because each topic is a course in itself, the next few chapters will be an in-depth study of some of the topics covered in this chapter. It is hoped that this will allow the microcomputer programmer to develop a good programming style and allow him or her to make the right decisions when selecting the many software development tools currently available.

REVIEW QUESTIONS AND PROBLEMS

1. Write a block-move program (similar to the one discussed in Section 8-2) to move a block of memory larger than 256 bytes. Start by constructing general, algorithmic, and instruction flowcharts and then develop the 8085 program.

2. What is the function of an assembler? Can a program be developed without the use of an assembler? Why?

3. What is the difference between resident and cross assemblers?

4. What is the difference between absolute- and relocatable-code-producing assemblers?

5. How does the operation of a compiler differ from the operation of an assembler?

6. Explain the differences between relocatable and absolute object code. Why must relocatable object code be located?

7. Explain some of the advantages of linkage.

8. How does the operation of an interpreter differ from the operation of a compiler?

9. What factors distinguish a simulator from a dynamic debugging tool (DDT)?

10. What is the purpose of having an operating system? Discuss the features of the different types of operating systems available.

CHAPTER 9

Introduction to Assembly Language Programming

9-1

Introduction

Chapter 8 introduced the reader to a software development tool called the assembler and also illustrated some of the advantages of using the assembler during the development of machine-language programs for the microprocessor. Some of the major advantages of using an assembler over hand assembling a program are particularly apparent during the development of extremely long programs. The probability of making an error during hand assembly is high. Furthermore, modifying a hand-assembled program, such as adding or deleting instructions, can be time-consuming, as almost all address references must be checked and modified to reflect any changes. Hand assembly is best suited for application programs that are fairly small and contain few program transfer instructions such as JMPs and CALLs and other address references.

To illustrate the disadvantage of hand assembling a program, consider the program example in Figure 9-1. The program is a simple 1-sec counter that counts sequentially from 00 to FF on a set of seven-segment LED displays. Note that the starting count of the program will depend on the contents of the accumulator before the program is executed. Also notice the address references in lines 3, 6, and 11.

LINE	ADDRESS	CODE	LABEL	MNEMONIC		COMMENTS
1	0000	D305	START:	OUT	05	; OUTPUT TO LED
2	0002	F5		PUSH	PSW	; SAVE COUNT
3	0003	CD0B00		CALL	DELAY	; DELAY 1 SECOND
4	0006	F1		POP	PSW	; RESTORE COUNT
5	0007	3C		INR	A	; COUNT = COUNT + 1
6	0008	C30000		JMP	START	; NEXT COUNT
7	000B	21FF01	DELAY:	LXI	H,01FF	; DELAY COUNT
8	000E	2B	D1:	DCX	H	; COUNT DOWN
9	000F	7C		MOV	A,H	; GET HIGH BYTE
10	0010	B5		ORA	L	; CHECK WITH LOW
11	0011	C20E00		JNZ	D1	; 1 SECOND UP ?
12	0014	C9		RET		; RETURN IF SO

FIGURE 9-1.

In order to modify the program in Figure 9-1 to force the count to start at 00, an instruction must be added to the program to clear the accumulator before its contents is sent to the output port. This is done by inserting an XRA A instruction as the first byte of the program. The modified program is shown in Figure 9-2. Note that all the other instructions have been shifted down by one memory location.

In Figure 9-2, notice that one change, the addition of the XRA A instruction, required that three address references in lines 3, 6, and 11 be changed to reflect the new values of the labels START, DELAY, and D1. Visualize the number of modifications that would have to be made to a similar program ten times longer with many more such address references!

When the programmer uses an assembler, minor and major modifications to a program are much easier to make, as all adjustments required are made automatically by the assembler. Because the development of a machine-language program often requires many modifications during testing and debugging, an assembler is a useful tool to aid the programmer in speeding up software de-

LINE	ADDRESS	CODE	LABEL	MNEMONIC		COMMENTS
	0000	AF		XRA	A	; CLEAR COUNT
1	0001	D305	START:	OUT	05	; OUTPUT TO LED
2	0003	F5		PUSH	PSW	; SAVE COUNT
3	0004	CD0C00		CALL	DELAY	; DELAY 1 SECOND
4	0007	F1		POP	PSW	; RESTORE COUNT
5	0008	3C		INR	A	; COUNT = COUNT + 1
6	0009	C30100		JMP	START	; NEXT COUNT
7	000C	21FF01	DELAY:	LXI	H,01FF	; DELAY COUNT
8	000F	2B	D1:	DCX	H	; COUNT DOWN
9	0010	7C		MOV	A,H	; GET HIGH BYTE
10	0011	B5		ORA	L	; CHECK WITH LOW
11	0012	C20F00		JNZ	D1	; 1 SECOND UP ?
12	0015	C9		RET		; RETURN IF SO

FIGURE 9-2.

velopment time, with greater accuracy, lower probability of errors, and consequently lower costs.

Chapter 8 also introduced the reader to two types of techniques used in assembly language software development: absolute and relocatable assembly. This chapter deals with microprocessor software development using an absolute-code-producing assembler. Note that the assembler described in this chapter deals with the operation of a typical 8080/8085 assembler. There is a variety of assemblers available for the 8080/8085 microprocessors whose operations and functions may differ slightly from the assembler described in this chapter. The objective of this chapter is therefore not to describe the operation of a specific assembler but to enforce the concepts used in assembly language software development.

Operation of the Assembler

The primary job of the assembler is translation. The assembler is a software development tool that takes a program written in mnemonics (often called the *assembly language program*) and converts it into code suitable for execution by the computer (often called the *machine language program*). This process of translation is called assembly. The assembler itself is a program written specifically to provide this translation. Figure 9-3 illustrates the function of the assembler in a block diagram.

The input to the assembler is the assembly language program called the *source file*. The source file contains the program written in mnemonics in a form specified by the rules of the assembler (as introduced in earlier chapters and to be studied in more depth in a later section). A typical source file for the program example in Figure 9-1 is shown in Figure 9-4.

Note that the program in Figure 9-4 looks similar (with a few exceptions to be seen later) to the first phase in the hand-assembly process. In other words, the program is written in mnemonic form with symbolic address references

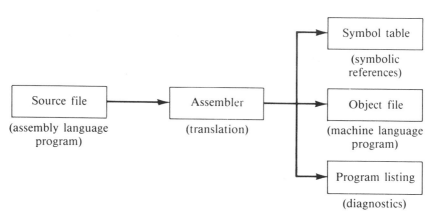

FIGURE 9-3. **Operation of the assembler.**

```
        ORG   0000H
START:  OUT   05H        ; Output to led
        PUSH  PSW        ; Save count
        CALL  DELAY      ; Delay 1 second
        POP   PSW        ; Restore count
        INR   A          ; Count = count + 1
        JMP   START      ; Next count
DELAY:  LXI   H,01FFH    ; Delay count
D1:     DCX   H          ; Count down
        MOV   A,H        ; Get high byte
        ORA   L          ; Check with low
        JNZ   D1         ; 1 second up?
        RET              ; Return if so

        END
```

FIGURE 9-4. Assembler source file.

before the code is assembled. This program is submitted to the assembler as the source file. The source file can be an area in memory or in most cases a file on disk. Once the source file is written, the programmer's task is complete.

From the source file written by the programmer the assembler translates each instruction and symbolic reference to machine code represented in hexadecimal. This machine language program is called the *object file*. For the program in Figure 9-4, the assembler would produce the machine language program shown in Figure 9-5.

The object file in Figure 9-5 is one of the outputs of the assembler after the source file has been translated. Besides the machine code for the instructions, the object file also contains other information (to be seen in Section 9-8), such as load addresses and checksums. However, by briefly scanning through the hexadecimal numbers in Figure 9-5, one can see that there is a close correspondence to the code assembled in Figure 9-1.

Most assemblers are *two-pass assemblers*, which means that the assembler goes through the assembly language program (source file) twice before the final machine code (object file) is generated. During the first pass through the source file, the assembler uses a *location counter* (not to be confused with the MPU's program counter) to count the number of bytes for each instruction. As each instruction is encountered, the value of the location counter is increased by one, two, or three, depending on the number of bytes required for the type of instruction scanned. If a symbolic address reference is encountered for a particular instruction, the value of the location counter is assigned to that symbol. When a complete pass is made through all the instructions, the assembler creates a *symbol table* that contains a list of symbols, such as symbolic address references, with their corresponding values.

```
:10000000D305F5CD0B00F13CC3000021FF012B7C93
:05001000B5C20E00C99D
:000000001FF
```

FIGURE 9-5. Assembler object file.

```
START    = 0000H
DELAY    = 000BH
D1       = 000EH
```

FIGURE 9-6. Assembler symbol table.

For example, in the source file in Figure 9-4, there are three symbolic address references—START, DELAY, and D1—in the program. The assembler counts each location starting with the first instruction and assigns a numeric address to each symbol. These symbols and their values are stored in a symbol table. For example, the symbol table for the program in Figure 9-4 is shown in Figure 9-6. When the assembler encounters the end of the source file, the first pass is complete, and the symbol table either is stored on a file on disk or is displayed on the computer screen.

The second pass of the assembler is dedicated to producing the machine language program. Each instruction in the program starting with the first is scanned and translated into its corresponding machine code. The technique used by the assembler is similar to the "look-up-table" approach used in hand assembly. When the assembler encounters an instruction with a symbolic operand, for example, CALL DELAY, the value of the symbol DELAY is obtained from the symbol table and assembled with the machine code for the CALL instruction.

As each line in the source file is assembled during the second pass, the assembler lists the address and the machine code produced for the instruction on the line. This results in another output, which gives the programmer a cross-reference of the mnemonics, the machine code, and the address at which each instruction will be stored in memory (called the load address). This is the *listing file* and is either stored on disk or displayed on the screen. The listing file for the program example in Figure 9-4 is similar to the final phase in a hand-assembled program and is shown in Figure 9-7.

Observe that the listing file is an exact duplicate of the source file but contains the machine code in hexadecimal for each instruction on the left-hand side,


```
                              ORG  0000H

0000   D305    START:  OUT  05H          ; Output to led
0002   F5              PUSH PSW          ; Save count
0003   CD0B00          CALL DELAY        ; Delay 1 second
0006   F1              POP  PSW          ; Restore count
0007   3C              INR  A            ; Count = count + 1
0008   C30000          JMP  START        ; Next count
000B   21FF01  DELAY:  LXI  H,01FFH      ; Delay count
000E   2B      D1:     DCX  H            ; Count down
000F   7C              MOV  A,H          ; Get high byte
0010   B5              ORA  L            ; Check with low
0011   C20E00          JNZ  D1           ; 1 second up?
0014   C9              RET               ; Return if so

0015                   END
```

FIGURE 9-7. Assembler listing file.

together with the load addresses. The listing is extremely useful during the testing and debugging of an assembly language program.

Syntax of the Assembly Language

Just as every spoken language has syntax rules that specify the arrangement of words in sentences, so does a computer programming language. Assembly language programs must conform to certain syntactical rules before they are submitted to the assembler for translation. These syntactical rules specify the manner in which a "vocabulary" of instruction operation codes and operands is written, the legal use of symbolic references, and the constraints of the language itself. A knowledge of these syntax rules often prevents frustrating errors generated during assembly.

When the programmer prepares an assembly language program for input to the assembler, program instructions are written sequentially and on separate lines; this form of coding was followed in hand assembly (in earlier chapters) and can be seen in the program example in Figure 9-4. During assembly, the assembler scans each line as three separate fields. These fields identify and separate symbolic address references (*labels*), instructions, and comments. For example, in Figure 9-4, the first line in the program can be divided into three fields, as follows:

```
START:  OUT 05H       ; Output to LED
label:  instruction   ; Comment field
```

The *label field* is an optional field and is used to reference symbolically a location in memory. Not every line in the program has to have a label field, as can be seen in Figure 9-4. Labels are used when the programmer wishes to refer to a particular location in the program, using a symbol rather than a numeric address. The labels used in assembly language programs can be alphanumeric but must start with an alphabetic character and cannot contain any spaces. The ":" (colon) used immediately following the label is not part of the label but is used to separate the label field from the instruction field. Such a symbol that is used to separate two fields is called a *delimiter*.

The *instruction field* contains an executable instruction and must be part of the MPU's instruction set. There is one exception to this, which will be seen in the next section. The instruction field contains the *operation code* and, in some cases for multibyte instructions, the *operand*. The op code and operand are separated from each other by one or more spaces.

The *comment field* is an optional field and is used to document each line in the program. The ";" (semicolon) character serves as a delimiter between the instruction field and the comment field. The assembler simply ignores anything written in the comment field and reproduces it verbatim in the listing file. Even though comments are optional, it is good programming practice to use a lot of comments during the development of assembly language programs, as they can be of aid during testing and debugging.

The assembler does allow some flexibility in constructing programs. For example, a label that references an instruction need not be placed on the same line as the instruction itself. Thus

```
START:
            OUT 05H   ; OUTPUT TO LED
```

would have the same meaning to the assembler as would one line containing all three fields.

Comments can also be isolated on single or multiple lines. It may be important to emphasize that whenever the assembler detects a ''; '' during the assembly process, it ignores everything to the end of the line. The major constraint in the syntax of the assembly language is that fields cannot be broken up into multiple lines.

9-4

Location Control

Before a programmer codes a program for input to an absolute-code-producing assembler, he or she must have an idea of the computer system's memory map. If the system has a RAM and ROM area, the exact boundaries of these areas must be known, so that the assembler can locate the machine language program at the right starting address. This starting address at which the first executable instruction of the program is located is also called the *base address* of the program. The base address of the program is specified in the program itself by means of an *assembler directive* (ORG).

A *directive* is an instruction to the assembler that directs the assembly process. These directives are also called *pseudo-operations* because they "look" like MPU instructions in the program but have absolutely no meaning to the MPU. The purpose of these directives is to control the operation of the assembler.

In Figure 9-4, the first line in the program is a directive to the assembler, instructing it to start assembling the program at location 0. This directive is called the *origin* directive and sets the value of the assembler's location counter to a specified value. Notice in Figure 9-7 that the listing file shows the address of the first byte assembled at location 0000. The assembler's location counter is initially always set at zero. The ORG directive is used to change its value. As each byte in the program is assembled, the value of the location counter is incremented sequentially until another ORG directive is encountered or the end of the program is reached.

An assembly language program can have many ORG directives. A typical example is in interrupt-driven programs as shown in Figure 9-8. The program in Figure 9-8 uses ORG directives to instruct the assembler to assemble appropriate jump instructions at the MPU reset location, and the RST 1 and 7 interrupt restart locations. The first ORG directive sets the assembler's location counter to zero. Note that because the assembler's location counter is initially set to zero, this directive is optional. The second ORG directive sets the location counter to 0008H and causes the assembler to locate the following three-byte

```
            ORG    0000H
            JMP    MAIN      ; Jump to main program
            ORG    0008H
            JMP    SERV1     ; Service for RST 1
            ORG    0038H
            JMP    SERV7     ; Service for RST 7
            ORG    1000H
MAIN:                       ; Main program starts
            .
            .
            .

SERV1:                      ; Service Routine
            .
            .
            .
```

FIGURE 9-8.   **Example of a program containing serveral ORG directives.**

jump instruction at 0008H. The third ORG directive is similar to the first but locates the following jump instruction at 0038H.

The ORG directives can also be used to separate the assembly language program into *segments*. In software, the area in memory where the program is stored is called the *code segment*. This area can be located in ROM if the application so demands, as it contains the program code itself as well as permanent (nonvariable) data. At this point it should be noted that the programmer must ensure that no temporary data storage is referenced to the code segment if this segment is to be placed in ROM. The area in memory where temporary data and stack data is stored is called the *data segment* (always RAM). The use of the ORG directive together with segment allocation will be seen along with other directives in Section 9-7 and Chapter 10.

The program in Figure 9-4 contains another directive included as the last line of the program. Although this directive has no relationship to location control, it is worth mentioning at this stage. The END directive signals the assembler to stop assembly. It identifies the logical END of the source file. When the assembler encounters the END directive, it terminates assembly. Anything placed after this directive does not exist for all practical purposes and will be ignored by the assembler. Also, in Figure 9-7 observe the value of the location counter at the end of assembly; its value is one greater than the address of the last byte assembled.

9-5

Symbols and Constants

The assembler recognizes five types of numeric *constants* used in operands or address references. These are binary (B), decimal (D), octal (Q), hexadecimal (H), and ASCII constants. When any of the first four types of constants are used in an assembly language program, the programmer must specify a base

(B, D, Q, or H) immediately following the constant. For example, in Figure 9-7, the instruction

```
LXI H,01FFH
```

caused the assembler to assemble a three-byte instruction as 21FF01: 21 was the op code for the LXI H instruction, and 01FFH was a numeric operand specified to be a hexadecimal number. If the following instruction were substituted,

```
LXI H,511D
```

the assembler would assemble the same code as before, as the constant 511 in decimal is 01FF in hexadecimal.

Similarly,

```
LXI H,777Q
```

and

```
LXI H,0000000111111111B
```

would be assembled into the same code, as

511 decimal = 01FF hexadecimal = 777 octal = 000000011111111 binary

If a base is not specified with a constant, the assembler will assume that the constant is a decimal number. For example, the code assembled for the instruction

```
LXI H,777
```

would be 210903, as 777 is assumed to be a decimal number and evaluates to 0309 hexadecimal. Refer to Appendix D for hexadecimal–decimal conversion tables.

Note that the instruction

```
LXI H,01FF
```

would cause the assembler to signal an error condition, as 01FF is an invalid decimal number.

Hexadecimal numbers that start with alphabetic characters such as FF03H, F2, and so on, must be preceded by a zero. This is because all labels and symbols start with an alphabetic character and can easily cause the assembler to confuse labels and symbols with hexadecimal constants. Thus the instruction LXI H,F200H would be invalid unless F200H were a label or symbol. However, if the programmer intended to load H&L with the constant F200H, the instruction LXI H, 0F200H would be valid.

ASCII constants are represented by ASCII graphic characters enclosed in single quotation marks. Any single ASCII graphic character enclosed in single quotation marks will cause the assembler to assemble its corresponding 7-bit ASCII code. For example, the instruction

```
MVI A,'E'
```

would assemble as 3E, the op code for the MVI A instruction, and 45, the 7-bit ASCII code of the graphic character 'E' (refer to Appendix B), which becomes the operand of the MVI instruction. Similarly, the instruction

```
LXI H,'12'
```

would assemble as 213231. The op code for LXI H is 21H, the ASCII code for "2" is 32H, and the ASCII code for "1" is 31H (note that the low-order byte is assembled first).

The assembly language allows identifiers called *symbols* to be used in place of constants anywhere in the program. Symbols are similar to labels. A *label* identifies a location in memory, whereas a symbol identifies a location in memory and/or a constant. As an example, consider the program example in Figure 9-7 rewritten with symbols and shown in Figure 9-9.

Figure 9-9 introduces another assembler directive, *equate*. The EQU or equate directive is used to assign a constant to a symbol. Like any assignment statement, the constant on the right-hand side of the EQU is assigned to the symbol on the left-hand side. The symbols LED and DCOUNT are assigned the values 05H and 01FFH, respectively, during the first pass of the assembler and the generation of the symbol table. Now during the second pass, whenever the assembler encounters any of the previously equated symbols, it assembles the symbols' assigned value.

```
                          ORG   0000H
0005  =        LED     EQU   05H          ; LED output port
01FF  =        DCOUNT  EQU   01FFH        ; 1 second delay count

0000  D305     START:  OUT   LED          ; Output to LED
0002  F5               PUSH  PSW          ; Save count
0003  CD0B00           CALL  DELAY        ; Delay 1 second
0006  F1               POP   PSW          ; Restore count
0007  3C               INR   A            ; COUNT = count + 1
0008  C30000           JMP   START        ; Next count

000B  21FF01   DELAY:  LXI   H,DCOUNT     ; Delay count
000E  2B       D1:     DCX   H            ; Count down
000F  7C               MOV   A,H          ; Get high byte
0010  B5               ORA   L            ; Check with low
0011  C20E00           JNZ   D1           ; 1 second up?
0014  C9               RET                ; Return if so
                       END
```

FIGURE 9-9.

The advantages of using symbols in place of constants are obvious in large programs in which a single constant is used over and over again. For example, assume that the program in Figure 9-7 were much larger in size and had many output instructions to port 05H. If for some reason the port number had to be changed to another value, all the OUT instructions in the program would have to have their operands changed. This could be time-consuming, and the chances of missing a few changes are great. However, equating the device number to a symbol as in Figure 9-9 would require that only the equate value be changed. On reassembling the program, the assembler would take care of changing all the OUT instruction operand values from 05H to another value. Symbols are also more descriptive than constants. In Figure 9-9, the instruction OUT LED "tells" a person inspecting the program more about what the output port 05H is than does the instruction OUT 05H.

In assembly language programs, arithmetic expressions can also be used together with or in place of symbols and constants. For example, if the program in Figure 9-9 had the line

                    DCOUNT   EQU   01FFH + 10H

the symbol DCOUNT would be assigned the value 020FH. Similarly, the directive

                    DCOUNT   EQU   256*2−1

would direct the assembler to evaluate the expression 256*2-1 = 511 = 01FFH and assign the value to the symbol DCOUNT.

Arithmetic expressions can also be used in operands of instructions. For example, if Figure 9-9 contained the instruction

                    OUT   LED + 3

the operand of the OUT instruction would be 05H + 3 = 08H. Similarly, the JNZ D1 instruction in Figure 9-9 could be replaced with JNZ DELAY + 3, as the label D1 will always evaluate to DELAY + 3 (as LXI H is a three-byte instruction). This eliminates having an extra label D1.

Once a symbol has been assigned a value by means of an EQU directive, its value is fixed and cannot be changed through another EQU directive at a later step in the program. However, the assembler recognizes another directive very similar to the EQU directive. The *set directive* (SET) can be used in place of the EQU directive and has exactly the same functions. The difference between the two is that a symbol defined with a SET directive can have its value changed any number of times in the program. Unlike the EQU directive, which operates during the first pass of the assembler, the SET directive operates during the second pass. Each time a SET directive that changes the value of a symbol is detected, the symbol-table entry is adjusted appropriately. SET directives are extremely useful when used with macros (discussed in Chapter 11).

The assembler has a special reserved symbol, "$," whose value is always equal to the current value of the location counter. Thus if a user-defined symbol is equated with the $, the symbol is assigned the current value of the location counter. For example, in Figure 9-9, if the directive

LAST   EQU $

were inserted just before the END directive, the symbol LAST would be assigned the value 0015H, which would be the current value of the location counter (that is, the value of the location counter after the RET instruction is assembled). If, for example, the directive

SIZE   EQU $-DELAY

were used in the same place in Figure 9-9, the symbol SIZE would evaluate to 0015H − 000BH = 000AH, the size in bytes of the DELAY subroutine. The $ symbol is extremely useful in string-size calculations, as will be seen in later programs.

Deciding whether to use constants or symbols or both in an assembly language program is left entirely up to the programmer. Although using plenty of symbols always makes good programming practice, there may be some situations when constants seem more appropriate. These situations will become evident in the course of the book and as the reader gains practice in understanding and writing assembly language programs.

9·6

Data Storage

As previously stated, the primary function of the assembler is to translate mnemonic instructions and symbolic references into machine code. Consequently, the machine code assembled is loaded into the computer for execution. In many software applications it is necessary to load into the computer's memory different types of data together with the program code. Examples of such applications are programs that require look-up tables, character string messages, and other forms of data that must be kept permanently (for example, in ROM) together with the machine instructions. The assembler must therefore give the programmer a technique by which these forms of data can be assembled together with the rest of the program. This is done by means of two *data storage directives:* the define byte (DB) and the define word (DW) directives.

For the 8251 microcomputer interface developed in Chapter 7, consider the following application program to print a message (character string) on the screen of the terminal connected to the 8251 USART. To implement this specification, a number of considerations have to be taken into account:

1. The message to be displayed on the screen has to be stored together with the program in ROM so that it is not lost when the system is shut down.
2. Each character in the message must be stored in its 7-bit ASCII code, as the terminal recognizes only this code.

3. The starting address of the first character in the message must be known so that the entire message is printed out.
4. The number of characters in the message must be known so that the program can stop when the entire message has been displayed.

The flowchart to implement this program specification is shown in Figure 9-10. The program to implement the flowchart of Figure 9-10 is shown in Figure 9-11 as the output listing file of the assembler.

With reference to Figure 9-11, observe the use of the DB directive to store the ASCII code for each character in the message immediately following the last instruction in the program. The label MESS is assigned the address of the first character in the message, and the length of the message is calculated by the assembler by subtracting the value of MESS with the current value of its

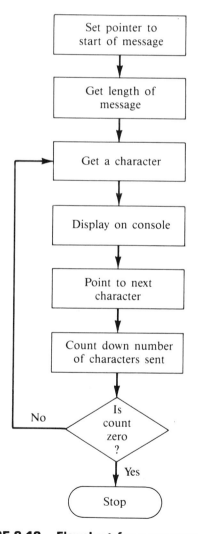

FIGURE 9-10. Flowchart for a message print routine.

```
0100                          ORG   0100H
                    ; MESSAGE PRINT PROGRAM
0100   210F01               LXI   H,MESS      ; Pointer to start of message
0103   060D                 MVI   B,LENGTH    ; Length of message
0105   4E       LOOP:       MOV   C,M         ; Get a character
U0106  CD0000               CALL  CONOUT      ; Display on console
0109   23                   INX   H           ; Point to next character
010A   05                   DCR   B           ; Count down # of chars sent
010B   C20501               JNZ   LOOP        ; Continue if count not zero
010E   76                   HLT               ; Else stop
                    ; MESSAGE STORAGE
010F   48454C   MESS:       DB    'HELLO TESTING'
0112   4C4F20
0115   544553
0118   54494E
011B   47
000D   =        LENGTH EQU   $-MESS
011C                        END
```

FIGURE 9-11. Message print program.

location counter (as discussed in Section 9-5). The result is assigned to the symbol LENGTH.

Referring to Figures 9-10 and 9-11 (note how the blocks in the flowchart of Figure 9-10 correspond to the comments in the program in Figure 9-11), the first instruction in the program sets RP H&L to the starting address of the message (MESS). The length of the message (LENGTH) is moved into register B; this will be used as a tally to keep track of how many characters have been displayed. The first character in the message is loaded into register C (preparation for the console output subroutine), and then CONOUT is called to send the character to the terminal. RP H&L is incremented to point to the next character in the message, the number of characters in the message is decremented (counted down to zero), and a test is made to see if the count has reached zero. If not, the next character will be loaded into register C, and the process will be repeated. The loop continues until all the characters in the message have been displayed, at which point the contents of register B is zero. The program then terminates.

Note that the assembler signaled an error condition during assembly by displaying a U on the left-hand side of the line containing the CALL to CONOUT. This error indicates that the address of the CONOUT subroutine is undefined, as the routine itself was not included as part of the program, and consequently, the assembler was not able to assemble the address operand of the CALL instruction. To ensure that the program is complete, the CONOUT subroutine (from Chapter 7) must be included in the program either before or after the DB directive.

The use of the DB directives to store data bytes does not have to be limited to ASCII constants or character strings but can contain any of the other numeric constants or symbols discussed in Section 9-5. For example,

$$DB\ 122,56H,326Q,'A','012'$$

would direct the assembler to assemble the following data:

$$7A,56,D6,41,30,31,32$$

at the current value of the location counter.

The DW directive is similar to the DB directive and is used to direct the assembler for data assembly. However, the DW directive is used to store 16-bit data instead of 8-bit data, as did the DB directive. The 16-bit data is stored least significant byte first, and this makes it ideal for the storage of addresses used by an application program.

A common application program used in many types of computer systems is called a *console command processor* (CCP). The function of the CCP is to get a single character from the console keyboard and interpret the character received as a command. The CCP must detect the command and branch off to a routine to implement the command—the *command implementing routine* (CIR). If an invalid command is entered, the CCP will branch off to a routine that prints an error message on the screen. The CCP is thus structured like the menu-driven program discussed in Chapter 8.

The flowchart of Figure 9-12 describes the operation of the CCP, and the program shown in Figure 9-13 implements the CCP. Notice that Figure 9-13 contains a look-up table consisting of DB and DW directives. The table has four sets of entries, each entry consisting of a DB directive that stores the valid command character and, immediately following, a DW directive that stores the address of transfer, on detection of that command. The program is designed to detect and implement any of the following four commands entered from the keyboard: A, Q, D, or X.

Because each three-byte entry in the table corresponds to one command, that is, one byte for the command character and two bytes for the address of the routine that implements the command, the number of commands is calculated by the assembler by the last EQU directive in Figure 9-13. The number of commands in the table is therefore the number of bytes in the table divided by 3, which in this case is four commands. Obviously, in this example the number 4 could be EQUated to the symbol NCMDS directly without requiring the assembler to do the calculation. But think of a situation in which the CCP has to be modified to recognize a few more commands. It would be quite easy to forget to change the NCMDS equate. Using this technique, any addition of table entries (addition of new commands) will automatically adjust the value of NCMDS. Note that additional commands can be added to the CCP's table simply by adding the command character and the address of the command implementing routine for each command.

With reference to Figures 9-12 and 9-13 (again notice the close correspondence between the flowchart and the program), RP H&L is set to point to the start of the command table "TABLE," and register B is loaded with a count of the number of commands. This count will be used to detect when the end of the table is reached. The console input routine (from Chapter 7) is called to get a command character from the terminal keyboard.

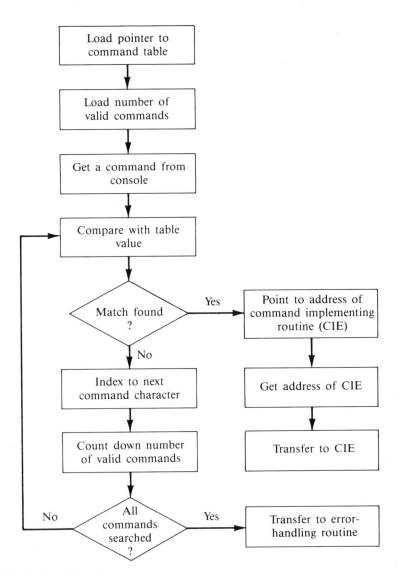

FIGURE 9-12. Flowchart for a console command processor.

On receiving the command character from the console, the character is compared with the first byte in the table. If a match is not found, RP H&L will be incremented three times to index over the address of the previous command implementing routine, and the next command character in the table will be compared with the character entered at the console. Each time through, the value of register B is decremented, to keep track of the number of commands searched. When the value of register B reaches zero, all the commands in the table have been searched, no match has been found, and control transfers to an error-handling routine labeled ERROR.

If a match is found during the search, control will transfer to the address "MATCH." Here, RP H&L is indexed to point at the CIR's low-order address. The low address is loaded into register E and the high address into register D,

```
00C8                    ORG    200
                ; Console command processor

00C8  21E400   CCP:     LXI    H,TABLE     ; Point to command table
00CB  0604              MVI    B,NCMDS     ; Number of valid commands
00CD  CDF000            CALL   CONIN       ; Get command from console
00D0  BE       SEARCH:  CMP    M           ; Compare with table value
00D1  CADE00            JZ     MATCH       ; Branch if match found
00D4  23                INX    H           ; Else index to next command
00D5  23                INX    H           ; Character in the table
00D6  23                INX    H
00D7  05                DCR    B           ; Count number of valid commands
00D8  C2D000            JNZ    SEARCH      ; Search until match found
00DB  C3F500            JMP    ERROR       ; Error if entire table search
00DE  23       MATCH:   INX    H           ; Point to cir (low byte)
00DF  5E                MOV    E,M         ; Low address to register E
00E0  23                INX    H           ; Point to cir (high byte)
00E1  56                MOV    D,M         ; High address to register D
00E2  EB                XCHG               ; Cir address to H&L
00E3  E9                PCHL               ; Execute the cir

                ; Table of valid commands and their implementing routine addresses

00E4  41       TABLE:   DB     'A'         ; A command character
00E5  F100              DW     ACMD        ; A CIR address
00E7  51                DB     'Q'         ; Q command character
00E8  F200              DW     QCMD        ; Q CIR address
00EA  44                DB     'D'         ; D command character
00EB  F300              DW     DCMD        ; D CIR address
00ED  58                DB     'X'         ; X command character
00EE  F400              DW     XCMD        ; X CIR address
0004  =        NCMDS    EQU    ($-TABLE)/3 ; Number of table commands
                ; The following routine must be added to the program

00F0  00       CONIN:   NOP

                ; The following are the CIRs for each of the table commands
                ; Actual operation of these routines will depend on the application

00F1  00       ACMD:    NOP
00F2  00       QCMD:    NOP
00F3  00       DCMD:    NOP
00F4  00       XCMD:    NOP
00F5  00       ERROR:   NOP
00F6                    END
```

FIGURE 9-13. Console command processor program.

so that RP D&E contains the CIR's address. The contents of RP D&E are then moved to RP H&L. Finally the contents of RP H&L is loaded into the PC, and control transfers to the appropriate CIR.

Note that because the CCP is a program that works in conjunction with other programs, the CIRs have not been included with the program in Figure 9-13. The exact code for these routines will depend on the application at hand.

9-7

Storage Allocation

In Section 9-4 the reader was introduced to the concept of coding most application programs in the assembly language in two distinct segments: the code segment and the data segment. The *code segment* is the area in memory that will hold the program itself as well as the character-string messages, look-up tables, and other constants. The *data segment* is the area in memory that holds temporary data for the stack, buffers, and other variables. For systems with ROM and RAM hardware, the code and data segments correspond to the ROM and RAM memory, respectively, and therefore it is necessary to organize the software in a similar manner. For disk-based systems that contain only RAM memory, this organization is desirable but not essential.

Section 9-4 also described the use of the ORG directive to set the value of the assembler's location counter to a specified value, thus causing assembly of the program starting at that location in ROM. A second ORG directive could also be used to reset the location counter to an area of RAM so that symbolic references to RAM storage in the program could be assembled by the assembler. Figure 9-14 illustrates a typical program organization for ROM/RAM systems.

The partial program in Figure 9-14 is written for a system that has ROM starting at location 0000H and 256 bytes of RAM at locations 1000H through 10FFH. Note the organization of the program into the code and data segments to correspond with the hardware memory map. The first instruction in the program sets up the stack pointer. Because the label STACK is in the data segment and the stack is usually set to the top of RAM, the ORG RAM + 255 directive is used to set the location counter to location 10FFH (top of RAM). The label STACK is set to this value and, during the second pass, assembled as the operand of the LXI SP instruction. This particular example illustrated only one portion of the data segment being used for stack storage allocation, but the next example in this section will broaden the use of storage allocation.

Consider a program that reads characters entered from a terminal keyboard and stores the characters obtained in a buffer in the data segment (RAM). The program is to keep on filling the buffer until the buffer is full, at which point the program will terminate. The buffer must be capable of holding eighty characters. Assume the same hardware memory map as in the program shown in Figure 9-14. The program to implement this specification is shown in Figure 9-15.

The operation of the program in Figure 9-15 is fairly simple. After the stack pointer is set, RP H&L is set to the start of the buffer area in the data segment,

```
0000 =        ROM     EQU   0000H      ; Start of ROM area
1000 =        RAM     EQU   1000H      ; Start of RAM area

0000                  ORG   ROM        ; Assemble in code segmen·

0000 31FF10           LXI   SP, STACK  ; Set up stack pointer
   .    .                       .                    .
                   <rest of program>
   .    .                       .                    .
10FF                  ORG   RAM+255    ; Assemble in data segment

10FF =        STACK   EQU   $          ; Stack starts here
                      END
```

FIGURE 9-14. Program organized for a ROM/RAM environment.

```
0000  =            ROM     EQU    0000H    ; Start of ROM area
1000  =            RAM     EQU    1000H    ; Start of RAM area

0000                       ORG    ROM      ; Assemble in code segment

0000  31FF10               LXI    SP,STACK ; Set up stack pointer
0003  21                   LXI    H,BUFFER ; Pointer to data buffer
0006  0650                 MVI    B,LENGTH ; Length of buffer
0008  CD1200       GET:    CALL   CONIN    ; Get a keyboard character
000B  77                   MOV    M,A      ; Store in buffer
000C  23                   INX    H        ; Next buffer location
000D  05                   DCR    B        ; Count down length
000E  C20800               JNZ    GET      ; Next if not full
0011  76                   HLT             ; Else stop program

0012                CONIN:          ; Place CONIN subroutine here

1000                       ORG    RAM      ; Assemble in data segment

1000         BUFFER  DS     80       ; Reserve 80 bytes buffer
0050  =      LENGTH  EQU    $-BUFFER ; Length of buffer
1050                 DS     6        ; Reserve 6 bytes for stack
1056  =      STACK   EQU    $        ; Stack starts here

1056                END
```

FIGURE 9-15. **Application of the DS directive for storage reservation.**

and register B is set to the length of the buffer. The CONIN subroutine (not shown) is called to get a character from the keyboard. The character is stored in memory, H&L set to point at the next buffer location, and the count in register B is decremented. The next character is then read from the keyboard and stored in the buffer. This continues till the count reaches zero, at which point the buffer is full and the program will terminate.

Notice in Figure 9-15 that a data storage (DS) directive has been used to reserve space for two areas in the data segment: the buffer area and the stack areas. Unlike the DB and DW directives, the DS directive does not instruct the assembler to assemble any code but merely causes a specified offset to be added to the location counter so as to reserve a portion of memory.

In Figure 9-15, the label BUFFER is assigned the value of 1000H (start of the data segment). Eighty bytes are then reserved for the buffer, from 1000H to 1050H, by using the DS 80 directive. The length of the buffer is then calculated by subtracting the value of buffer from the current value of the location counter. Then six bytes are reserved for the stack (this is arbitrary) using the DS 6 directive, which causes the location counter to be set at 1056. The label STACK is set to this value. The program thus has six bytes of stack space and eighty bytes of buffer space in the data segment, allowing for efficient storage allocation.

The DS directive is not limited to the data segment but can also be used in the code segment, to bypass certain areas of the memory map, such as interrupt restart locations, or to leave a blank area in the memory map for memory-mapped I/O systems. Appropriate use of the DS directive can lead to memory-efficient software design.

The Object File

In Section 9-2 the operation of the assembler was described as being the translation of an assembly language program into a machine language program. The machine language program is the actual sequence of machine instructions (and data) that is processed by the CPU. One of the outputs of the assembler is the object file that contains the machine language program.

Figure 9-5 illustrates a typical object file produced by an assembler. This object file is a sequence of hexadecimal digits organized into *records*. As shown in Figure 9-5, a record starts with a ":" (colon) and ends with a *checksum*, which is a two-digit hexadecimal number. The number of records in an object file will depend on the size of the program assembled. Thus in Figure 9-5, the object file has three records ending with checksums 93, 9D, and FF from first to last record, respectively. The contents of an object file record is mostly the instruction codes and/or data of the assembled program. However, records do contain some additional information. This additional information in the object file is often required, as the object file is often passed through a special program called a *loader*. The function of the loader is to read each record and to determine where in the computer's memory each instruction is to be loaded and whether there are any errors in the object file.

Figure 9-16 shows a dissected view of the first record of the object file in Figure 9-5. Observe that the record is divided into six fields.

Field 1, as mentioned before, is a special character intended to identify the start of an object file record.

Field 5 contains the instructions and/or data (program bytes) in hexadecimal bytes that were translated from the source file. For example, the first two bytes, D305, represent the OUT 05 instruction; the next byte, F5, represents the PUSH PSW instruction; and so on.

Field 2 is a hexadecimal number that identifies the number of program bytes in field 5. In Figure 9-16, the record contains sixteen (ten hex) program bytes. The number of program bytes in a record will depend on the type of assembler being used.

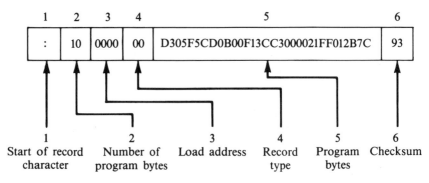

FIGURE 9-16. Object file record format.

Field 3 is a four-digit hexadecimal number that identifies the address at which the first program byte will be loaded into the computer's memory (load address). For example, the first program byte D3 will be loaded at location 0000, 05 at location 0001, F5 at location 0002, . . . , 7C at location 000F. Notice in Figure 9-5 that the load address of the next record is 0010.

Field 4 is the "record type." It is usually set to zero for all records except the last, which is set to one. It can be used by the loader to detect the last record in the object file.

Field 6 is two-digit hexadecimal checksum used to detect any errors that may have occurred in fields 2 through 5. This format for each record was developed during the early years of computers. At the time, paper-tape strips were used to store object file information. These paper tapes were prone to many errors when read. As a result, some means of error detection was necessary during the reading of paper tape by the loader. The checksum is calculated by taking the modulo 256 sum of *all* the bytes in the record and then its two's complement. Figure 9-17 shows the calculation of the checksum for the record in Figure 9-16. Because the checksum is the two's complement of the modulo 256 sum of all the bytes in the record, if *all* the bytes in the record are added modulo 256 (including the checksum), the result should be zero.

In Figure 9-17, by adding all the bytes in fields 2 through 5, the result obtained is 066D. Considering only the least significant eight bits of this number yields

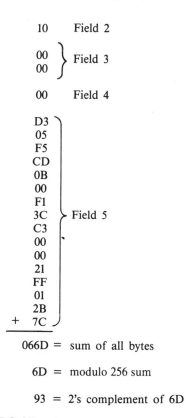

066D = sum of all bytes

6D = modulo 256 sum

93 = 2's complement of 6D

FIGURE 9-17.   Checksum calculation.

a modulo 256 sum of 6D. The two's complement of 6D is 93, which is the checksum for the record.

As the loader reads in each byte in the record, it also calculates its own checksum based on the preceding algorithm. When all the bytes of the record are read, the loader compares its checksum with the checksum in the record. If they do not match, an error condition was encountered during the read. Chapter 10 deals with the actual implementation of a loader.

At this point it is important to realize that even though the object file contains the machine language program in hexadecimal representation, it is merely a representation of the program in binary form. The CPU "understands" only binary instructions. Hexadecimal representation is used only for convenience and for economical purposes, as it greatly reduces the number of digits when printed or displayed. Ultimately, every instruction and data byte is loaded into the computer in binary. Each hexadecimal digit in an object file also is represented by its ASCII code. Again, this is done so that the object code can be "stored" on a 7-bit storage medium such as paper tape or be transmitted over a 7-bit ASCII serial data link.

9-9

Summary

The assembler was introduced as a software development tool that can translate an assembly language program into a form suitable for execution by the computer. Besides translating instructions, the assembler can also be used to store data tables and character strings and to reserve specified memory locations for temporary data storage. The user can control the location at which the code and data segments are assembled, so that the software organization corresponds with the hardware environment. The most important feature of the assembler is its ability to allow symbolic references to data and memory locations, thus eliminating a lot of overhead during program development. Finally, the assembler produces the machine language program in the form of an absolute object file; the location at which the machine language program is loaded and eventually executed is fixed after assembly and cannot be executed at a different memory address.

This chapter discussed the use of an extremely important tool used in developing assembly language programs. The material covered in this chapter serves only as an introduction to assembly language programming and the basic directives for controlling assembly. The next two chapters deal with some of the more advanced features of assembly language programming and features of the assembler.

REVIEW QUESTIONS AND PROBLEMS

1. Describe some of the advantages of using an assembler over hand assembly.

2. Briefly describe the functions of the following:

(a) Source file. (b) Symbol table.
(c) Object file. (d) Program listing.

3. Describe the operation of a two-pass assembler.

4. The following sequence of hexadecimal bytes (shown as an object file record) represents a machine language program for the 8085. Disassemble (that is, convert each machine instruction to mnemonics) the program into assembler format.

:132000000E7B3A502006559180D3303250200DCA0220761A

5. What is an assembler directive? What is the purpose of having an ORG directive to the assembler?

6. Identify the invalid constants in the following list and explain why they are considered invalid:
(a) 0F3H   (b) '3CH'   (c) 3C05
(d) 378   (e) 'HELLO'   (f) 512Q
(g) 1010B   (h) 1010   (i) 823Q
(j) 11011021B (k) '13'   (l) 753D

7. What is the function of the special reserved symbol "$"?

8. Compare the operation of the two data storage directives DB and DW. How does the DS directive differ from the DB and DW directives?

9. The following program is written in assembler format. Assuming that you are the assembler, fill in the addresses and object code on the left-hand side of the listing.

```
5010                   ORG    5010H
  35 =          PANEL   EQU    35H           ; Display port
5010  31                LXI    SP,STACK      ; Set up stack
                                             ;   pointer
5013  21                LXI    H,TABLE       ; Point to table

5016  7E        OVER:   MOV    A,M           ; Get table value
5017  FE                CPI    '$'           ; End of table?
5019  CA 22 50           JZ    QUIT          ; Quit if so

501C  D3 35             OUT    PANEL         ; Else display it
501E  23                INX    H             ; Next table value
501F  C3 16 50          JMP    OVER          ; Do it again

5022  76        QUIT:   HLT                  ; Quit
5023            TABLE:  DB     '9876543210$'
                        DS     12 ;12 bytes for stack
                STACK   EQU    $
                        END
```

10. The following program contains five syntax errors that will be flagged by the assembler. Identify and explain these errors.

```
                    ORG    1000
        REF         EQU    2000H

                    LXI    H,REF
        START:      MVI    C,F0
                    IN     SWT
                    CMP    'A'
                    JZ     TERM
                    ADD    M
                    INX    H
                    JMP START
        REF:        DS     12H,'B',5EH, 'CCCC'
        TERM:       HLT
                    END
```

CHAPTER 10

Relocatable Assembly and Utility Subroutines

Introduction

Relocatable assembly is a process that aids the development of an assembly language program that requires programming in several modular steps. To illustrate the difference between absolute assembly (described in Chapter 9) and relocatable assembly, consider the operation of the assembler in Figure 9-3. The process of assembly involved only one development stage: the assembler translated the source file into the object file. Once assembled, the object file was ready to be loaded into the computer. Relocatable assembly requires an additional step in the software development process, linkage and location. This may seem disadvantageous at first thought, but it does provide a more flexible technique of developing programs, as will be seen in this chapter.

The process of relocatable assembly is shown in Figure 10-1. By comparing the diagram of Figure 10-1 with the function of the absolute assembler (Figure 9-3), one can see that the end result of the assembly is the same—the object file. However, the intermediate steps in the development of the program are quite different.

The input to the assembler consists of one or more source files constructed

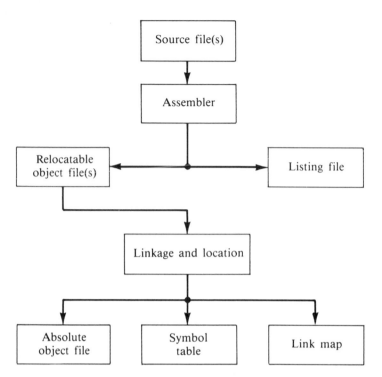

FIGURE 10-1. Process of relocatable assembly.

in a manner similar to the source files in Chapter 9. The assembler translates these source files into *relocatable object files*. Relocatable object files are similar to absolute object files except that all symbolic address references are variable. For example, any JMP or CALL instructions have operands that reference a location relative to the base of the program rather than an absolute location in memory. Thus, after assembly, these object files can be located anywhere in memory by the linking and locating process.

The relocatable object files (*modules*) are then submitted to a linkage editor, which combines all the object files into a single absolute object file with absolute address references, for loading into the computer. The linkage editor also produces a *link map*, which tells the programmer the absolute addresses of the program modules, and a symbol table, with all the symbols and their absolute values. The process of combining the relocatable object files (modules) into a single module is called *linkage*. The process of adding absolute addresses to the resultant object file so that the machine code is ready for execution at a specified address is called *location*. Linkage and location are usually (but not always) done in a single step in the development stage.

All the directives discussed in Chapter 9 for absolute assembly are applicable to relocatable assembly. There are, however, certain directives used exclusively for relocatable assembly, as will be seen in the following sections.

Structured Assembly Language Programs

A *structured program* is one that is constructed on various levels. A hierarchical tree illustrating these levels of a structured program is shown in Figure 10-2. Notice in the figure that the main program (first level) consists of CALLs to various subroutines (or modules) in the second level, as represented by the arrows. Subroutines in the second level may have calls to a third level, and so on. What this illustrates is a program structure that is divided into separate sections or subprograms. Subprograms at the highest level of the tree are dependent on subprograms at the lower levels, whereas lower-level subprograms are essentially independent of upper-level programs. The advantage of such a scheme of program organization is that lower-level subprograms can be tested independently and used when required during the development of the main program. These lower-level subprograms are usually used over and over again in application programs and are hence termed *utility subroutines*.

Consider some of the program examples in Chapter 9. Most of those programs required the use of two subroutines: CONIN (console input) and CONOUT (console output). Each time a program was written that required one or both of these subroutines, the programmer had to include the source code for the subroutines in the program being written (main program). It would be convenient if these subroutines were written and assembled separately (into relocatable modules) and then included in the final absolute object file during linkage and location. This would preclude the need for including the subroutines at the source level, and this is exactly the concept behind relocatable assembly, as shown in Figure 10-3.

The main program is constructed in a organization similar to that of the hierarchical tree structure shown in Figure 10-2. Because a major portion of the main program consists of calls to subroutines, the size of the main program is relatively small at the source level. The programmer does not have to include the source code for the subroutines in the main program. (*Note:* Normally, an absolute assembler would signal an error if a call were made to a subroutine that did not exist in the source file, but a relocatable assembler does not do this.)

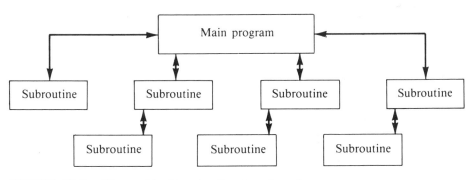

FIGURE 10-2. Hierarchical levels of a structured program.

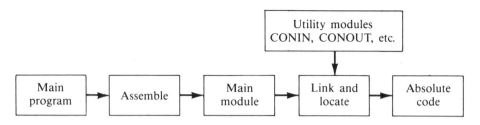

FIGURE 10-3. Development of an assembly language program.

The subroutines used in the main program are assembled separately. Finally, the linkage editor is used to combine the main program with its referenced subroutines. The final combined code is then located at a specified location.

The real advantage of this technique of software development is seen during the development of later application programs that require the same modules developed before. Because these modules have been previously developed, all the programmer has to do is construct the main program without being concerned about the subroutines, and the linkage editor takes care of the rest. These utility subroutines (commonly used subroutines) are usually kept in a file (in relocatable form) called a utility library. During the linkage stage, the library is searched for modules that are needed in the main program. Only the modules that are referenced in the main program are included in the final object code.

10-3

Subroutine Modules

There are four basic types of subroutines: subroutines with no parameters, subroutines with input parameters, subroutines with output parameters, and subroutines with both input and output parameters.

A *subroutine with no parameters* is one that is called to perform a task, without sending it any data or receiving any data from it. Such a subroutine can be an interrupt subroutine that is independent of the main program.

A *subroutine with input parameters* is one that must have data passed to it in order to operate properly. A good example of this type of subroutine is the console output subroutine (CONOUT) for the 8251 UART. Before CONOUT is called, register C is loaded with the character that is to be displayed on the terminal. The character in register C is the input parameter to the CONOUT subroutine. If register C is not loaded with the character (data), the subroutine will not work as intended. Note that CONOUT does not return any data to the main program.

A *subroutine with output parameters* always returns data to the main program. An example of such a subroutine is the console input subroutine (CONIN). CONIN is called without sending any data to it (no input parameter) but it returns the ASCII code of the key (in register A) entered on the keyboard. The ASCII code returned in register A by the CONIN subroutine is the output parameter of the subroutine. A subroutine with output parameters always returns data to the main program, and in most cases the main program always expects this data to be returned.

A *subroutine with both input and output parameters* accepts input data and returns output data. For example, consider a subroutine to multiply two numbers. Before the subroutine is called, the two numbers to be multiplied will be loaded into appropriate registers. Then the subroutine is called; the subroutine performs the multiplication and returns the product of the two numbers in an appropriate register. The data contained in the two registers before the subroutine was called are the input parameters to the subroutine, and the result (the product of the two numbers) returned by the subroutine is the output parameter.

The process of sending and returning parameters to and from a subroutine is known as *parameter passing*. Passing of input and output parameters does not have to be limited to being passed in CPU registers but can be extended to memory locations and status flags as well.

In writing utility subroutines, it is important to document the input and output parameters (if any) of a subroutine. When these subroutines are used in a main program, the user often has to know what these parameters are so that the code in the main program will comply with the subroutine calls. For example, if a main program called CONOUT with the input parameter in register D, the subroutine would be ineffective. The main program must therefore follow the *parameter-passing conventions* of the subroutine. If the subroutine requires that a particular piece of information be passed in a particular register, the main program must conform to the specification; similarly, if a subroutine returns information in a particular register, the main program can expect the data to be there.

Besides documenting parameter-passing rules in a subroutine, it is also important to document the registers used (if any) by the subroutine. For example, if a main program is using a particular register, and a call is made to a utility subroutine that destroys the original contents of the register, the operation of the main program could be affected. In order for the programmer to know what registers are used by the subroutine so that they may be saved (if necessary) before the subroutine is called, these registers should be documented as a part of writing utility subroutines.

Finally, if a subroutine CALLs another subroutine, it is important to document the subroutine(s) that are called, so that they can be linked into the final object code.

In many cases, glancing through an undocumented subroutine will provide the information mentioned. However, in lengthy and complex subroutines, it is easy to miss vital information about the subroutine.

As an example of subroutine documentation and preparation for relocatable assembly, Figures 10-4 and 10-5 show the CONIN and CONOUT subroutines, respectively. Subroutine documentation is shown as comments before the actual subroutine.

Notice in Figures 10-4 and 10-5 that each subroutine contains header information on the calling name of the subroutine, the inputs (input parameters) to the subroutine, the outputs (output parameters) from the subroutine, the registers destroyed (used up) by the subroutine, any other subroutines called by the subroutine, and a brief description of the subroutine. A programmer who requires

```
;  ****************************************************************  *
;                                                                    *
;  NAME:          CONSOLE INPUT (CONIN)                              *
;  INPUTS:        NONE                                               *
;  OUTPUTS:       REG A = CHARACTER RECEIVED FROM KEYBOARD           *
;  DESTROYS:      NOTHING                                            *
;  CALLS:         NOTHING                                            *
;  DESCRIPTION:   THE CONSOLE INPUT SUBROUTINE WAITS FOR A           *
;                 CHARACTER TO BE ENTERED ON THE CONSOLE             *
;                 KEYBOARD AND RETURNS THE ASCII CODE OF THE         *
;                 CHARACTER IN REG A.                                *
;                                                                    *
;  ****************************************************************  *

                        PUBLIC    CONIN

0002 =      DATA    EQU     02H         ; 8251 data port
0003 =      STATUS  EQU     03H         ; 8251 status port

0000 DB03   CONIN:  IN      STATUS      ; Get UART status
0002 E602           ANI     00000010B   ; See if receiver ready
0004 CA0000'        JZ      CONIN       ; Wait until ready
0007 DB02           IN      DATA        ; Get received character
0009 E67F           ANI     01111111B   ; Strip parity bit
000B C9             RET

000C                END
```

FIGURE 10-4. Console input subroutine.

such a subroutine in a main program needs only to glance at the header documentation (without inspecting the actual code) to know what to expect from the
subroutine.

There are many variations used by programmers when documenting subroutines with header information. Besides the information shown in Figures 10-4
and 10-5, the programmer may also wish to include his or her name, the date
of completion, and the revision number. The date of completion and revision
number enable the programmer to keep track of the most current revision, often
the one that has been most field proven; programmers can often lose track of
which routine was the latest revision.

Some programmers may choose to omit the "destroys" information from the
subroutine documentation, by preserving the contents of all CPU registers (on
the stack) that are used locally by the subroutine. Just before the subroutine
returns to the calling program, the contents of the registers used can be restored,
allowing local register usage to be transparent to the user. This technique relieves
the programmer from the burden of saving appropriate registers in the main
program before calls are made to the utility subroutines; this is particularly
helpful when a programmer has built a large collection of utility subroutines.
Saving the contents of locally used registers could, however, waste a small
amount of memory space.

Figures 10-4 and 10-5 also introduce a new directive used in relocatable
assembly, the *public directive* (PUBLIC). The PUBLIC directive instructs the

```
;  ****************************************************************  *
;                                                                   *
;  NAME:           CONSOLE OUTPUT (CONOUT)                          *
;  INPUTS:         REG C = CHARACTER TO BE TRANSMITTED              *
;  OUTPUTS:        NONE                                             *
;  DESTROYS:       REG A                                            *
;  CALLS:          NOTHING                                          *
;  DESCRIPTION:    THE CONSOLE OUTPUT SUBROUTINE WAITS FOR          *
;                  THE UART TRANSMITTER TO BE READY BEFORE          *
;                  SENDING THE CHARACTER IN REG C TO THE            *
;                  CONSOLE.                                         *
;                                                                   *
;  ****************************************************************  *

                         PUBLIC   CONOUT

0002 =         DATA     EQU      02H        ; 8251 data port
0003 =         STATUS   EQU      03H        ; 8251 status port

0000 DB03      CONOUT:  IN       STATUS     ; Get UART status
0002 E602               ANI      00000001B  ; See if transmitter ready
0004 CA0000'             JZ       CONOUT     ; Wait until ready
0007 79                 MOV      A,C        ; Get character
0008 D302               OUT      DATA       ; Transmit character
000A C9                 RET

000B                    END
```

FIGURE 10-5.   Console output subroutine.

assembler that the following symbol is to be made available for access by other modules (main program or other subroutines). Because the symbol referenced in the PUBLIC directive is the name of the subroutine, the subroutine becomes accessible by other subroutines or main programs. The PUBLIC directive is also used to identify all the modules in a utility subroutine library, consisting of concatenated modules.

Note that the subroutines in Figures 10-4 and 10-5 do not contain ORG directives, because the ORG directive implies assembly at an absolute memory location. And because the assembled code for the subroutines will be located elsewhere at link time, the ORG directive is no longer needed. Even though the assembler ''seems'' to assemble the subroutines at a base address of 0, the actual location of the subroutines will be determined when the subroutine and main program are linked and located. Operands of instructions that have relocatable addresses (which will be changed at link time) are identified by the assembler by the single quotation mark (') shown to the immediate right of the assembled code, such as for the JZ CONOUT instruction in Figure 10-5.

10-4

Utility Subroutines

This section deals with the development of five utility subroutines that will be used with the CONIN and CONOUT subroutines in the construction of an absolute object file loader. The operation of each subroutine will be explained by means of a flowchart, followed by a discussion of the linkage directives.

PRINT Utility

In Figure 9-10, a flowchart for a message print program (Figure 9-11) was developed. The program displayed an ASCII character string on the console. Because this type of program is used fairly often in application programs, it is best to rewrite the program as a utility subroutine. In rewriting the PRINT subroutine, one major change will be made—instead of supplying the subroutine with a count of the number of characters in the string, the string will be terminated with the ASCII nongraphic null character (00H) so that the subroutine can automatically detect the end of the string.

The flowchart for the PRINT utility is shown in Figure 10-6. Assume that a pointer has already been set to the start of the string before the subroutine is called.

Notice that the flowchart in Figure 10-6 is similar to the flowchart in Figure 9-10. In Figure 9-10 the program determined when the entire string was displayed, by decrementing a count that was initially the length of the string. In Figure 10-6 the subroutine does not require a count set to the length of the string. Instead, the requirement of the subroutine is that the string be terminated with an ASCII *null* character. The program gets each character from memory and checks to see if it is a null. If it is, the entire string has been displayed; if not, the character is displayed, the pointer set to the next character in the string, and the process continued.

Figure 10-7 shows the implementation of the flowchart in Figure 10-6 as a utility subroutine. Before the subroutine in Figure 10-7 is called, RP D&E must be set to the starting address of the string (input parameter). The string can be stored along with the calling program by using a DB directive. The string *must* be terminated by an ASCII NULL character.

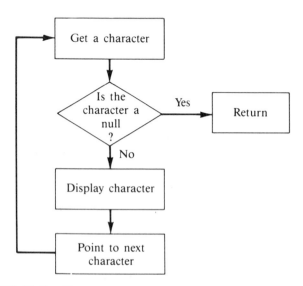

FIGURE 10-6. Flowchart for the PRINT subroutine.

```
;  ************************************************************ *
;                                                              *
; NAME:           PRINT STRING (PRINT)                         *
; INPUTS:         RP DE = ADDRESS OF STRING TO BE PRINTED      *
; OUTPUTS:        NONE                                         *
; DESTROYS:       REGS A,C,D,E                                 *
; CALLS:          CONOUT                                       *
; DESCRIPTION:    THE PRINT STRING SUBROUTINE PRINTS THE       *
;                 STRING WITH STARTING ADDRESS SPECIFIED IN    *
;                 RP DE ON THE CONSOLE. THE STRING MUST BE     *
;                 TERMINATED WITH AN ASCII NULL (00).          *
;                                                              *
;  ************************************************************ *
;

                        PUBLIC  PRINT

                        EXTRN   CONOUT

0000 =        NULL      EQU     00H       ; ASCII code for null

0000 1A       PRINT:    LDAX    D         ; Get a character
0001 FE00               CPI     NULL      ; See if end of string
0003 C8                 RZ                ; Return if so
0004 4F                 MOV     C,A       ; Else prepare for CONOUT
0005 CD0000'            CALL    CONOUT    ; Display it
0008 13                 INX     D         ; Point to next character
0009 C30000'            JMP     PRINT     ; Continue until end

000C                    END
```

FIGURE 10-7. PRINT subroutine.

Notice in Figure 10-7 that the PRINT subroutine calls CONOUT to display each character in the string. Because CONOUT is another subroutine external to the PRINT subroutine, the EXTRN directive is used, telling the assembler that the absolute address of the CONOUT routine will be determined and filled in at link time. Also notice that before the CONOUT subroutine is called, the character to be displayed is moved to register C (as register C must contain the input parameter) in preparation for CONOUT.

VALDGT Utility

In many application programs it is necessary to accept numeric ASCII graphic characters from the console keyboard for various types of arithmetic and numeric processing. When a numeric ASCII character is entered at the keyboard, it is important to check the validity of the character entered to make sure that the user did type a numeric key and not any other key. This check ensures that the arithmetic or numeric processing done on the numbers is not erroneous. The VALDGT subroutine checks the validity of hexadecimal numbers (0 through 9, A through F) entered on the keyboard and returns a flag set if the character entered was a valid hex digit, or reset if it was an invalid hex digit. The flowchart to implement the VALDGT subroutine is shown in Figure 10-8.

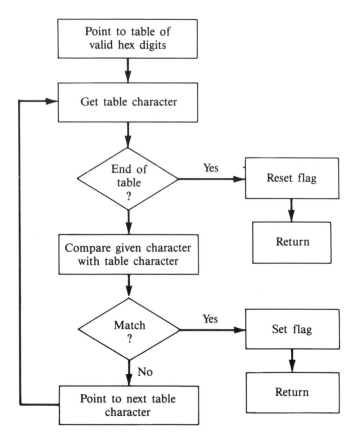

FIGURE 10-8. Flowchart for the VALDGT subroutine.

The flowchart in Figure 10-8 uses a look-up table to determine whether the given character is a valid ASCII hex digit. The table contains all the valid ASCII hexadecimal digits stored in hexadecimal representation. The program compares each byte in the table with the given character until a match is found; on finding a match, a flag is set to indicate success. If the search is exhausted and the end of the table is reached (no match has been found), the given character is invalid and the flag will be reset, indicating failure. The program implementation of the flowchart is shown in Figure 10-9.

The subroutine in Figure 10-9 has both input and output parameters. The input parameter is the ASCII digit (in hexadecimal representation) to be checked and has to be loaded into register C before calling the subroutine. The output parameter is the carry flag, which is set to indicate that the contents of register C is a valid digit and reset to indicate that the character is an invalid digit. The table of valid digits (HEXTBL) is stored using a DB directive and is terminated with a "$." The $ will be used in the program to check for an end-of-table condition.

RP H&L is set to the start of the table, and the first table character is brought into register A. The table character is checked to see if it is a $. If it is not a $, the table character will be compared with the given character in register C.

```
;   ********************************************************** *
;                                                             *
; NAME:           DETERMINE IF VALID HEX DIGIT (VALDGT)       *
; INPUTS:         REG C = ASCII CHARACTER TO BE CHECKED       *
; OUTPUTS:        CARRY = 1 IF CHAR IS A VALID HEX DIGIT      *
;                 CARRY = 0 IF CHAR IS AN INVALID HEX DIGIT   *
; DESTROYS:       H,L,A                                       *
; CALLS:          NOTHING                                     *
; DESCRIPTION: THE VALDGT SUBROUTINE CHECKS THE ASCII         *
;                 CHARACTER IN REGISTER C AND DETERMINES IF   *
;                 IT LIES WITHIN THE RANGE '0'-'9', 'A'-'F'   *
;                 (30-39, 41-46). IF IT IS WITHIN THIS RANGE, *
;                 THE CARRY FLAG IS SET TRUE INDICATING       *
;                 SUCCESS. IF IT IS NOT WITHIN THE RANGE THE  *
;                 CARRY FLAG IS SET FALSE INDICATING          *
;                 FAILURE.                                    *
;                                                             *
;   ********************************************************** *

                        PUBLIC VALDGT,ERR,OK,HEXTBL

0000 211600'    VALDGT: LXI  H,HEXTBL  ; Point to valid hex table
0003 7E         NXT:    MOV  A,M       ; Get table character
0004 FE24               CPI  '$'       ; End of table?
0006 CA1100'            JZ   ERR       ; No match . . . error
0009 B9                 CMP  C         ; Else compare with given char
000A CA1400'            JZ   OK        ; Match? . . . success
000D 23                 INX  H         ; Point to next table char
000E C30300'            JMP  NXT       ; Loop until end of table
0011 37         ERR:    STC            ; First set carry true
0012 3F                 CMC            ; Now make it false
0013 C9                 RET            ; and return error code C = 0
0014 37         OK:     STC            ; Set carry true
0015 C9                 RET            ; and return success code C = 1

0016 303132     HEXTBL: DB   '0123456789ABCDEF','$'
0019 333435
001C 363738
001F 394142
0022 434445
0025 4624

0027                    END
```

FIGURE 10-9. VALDGT subroutine.

If a match is found, control will be transferred to the portion of the program (OK) that sets the carry flag and returns. If no match is found, H&L will be set to the next table character, and the process will be repeated until the table search is exhausted. When the entire table has been searched (a $ is detected), control transfers to ERR, the carry flag is reset, and the subroutine returns.

Note that because VALDGT does not call any other subroutine, no externals have been defined. Besides using the PUBLIC directive to make the VALDGT subroutine accessible, the labels ERR, OK, and HEXTBL have also been made public. This is because these symbolic addresses will be used again by some of the following utility subroutines and will prevent any duplication of code.

ASCHEX Utility

When numeric digits are entered on the console keyboard, the CONIN subroutine always returns the ASCII representation (in hexadecimal) of the numeric digit. For example, if the ''3'' key is depressed, the value returned is 33H, which is the ASCII code for a ''3.'' Similarly, if the hexadecimal digit ''B'' is depressed on the keyboard, the ASCII code 42H is returned. Because arithmetic and numeric processing require hex key values rather than ASCII codes (that is, we would like to see a 03H instead of a 33H, and a 0BH instead of a 42H) a utility subroutine to convert the ASCII representation of a hex digit to its hex value is needed. The ASCHEX utility performs this conversion. The flowchart for the ASCHEX subroutine is shown in Figure 10-10.

The flowchart for the ASCHEX subroutine in Figure 10-10 is similar to the operation of the VALDGT subroutine. The only difference is that a count is maintained to keep track of the position of the character scanned in the table of valid hex digits. When a match is found, the subroutine will return this count as the hexadecimal value of the ASCII character. The manner in which this is done can be seen in the implementation of the ASCHEX subroutine in Figure 10-11.

Notice that the ASCHEX subroutine in Figure 10-11 uses three portions of the VALDGT subroutine. These are HEXTBLE, ERR, and OK and are declared to be external to the subroutine. Because these three portions already exist in another subroutine, there is no point duplicating the code; the linkage editor will automatically fill in any address references to those labels. The subroutine checks for errors on the input parameter in register C and returns the same codes as in the VALDGT subroutine.

Notice that the position of each character in the HEXTBL (Figure 10-9) corresponds to the hexadecimal value of the character. This can be seen as follows:

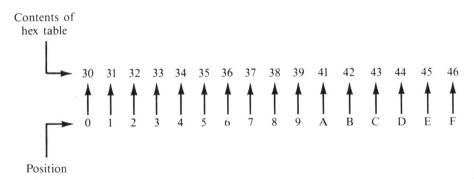

Register B is used to keep track of the position of the table value scanned. If a match is found between the table value and the given character, register B contains the hex value of the character. The ASCII representation of the character has thus been converted to its hex value and returned in register A with the carry flag set to indicate success. If no match is found, the subroutine will

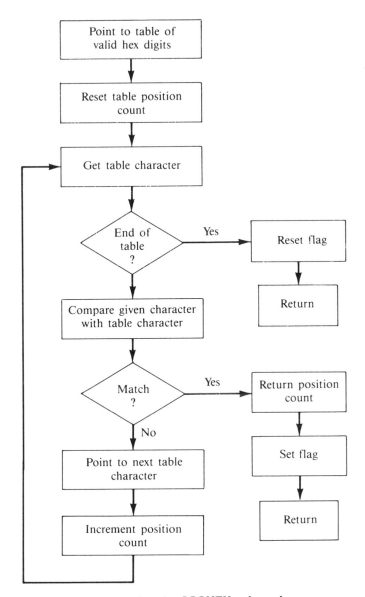

FIGURE 10-10. Flowchart for the ASCHEX subroutine.

reset the carry flag and return; the contents of register A is unpredictable. It is thus up to the calling program to check the state of the carry flag before accepting as valid the converted number in register A.

GET2HX Utility

In application programs that require 8-bit (two hex digits) numeric processing, a subroutine is often required that reads two hex digits from the console keyboard and returns an assembled byte. For example, the subroutine would read two keystrokes, "5," "C," in sequence and return in a register the assembled byte 5CH. Remember that when these two keys are depressed, the ASCII codes 35H

```
; **************************************************************** *
;                                                                 *
; NAME:          ASCII TO HEXADECIMAL CONVERSION (ASCHEX)         *
; INPUTS:        REG C = ASCII CHARACTER TO BE CONVERTED          *
; OUTPUTS:       REG A = CONVERTED HEXADECIMAL NUMBER             *
;                CARRY = 0 IF INVALID ASCII CHAR                  *
;                CARRY = 1 IF VALID ASCII CHAR                    *
; DESTROYS:      H,L,B                                            *
; CALLS:         ERR,OK,HEXTBL (references)                       *
; DESCRIPTION:   THE ASCHEX SUBROUTINE CONVERTS THE ASCII         *
;                REPRESENTATION OF THE HEXADECIMAL                *
;                CHARACTER IN REG C INTO ITS HEXADECIMAL          *
;                VALUE. ASCHEX CHECKS THE VALIDITY OF THE         *
;                CHARACTER IN REG C TO DETERMINE IF IT LIES       *
;                IN THE VALID RANGE.                              *
;                                                                 *
; **************************************************************** *

                     PUBLIC  ASCHEX
                     EXTRN   ERR,OK,HEXTBL

0000 210000' ASCHEX: LXI     H,HEXTBL  ; Point to valid hex table
0003 0600            MVI     B,0       ; Table position count
0005 7E      NXT:    MOV     A,M       ; Get table character
0006 FE24            CPI     '$'       ; End of table?
0008 CA0000'         JZ      ERR       ; Error . . . no match
000B B9              CMP     C         ; Compare with given character
000C CA1400'         JZ      NUM       ; Match? . . . found number
000F 23              INX     H         ; Else next table character
0010 04              INR     B         ; Next position
0011 C30500'         JMP     NXT       ; Loop until table end
0014 78      NUM:    MOV     A,B       ; Register B contains number
0015 C30000'         JMP     OK        ; Return success

0018                 END
```

FIGURE 10-11.   ASCHEX subroutine.

and 43H are transmitted from the terminal. It is therefore up to the GET2HX subroutine to read two digits from the keyboard, convert the ASCII codes of the two characters entered into their hexadecimal values, assemble the two hexadecimal values into a byte, and return the result. The GET2HX subroutine must also check the validity of the two digits entered. The flowchart for the GET2HX subroutine is shown in Figure 10-12.

The subroutine to implement the flowchart of Figure 10-12 is shown in Figure 10-13. Observe that the GET2HX subroutine in Figure 10-13 calls CONIN, VALDGT, and ASCHEX. The subroutine also returns the same error code as the previous subroutines in cases in which invalid digits are entered on the keyboard.

The subroutine in Figure 10-13 implements the flowchart of Figure 10-12 as follows. The CONIN routine is called to get the first digit entered at the console keyboard. CONIN returns the ASCII value of the character in register A. Next, VALDGT is called with the ASCII character in register C, to check if the entered

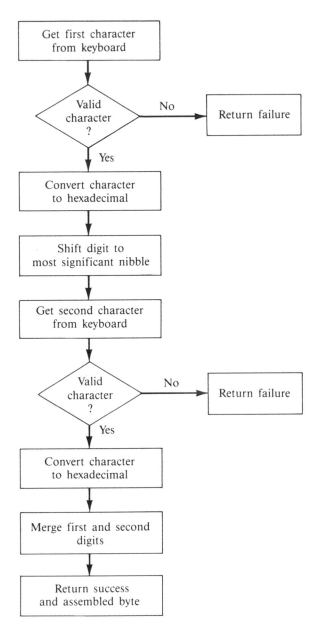

FIGURE 10-12.   Flowchart for the GET2HX subroutine.

character is valid. If an invalid digit was entered, VALDGT returns the carry flag reset, and the subroutine returns with the carry flag preserved. If the digit entered is valid, ASCHEX is called to convert the ASCII representation of the digit to its corresponding value. The digit value is returned in the least significant nibble of register A; the contents of register A are shifted left four times to get the first digit in the most significant 4-bit position. The first digit is saved in register D. CONIN is then called to get the second digit from the keyboard.

```
; ****************************************************************  *
;                                                                   *
; NAME:          GET 2 HEX DIGITS FROM CONSOLE (GET2HX)             *
; INPUTS:        NONE                                               *
; OUTPUTS:       REG A = ASSEMBLED HEX BYTE                         *
;                CARRY=1 IF VALID BYTE ENTERED                      *
;                CARRY=0 IF INVALID BYTE ENTERED                    *
; DESTROYS:      B,C,H,L,D                                          *
; CALLS:         VALDGT,CONIN,ASCHEX                                *
; DESCRIPTION:   THE GET2HX SUBROUTINE READS TWO HEXA-              *
;                DECIMAL CHARACTERS (REPRESENTED IN ASCII)          *
;                FROM THE CONSOLE, CHECKS THE VALIDITY OF           *
;                EACH, AND ASSEMBLES THEM INTO A HEXA-              *
;                DECIMAL BYTE IN REG A.                             *
;                                                                   *
; ****************************************************************  *

                          PUBLIC   GET2HX
                          EXTRN    CONIN,VALDGT,ASCHEX

0000 CD0000'  GET2HX:  CALL    CONIN   ; Get a character
0003 4F                 MOV     C,A     ;
0004 CD0000'            CALL    VALDGT  ; Check its validity
0007 D0                 RNC             ; Error if invalid character
0008 CD0000'            CALL    ASCHEX  ; Convert to hexadecimal
000B 07                 RLC             ; Get in M.S. nibble position
000C 07                 RLC
000D 07                 RLC
000E 07                 RLC
000F 57                 MOV     D,A     ; Save in register D
0010 CD0000'            CALL    CONIN   ; Get next character
0013 4F                 MOV     C,A     ;
0014 CD0000'            CALL    VALDGT  ; Check its validity
0017 D0                 RNC             ; Error if invalid character
0018 CD0000'            CALL    ASCHEX  ; Convert to hexadecimal
001B B2                 ORA     D       ; Merge two numbers
001C 37                 STC             ; Success carry = 1
001D C9                 RET             ; Return result

001E                    END
```

FIGURE 10-13. GET2HX subroutine.

The same process is repeated to check the validity of the character and then to convert the character to its hexadecimal value. The second digit is now in the least significant four bits of register A. The contents of register D (temporary storage of first digit) is ORed with register A to obtain the assembled byte as a result. The subroutine then returns with the carry flag set to indicate success. Thus if the following keystrokes "A," "5" were entered in sequence on the keyboard, GET2HX returns register A = A5H.

GET4HX Utility

The GET4HX subroutine is similar to the GET2HX subroutine except that GET4HX waits until four valid digits have been entered on the keyboard and returns the assembled word in a 16-bit register. This type of subroutine is useful for accepting four-digit hex numbers from the keyboard for numeric processing. Because most of the work for the GET4HX subroutine was done in the GET2HX subroutine, implementing GET4HX is fairly simple and is shown in Figure 10-14.

The subroutine in Figure 10-14 first calls GET2HX to input two digits assembled into a byte (most significant) in register A. If any invalid character was entered, the carry flag is reset by GET2HX, and the subroutine returns with the value of the flag preserved. The most significant byte is saved in register H. GET2HX is then called again to get the least significant byte. Because GET2HX destroys H&L (recall that register H contains the most significant byte), the contents of H&L is saved on the stack before the second call. On return from GET2HX, the value of H&L is restored, and the carry flag is tested again to make sure that no invalid digits have been entered for the least significant digits. If the carry flag is set (indicating valid digits), the least significant two digits are moved into register L, so that RP H&L now contains the four-digit assembled word. The subroutine then returns with the carry flag preserved (set). For example, if the keystrokes "1," "B," "D," "5" were entered on the keyboard, GET4HX would return RP H&L = 1BD5H.

```
; *************************************************************** *
;                                                                 *
; NAME:          GET 4 HEX DIGITS FROM CONSOLE (GET4HX)           *
; INPUTS:        NONE                                             *
; OUTPUTS:       RP HL = ASSEMBLED HEX WORD                       *
;                CARRY=1 IF VALID BYTE ENTERED                    *
;                CARRY=0 IF INVALID BYTE ENTERED                  *
; DESTROYS:      B,C,D                                            *
; CALLS:         GET2HX                                           *
; DESCRIPTION:   THE GET4HX SUBROUTINE READS FOUR HEXA-           *
;                DECIMAL CHARACTERS (REPRESENTED IN ASCII)        *
;                FROM THE CONSOLE, CHECKS THE VALIDITY OF         *
;                EACH, AND ASSEMBLES THEM INTO A HEXA-            *
;                DECIMAL WORD IN RP HL.                           *
;                                                                 *
; *************************************************************** *

                     PUBLIC   GET4HX
                     EXTRN    GET2HX

0000 CD0000' GET4HX: CALL     GET2HX   ; Get M.S. byte
0003 D0              RNC               ; Error if invalid
0004 67              MOV      H,A      ; Store in register H
0005 E5              PUSH     H        ; Save M.S. byte
0006 CD0000'         CALL     GET2HX   ; Get L.S. byte
0009 E1              POP      H        ; Get M.S. byte
000A D0              RNC               ; Error if invalid
000B 6F              MOV      L,A      ; Save L.S. byte in register L
000C C9              RET               ; Success return

000D                 END
```

FIGURE 10-14.   GET4HX subroutine.

Main Program

Sections 10-3 and 10-4 discussed the operation of seven utility subroutines that were developed as relocatable modules. These utilities will now be used in an application program (main program) structured in a form similar to the hierarchical tree in Figure 10-2. The application program is a *loader*, which will read individual object file records from an absolute object file (refer to Chapter 9), load the program bytes in each record at their respective load addresses, and determine whether the records contain any errors. With the description of the object file format in Chapter 9 and the subroutines in Section 10-4, the reader should have a fairly clear picture of the solution to the specification.

The flowchart in Figure 10-15 describes the implementation of the loader. The second record of the object file in Figure 9-5 will be used to illustrate the manner in which each field of the record is detected and interpreted by the loader. These fields are shown on the left-hand side (in parentheses) of each block in the flowchart where the data is read in. Note that this program reads each record in the object file from the console keyboard. However, the input device need not be limited to a console keyboard but can be any serial device attached to the 8251 chip (such as a paper-tape reader, cassette, or modem). The program can easily be modified (by changing CONIN) to read the object file from disk.

The program to implement the flowchart of Figure 10-15 is shown in Figure 10-16. The program illustrated in Figures 10-15 and 10-16 reads in each field of an object file record: the starting character (:), the number of program bytes, the load address, the record type, the program bytes, and the checksum. As each field is read in, the program adds each of the bytes in the field to an 8-bit memory location. Just before the record checksum is read in, the program calculates the modulo 256 checksum of all the fields and compares it with the record checksum. If a match is found, control transfers to the start of the program to read the next record. Each record is read in until the last record in the object file indicates a record count of 00, at which time the program terminates.

The steps in the flowchart and program in Figures 10-15 and 10-16 can be explained as follows. The first part of the main program sets up the stack pointer and clears the memory location that will hold the modulo 256 sum of all the fields in the object file record. Next, the program waits until it receives the ":" character, which indicates the start of a record. On receiving the ":" the program calls GET2HX to input the program byte count from the record. If any invalid character is entered, GET2HX will reset the carry flag, and the program will print an error message (CERR) and prompt the user to reenter the entire record. The program byte count is checked and, if zero, indicates that all the records in the object file have been read in, and the program terminates. If the count is not zero, the count is added to the modulo 256 sum (CKSUM) and saved on the stack for future use.

The subroutine GET4HX is then called to read in the load address of the record. GET4HX will return the carry flag reset if any invalid characters have been entered; control is transferred to CERR, and the process in the preceding

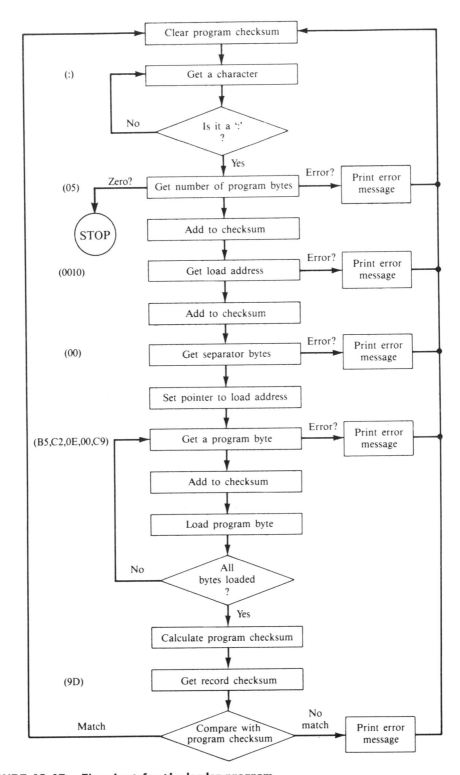

FIGURE 10-15. Flowchart for the loader program.

```
              ; ****************************** *
              ;                               *
              ; ABSOLUTE OBJECT FILE LOADER   *
              ;         MAIN PROGRAM          *
              ;                               *
              ; ****************************** *

              ; Assemble in the code segment

                    CSEG

              ; External utility subroutines

                    EXTRN  GET2HX,GET4HX,PRINT,CONIN

              ; Nongraphic ASCII characters

0000 =        NULL    EQU   00H      ; Null
000D =        CR      EQU   0DH      ; Carriage return
000A =        LF      EQU   0AH      ; Line feed

              ; Start of main program

0000 311500'          LXI   SP,STACK ; Set up stack area in DSEG
0003 3E00     START:  MVI   A,0      ; Set program checksum to zero
0005 320000'          STA   CKSUM

              ; Wait for ':' to indicate start of record

0008 CD0000'  WAIT:   CALL  CONIN    ; Get a character
000B FE3A             CPI   ':'      ; Record started?
000D C20800'          JNZ   WAIT     ; Wait until ':' received

              ; Now get number of program bytes

0010 CD0000'          CALL  GET2HX   ; Get program byte count
0013 D26700'          JNC   CERR     ; Error if invalid
0016 FE00             CPI   00H      ; Is it zero?
0018 CA6600'          JZ    STOP     ; All records loaded—stop
001B 5F               MOV   E,A      ; Save count in register E
001C D5               PUSH  D        ; Save it for now
001D 3A0000'          LDA   CKSUM    ; Get program checksum
0020 83               ADD   E        ; Add to checksum
0021 320000'          STA   CKSUM    ; Save new checksum

              ; Get load address

0024 CD0000'          CALL  GET4HX   ; Get the load address
0027 D26700'          JNC   CERR     ; Error if invalid
002A E5               PUSH  H        ; Save the address
002B 3A0000'          LDA   CKSUM    ; Get the program checksum
002E 84               ADD   H        ; Add high address
002F 85               ADD   L        ; Add low address
0030 320000'          STA   CKSUM    ; Save the checksum

              ; Index over record type

0033 CD0000'          CALL  GET2HX   ; Get record type
0036 D26700'          JNC   CERR     ; Error if invalid

              ; Get and load the program bytes

0039 E1               POP   H        ; Restore the load address
003A D1               POP   D        ; Restore program byte count
003B E5       DBYTES: PUSH  H        ; Save address
```

FIGURE 10-16. Implementation of the loader.

```
003C D5                        PUSH  D          ; Save count
003D CD0000'                   CALL  GET2HX     ; Get a program byte
0040 D1                        POP   D          ; Restore address
0041 E1                        POP   H          ; Restore count
0042 D26700'                   JNC   CERR       ; Error if invalid
0045 77                        MOV   M,A        ; Save the program byte
0046 3A0000'                   LDA   CKSUM      ; Get program checksum
0049 86                        ADD   M          ; Add to sum
004A 320000'                   STA   CKSUM      ; Save checksum
004D 23                        INX   H          ; Next load location
004E 1D                        DCR   E          ; Count down number of program bytes
004F C23B00'                   JNZ   DBYTES     ; Loop until all bytes loaded

               ; Get the record checksum

0052 CD0000'                   CALL  GET2HX     ; Get record checksum
0055 D26700'                   JNC   CERR       ; Error if invalid character
0058 5F                        MOV   E,A        ; Save record checksum

               ; Calculate the program checksum

0059 3A0000'                   LDA   CKSUM      ; Get program checksum
005C 2F                        CMA              ; One's complement
005D C601                      ADI   1          ; Two's complement

               ; Compare record checksum with program checksum

005F BB                        CMP   E          ; Compare the two checksums
0060 C27000'                   JNZ   ERROR      ; Error if no match
0063 C30300'                   JMP   START      ; Read next record if match

               ; Enter this point when entire object file is loaded

0066 76        STOP: HLT

               ; Enter this point for invalid character error

0067 117900'   CERR: LXI   D,ICERR  ; Point to error message
006A CD0000'         CALL  PRINT    ; Print the error message
006D C30300'         JMP   START    ; Read record again

               ; Enter this point for checksum error

0070 119F00'   ERROR: LXI   D,CKERR  ; Point to error message
0073 CD0000'          CALL  PRINT    ; Print the error message
0076 C30300'          JMP   START    ; Read record again

               ; Error messages

0079 0D0A494E ICERR: DB    CR,LF,'INVALID CHARACTER-RETYPE',CR,LF,NULL
009F 0D0A4348 CKERR: DB    CR,LF,'CHECKSUM ERROR-RETYPE',CR,LF,NULL

               ; Data segment in RAM

                             DSEG

0000           CKSUM: DS   1          ; Reserve 1 byte for checksum storage
0001                  DS   20         ; 20 bytes for stack
0015 =         STACK  EQU  $          ; Stack starts here

0015                  END
```

FIGURE 10-16. (Continued)

step is repeated. Each byte of the load address is added to the checksum and then saved on the stack for future use. GET2HX is again called to get the record type field (00) between the load address and the program bytes. Nothing is done with these numbers as they serve only as a separator.

Finally, the program goes through a loop to read and load each program byte in the record. This is done by setting RP H&L to the load address (previously saved) and register E to the count of the number of program bytes (previously saved). As each byte is read in by GET2HX (error checking is done as before), it is stored at the address pointed to by RP H&L; for each byte read in, the count is decremented. This continues until the count is zero, at which time all the program bytes have been read from the record. The loop also adds each byte read to the modulo 256 checksum.

The last step in the program recalls the final modulo 256 sum and, by taking its two's complement, generates a checksum for all the bytes previously read in. The checksum appended to the end of the object file record is read in (again, by calling GET2HX), and the calculated checksum is compared with the record checksum. If they match, the record has been loaded properly, and control transfers to the start of the program to read the next record. If they do not match, an error has been read in somewhere in the record; the program prints an error message, prompting the user to reenter the record, and transfers control to the start of the program to read the record again.

Notice in Figure 10-16 that all the subroutines that are used in the program—GET2HX, GET4HX, PRINT, and CONIN—are declared to be external and will be linked into the main program during linkage and location. These subroutines are the first-level subroutines (refer to Figure 10-2). The second-level subroutines, CONOUT, VALDGT, and ASCHEX, will automatically be linked in, as they are declared external in the first-level subroutines. Also notice in Figure 10-16 that two new directives used in relocatable assembly have been introduced in the main program: the CSEG (code segment) and the DSEG (data segment) directives. The use of these directives can be related to the discussion of program segments from Chapter 9. The CSEG and DSEG directives will ultimately instruct the linkage editor to locate the following code in the code and data segments of memory, respectively. The manner in which this is done will be seen in the next section.

10-6

Linkage and Location

At this point in the development of the assembly language application program there are seven relocatable utility modules—CONIN, CONOUT, PRINT, VALDGT, ASCHEX, GET2HX, and GET4HX—and one main module—LOADER. The next step in the development process is to use the linkage editor to "bind" (link) all these modules into an absolute object code file at specified addresses for the code and data segments.

The linkage editor must be instructed to link all the relocatable utility subroutines with the main program and to locate the code and data segments at specified addresses. For example, Figure 10-17 shows a link map produced by

```
GET2HX  111C    GET4HX  113A    PRINT 10D1    CONIN 10BA
CONOUT  10C6    VALDGT  10DD    ERR   10EE    OK    10F1
HEXTBL  10F3    ASCHEX  1104

CODE SIZE        0147 (1000-1146)
DATA SIZE        0015 (5000-5014)
```

FIGURE 10-17. Link map produced by linkage editor.

the linkage editor when instructed to link the previously mentioned utility modules with the main module; the location specified for the code segment is 1000H, and the location specified for the data segment is 5000H. (*Note:* Other values could be specified.)

From the link map in Figure 10-17 one can get a picture of how the linkage editor organizes the modules. The interpretation of the link map in Figure 10-17 can be explained as follows. The application program is located in two segments in memory: a code segment of 0147H bytes starting at location 1000H and ending at location 1146H, and a data segment of 0015H bytes starting at location 5000H and ending at 5014H.

The code segment contains all the code assembled for the main program at locations 1000H through 10B9H. The other utility modules are located directly below the main program in the following sequence:

```
1000H-10B9H—main program
10BA-CONIN
10C6-CONOUT
10D1-PRINT
10DD-VALDGT
1104-ASCHEX
111C-GET2HX
113A-GET4HX
```

The data segment simply contains the stack area defined in the main program and the storage location for the checksum (CKSUM). Thus the label CKSUM will have a value of 5000H, and the label STACK will have a value of 5015H.

At this point it may be important to point out that how the linkage editor is commanded to link the modules and how the modules are organized will depend entirely on the type of linkage editor being used. The example given in this section describes the operation of most linkage editors.

10-7

Summary

The purpose of this chapter was to introduce the reader to the concept of relocatable assembly and the techniques used in developing suitable assembly language programs. The construction of structured programs is extremely important to relocatable assembly. Structured programs often lead to the production of more efficient machine code, and also reduce the amount of development time spent on an application program. This is true not only for assembly language programs but also for programs written in higher-level languages (to be seen later). By using many relocatable utility modules, the programmer can eventually build a utility library consisting of well-documented, commonly used subroutines. When an application program requires one or more of the utility subroutines, all the programmer needs to do is to link the required module into the main program, without spending the time required to develop the subroutines at the source level. Another advantage is that the subroutines are "mature"; that is, they have been previously checked and tested, and if the application program does not work as intended, the problem can be narrowed down to the main program. Because the main program is relatively short (a major portion of the main program consists of calls to utility subroutines), debugging the main program is much easier.

This chapter has illustrated one complete example of the development of an assembly language application program using relocatable assembly. However, any well-structured program can fit this scheme.

REVIEW QUESTIONS AND PROBLEMS

1. Compare relocatable assembly with absolute assembly.

2. What are the differences among the four basic types of subroutines in regard to parameters?

3. What is the purpose of the PUBLIC and EXTRN directives to the assembler?

4. Modify the utility subroutines developed in this chapter so that each subroutine preserves the contents of the CPU registers (does not destroy any register). Change the LOADER program to access these modified utilities.

5. What is the process of linkage and location? Briefly describe the operation of the linkage editor.

6. What is the purpose of the CSEG and DSEG directives?

7. Develop a utility subroutine, HEXASC, to convert a hexadecimal number in the range 00–0F to its ASCII representation. The input to the subroutine will be register C (hex number in the range 00–0F), and the outputs will be register A (ASCII representation of the number), CARRY = 0 if the input hex number if invalid, and CARRY = 1 if the conversion was performed correctly. Note that this subroutine will function in a manner opposite to that of the ASCHEX subroutine.

8. Develop a utility subroutine, PUT2HX (function opposite to GET2HX), to display two hex digits in the range 00–FF on the console. The inputs to the subroutine will be register A (hex byte in the range 00–FF). No outputs are required.

9.   Develop a utility subroutine, PUT4HX (function opposite to GET4HX), to display four hex digits in the range 0000–FFFF on the console. The inputs to the subroutine will be RP H&L (hex address in the range 0000–FFFF). No outputs are required.

10. The LOADER program discussed in the chapter read in object file records and stored the data bytes in memory. Write a program called DUMP that will operate in reverse. The DUMP program will display on the console a specified range of memory locations in the form of object file records. Each record should have ten data bytes, together with the remaining five fields.

CHAPTER 11

Macros and
Conditional Assembly

11-1

Introduction

The preceding two chapters dealt with software development using absolute- and relocatable-code-producing assemblers. Both these assemblers usually give the programmer additional facilities to aid in software development. Programming with macros also gives the programmer greater flexibility in writing segments of code and allows the programmer to expand superficially the microprocessor's instruction set. Another facility provided by most assemblers is conditional assembly. By using certain conditional assembly directives, a single "generic" program can be written that includes several possible segments of code, only a few of which are selectively included for assembly. This chapter discusses the applications of macros and conditional assembly during assembly language software development.

11-2

Macros

Consider a program that is to accept four 4-bit numbers from an input port and assemble the numbers into a 16-bit word. This type of a program is known as *word assembly* and is shown in Figure 11-1.

```
1000              ORG   1000H

1000 DB00   IN    0              ; Get first number
1002 07     RLC                  ; Move to M.S. position
1003 07     RLC
1004 07     RLC
1005 07     RLC
1006 E6F0   ANI   11110000B      ; Clear L.S. bits
1008 47     MOV   B,A            ; Save first number
1009 DB00   IN    0              ; Get second number
100B E60F   ANI   00001111B      ; Clear M.S. bits
100D B0     ORA   B              ; Merge with first number
100E 67     MOV   H,A            ; Save first and second numbers
100F DB00   IN    0              ; Get third number
1011 07     RLC                  ; Move to M.S. position
1012 07     RLC
1013 07     RLC
1014 07     RLC
1015 E6F0   ANI   11110000B      ; Clear L.S. bits
1017 47     MOV   B,A            ; Save third number
1018 DB00   IN    0              ; Get fourth number
101A E60F   ANI   00001111B      ; Clear M.S. bits
101C B0     ORA   B              ; Merge with third number
101D 6F     MOV   L,A            ; Save third and fourth numbers
101E 76     HLT                  ; RP H&L contains word

101F              END
```

FIGURE 11-1. Word assembly program.

The program in Figure 11-1 reads each number from input port 0; the numbers arrive in the least significant four bits of the accumulator. Assuming that the 4-bit numbers are brought in most significant digit first, the final four-digit number is assembled in register pair H&L when the program terminates.

The program begins execution by an input from port 0 to bring in the first number. Because the number brought in is positioned in the least significant four bits of the accumulator, the four RLC instructions shift the four bits into the most significant four bits of the accumulator. The contents of the least significant four bits of the accumulator is then cleared by ANDing it with 11110000B. The first entered number is then saved in register B. The second 4-bit number is then brought in from port 0, and the most significant four bits are cleared (in case there are erroneous bits brought in from the 4-bit port) by ANDing the contents of the accumulator with 11110000B. The contents of register B (first number in the most significant four bits) is then "merged" with the contents of the accumulator (second number in the least significant four bits), by ORing the two registers. The accumulator now contains the first and second numbers brought in from port 0 as a two-digit byte. This byte is saved in register H.

The process described above is repeated for the third and fourth numbers brought in from port 0. The third and fourth numbers are assembled as a byte and stored in register L. Thus, when the program completes execution, register pair H&L contains the assembled four digits as a single word.

In developing the program shown in Figure 11-1, one can see that it would be nice if the 8085 instruction set included an instruction that would automatically shift 4 bits at a time. In other words, if the 8085 had a single instruction, say SLN (shift left nibble), that would automatically perform four single-bit left shifts and pad the least significant four bits of the accumulator with zeros. Because there is no means to expand the processor's instruction set (through hardware), the assembler offers a facility to do this superficially by means of a *macro definition*.

In Figure 11-1, the sequence of four RLC instructions and the ANI 11110000 instruction could be "defined" as a MACRO called SLN:

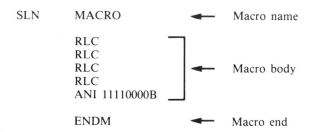

This macro definition consists of three parts. The first line in the definition identifies the name of the macro. In this case the name of the macro is SLN. The *macro name* is defined in the label field of the source file, and the MACRO directive is used to identify the name. Immediately following the name definition is the *macro body*. The macro body consists of several instructions in sequence. Now whenever the assembler identifies a macro name during the assembly process, the entire body is inserted at that point. This process will be seen in another example. Finally, the ENDM directive identifies the end of the macro definition.

Figure 11-2 shows the source file of the same program in Figure 11-1, with a macro definition for SLN. Notice that the SLN macro is defined before the actual program, which allows the assembler to encounter (and thus remember) the macro definition before the program is assembled. The actual program in Figure 11-2 resembles the program in Figure 11-1, except that it appears smaller in size and includes a new "instruction," SLN.

When the source program of Figure 11-2 is assembled, the assembler "remembers" the macro definition for the macro SLN during its first pass. During the second pass, every time the SLN "instruction" is encountered in the program sequence, a *macro expansion* takes place, as shown in Figure 11-3. A macro expansion is a process by which the assembler inserts the entire macro body of a defined macro every time the name of the macro is encountered during the second pass of assembly. In Figure 11-3, these macro expansions are identified by the assembler with " + " signs between the address and instruction bytes. Notice in Figure 11-3 that two expansions have taken place, one for each SLN instruction encountered. During each expansion the entire macro body has been inserted at the position of the SLN instruction.

If the code generated by the program in Figure 11-1 is compared with the code generated by the program in Figure 11-3, one can see that they are identical. Thus both programs will execute in the same manner, the difference between the two programs being at the source level. The program portion of Figure

```
; Macro:          Shift left nibble (SLN)
; Description:    The SLN macro moves the least significant 4
;                 bits of the accumulator into the most
;                 significant 4-bit position. The L.S. 4 bits
;                 are padded with zeros.

SLN    MACRO
       RLC                    ; Shift 4 bits left
       RLC
       RLC
       RLC
       ANI     11110000B  ; Clear L.S. 4 bits
       ENDM

       ORG     1000H

       IN      0          ; Get first number
       SLN                    ; Move to M.S. position
       MOV     B,A        ; Save first number
       IN      0          ; Get second number
       ANI     00001111B  ; Clear M.S. bits
       ORA     B          ; Merge with first number
       MOV     H,A        ; Save first and second numbers
       IN      0          ; Get third number
       SLN                    ; Move to M.S. position
       MOV     B,A        ; Save third number
       IN      0          ; Get fourth number
       ANI     00001111B  ; Clear M.S. bits
       ORA     B          ; Merge with third number
       MOV     L,A        ; Save third and fourth numbers
       HLT                    ; RP H&L contains word

       END
```

FIGURE 11-2. Word assembly with SLN macro.

11-3 is much shorter than Figure 11-1. As far as the programmer is concerned, the SLN macro is simply another 8085 instruction and is used as one during program development.

Thus, by using macros at the source level in assembly language programs, the programmer can "create" new instructions for the microprocessor. These new instructions do not have any meaning to the microprocessor but are simply a sequence of existing instructions organized to simulate a new instruction. Hence macros can be used to expand superficially the instruction set of the microprocessor. For example, the following macro definition defines a new instruction, SRN, which is similar to the SLN instruction except that it shifts the most significant nibble into the least significant position.

```
; Macro:          Shift right nibble (SRN)
; Description:    The SRN macro moves the most significant 4
;                 bits of the accumulator into the least
;                 significant 4-bit position. The MS 4 bits
;                 are padded with zeros.
```

```
SRN     MACRO
        RRC                         ; Shift 4 bits right
        RRC
        RRC
        RRC
        ANI     00001111B   ; Clear MS 4 bits
        ENDM
```

The existence of a macro name as part of the sequence of instructions in a program is known as a macro call. Macro calls should not be confused with subroutine calls. A *macro call* signals the assembler that a previously defined macro is to be expanded. A *subroutine call* transfers control of the CPU to another portion of the program. Thus, each time a macro is called, the entire code for that macro is inserted at that point, and each time a subroutine is called, control transfers to a common area in memory during execution. The use of macros therefore leads to the generation of code that is very inefficient in memory requirements but very efficient in execution speed.

Another application of macros is in expanding the assembler's translation capabilities. Most assemblers are designed to assemble instructions of one particular microprocessor. If any instructions that are not part of the microprocessor's instruction set are included in a program for assembly, the assembler will signal an error condition.

It was pointed out in Chapter 2 that the instruction set of the 8085 microprocessor is upward compatible with its predecessor, the 8080 microprocessor's instruction set. Therefore, an assembler that is designed to assemble 8080 mnemonics can also handle 8085 mnemonics, with two exceptions—the RIM and SIM instructions. These two instructions are part of the 8085 instruction set that cannot be executed by the 8080 microprocessor and consequently cannot be assembled by an 8080 assembler. An 8080 assembler can therefore assemble any 8085 program that does not contain the RIM and SIM instructions. Because there are several 8080 assemblers in existence, it would be desirable somehow to "force" an 8080 assembler to assemble these two additional 8085 instructions, and this can easily be done by defining the RIM and SIM instructions of the 8085 as macros.

Recall that during the assembly process, as each instruction is assembled by the assembler, the mnemonics are translated into their corresponding machine code. Thus whenever a RIM or SIM mnemonic is encountered in the program, we would like the appropriate machine codes (20H and 30H, respectively) assembled for each instruction. To do this, two macros are defined for the RIM and SIM instructions as follows:

```
RIM     MACRO
        DB      20H   ; Code for RIM
        ENDM
```

```
            SIM     MACRO
                    DB        30H     ; Code for SIM
                    ENDM
```

In both the RIM and SIM macros, the macro body consists of a single DB directive that includes the machine code for the respective instruction. Now assuming that these macros have been defined in the 8085 program, whenever the assembler encounters either the RIM or SIM instruction in the sequence of instructions that make up the program, it substitutes a 20H or 30H at the current value of the location counter. The effect is thus the same as having an 8085 assembler.

```
            ; Macro:              Shift left nibble (SLN)
            ; Description:        The SLN macro moves the least significant 4
            ;                     bits of the accumulator into the most
            ;                     significant 4-bit position. The L.S. 4 bits
            ;                     are padded with zeros.

       SLN  MACRO
            RLC                              ; Shift 4 bits left
            RLC
            RLC
            RLC
            ANI     11110000B                ; Clear L.S. 4 BITS
            ENDM

1000                ORG     1000H

1000  DB00          IN      0                ; Get first number
                    SLN                      ; Move to M.S. position
1002+ 07            RLC                      ; Shift 4 bits left
1003+ 07            RLC
1004+ 07            RLC
1005+ 07            RLC
1006+ E6F0          ANI     11110000B        ; Clear L.S. 4 bits
1008  47            MOV     B,A              ; Save first number
1009  DB00          IN      0                ; Get second number
100B  E60F          ANI     00001111B        ; Clear M.S. bits
100D  B0            ORA     B                ; Merge with first number
100E  67            MOV     H,A              ; Save first and second numbers
100F  DB00          IN      0                ; Get third number
                    SLN                      ; Move to M.S. position
1011+ 07            RLC                      ; Shift 4 bits left
1012+ 07            RLC
1013+ 07            RLC
1014+ 07            RLC
1015+ E6F0          ANI     11110000B        ; Clear L.S. 4 bits
1017  47            MOV     B,A              ; Save third number
1018  DB00          IN      0                ; Get fourth number
101A  E60F          ANI     00001111B        ; Clear M.S. bits
101C  B0            ORA     B                ; Merge with third number
101D  6F            MOV     L,A              ; Save third and fourth numbers
101E  76            HLT                      ; RP H&L contains word

101F                END
```

FIGURE 11-3. Macro expansion of word assembly program.

Macros with Parameters

In Section 11-2 the examples illustrated the use of macros without parameters. Just as one can pass parameters to a subroutine, one can also pass parameters to a macro. For example, the block-move program in Chapter 8 could be converted into a macro with parameters. The parameters passed to the macro would be the source address of the move, the destination address of the move, and the count of the number of bytes to be moved. The manner in which this is done is shown in Figure 11-4.

The macro definition for the block-move program segment in Figure 11-4 is similar to the definitions discussed for macros without parameters. The definition starts with the macro directive and ends with the ENDM directives. However, notice that the first line in the macro definition (the line containing the MACRO directive) contains a parameter list consisting of three symbols: SOURCE, DEST, and COUNT. These symbols are called *dummy parameters* and will be used to pass values to the macro body during an expansion. The dummy parameters SOURCE, DEST, and COUNT are also included in the macro body as operands of the LXI H, LXI D, and MVI B instructions, respectively. The name of the macro is MOVE.

Figure 11-5 shows two expansions of the MOVE macro in a skeleton program. Notice that the macro definition appears before the program itself, as was the case in examples discussed previously.

In Figure 11-5, the first macro call, MOVE 1000H,2000H,50H, initiates an expansion of the MOVE macro. The value 1000H (SOURCE) is assigned to the operand of the LXI H instruction, the value 2000H (DEST) is assigned to the operand of the LXI D instruction, and the value 50H (COUNT) is assigned to

```
; Definition for move macro

MOVE      MACRO       SOURCE,DEST,COUNT

          LOCAL       M1

          LXI         H,SOURCE     ; Get source address
          LXI         D,DEST       ; Get destination address
          MVI         B,COUNT      ; Number of bytes to be moved
M1:       MOV         A,M          ; Get source byte
          XCHG                     ; Exchange pointers
          MOV         M,A          ; Put in destination
          XCHG                     ; Restore pointers
          INX         H            ; SOURCE = SOURCE + 1
          INX         D            ; DEST = DEST + 1
          DCR         B            ; Count down bytes moved
          JNZ         M1           ; Continue until done

          ENDM
```

FIGURE 11-4. Macro definition for block move.

```
        MOVE        MACRO       SOURCE,DEST,COUNT
                    LOCAL       M1
                    LXI         H,SOURCE            ; Get source address
                    LXI         D,DEST              ; Get destination address
                    MVI         B,COUNT             ; Number of bytes to be
                                                      moved
        M1:         MOV         A,M                 ; Get source byte
                    XCHG                            ; Exchange pointers
                    MOV         M,A                 ; Put in destination
                    XCHG                            ; Restore pointers
                    INX         H                   ; SOURCE = SOURCE + 1
                    INX         D                   ; DEST = DEST + 1
                    DCR         B                   ; Count down bytes moved
                    JNZ         M1                  ; Continue until done
                    ENDM

0500                ORG         0500H               ; Main program
                    .
                    .
                    MOVE        1000H,2000H,50H     ; First call
050F+210010         LXI         H,1000H             ; Get source address
0512+110020         LXI         D,2000H             ; Get destination address
0515+0650           MVI         B,50H               ; Number of bytes to be
                                                      moved
0517+7E     ??0001: MOV         A,M                 ; Get source byte
0518+EB             XCHG                            ; Exchange pointers
0519+77             MOV         M,A                 ; Put in destination
051A+EB             XCHG                            ; Restore pointers
051B+23             INX         H                   ; SOURCE = SOURCE + 1
051C+13             INX         D                   ; DEST = DEST + 1
051D+05             DCR         B                   ; Count down bytes moved
051E+C21705         JNZ         ??0001              ; Continue until done
                    .
                    .
                    .
                    MOVE        5000H,1070H,10      ; Second call
0539+210050         LXI         H,5000H             ; Get source address
053C+117010         LXI         D,1070H             ; Get destination address
053F+060A           MVI         B,10                ; Number of bytes to be
                                                      moved
0541+7E     ??0002: MOV         A,M                 ; Get source byte
0542+EB             XCHG                            ; Exchange pointers
0543+77             MOV         M,A                 ; Put in destination
0544+EB             XCHG                            ; Restore pointers
0545+23             INX         H                   ; SOURCE = SOURCE + 1
0546+13             INX         D                   ; DEST = DEST + 1
0547+05             DCR         B                   ; Count down bytes moved
0548+C24105         JNZ         ??0002              ; Continue until done
                    .
                    .
                    .
0555                END
```

FIGURE 11-5. Two expansions of the MOVE macro.

the operand of the MVI B instruction. Notice that the symbols SOURCE, DEST, and COUNT do not appear in the expansion. Similarly, in the second macro expansion, the macro body is exactly the same as before except that the values of SOURCE, DEST, and COUNT are now 5000H, 1070H, and 10, respectively. Thus, each time a macro with parameters is called, the parameter values can be changed as required, allowing for a modified macro expansion each time.

In Figure 11-4 notice that within the macro body, a new directive, the *local directive* (LOCAL), has been used. The LOCAL directive in Figure 11-4 identifies the label M1 as being local (that is, to exist only in the macro definition) to the MOVE macro and allows its value to change during each expansion, as shown in Figure 11-5.

In Figure 11-5 during the first expansion of the macro, the original label M1 was renamed ??0001 and obtained a value of 0517H during assembly. During the second expansion, the label was referenced as ??0002 and obtained a value of 0541H during assembly. Now if the label M1 were not renamed in each expansion, there would be a multiple-label definition in the program; in other words, both expansions would contain the label M1, and the assembler would have to keep track of the value of M1 during each expansion. Therefore, the label M1 is defined to be local only to the macro definition and does not exist in the program.

11-4

An Application of Macros

Consider an application program to control a set of traffic lights at the intersection of two streets: Main Street (north and south), and Third Street (east and west). Two output ports are used to turn the lights on or off as follows:

output port 50H = Main Street (north/south)

output port 60H = Third Street (east/west)

Three bits of each port are used to turn on or off the red, yellow, and green lights:

bit 0 = red

bit 1 = yellow

bit 2 = green

Assuming that a logic 1 turns a light on and a logic 0 turns a light off, the following are some of the instructions that could be used to control the state of the lights at the intersection.

1. Turn on red light for Main Street (yellow and green off).

```
MVI  A,00000001B
OUT  50H
```

2. Turn on green light for Third Street (red and yellow off).

```
MVI  A,00000100B
OUT  60H
```

3. Turn on yellow light for Main Street (green and red off).

```
MVI  A,00000010B
OUT  50H
```

Thus to turn on a specific light (note that only one of the three lights for a particular street is on at a given time), a specific bit pattern is sent to the output port assigned to a particular street. These values are assigned to symbols as follows:

MAIN = 50H   RED   = 00000001B

THIRD = 60H   YELLOW = 00000010B

                GREEN   = 00000100B

The requirements for the software controlling the traffic lights are shown in the flowchart of Figure 11-6.

The program starts by switching the traffic lights on Main Street to green and the Third Street lights to red. A 50-sec delay is then initiated. After the delay, Main Street is switched to yellow and, after a further 5-sec delay, to red, and Third Street is switched to green. Another 20-sec delay is initiated. After the delay Third Street is now switched to yellow, and after another 5-sec delay, the cycle is repeated.

The program to implement the flowchart of Figure 11-6 will be constructed using only macros. In order to do this, three macros will be written as follows:

1. A macro called SWITCH, which will switch the lights on a specified street to a specified color.
2. A macro called WAIT, which will delay the CPU a specified number of seconds.
3. A macro called BEGIN, which will be used to transfer control to the start of the program on completion of a cycle.

Figure 11-7 shows the definition for the three macros SWITCH, WAIT, and BEGIN.

The SWITCH macro simply sets the accumulator to the specified bit pattern (dummy parameter COLOR) and outputs this to the specified port (dummy parameter STREET). Thus the macro call

```
SWITCH    MAIN,RED
```

(assuming that MAIN and RED have been equated to 50H and 00000001B, respectively) will turn the red light on for Main Street by means of the following instructions:

```
MVI  A,01H
OUT  50H
```

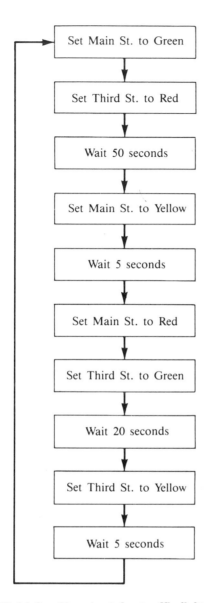

FIGURE 11-6.   Flowchart for traffic light controller.

The WAIT macro initiates a calculated delay loop that delays the CPU for a period of time (in seconds) specified by the dummy parameter SECONDS. For example, the macro call

WAIT 6

would cause the operand of the MVI D instruction to assemble as 24 and thus delay the CPU approximately 6 sec.

```
SWITCH    MACRO    STREET,COLOR
          MVI      A,COLOR        ; Light code
          OUT      STREET         ; Street code
          ENDM

WAIT      MACRO    SECONDS
          LOCAL    W1,W2,W3
          MVI      D,4*SECONDS    ; Basic loop value
W1:       MVI      B,250          ; 250 msec * 4 = 1 sec
W2:       MVI      C,182          ; 182*5.5 µsec = 1 msec
W3:       DCR      C              ; 1 cy = 0.5 µsec
          JNZ      W3             ; +10 cy = 5.5 µsec
          DCR      B              ; Count 250, 249, . . .
          JNZ      W2             ; Loop on register B
          DCR      D              ; Basic loop control
          JNZ      W1             ; Loop on register D
          ENDM

BEGIN     MACRO    WHERE
          JMP      WHERE
          ENDM
```

FIGURE 11-7. Macro definitions for traffic light controller.

The BEGIN macro is used to transfer control of the program to a specified label. The manner in which this is done will be seen in the macro expansion.

The program to implement the flowchart of Figure 11-6 using the macros of Figure 11-7 is shown in Figure 11-8. Notice that a major portion of the program consists of macro calls. In fact, the program in Figure 11-8 barely resembles an

```
MAIN      EQU      50H            ; Output port for Main St.
THIRD     EQU      60H            ; Output port for Third St.
RED       EQU      01H            ; Red-light control
YELLOW    EQU      02H            ; Yellow-light control
GREEN     EQU      04H            ; Green-light control

CYCLE:    SWITCH   MAIN,GREEN     ; Set Main St. Green
          SWITCH   THIRD,RED      ; Set Third St. Red
          WAIT     50             ; Delay 50 seconds

          SWITCH   MAIN,YELLOW    ; Set Main St. Yellow
          WAIT     5              ; Wait 5 seconds

          SWITCH   MAIN,RED       ; Set Main St. Red
          SWITCH   THIRD,GREEN    ; Set Third St. Green
          WAIT     20             ; Delay 20 seconds

          SWITCH   THIRD,YELLOW   ; Set Third St. Yellow
          WAIT     5              ; Delay 5 seconds

          BEGIN    CYCLE          ; Start all over again

          END
```

FIGURE 11-8. Traffic light controller program: source file.

8085 assembly language program. Also, by simply scanning through the program one can get a clear picture of the program's operation, another advantage of using macros in assembly language programs. Notice that each macro implements the corresponding step in the flowchart of Figure 11-6.

Figure 11-9 shows the macro expansion initiated during the assembly of the program of Figure 11-8. Notice in Figure 11-9 that the MVI D instruction in each expansion of the WAIT macro changes to reflect the amount of time delay. Also notice that the assembler renames the local labels W1, W2, and W3 during each expansion of the WAIT macro. The BEGIN macro at the end of the program simply contains a JMP instruction to the start of the program, which causes the entire monitoring cycle to be repeated over and over again.

```
0050 =          MAIN    EQU    50H        ; Output port for Main St.
0060 =          THIRD   EQU    60H        ; Output port for Third St.
0001 =          RED     EQU    01H        ; Red-light control
0002 =          YELLOW  EQU    02H        ; Yellow-light control
0004 =          GREEN   EQU    04H        ; Green-light control

                CYCLE:  SWITCH MAIN,GREEN ; Set Main St. Green
0000+3E04               MVI    A,GREEN    ; Light code
0002+D350               OUT    MAIN       ; Street code
                        SWITCH THIRD,RED  ; Set Third St. Red
0004+3E01               MVI    A,RED      ; Light code
0006+D360               OUT    THIRD      ; Street code
                        WAIT   50         ; Delay 50 seconds
0008+16C8               MVI    D,4*50     ; Basic loop value
000A+06FA     ??0001: MVI      B,250      ; 250 msec * 4 = 1 sec
000C+0EB6     ??0002: MVI      C,182      ; 182 * 5.5 µsec = 1 msec
000E+0D       ??0003: DCR      C          ; 1 cy = 0.5 µsec
000F+C20E00             JNZ    ??0003     ; +10 cy = 5.5 µsec
0012+05                 DCR    B          ; Count 250, 249, . . .
0013+C20C00             JNZ    ??0002     ; Loop on register B
0016+15                 DCR    D          ; Basic loop control
0017+C20A00             JNZ    ??0001     ; Loop on register D

                        SWITCH MAIN,YELLOW ; Set Main St. Yellow
001A+3E02               MVI    A,YELLOW   ; Light code
001C+D350               OUT    MAIN       ; Street code
                        WAIT   5          ; Wait 5 seconds
001E+1614               MVI    D,4*5      ; Basic loop value
0020+06FA     ??0004: MVI      B,250      ; 250 msec * 4 = 1 sec
0022+0EB6     ??0005: MVI      C,182      ; 182 * 5.5 µsec = 1 msec
0024+0D       ??0006: DCR      C          ; 1 cy = 0.5 µsec
0025+C22400             JNZ    ??0006     ; +10 cy = 5.5 µsec
0028+05                 DCR    B          ; Count 250, 249, . . .
0029+C22200             JNZ    ??0005     ; Loop on register B
002C+15                 DCR    D          ; Basic loop control
002D+C22000             JNZ    ??0004     ; Loop on register D

                        SWITCH MAIN,RED   ; Set Main St. Red
0030+3E01               MVI    A,RED      ; Light code
0032+D350               OUT    MAIN       ; Street code
```

FIGURE 11-9. Macro expansion of traffic light controller program.

```
                             SWITCH   THIRD,GREEN   ; Set Third St. Green
0034 + 3E04                  MVI      A,GREEN       ; Light code
0036 + D360                  OUT      THIRD         ; Street code
                             WAIT     20            ; Delay 20 seconds
0038 + 1650                  MVI      D,4*20        ; Basic loop value
003A + 06FA     ??0007: MVI           B,250         ; 250 msec * 4 = 1 sec
003C + 0EB6     ??0008: MVI           C,182         ; 182 * 5.5 μsec = 1 msec
003E + 0D       ??0009: DCR           C             ; 1 cy = 0.5 μsec
003F + C23E00                JNZ      ??0009        ; +10 cy = 5.5 μsec
0042 + 05                    DCR      B             ; Count 250, 249, . . .
0043 + C23C00                JNZ      ??0008        ; Loop on register B
0046 + 15                    DCR      D             ; Basic loop control
0047 + C23A00                JNZ      ??0007        ; Loop on register D

                             SWITCH   THIRD,YELLOW; Set Third St. Yellow
004A + 3E02                  MVI      A,YELLOW      ; Light code
004C + D360                  OUT      THIRD         ; Street code
                             WAIT     5             ; Delay 5 seconds
004E + 1614                  MVI      D,4*5         ; Basic loop value
0050 + 06FA     ??0010: MVI           B,250         ; 250 msec * 4 = 1 sec
0052 + 0EB6     ??0011: MVI           C,182         ; 182 * 5.5 μsec = 1 msec
0054 + 0D       ??0012: DCR           C             ; 1 cy = 0.5 μsec
0055 + C25400                JNZ      ??0012        ; +10 cy = 5.5 μsec
0058 + 05                    DCR      B             ; Count 250, 249, . . .
0059 + C25200                JNZ      ??0011        ; Loop on register B
005C + 15                    DCR      D             ; Basic loop control
005D + C25000                JNZ      ??0010        ; Loop on register D

                             BEGIN    CYCLE         ; Start all over again
0060 + C30000                JMP      CYCLE

0063                         END
```

FIGURE 11-9. (Continued)

The application program example given in this section also illustrates the use of macros in writing "RAM-less" programs. If the expanded program of Figure 11-9 is examined carefully, it can be seen that there are no references to RAM memory and no instructions such as CALL, RET, POP, and PUSH that require the use of a stack. Programs such as these can be implemented entirely in a "RAM-less" microprocessor system (that is, a system containing only ROM).

11-5

Repetitive Macros

In many assembly language application programs, a sequence of instructions may often be repeated many times in the course of the program. A good example of this is in the program shown in Figure 11-1. Notice in Figure 11-1 that the RLC instruction sequence is repeated twice in the program. In developing programs that contain such repetitive instruction sequences, it would be nice to have some facility that instructs the assembler to assemble a certain instruction (or sequence of instructions) a specified number of times. In other words, instead of the programmer's typing in four RLC instructions each time in Figure 11-1, a directive to the assembler could instruct it to assemble the code for the RLC instruction four times. Such a directive is available in most assemblers and is a macro directive known as the *REPT directive*.

Figure 11-10 illustrates the implementation of the program in Figure 11-1 with the REPT directive. Notice in Figure 11-10 that the four RLC instructions have been replaced with a REPT directive instructing the assembler to repeat assembly of the following instruction (between the REPT and ENDM) four times. This is done in both sections in the program where there previously were four individual RLC instructions (refer to Figure 11-1). The program in Figure 11-10 is the source program before assembly, and Figure 11-11 shows the operation of the REPT directive by illustrating the macro expansions after assembly.

In Figure 11-11 notice that for each REPT directive, four RLC instructions were assembled (inserted as in a MACRO). By comparing the programs in Figures 11-1, 11-3, and 11-11, one can see that they are identical in the machine code generated but different at the source level. The three programs also illustrate different ways of writing the same program and should help when deciding which of the assembler's facilities to use.

Another application of the REPT macro directive is in the automatic generation of look-up data tables for various application programs. When the REPT directive is used in conjunction with the DB or DW and SET directives, it can be of tremendous aid to the programmer.

```
ORG     1000H

IN      0               ; Get first number
REPT    4               ; Move to M.S. position
RLC
ENDM
ANI     11110000B       ; Clear L.S. bits
MOV     B,A             ; Save first number
IN      0               ; Get second number
ANI     00001111B       ; Clear M.S. bits
ORA     B               ; Merge with first number
MOV     H,A             ; Save first and second numbers
IN      0               ; Get third number
REPT    4               ; Move to M.S. position
RLC
ENDM
ANI     11110000B       ; Clear L.S. bits
MOV     B,A             ; Save third number
IN      0               ; Get fourth number
ANI     00001111B       ; Clear M.S. bits
ORA     B               ; Merge with third number
MOV     L,A             ; Save third and fourth numbers
HLT                     ; RP H&L contains word

END
```

FIGURE 11-10.   Word assembly program implemented with the REPT macro.

```
1000            ORG   1000H

1000  DB00      IN    0              ; Get first number
                REPT  4              ; Move to M.S. position
                RLC
                ENDM
1002+07         RLC
1003+07         RLC
1004+07         RLC
1005+07         RLC
1006  E6F0      ANI   11110000B      ; Clear L.S. bits
1008  47        MOV   B,A            ; Save first number
1009  DB00      IN    0              ; Get second number
100B  E60F      ANI   00001111B      ; Clear M.S. bits
100D  B0        ORA   B              ; Merge with first number
100E  67        MOV   H,A            ; Save first and second numbers
100F  DB00      IN    0              ; Get third number
                REPT  4              ; Move to M.S. position
                RLC
                ENDM
1011+07         RLC
1012+07         RLC
1013+07         RLC
1014+07         RLC
1015  E6F0      ANI   11110000B      ; Clear L.S. bits
1017  47        MOV   B,A            ; Save third number
1018  DB00      IN    0              ; Get fourth number
101A  E60F      ANI   00001111B      ; Clear M.S. bits
101C  B0        ORA   B              ; Merge with third number
101D  6F        MOV   L,A            ; Save third and fourth numbers
101E  76        HLT                  ; RP H&L contains word

101F            END
```

FIGURE 11-11.   Macro expansion of the REPT macro directive.

For example, assume that an application program requires a look-up table of bytes in the following sequence:

01H,02H,04H,08H,10H,20H,40H,80H

Instead of defining each byte with a DB directive in the source program, the programmer simply writes the following sequence of code:

```
NEXT    SET    1              ; First table value

TABLE:  REPT   8              ; Make eight table entries
        DB     NEXT           ; Table byte
NEXT    SET    NEXT*2         ; Next table entry
        ENDM

        END
```

```
0001  #    NEXT     SET    1          ; First table value

           TABLE:   REPT   8          ; Make 8 table entries
                    DB     NEXT       ; Table byte
           NEXT     SET    NEXT*2     ; Next table entry
                    ENDM
0000+01             DB     NEXT       ; Table byte
0001+02             DB     NEXT       ; Table byte
0002+04             DB     NEXT       ; Table byte
0003+08             DB     NEXT       ; Table byte
0004+10             DB     NEXT       ; Table byte
0005+20             DB     NEXT       ; Table byte
0006+40             DB     NEXT       ; Table byte
0007+80             DB     NEXT       ; Table byte

0008                END
```

FIGURE 11-12.   Automatic generation of data table.

Recall that the SET directive can be used to define the value of a symbol as well as have the value of the symbol changed during assembly. Initially, the value of the symbol NEXT is set to 1. The REPT directive is used to repeat assembly of the following DB directive eight times. The first time the DB directive is assembled, the value of NEXT is 1, and therefore the first byte in the table is assembled as a 01H. The value of NEXT is then set to the old value of NEXT (01) times 2; the new value is now 2. When the DB directive is assembled the second time, a 02H is stored in the table, and the value of NEXT becomes 2 × 2, or 04H. This is then stored as the third table entry, and so on, until eight table entries have been created. The table generated by the assembler is shown in Figure 11-12.

In the expansion shown in Figure 11-12, notice that eight table entries have been created using the DB directive. However, for each entry in the table the value of the symbol NEXT is different (two times greater). This scheme for generating tables with data values following mathematical progressions is very convenient in assembly language programming, especially when such tables are extremely long.

11-6

Conditional Assembly

When a programmer develops "universal" assembly language programs (that is, programs that have to be adapted to a wide variety of systems), these programs must be geared to the hardware environment of the system on which they are being run. For example, the console input subroutine in Figure 10-4 is compatible only with an 8251 chip. Also, for the subroutine to execute properly, the hardware scheme must be designed so that the data port is addressed as device 02H and the status port as device 03H. If any of these requirements are

```
FALSE      EQU    0000H        ; False variable
TRUE       EQU    NOT FALSE    ; True variable

U8251      EQU    TRUE         ; Set true for 8251 UART
U1602      EQU    NOT U8251    ; Set false for 1602 UART

           IF     U8251
DATA       EQU    02H          ; 8251 data port
STATUS     EQU    03H          ; 8251 status port
MASK       EQU    00000010B    ; 8251 receiver mask
           ENDIF

           IF     U1602
DATA       EQU    05H          ; 1602 data port
STATUS     EQU    06H          ; 1602 status port
MASK       EQU    00010000B    ; 1602 receiver mask
           ENDIF

CONIN:     IN     STATUS       ; Get UART status
           ANI    MASK         ; See if receiver ready
           JZ     CONIN        ; Wait until ready
           IN     DATA         ; Get data
           RET
```

FIGURE 11-13. CONIN subroutine written for two UARTs.

not met, the subroutine will not execute properly, and consequently, the program that CALLs the subroutine will not work as intended.

Thus the problem of adapting software to the hardware environment often arises. If a program that is designed for a particular hardware environment is to be executed on another system with a different hardware scheme, the program has to be modified to reflect the characteristics of the new hardware. This can be done by searching through the program for hardware-dependent code and modifying those segments of code appropriately. To make such modifications to a program easier for the programmer, most assemblers have conditional assembly directives. These directives can be used to define segments of code that can be included or excluded during assembly. The programmer can control the assembly of these segments through a simple process.

Consider the 8251 console input routine discussed in previous chapters. As mentioned before, the CONIN routine is a hardware-dependent routine and works only with the 8251 UART chip. Assuming that the CONIN routine is to be modified for another UART with characteristics that are different from those of the 8251, three modifications must be made to the routine: the addresses of the data and status ports, and the receiver mask word. To make these modifications easier it would be convenient to have a directive that would instruct the assembler to assemble CONIN for either the 8251 or some other chip. This can be done in assembly language programming, as shown in Figure 11-13.

In Figure 11-13, two symbols, TRUE and FALSE, are equated as complements of each other. That is, the symbol FALSE is set to zero, and the symbol TRUE is set to the complement of FALSE (NOT FALSE) so as to give it the value FFFFH. Similarly, the symbol U8251 is set to the value of the symbol TRUE (FFFFH), and U1602 is set to the complement of U8251 (NOT U8251) to yield a value of 0000H. After the program in Figure 11-13 is assembled, the result of the conditional assembly directives is shown in Figure 11-14.

The program in Figure 11-14 can be assembled as a CONIN routine for either the 8251 UART or the 1602 UART. Notice the differences in the 8251 and 1602 address and mask words. The value of U8251 is set TRUE to direct assembly of the subroutine for the 8251. When the assembler encounters the IF directive, it examines the operand of the directive; if the value of the operand is FFFFH (TRUE), it will accept all code between the IF and ENDIF directives. If the value of the operand is 0000H (FALSE), it will ignore everything between the IF and ENDIF directives. In Figure 11-14, because the value of U8251 is TRUE, the DATA, STATUS, and MASK symbols are set to the appropriate values for the 8251. Because U8251 is TRUE in this case, U1602 is automatically equated FALSE, as they complement each other in value. The EQUates for the 1602 are thus ignored. Finally, when the actual code for the subroutine is assembled, the values used for DATA, STATUS, and MASK are specific to the 8251 UART.

Figure 11-15 illustrates the same CONIN subroutine of Figure 11-13 assembled for the 1602 UART (U8251 set FALSE). When the programs of Figures 11-14 and 11-15 are compared, one can see that if the programmer wanted to change the subroutine for either the 1602 or 8251 UARTs, a single byte would be all that had to be modified. By adding more conditional blocks, the CONIN subroutine could be modified to include many other types of UARTs and addressing schemes.

```
0000 =        FALSE  EQU   0000H      ; False variable
FFFF =        TRUE   EQU   NOT FALSE  ; True variable

FFFF =        U8251  EQU   TRUE       ; Set true for 8251 UART
0000 =        U1602  EQU   NOT U8251  ; Set false for 1602 UART

              IF     U8251
0002 =        DATA   EQU   02H        ; 8251 data port
0003 =        STATUS EQU   03H        ; 8251 status port
0002 =        MASK   EQU   00000010B  ; 8251 receiver mask
              ENDIF

              IF     U1602
              DATA   EQU   05H        ; 1602 data port
              STATUS EQU   06H        ; 1602 status port
              MASK   EQU   00010000B  ; 1602 receiver mask
              ENDIF

0000 DB03     CONIN: IN     STATUS    ; Get UART status
0002 E602            ANI    MASK      ; See if receiver ready
0004 CA0000          JZ     CONIN     ; Wait until ready
0007 DB02            IN     DATA      ; Get data
0009 C9             RET
```

FIGURE 11-14.   CONIN subroutine assembled for the 8251 UART.

```
0000 =          FALSE  EQU  0000H       ; False variable
FFFF =          TRUE   EQU  NOT FALSE   ; True variable

0000 =          U8251  EQU  FALSE       ; Set true for 8251 UART
FFFF =          U1602  EQU  NOT U8251   ; Set false for 1602 UART

                       IF   U8251
                DATA   EQU  02H         ; 8251 data port
                STATUS EQU  03H         ; 8251 status port
                MASK   EQU  00000010B   ; 8251 receiver mask
                       ENDIF

                       IF   U1602
0005 =          DATA   EQU  05H         ; 1602 data port
0006 =          STATUS EQU  06H         ; 1602 status port
0010 =          MASK   EQU  00010000B   ; 1602 receiver mask
                       ENDIF

0000 DB06       CONIN: IN   STATUS      ; Get UART status
0002 E610              ANI  MASK        ; See if receiver ready
0004 CA0000            JZ   CONIN       ; Wait until ready
0007 DB05              IN   DATA        ; Get data
0009 C9                RET
```

FIGURE 11-15. CONIN subroutine assembled for the 1602 UART.

The use of conditional assembly does not have to be limited to the development of universal programs. One of the most useful features of conditional assembly is when it is used together with macros. For example, assume that a programmer wants to create four new instructions for the 8085 by using macro definitions. The mnemonics for these new instructions are as follows:

- COM B   Complement the contents of register B
- COM C   Complement the contents of register C
- COM D   Complement the contents of register D
- COM E   Complement the contents of register E

Instead of writing four separate macros for each instruction (each one containing the appropriate 8085 instructions to implement the macro), the programmer can define a single macro that will conditionally expand a section of code, depending on a macro parameter. This technique is shown in Figure 11-16.

The name of the macro in Figure 11-16 is COM, and the macro will be called with a single parameter, which can be B, C, D, or E. One of these symbols will be assigned to the dummy parameter REG. Notice that the first and last instructions in the macro body are a PUSH and POP, respectively; these instructions are used to preserve the contents of the accumulator and will always be the first and last instructions of each macro expansion.

For example, if the macro call COM B is encountered during assembly, a macro expansion will be initiated. Because the dummy parameter REG is equal to the symbol B, the instructions within that block are expanded, and all other blocks are ignored. Figure 11-17 shows the macro expansions for each macro call.

Notice in Figure 11-17 that each macro call initiates a different set of instructions for assembly. The set of instructions assembled depends on the macro parameter used in the calling macro.

The ELSE directive can also be used with the IF and ENDIF directives to assemble conditionally certain segments of code. For example, Figures 11-18 and 11-19 illustrate the implementation of the console output routine (CONOUT) for the 8251 or 1602 UARTs.

Figure 11-18 shows the CONOUT subroutine assembled for the 8251 (U8251 set TRUE). The use of the ELSE directive in the CONOUT subroutine illustrates an alternative means of developing a universal program. In Figure 11-18, instead of including the mask word as a group condition (as was done for CONIN), the symbol U1602 is tested during the assembly of the subroutine code. In this case, because U1602 evaluated FALSE, the ANI 00100000B instruction was ignored, and the ANI 00000001B instruction assembled at the current value of the location counter.

Figure 11-19 illustrates the CONOUT subroutine assembled for the 1602 UART (U8251 set FALSE). Notice in Figure 11-19 that because U8251 is set FALSE, the assembler assembles the instruction immediately following the ELSE directive and ignores the assembly of the preceding instruction.

```
COM     MACRO       REG

        PUSH        PSW         ; Save original contents

        IF          REG=B       ; Complement register B
        MOV         A,B
        CMA
        MOV         B,A
        ENDIF

        IF          REG=C       ; Complement register C
        MOV         A,C
        CMA
        MOV         C,A
        ENDIF

        IF          REG=D       ; Complement register D
        MOV         A,D
        CMA
        MOV         D,A
        ENDIF

        IF          REG=E       ; Complement register E
        MOV         A,E
        CMA
        MOV         E,A
        ENDIF

        POP         PSW

        ENDM
```

FIGURE 11-16.   Definition for the 'COM r' macro.

```
                          COM         B
        0000 + F5         PUSH        PSW         ; Save original contents
        0001 + 78         MOV         A,B
        0002 + 2F         CMA
        0003 + 47         MOV         B,A
        0004 + F1         POP         PSW


                          COM         C
        0005 + F5         PUSH        PSW         ; Save original contents
        0006 + 79         MOV         A,C
        0007 + 2F         CMA
        0008 + 4F         MOV         C,A
        0009 + F1         POP         PSW


                          COM         D
        000A + F5         PUSH        PSW         ; Save original contents
        000B + 7A         MOV         A,D
        000C + 2F         CMA
        000D + 57         MOV         D,A
        000E + F1         POP         PSW


                          COM         E
        000F + F5         PUSH        PSW         ; Save original contents
        0010 + 7B         MOV         A,E
        0011 + 2F         CMA
        0012 + 5F         MOV         E,A
        0013 + F1         POP         PSW
```

FIGURE 11-17. Macro expansions for the COM r macros.

```
        0000 =            FALSE       EQU     0000H       ; False variable
        FFFF =            TRUE        EQU     NOT FALSE   ; True variable

        FFFF =            U8251       EQU     TRUE        ; Set true for 8251 UART
        0000 =            U1602       EQU     NOT U8251   ; Set false for 1602 UART

                          IF          U8251
        0002 =            DATA        EQU     02H         ; 8251 data port
        0003 =            STATUS      EQU     03H         ; 8251 status port
                          ENDIF


                          IF          U1602
                          DATA        EQU     05H         ; 1602 data port
                          STATUS      EQU     06H         ; 1602 status port
                          ENDIF

        0000 DB03         CONOUT:  IN         STATUS      ; Get UART status
                          IF          U1602
                          ANI         00100000B   ; See if 1602 TX ready
                          ELSE
        0002 E601         ANI         00000001B   ; See if 8251 TX ready
                          ENDIF
        0004 CA0000       JZ          CONOUT      ; Wait until ready
        0007 79           MOV         A,C         ; Get character
        0008 D302         OUT         DATA        ; Transmit character
        000A C9           RET
```

FIGURE 11-18. CONOUT subroutine assembled for the 8251 UART.

```
0000  =        FALSE   EQU    0000H        ; False variable
FFFF  =        TRUE    EQU    NOT FALSE    ; True variable

0000  =        U8251   EQU    FALSE        ; Set true for 8251 UART
FFFF  =        U1602   EQU    NOT U8251    ; Set false for 1602 UART

               IF      U8251
      DATA     EQU     02H                 ; 8251 data port
      STATUS   EQU     03H                 ; 8251 status port
               ENDIF

               IF      U1602
0005  =        DATA    EQU    05H          ; 1602 data port
0006  =        STATUS  EQU    06H          ; 1602 status port
               ENDIF

0000  DB06     CONOUT: IN     STATUS       ; Get UART status
                       IF     U1602
0002  E620             ANI    00100000B    ; See if 1602 TX ready
                       ELSE
                       ANI    00000001B    ; See if 8251 TX ready
                       ENDIF
0004  CA0000           JZ     CONOUT       ; Wait until ready
0007  79               MOV    A,C          ; Get character
0008  D305             OUT    DATA         ; Transmit character
000A  C9               RET
```

FIGURE 11-19. CONOUT subroutine assembled for the 1602 UART.

To summarize the use of the IF, ELSE, and ENDIF directives, the following points should be noted:

1. When the assembler encounters an IF directive during assembly, it examines the operand of the IF directive. The operand can be a symbol or expression that evaluates to a TRUE (FFFFH) or FALSE (0000H) result.
2. If the operand of the IF directive evaluates TRUE, the assembler will assemble all following instructions (or directives) until an ENDIF or ELSE directive is encountered. If an ELSE directive is encountered, all instructions between the ELSE and ENDIF directives will be ignored.
3. If the operand of the IF directive evaluates FALSE, the assembler will ignore all following instructions (or directives) until an ENDIF or ELSE directive is encountered. If an ELSE directive is encountered, all instructions between the ELSE and ENDIF directives will be assembled.

11-7

Summary

The use of macros in assembly language programming often is of tremendous aid to the programmer, but there are always advantages and disadvantages of using macros in application programs. A major trade-off lies between execution speed and memory requirements. Because the macro body is expanded "in-line'' each time the assembler encounters a macro call, the memory requirements of the final program are very high. Most of the code for macros can be implemented with subroutines, although the execution time of CALL and RET instructions increases the overall execution time of the program. In this chapter it was also seen that by using macros, the programmer could create ''RAM-less'' programs. These programs are frequently used in ROM-only systems and therefore cannot have any CALL or RET instructions.

The use of macros also changed the ''appearance'' of the assembly language program. An assembly language program implemented only with macros was more descriptive at the source level in terms of its operation. Many assemblers provide facilities for storing macros in files called macro libraries. These libraries are used in a manner similar to the subroutine library discussed in Chapter 10. The programmer stores various utility macros in a library, and the assembler automatically references the library for the macro definitions. This technique allows the programmer to treat macros as if they were mnemonic instructions.

Perhaps the greatest advantage of using macros in assembly language programming is in creating new instructions for the microprocessor. By using the right sequence of code in macros, the programmer can simulate the instruction set of large computers. Macros can also be used to force the assembler to recognize instructions of upwardly compatible microprocessors. In fact, by creating a library of macros, one can make the assembler recognize and assemble instructions for any microprocessor.

Conditional assembly is an easy way of changing the operation of a program. It allows the programmer to create a single ''generic'' program with a number of alternative program segments, which are included or excluded as part of the final assembled code. The conditional segments of a program are controlled by simply setting a symbol TRUE or FALSE and thus eliminating the need for searching through a program during modification.

The use of conditional assembly directives in macros allows the programmer to develop a single macro that will change its function depending on the value of an operand (dummy parameter). This application is used extensively in superficially expanding the instruction set of the microprocessor.

Macros and conditional assembly are optional features provided by most 8080/85 assemblers, although all assembly language programs can be developed without such features. The use of macros and conditional assembly in application programs will depend on the type of program being designed. It is up to the programmer to decide when a program can be implemented more efficiently with macros and/or conditional segments or without such code.

REVIEW QUESTIONS AND PROBLEMS

1. How does a macro differ from a subroutine? Give examples.

2. Describe briefly two applications of macros in assembly language programming.

3. By means of an example, describe how a macro definition is constructed.

4. How are parameters used with macros?

5. What is the purpose of defining a label LOCAL within the macro body?

6. Convert to macros the utility subroutines developed in Chapter 10.

7. Use the macros developed in Problem 6 to implement the LOADER program of Chapter 10.

8. Compare the loader program of Problem 7 with the LOADER program developed in Chapter 10.

9. Define a macro to generate automatically a data table containing the following 16-bit words:

```
0001H,0003H,0009H,001BH,0051H,00F3H,
02D9H,088BH,19A1H,4CE3H
```

10. What is conditional assembly? How is it used in the development of assembly language programs?

11. Without using an assembler, identify the instructions that will be assembled in the following program segment:

```
YES       EQU      OFFFFH
NO        EQU      NOT YES
STEP      EQU      NO
ALTER     EQU      NOT STEP
NOW       EQU      YES
          LXI      SP,STACK
          IF       STEP
          LXI      H,DATA
          ELSE
          LXI      H,TABLE
          ENDIF
          IF       NOW
          IF       NOT ALTER
          MOV      A,M
          OUT      LED
          ENDIF
          MOV      C,M
          ENDIF
          IF       STEP AND NOW
          INX      H
          DCR      C
          ENDIF
```

12. Repeat Problem 11 by setting the label STEP to YES.

13. Define a new instruction for the 8085 using macros and conditional assembly. The general form of the instruction should be

$$BIT \quad p,r$$

where p is the position (0 through 7) of a bit to be set in an 8-bit register "r" (A,B,C,D,E,H, or L). For example, if it were desired to set the most significant bit of register C (without affecting any other bits), the instruction BIT 7,C could be used.

CHAPTER 12

Introduction to the C Compiler

12-1

Introduction

Chapter 8 introduced the reader to the use of the assembler in developing programs in assembly language. This chapter introduces the reader to the use of a compiler in the development of programs written in a higher-level language.

The programming language used to illustrate the applications of a compiler for microcomputer software development is the "C" programming language. C was chosen because it is a general-purpose language that has become extremely popular for use with microcomputers. Also, C is flexible enough to be used for relatively low-level control programs, as well as for the more sophisticated "systems" and "applications" programming. Another reason for the popularity of C is its *portability*. One of the main disadvantages of assembly language programming is its restriction to the CPU's instruction set; that is, an assembly language program can be developed only for a specific computer, as the instruction set differs in each CPU. Therefore, in order to execute on a CPU an assembly language program designed for another CPU, the programmer must become familiar with another instruction set and perhaps be forced to rewrite the entire program. But a C program can easily be transported from one computer to another with few or no modifications. C also allows a programmer to extend its features to the same level as some of the more sophisticated languages such as FORTRAN, Pascal, and PL/I.

The C programming language is based on the language B, an adaptation of BCPL (Basic Combined Programming Language). The name C stems from the fact that it is the second adaptation of BCPL and that C is the second letter in BCPL.

This chapter will serve only as an introduction to the C programming language and the C compiler, as it is beyond the scope of this book to study it in detail.

12-2

The Operation of a Compiler

The notion of developing software with a compiler was discussed briefly in Chapter 8. Now we shall explain the differences between assembly language software and compiler language software, as well as the differences between an assembler and a compiler.

The building blocks of a higher-level language consists of "English-like" program *statements,* rather than mnemonics. A single statement can be used to perform a number of machine instructions, hence the term *higher-level language.* In the development of higher-level programs, the user codes the program as a sequence of tasks rather than as a sequence of mnemonics. This therefore leads to the concept of a higher-level language being task oriented versus an assembly language being machine oriented. In an assembly language program, a software tool, an assembler, is used to translate the sequence of mnemonic instructions into machine code. Similarly, a software tool, a compiler, is used to translate a higher-level language into a sequence of machine instructions. Higher-level languages are therefore also known as *compiler-level languages.* Figure 12-1 shows the software development process using both an assembler and a compiler.

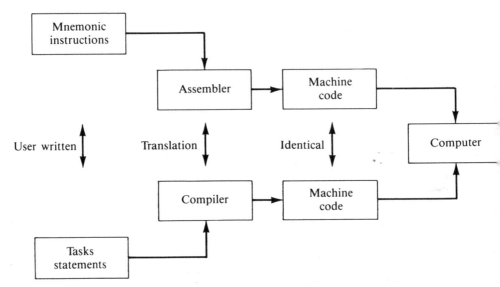

FIGURE 12-1. Software development using assemblers and compilers.

Note that in Figure 12-1 the only difference in the development of a program at the compiler level and at the assembler level is how the programs are written. As far as execution of the translated machine code is concerned, the computer cannot distinguish between the machine code generated by a compiler and the machine code generated by an assembler; for all practical purposes, they are identical.

12-3

The General Form of a C Program

To illustrate the general form of a C program, a simple program specification will be implemented in both assembly language and C.

A microcomputer has three parallel I/O ports. Two of the ports are 8-bit input ports connected to sets of eight switches. The third port is an output port connected to a set of seven-segment LED displays. A program is to be written that gets the data bytes from these two switches, computes the sum of the two bytes, and displays the result on the LEDs. The port numbers for the switches are 54H and 55H, the port number for the LED is 60H, and the assembly language implementation of this specification is shown in Figure 12-2.

The assembly language implementation of the program specification is fairly straightforward, as can be seen in Figure 12-2. The C implementation of the program specification is shown in Figure 12-3. Line numbers have been added to the program in order to reference the individual statements for explanation. Note that these numbers are not part of the C program.

It is conventional to use lowercase letters throughout a C program, except for symbolic names and constants which are usually entered in uppercase letters. This convention is shown in the C program of Figure 12-3. C programs can also be written in a *free-format* style, which means that spaces and blank lines can be used freely in the program without any rigid formatting restrictions.

Figure 12-3 also illustrates the general flow and characteristics of a C program, which here contains seven statements (numbered 5–7, 10–13). A statement is always terminated with a ";" and does not have to be limited to a single line. The seven statements can be divided into two types, *nonexecutable statements*

```
; CALCULATE THE SUM OF TWO BYTES

SWITCH1 EQU 54H      ; Port number for switch 1
SWITCH2 EQU 55H      ; Port number for switch 2
LED     EQU 60H      ; Port number for LED

        IN  SWITCH1  ; Get data from switch 1
        MOV B,A      ; Save it in reg B
        IN  SWITCH2  ; Get data from switch 2
        ADD B        ; Add the two values
        OUT LED      ; Output result to LED
        HLT

(9 BYTES ASSEMBLED
```

FIGURE 12-2. Assembly language program to calculate a sum.

```
Line
1          /*    Calculate the sum of two numbers */

2          #define SWITCH1  0x54
3          #define SWITCH2  0x55
4          #define LED      0x60

5          char data1;
6          char data2;
7          char sum;

8          main()
9          {
10                 data1 = input (SWITCH1);
11                 data2 = input (SWITCH2);
12                 sum = data1 + data2;
13                 output (LED,sum);
14         }
```

FIGURE 12-3.   C program to calculate a sum.

(numbered 5 through 7) and *executable statements* (numbered 10 through 13). The nonexecutable statements can be thought of as "directives" to the compiler and are used only at *compile time* (that is, while the program is being compiled), whereas the executable statements can be considered the actual "tasks" that are translated into machine code by the compiler and are executed at *run time* (while the program is being executed). Henceforth, whenever a reference is made to the *execution of a statement,* what is meant is the *execution of the machine code compiled for that statement.*

By viewing the general form of the C program, one can see that hardware registers are no longer used to represent the storage of numeric data; instead, unique names called *identifiers* are used to reference a numeric quantity. Examples of such identifiers used in the C program of Figure 12-3 are *data1, data2, sum,* SWITCH1, SWITCH2, and LED. An identifier can be a unique reference to a memory location or a symbol that is associated with a numeric constant. With a few exceptions, any references made to an identifier refer indirectly to the contents of the memory location allocated for the identifier. Similarly, the *value* of an identifier (that is not a symbolic constant) refers to the data stored at the identifier's memory location. If an identifier allows the content(s) of its memory location(s) to be modified, it is known as a *variable.*

Variables are referred to by names that can be of any length and are not restricted to alphabetic characters. However, the first character in the identifier must be alphabetic or an underscore "_". Spaces are not permitted between the characters that make up the identifier's name, but the underscore ("_") has the effect of improving readability in extremely long identifier names. Even though the length of an identifier's name is not restricted, the C compiler will use only the first eight characters. The case of the letters used in the names of identifiers is significant. For example, DATA1 and *data1* are not the same identifiers. As was mentioned before, lowercase letters should be used throughout a C program except for the names of symbolic references. And identifier names cannot be one of the C compiler's *keywords.* These keywords have a special meaning in the compilation process and therefore cannot be used as identifier names. The list of C keywords (reserved words) is listed in Table 12-1.

Line 1 of the C program in Figure 12-3 is a comment string. In C, two delimiters are required to enclose a comment string, a left delimiter pair ''/*'' and a right delimiter pair ''*/''. The text within the delimiters serves only as documentation and is completely ignored by the compiler. A comment does not have to be limited to a single line but can extend to a paragraph or even a page, as long as the comment starts and ends with these delimiter pairs. Comments can be used anywhere in the C program.

Lines 2, 3, and 4 are nonexecutable statements, known as *macro preprocessor directives*. During the compilation (translation) process, whenever the compiler encounters a symbol defined with the #*define* directive, it will substitute the specified value for the symbol. For example, whenever the symbol LED is encountered, the compiler will substitute (sometimes called a *macro substitution*) the hexadecimal constant 60. The #*define* directive can be thought of as the EQUates used in assembly language programming, although the substitution process is similar to the macro expansions discussed in Chapter 11. The use of symbols in place of numeric values is desirable, as it makes the program much easier to interpret. Recall that assembly language programs also use symbols. Notice that the symbols SWITCH1, SWITCH2, and LED are written in upper-case letters, as is conventional in C programs. The preprocessor directives in lines 2 through 4 assign the hexadecimal constants 54, 55, and 60 to the symbols SWITCH1, SWITCH2, and LED, respectively. Notice that the syntax used to define a hexadecimal constant is different from the assembly language syntax: the prefix 0x is used instead of the base specifier suffix H. In C, numeric values can be expressed in one of three bases—decimal, hexadecimal, or octal. Hexadecimal numbers must have the prefix 0x, as just mentioned, whereas numbers preceded by a zero are interpreted as octal numbers. A number that does not have one of these prefixes is assumed to be a decimal number, in accordance with assembler conventions. Therefore the number 0x54 (hexadecimal) can also be written as 0124 (octal) or 84 (decimal). The C programming language also recognizes *character constants,* which are defined by enclosing an ASCII character in single quotation marks (according to assembly language conventions). These character constants are used in character and string operations and also in arithmetic and logical operations.

Lines 5, 6, and 7 in Figure 12-3 are also nonexecutable statements, known as *declarations.* These declarations are used to identify the characteristics of

TABLE 12-1. Reserved Words in the C Language

auto	break	case	char
continue	default	do	double
else	entry	extern	float
for	goto	if	int
long	register	return	sizeof
short	static	struct	switch
typedef	union	unsigned	while

variables used in the C program. A declaration is used to indicate to the compiler the properties of a variable, such as its type or size. If a declaration causes the compiler to allocate storage for a variable, that declaration will become a *definition*. The difference between a declaration and a definition will be described in Chapter 13. For now we shall assume that all declarations cause the compiler to allocate storage for the specified variable. Henceforth, whenever a reference is made to the *value of a variable,* this actually means the *content(s) of the memory location(s) allocated to that variable.* There is one exception that will be discussed in Chapter 13.

Line 5 declares the variable *data1* to be of the *character* (char) type. A character type variable is allocated 8 bits (one byte) of storage and can hold a signed value in the range − 128 (80H) to + 127 (7FH) when used in arithmetic operations. The character-type variable, however, is usually used to represent the ASCII codes of the various character constants used in the program. The character type variable is the smallest-sized variable used in the C programming language. There is another data type called the *integer* (int) type variable, which requires two bytes of storage and is usually used for arithmetic operations. More will be said in Section 12-4 about the integer type variable. Thus, each variable declared in lines 5 through 7 is of the character type and will be allocated one byte of storage by the compiler. Any reference made to the name of the variable will indirectly refer (with a few exceptions, to be discussed in Chapter 13) to the contents of the memory location allocated to the variable. Every variable used in a C program must be declared before it is referenced in an executable statement later in the program. Similar types of variables do not have to be declared in separate declarations. For example, lines 5, 6, and 7 can be replaced with the single declaration

```
char data1,data2,sum;
```

Line 8 marks the entry point of the C program. This is the point at which the C program begins execution. The *main()* is a special *function* that identifies the start of the program. A C program is usually constructed in a hierarchical top-down structured form (as discussed in Chapter 10) as a sequence of functions that specify the various operations that the program is to perform. These functions are similar to the utility subroutines discussed in Chapter 10. The main program identified by *main()* is also considered a special function at which program execution begins. The main function can call other user-written functions that must be externally linked with the main program or that must be included following the main program. The parentheses "()" following the function name *main* can be used to pass *arguments* (parameters) to the function. The design of C functions will be discussed in Chapter 13. The C program of Figure 12-3 has no arguments and therefore contains no information within the parentheses. Every C program must have a main() function.

The braces on lines 9 and 14 define the limits of the *function body,* which in this case is the main program body. The opening brace "{" on line 9 identifies the beginning of the function body—the start of the program—and the closing brace "}" on line 14 identifies the end of the function body—the end of the program. The function body can consist of executable or nonexecutable program statements. In Figure 12-3, lines 10 through 13 make up the executable statements of the program (function body). The free-format syntax of C allows the entire main program to be written as one line enclosed by the opening and closing braces, as follows:

```
main() {data1=input(SWITCH1); data2=input(SWITCH2);
     sum=data1+data2; output(LED,sum);}
```

A C program constructed in this way compiles and executes in exactly the same way as the program in Figure 12-3 does. But the program is much more difficult to read, and therefore the style used in Figure 12-3 and the following examples should be followed.

Lines 10 and 11 are executable statements, called *assignment statements.* After the program has been compiled and when it is being executed (at run time), the variable *data1* is assigned the data at input port 54H, and the variable *data2* is assigned the data at input port 55H. In other words, the byte of storage allocated to *data1* contains the data from input port 54H; similarly, the byte of storage allocated to *data2* contains the data from input port 55H. An assignment statement assumes a right-to-left orientation; that is, the variable, constant, or expression (to be seen later) on the right-hand side of the " = " is assigned to the variable on the left-hand side. For example, *input*(SWITCH1) (line 10) can be thought of as a variable that holds the value of an input port. This value is then assigned to *data1*. Similarly, in line 11, the data from input port 55H is assigned to the variable *data2*. Thus, an assignment statement can be thought of as one used to alter the contents of the memory location allocated to a variable. It is important to note that the " = " symbol does not indicate algebraic equality but, rather, the assignment of data on the right-hand side of the statement to the memory location allocated to a variable on the left-hand side. The assignment statements in lines 10 and 11 on the right-hand side are actually "calls" to the external functions (subroutines) responsible for reading the data from a specified input port (the port number is specified as a parameter) and returning the result in the memory location allocated to the variable on the left-hand side. The manner in which this is done will be described in Chapter 13.

Line 12 is also an executable assignment statement, but the right-hand side of the statement contains a construct in C called an *expression,* in this case, an *arithmetic expression.* The construct

```
data1 + data2
```

indicates the arithmetic sum of the variables *data1* and *data2*. The result of the arithmetic operation, that is, the sum of *data1* and *data2*, is then assigned to the variable *sum*.

Line 13 is another function call to the external function "output." The responsibility of the output function is to use the arguments (parameters) LED and *sum* to send the contents of the memory location allocated to the variable *sum* to the output port LED. The code to implement this function will also be discussed in Chapter 13.

In comparing the programs in Figures 12-2 and 12-3, it can be observed that both perform exactly the same function, although there is a considerable syntactical difference in their construction. Note that the C program in Figure 12-3 has no direct references to any CPU registers or absolute memory locations; the only hardware references made are to the I/O ports. As we shall see in this chapter and the next, the programmer need not be aware of the hardware environment when coding programs in C, although he or she must know this when developing assembly language software.

The tremendous task of compiling each statement in the source program into a sequence of related machine code often leads to the generation of code inefficient in both speed and memory requirements. This is particularly true during the translation of very simple tasks, such as in the previous example. To show how the code is compiled, let us examine the code generated by the compiler for the previous example.

```
                    EXTRN input,output  ;User-provided subroutines
                    CSEG
0000 311500         LXI   SP,STACK      ;Initialize stack area
0003 CD0700         CALL  main          ;Execute main program
0006 76             HLT                 ;Stop
          ; main()
          main:
          ; {
          ; data1 = input(SWITCH1);
0007 215400         LXI   H,54H         ;Input port # to HL
000A E5             PUSH  H             ;Port # to top of stack
000B CD0000         CALL  input         ;Get byte from input port
000E C1             POP   B             ;Restore stack pointer
000F 7D             MOV   A,L           ;Get input port data
0010 320000         STA   data1         ;Save input port data
          ;data2 = input(SWITCH2);
0013 215500         LXI   H,55H         ;Input port # to HL
0016 E5             PUSH  H             ;Port # to top of stack
0017 CD0000         CALL  input         ;Get byte from input port
001A C1             POP   B             ;Restore stack pointer
001B 7D             MOV   A,L           ;Get input port data
001C 320100         STA   data2         ;Save input port data
          ;sum = data1 + data2;
001F 3A0000         LDA   data1         ;Get first value
0022 2600           MVI   H,0           ;Clear high byte
0024 6F             MOV   L,A           ;HL=data1
0025 E5             PUSH  H             ;Save it
0026 3A0100         LDA   data2         ;Get second value
0029 2600           MVI   H,0           ;Clear high byte
002B 6F             MOV   L,A           ;HL=data2
002C D1             POP   D             ;Recall first value to DE
002D 19             DAD   D             ;Add to second
002E 7D             MOV   A,L           ;Get 8-bit result
002F 320200         STA   sum           ;Save result
```

FIGURE 12-4. Machine code generated for each compiler statement.

```
                    ; output (LED, sum);
0032 218000         LXI   H,80H          ;Output port # to HL
0035 E5             PUSH  H              ;Save port #
0036 3A0200         LDA   sum            ;Get the sum
0039 2600           MVI   H,0            ;Clear high byte
003B 6F             MOV   L,A            ;HL=sum
003C E5             PUSH  H              ;Save the sum
003D CD0000         CALL  output         ;Output the sum
0040 C1             POP   B              ;Restore the stack
0041 C1             POP   B              ;
            ; }
0042 C9             RET                  ;End of program
                    DSEG
0000        data1:  DS    1              ;Character data1 storage
0001        data2:  DS    1              ;Character data2 storage
0002        sum:    DS    1              ;Character sum storage
0003                DS    18             ;Stack area
0015 =      STACK   EQU   $
0015                END
(67 Bytes Compiled)
```

FIGURE 12-4. Cont.   Machine code generated for each compiler statement.

Figure 12-4 shows the machine code generated by the C compiler in mnemonic form. Recall from Figure 12-1 that the compiler's output is usually machine code and not mnemonic code and is similar to the assembler's output. This machine code has been converted to mnemonic form (for clarity) and is shown in Figure 12-4. The C statement corresponding to each set of machine instructions or directives is also shown in commented form.

Notice in Figure 12-4 that each executable statement has been compiled into a sequence of machine instructions (represented in mnemonics). For example, the statement

$$data1 = input(SWITCH1);$$

caused the compiler to generate the following six machine instructions to perform the task of assigning to the variable *data1*, the data from input port 54H:

```
LXI   H,54H
PUSH  H
CALL  input
POP   B
MOV   A,L
STA   data1
```

The first two instructions load the top of the stack, with the input port number as a parameter for the "input" subroutine. It is assumed that the input subroutine will take this port number from the top of the stack, access the input port, and return the data from the port in register L. These are the parameter-passing conventions used by the C compiler and will be discussed in more detail in Chapter 13. The last instruction then stores the contents of register L in memory location *data1*. Notice in Figure 12-4 that the variable *data1* has been allocated one byte of storage in the *data segment*.

Similar code is generated for the next executable assignment statement

```
data2 = input(SWITCH2);
```

Notice that the code generated for the statement

```
sum = data1 + data2;
```

first takes the contents of the memory location allocated to the variable *data1* and loads it as an extended 16-bit number into register pair HL. This number is saved on the stack, and the same process is repeated for the variable *data2*. The first number is retrieved from the stack into register pair DE and then added to the contents of register pair HL to obtain the resulting sum in HL. Because the sum is assumed to be 8 bits (SUM was declared to be a *char*acter type of variable), the contents of register L is then saved in the memory location allocated to *sum*. Notice that the compiled C program performs 16-bit arithmetic, even though it was not required. This is because all arithmetic operations in C are performed with 16-bit numbers.

The statement

```
output(LED,sum);        .
```

initiates a call to the user-written (assembly language) output subroutine, and again, parameters are passed to the subroutine. In this case two parameters, the output port number and the data to be sent to the output port, are loaded on the stack (the first parameter, followed by the second parameter) before the subroutine is called. It is the responsibility of the output subroutine to send the given data to the specified output port. Notice that the output subroutine does not (and is not expected to) return any data to the main program. More will be said about the output subroutine in Chapter 13.

Figure 12-4 clearly illustrates some of the redundancies in the code generated by the compiler to perform the simple task of adding two numbers. By comparing the equivalent assembly language program in Figure 12-2 and the compiled code in Figure 12-4, it can be seen that the size of the code generated by the compiler is large (sixty-seven bytes compiled as compared with nine bytes assembled). Consequently, the execution speed of the compiled program increases. Also notice that the programmer does not have much control over the machine code generated by the compiler. For example, in this program, simple 8-bit arithmetic would suffice in obtaining the sum of the two numbers. But because the compiler is designed for integer (16-bit) arithmetic, a few extra operations are required, and so the complexity of the machine code is increased. Also, because C is not a machine-dependent language, the compiler offers no direct I/O facilities (such as access to IN and OUT instructions). This means that the programmer must access hardware I/O units through function calls, which again contributes to the bulk of the code generated by the compiler.

Because a compiler sometimes makes a simple programming task fairly complex, such simple tasks are much easier to perform in assembly language. On the other hand, complex programming is much more easily performed by a compiler-level language, as will be shown later in this and the following chapter.

12·4

Integer Variables and Initializations

In the C program example shown in Figure 12-3, all the variables declared were of the character type. These variables were allocated one byte of storage, as shown in Figure 12-4. But because most arithmetic operations in C are performed on 16-bit numbers, the C programing language gives the programmer the *integer data type*.

The compiler allocates two bytes of contiguous storage to an integer type variable. An integer type variable can therefore hold a signed number in the range -32768 (8000H) to +32767 (7FFFH).

The C program in Figure 12-3 has been modified to use integer variables and is shown in Figure 12-5. Notice that the only difference between the two programs is that the variables *data1, data2,* and *sum* have been declared as integers *int*. Also, the three variables have been declared through only one statement instead of three separate declarations. The program in Figure 12-5 executes in exactly the same manner as does the program in Figure 12-3, although, the code generated by the compiler for the program in Figure 12-5 is different.

Figure 12-6 shows the machine code produced by the compiler when the C program of Figure 12-5 is compiled. Notice that the size is somewhat shorter: fifty-five bytes long, as compared with sixty-seven bytes for the program shown in Figure 12-3. The slight reduction in length is due to the use of integer variables, a more natural data type for arithmetic operations. Also notice in Figure 12-6 that two bytes of storage have been allocated to each of the integer variables, *data1, data2,* and *sum*. The rest of the program is similar in operation to the program shown in Figure 12-4.

```
/*   Calculate the sum of two numbers */
#define SWITCH1 0x54
#define SWITCH2 0x55
#define LED     0x60

int data1,data2,sum;

main( )
{
        data1 = input(SWITCH1);
        data2 = input(SWITCH2);
        sum = data1 + data2;
        output(LED,sum);
}
```

FIGURE 12-5.   C program with integer variables.

```
                    EXTRN input,output  ;User-provided subroutines
                    CSEG
0000 311800         LXI   SP,STACK      ;Initialize stack area
0003 CD0700         CALL  main          ;Execute main program
0006 76             HLT                 ;Stop
            ; main()
            main:
            ; {
            ; datal = input(SWITCH1);
0007 215400         LXI   H,54H         ;Input port # to HL
000A E5             PUSH  H             ;Port # to top of stack
000B CD0000         CALL  input         ;Get byte from input port
000E C1             POP   B             ;Restore stack pointer
000F 220000         SHLD  datal         ;Save input port data
            ; data2 = input(SWITCH2);
0012 215500         LXI   H,55H         ;Input port # to HL
0015 E5             PUSH  H             ;Port # to top of stack
0016 CD0000         CALL  input         ;Get byte from input port
0019 C1             POP   B             ;Restore stack pointer
001A 220200         SHLD  data2         ;Save input port data
            ; sum = datal + data2;
001D 2A0000         LHLD  datal         ;Get first value
0020 E5             PUSH  H             ;Save it
0021 2A0200         LHLD  data2         ;Get second value
0024 D1             POP   D             ;Recall first value
0025 19             DAD   D             ;Add to second
0026 220400         SHLD  sum           ;Save result
            ; output(LED,sum);
0029 218000         LXI   H,80H         ;Output port # to HL
002C E5             PUSH  H             ;Save port #
002D 2A0400         LHLD  sum           ;Get the sum
0030 E5             PUSH  H             ;Save the sum
0031 CD0000         CALL  output        ;Output the sum
0034 C1             POP   B             ;Restore the stack
0035 C1             POP   B
            ; }
0036 C9             RET                 ;End of program
                    DSEG
0000        datal:  DS    2             ;Integer datal storage
0002        data2:  DS    2             ;Integer data2 storage
0004        sum:    DS    2             ;Integer sum storage
0006                DS    18            ;Stack area
0018 =      STACK   EQU   $
0018                END
(55 Bytes Compiled)
```

FIGURE 12-6.   Machine code generated for a program with integer variables.

Variables defined through a declaration statement are allocated storage by the compiler in the program's data segment. By default, the compiler initializes their values to zero, although the programmer can change this default condition by initializing the value of a variable at the time it is declared. For example the declaration

```
char p;
```

may cause the compiler to allocate one byte of storage to the variable *p* and initialize its contents to zero. However, the declaration

```
char p = 3;
```

allocates one byte of storage to the variable *p* but initializes its content to 3.

The compiler always allocates storage to a variable in the program's data segment. Thus if the program is to be run in a ROM/RAM environment, caution should be exercised with *compile-time initializations* such as these, as the compiler cannot initialize the actual contents of RAM. In order to initialize the value of a variable without using a compile-time initialization, such as in the preceding example, one could use an assignment statement such as

```
p = 3;
```

which would cause the value of the variable *p* to be initialized while the program is in execution—a *run-time initialization*.

The C compiler performs automatic *type conversions* on those assignment statements that contain a mismatch of data types. This means that if a character variable or constant is assigned to an integer variable, it will actually be assigned to the low-order byte allocated to the integer variable—the high-order byte is set to zero. If, however, an integer variable or constant is assigned to a character variable, the value of the character variable will be set to the low-order byte of the integer, and the high order byte of the integer will be discarded.

The full implementation of the C programming language also supports other data types besides *int*eger and *char*acter. Data types such as *float* and *double* are usually available on C compilers that provide floating point and double precision arithmetic. These data types will not be discussed in this book.

12-5

Manipulation of Tabular Data

Array variables are used in C to reference tables of data. These variables can be thought of as a collection of similar variables that can be referenced by a common name. The data can be 8-bit data (character type) or 16-bit data (integer type), depending on the type of array variable declared. An array variable can be used to reference by a unique name a group of contiguous memory locations. When an array variable is defined by a declaration, the compiler allocates a certain amount of storage, which will depend on the type of variable as well as on the *dimension* of the array variable. For example, the declaration.

```
char table[10];
```

declares an array variable *table* of character type having a dimension of 10. This means that the variable *table* can be associated with ten different character (8-bit) values. The compiler allocates ten bytes of storage to the variable *table*. The first byte allocated to the variable *table* is referenced as *table*[0]; the second byte allocated for *table* is referenced as *table*[1]; the third byte as *table*[2]; and so on. In simple terms, one can allocate space to ten character variables, named *table*[0], *table*[1], . . . *table*[9]. The number within the brackets "[]" is called the *subscript* of the array. Thus an array variable must be referenced by its name and its subscript; its subscript indicates its relative position in memory. Each unique variable that references a part of the array is called an *array member*.

An array can also be declared as being of the *integer* type. For example the declaration

```
int table[10];
```

causes the compiler to allocate twenty bytes of storage to the array variable *table*. Each member of the array is of the integer type and occupies two bytes of memory. The array members can be referenced as before by the variable name *table* and the subscript.

Array variables are useful for holding tables of data or ASCII character strings. For example, if a program had to reference a table of data bytes without using an array variable, each data byte would have to be assigned to a unique character type variable that had been previously declared in the program. A specific data byte could then be referenced by its variable's name. The number of variables that would have to be declared would be equal to the number of data bytes in the table. Using an array variable, a single character type variable could be declared with a dimension equal to the number of data bytes in the table. Each data byte could then be referenced by the same array variable name, but with a different subscript. There is an example of how this is done in Section 12-6.

When a defined array is allocated storage, the compiler automatically allocates storage to each member in the array and initializes their values to zero. This process of initialization was seen in the previous section for nonarray variables. However, the programmer can explicitly force the compiler to initialize the members of the array at compile time, by including a list of values with the declaration, as follows:

```
int table[5] ={ 32, 10, 5, 2, 64 };
```

In the preceding declaration, the array table has been declared an integer type, and its five members, *table*[0] through *table*[4], have been initialized to the numbers (decimal) 32, 10, 5, 2, and 64, respectively. This initialization is similar to that performed by an assembler using the DB and DW directives. Declared array members, like variables, can also be initialized through assignment statements at run time. For example, instead of initializing the array members at compile time through the preceding declaration, the following assignment statements could perform the same task at run time (while the program is in execution):

```
table[0] = 32;
table[1] = 10;
table[2] =  5;
table[3] =  2;
table[4] = 64;
```

As mentioned before, if a C program is compiled for a ROM/RAM environment, then it is advisable to initialize the array members at run time by using assignment statements, as arrays are always allocated storage in the data segment where compile-time initializations are ineffective.

The full implementation of the C programming language also supports the more complex two-dimensional arrays, though a discussion of these types of arrays are beyond the scope of this book and so will not be discussed.

12-6

Controlling the Flow of a C Program

The programs in the previous examples did not illustrate the advantages of programming in C. In fact, by comparing the two programs shown in Figures 12-2 and 12-3, one can see that it would be easier to write such a simple program in assembly language rather than in C. Indeed, a simple program specification such as that mentioned in Section 12-3 would be more efficient in execution speed and memory requirements if it were implemented in assembly language. However, when the complexity of the program specification is increased, coding the program in C is much easier than coding it in assembly language.

Consider a program to monitor the temperature of an industrial oven and to maintain this temperature at 90°C. The oven temperature is obtained through an input port connected to an analog-to-digital converter (ADC) and a thermistor. The program has to make a decision based on the temperature read from the oven. The flowchart for the program is shown in Figure 12-7.

Two bits of an output port are used to control the state of the oven and an alarm. The hardware scheme for the I/O ports can be summarized as follows:

Input port 12H: ADC/thermistor (oven temperature)

  0°C converted to 00000000B
  100°C converted to 01100100B (100 decimal = 64 hexadecimal)

Output port 78H: oven/alarm control

  Bit 1: 1 = oven on
       0 = oven off
  Bit 0: 1 = alarm on
       0 = alarm off

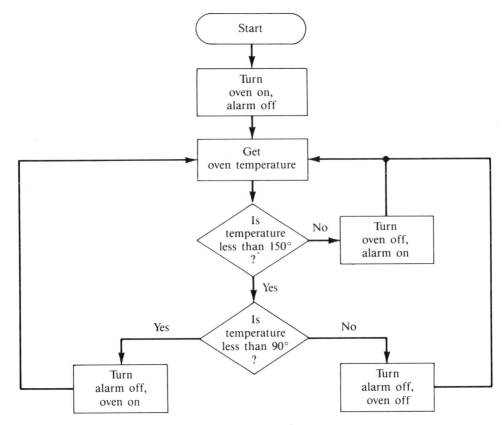

FIGURE 12-7. Flowchart for temperature monitor.

With reference to the flowchart of Figure 12-7, the logic of the required program can be explained as follows: The initialization sequence turns on the oven and turns off the alarm. The CPU then inputs the temperature from the ADC and checks to see if the oven is overheating (temperature greater than 150°C). If this happens, the alarm is turned on, and the oven is turned off. The temperature is then continuously monitored until it reaches below 150°C. When this happens, the alarm is turned off, and a check is made to see if the temperature is lower than 90°C. If it is lower, the oven is turned on; if it is higher, the oven is turned off. The entire sequence is then repeated. The C program to implement the flowchart of Figure 12-7 is shown in Figure 12-8.

With reference to Figure 12-8, notice that the C program has the same structure as the C programs shown in Figures 12-3 and 12-5. That is, the program starts with the definitions of various symbolic names and the declarations of program variables and follows with the main program (enclosed in braces). The main program incorporates several statements that are used to control the flow of the C program. These *flow control* statements are described in conjunction with the program's function, as follows:

```
 1  /* Temperature-monitoring program */
 2  #define OV0AL0   0x00           /* CONTROL BYTES */
 3  #define OV0AL1   0x01
 4  #define OV1AL0   0x02
 5  #define OV1AL1   0x03

 6  #define ADC      0x12           /* SYSTEM I/O PORTS */
 7  #define CONTROL  0x78

 8  char temperature;

 9  main()
10  {
11        output(CONTROL,OV1AL0);

12  monitor:
13      temperature = input(ADC);
14      if (temperature < 150)
15          goto maintain;
16      output (CONTROL,OV0AL1);
17      goto monitor;

18  maintain:
19      if (temperature < 90)
20          output(CONTROL,OV1AL0);
21      else;
22          output(CONTROL,OV0AL0);
23      goto monitor;
24  }
```

FIGURE 12-8. **Temperature-monitoring program in C.**

Lines 2 through 4 define the four combinations of control bits used to control the state of the oven and the alarm. Each constant, when sent to the output port (CONTROL) that controls the alarm and oven, will turn on or off the alarm, the oven, or both. The function of each symbol can be summarized as follows:

$$OV0AL0 = \text{Turn oven off, alarm off}$$
$$OV0AL1 = \text{Turn oven off, alarm on}$$
$$OV1AL0 = \text{Turn oven on, alarm off}$$
$$OV1AL1 = \text{Turn oven on, alarm on}$$

Lines 6 and 7 define the I/O port numbers for the ADC and the oven/alarm control port, respectively. Line 8 is a declaration for the variable *temperature* which causes the compiler to allocate one byte of storage. This variable is used to hold the data obtained from the ADC.

As before, line 9 identifies the main program contained within the opening and closing braces shown on lines 10 and 24, respectively.

The first executable statement in the main program is shown on line 11. This statement sends the control word OV1AL0 to the CONTROL port and causes the oven to be turned on and the alarm to be turned off.

Lines 12 and 18 contain an identifier called a *label*. A label in C has the same function as does a label in assembly language, to reference a point in the program. Just as labels were used with JMP and CALL instructions in assembly language programs to transfer control to a specified symbolic address, labels are used with **goto** statements in C to reference a particular portion of the program. In its simplest form, a label is an identifier that has the value of a location in memory. Labels must conform to the rules specified for naming variables and must be terminated with a ":" (colon). The use of labels in conjunction with the **goto** statement will be seen in the following paragraphs.

Line 13 is an assignment statement that assigns the data from input port 12H (ADC) to the variable *temperature*. The current value of the oven temperature is stored in the memory location allocated to the variable *temperature* and is updated every time the statement in line 13 is executed.

Lines 14 and 15 make up a *program flow control statement,* known as an **if** statement. This statement checks the contents of the memory location allocated to the variable *temperature*. If the contents is lower than 150°C, the program control will transfer to the statement on line 19 following the label *maintain* (line 18), and the statements on lines 16 and 17 are not executed. However, if the value of the variable *temperature* is higher than or equal to 150°C, the program control will transfer to line 16. Line 16 contains a statement to send the control byte OV0AL1 to the CONTROL port, thereby turning the oven off and the alarm on; control is then transferred (unconditionally) to the label *monitor* by the **goto** statement in Line 17. The monitoring process then continues as before.

When used in conjunction with the **goto** statement in line 15, the **if** statement in line 14 is called a *conditional program transfer statement.* For example, if the condition specified within the parentheses following the **if** keyword is satisfied, then the statement on line 15 will be executed; otherwise the statement in line 15 will be ignored, and control will be transferred to the statement on line 16. The "condition" within the parentheses can be any expression, variable, or constant that evaluates to (produce) a true or false result. In the C programming language, a *true* result is defined as any nonzero value, and a *false* result is defined as a zero value. In line 14 the expression within parentheses is known as a *relational expression* and always evaluates to a true or false result. The "<" is a *relational operator* that is used to check the value of *temperature* and determine whether it is lower than 150°C. More will be said about relational operators and expressions in Chapter 13. The statement following the "condition" will always be executed if the condition evaluates to a true result. If the condition evaluates false, the following statement will be skipped, and control will transfer to the next statement in sequence.

The label *maintain* on line 18 references the statements that will be executed if the temperature is lower than 150°C. Line 19 contains another conditional program transfer instruction that checks the variable *temperature* for a value of less than 90. If the value of *temperature* is less than 90°C, then the statement on line 20 will be executed, and the oven will be turned on (alarm off). Control then transfers to line 23, which contains a **goto** statement that transfers control to the label *monitor,* and the monitoring process begins all over again. However, if the value of *temperature* is greater than or equal to 90°C, the statement on line 21 will be executed. Line 21 contains the **else** statement that is used in conjunction with the **if** statement to force execution of the following statement. If the **else** statement did not exist, line 22 would be executed, regardless of whether the temperature was lower than, higher than, or equal to 90°C, and the program would not therefore execute properly. The statement on line 22 will therefore turn off the oven (alarm off) if *temperature* is higher than or equal to 90°C. As before, control is then transferred to the **goto** statement on line 23, and the monitoring process continues.

Notice how closely each executable statement in the C program of Figure 12-8 corresponds to each step of the flowchart in Figure 12-7. Also observe that the C program to implement the oven control specification is very descriptive (when compared with an assembly language implementation) and requires few comments. This self-documenting characteristic of compiler-level languages is apparent in most C programs. The C program of Figure 12-8, however, would not be considered a very "structured" program, as it does not use some of the more structured constructs of the C programming language. The programmer should try to avoid using **goto** statements, as they often obscure the logic of the program's function. A more refined version of the same program can be constructed without using **goto** statements, by using another type of flow control statement—the **while** statement. This version is shown in Figure 12-9.

The program shown in Figure 12-9 functions in exactly the same manner as does the program in Figure 12-8. The program in Figure 12-9, however, is better organized and the "flow" of the program is easier to visualize because of its structured (or modular) construction.

```
1   /* Temperature-monitoring program (structured version) */
2   #define OVOALO 0x00                  /* CONTROL BYTES */
3   #define OVOAL1 0x01
4   #define OV1ALO 0x02
5   #define OV1AL1 0x03

6   #define ADC     0x12                  /* SYSTEM I/O PORTS */
7   #define CONTROL 0x78

8   char temperature;
9   main()
10  {
11          output(CONTROL,OV1ALO);

12      while(1) {
13          temperature = input(ADC);
14          if (temperature >=150)
15              output(CONTROL,OVOAL1);
16          if (temperature < 90)
17              output(CONTROL,OV1ALO);
18          else if (temperature < 150)
19              output(CONTROL,OVOALO);
20      }
21  }
```

FIGURE 12-9.   Structured version of the temperature-monitoring program.

Lines 1 through 11 (in Figure 12-9) serve the same purpose as discussed earlier. The main program is again contained within the braces on lines 10 and 21, and as before, these define the body of the main program. Line 12 contains a flow control statement called a *while statement*. The function of this statement is to test a condition enclosed in the parentheses that follow and repetitively execute the statement that follows, as long as the condition evaluates to a true result. When (or if) the condition is evaluated as false, execution of the statement that follows is terminated and control transfers to the next executable statement. As in the **if** statement, this condition can be a constant, a variable, or an expression that evaluates to a true or false result.

In the C programming language a group of statements enclosed in braces "{}" is a *compound statement*. A compound statement can be used in place of a single (simple) statement and is executed as if it were a single statement. Compound statements can be used to define a *block*, or a group, of statements to be treated as a single statement. A compound statement can be used in any C construct that specifies a simple statement.

The condition for the **while** statement in line 12 is always true, as it is set permanently to a 1. This means that the statement that follows will be executed continuously without any provisions for exit. The statement that follows however, is a compound statement defined by the opening and closing braces on lines 12 and 20, respectively. This means that all the statements within this block will be executed continuously. Because the temperature-monitoring program is a continuous loop, this is ideally suited for the application. The compound statement therefore comprises the actual monitoring routine.

As before, line 13 obtains the data from the ADC and assigns it to the variable *temperature*. Line 14 now checks to see if the temperature is higher than or equal to 150°C. The relational operator ">=" tests for this condition. If the temperature is higher than or equal to 150°C the oven will be turned off, the alarm will be turned on, and the monitoring process will continue. If the temperature is lower than 90°C, then line 17 will turn on the oven, and control will transfer to line 13. However, if the temperature is higher than (or equal to) 90°C, control will transfer to the **else if** statement on line 18. The **else if** statement determines whether the temperature is lower than 150°C, and, if so, will turn off the oven; control then transfers to line 13, and the monitoring is repeated.

The C programming language allows the *nesting* of **if** statements in a program. For example, in the statement

```
if (a > 0)
    if (b > 0)
        x = 5;
```

the variable x will be assigned the value of 5 if the variables a and b are both greater than zero. This example illustrates one **if** statement "nested" into another. The level of nesting allowed depends on the type of C compiler being used. A problem arises when nested **if** statements are used along with the **else** statement. For example, in the following statements

```
if (a > 0)
    if (b > 0)
        x = 5;
    else
        x = 4;
```

it is difficult to determine with which **if** statement the **else** statement is associated. If the **else** statement is associated with the outer **if,** then if the variable *a* is less than or equal to zero, the variable *x* will be set to 4. But if the **else** statement is associated with the inner **if,** then if the variable *a* is greater than zero, but the variable *b* is less than or equal to zero, the variable *x* will be set to 4. This ambiguity is resolved in C by specifying that for nested **if** statements, only one **else** is allowed, and that **else** is always associated with the innermost **if** statement. The indentation in the preceding example clarifies this association and should be used in all C programs.

One can clearly see that the C program of Figure 12-9 is more structured and easier to interpret than is the C program of Figure 12-8. In Figure 12-9, the entire monitoring process is performed in one continuous loop, (and not in two, as was the case in the program of Figure 12-8), giving the program a more structured and logical appearance. Even though the C programs can be written in a free-format syntax, it is advisable to use indentations to highlight the various levels in the program. This technique can be seen in the C program examples discussed earlier in this chapter. The syntax of the C programming language is such that a program can be made extremely difficult to read, simply by avoiding indentations or misusing them.

At this point the reader has been introduced to the basic flow control statements available in the C programming language for elementary programming. But there are several other similar statements available in C that provide more flexible alternatives to the statements discussed in these sections.

The **do while** statements in C functions in a manner similar to that of the **while** statement. The difference between the two is a subtle one. For example, in the following statement

```
while (a > 5)
    a = b - 1;
```

the variable *a* is assigned a value that is decreased by one each time the statement is executed, and this continues until the value of *a* reaches 5. However, if the value of *a* is less than or equal to 5 before the **while** statement is executed, the following statement

```
a = b - 1;
```

will be ignored. In the following **do while** statement

```
do
    a = b - 1;
while (a > 5);
```

exactly the same function is performed except that if the value of *a* is less than or equal to 5 before the **do** statement is executed, the statement

$$a = b - 1;$$

will be executed only once. The difference, then, between the **while** statement and the **do while** statement is the point at which the relational expression is tested—the **while** statement tests first and then executes, whereas the **do while** statement executes first and then tests. In both cases the statement that is repetitively executed can be replaced by a compound statement.

Certain applications may require iterations of the values of variables used in a program. These iterations can be performed by the flow control statements mentioned in this section, by incrementing or decrementing the value of a variable through an assignment statement. For example, if an application required ten data bytes to be sent to an output port in the order 2,3,4,5,6,7,8,9,10,11, the following **while** statement could perform the task:

```
data = 2;
while (data <= 11) {
        output(PORT,data);
        data = data + 1;
}
```

In this example, the value of *data* is initially set to 2, as this is the first data byte to be sent to the output port, PORT. The compound statement within the braces is then executed repetitively, and each time the value of *data* is incremented by one. Note that the assignment statement

$$data = data + 1;$$

is algebraically incorrect but takes on an entirely different meaning as an assignment statement in C: the statement will increment and update the contents of the memory location allocated to the variable *data*. When the value of *data* reaches 12, the **while** statement terminates.

The same function could have been performed by a simpler construct available in C—the **for** loop.

```
for (data = 2; data <= 11; data++)
        output(PORT,data);
```

The **for** loop consists of three expressions enclosed in parentheses. The first expression is used to initialize the value of a variable, the second to test the value of the variable, and the third to modify the value of the variable. The statement (simple or compound) following the **for** is executed over and over until the second expression (always a relational expression) evaluates false. In the preceding example, *data* is initially set to 2. The following *output* statement is executed, and each time the value of *data* is incremented by one. The value of *data* is incremented through the use of the *increment operator* " + + "; more will be said about this operator in Chapter 13. The value of *data* is incremented and tested each time until it reaches 12, at which time the **for** loop terminates. Any of the three expressions in the parentheses may be left out, but the semi-colons must remain. If the second expression (the test) is omitted, it is assumed to be permanently true, and so the loop becomes "infinite." If the first expression is omitted, there is no initialization, and if the third expression is omitted, the variable's value is not changed each time through the loop. For example, the statement

```
for (;;)
    ;
```

produces an infinite loop with no exit. While in the loop, nothing is executed. But the C compiler gives the programmer a means of escaping from a continuous loop, through the **break** statement. For example, in the following **for** loop

```
p = 0;
for (; ; p++) {
        if (p > 60000)
                break;
}
```

the compound statement enclosed in braces consists of an **if** statement that tests the value of the variable p. The compound statement is set up by the **for** loop to execute continously each time, incrementing the value of p. When the value of p reaches 60001, the **break** statement is executed, which causes the **for** loop to terminate.

The same effect could also be achieved by using the **continue** statement:

```
p = 0;
for (; ; p++) {
        if (p < 60001)
                continue;
        break;
}
```

In this example, the **if** statement will *continue* executing the **for** loop (the **break** statement will be ignored) until the value of the variable p reaches 60001. When this occurs, the **break** statement is executed, and the **for** loop terminates. Execution of the **continue** statement therefore causes the next iteration to take place in a **for** loop, and the statements following the **continue** are ignored. In a **while** or **do while** loop, the **continue** statement returns control to the start of the loop.

Even though the **break** and **continue** statements are related in function and can be used for the same purpose, the **break** statement is often used in C to interrupt the execution of a continuous loop, as was seen in the previous example. However, the **continue** statement is often used to bypass a section of following code (on a certain condition) and to continue processing a program loop.

As this point, we have examined several constructs in C, called *program loops*. Loops are particularly useful when they are used in conjunction with the array variables mentioned in Section 12-5. For example, consider a C program to print the message "hello" on the console device attached to a computer. The C program to accomplish the task is shown in Figure 12-10. This program uses a function called *conout* that implements the standard console output subroutine discussed in Chapter 7. The actual implementation of *conout* will be examined in Chapter 13; for now, assume that the *conout* function displays the given character (specified within the parentheses) on the console device.

In Figure 12-10, an array *string* of *char*acter type is declared with five members. The compiler allocates five bytes of storage and initializes each member of the array *string* to the characters specified in the initialization list. Thus the values of the members of the array *string* before the program starts execution are

```
string[0] = 'h'
string[1] = 'e'
string[2] = 'l'
string[3] = 'l'
string[4] = 'o'
```

Because the characters within the quotation marks are considered character constants, each member actually contains the ASCII code for the respective character.

The variable x is defined as an integer variable and is used to reference each array member. The **for** loop causes the following statement to execute repetitively. Each time the statement is executed, the value of x is incremented, so that the array member referenced by the *conout* function changes sequentially from 0 to 4. The value of each array member is then sent to the console, until x reaches 5, at which point the program terminates.

The program in Figure 12-10 thus illustrates the flexibility of using array variables in a C program. The technique used in the program to print a message on the screen is not the best; a more convenient program to provide the same function will be examined in Chapter 13.

The C programming language also offers the programmer a construct that allows control to be transferred to one of several points in a block of statements. For example, the console command processor (CCP) implemented in assembly language and shown in Figure 9-13 can be easily implemented in C, as shown in Figure 12-11. Recall from Chapter 9 that the CCP's function is to input a single character command from the console, decode the command, and then transfer control to the appropriate command implementing routine (CIR). If the

```
char string[5] = {'h','e','l','l','o'};
int x;

main()
{
    for (x = 0; x < 5; x++)
        conout(string[x]);
}
```

FIGURE 12-10. Message display program.

```
1       char command;
2       main( )
3       {
4            while (1) {
5                 command = conin( );
6                 switch (command) {
7                 case 'A':
8                      acmd( );
9                      break;
10                case 'Q':
11                     qcmd( );
12                     break;
13                case 'D':
14                     dcmd( );
15                     break;
16                case 'X':
17                     xcmd( );
18                     break;
19                default:
20                     error( );
21                     break;
22                }
23           }
24      }
```

FIGURE 12-11. C implementation of a console command processor.

command obtained from the console is invalid, control will transfer to an error-handling routine. After each CIR is executed, control returns to the CCP to await and interpret the next command entered at the console.

Line 1 in Figure 12-11 defines the variable *command* to be of character type, and this variable is used to hold the data (command) obtained from the console. The main program is identified on line 2, and its body is enclosed by the opening and closing braces shown on lines 3 and 24, respectively.

The **while** on line 4 causes continuous execution of the following compound statement, defined by the opening and closing braces on lines 4 and 23, respectively. The actual statements that make up the console command processor are contained in this compound statement. Several of these statements contain function calls considered to be "calls" to external subroutines. As indicated earlier, these functions will be examined in the following chapter; at this stage we shall assume that these undefined subroutines perform the appropriate tasks.

Line 5 initiates a call to the *conin* subroutine which returns the console character and assigns it to the variable *command*.

Line 6 contains the **switch** statement that examines the value of the variable *command* and, depending on its value, transfers control to one of five labels within the block, defined by the opening and closing braces on lines 6 and 22, respectively. If the value of *command* is 'A', control will transfer to line 7 where a call to the subroutine *acmd* (CIR) will be initiated. If the value of *command* is 'Q', control will transfer to line 10, and the CIR *qcmd* will be called. Similarly, *dcmd* will be called if the value of *command* is 'D', and *xcmd* will be called if the value of *command* is 'X'. If the value of *command* is not

A, Q, D, or X, control will transfer to the label **default,** where it will call the subroutine *error* (error-handling subroutine).

After returning from each one of the subroutines (CIRs or error-handling subroutine), the **break** statement is executed, which transfers control out of the block defined by the **switch** statement (lines 6–22). Control then resumes at line 5, and the process continues. If the **break** statement is not included after the execution of each function, control will be passed on to the next statement in sequence until the end of the block is reached. When this occurs, there is an automatic break, and control is transferred out of the block.

One can see that the C implementation of the CCP is logically performed by the **switch** statement. In general, the **switch** statement always evaluates the expression, or variable (in parentheses), following the **switch** keyword and transfers control to the **case** label followed by a constant that is equal to the evaluated expression; this constant can be either an integer or a character constant. The number of *cases* that the **switch** statement can handle depends on the characteristics of the compiler being used.

As a final note, observe in Figure 12-11 the use of indentations to point up the logical structure of the program. Notice that the C program is made up of various blocks nested within other blocks so as to structure the program into several levels. The main program is enclosed by the first set of braces on lines 3 and 24. Along with the function name *main( )*, these braces are entered at the first column and represent the first level in the program. Within the main program, the **while** loop encloses a group of statements defined by the braces on lines 4 and 23: the brace on line 23 is lined up with the **while** on line 4 to indicate the second level in the program. Within the **while** loop, the **switch** statement encloses another group of statements defined by the braces on lines 6 and 22. Again, the brace on line 22 is lined up with the **switch** on line 6 to indicate the third level in the program. The use of indentations therefore clarifies the number of nested statements or blocks and also may help identify any missing braces.

12-7

Summary

This chapter introduced the C programming language, a compiler-level language, and illustrated the similarities and differences between assembly language programming and higher-level programming.

From the material covered in this chapter, one can see that the building blocks of the C programming language are fairly easily grasped and do not require a detailed understanding of microprocessor hardware. The capability of hardware independence is one of the main goals of the C programming language and other higher-level languages and is one of the factors that make a programming language portable, but this is not the case in assembly language programming. However, there is always a trade-off—ease of programming and portability or compact machine code and fast execution speed.

Designing a program in C can be much simpler than designing the same program in assembly language, as seen in many of the program examples introduced in this chapter. Some of the compiler's inefficiencies were also illustrated in this chapter, particularly in cases when the task was extremely simple. These inefficiencies were particularly evident in the size of the code generated by the compiler, which consequently slows the program's execution speed. In some cases it may be more efficient to write a program in a higher-level language such as C, whereas in other cases a program may be better written in assembly language. The decision as to which language to use should be made after investigating the program's application. Speed and memory requirements are the primary considerations. Certain parts of a program can be written in a higher-level language, and speed-critical segments can be implemented in assembly language. The C programming language provides such a facility through the use of external function calls.

REVIEW QUESTIONS AND PROBLEMS

1. Compare the features of assembly language programs and compiler-level programs in terms of the source code written and its translation.

2. What are nonexecutable program statements? How do they differ from executable program statements?

3. What is the purpose of a declaration in the C programming language?

4. What is the difference between a macro preprocessor directive and a declaration?

5. What is the purpose of an integer variable? How does the integer variable differ from the character variable?

6. Write a complete C program to read ten data bytes from input port 50H and store the bytes in a buffer. When all ten bytes have been read in, display them at output port 60H in reverse order.

7. For the following C program segment, determine the value of the variable *result* after the last statement in the segment is executed:

```
data = 3;
result = 0;
if (data < 'A')
     data = data + 0x30;
if (data > 65)
     data = data - 0x30;
result = result + data;
```

8. Repeat Problem 7 by changing the assignment statement

```
data = 3;
```

    to

    (a) data = 0x41   **(b)** data = 'Z'

9. What is the difference between a run-time initialization and a compile-time initialization?

10. Write a C program segment to initialize the two hundred members of an array *tab* to zero, by using
(a) a **while** statement.
(b) a **for** statement.

11. If the variables *p* and *g* are declared as character and integer types, respectively, and have the values 37 and 513, respectively, determine the values of the variables after each of the following assignment statements has been executed:

(a) p = q   (b) q = p

12. For the following values of the variable *test,*

(a) test = 0x12   (b) test = 20   (c) test = 0x23

determine the value of the variable *result* after the following sequence of statements has been executed:

```
if (test > 5)
    if (test < 30)
        if (test <= 18)
            result = 29;
        else
            result = 19;
```

13. For the given values of the variable *a*, what is the value of the variable *eqt* (initially 17) after the following sequence of statements has been executed?

```
switch(a−3) {
case 0:
        eqt = a;
        break;
case 1:
        eqt = a+a;
        break;
case 2:
        eqt = a−3;
        break;
case 4:
        eqt = a+3;
        break;
default:
        break;
}
```

(a) *a* = 17   (b) *a* = 3   (c) *a* = 6   (d) *a* = 4   (e) *a* = 1

CHAPTER 13

Advanced C Concepts

Introduction

This chapter expands on the previously learned concepts of the C programming language and illustrates some of its more sophisticated features. As mentioned in Chapter 12, a thorough study of the C programming language is beyond the scope of the book, and so we shall consider only those features that are necessary to understand the concepts of programming in a higher-level language such as C and those features that make the C programming language ideal for a microcomputer environment.

A study of the C programming language cannot be complete without a discussion of one of its building blocks: functions. Functions give the programmer a means of extending the capabilities of the language while maintaining its simplicity. Functions also enhance the structure of a C program. Certain data types known as *pointers* are another feature of the C programming language. Pointers allow the programmer to manipulate memory locations through the use of variables and therefore provide an "assembly language" environment. The large repertoire of operators and their associated expressions also gives the C programmer enormous flexibility in constructing programs. In addition, we shall discuss how the C compiler allocates storage to its variables, as well as some of its limitations for the programmer. We shall conclude by developing a structured C program with many of the constructs covered in this chapter and in Chapter 12.

C Operators and Expressions

Chapter 12 introduced the use of expressions in assignments statements and in statements testing a particular condition. An expression in C can be one of four types: arithmetic expressions, logical expressions, relational expressions, and conditional expressions. A statement can also contain a mixture of these expressions. Expressions in C are made up of operands and operators and often resemble conventional algebraic expressions. For example, in the expression

$$a + b - c - 5$$

the operands are the variables a, b, c, and the constant 5. The operators are the arithmetic symbols " + " for addition and " − " for subtraction.

There are six *arithmetic operators* in the C programming language, which are listed in order of precedence in Table 13-1. The order of precedence is important to the compiler to determine how the equivalent code for an expression should be compiled. As illustrated in Table 13-1, *, /, and % operators have the highest precedence (indicated by 1). The + and − operators have the next highest precedence.

These precedence rules can be illustrated as follows. Consider the arithmetic expression

$$a + b * c + d$$

Because the * operator has the highest precedence, the subexpression $b * c$ is evaluated first, and its result is added to a and d.

The C programming language uses parentheses to force precedence during the evaluation of an expression. For example, in the following expression

$$(a + b) * (c + d)$$

the subexpressions $a + b$ and $c + d$ are evaluated first and then multiplied together. These precedence rules are exactly the same for the evaluation of algebraic expressions.

TABLE 13-1. Arithmetic Operators

Precedence	Operator	Function
1	*	multiplication operator
1	/	division operator
1	%	modulo operator (remainder of division)
2	+	addition operator
2	−	subtraction operator

The operators shown in Table 13-1 are known as *binary operators*, as they require (or operate upon) two operands. The C programming language also has a single arithmetic *unary operator* that can be used to negate the value of a variable. This operator is the *unary minus* and is used with only one operand, as illustrated in the following assignment statement:

$$a = - b;$$

In this assignment statement, the variable *a* is assigned the negative representation (two's complement) of the variable *b*. A unary operator always has a precedence higher than that of any binary operator.

Logical operators in the C programming language are used to perform Boolean operations on their operands. The seven logical operators supported by C are listed in order of precedence in Table 13-2.

The logical operator set shown in Table 13-2 includes two operators, "<<" and ">>," for the left and right shifts, respectively. The shift operators shift the left operand the number of bit positions specified by the right operand. For example,

$$mask << 3$$

shifts the value of the variable *mask* left by three positions, and the expression

$$mask >> 1$$

shifts the value of *mask* right by one position.

Unlike rotates, the shift operations do not "rotate" bits but simply pad the vacated bits with zeros and discard the bits shifted out.

The bitwise logical operators shown in Table 13-2 are used to perform the Boolean operations AND, OR, and XOR on binary numbers on a bit-to-bit basis. For example, in the assignment statement

$$x = a \mid b$$

if the variable *a* has the value 0x46 and the variable *b* has the value 0xA9, then the variable *x* will be assigned the value 0xEF.

TABLE 13-2. Logical Operators

Precedence	Operator	Function
3	<<	shift-left operator
3	>>	shift-right operator
6	&	bitwise AND operator
7	^	bitwise exclusive OR operator
8	|	bitwise OR operator
9	&&	AND operator
10	||	OR operator

The AND operator "&&" and the OR operator "||" differ from their bitwise counterparts and do not perform bitwise Boolean operations. Instead they are used in conjunction with relational expressions to test certain conditions, as will be seen later in this section.

The C programming language also supports another unary operator that can be used for binary negation. The "~" unary operator can be used to obtain the one's complement of its operand. For example, in the following statement, the variable *yes* is set to the complement of the variable *no*

$$yes = \sim no;$$

Another logical unary operator used in conjunction with relational expressions is the "!" (NOT) operator. This is a logical negation operator used to negate the logic of a relational expression, as will be seen later in this section.

The precedence rules for the evaluation of Boolean expressions are similar to those for the evaluation of any expression in Boolean algebra. Note that the logical operators have a precedence lower than that of arithmetic operators. Thus when arithmetic and logical operators are mixed in expressions, the arithmetic operators are always evaluated first. As before, parentheses can be used to force the precedence of evaluation. For example, the expression

$$(2 \& 3) * 4 | 3 - 2$$

is evaluated in precedence as follows:

(2 & 3) evaluates to 2; the expression becomes

$$2 * 4 | 3 - 2$$

2 * 4 evaluates to 8; the expression becomes

$$8 | 3 - 2$$

3 − 2 evaluates to 1; the expression becomes

$$8 | 1$$

8 | 1 evaluates to 9; the final evaluation is

$$9$$

Chapter 12 introduced the use of *relational operators* and *relational expressions*. Recall that relational expressions always evaluate to a true (nonzero) or false (zero) result. For example, consider the following relational expressions:

$$test = (5 > 4)$$
$$test = (4 >= 5)$$

In the first case, the variable *test* is assigned a nonzero value, as 5 *is* greater than 4. In the second case, however, because 4 is *not* less than or equal to 5, the variable *test* is assigned a value of zero.

Table 13-3 lists the six binary relational operators supported by the C compiler. Notice that the operator "= =" is used to test equality instead of the "=" used by most programming languages. The "=" is used in assignment statements to assign the expression on the right-hand side to the variable on the left-hand side, whereas the "= =" operator is used in a relational expression to test the operands for equality. Similarly, the "! =" operator is used to test for inequality. For example, both of the following expressions will evaluate true if the variable *a* has the value 5:

$$a == 5$$
$$a != 4$$

As mentioned earlier in this section, relational operators can be used in conjunction with the logical operators "&&" and "||" in relational expressions. For example, in the following expression

$$(a > b) \&\& (c == d)$$

if *a* is greater than *b* and if *c* is equal to *d,* then the expression will evaluate true. Therefore both subexpressions (*a* > *b*) and (*c* = = *d*) must evaluate true in order for the expression to evaluate true. Notice that this is similar to the bitwise AND operation discussed earlier in the section.

Similarly, the expression

$$(a > b) || (c == d)$$

will evaluate true if either subexpression (*a* > *b*) or (*c* = = *d*) evaluates true.

Thus, in the following expression

$$(x != 10) || (y >= 20)$$

if the variable *x* has the value 10 and the variable *y* has the value 20, the expression will evaluate true. Note that because the relational operators have a

TABLE 13-3. Relational Operators

Precedence	Operator	Function
4	<	less-than operator
4	< =	less-than or equal-to operator
4	>	greater-than operator
4	> =	greater-than or equal-to operator
5	= =	equal-to operator
5	! =	not-equal-to operator

higher precedence than do the logical operators, the parentheses are not really required but are included to emphasize the order of evaluation.

The logical negation operator "!" introduced earlier can be used to negate the logic of a relational expression. For example, the expression

$$a == 5$$

will evaluate true if the variable *a* is equal to 5. However, the following expression

$$!(a == 5)$$

evaluates false, as the "!" operator negates the true condition to a false one. Note that parentheses must enclose the relational expression when used with the "!" operator, as the "!" operator has a higher precedence than does a logical operator. The "!" operator can also be used to operate on a variable. For example, the following **while** statement

```
while (yes)
```

causes repetitive execution of a statement as long as the variable *yes* holds a *true* value. However, the following **while** statement

```
while (!yes)
```

causes repetitive execution of a statement as long as the variable *yes* holds a *false* value.

The C compiler supports two other unary operators that are used to increment or decrement the value of a variable. Like all other unary operators, these operators have a precedence higher than the precedence of a binary operator. The *increment operator* "++" increments the value of a variable, and the *decrement operator* "−−" decrements the value of a variable. For example, if the value of the variable *count* is 32, the expression

```
count++
```

will increment *count* to 33, and the expression

```
count−−
```

will decrement *count* to 31.

Placing the "++" and "−−" operators after the variable name, as shown above, or before the variable name, as shown below,

```
−−count
```

will produce the same result if used as an isolated statement. However, if these operators are used in an assignment statement, then the placement of the operators will make a difference. For example, in the assignment statement

$$p = count++;$$

the variable p is set to the value of the variable count, and then the value of *count* is incremented. However, in the assignment statement

$$p = ++count;$$

the value of *count* is incremented first and then assigned to the variable p.

A special *conditional operator* is also supported by the C compiler. The *ternary* operator "?:" requires *three* operands, unlike binary and unary operators, and is used in *conditional expressions*. For example, consider the following C statement:

```
if (x < y)
        z = a;
else
        z = b;
```

The variable z will be assigned the value of a if the variable x is less than the variable y. Otherwise, z will be assigned the value of the variable b. The same assignment for the variable z can be accomplished by using the conditional statement

$$z = (x < y) ? a : b;$$

In this statement, the variable z will be assigned the value of a if the relational expression $(x < y)$ evaluates true. If the relational expression evaluates false, z will be assigned the value of b. A conditional statement using the "?:" operator therefore has the form

$$var = expr1 ? expr2 : expr3;$$

where expression *expr1* is evaluated first, and if true (nonzero), the expression *expr2* will be evaluated and assigned to the variable *var*. But if *expr1* evaluated false (zero), then the expression *expr3* will be evaluated and assigned to the variable *var*.

Finally, the assignment operator " = " is used in the C programming language to assign the variable, expression, or constant on the right-hand side of the operator to the variable on the left-hand side. For example, the assignment statement

$$x = x + 3;$$

adds the constant 3 to the value of the variable x and assigns the result to the same variable x. The same statement can also be written as

$$x \mathrel{+}= 3;$$

Similarly, the "$=$" operator can be used with any of the following binary arithmetic operators: $+$, $-$, $*$, $/$, and $\%$ or the following binary logical operators: $<<$, $>>$, $\&$, $\verb|^|$, and $|$.

Thus the expression

$$x \mathrel{*}= x;$$

is equivalent to

$$x = x * x;$$

and the expression

$$y \mathrel{+}= x * 2;$$

is equivalent to

$$y = y + (x * 2);$$

The C programming language supports other special-purpose operators besides the ones discussed in this section, and a few of them will be examined in this chapter.

13-3

Pointers and String Constants

Every variable defined in a C program is allocated one or more memory locations for storage. Recall from Chapter 12 that when a reference is made to the value of a variable, the value is actually the contents of the memory location(s) allocated to the variable—the *rvalue* (right value). A variable also has another value associated with it, called the *lvalue* (left value), and refers to the address of the memory location allocated to the variable. For example, if the declaration

$$\verb|char x;|$$

causes the compiler to allocate one byte of storage to the variable x at memory location 0x1000, then the lvalue of the variable x will be 0x1000. The assignment statement

$$x = 25;$$

sets the content of memory location 0x1000 to the value 25, and the value, or rvalue of the variable x, is 25.

The C programming language provides the programmer with a special type of variable called a *pointer*. A pointer is simply a variable that holds the address (lvalue) of another variable. The value held by a pointer is therefore a location in memory. This location can be specified absolutely, through an assignment statement, or by making the pointer point to a character or integer type of variable. In the latter case, the value of the pointer is equal to the memory location allocated to the variable. Because integer variables are allocated two memory locations, the pointer points to the first memory location allocated to the integer.

A pointer can be declared in C by using the ''*'' operator before the variable's name. For example, the declaration

```
char *index;
```

identifies the variable *index* to be a pointer that points to a character variable. Similarly, the declaration

```
int *key;
```

identifies the variable *key* to be a pointer that points to an integer variable.

Pointers must always point to some variable or memory location. A pointer that has been declared can be made to point to a variable by using the special unary operator ''&''. For example, consider the following statements

```
char *index;
char val;

val = 48;
index = &val;
```

Here the variable *index* is declared to be a pointer variable, and the variable *val* is declared to be a character variable. Note that the declarations have not established the relationship between *index* and *val*. The variable *val* is set to the value of 48 through an assignment statement, and the pointer *index* is set to the memory location allocated to the variable *val* through the last assignment statement. Thus the value of *index* is not 48 but is equal to the lvalue of *val*; a change in the value *rvalue* of *val* does not affect the value of *index*.

Notice that when the ''&'' operator is used as a unary operator, it provides the address (lvalue) of a variable. But when it is used as a binary operator, it performs the bitwise AND operation.

A pointer can have its value changed by assigning it a constant or the value of another pointer. For example, if *index* and *key* both are pointers, the assignment statement

```
index = 0x1B50;
```

will set the pointer *index* to point to memory location 0x1B50, and the assignment statement

```
key = index;
```

will set the pointer *key* to 0x1B50.

The "*" operator can be used to reference the memory location pointed to by a pointer variable. For example, the statement

$$*key = 12;$$

sets the contents of memory location 0x1B50 (location pointed to by *key*) to 12. Similarly, the statement

$$x = *key;$$

sets the variable *x* to 12 (the contents of the memory location pointed to by *key*).

The block-move algorithm developed in Chapter 8 can be used to illustrate the use of pointers. For example, consider a C program that is to move a 300-byte (count) block of memory from address 0x2000 (source) to address 0x8000 (destination). The program that does this is shown in Figure 13-1.

Lines 3 and 4 in Figure 13-1 declare two pointers, *source* and *destination*, that will be used to point to character variables. Note that the pointers do not point to an actual variable in this example, but simply to a byte of storage. The variable *source* is used as a pointer to the source block, and the variable *destination* is used as a pointer to the destination block. The variable *count* declared as an integer variable in line 5 is used to keep track of the number of bytes that have been moved.

The assignment statements in lines 7 and 8 set the values of the source and destination pointers to the starting address of the source (0x2000) and destination (0x8000) blocks, respectively.

The **for** loop in line 10 that encloses the block of statements within the braces initiates execution of the block 300 times. Line 11 sets the contents of the memory location pointed to by *destination* equal to the contents of the memory location pointed to by *source* and thus transfers one byte of data. Lines 12 and 13 increment the destination and source pointers, respectively. The process then

```
1       main()
2       {
3               char *source;
4               char *destination;
5               int count;
6
7               source = 0x2000;
8               destination = 0x8000;
9
10              for (count=0; count<300; count++) {
11                      *destination = *source;
12                      destination++;
13                      source++;
14              }
15      }
```

FIGURE 13-1.   Memory block-move program.

continues for the next memory location referenced by the pointers, until the value of *count* reaches 300.

Pointers can also be made to point to array variables. For example, if an array variable of an integer type called *table* is declared with a dimension of 12, then a pointer *p* can be made to point to, for example, the fourth member of the array through the following assignment statement:

```
p = &table[3];
```

The use of pointers with array variables will be discussed later in this chapter.

The real utility of pointers is evident when they are used with *string constants*. In the C programming language, a string constant is defined as an ASCII character string that is enclosed in double quotation marks (''). For example,

```
"This is a C program"
```

causes the compiler to store the ASCII representation of each character in the string in the program's *code segment*. The compiler always appends an ASCII NUL (0) to the end of a string. String constants are used in C in a manner similar to the ASCII strings assembled through the assembly language DB directive. String constants should not be confused with the character constants introduced in Chapter 12. Character constants are single characters enclosed in single quotation marks (') and represented by character variables. String constants, however, are character strings enclosed in quotation marks ('') and represented by pointers. For example, if the variable *messg* is declared as a pointer,

```
char *messg;
```

then the assignment statement

```
messg = "This is a C program";
```

will assign to the pointer *messg* the starting address of the string constant, that is, the address at which the first character in the string, "This is a C program," is stored. This is a useful feature that can be used by programs that need to display character strings (or messages). For example, consider a C program similar in function to the PRINT assembly language subroutine in Figure 10-7, which displays an ASCII string on the console of a microcomputer. The program to implement this task is shown in Figure 13-2 and is similar in function to the program in Figure 12-10. The program is to print the message "This is a C program" on the console.

Line 1 in Figure 13-2 defines the symbol NUL as holding a value equal to the code for the nongraphic ASCII character "NUL" (see Appendix B). Several of the nongraphic ASCII codes can be evaluated by the C compiler by using the special *escape sequence* "\" in a string or character constant. For example, on line 1, the escape sequence '\0' represents the ASCII code for NUL. The escape sequences supported in C are listed in Table 13-4. More will be said about them later in this section.

```
1       #define NUL '\0'
2
3       main( )
4       {
5            char *message;
6
7            message = "This is a C program";
8
9            while (*message != NUL) {
10                conout(*message);
11                message++;
12           }
13      }
```

FIGURE 13-2. Message print program.

Line 5 declares the variable *message* to function as a pointer to a byte (character type) of storage, and line 7 sets *message* to point to the first character in the ASCII string "This is a C program." Recall that the compiler compiles the string along with the code in the code segment and appends a zero (ASCII NUL) to the string.

The **while** statement in line 9 will initiate continuous execution of the enclosed block (lines 10 and 11) as long as the contents of the memory location pointed to by *message* is not a NUL. Within the block, line 10 sends the contents of the memory location pointed to by *message* to the console, and thus a character in the string is displayed. Line 11 increments the pointer *message* to point to the next string character to be displayed. This continues until the next string character to be displayed is a NUL, at which point the program terminates.

The escape sequences shown in Table 13-4 can be used to insert some of the nongraphic ASCII characters into string constants. For example, the data compiled for the string

```
"hello\n"
```

can be terminated with a LF (line feed) and, of course, the NUL. Similarly,

```
"hello\n\r"
```

has LF, CR, and NUL appended to the ASCII characters "hello".

The escape sequence character "\" can also be used to insert a single quote or a backslash, as shown in Table 13-4. The escape sequence character followed by a (octal represented) three-digit number can be used to insert any data byte (bit pattern) the programmer desires. For example,

```
"hello\030"
```

causes the compiler to append the ASCII code "CAN" to the string "hello".

One can see that string constants are similar to arrays. In fact, a string constant can be considered an array of characters. The difference is that the characters

TABLE 13-4. Escape Sequences

Character	ASCII mnemonic	ASCII code	Function
\n	LF	0x0A	Line feed
\t	HT	0x09	Horizontal tab
\b	BS	0x08	Back space
\r	CR	0x0D	Carriage return
\f	FF	0x0C	Form feed
\0	NUL	0x00	No operation
\\	\	0x5C	Backslash
\'	'	0x27	Single quote
\xxx	xxx	xxx	Bit pattern

in a string *must* be accessed through pointers, whereas the characters in an array *can* be accessed through pointers or subscripts.

13·4

Functions

The concept of functions was briefly discussed in Chapter 12 and at the beginning of this chapter. A function is simply a subroutine in the C programming language. However, unlike assembly language subroutines, functions offer a sophisticated mechanism for passing information (parameters) to and from a program. The use of functions in a C program greatly enhances the program's structure and also leads to the generation of various utilities that can be used in other programs; this type of software design was seen in the assembly language program developed in Chapter 10. Functions that are referenced by a C program can be written in C or in assembly language or even in another compiler-level language. If a main program calls a function, the function can be compiled either with the main program or separately and can then be linked in by the linkage editor. The compiler will automatically assume that a reference to a function is *external* if the function does not exist along with the main program, as seen in the compiled code shown in Figures 12-4 and 12-6. Notice that because the actual code for the *input* and *output* functions were not included as part of the program, the compiler assumed that their code would be linked in by the linkage editor and therefore identified them as EXTRN subroutines. The actual implementation of these assembly language functions will be described in the following section.

Consider the implementation of a delay function that is to simply produce a delay for a *fixed* amount of time. In other words, when this function is called, the program delays a certain amount of time, which remains the same each time the function is executed: no parameters are passed to the function, and no parameters are returned by the function. The implementation of the *delay* function is shown in Figure 13-3.

Notice in Figure 13-3 that the *delay* function is identified in a manner similar to the identification of the main function. That is, on line 1, *delay()* identifies

```
1      delay()
2      {
3            int x;
4
5            for (x=0; x < 30000; x++)
6                  ;
7      }
```

FIGURE 13-3.   The *delay* function.

the *function name,* and the statements enclosed within the opening and closing braces in lines 2 and 7, respectively, make up the *function body.* Within the function body, line 3 declares the integer variable x which will be used to maintain a delay count; any variables used locally within a function must be declared. Line 5 sets up a **for** loop that executes the statement on line 6 (null statement) until the value of x reaches 30000. When the loop terminates, the logical end of the function is encountered, and control is returned to the statement following the call to the *delay* function.

The *delay* function can be called by the main program or by another function by using the statement

```
delay();
```

Notice that no explicit "call" keyword is required, like the CALL instruction used in assembly language programs. The name of the function followed by a semicolon causes the compiler to generate a call to the appropriate function. This can be seen for the *input* and *output* functions in Figures 12-4 and 12-6.

The parentheses "()" following the function name can be used to pass parameters to the function. These parameters are called *arguments* in the C programming language. Because no data was passed to the delay function, thè call to the function did not include any arguments. To illustrate the use of arguments in a C function, consider the C implementation of the 8251 UART console output subroutine, whose assembly language implementation is shown in Figure 10-5.

The console output function is to send an input parameter (the character to be transmitted to the console) to the console after checking the UART's transmitter status. The C implementation of this function is shown in Figure 13-4. The *conout* function in Figure 13-4 can be called by the statement

```
conout(val);
```

where *val* is the data passed to the function and can be any constant of character type, or a variable, or expression that evaluates to a character type.

Line 1 in Figure 13-4 identifies the name of the *conout* function and the argument *data.* The calling statement passes a value to the variable *data,* and this value is sent to the console. The argument *data* must be declared immediately following the name of the function in order to identify its data type, as shown in line 2. The character variable *data* thus becomes a variable that is

```
1        conout(data)
2        char data;
3        {
4             char status;
5
6             do {
7                   status = input(0x03);
8                   status = status & 0x01;
9             } while (status == 0);
10            output(0x02,data);
11       }
```

FIGURE 13-4. The *conout* function.

used locally to hold the character that is to be transmitted to the console. The braces on lines 3 and 11 enclose the code for the *conout* function. The locally used character variable *status* is declared on line 4 and is used to hold the UART's transmitter status. Lines 6 through 9 initiate a **do** loop that checks the status of the transmitter. A **do** is used instead of a **while** to force execution of the statement on line 7 at least once before the data is sent to the console. The statement on line 7 inputs the data from the UART's status port 0x03 and assigns it to the variable *status*. The statement on line 8 then masks (ANDs) the UART status with the mask word 0x01 in order to check the TxRDY bit, and the result is assigned to the same variable *status*, whose value will be a zero if the transmitter is not ready or a one if the transmitter is ready. Note that the statement on line 8 can also be written as

$$status \&= 0x01;$$

The statements on lines 7 and 8 are therefore executed over and over until the transmitter is ready and the variable *status* has a nonzero value. When the **do** loop terminates, the data to be transmitted to the console (data) is sent to the UART's data port (0x02) through the execution of the *output* function in line 10. Notice that the *output* function is passed two parameters—the port number and the data to be sent to that port. An example of a function with more than one parameter will be shown later in this section. Also notice in line 7 that the data from input port 0x03 is obtained through another function call to the *input* function, which returns a value and is called through an assignment statement.

Functions that return data to the calling program are usually used in assignment statements in which the variable on the left-hand side is assigned the data returned by the function. For example, in Figure 13-4, the *input* function is called in line 7 through the assignment statement

$$status = input(0x03);$$

The right-hand side of the assignment statement initiates a call to the *input* function and passes to it the port number (argument) 0x03. The *input* function then returns the data from input port 0x03 to the variable *status*. Any function that returns data can be treated as a variable that holds a value and can be used

```
1       conin()
2       {
3             char status,data;
4
5             do
6                   status = input(0x03) & 0x02;
7             while (status == 0);
8             data = input(0x02);
9             return(data);
10      }
```

FIGURE 13-5.   The *conin* function.

in an expression or assignment statement as any variable would. For example, in Figure 13-4, the statements in lines 7 and 8 could be combined into one statement

$$status = input(0x03) \& 0x01;$$

In order to examine how data is returned by a function, consider the C implementation of the 8251 console input subroutine, whose assembly language implementation is shown in Figure 10-4. The function is to wait until a character has been received by the UART and then return the received character to the calling program or function. The *conin* function is shown in Figure 13-5.

Note in Figure 13-5 that there are no input arguments to the *conin* function, as no data is sent to the function. Within the body of the function, on line 3, two character variables, *status* and *data,* have been declared for local use. The variable *status* is used to hold the UART receiver status, and the variable *data* is used to hold the character obtained from the console.

The **do-while** loop in lines 5 through 7 initiates a continuous loop until the RxRDY bit is true, indicating that a character has been received by the UART; As in the *conout* function, this is done by calling the *input* function and masking the data obtained from the UART status port with the mask word, 0x02. When the RxRDY bit is true, the loop terminates, and control transfers to line 8. At line 8, the assignment statement sets the value of the variable *data* to the contents of input port 0x02 (UART data port). Line 9 contains a **return** statement that returns the value of the variable *data* to the calling program or function. The reference to the *conin* function in the calling statement therefore is replaced by the value of the variable *data.* For example, in the calling statement

$$a = conin();$$

the variable *a* is set to the value of the variable *data.*

Arguments passed to functions can be of character or integer type. The type of the arguments passed must be declared before the body of the function begins. Arguments passed to functions are not limited to one, as was seen in the *output* function. The maximum number of arguments passed depends on the characteristics of the C compiler being used. However, only one result can be returned by a function. To illustrate the design of functions that have more than one

```
1      average(a,b)
2      int a,b;
3      {
4          int avg;
5
6          avg = (a + b)/2;
7          return(avg);
8      }
```

FIGURE 13-6. The *average* function.

input parameter and return a result, consider the implementation of a function that calculates the average of two integers. The function *average* is to be called through the statement

$$var = average(arg1,arg2);$$

where *arg1* and *arg2* are variables, constants, or expressions that evaluate to the two numbers to be averaged and *var* is the variable that is to be assigned the average of *arg1* and *arg2* (result). For example, the sequence of statements

$$x = 35;$$
$$y = 51;$$
$$z = average(x,y);$$

calculates the average value of the variables x and y and assigns the result (43) to the variable z. The implementation of the *average* function is shown in Figure 13-6.

The arguments a and b for the *average* function in Figure 13-6 are identified on line 2 as integers. The variable *avg* declared on line 4 is used to hold the average value of the variables a and b, and the assignment statement on line 6 calculates this value. Finally, the statement on line 7 returns the value of the variable *avg* to the calling program or function. Actually, the data that is to be returned to the calling program (through the use of the **return** statement) can be a constant, the value of a variable (such as *avg*), or an evaluated expression. Thus lines 4 through 7 in Figure 13-6 could be replaced by the single **return** statement

$$return ((a + b)/2);$$

Data is passed to a function by *value*, which means that when a variable is passed as an argument for a function, the value of the variable does not change. For example, if the *average* function in Figure 13-6 is called to calculate the average value of the variables p and q and assign the result to the variable z, through the statement

$$z = average(p,q);$$

the values p and q will be assigned to the local variables a and b, respectively, when the *average* function is executed. If the *average* procedure happened to

```
1       offset(list)
2       int list[];
3       {
4           int p;
5
6           for (p=0; ;p++) {
7               if (list[p] = 0)
8                   break;
9               list[p] += 2;
10          }
11      }
```

FIGURE 13-7. Function with an array argument.

change the values of *a* and *b*, the values of *p* and *q* would not be affected. This is known as the *privacy rule* and pertains to how storage is allocated by the compiler (see Section 13-6). The passing of array variables is an exception to the privacy rule.

When an array variable is passed as an argument to a function, it is passed by location rather than by value. This means that a pointer to the array is passed to the function rather than a copy of the array members. Therefore, if the function modifies the value of any array member, the original array member's value will be affected. For example, consider a function called *offset* that is to add the number 2 to each member of a specified array (of integer type) whose last member has a value of 0. The implementation of this function is shown in Figure 13-7.

Assuming that in some program an array called *index* must have its members offset by a value of 2, the statement

offset(index);

initiates a call to the offset function in Figure 13-7 and passes a pointer to the array *index*. The declaration on line 2 identifies the argument as a pointer to an array of integer type. Even though it may appear that the values of the members of the array *index* have been assigned to the members of the local array *list*, this is not the case; only a pointer has been passed. Any reference made to the local array *list* actually references the array *index*. Therefore any change made to the members of the array *list* also changes the corresponding member of the array *index*. The **for** loop in lines 6 through 9 therefore adds 2 to each member of the array *index*, starting with member 0. When the last array member (whose value is zero) is accessed, the **break** statement is executed, the **for** loop terminated, and control returned to the calling program.

Pointers can be passed as arguments to functions that require access to string constants. For example, if it were required to convert the program in Figure 13-2 to a utility function called *print* that would display a specified character string on the console, a pointer to the string could be passed to the function. This can be seen in the implementation of the *print* function in Figure 13-8. For

```
1        print(message)
2        char *message;
3        {
4              while (*message != '\0') {
5                    conout(*message);
6                    message++;
7              }
8        }
```

FIGURE 13-8.   The *print* function.

example, in order to print the character string "Hello," a predeclared pointer *h* is set to point to the string, as follows:

$$h = \text{"Hello"};$$

and then the print function is called by the statement

$$\text{print}(h);$$

Because the variable *h* is a pointer to the string "Hello," the statement

$$\text{print("Hello")};$$

eliminates the need of the previous assignment statement and produces the same result.

Line 2 in Figure 13-8 identifies the argument being passed as a pointer. When the *print* function is called, the variable *message* points to the string that is to be printed. The statements in lines 4 through 6 are then used to access each character in the string and display the character on the console, as was explained in Section 13-3. Notice that because pointers are used to pass array arguments, the same function can be used to display the members of an array. For example, if the character type array variable *table* contained the following data

```
table[0] = 'H'
table[1] = 'e'
table[2] = 'l'
table[3] = 'l'
table[4] = 'o'
table[5] = 0
```

then the calling statement

$$\text{print(table)};$$

would pass to the *print* function a pointer to the array *table* which would cause the string "Hello" to be printed on the console. Notice that the last member in the array *table* is a zero, which is required by the *print* function.

Assembly Language Linkage

In Chapter 12, it was stated that the C programming language is essentially a hardware-independent language. Hardware independency means that the language does not support microcomputer-specific features such as access to I/O ports addressed by an isolated I/O addressing scheme, for isolated I/O addressing is not a feature inherent in all microprocessors. This means that the burden of writing hardware-dependent code to access such specific functions of the microprocessor falls on the programmer. Fortunately, the C programming language allows a program to access external functions that can be written in assembly language.

In Chapter 12 and in this chapter it was seen that many programs and functions accessed an 8085 I/O port by calling the *input* and *output* functions. These two functions must be written by the programmer in assembly language and then must be linked by the linkage editor with the compiled C program. The functions written in assembly language must be able to accept arguments from the C program and also to return data to the C program. In order to write such assembly language functions, the programmer must be aware of the paremeter-passing conventions used by the compiler.

In Figure 12-4, notice that the code compiled for the statement

```
data1 = input(SWITCH1);
```

consists of the following machine instructions:

```
LXI     H,54H
PUSH    H
CALL    input
POP     B
MOV     A,L
STA     data1
```

The statement therefore initiates a call to the external function *input* and passes the port number SWITCH1 (54H) as an argument. The *input* function returns the data from port 54H and assigns it to the variable *data1*.

Notice that the port number 54H is pushed on the stack before the *input* subroutine is called. The *input* subroutine therefore can expect the port number of the input port to be accessed, to be stored on the stack. Also note that the main program expects the *input* subroutine to return the data from the input port in register L, as the instructions

```
MOV     A,L
STA     data1
```

save the contents of register L (on return from the *input* subroutine) in the memory location allocated to the variable *data1*.

```
              PUBLIC    input
   input:
              POP       B            ;get the return address
              POP       H            ;get the port number
              MOV       A,L
              STA       P1+1         ;modify the "IN" instruction
   P1:        IN        0            ;input from specified port
              PUSH      H            ;restore port number
              MOV       L,A          ;result in Reg L
              PUSH      B            ;restore return address
              RET

              END
```

FIGURE 13-9.   Assembly language *input* function.

The parameter-passing conventions of an 8085 C compiler therefore specify that input arguments be loaded on the stack before the function is called and that output results be returned by the function in register L, if the result is of character type, or register pair HL, if the result is an integer; there is no standard 8085 C compiler, and therefore these conventions may differ from one compiler to the next.

Therefore in order to implement a subroutine in assembly language (called *input*), that is, to read the data from a specified input port and return the result to the program, the compiler's parameter-passing conventions must be known. The assembly language implementation of the *input* function is shown in Figure 13-9. The *input* subroutine is declared PUBLIC so that the linkage editor can identify the module for linkage.

Notice in Figure 13-9 that on entry to the *input* subroutine, the return address is stored on the top of the stack. Therefore, the first instruction "pops" this return address so that the stack pointer points to the port number. The POP H instruction then loads the port number from the stack into register pair HL (the port number is actually in register L). The port number is then stored at address P1+1, which is the memory location that contains the operand of the IN instruction at address P1. The IN 0 instruction is thus dynamically changed to the appropriate IN instruction needed to access the specified port. After the IN instruction is executed, the following PUSH H instruction restores the stack pointer by loading HL back on the stack. The data from the input port is then moved into register L, as this is where the calling program expects to find the data, and the return address is pushed back on the stack so that control can transfer back to the calling program. The implementation of the *output* function is slightly different from the *input* function because two arguments are passed to the function and no results are returned. For example, Figure 12-4 illustrates the compilation of the statement

```
                     output(LED,sum)
```

into the following sequence of machine instructions:

```
LXI     H,80H
PUSH    H
LDA     sum
MVI     H,0
MOV     L,A
PUSH    H
CALL    output
POP     B
POP     B
```

Recall that the *output* function sends the value of the second argument *sum* to the output port specified by the first argument LED (80H). The *output* function does not return any result.

For functions that are passed more than one argument, the first argument in the list is loaded onto the stack first, and then the next argument, and so on. Thus for the *output* function, because the first argument passed is the output port number, it is first loaded into register pair HL and then pushed on the stack. Next the second argument, which is the data to be sent to the output port, is retrieved from the memory location allocated to the variable *sum* and pushed on the stack. Note that because *sum* is a character variable, register L actually contains its value, and register H is cleared. On entry to the *output* subroutine, the top of the stack contains the return address, followed by the data to be sent to the output port, and then the output port number. The assembly language implementation of the *output* subroutine is shown in Figure 13-10.

On entry to the *output* subroutine in Figure 13-10, the subroutine return address, data, and output port number are loaded from the stack into register pairs BC, DE, and HL, respectively. As usual, these values are retrieved from the stack in a sequence that is the opposite of that used to store the values on the stack. As before, the port number is retrieved from register L and stored at address P1 + 1, the operand of the OUT instruction. The OUT instruction at address P1 is therefore modified to output data to the specified output port. The data to be sent to the output port is then retrieved from register E and loaded into the accumulator. The OUT instruction then sends the content of the accumulator to the appropriate output port. Finally, the data on the stack and the

```
        PUBLIC  output
output:
        POP     B       ;get the return address
        POP     D       ;get the data
        POP     H       ;get the port number
        MOV     A,L
        STA     P1+1    ;modify the "OUT" instruction
        MOV     A,E     ;get the data to be output
P1:     OUT     0       ;output to the specified port
        PUSH    H       ;restore port number
        PUSH    D       ;restore data
        PUSH    B       ;restore return address
        RET

        END
```

FIGURE 13-10. Assembly language *output* function.

return address is restored in the correct sequence, and the subroutine returns to the calling program.

The assembly language implementations of the *input* and *output* functions give the programmer an easy means to access an I/O port, by simply specifying the I/O port number as an argument. However, there is one major restriction to using these two subroutines. Because each time the subroutine is called, the subroutine dynamically modifies one of its own instructions, these subroutines cannot be used in a program that is to be stored in ROM. Owing to the limitation of the 8085 instruction set to only two I/O instructions, both of which require an immediate operand, there is no way to implement the *input* and *output* functions for a ROM environment. An alternative would be to create a separate function for each port being accessed in a program, which would perform I/O to absolute I/O port addresses and would not require a port number passed as a parameter. For example,

$$a = input5();$$

would return the data from input port 5 to the variable *a* and

$$a = input12();$$

would return the data from input port 12 to the variable *a*.
    Similarly,

$$output0(a);$$

would output the value of variable *a* to output port 0 and

$$output9(a);$$

would output the value of variable *a* to output port 9.

The assembly language implementation of these "ROMable" functions is left as an exercise for the reader.

The assembly language linkage can therefore offer a C program a means of accessing certain nonstandard or unique characteristics of a microcomputer system. Besides accessing the computer's I/O structure, assembly language functions can be used to implement other hardware-dependent portions of code, such as interrupt service routines and complex memory management routines for bank switching. The use of linkage in combining the compiled C programs with assembled programs gives the user an efficient interface between the two areas of software development.

13-6

Scope and Longevity of Variables

In previous examples of programs and functions we found that every variable had to be declared before it was actually referenced in statements. As indicated in Chapter 12, the declaration of a variable simply identifies to the compiler the characteristics of the variable so that the compiler may (if necessary) allocate the correct amount of storage to hold the value of that variable. But the declaration of a variable does not always cause the compiler to allocate storage to the variable; examples of such variables are the arguments declared when passing arrays to a function or the declaration of an external variable (to be discussed later in this section). When storage is allocated to a declared variable, that declaration is known as a *definition*.

The accessibility of (the value of) a variable in a C program is called its *scope*. The value of a variable is accessible only within the block in which it is declared. For example, consider the skeletal program shown in Figure 13-11, which illustrates the typical structure of a complete C program. The program is organized into three different blocks, the *main* program being the first block and the two functions, *func1* and *func2*, making up the second and third blocks of the program, respectively.

In Figure 13-11, the integer variable *x* that has been declared outside the main program can have its value accessed and modified anywhere (with one exception) in the program. The value of *x* is said to be *globally* accessible, and therefore

```
int x;
main()
{
            int y;
            .
            .
            x = 3;
            y = 4;
            .
            .

}
func1()
{
            int y;
            .
            .
            x = 5;
            y = 6;
            .
            .

}
func2()
}
            int x;
            .
            .
            x = 7;
            y = 8;
            .
            .

}
```

FIGURE 13-11. Scope of variables.

x is known as a *global variable*. In C, a global variable is also known as an *external variable*. Recall from Chapter 10 that an external subroutine or address (defined by the EXTRN directive) is accessible from any point in the assembly language program. In the main program, the assignment statement

$$x = 3;$$

changes the value of the external variable x to 3. Similarly, in the function *func1*, the assignment statement

$$x = 5;$$

modifies the value of the same variable x to 5.

Within the main program in Figure 13-11, the integer variable y is a *local variable*, which means that its value can be accessed only within the main program block. In the C programming language, a local variable is also known as an *automatic variable*. Thus in the main program, the assignment statement

$$y = 4;$$

sets the value of y to 4. No reference to y outside the main program affects its value.

Notice in *func1* that another integer variable, y, has been declared. Even though this variable is referenced by the same name as the variable declared locally within the main program, the two variables are treated as different variables and have no relationship. The assignment statement

$$y = 6;$$

in func1 therefore changes the value of the local variable y but does not affect the variable y declared in the main program.

In the function *func2*, the assignment statement

$$y = 8;$$

causes the‚compiler to generate an error message, as the variable y has not been declared locally (automatic) or globally (external).

Notice in *func2* that the automatic variable x has been declared within the function body. In the same program there also exists an external variable x. Therefore, in the assignment statement

$$x = 7;$$

that is located within *func2*, which variable x is set to the value of 7? The compiler resolves this ambiguity by making the automatic variable declaration overeride the external variable declaration. Thus, in the preceding assignment statement, the value of the local variable x is changed, but the value of the global variable x is not affected.

C programs therefore maintain *privacy* between automatic variables having the same name. That is, even though two automatic variables may have the same name, their values are maintained independently.

Any variable that is declared outside the blocks that make up a C program is assumed by the compiler to be an external variable. However, for separately compiled C programs, the programmer can specify that a particular variable be handled as an external variable. This allows a C program or function to access global variables that have been defined in other (separately compiled or assembled) programs or functions. For example, the declaration

```
extern int x;
```

identifies the integer variable *x* that is defined in another program or function. The linkage editor will then link in the appropriate address for this variable.

The C compiler usually allocates permanent storage to external variables and temporary storage to automatic variables. This means that the value of an external variable is maintained throughout the execution of a program. For example, the permanent memory allocation of the external variables (*data1, data2,* and *sum* in the C program of Figure 12-3 can be seen in the compiled code shown in Figure 12-4. Automatic variables are allocated storage dynamically. That is, on entry to a function or a main program, storage is allocated (at run time) to the automatic variable (for example, on the stack), and on exit from the function or main program, the memory location(s) allocated to the variable is made available for something else (deallocated). An automatic variable therefore "lives" only while the block in which it is declared is being executed and "dies" after the block's execution is complete. An external variable is allocated permanent storage and "lives" throughout the execution of the entire program. The "life" of a variable in a C program is also known as its *longevity*.

Because the longevity of an automatic variable is limited to the block in which it was defined, then on entry to the block, the value of the variable is undefined, as a new memory location can be allocated to that variable. Therefore the value of an automatic variable may not be the same on reentry into the block. The programmer can override this condition by forcing the compiler to allocate permanent storage to an automatic variable, so that the value of the variable is maintained each time the block is executed. This is done by specifying the local variable to be a *static variable*. For example, the declaration

```
static int x;
```

defines the integer variable *x* by allocating two bytes of permanent storage. Every time the block that contains this declaration is executed, any reference made to the variable *x* will reference these permanent memory locations. Thus the previous value of the variable *x* will be maintained on reentry to the block. The longevity of a static variable is therefore the same as the longevity of an external variable.

The scope and privacy rules of the C programming language, as well as the storage allocation techniques used by the compiler, offer efficient code generation and memory management. The scope and privacy of variables and function arguments can prevent any undesirable effects from occurring in a C program. For example, changing the value of a variable in one part of the program does not affect the value of another variable in another part of the program, although this does happen in some of the other programming languages. And the programmer does not have to keep track of a multitude of variable names, as is the case in languages that offer only global variables. Even though the storage allocation is maintained by the compiler and is "transparent" to the programmer, an understanding of the techniques used by the compiler to maintain variables can help in constructing efficient C programs.

13-7

A C Program Example

In order to tie together many of the concepts and constructs of the C programming language examined in Chapter 12 and this chapter, this section will implement a C program. The program developed in this section will also illustrate the structure of a typical C program and its adherence to the concepts of structured top-down programming discussed in Chapter 10.

This program will be required to input an ASCII character string from a computer console, sort the string in increasing order, and display the sorted string on the console. The program is shown in Figure 13-12.

This program is organized into seven logical blocks. The first block is the main program where the program execution starts; the next three blocks represent the functions that are referenced by the main program; and the last three blocks represent the functions that are referenced by the main program and other functions. Notice the simplicity of the code implemented at the main program level. In accordance with hierarchical top-down program design, the main program uses function calls to handle the specific tasks that the program is to perform.

The C program in Figure 13-12 begins by defining the various symbolic constants used in the main program and functions. The symbol MAXSIZE is assigned the value 40, which is the maximum length of the string that will be entered from the console. The symbol CR is assigned its appropriate ASCII code through the escape sequence '\r' (carriage return), and the carriage return will be used to terminate the keyboard entry of the string to be sorted and to detect the end of the string during the sorting and displaying processes. The next five symbols define the data and status ports and the mask words for the UART connected to the console device; these values are the same as those used in the CONIN and CONOUT subroutines in Figures 10-4 and 10-5, respectively.

Note that no external variables (global variables) have been defined in the program. This is good programming practice, as it essentially makes each module or function operate independently and not have to depend on external variables for local storage. External variables should be used only when absolutely necessary.

The main program defines an array variable of character type called *buffer* that has forty-one members. The extra member holds the CR that will be stored

```
/ ****************************************************************
*                                                                *
*              String-sorting program in C                       *
*                                                                *
* The following program reads an ASCII character string from     *
* the console and stores it in an array. The string              *
* is then sorted in ascending order, and the sorted string is    *
* displayed on the console.                                      *
*                                                                *
******************************************************************/

#define MAXSIZE 40              /* maximum buffer (array) size */
#define CR        '\r'                  /* ASCII carriage return */

#define DPORT    0x02                        /* UART data port */
#define SPORT    0x03                      /* UART status port */
#define RMASK    0x02                /* Receiver Ready bit mask */
#define TMASK    0x01             /* Transmitter Ready bit mask */
#define PMASK    0x7F                        /* Parity bit mask */

main()
{
        char buffer[MAXSIZE+1];

        print("Sorting Program in C \r\n);
        while (buffer[0] != CR) {
                print("\r\n Enter String:  ");
                if (get(buffer,MAXSIZE) == 1) {
                        print("\r\n Buffer Overflow \r\n");
                        continue;
                }
                sort(buffer);
                print("\r\n Sorted String: ");
                put(buffer);
        }
}
```

FIGURE 13-12.   A sorting program.

```
/ ****************************************************************
*                       The get function                       *
*                                                              *
* arguments:    array containing string                        *
*               maximum array (buffer) size                    *
* returns:      1 if buffer overflow                           *
*               0 if no overflow                               *
* description: The get function fills each array member with a  *
*               character from the console. The function will   *
*               return a 0 if a carriage return was entered     *
*               and the maximum buffer size was not exceeded.   *
*               If the maximum buffer size is exceeded, the     *
*               function will return a 1 (without waiting for a  *
*               carriage return).                               *
*                                                              *
**************************************************************** /

get(string,max)
char string[];
int max;
{
        int p;

        for (p=0; p <= max; p++) {
                string[p] = conin();
                if (string[p] == CR)
                        return(0);
        }
        return(1);
}




/ ****************************************************************
*                       The put function                       *
*                                                              *
* arguments:    array containing string                        *
* returns:      nothing                                        *
* description: The put function prints each member of the       *
*               specified array on the console. The function   *
*               returns when it detects a carriage return       *
*               in the array.                                  *
*                                                              *
**************************************************************** /

put(string)
char string[];
{
        int p;

        for (p=0; ; p++) {
          conout(string[p]);
          if (string[p] == CR)
                break;
        }
}
```

FIGURE 13-12. (Continued).

```
/ ****************************************************************
*                        The sort function                      *
*                                                                *
* arguments:    array containing string                         *
* returns:      nothing                                         *
* description:  The sort function sorts the members of the      *
*               specified array in ascending order. The array   *
*               is scanned from first member to last for any    *
*               misplaced elements. When a misplaced pair is    *
*               found, their positions are switched and a flag is *
*               set. This continues until no interchanges are   *
*               made, which indicates that the members of the   *
*               array have been completely sorted.              *
*                                                                *
* ****************************************************************/

sort(string)
char string[];
{
        int p;
        int iflag;
        char temp;

        do {
            iflag = 0;
                for (p=0; ;p++) {
                        if (string[p]==CR || string[p+1]==CR)
                                break;
                        if (string[p] > string[p+1]) {
                                temp = string[p];
                                string[p] = string[p+1];
                                string[p+1] = temp;
                                iflag = 1;
                        }
                }
        } while(iflag);
}
```

FIGURE 13-12. (Continued).

```
/ ****************************************************************
 *                     The print function                       *
 *                                                              *
 * arguments:   pointer to start of string constant             *
 * returns:     nothing                                         *
 * description: The print function prints the given ASCII        *
 *              string constant on the console.                  *
 *                                                              *
 **************************************************************** /

print(message)
char *message;
{
        while (*message != '\0') {
                conout(*message);
                message++;
        }
}

/ ****************************************************************
 *                     The conin function                       *
 *                                                              *
 * arguments:   none                                            *
 * returns:     character entered at console                    *
 * externals:   input                                           *
 * description: The conin function waits for a character to be   *
 *              entered at the console (checks UART receiver      *
 *              status), inputs the character, strips the         *
 *              parity bit, echoes the character to the console,  *
 *              and returns the ASCII code of the character.      *
 *                                                              *
 **************************************************************** /

conin()
{
        char data,status;

        do
            status = input(SPORT) & RMASK;
        while (status == 0);
        data = input(DPORT) & PMASK;
        conout(data);
        return(data);
}
```

FIGURE 13-12. (Continued).

```
/ ****************************************************************
 *                                                              *
 *                   The conout function                        *
 *                                                              *
 * arguments:    character to be displayed on console           *
 * returns:      nothing                                        *
 * externals:    input, output                                  *
 * description: The conout function waits till the UART is      *
 *               ready to transmit the specified character and  *
 *               then transmits it to the console.              *
 *                                                              *
 **************************************************************** /
conout(data)
char data;
{
        char status;

        do
            status = input(SPORT) & TMASK;
        while (status == 0);
        output(DPORT,data);
}
```

FIGURE 13-12. (Continued).

at the end of the ASCII string. The first executable statement in the program calls the *print* function to print the message

$$\text{"Sorting Program in C"}$$

on the console. Notice that the string constant is terminated with an "\r" carriage return and an "\n" linefeed code so that the console is positioned at the start of the next line.

A **while** loop is set up in the main program to cause continuous execution until the user enters an isolated carriage return, which is detected by examining the first array member *buffer[0]* for a value of CR. The first statement executed within the loop prints on the console the prompt message

$$\text{"Enter String:"}$$

This prompts the user to enter the ASCII string on the console keyboard. The following **if** statement initiates a call to the *get* function that is passed two arguments—the maximum buffer size and a pointer to the array *buffer*. The function of *get* is to read the characters entered at the console keyboard and fill the array *buffer* with them. The *get* function must also detect if there is a "buffer overflow" condition, that is, if there has been an attempt to enter more characters than the array *buffer* can handle. The *get* function returns a 0 when a CR is entered and there is no buffer overflow, and a 1 if there is a buffer overflow. The latter condition is tested by the **if** statement, and the message

$$\text{"Buffer Overflow"}$$

is displayed; control then transfers to the beginning of the **while** loop through execution of the **continue** statement. If there is no buffer overflow, the array *buffer* will be sorted in ascending order by calling the function *sort* and passing to the function a pointer to the array *buffer*. The message

"Sorted String:"

is then displayed by the *print* function, and finally the function *put* is called to display the members of the array *buffer* on the console. Control then resumes at the start of the **while** loop. When the user enters only a CR (empty buffer) while the *get* function is in execution, the CR is assigned to the first array member *buffer[0]*. Because this member is checked by the **while** statement, the program exits the **while** loop and terminates when the user enters a single CR at the "Enter String:" prompt.

The *get* function accepts two arguments from the main program. The first is a pointer to the array *buffer,* and the second is the maximum number of characters accepted from the keyboard (the maximum size of the array). Recall from Section 13-4 that because pointers are passed for array arguments, changing the value of a member of the array *string* in the *get* function actually changes the value of the corresponding member in the array *buffer*. The *get* function initiates a **for** loop that reads a character entered at the console (through a call to the *conin* function) and assigns this character to sequential members of the array *string*. This continues until the character entered at the console is a CR, or the number of array members filled is equal to the maximum size specified in the argument. If a CR is entered, then the **if** statement will terminate execution of the function and return a 0 to the main program; the **for** loop terminates when a buffer overflow occurs and returns a 1 to the main program.

The *put* function receives as a single argument a pointer to the array variable whose member values are to be displayed on the console. The **for** loop in the put function uses the *conout* function to display each array member starting with member 0. Each time within the loop, the value of the array member is checked for a carriage return (CR). Because the last array member always has a value of CR, the **break** statement terminates execution of the **for** loop and the function, and control then returns to the main program.

Like the *get* and *put* functions, the *sort* function receives as an argument a pointer to the buffer that is to be sorted in ascending order. The purpose of the *sort* function is to organize each member of the array *string* (actually *buffer*) in the appropriate sequence (with the exception of the last member, whose value is a CR) and return to the main program when the sorting has been completed.

The technique used to sort the array is based on an algorithm called a *bubble sort*. The sorting process can be described as follows. A flag called *iflag* (initially set to 0) is used to keep track of completion of the sorting process. The members of the array *string* are scanned in pairs, starting from the first member of the array. If the pairs scanned are out of order, the values of the two members will be switched, and the interchange flag *iflag* will be set to indicate the switch. The next consecutive pairs are then scanned and will be switched if out of order; *iflag* is set each time there is an interchange (or switch). This continues until all the members of the array have been scanned. The entire process is then

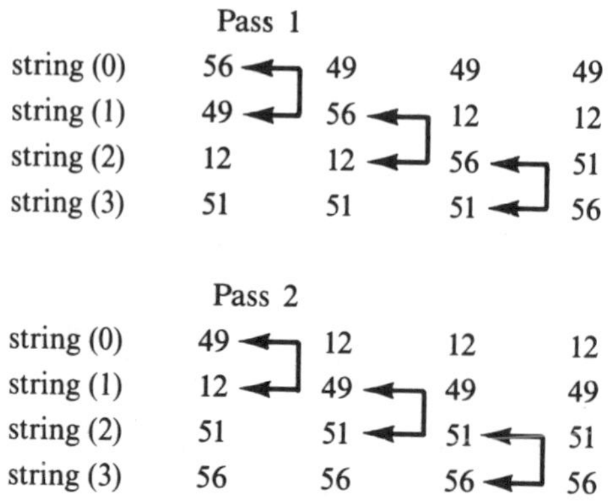

FIGURE 13-13. Trace of the array "string" in bubble sort.

repeated continuously until no more interchanges have taken place (*iflag* = 0). At this point the array *string* has been completely sorted. As the program sorts through the array, the smaller values seem to "bubble" up to the top of the list, hence giving the algorithm the name *bubble sort*. A trace of the array *string* is shown in Figure 13-13 during the sorting of four members of the array.

The *sort* function in Figure 13-12 contains a **do** loop that continuously executes the enclosed block while the value of *iflag* is true, that is, while an interchange takes place during one scan of the array. Each time through the loop, the value of *iflag* is cleared at the beginning and then tested at the end of the loop. Within the **do** loop, the **for** loop initiates a scan through the array and interchanges any array members that are out of order. The first **if** statement in the **for** loop will terminate execution of the **for** loop if the member being scanned or the next sequential member has a value of CR. Recall that the CR is the last character in the string. The second **if** statement compares two members and, if out of order, switches them and sets *iflag*; the switch is made by assigning the value of the first member to a temporary variable *temp,* assigning the value of the second member to the first, and then assigning the value of *temp* to the second member. If there are no interchanges, the value of *iflag* will be preserved (reset), and the **do** loop will terminate. The string is then completely sorted, and control returns to the main program.

The remaining three utility functions, *print, conin,* and *conout,* operate as described in Section 13-4. The *conin* function, however, has been modified slightly to clear the parity bit in the received character and echo it to the console display. If the console device provides a built-in echo, the function call to *conout* can be removed.

The program in Figure 13-12 can be compiled by the C compiler as one complete program or, by using a technique similar to the one discussed in Chapter 10, can be compiled and linked separately. The advantage of separate compilation, of course, is that the functions can be used as utilities in other main programs and, because they have already been compiled into relocatable object code, will reduce the development and testing time required for the application program.

Summary

The study of the C programming language in this chapter has illustrated some of the more sophisticated constructs provided by the compiler. These constructs are largely responsible for the popularity of the C programming language, as they often simplify the software development process. For example, the large collection of operators available in C offers many alternatives to the programmer during the development of a program. The availability of pointers allows low-level (machine-oriented) code to be implemented at the compiler level and also provides a powerful mechanism for manipulating program data. The use of functions in a C program has several advantages. Functions allow the programmer to take a more logical and structured approach to program design and to extend the language's capabilities through the creation of utilities. Finally, hardware-dependent functions can be implemented in assembly language, thereby making the language more portable.

The C programming langauge is a natural transition from assembly language to a higher-level language. Many of the concepts of assembly language programming are applicable to programs written in C, and for this reason, C has often been referred to as a *medium-level language*. However, this term can be misleading, as C in its full implementation provides most of the constructs available in true high-level languages such as PL/I and FORTRAN.

REVIEW QUESTIONS AND PROBLEMS

1. Evaluate the following C arithmetic expressions if $sum = 5$, $x = 10$, and $y = 12$. In each case, determine whether the expression evaluates to a character or an integer value.
(a) $x + sum * sum - y + sum$
(b) $(x + sum) * (sum - y) + sum$
(c) $x / sum * sum + (y - x)$

2. Evaluate the following C logical expressions if $a = 0x50$, $b = 0x27$, $c = 0x36$, and $d = 0xF3$.
(a) $a \& b \mid b \& c \mid \sim d$
(b) $a \& (b \mid b) \& (c \mid \sim d)$
(c) $\sim d \char`^ \sim c \& (b \mid a)$

3. Evaluate the following C relational expressions if $x = 3$, $y = 24$, and $z = 6$:
(a) $(x == 3) \&\& (z > 3)$
(b) $!(x < 7) \mid\mid (y == 23)$
(c) $(y < 3) \mid\mid 1 \mid\mid (z != 7)$

4. Evaluate the following C statements if $one = 12$, $two = 0x34$, $three = 500$, and $result = 1$:
(a) $result = three--$

(b) *result = (one > two) ? three + one : three − two*
(c) *result *= one + three*
(d) *result = + +two*

5. Describe the differences between an external variable and an automatic variable in the C programming language.

6. Write a C function called *lowest* that returns the lowest value of two integers passed to the function. For example, if

```
a = 5;
b = 10;
c = lowest(a,b);
```

the variable *c* will be set to 5. Note that if the values of *a* and *b* are equal, the returned value should be that value.

7. Write a C program to read data from input port 1 and store each data byte at consecutive memory locations, starting at location 0x4000. Stop reading the data when a 0 is read from the input port.

8. What is the function of the unary operator "&"? How does it differ from the binary operator "&"?

9. Write a function called *exchange* that will exchange the values of two variables supplied as arguments. For example, if $x = 5$, and $y = 9$, the function call

```
exchange(x,y)
```

will assign the value 9 to the variable *x* and the value 5 to the variable *y*. No result is returned!

10. Write an assembly language subroutine *output10* that will send a specified character to output port 10.

11. Write an assembly language subroutine *input5* that will return the data from input port 5.

12. The Z80 microprocessor is upward compatible with the 8085 microprocessor's instruction set. It has a few additional I/O instructions, two of which are

```
IN   A,(C)
OUT  (C),A
```

The first instruction will input a byte into the accumulator from the input port, whose address is specified in register C. The second instruction will output a byte from the accumulator to the output port, whose address is specified in register C. Using these two instructions, write the assembly language subroutines

ADVANCED C CONCEPTS

to implement the *input* and *output* functions discussed in Section 13-5, so that the functions are now "ROMable."

13. Convert the utility subroutines developed in Chapter 10 into C functions. Then write the C implementation of the "loader" program using these utility functions. Compare the C implementation of the loader with the assembly language implementation.

CHAPTER 14

8085 Microprocessor System Design

Introduction

The interface between the 8085 microprocessor and various standard memory and I/O devices was examined in Chapters 3 and 4. An address latch and a few logic gates usually are all that is required for an interface for a minimum microprocessor system. However, recall that the number of components and their interconnections in a typical system is fairly high. But for most simple microprocessor system applications, it is often desirable to keep the component (and hence the interconnection) count as low as possible, which is one of the bases on which the 8085 microprocessor was designed.

The pin configuration of the 8085 microprocessor is designed to provide a simple interface with certain memory and I/O components designed specifically for 8085 support. The interface usually involves relatively few components and a minimum amount of interconnections between them. Two of these components, the 8755 and the 8155 integrate memory, I/O, and other functions on a single chip and provide a direct interface to the multiplexed 8085 address and data bus without the need for an address latch. A minimum three-chip, 8085-based microprocessor system can therefore be constructed quite easily with a minimum number of interconnections.

This chapter considers the 8085 microprocessor's memory and I/O support chips, the 8755 and the 8155, and their integration into a system, as well as a simple "real-world" application of the 8085 microprocessor system—a security system.

14-2

The 8755 EPROM with I/O

The 8755 chip is an erasable and programmable ROM (EPROM) that also contains two 8-bit bidirectional I/O ports. Because the 8755 contains an internal address latch, the 8085's multiplexed address and data bus can be directly connected without the need for external hardware. The 8755's read/write control signals are also designed for direct interface to the 8085 microprocessor. The pin configuration and block diagram of the 8755 is shown in Figure 14-1.

With reference to the block diagram of the 8755 shown in Figure 14-1, notice that the chip contains 2K bytes of EPROM; a MROM version, called the 8355, is also available. The 8755 also provides two 8-bit I/O ports—port A and port B. The interface between the 8085 and the 8755 is accomplished by twenty-one lines, whose functions are briefly described, as follows:

AD_0–AD_7. These multiplexed address/data lines allow for data transfers to and from the chip's EPROM and I/O section. The least significant eight bits of an EPROM memory address appear on these lines when ALE is at the high state and are also used to select I/O ports A or B during an I/O cycle.

PIN CONFIGURATION   BLOCK DIAGRAM

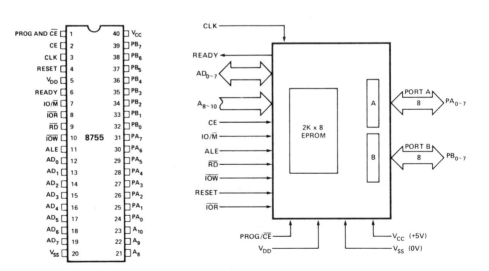

FIGURE 14-1.   8755 pin configuration and block diagram. (Courtesy of Intel Corp.)

A_8–A_{10}. These lines provide the high-order three bits for the EPROM address. These lines do not affect the 8755's I/O operations.

ALE. The address latch enable line (when high) is used to enable the internal address latch of the 8755 in order to demultiplex the address and data lines from the address/data bus (AD).

$\overline{CE}$/*PROG*. This line serves two purposes. Under normal operation of the 8755, it is used, when at the low state, to enable the EPROM and I/O section. And when the 8755 EPROM is being programmed, a high voltage on this pin is used to program each EPROM location.

CE. This chip enable line must be active (high state) in order to enable the 8755's EPROM and I/O section.

IO/$\overline{M}$. The 8755 EPROM section or the I/O section is accessed when IO/$\overline{M}$ is at the low or high state, respectively.

$\overline{RD}$. When the chip has been selected, this line can be used to READ data from a selected I/O port or EPROM location, depending on the state of IO/$\overline{M}$.

$\overline{IOR}$. This line performs the same function as does the combination of $\overline{RD}$ and IO/$\overline{M}$ and provides the standard I/O read operation. When the chip is selected, a low on this line will cause data to be read from a selected I/O port. Either this line or $\overline{RD}$ and IO/$\overline{M}$ should be used; if $\overline{IOR}$ is not used, it should be conditioned at the high state.

$\overline{IOW}$. This line provides the standard I/O write operation and is used to write data to a selected I/O port when the chip is selected. Because it is not possible to write to an EPROM location (during system operation), no $\overline{WR}$ line is provided, as the only write operation can be to an I/O port. The state of the IO/$\overline{M}$ line is therefore ignored during a write operation.

READY. The 8755 EPROM section contains the necessary logic to generate an (optional) wait state to the 8085 microprocessor during memory cycles. This line can be tied to the CPU's READY line to generate a wait state if the 8755's access time is relatively slow.

CLK. This line provides the basic timing for the 8755 during wait states. It is usually tied to the CLK (OUT) line of the 8085 microprocessor to synchronize the two devices if an optional wait state is used during memory cycles.

RESET. The function of the RESET line is to initialize the 8755's two I/O ports. Because the I/O ports are bidirectional, this line, when activated, will initialize both ports to the input mode.

The 8755 pins PA_0–PA_7 and PB_0–PB_7 provide the connections to the 8755's bidirectional I/O ports A and B, respectively.

The 8755 also requires a 5-V power supply that is provided by the V_{cc} (+5 V) and V_{ss} (ground reference) pins. The V_{DD} pin is the programming voltage used during EPROM programming and is tied to +5 V during normal operation.

The 8755's EPROM section is accessed by the address/data lines AD_0–AD_7, the high-order address lines A_8–A_{10}, the two chip enable lines $\overline{CE}$ and CE, and the memory read control lines IO/$\overline{M}$ and $\overline{RD}$. When ALE is active, the latched low-order address byte A_0–A_7, along with the high-order address lines A_8–A_{10},

TABLE 14-1. 8755 I/O Selection

AD$_1$	AD$_0$	Selection
0	0	Port A
0	1	Port B
1	0	Port A Data Direction Register (DDRA)
1	1	Port B Data Direction Register (DDRB)

are used to address the 2048 bytes of EPROM memory. At this time, the EPROM section must be enabled by both the chip enable lines $\overline{CE}$ and CE. Data from the addressed memory location is then loaded onto the data bus when both IO/$\overline{M}$ and $\overline{RD}$ are at the low state. The EPROM section thus operates in a manner similar to that of a standard memory chip.

The 8755's I/O section is accessed by the address/data lines AD$_0$ and AD$_1$, the chip enable lines $\overline{CE}$ and CE, and the I/O read/write control lines $\overline{RD}$, $\overline{IOW}$, and IO/$\overline{M}$. The address/data lines AD$_0$ and AD$_1$ are used to select either port A or port B for I/O operations and also to establish the direction of each bit (input or output) for a particular port. Table 14-1 illustrates the use of the two address/data lines for port and direction selection.

Note in Table 14-1 that when AD$_0$ and AD$_1$ are at the low state, port A is accessed, and data can be either read from or written to the port. Similarly, when AD$_0$ is at the high state and AD$_1$ is at the low state, port B is accessed for I/O operations.

The 8755's two I/O ports are bidirectional and can be programmed for an input or output mode. Furthermore, each bit in a particular port can be programmed to be either an input or an output. The 8755's I/O ports are said to be *bit programmable,* and this programming is accomplished through the *data direction registers* (DDR) for each port.

The DDRs for ports A and B are accessed when AD$_1$ is at the high state, as shown in Table 14-1. The data direction registers (DDRA) and (DDRB) are write-only registers (their contents cannot be read) and establish the direction (input or output) of each bit of port A or port B, respectively. Each bit in the DDR corresponds to a bit in the I/O port. If a bit in the DDR is set to a one, then the corresponding bit in the I/O port will be set for an output mode. If, however, the bit in the DDR is set to a zero, then the corresponding bit in the I/O port will be set for an input mode. For example, to initialize the entire port B as an input port, all bits in DDRB must be set to zeros. To set bits 0 through 3 of port A as output bits and bits 4 through 7 as input bits, the byte 00001111B must be loaded into DDRA. Similarly, to initialize port B bits 0, 2, 4, 6 to the input mode and all other bits to the output mode, the byte 10101010B must be loaded into DDRB. When the 8755 is RESET, the contents of both DDRA and DDRB are cleared, and therefore ports A and B are initialized as 8-bit input ports.

Any I/O operation to or from the DDRs or ports listed in Table 14-1 can be conducted only when the chip enable lines CE and $\overline{CE}$ are active. In order to read data from either port A or port B, the address/data lines AD$_0$ and AD$_1$

must be conditioned as shown in Table 14-1, and the $IO/\overline{M}$ and $\overline{RD}$ lines must be set high and low, respectively, to select an I/O read function. Recall that the $\overline{IOR}$ line can also be used instead of $IO/\overline{M}$ and $\overline{RD}$ to read data from an addressed port.

In order to write data to port A or B or to the data direction registers, DDRA or DDRB, the address/data lines AD_0 and AD_1 must be conditioned, as shown in Table 14-1, and the $\overline{IOW}$ line must be active in order to select an I/O write operation. When this occurs, data from the data bus is written to a DDR or an I/O port. Recall that the state of $IO/\overline{M}$ is ignored because data cannot be written into EPROM, and therefore because no distinction is required between a memory and I/O write operation, the 8085 $\overline{WR}$ line can be directly connected to the 8755 $\overline{IOW}$ line.

Figure 14-2 illustrates a typical interface between the 8755 and the 8085 microprocessor. By connecting the $IO/\overline{M}$ line of the 8755 to an 8085 address line (A_{15}) or the 8085 $IO/\overline{M}$ line, the addressing scheme can be either memory mapped or standard (isolated) input/output.

Isolated (Standard) I/O

If in Figure 14-2 the $IO/\overline{M}$ line of the 8755 is connected to the $IO/\overline{M}$ line of the 8085 microprocessor, the 8085 will distinguish between I/O and memory operations. The interface will then allow access to the DDRs and I/O ports through the standard IN and OUT instructions. Because the $\overline{CE}$ line is connected to address line A_{11}, the 8755 is enabled for I/O or memory operations only when A_{11} is low. Notice that the other chip enable line CE is not used and is conditioned high. Linear addressing is used to eliminate the need for an I/O and memory decoder. The $\overline{IOR}$ line in this example is not used and is conditioned high. The 8085 control lines $\overline{RD}$, $\overline{WR}$, and $IO/\overline{M}$ provide access to the EPROM or I/O sections of the 8755.

In order to access the 8755 EPROM, address line A_{11} must be low; address lines A_0 through A_{10} address the 2048 bytes of EPROM during this time. The 8755 EPROM therefore occupies memory addresses 0000H through 07FFH. Memory foldback will occur whenever address line A_{11} is low during higher addresses. A particular EPROM location is then actually read (loaded onto the data bus) when $\overline{RD}$ and $IO/\overline{M}$ are at the low state.

In order to access the 8755 I/O section (port A, port B, DDRA, and DDRB), the chip must be selected, and so address line A_{11} must be low again. Because the address mirror effect takes place during an I/O operation (the upper half of the address bus has the same contents as the lower half does), address line A_{11} will be low if address line A_3 is low. Therefore the I/O device address for accessing the 8755 I/O section must have address line A_3 low. Each of the four I/O units of the 8755 illustrated in Table 14-1 can be addressed by a unique I/O device address, as shown in Table 14-2. Thus the 8755 I/O ports can be accessed by the IN 0 and OUT 0 (port A) instructions and the IN 1 and OUT 1 (port B) instructions. Similarly, DDRA and DDRB can be accessed by the OUT 2 and OUT 3 instructions, respectively. Because linear addressing is used, I/O foldback will occur whenever address line A_3 is at the zero state during higher I/O addresses.

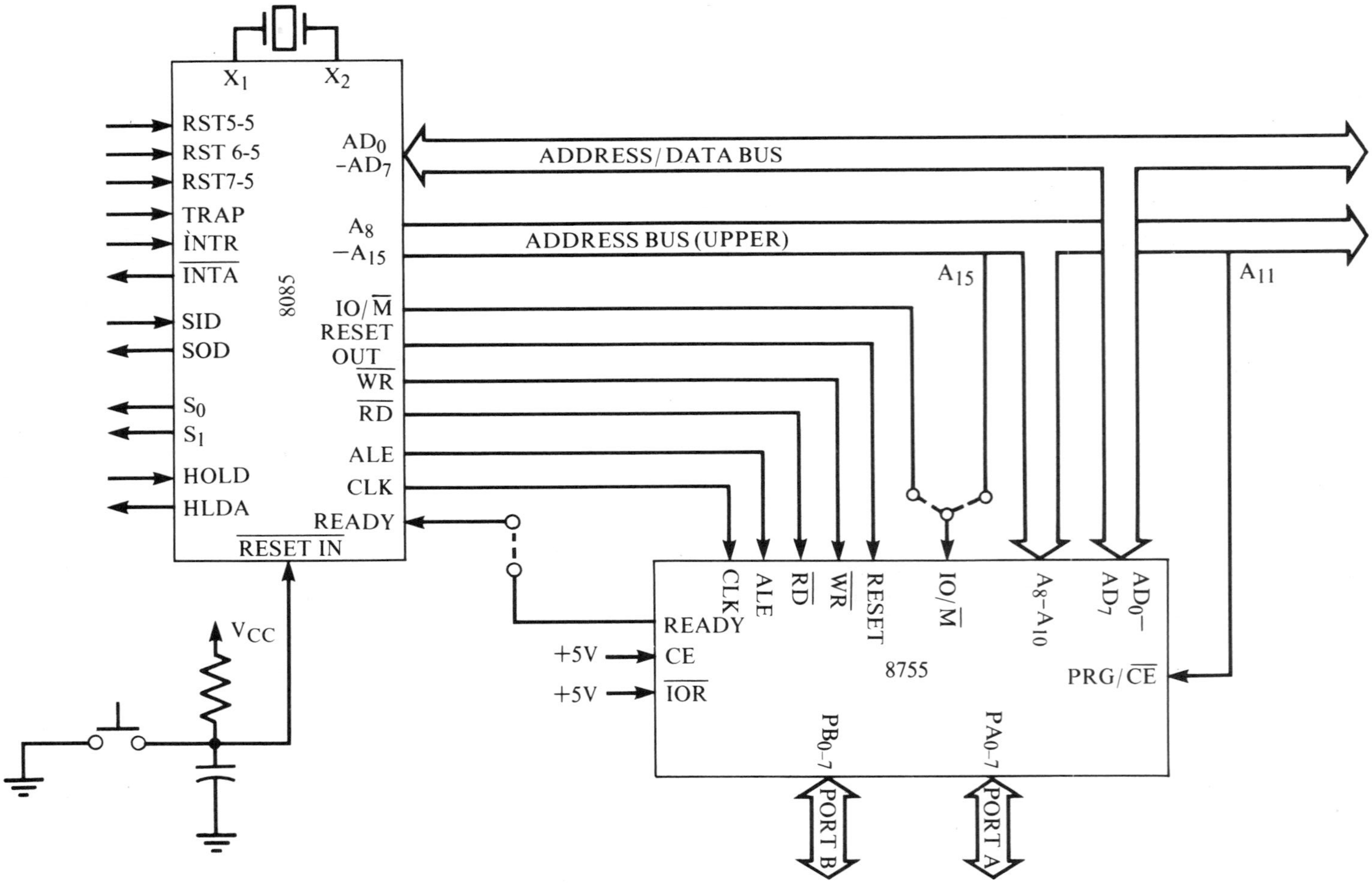

FIGURE 14-2. 8755 interface with the 8085 microprocessor.

TABLE 14-2. 8755 I/O Addressing Scheme

A_7	A_6	A_5	$\overline{CE}$ $\downarrow$ A_4	A_3	A_2	See Table 14-1 A_1	A_0	Port	Function
0	0	0	0	0	0	0	0	00H	Port A
0	0	0	0	0	0	0	1	01H	Port B
0	0	0	0	0	0	1	0	02H	DDR A
0	0	0	0	0	0	1	1	03H	DDR B

Memory-mapped I/O

If the 8755's IO/$\overline{M}$ line is connected to the 8085's address line A_{15}, the interface in Figure 14-2 will become memory mapped. This is because the 8085's IO/$\overline{M}$ line is no longer used to distinguish between a memory or I/O operation, but instead this distinction is made with an address line (A_{15}) that can be made active during both memory and I/O operations. This addressing scheme allows the 8755's EPROM section to be accessed in the same way as before, but the I/O section can now be accessed by memory reference instructions instead of I/O instructions. Address line A_{15} therefore maps the entire 64K memory address range into two areas: memory and I/O. The 8755 EPROM section is accessed when address line A_{15} is at the low state (addresses 0000H through 7FFFH), and the 8755 I/O section is accessed when address line A_{15} is at the high state (addresses 8000H through FFFFH). Table 14-3 illustrates the memory-addressing scheme used to access the 8755.

Note in Table 14-3 that the 8755 EPROM section will be addressed from 0000H through 07FFH, as the chip is enabled by address line A_{11} and address line A_{15} selects a memory operation. As before, memory foldback will occur when address lines A_{11} and A_{15} are at the low state for higher addresses.

When address line A_{15} is high, the 8755 is selected for an I/O operation, and a memory address can then be used to access a port or DDR of the 8755. As before, address line A_{11} must be low in order to enable the chip. Thus in Table 14-3 it can be seen that port A, port B, DDRA, and DDRB will be addressed at locations 8000H through 8003H. Again, because linear addressing is used, I/O foldback will occur whenever address line A_{15} is high and A_{11} is low for higher addresses. Also observe that because the 8085 IO/$\overline{M}$ line is not used to distinguish between an I/O or memory operation, the same four I/O units of the 8755 (Table 14-1) can also be addressed by IN and OUT instructions when an I/O address appears on the address bus. When an I/O address appears on the low-order address bus (owing to the execution of an IN or OUT instruction), the address mirror effect will cause A_{15} to go high whenever A_7 is high, which will enable the 8755 for I/O operations. Similarly, the 8755 chip enable line will be active when address line A_3 is low. The 8755's port A, port B, DDRA, and DDRB can then be addressed by I/O addresses 80H, 81H, 82H, and 83H, respectively. Similarly, performing an I/O read from any address that causes A_3

TABLE 14-3. 8755 Memory Addressing Scheme

CE → points to A11. "8755 address lines" spans A10 through A0.

IO/M̄	A15	A14	A13	A12	A11 (CE)	A10	A9	A8	A7	A6	A5	A4	A3	A2	A1	A0	Location	
0	0	0	0	0	0	0	0	0	0	0	0	0	0	0	0	0	0000H	⎫
·	·	·	·	·	·	·	·	·	·	·	·	·	·	·	·	·	·	⎬ 8755 ROM
0	0	0	0	0	0	1	1	1	1	1	1	1	1	1	1	1	07FFH	⎭
0	0	0	0	0	1	0	0	0	0	0	0	0	0	0	0	0	0800H	⎫
·	·	·	·	·	·	·	·	·	·	·	·	·	·	·	·	·	·	⎬ Unused area and memory foldback
0	0	1	1	1	1	1	1	1	1	1	1	1	1	1	1	1	7FFFH	⎭
1	0	0	0	0	0	0	0	0	0	0	0	0	0	0	0	0	8000H	Port A ⎫
1	0	0	0	0	0	0	0	0	0	0	0	0	0	0	0	1	8001H	Port B ⎬ 8755 I/O
1	0	0	0	0	0	0	0	0	0	0	0	0	0	0	1	0	8002H	DDR A ⎪
1	0	0	0	0	0	0	0	0	0	0	0	0	0	0	1	1	8003H	DDR B ⎭
1	0	0	0	0	0	0	0	0	0	0	0	0	0	1	0	0	8004H	⎫
·	·	·	·	·	·	·	·	·	·	·	·	·	·	·	·	·	·	⎬ Unused area and I/O foldback
1	1	1	1	1	1	1	1	1	1	1	1	1	1	1	1	1	FFFFH	⎭

and A_7 to go low obtains data from an EPROM location. This procedure, however, should not be used to read the EPROM.

Incorporating the 8755 into an 8085-based microprocessor system is therefore relatively simple. Because the 8755 incorporates both EPROM and I/O, two necessary functions are performed by one chip, thereby reducing the size of the system and also the interconnection between components.

14-3

The 8155 RAM with I/O and Timer

The 8155 is a component that is also designed to interface directly with the 8085 microprocessor. It provides a system with Read/Write memory as well as programmable I/O ports and a programmable binary counter/timer. Figure 14-3 illustrates the pin configuration and block diagram of the 8155. Notice that the address/data bus and the read/write control signals are designed for a direct interface with the 8085 microprocessor.

Like the 8755, the 8155 has two functional sections—the memory section and the I/O section. The memory section consists of 256 bytes of static RAM. The I/O section contains two 8-bit programmable ports (ports A and B), one 6-bit programmable I/O port (port C), and a 14-bit programmable counter/timer that can be used for either a square wave or a terminal count pulse, depending on how it is programmed. The memory and I/O section of the 8155 is controlled and accessed by fourteen lines that function as follows:

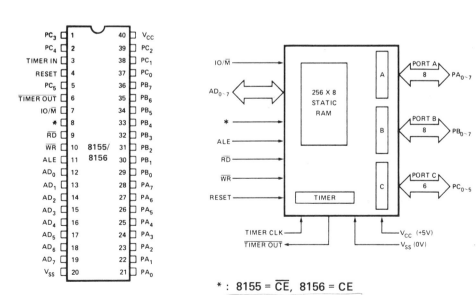

FIGURE 14-3. 8155 pin configuration and block diagram. (Courtesy of Intel Corp.)

AD_0–AD_7. These multiplexed address/data lines allow for data transfers to and from the chip's RAM and I/O section. During a memory or I/O cycle, the least significant 8-bit address appears on these lines when ALE is at the high state and is used to access one of 256 RAM locations, an I/O port, or an I/O register.

ALE. The address latch enable line (when high) is used to enable the 8155's internal address latch in order to demultiplex the address and data lines from the address/data bus (AD).

$\overline{CE}$. This line enables the 8155 for I/O and memory operations. It must be in the low state before any data transfer can take place between the CPU and the 8155. A modified version of the 8155 chip (the 8156) provides an *active-high* chip enable line.

$IO/\overline{M}$. This line selects the 8155 for either an I/O ($IO/\overline{M} = 1$) or memory ($IO/\overline{M} = 0$) operation.

$\overline{RD}$. The READ line is used to obtain data from the 8155's memory or I/O section, depending on the state of $IO/\overline{M}$. The $\overline{CE}$ line must be enabled in order to read from the 8155.

$\overline{WR}$. The WRITE line is used to send data to the 8155's memory or I/O section, depending on the state of $IO/\overline{M}$. The $\overline{CE}$ line must be enabled in order to write to the 8155.

RESET. A high level on this line used to initialize the 8155's three I/O ports to the input mode. The RESET line, when active, will also stop the timer from counting if the timer was started before the occurrence of the RESET pulse.

Ports A, B, and C are accessed through the PA_0–PA_7, PB_0–PB_7, and PC_0–PC_5 lines, respectively. The 8155 timer is accessed through the TIMER CLK and $\overline{\text{TIMER OUT}}$ lines. The 8155 requires a single 5-V power supply that is provided at pins V_{cc} (+ 5 V) and V_{ss} (ground reference).

When the 8155 is enabled ($\overline{CE} = 0$), the RAM section is selected when the $IO/\overline{M}$ line is at the low state. The $\overline{RD}$ and $\overline{WR}$ lines allow the CPU to read or write, respectively, from and to an addressed memory location. A RAM location is addressed by an 8-bit address that appears on AD_0–AD_7 when ALE is at the high state. This 8-bit address can uniquely reference one of 256 RAM locations, and hence no additional address lines are required, as in the 8755.

The 8155's I/O section is selected when $IO/\overline{M}$ is at the high state. As before, the 8155 must be enabled by conditioning the $\overline{CE}$ line low before any I/O operations can take place. The $\overline{RD}$ and $\overline{WR}$ control lines then establish the direction of data flow either to or from an I/O port or internal register. The 8155's I/O section is made up of six registers, three of which are I/O ports. A particular register is selected by conditioning AD_0, AD_1, and AD_2, as shown in Table 14-4.

The 8155 command/status (C/S) register is used to define the mode of operation for each port, enable and disable interrupts from ports A and B, and control the operation of the timer; this is done by writing a byte to the 8155 when the AD_0–AD_2 lines are set to zeros (as illustrated in Table 14-4). The bit assignments for the C/S register is shown in Figure 14-4.

TABLE 14-4. 8155 I/O Selection

AD_2	AD_1	AD_0	Selection
0	0	0	Command/Status Register (C/S)
0	0	1	Port A
0	1	0	Port B
0	1	1	Port C
1	0	0	Timer count register (LSB)
1	0	1	Timer count register (MSB) and mode

With reference to Figure 14-4, bits 0 and 1 of the C/S register define the mode of operation for ports A and B, respectively. A one in this bit position will program the port for output, and a zero will program the port for input. Bits 2 and 3 of the C/S register establish the mode of operation for port C, which functions in a manner similar to the 8255 PPI discussed in Chapter 7. If bits 2 and 3 are conditioned for ALT 1 and ALT 2, as shown in Figure 14-4, then port C will be programmed as a simple 6-bit input port (ALT 1) or output port (ALT 2). Port C also can give ports A and B interrupt and handshaking capabilities when bits 2 and 3 of the C/S register are conditioned for ALT 2 and ALT 3. The definitions of the 6 bits that make up port C for ALT 2 and ALT 3 operations are shown in Table 14-5.

When port C is programmed for ALT 3, the low-order 3 bits PC_0–PC_2 are used as control signals for port A, as shown in Table 14-5. The remaining 3 bits PC_3–PC_5 are used as a simple latched 3-bit output port. The INTR, BF,

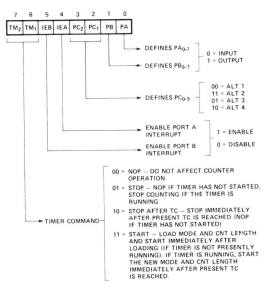

FIGURE 14-4. 8155 command/status register bit assignments. (Courtesy of Intel Corp.)

TABLE 14-5. Port C bit assignments

Pin	ALT 3	ALT 4
PC_0	A INTR (port A interrupt)	A INTR (port A interrupt)
PC_1	A BF (port A buffer full)	A BF (port A buffer full)
PC_2	A STB (port A strobe)	A STB (port A strobe)
PC_3	Output port	B INTR (port B interrupt)
PC_4	Output port	B BF (port B buffer full)
PC_5	Output port	B STB (port B strobe)

and STB can be used in conjunction with port A to handshake with an external device, to generate an interrupt to the CPU, or to function as a strobed input port. The function of these three lines was explained in Section 7-3.

When port C is programmed for ALT 4, the low-order 3 bits (PC_0–PC_2) are used as control signals for port A (as for ALT 3), but the remaining 3 bits (PC_3–PC_5) are now used as similar control signals for port B. Thus when it is programmed for ALT 4, port C can be used in conjunction with both ports A and B.

Bits 4 and 5 of the C/S register (Figure 14-4) can be used to enable or disable interrupts from ports A and B, respectively, if port C is programmed for ALT 3 or ALT 4. The most significant two bits in the C/S register are used to control the timer. The operation of the timer and how these two bits affect it will be discussed at a later point in this section.

When an attempt is made to read from the C/S register, the 8155 supplies the CPU with status information. The bit definitions of the C/S register status word is illustrated in Figure 14-5.

The status word shown in Figure 14-5 can be used by the CPU to obtain status information on ports A and B when port C is programmed for ALT 3 or ALT 4. Bits 0 through 5 provide the states of port C lines A INTR, B INTR, A BF, B BF, as well as on the interrupt states of port A and B (enabled or

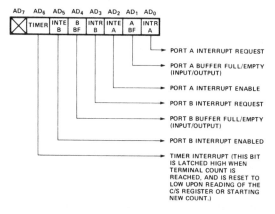

FIGURE 14-5. 8155 command/status register status word.
(Courtesy of Intel Corp.)

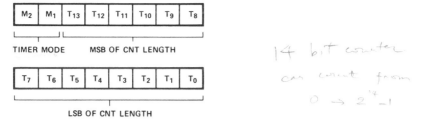

FIGURE 14-6. 8155 timer register format. (Courtesy of Intel Corp.)

disabled). Bit 6 of the status word offers information on the timer, and its function will be discussed in conjunction with the operation of the timer.

In order to access ports A, B, or C, the address/data lines AD_0–AD_2 must be conditioned, as shown in Table 14-4. Once a particular port has been programmed for input, output, or the control mode, data can be sent or retrieved by addressing the ports, as shown in Table 14-4.

When address lines AD_0, AD_1, and AD_2 are conditioned, as shown in the fifth and sixth entry in Table 14-4, the CPU can access the 8155 timer. The timer section of the 8155 is a 14-bit programmable counter that counts the pulses on the TIMER CLK line and produces either a square wave or a pulse when a programmed *terminal count* (TC) is reached. The timer can be programmed to produce a single square wave or pulse output when the TC is reached or to provide a continuous square wave or pulse stream. The output of the timer is obtained from the TIMER OUT line. The TC and the mode of operation can be programmed via the two I/O registers shown in Table 14-4. The format of the two timer registers is shown in Figure 14-6.

The 14-bit terminal count is loaded into the two registers shown in Figure 14-6. This 14-bit number is broken up into a least significant part that is loaded into one register and a 6-bit, most significant part that is loaded into the other register. The value loaded into these register(s) can have any value, from 0002H to 3FFFH, The most significant two bits of the timer count register (MSB) define the mode of operation for the timer. These two bits, M_2 and M_1, cause the timer to function, as shown in Table 14-6.

The timing diagram in Figure 14-7 illustrates the timer's output for each mode of operation shown, in relation to a periodic clock supplied at the TIMER CLK line. It is assumed that the timer count register(s) have been programmed for a TC of 6. Each timer mode listed in the preceding table will be discussed with reference to the timing diagram of Figure 14-7.

TABLE 14-6. 8155 Timer Operating Modes

Mode	M_2	M_1	Function
0	0	0	single square wave
1	0	1	continuous square wave
2	1	0	single pulse
3	1	1	continuous pulses

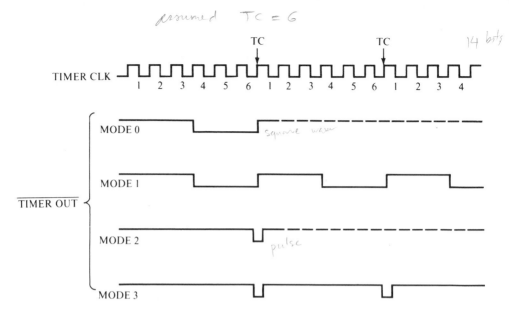

FIGURE 14-7. Timing diagram of 8155 timer operating modes.

Timer Mode 0

When the 8155 timer is programmed for mode 0, it produces a single square wave that is initially high for the first half of the TC and then low for the second half of the TC. Once the TC has been reached, the output remains high until the timer is started again. In the case of an odd-numbered terminal count, the first half-cycle of the square wave that is high is one count longer than the second (low) half-cycle is, and so the output is asymmetrical.

Timer Mode 1

Mode 1 is similar to mode 0 except that the timer produces a continuous square wave instead of a single one. When the TC is reached, the timer starts the count again, thus producing another cycle. The process continues until the timer is stopped. As in mode 0, if the TC is an odd number, the first half-cycle (high) will be one count longer than the second (low) half-cycle. Notice in Figure 14-7 that in mode 1 the timer essentially divides the TIMER CLK frequency by the terminal count, in this example, a divide-by-six counter.

Timer Mode 2

When programmed for mode 2, the timer will produce a single pulse when the TC is reached. As in mode 0, once the terminal count is reached, the timer stops counting and holds its output at the high state until the timer is started again. This mode is particularly useful in counting and detecting a programmed number of clock pulses in a waveform.

Timer Mode 3

Mode 3 causes the timer to produce a continuous stream of pulses. As in mode 2, each pulse is produced when the TC is reached, but the process repeats itself for each terminal count. The pulses are periodic and will continue until the timer is stopped. The pulse repetition rate in this mode can therefore be changed by changing the value of the timer count register.

Once the TC has been loaded into the timer count register and the mode of operation has been established, the timer can be started, stopped, or controlled by the command/status register bits 6 and 7, as illustrated in Figure 14-4. The status of the timer (terminal count reached?) can also be polled by reading the C/S register and checking bit 6 of the status word, as illustrated in Figure 14-5.

Figure 14-8 shows a typical interface between the 8155 and the 8085 microprocessor. Notice how similar the interface is to the 8755 interface shown in Figure 14-2. Like the 8755 interface, the addressing scheme can also be either memory mapped or standard (isolated) I/O. The type of addressing scheme used will again depend on the connection made to the IO/$\overline{\text{M}}$ line of the 8155.

Isolated (Standard) I/O

If the IO/$\overline{\text{M}}$ line of the 8155 is connected to the IO/$\overline{\text{M}}$ line of the 8085 microprocessor, the interface will have a standard isolated I/O addressing scheme, and the I/O section of the 8155 (Table 14-4) can be accessed by the 8085 IN and OUT instructions only. The 8155's I/O and memory sections will therefore be controlled by the 8085's I/O and memory cycles, respectively. Notice that the 8155 chip is enabled whenever address line A_{11} is at the one state, as the connection is made through an inverter. Thus all I/O and memory operations between the 8085 and the 8155 can take place only when A_{11} is at the high state. Read or write operations for memory or I/O are controlled by the $\overline{\text{RD}}$ and $\overline{\text{WR}}$ lines, respectively. Because the 8155 contains only 256 bytes of RAM, no additional address lines have to be connected to the 8085 address bus.

The 8155 RAM section is accessed whenever the IO/$\overline{\text{M}}$ line is at the low state and the chip is enabled. Because the chip can be enabled only when address line A_{11} is high, the RAM is located at addresses 0800H through 08FFH. This addressing scheme was chosen because in most systems, the lower portion of memory (0000H–07FFH in this case) is usually reserved for ROM. Because linear addressing is used, memory foldback occurs whenever address line A_{11} is high during higher addresses. When the 8155 RAM is enabled, the data flow into and out of memory can be controlled by the $\overline{\text{WR}}$ and $\overline{\text{RD}}$ lines, respectively.

The I/O section of the 8155 is accessed when the chip is selected (address line A_{11} is high) and the IO/$\overline{\text{M}}$ line is at the high state. Because the address mirror effect causes the I/O address to be "reflected" on the upper 8 bits of the address bus (A_8–A_{15}), address line A_{11} is set high whenever address line A_3 is high during an I/O cycle. The 8155's six I/O ports and registers can thus be addressed, as shown in Table 14-7. Note that I/O addresses 08H through 0DH cause address line A_3 to stay high and therefore enable the chip. Address lines A_0 through A_2 (when internally latched) are used to select the respective registers or I/O ports of the 8155, as was seen in Table 14-4. The 8155 I/O section thus occupies six addresses, and because linear addressing is used, I/O foldback occurs whenever address line A_3 is high during higher I/O addresses.

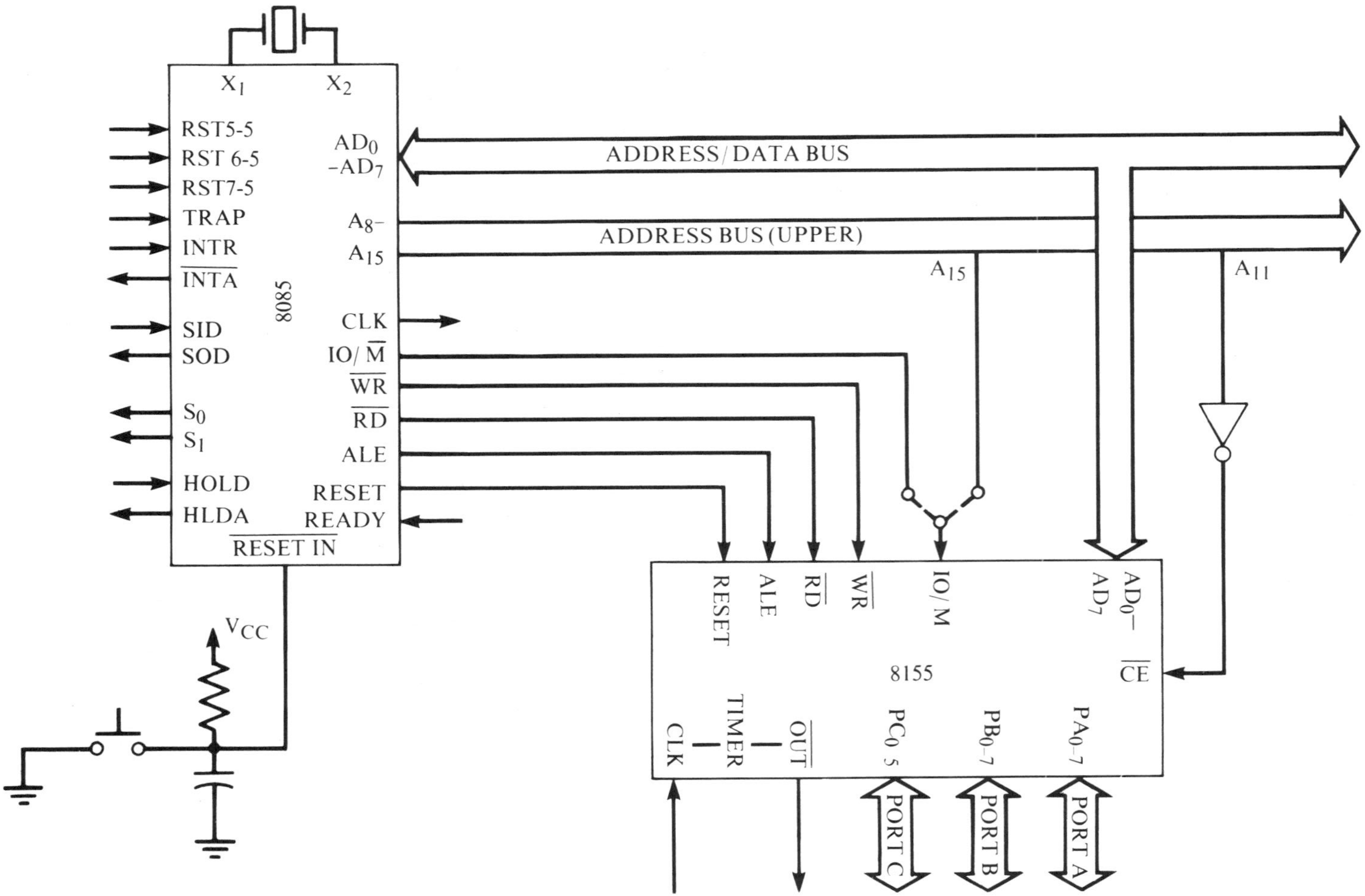

FIGURE 14-8. 8155 interface with the 8085 microprocessor.

TABLE 14-7. 8155 I/O Addressing Scheme

A_7	A_6	A_5	A_4	$\overline{CE}$ $\downarrow$ A_3	See Table 14-4 A_2	A_1	A_0	Port	Function
0	0	0	0	1	0	0	0	08H	C/S register
0	0	0	0	1	0	0	1	09H	Port A
0	0	0	0	1	0	1	0	0AH	Port B
0	0	0	0	1	0	1	1	0BH	Port C
0	0	0	0	1	1	0	0	0CH	TC (LSB)
0	0	0	0	1	1	0	1	0DH	TC (MSB) and mode

Memory-mapped I/O

The addressing scheme for the interface shown in Figure 14-8 becomes memory mapped when the 8155 IO/$\overline{M}$ line is connected to the 8085 address line A_{15}. The same scheme was used in Figure 14-2 to provide a memory-mapped I/O interface between the 8755 and the 8085 microprocessor. As before, because address line A_{15} now selects either the I/O or the memory section of the 8155, the I/O section now is addressed as memory locations instead of I/O ports, and the 8155 RAM is still addressed as before (isolated I/O addressing), as address line A_{15} is low for addresses 0800H through 08FFH.

Table 14-8 shows the memory addressing scheme for the memory-mapped interface of Figure 14-8. Notice that address line A_{15} again divides the memory map into a memory area (low) and an I/O area (high). The 8155 RAM resides (as before) from addresses 0800H through 08FFH, with memory foldback occurring at certain memory locations in the range 0900H through 87FFH. Locations 0000H through 07FFH are reserved for ROM. The 8155 I/O section is enabled when A_{15} is high and when the chip is selected (A_{11} is high). The six I/O ports or registers of the 8155 are then accessed by address lines A_0–A_2, as indicated in Table 14-4. Again, because linear addressing is used, I/O foldback occurs at certain memory locations in the range 8806H through FFFFH.

The I/O ports and registers of the 8155 chip can therefore be accessed by memory reference instructions of the 8085 (instead of the two IN and OUT instructions) in a memory-mapped I/O interface. Because the 8085 IO/$\overline{M}$ line is not used to distinguish between memory and I/O cycles performed on the 8155, the I/O section can also be accessed by I/O addresses appearing on the address bus. Because address lines A_{15} and A_{11} must be at the high state to access the 8155 I/O section, any I/O address that causes these address lines to go high can enable the I/O section. Owing to the address mirror effect, if address lines A_7 and A_3 are high, the corresponding address lines A_{15} and A_{11} will also be high. Thus during an I/O cycle, if addresses 88H through 8DH appear on the address bus, the respective 8155 I/O ports or register will be selected for read or write operations. Similarly, RAM locations can also be accessed by I/O instructions that cause address line A_{15} to go low when the chip is selected (A_{11} is high). This procedure, however, should not be used to read the RAM.

TABLE 14-8. 8155 Memory Addressing Scheme

IO/M̄ → A15 CE → A11

A15	A14	A13	A12	A11	A10	A9	A8	A7	A6	A5	A4	A3	A2	A1	A0	Location	
0	0	0	0	0	0	0	0	0	0	0	0	0	0	0	0	0000H	Unused area
.	.	.	.	.	.	.	.	.	.	.	.	.	.	.	.	.	
0	0	0	0	0	1	1	1	1	1	1	1	1	1	1	1	07FFH	
0	0	0	0	1	0	0	0	0	0	0	0	0	0	0	0	0800H	8155 RAM
.	.	.	.	.	.	.	.	.	.	.	.	.	.	.	.	.	
0	0	0	0	1	0	0	0	1	1	1	1	1	1	1	1	08FFH	
0	0	0	0	1	0	0	1	0	0	0	0	0	0	0	0	0900H	Unused area and memory foldback
.	.	.	.	.	.	.	.	.	.	.	.	.	.	.	.	.	
1	0	0	0	0	1	1	1	1	1	1	1	1	1	1	1	87FFH	
1	0	0	0	1	0	0	0	0	0	0	0	0	0	0	0	8800H	C/S Reg. ⎫
1	0	0	0	1	0	0	0	0	0	0	0	0	0	0	1	8801H	Port A ⎪
1	0	0	0	1	0	0	0	0	0	0	0	0	0	1	0	8802H	Port B ⎬ 8155 I/O
1	0	0	0	1	0	0	0	0	0	0	0	0	0	1	1	8803H	Port C ⎪
1	0	0	0	1	0	0	0	0	0	0	0	0	1	0	0	8804H	TC (LSB) ⎪
1	0	0	0	1	0	0	0	0	0	0	0	0	1	0	1	8805H	TC (MSB) ⎭
1	0	0	0	1	0	0	0	0	0	0	0	0	1	1	0	8806H	Unused area and I/O foldback
.	.	.	.	.	.	.	.	.	.	.	.	.	.	.	.	.	
1	1	1	1	1	1	1	1	1	1	1	1	1	1	1	1	FFFFH	

8155 address lines: A7–A0

Although the 8155 provides a more sophisticated I/O section, its operation and interface with the 8085 microprocessor are similar to the 8755. The 8155 offers a system with another essential "ingredient"—read/write memory (or RAM), while adding more I/O capabilities. When both the 8755 and the 8155 are integrated with the 8085 microprocessor into a microprocessor system, the result is a compact, three-chip interface that offers the optimum memory and I/O facilities for most small applications.

14-4

An 8085-based Microprocessor System

The interface among the 8755, the 8155, and the 8085 illustrated in Figures 14-2 and 14-8 can be combined to obtain a complete microprocessor system. This system is shown in Figure 14-9 and represents a *minimum* system, with ROM, RAM, and I/O integrated into three chips. Notice in Figure 14-9 that the same addressing scheme (discussed in Sections 14-2 and 14-3) is used for the interface between the 8085 microprocessor and the support chips. The 8085 microprocessor's IO/$\overline{\text{M}}$ line or A_{15} line can be used to select a memory-mapped configuration or an isolated I/O configuration, respectively. Notice that an 8156 chip is used instead of an 8155. Recall from Section 14-3 that the 8155 has an active low chip enable line ($\overline{\text{CE}}$), whereas the 8156 has an active high chip enable line (CE). Using an 8156 instead of an 8155 eliminates the need for an inverter and, hence, an additional chip. Also note that the READY line of the 8755 can be tied to the READY line of the 8085 if the CPU is being operated at a high clock rate or if the 8755 has a slower access time. In this example, we shall assume that no wait states are needed and that the CPU crystal frequency is 4 MHz. Because the crystal frequency is divided by 2 to obtain the internal operating frequency, the 8085 will be operating at a frequency of 2 MHz. The 2-MHz clock output (CLK) of the 8085 is also tied to the TIMER IN (or TIMER CLK) line of the 8155 to provide the basic input clock for the timer. The output of the timer ($\overline{\text{TIMER OUT}}$) is connected to the TRAP interrupt line of the 8085 and will be used to provide a *real-time clock* for the CPU. How this clock is used will be seen in the following example.

In order to illustrate the application of a typical minimum system, the 8085-based microprocessor system shown in Figure 14-9 will be used in the design of a simple security system. The general flowchart for the system is shown in Figure 14-10. The function of the security system is to monitor a series of switches (series switch circuit) connected to various doors and windows in a dwelling. If any of the doors or windows are opened while the system is armed, the system will trigger a warning alarm (prealarm) and wait for 20 sec for the system to be disarmed. If the system is disarmed within the 20-sec period, the prealarm will be turned off, and the system will idle until armed again. If the system is not disarmed within 20 sec, another alarm (main alarm) will be triggered and remain on until the system is disarmed. The system is armed or disarmed by a keyswitch (arm/disarm switch). When the system is armed, a time period of 50 sec will elapse before the doors and windows are actually monitored. The system will also incorporate a simple monitor mode that is activated by a switch (monitor switch). This mode allows monitoring of the

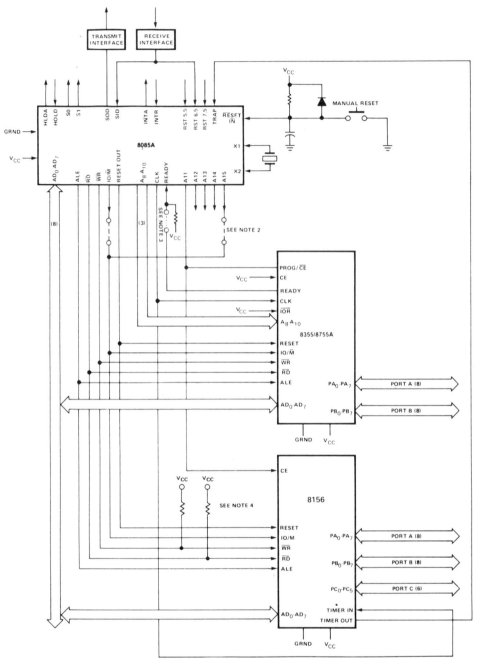

NOTE 1: TRAP, INTR, AND HOLD MUST BE GROUNDED IF THEY AREN'T USED.
NOTE 2: USE IO/M FOR STANDARD I/O MAPPING. USE A15 FOR MEMORY MAPPED I/O.
NOTE 3: CONNECTION IS NECESSARY ONLY IF ONE T$_{WAIT}$ STATE IS DESIRED.
NOTE 4: PULL UP RESISTORS RECOMMENDED TO AVOID SPURIOUS SELECTION WHEN $\overline{RD}$ AND $\overline{WR}$ ARE
3-STATED.

FIGURE 14-9. 8085-based microprocessor system (Courtesy of Intel Corp.)

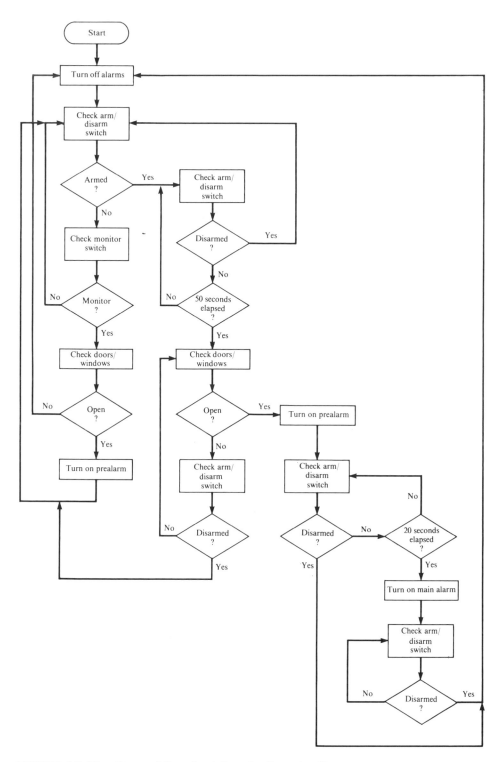

FIGURE 14-10.   General flowchart for the Security System.

doors and windows while the system is idling (while waiting to be armed). In this mode the prealarm will be turned on if any of the doors or windows are opened and turned off when all doors and windows are closed. The main alarm is not activated while in the monitor mode unless the system is armed.

For this application, the 8085-microprocessor system of Figure 14-9 will be operated at a internal clock frequency of 2 MHz and will be configured for isolated I/O. The addresses for the 8755 I/O and ROM will be as shown in Tables 14-2 and 14-3, respectively. The addresses for the 8155 I/O and RAM will be as shown in Tables 14-7 and 14-8, respectively. Only ports A and B of the 8155 will be used in the security system; the other ports can be reserved for possible expansion of the system's functions. The timer of the 8155 will also be used for determining elapsed time.

Figures 14-11 and 14-12 illustrate the real-world inputs and outputs for the 8085-based microprocessor system when used as a security system. The com-

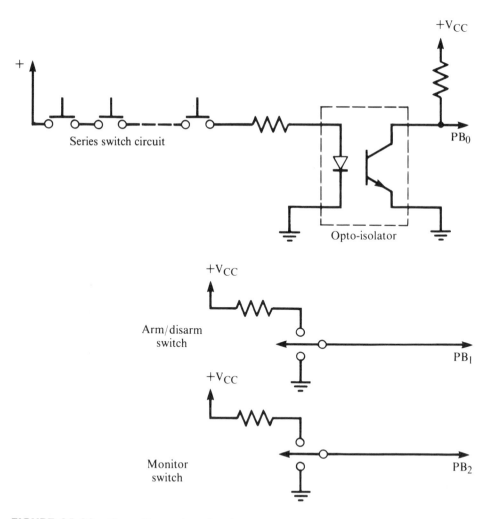

FIGURE 14-11. Security system inputs.

ponents shown in these illustrations will provide the interface between the system's I/O ports and the actual devices such as the alarms and switches that exist in the real world outside the microprocessor.

The three inputs to the security system shown in Figure 14-11 are applied to bits 0, 1, and 2 of the 8155's port B. The state of bit 0 will be affected by a series switch circuit installed for the doors and windows to be monitored. This bit is connected to the series switch circuit through an optoisolator (optocoupler) to isolate any noise that could be picked up over the typically long lengths of wire. The series switch circuit is normally closed when all the doors and windows are shut. When closed, current flows through the circuit and turns on the internal LED of the optoisolator. If the internal LED is on, the internal phototransistor is on, and the state of PB_0 is low. If the series switch circuit is open (because of an open door or window), no current will flow through the circuit, the LED and transistor will be off, and the logic state at PB_0 will be high. Thus PB_0 will be high if a door or window is open, and low if all doors and windows are closed. The system's remaining two inputs are used to detect the state of

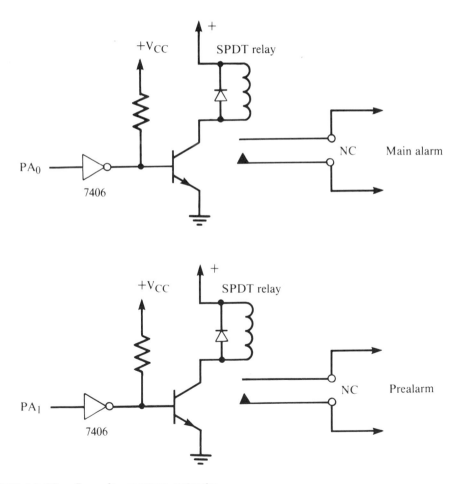

FIGURE 14-12. Security system outputs.

the arm/disarm command switch and the monitor switch. If the state of PB_1 is high, this will indicate that the system is to be armed; a low on PB_1 will be interpreted as a disarmed state. Similarly, a high on PB_2 will be used to initiate the monitor mode that allows the doors and windows to be monitored while the system is disarmed; a low on PB_2 will disable the monitor mode.

The security system outputs shown in Figure 14-12 are controlled by bits 0 and 1 of the 8155 port A. These two bits are used to activate or deactivate a relay that will control the main alarm and the prealarm. A logic 1 on PA_0 will produce a logic 0 at the output of the 7406 open collector inverter. This will turn off the transistor and deactivate the relay. Because the main alarm is connected to a set of normally closed contacts (NC), it will be turned on. A logic 0 on PA_0 will turn on the transistor, thereby activating the relay, and the main alarm will be turned off. Similarly, the state of the prealarm is controlled by PA_1. The control circuits shown in Figure 14-12 can be modified by using a noninverting open collector buffer (7407) instead of the 7406 and by connecting the alarm to the normally open (NO) contacts of the relay. A solid-state relay can also be substituted for these circuits.

The inputs and outputs of the security system are monitored and controlled by the microprocessor system, in particular the system's software. The assembly language program to implement the flowchart of Figure 14-10 is shown in Figure 14-13. The program occupies 216 bytes of ROM memory (0000H-00D7H) and is stored in the 8755 EPROM section so that it is executed during power-up or when the system is reset. The program also uses twenty-one bytes of 8155 RAM (0800H-0814H) for the stack area and temporary storage of variables used in the program.

The first few memory locations in EPROM are reserved for two "jump" vectors—a jump instruction at location 0000H to the main program (executed on powerup or reset) and a jump instruction to the timer service routine (executed when an interrupt is received on the TRAP line of the 8085). The main program (START) and the interrupt service routine (TIMER) begin at locations 0027H and 00A8H, respectively.

The first section of code in the main monitoring program performs the basic initialization of the hardware and various variables used in the program. After initializing a stack area in RAM, the 8155 timer count register is loaded with the TC 16000 (3E80H) and programmed for mode 1 (continuous square wave). The timer will therefore divide the 2-Mhz clock at the TIMER CLK input by 16000 and produce a symmetrical square wave at the TIMER OUT line and the TRAP interrupt line of the 8085. The 8085 will thus be interrupted 125 times every second. The real-time interrupt will be used to maintain the timing for the various delays required in the monitoring process. Two variables—TICK and SECOND—will be used to keep track of real time. The contents of memory location TICK will be used to keep track of the number of interrupts that have elapsed, and SECOND will be incremented after 125 interrupts have occurred and will therefore be incremented every second. The contents of memory location STATE will contain a toggle byte that will be complemented every second (00H or FFH), and this byte will be used to toggle an active alarm on and off for 1-sec durations (instead of sounding the alarm continuously). The contents of memory location AFLAG will contain the alarm control byte that will be

```
                ;**************************************************
                ;*    8085-based Microprocessor Security System    *
                ;*                                                 *
                ;**************************************************
                ;
                ;***    System memory map equates   ****
0000 =          ROM     EQU   0000H    ;8755 EPROM base address
0800 =          RAM     EQU   0800H    ;8155 RAM base address
0024 =          TRAP    EQU   0024H    ;Restart for TRAP interrupt
                ;
                ;****    System I/O port equates (8155)   ****
0008 =          CSREG   EQU   08H      ;8155 C/S register
0009 =          PORTA   EQU   09H      ;8155 port A
000A =          PORTB   EQU   0AH      ;8155 port B
000B =          PORTC   EQU   0BH      ;8155 port C (not used)
000C =          TIMRL   EQU   0CH      ;TC low byte
000D =          TIMRH   EQU   0DH      ;TC high byte & mode
                ;
                ;****    Program restart vectors   ****
0000                    ORG   ROM
0000 C32700             JMP   START    ;Enter the main program
0024                    ORG   TRAP
0024 C3A800             JMP   TIMER    ;Enter the timer service routine
```

FIGURE 14-13. Security system software.

```
                  ;     ****     The main monitoring program     ****
                  ;
0027 311408   START:   LXI   SP,STACK      ;Set up stack area in RAM
002A 21803E            LXI   H,16000       ;Terminal count (TC) 125 HZ
002D 7C                MOV   A,H           ;MSB of count
002E F640              ORI   01000000B     ;Make timer mode bits = 01 (mode 1)
0030 D30D              OUT   TIMRH
0032 7D                MOV   A,L           ;LSB of count
0033 D30C              OUT   TIMRL
0035 AF                XRA   A             ;Clear. . .
0036 320208            STA   AFLAG         ;   Alarm state flag
0039 320308            STA   STATE         ;   Interrupt toggle byte
003C 320008            STA   TICK          ;   Interrupt count
003F 320108            STA   SECOND        ;   One second count
0042 3EC1              MVI   A,11000001B   ;PA=output, PB=input, start timer
0044 D308              OUT   CSREG         ;Program the 8155 C/S register

                  ; Monitor the system

0046 AF        RESTRT:  XRA   A             ;Turn off both alarms
0047 320208            STA   AFLAG
004A DB0A      MONTR;   IN    PORTB         ;Get input status
004C 0F                RRC                 ;Monitor S/W to bit 1
004D 47                MOV   B,A           ;Save it
004E DB0A              IN    PORTB         ;Get input status
0050 07                RLC                 ;Series switch CKT status to bit 1
0051 A0                ANA   B             ;See if both bits are 1
0052 E602              ANI   00000010B     ;Clean out other bits
0054 D309              OUT   PORTA         ;Sound prealarm if needed
0056 DB0A              IN    PORTB         ;Get input status
0058 E602              ANI   00000010B     ;See if system armed
005A CA4A00            JZ    MONTR.        ;Wait till armed
```

```
                    ; Arm switch has been activated, now wait 50 secs before arming system

005D AF           TIMOUT:   XRA    A           ;Clear . . .
005E 320108                 STA    SECOND      ; One-second counter
0061 DB0A         WAIT:     IN     PORTB       ;Get input status
0063 E602                   ANI    00000010B   ;See if system disarmed
0065 CA4600                 JZ     RESTRT      ;Restart process if so
0068 3A0108                 LDA    SECOND      ;Get seconds count (interrupt)
006B FE32                   CPI    50          ;50 seconds elapsed ?
006D C26100                 JNZ    WAIT        ;No, wait

                    ; System is now armed, Now check series switch circuit & arm switch

0070 DB0A         ARMED:    IN     PORTB       ;Get input status
0072 E601                   ANI    00000001B   ;See if break in series switch CKT
0074 C28100                 JNZ    BREAK       ;Door or window open if nonzero
0077 DB0A                   IN     PORTB       ;Get input status
0079 E602                   ANI    00000010B   ;See if system has been disarmed
007B CA4600                 JZ     RESTRT      ;Restart process if so
007E C37000                 JMP    ARMED       ;Else continue checking

                    ; Series switch circuit is open, sound prealarm and wait 20 seconds

0081 3E02         BREAK:    MVI    A,00000010B ;Prealarm control byte
0083 320208                 STA    AFLAG       ;Alarm will be activated by trap service RTN
0086 AF                     XRA    A           ;Clear . . .
0087 320108                 STA    SECOND      ; One-second counter
008A DB0A         PRE:      IN     PORTB       ;Get input status
008C E602                   ANI    00000010B   ;See if system disarmed
008E CA4600                 JZ     RESTRT      ;Restart monitoring process if so
0091 3A0108                 LDA    SECOND      ;Else get seconds count (interrupt)
0094 FE14                   CPI    20          ;20 seconds elapsed ?
0096 C28A00                 JNZ    PRE         ;No, wait
```

FIGURE 14-13. continued

457

```
                ; 20 secs has elapsed and system has not been disarmed, sound main alarm

0099 3E03       MAIN:    MVI  A,00000011B   ;Pre/main alarm control byte
009B 320208              STA  AFLAG         ;Alarm will be activated by trap service RTN
009E DB0A       FOREVR:  IN   PORTB         ;Get input status
00A0 E602                ANI  00000010B     ;See if system disarmed
00A2 CA4600              JZ   RESTRT        ;Restart monitoring process if so
00A5 C39E00              JMP  FOREVR        ;Else wait forever. . .

;               ****  Real-time clock interrupt service routine (TRAP)  ****

00A8 F5         TIMER:   PUSH PSW           ;Save registers used locally
00A9 C5                  PUSH B
00AA 3A0008              LDA  TICK          ;Get interrupt count
00AD FE7C                CPI  124           ;See if 125 interrupts
00AF CAB900              JZ   ONESEC        ;One second has elapsed if so
00B2 3C                  INR  A             ;Else update interrupt count
00B3 320008              STA  TICK
00B6 C1         BACK:    POP  B             ;Restore registers
00B7 F1                  POP  PSW
00B8 C9                  RET                ;Return to main program

;  This point is entered every second

00B9 AF         ONESEC:  XRA  A             ;Clear. . .
00BA 320008              STA  TICK          ; Interrupt count
00BD 3A0108              LDA  SECOND        ;Get one-second count
00C0 3C                  INR  A             ;Update it
00C1 320108              STA  SECOND        ;Count to 255
```

```
            ; See if any alarm is to be activated

00C4 3A0308    ACHECK:  LDA  STATE   ;Get toggle byte
00C7 2F                 CMA          ;Complement it
00C8 320308             STA  STATE   ;Save it
00CB 3A0208             LDA  AFLAG   ;Get alarm control byte
00CE 47                 MOV  B,A     ;Else save control byte temporarily
00CF 3A0308             LDA  STATE   ;Get the toggle byte
00D2 A0                 ANA  B       ;Toggle the specified alarm (on/off)
00D3 D309               OUT  PORTA   ;Sound alarm for 1-second cycle
00D5 C3B600             JMP  BACK    ;And return to main program

            ;       ***** System variables in (8155) RAM *****

0800            ORG  RAM

0800    TICK:    DS   1      ;Interrupt count
0801    SECOND:  DS   1      ;One-second count
0802    AFLAG:   DS   1      ;Alarm control byte (bit 0=main, bit 1=pre)
0803    STATE:   DS   1      ;Toggle byte
0804             DS   16     ;Reserve 8 level stack
0814 =  STACK    EQU  $      ;Stack begins here

0814            END

SYMBOL TABLE

00C4 ACHECK   0802 AFLAG    0070 ARMED   00B6 BACK     0081 BREAK    0008 CSREG
009E FOREVR   0099 MAIN     004A MONTR   00B9 ONESEC   0009 PORTA    000A PORTB
000B PORTC    008A PRE      0800 RAM     0046 RESTRT   0000 ROM      0801 SECOND
0814 STACK    0027 START    0803 STATE   0800 TICK     00A8 TIMER    005D TIMOUT
000D TIMRH    000C TIMRL    0024 TRAP    0061 WAIT

ASSEMBLY COMPLETE, NO ERRORS
```

FIGURE 14-13. continued

459

used to turn a particular alarm on or off. The bits that represent the main and prealarms correspond to the connections of the main and prealarms to port A. That is, bit 0 will control the state of the main alarm, and bit 1 will control the state of the prealarm; a 1 in the respective bit position will turn the alarm on, and a zero will turn the alarm off. This byte is set by the main program whenever a particular alarm is to be turned on or off. The alarm is actually switched in the interrupt service routine to allow it to sound at a frequency of 1 Hz (instead of continuously). The initialization sequence clears the variables AFLAG, STATE, TICK, and SECOND. The last step in the initialization is to program the 8155's I/O section. By sending the byte C1H to the 8155's C/S register, port A is programmed as an output port, port B is programmed as an input port, and the timer is started. Note that interrupts on the TRAP line are enabled at all times and are not affected by the SIM or DI instructions. Therefore, once the timer is started, interrupts will start occurring on the TRAP line at a rate of 125 per sec.

The next section of code beginning at address RESTRT is entered after initialization and also whenever the system is disarmed during the monitoring process. First, both alarms are turned off by clearing AFLAG. The status of the monitor switch is then checked to determine whether the doors and windows are to be monitored. This is done by ANDing the monitor switch status bit with the series switch circuit status bit and sending the result (in bit position 1) to port A. If both bits are high, it will indicate that the monitor mode is active and that a door or window is open. Because the result of the ANDing is a 1, the byte sent to port A will activate the prealarm and keep it on as long as the monitor switch is set and the series switch circuit is open. If any of these bits is low, the prealarm will not sound. While in the loop, the program also checks the status of the arm/disarm switch. If the status of the arm/disarm switch bit of port B is low, the program will repeat the process and continue until the arm/disarm switch bit is set high to arm the system.

When the system is armed, control transfers to address TIMOUT. Here, the 1-sec counter SECOND is cleared, and the program waits for this memory location to reach a count of 50. Recall that this memory location is updated once every second by the interrupt service routine. While in the loop, the program also checks the status of the arm/disarm switch. If the bit is high, no action will be taken, but if the bit is low (disarm), control will transfer back to address RESTRT.

After 50 sec have elapsed and if the system is still armed, control will transfer to location ARMED. Here the series switch circuit is monitored for a break. As long as the series switch circuit status bit (bit 0) is low, the program remains in the loop. While in the monitoring loop, a check is also made on the arm/disarm switch bit. If this bit is 0 (disarmed), control will transfer back to address RESTRT. But if the series switch circuit status bit goes high, it will indicate a break in the circuit (a door or window has been opened while the system is armed), and control will transfer to address BREAK.

Once a break is detected, the prealarm bit in AFLAG is set so that the interrupt service routine turns on the prealarm. The SECOND counter is cleared, and the program enters a loop. While in the loop, the arm/disarm switch is monitored again. If low, (disarm) control transfers back to address RESTRT. If the arm/

disarm switch is high (system is still armed) and the SECOND count has read 20 (20 sec have elapsed), the program will exit the loop and transfer control to the final program segment at address MAIN.

At this point in the program (MAIN), the alarm control byte AFLAG is set to turn on the main alarm (the prealarm is also left on). Finally, the program enters a loop that monitors the arm/disarm switch. The program stays in this loop as long as the arm/disarm status bit is 1 (system still armed). When this bit goes low (system disarmed), control transfers back to address RESTRT, and the entire process is repeated.

The real-time clock interrupt service routine is entered at address TIMER each time an interrupt is received over the 8085 TRAP interrupt line. Recall that the 8155 timer is programmed to provide an interrupt rate of 125 Hz. Each time there is an interrupt, the service routine increments and checks the contents of memory location TICK (interrupt counter). As long as the contents of TICK is less than 124, the interrupt service routine simply returns control to the main program (BACK). When the contents of TICK reach 124, 1 sec of real time has elapsed, and control transfers to address ONESEC.

At address ONESEC, the contents of the toggle byte STATE is complemented. This byte will therefore be complemented every second. Next, a check is made on the alarm control byte AFLAG. The contents of AFLAG is ANDed with the contents of STATE, and the result is sent to port A to turn either or both alarms on or off. If AFLAG is zero (both alarms off), the result of the ANDing (irrespective of the value of STATE) will be a zero, and both alarms will remain off. But if AFLAG is either a 01H (main alarm on) or a 02H (prealarm on), the result of the ANDing will yield the same value of AFLAG if STATE is a FFH, and therefore the respective alarm will be turned on. If STATE is a 00H, the alarms will be turned off. Because STATE toggles every second, the selected alarm will be activated ON and OFF every second. This allows a distinction to be made between the monitor mode (when the prealarm is activated continuously as long as a door or window is open) and the armed mode (when the prealarm is activated at a rate of 1 Hz).

The 8085 microprocessor security system application described in this section is an elementary example of how a microprocessor can be used in a real-world control system. Notice that this application used only a small portion of the microprocessor system's capabilities: approximately 10 percent of EPROM memory and 8 percent of RAM memory. Two 8-bit I/O ports and one 6-bit I/O port are still available for use, as well as a serial I/O port and several additional interrupt lines. The application is therefore expandable, simply by adding a minimum amount of additional hardware and by making the appropriate software changes. This is one of the advantages in using a microprocessor system instead of conventional logic design.

14-5

Summary

In any microprocessor-based system, simplicity of hardware design is often an important consideration and is seen in the development of the newer 8-bit microcontrollers. From previous chapters we found that by integrating several functions on a single chip, the 8085 microprocessor required fewer external support components. Similarly, in this chapter, the 8755 and the 8155 provided all the necessary support components for a minimum microprocessor system.

The 8755 and 8155 chips discussed in this chapter give an 8085-based microprocessor system two essential ingredients—memory and I/O. Both these chips were designed for a simple interface with the 8085 microprocessor while providing flexibility in addressing. Even though these chips' memory and I/O sections are physically located on the same chip, they can be accessed independently. The programmable I/O sections of both chips allow different modes of operation and therefore can be used in a variety of applications.

When both the 8755 and the 8155 are integrated into an 8085 microprocessor system, the combined memory sections give the designer sufficient RAM and EPROM for most simple applications. Similarly, the number of I/O ports available in the system is usually adequate for a minimum system such as the one discussed in this chapter. The design of the security system discussed in this chapter illustrated the use of a minimum system in a real-world application. Recall that the system was expandable, as not all of its capabilities were used. The microprocessor application in this chapter also showed the use of the 8155's programmable timer for monitoring real time, essential to applications that have to interface with the "external world."

Whereas the previous chapters discussed the various techniques of using the 8085 microprocessor with standard I/O and memory components, this chapter illustrated a flexible alternative. It should be noted, however, that an 8085-based microprocessor system need not be limited to one of the two alternatives but can just as easily be designed with both standard memory and I/O components, as well as with chips such as the 8755 and the 8155.

REVIEW QUESTIONS AND PROBLEMS

1. What is the purpose of the 8755's data direction registers (DDRs)?

2. How is the 8755's I/O or memory section selected?

3. Obtain the instructions required to program the 8755's (in Figure 14-2) port A bits 0,1, and 2 for input, and bits 3–7 for output, in the following configurations:
   (a) memory mapped.
   (b) standard I/O.

4. How would the 8755 in Figure 14-2 be addressed if the IO/$\overline{\text{M}}$ line and the $\overline{\text{CE}}$ line were connected to address lines A_{13} and A_{12}, respectively? Construct a table similar to Table 14-3 to illustrate the addressing scheme for the EPROM and I/O sections.

5. Compare the operation of ports A and B of the 8755 with ports A and B of the 8155.

6. What is the purpose of the 8155 C/S register? What effect does it have when data is loaded into it? When data is read from it?

7. What bytes must be written into the two timer registers shown in Table 14-4 in order to divide the clock frequency at the TIMER CLK line by 64 and produce a continuous square-wave output at the $\overline{\text{TIMER OUT}}$ line of the 8155?

8. How would the 8155 in Figure 14-8 be addressed if the IO/$\overline{\text{M}}$ line and the $\overline{\text{CE}}$ line were connected to address lines A_{10} and A_8, respectively? Construct a table similar to Table 14-8 to illustrate the addressing scheme.

9. Expand the 8085 microprocessor system of Figure 14-9 to include an additional 8755 and an additional 8155 or 8156.

10. Modify the software for the security system (Figure 14-13) to monitor individually the states of eight doors and windows, instead of monitoring a series switch circuit. The states of the doors and windows should be read in from 8755 port A. A logic 1 state will indicate that a particular door or window is open, and a logic 0 will indicate that it is closed. The software should be implemented as shown in the flowchart of Figure 14-10. However, the system must continuously display the status of each door or window on a set of eight LEDs connected to port B of the 8755. All LEDs off will indicate that all doors and windows are closed. If any LED is on, it will indicate that the corresponding door or window is open.

CHAPTER 15

A Survey of the 6800 Microprocessor

15-1

Introduction

This text was written with the belief that by studying and understanding a specific microprocessor (in this case the 8085) the essence of all microprocessors could be learned. The same can also be said of microprocessor-based systems; that is, the same concepts hold for all microprocessor-based systems—only the details are different. This book has studied microprocessor concepts using as an example a general-purpose 8-bit microprocessor like the 8085. The 8085 microprocessor is by no means the most current microprocessor, nor is it the best suited for every application. Rather, in our opinion, its simplicity and associated systems make it an ideal example to illustrate the elementary concepts. And once these concepts are understood for the 8085, it is relatively easy to apply them to other microprocessors.

15-2

6800 Architecture and Pin Configuration

The architecture of the 6800 microprocessing unit (microprocessor) is shown in Figure 15-1. The architecture of the 6800 has three major differences from the

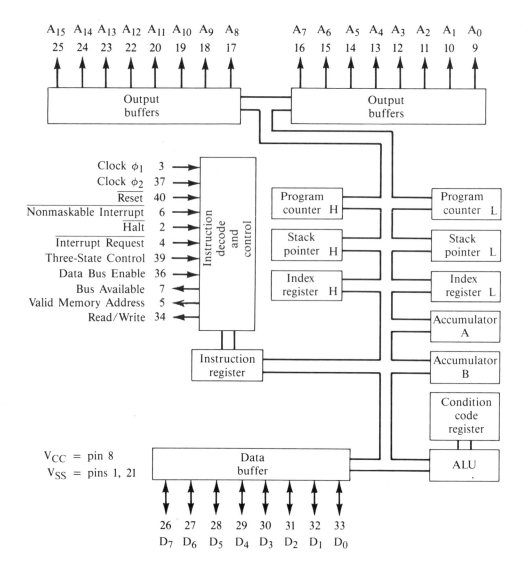

FIGURE 15-1. Architecture of the 6800 MPU. (Courtesy of Motorola, Inc.)

8085's architecture: the interrupt structure, the control signals, and the internal arrangement of registers.

Interrupt Structure. The 6800 microprocessing unit (MPU) has two interrupt inputs, which allow for multilevel interrupts. Each interrupt line to the MPU is capable of vectoring the MPU to a specified location in memory (to be discussed later). However, the difference between the two interrupts is that the state of the IRQ (interrupt request) line can be enabled or disabled via a 6800 instruction. The NMI (nonmaskable interrupt) line is "nonmaskable," and therefore no instruction can be used to control the state of this interrupt line. The NMI line is therefore very similar to the TRAP line of the 8085. The IRQ line

TABLE 15-1. Comparison of 8080/8085 and 6800 Register Set

6800 Registers		8080/8085 Registers	
Size	Function	Size	Function
8	A—accumulator A	8	A—accumulator
8	B—accumulator B		None
8	CCR—condition code register	8	PSW—flags
16	IX—index register	16	Register pair H&L
16	PC—program counter	16	Program counter
16	SP—stack pointer	16	Stack pointer

is similar to the INT line of the 8085 except that there is no equivalent RST N instruction to vector the MPU to different areas in memory; the 6800 uses another technique (described later) to accomplish this task.

Control Signals. The 6800 MPU has only two control signals to control the operation of external devices: VMA (valid memory address) and R/W (read/write). These two signals, together with the MPU's address lines, are used to select memory and I/O devices connected to the MPU. As the name suggests, the VMA control line is active whenever the MPU's address bus contains a valid memory address during a read or write operation to a memory or I/O device. The R/W line is used to distinguish between a read or write operation being performed on a memory or I/O device. If these are the only two control lines provided by the MPU, how does the MPU know whether it is accessing a memory or an I/O device? The answer to this question is: It does not distinguish a memory device from an I/O device; the 6800 MPU is designed for memory-mapped I/O, and unlike the 8085, does not provide a separate addressing scheme for memory and I/O devices (isolated I/O). Thus an I/O device is addressed in the same way as a location in memory, and the system's memory map will dictate the locations in memory that are assigned to I/O devices.

Internal Registers. The 6800 MPU contains six (user-accessible) general-purpose registers, compared with the ten registers of the 8085. Table 15-1 lists the 6800's registers together with the equivalent 8085 register.

The stack pointer (SP) and program counter (PC) are 16-bit registers that are similar in function to the 8085's SP and PC. The index register (IX) is a 16-bit register that is used as a data counter and functions in a manner similar to the 8085's register pair H&L. The condition code register (CCR) is an 8-bit register containing six condition flags and provides the same function as the 8085's PSW. The 6800 MPU has two 8-bit accumulators: accumulator A and accumulator B. Both of these accumulators are capable of holding the results of arithmetic and logic operations. Note that in the 8085, only register A is used to hold the result of an arithmetic or logic operation. Even though the 6800 MPU seems to be limited in the number of internal registers (when compared to the 8085), the instruction set of the 6800 contains various memory instructions that compensate for this shortage. These instructions can be used to treat memory

1	V$_{SS}$	$\overline{Reset}$	40	
2	$\overline{HALT}$	TSC	39	
3	ϕ_1	N.C.	38	
4	$\overline{IRQ}$	ϕ_2	37	
5	VMA	DBE	36	
6	$\overline{NMI}$	N.C.	35	
7	BA	R/W	34	
8	V$_{CC}$	D$_0$	33	
9	A$_0$	D$_1$	32	
10	A$_1$	D$_2$	31	
11	A$_2$	D$_3$	30	
12	A$_3$	D$_4$	29	
13	A$_4$	D$_5$	28	
14	A$_5$	D$_6$	27	
15	A$_6$	D$_7$	26	
16	A$_7$	A$_{15}$	25	
17	A$_8$	A$_{14}$	24	
18	A$_9$	A$_{13}$	23	
19	A$_{10}$	A$_{12}$	22	
20	A$_{11}$	V$_{SS}$	21	

FIGURE 15-2.   Pin configuration of the 6800 MPU. (Courtesy of Motorola, Inc.)

locations as temporary storage registers, thus using external memory for "scratch-pad" operations.

Besides the previously discussed differences, the 6800 has many similarities with the 8085 microprocessor, which are best understood by an examination of the pin configuration of the 6800, shown in Figure 15-2.

Φ_1 *and* Φ_2: These inputs to the 6800 chip are the phase 1 and phase 2 clock pulses that are nonoverlapping and must be provided by an external clock generator. The logic levels required for these clocks are TTL, and the maximum clock rate is 1 MHz.

A_0–A_{15}: These sixteen outputs are the address lines of the 6800 that form the address bus and are similar in function to the 8085's address lines. These address lines allow for accessing a combination of up to 65,536 memory locations and I/O devices. Because the 6800 uses memory-mapped I/O, the total number of memory locations and I/O devices cannot exceed 65,536. The address lines are tristated for DMA operations.

D_0–D_7: The eight bidirectional data lines of the 6800 are similar to the 8085's data lines and are used to transfer 8-bit data to and from memory or I/O devices. These lines form the data bus and are tristated for DMA.

$\overline{HALT}$: This line can be used to put the MPU into a HALT state. When the $\overline{HALT}$ line is set low, the MPU enters an idle mode after completion of the current instruction. In the HALT state, all activity is stopped while the data and address lines are tristated. Note that the 8085 does not have the facility to put the CPU into a HALT state via a hardware line but can do so only through the execution of a HLT instruction.

TSC: The TSC (tristate control) input to the MPU is similar to the HOLD input of the 8085 and is used for DMA operations. When the TSC input is in the high state, the MPU sets the address bus and R/W line to a high-impedance state, allowing for an external device to gain control of memory. The data bus is not affected by the TSC control but has a separate control (DBE).

DBE: The data bus enable line (DBE) is used to control the state of the data bus during DMA operations. The data bus drivers are enabled when DBE is high, and put into a high-impedance state (disabled) when DBE is low.

R/W: The read/write (R/W) line is an output from the MPU used to signal a memory or I/O device whether the MPU is in a read (R/W = high) or write (R/W = low) state. In the read state, the MPU's data bus is in the input mode and in the write state, is in an output mode. Because the 6800 uses memory-mapped I/O, this line *cannot* be used to distinguish between a memory or I/O device.

VMA: This output (when high) indicates to memory and I/O devices that there is a valid memory address on the MPU's address bus. When this output is used in conjunction with selected address lines and the R/W line, it can be used to select a memory or I/O device for read or write operations.

BA: The bus available (BA) output, when high, indicates that the MPU is in a HALT state and that the address bus is available. This line is similar in function to the HLDA line of the 8085, except that it is also active when the MPU is in a WAIT state.

$\overline{IRQ}$: The interrupt request ($\overline{IRQ}$) input to the MPU is a level-sensitive signal that causes an interrupt sequence to be generated within the machine. Interrupts on this line can be masked by means of a 6800 instruction. More will be said about interrupts in a later section.

$\overline{NMI}$: The nonmaskable interrupt ($\overline{NMI}$) causes a similar interrupt (as for $\overline{IRQ}$) sequence to be generated by the MPU, except that interrupts arriving at the $\overline{NMI}$ line cannot be masked by the MPU. This line is similar in function to the TRAP line of the 8085.

RESET: This input is used to reset the MPU for initial startup. The function of the $\overline{\text{RESET}}$ input is similar to the 8085's reset line in regard to initial startup. However, the reset sequence generated by the MPU is very different from the 8085's reset sequence. Recall that on receiving a reset, the 8085 sets its program counter to 0000H; the CPU then accesses memory location 0, where it expects to find the first program instruction. On receiving a reset, the 6800 MPU automatically accesses the last two memory locations (FFFE, FFFF) to obtain the address at which the MPU will begin program execution. These two memory locations *must* contain the starting address of the program. This scheme is much more flexible, as it allows the MPU to begin execution at any address rather than being limited to one address (as in the 8085). For example, if memory locations FFFE and FFFF contain the bytes 85 and 40, respectively, on receiving a reset, the MPU will start program execution at location 8540. Like the 8085, the 6800 disables interrupts (on the $\overline{\text{IRQ}}$ line only) upon being reset.

Notice in Figure 15-2 that like the 8085, the 6800 chip requires only a single 5-V power supply, which is provided to the V_{CC} and V_{SS} pins. Also notice that the 6800 microprocessor has a separate 16-bit address bus and an 8-bit data bus. The lower eight address lines are not multiplexed with the data lines, as in the 8085 microprocessor.

A study of the pin-outs of the 6800 MPU illustrates some interesting similarities and differences with the 8085 CPU. Because it would be redundant to investigate the similarities, the remainder of the chapter will deal with the three major differences between the 8085 and 6800 that were mentioned in this section.

15-3

6800 Interrupt Structure

The 6800 MPU can be viewed as a microprocessor that has four levels of interrupts: a restart interrupt, a nonmaskable interrupt, a software interrupt, and an interrupt request. On receiving any one of these interrupts, the MPU fetches a vector address from a predetermined memory location and transfers control to that location. The memory map for interrupt vectors is shown in Table 15-2.

Restart Interrupt

A restart interrupt is initiated when the MPU's $\overline{\text{RESET}}$ line is activated. In a 6800 system a reset is considered to be an interrupt, as it stops execution of the MPU and transfers control to the address stored in memory locations FFFE and FFFF. But it is not a true interrupt as control can never transfer back to the point of interruption (no return address is stored on the stack). The restart interrupt sequence for the 6800 MPU is shown in Figure 15-3.

As mentioned in Section 15-2, on receiving a reset, the MPU disables interrupts (on the IRQ line) by setting an internal interrupt mask (I_m). The program counter is then loaded with the contents of memory locations FFFE (high byte of PC) and FFFF (low byte of PC), and control transfers to that address. Notice

TABLE 15-2. Memory Map for Interrupt Vectors

Vector		
MS	**LS**	**Description**
FFFE	FFFF	Restart
FFFC	FFFD	Nonmaskable interrupt
FFFA	FFFB	Software interrupt
FFF8	FFF9	Interrupt request

Contents	Address
$\overline{RES}$ (Low Byte)	FFFF
$\overline{RES}$ (High Byte)	FFFE
$\overline{NMI}$ (Low Byte)	FFFD
$\overline{NMI}$ (High Byte)	FFFC
SWI (Low Byte)	FFFB
SWI (High Byte)	FFFA
$\overline{IRQ}$ (Low Byte)	FFF9
$\overline{IRQ}$ (High Byte)	FFF8

that no return address is stored on the stack when the $\overline{RESET}$ line is activated. The MPU can therefore never return to the point of interruption before it was reset (received a restart interrupt).

Nonmaskable Interrupt

The $\overline{NMI}$ line to the MPU is used to generate a ''high-priority'' interrupt that cannot be disabled by means of software. The NMI interrupt sequence is shown in Figure 15-4. With reference to Figure 15-4, notice that when the $\overline{NMI}$ line

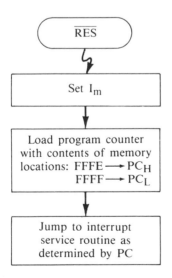

FIGURE 15-3. Restart interrupt sequence. (Courtesy of Motorola, Inc.)

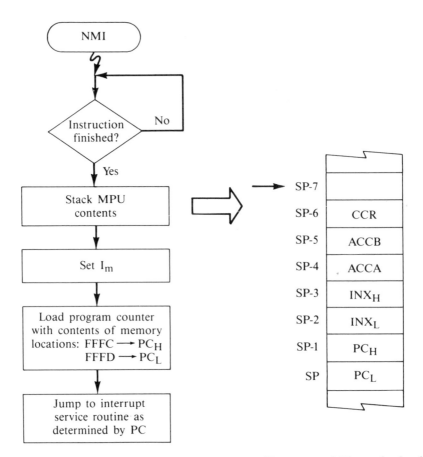

FIGURE 15-4. **Nonmaskable interrupt sequence. (Courtesy of Motorola, Inc.)**

of the MPU is activated, the MPU completes execution of the current instruction and then services the interrupt. The first interrupt operation is to store the contents of the MPU registers on the stack. Unlike the 8085 interrupt sequence, in which a series of PUSH instructions has to be used to stack the CPU registers, the 6800 MPU does this automatically. First, the contents of the PC is stored on the stack, then the IX, the accumulators, and the CCR, in the order shown. The interrupt mask is then automatically set to prevent any interrupts from being acknowledged over the IRQ line. The MPU then examines memory locations FFFC and FFFD (refer to Table 15-2) and obtains the vector address for the interrupt service routine. The data at memory locations FFFC and FFFD is stored in the high and low (respectively) bytes of the PC, and control is transferred to that memory location.

On completion of the NMI interrupt sequence, the MPU must execute the RTI (return from interrupt) instruction. The RTI instruction restores the contents of the MPU registers in the order in which they were saved, resets the interrupt mask to allow for following interrupts, and returns control to the point of interruption.

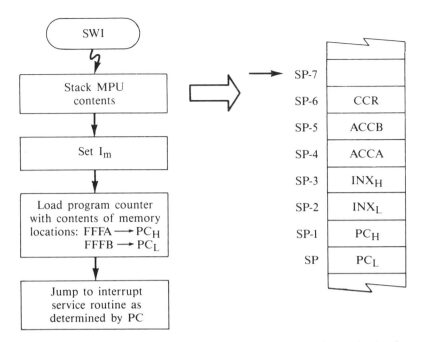

FIGURE 15-5. Software interrupt sequence. (Courtesy of Motorola, Inc.)

Software Interrupt

The 6800 MPU has a facility to generate a software interrupt by means of a special instruction, the SWI instruction. On execution of the SWI instruction, an interrupt sequence is "simulated" by the MPU. The software interrupt sequence conducted by the MPU is shown in Figure 15-5.

The sequence of events for a software interrupt as shown in Figure 15-5 is similar to that of the NMI interrupt. On execution of the SWI instruction, the contents of the MPU registers is saved on the stack in the same way as was done for an NMI interrupt. The interrupt mask is set to block any other interrupts (excluding NMI). This time, however, the vector address for the SWI service routine (refer to Table 15-2) is taken from memory locations FFFA and FFFB and loaded into the high and low bytes of the PC, respectively. Control then transfers to the address stored in the PC. Return from a SWI service routine is also accomplished by the RTI instruction, as the contents of the MPU registers must be restored, the interrupt mask reset, and control returned in the instruction following the SWI.

The SWI interrupt is therefore similar to the NMI hardware interrupt and is extremely useful as a breakpoint during the debugging of 6800 programs. Note that the RST N instruction of the 8085 can also be used to generate a somewhat similar software interrupt to the 8085 CPU.

Interrupt Request

The $\overline{\text{IRQ}}$ line to the 6800 MPU causes the interrupt sequence shown in Figure 15-6 to be conducted by the MPU. The sequence of events during the IRQ

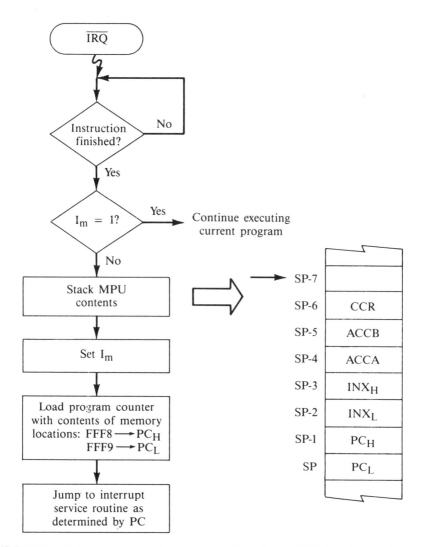

FIGURE 15-6. Interrupt request sequence. (Courtesy of Motorola, Inc.)

interrupt request is similar to the NMI and SWI sequence except that on completion of the current instruction, the interrupt mask (I_m) is tested for a set or reset condition. If I_m is set by means of a SEI (set interrupt mask) instruction (or a previous interrupt), the interrupt will not be acknowledged and the MPU will continue executing the current program. If I_m is reset, the MPU will acknowledge the interrupt by stacking the contents of the MPU registers (as before), and blocking further interrupts over the $\overline{IRQ}$ line by setting I_m. The MPU then accesses memory locations FFF8 and FFF9 (refer to Table 15-2) to obtain the vector address of the service routine. Control then transfers to the address referenced by the PC. As before, the last instruction in the IRQ service routine should be an RTI instruction.

To summarize the interrupt structure of the 6800 MPU, one can think of the MPU as having four level of interrupts, two of them (IRQ and NMI) being true hardware interrupts. Each type of interrupt causes the MPU to load the contents of predetermined memory addresses into its PC, as shown in Table 15-2. Control is then transferred to the memory location whose address is stored in the PC. Because memory locations FFF8 through FFFF (inclusive) are always used to store these vector address, most 6800-based systems usually have ROM located in this area.

15·4

6800 Microprocessor System

As with any type of microprocessor, the control signals and the address bus often dictate the design of a microprocessor system that encompasses the microprocessor and other memory and I/O chips. Figure 15-7 shows the design scheme of a simple 6800-based microprocessor system. The system includes 128 bytes of RAM (6810 chip), 1024 bytes of ROM (6830 chip), two parallel ports (6820 chip), and one serial port (6850 chip). System timing is provided by the 6871 clock generator.

6810 RAM Interface

With reference to Figure 15-7, notice that the 6810 RAM has six chip select inputs; CS3 and CS0 are active high; and the others are active low. Seven address inputs (A_0–A_6) are connected to the MPU's address bus to allow for 128 bytes of storage. The data I/O pins of the 6810 (D_0–D_7) are connected to the MPU's data bus to allow storage and retrieval of data. The R/W pin of the 6810 establishes the direction of data flow within the chip and is therefore connected to the R/W line of the MPU. CS0 is connected to the MPU's VMA line so that the chip is selected when a valid memory address appears on the address bus. The 6810 is addressed by using the high-order address lines of the MPU—A_{15}, A_{14}, A_{13}, A_{12}—to select the chip. The addressing scheme is shown in Table 15-3.

The six chip select lines provided by the 6810 RAM make the interface with the MPU ideal for linear addressing, as can be seen in Table 15-3. In Table 15-3, assuming that the "x" (unconnected) bits are zeros, the addressing scheme locates the 6810 at hexadecimal addresses 0000–007F. This is done by connecting address lines A_{15}–A_{12} to the active-low chip select lines shown. Because these address lines will be in the low state for addresses 0000–007F, the 6810 will be selected by the MPU when these addresses appear on the address bus and when the VMA line is active.

TABLE 15-3. RAM Addressing Scheme

$\overline{CS_1}$	$\overline{CS_2}$	$\overline{CS_4}$	$\overline{CS_5}$						Connected to A_0–A_6							
↓	↓	↓	↓													
A_{15}	A_{14}	A_{13}	A_{12}	A_{11}	A_{10}	A_9	A_8	A_7	A_6	A_5	A_4	A_3	A_2	A_1	A_0	Location
0	0	0	0	x	x	x	x	x	0	0	0	0	0	0	0	0000
0	0	0	0	x	x	x	x	x	1	1	1	1	1	1	1	007F

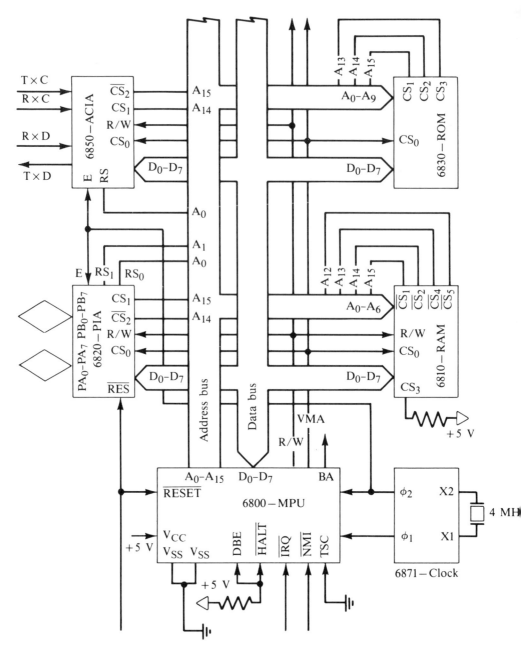

FIGURE 15-7. 6800-based microprocessor system.

Notice in Table 15-3 that because address lines A_7–A_{11} are not used in the addressing scheme, the same memory locations in the 6810 RAM chip could also be selected when addresses 0080 through 0FFF appear on the address bus. Recall from previous chapters that this area in memory (0080–0FFF) where the RAM chip could be accessed again is called the *foldback area* and serves no

TABLE 15-4. ROM Addressing Scheme

CS$_1$ ↓ A$_{15}$	CS$_2$ ↓ A$_{14}$	CS$_3$ ↓ A$_{13}$	A$_{12}$	A$_{11}$	A$_{10}$	A$_9$	A$_8$	A$_7$	A$_6$	A$_5$	A$_4$	A$_3$	A$_2$	A$_1$	A$_0$	Location
						Connected to A$_0$–A$_9$										
1	1	1	x	x	x	0	0	0	0	0	0	0	0	0	0	FC00
1	1	1	x	x	x	1	1	1	1	1	1	1	1	1	1	FFFF

practical purpose. Observe that the 6810 addressed in this manner would never be selected if an address greater than 0FFF appeared on the address bus.

6830 ROM Interface

The 6830 ROM chip is connected to the MPU (in Figure 15-7) in a manner similar to the 6810 RAM. The 10 address inputs (A$_0$–A$_9$) to the 6830 are connected to the MPU's address bus to allow 1024 bytes of memory to be accessed. Because the 6830 ROM can only have data read from it, no R/W input is provided. As before, the MPU's VMA line is connected to the active-high chip select input (CS0) to select the chip only when a valid memory address appears on the address bus. The 6830 ROM is addressed at hexadecimal locations FC00–FFFF as shown in Table 15-4.

Notice in Table 15-4 that the high-order address lines of the MPU—A$_{15}$, A$_{14}$, and A$_{13}$—are connected to the active-high chip select inputs CS1, CS2, and CS3, respectively. Thus whenever these three address lines are at the logic-high state (and VMA is active), the 6830 ROM will be selected. Then assuming that the unconnected address lines (A$_{12}$–A$_{10}$) are at the logic-high state, the 6830 ROM will be selected when the addresses FC00–FFFF appear on the address bus. As before, because address lines A$_{12}$, A$_{11}$, and A$_{10}$ are not included in the addressing, foldback will appear at addresses E000–FBFF.

6820 PIA Interface

The 6820 peripheral interface adapter (PIA) is a programmable chip that provides the means of interfacing parallel-communicating external I/O devices to the MPU. The 6820 is similar in function to the 8255 PPI discussed in Chapter 7. Like the 8255 (with reference to Figure 15-7), the 6820 PIA can be addressed as four ports via the register select, RS0, and RS1 inputs (similar to the A$_0$ and A$_1$ inputs to the 8255). Each of the four logic combinations of RS$_0$ and RS$_1$ will select an internal register or I/O port of the PIA. Because the PIA is capable of input and output, the R/W pin is connected to the R/W signal of the MPU to establish the direction of data flow. The reset signal to the MPU is also connected to the $\overline{\text{RES}}$ line of the PIA to initialize the internal registers during startup. The enable pulse (E) input to the PIA is used to maintain internal timing and synchronization and is provided by the Φ$_2$ clock pulse of the clock generator.

The addressing scheme used to interface the 6820 PIA to the MPU connects the chip select lines and the register select lines to the MPU's address bus, as shown in Table 15-5. Observe in Figure 15-7 that the VMA line of the MPU

TABLE 15-5. PIA Addressing Scheme

CS_1 $\downarrow$ A_{15}	$\overline{CS_2}$ $\downarrow$ A_{14}	A_{13}	A_{12}	A_{11}	A_{10}	A_9	A_8	A_7	A_6	A_5	A_4	A_3	A_2	RS_1 $\downarrow$ A_1	RS_0 $\downarrow$ A_0	Location
1	0	x	x	x	x	x	x	x	x	x	x	x	x	0	0	8000
1	0	x	x	x	x	x	x	x	x	x	x	x	x	0	1	8001
1	0	x	x	x	x	x	x	x	x	x	x	x	x	1	0	8002
1	0	x	x	x	x	x	x	x	x	x	x	x	x	1	1	8003

is connected to the active-high chip select line CS_0, so that the PIA is selected only when there is a valid memory address on the address bus.

Referring to Table 15-5, notice that the 6820 PIA will be selected only when the MPU's address line A_{15} is at a logic-high state and address line A_{14} is at a logic-low state (and VMA is active). Because the register select bits RS_0 and RS_1 are connected to A_0 and A_1, respectively (assuming that the unconnected address lines are low), the PIA will occupy four locations in memory, 8000–8003. As in the previous memory interface, because linear addressing is used, and address lines A_{13}–A_2 are not included in the addressing scheme, foldback will exist from memory locations 8004–BFFF.

6850 ACIA Interface

The 6850 asynchronous communications interface adapter (ACIA) is an I/O chip that allows the 6800 MPU to communicate with external serial I/O devices. The operation of the 6850 ACIA is very similar to the 8251 UART discussed in Chapter 7. Like the 8251, the 6850 ACIA is a two-port device and will thus occupy two locations in memory. Referring to Figure 15-7, observe that the register select (RS) input to the ACIA allows the MPU to select the ACIA for data or control information (similar to the C/D line of the 8251). As in the 6820 PIA, the R/W and E inputs to the 6850 ACIA are connected to the R/W and Φ_2 (respectively) lines of the MPU. The VMA line of the MPU is tied to the active-high chip select line (CS0) to select the ACIA only when a valid address appears on the address bus. The high-order address lines of the MPU (A_{15} and A_{14}) are tied to the remaining chip select lines of the ACIA ($\overline{CS_2}$ and CS_1) to provide the addressing scheme shown in Table 15-6.

TABLE 15-6. ACIA Addressing Scheme

$\overline{CS_2}$ $\downarrow$ A_{15}	CS_1 $\downarrow$ A_{14}	A_{13}	A_{12}	A_{11}	A_{10}	A_9	A_8	A_7	A_6	A_5	A_4	A_3	A_2	A_1	RS $\downarrow$ A_0	Location
0	1	x	x	x	x	x	x	x	x	x	x	x	x	x	0	4000
0	1	x	x	x	x	x	x	x	x	x	x	x	x	x	1	4001

Notice in Table 15-6 that the ACIA will be selected only when the MPU's address line A_{15} is at a logic-low state and address line A_{14} is at a logic-high state. Because address line A_0 is used to select one of the two ACIA's internal registers, the ACIA will occupy memory locations 4000 and 4001 (assuming that the unconnected address lines A_{13}–A_1 are at the logic-low state). Again, because the unconnected address lines are not used in the addressing scheme, foldback will occur from memory locations 4002–7FFF.

The memory map for the basic 6800-based system is shown in Figure 15-8. Even though the term *memory map* is used, the map includes the addresses for memory as well as for I/O, as the 6800 can have only memory-mapped I/O.

The 6800-based microprocessor system shown in Figure 15-7 is a minimum system designed with the basic support chips in the 6800 family. The design incorporates only the simple concepts of interfacing memory and I/O devices to the MPU. As a result, it can be seen in Figure 15-8 that a considerable amount of memory space is wasted in foldback areas. No other memory or I/O device can be addressed in these foldback areas unless the addressing schemes are altered to prevent an addressing conflict. The linear addressing used to interface the support chips to the MPU led to the generation of foldback areas, but it did save a considerable amount of hardware in the form of logic gates and address decoders. Foldback does not provide any disadvantages in a simple design such as this if it is anticipated that the system will never be expanded. If expansion is desired, the same concepts of address decoding used for the 8085 system design can be applied to the 6800 to reduce the foldback areas.

Hexadecimal
locations

Location	Device
0000–007F	6810 RAM
0080–0FFF	6810 Foldback
4000–4001	6850 ACIA
4002–7FFF	6850 Foldback
8000–8003	6820 PIA
8004–BFFF	6820 Foldback
E000–FBFF	6830 Foldback
FC00–FFFF	6830 ROM

FIGURE 15-8. System memory map.

6800 Instruction Set

Because the 6800 microprocessor is designed for memory-mapped I/O and the internal registers of the MPU are limited in number, the instruction set of the 6800 is made up of extensive memory manipulation instructions. Recall that the 8085 microprocessor has only two I/O instructions that can be used in an isolated I/O hardware scheme—IN and OUT. However, in a 6800 system, all the memory reference instructions can be used for I/O devices, as all I/O devices are mapped to memory locations.

Programming Model

Before examining the instruction set of the 6800 MPU, it is important to investigate the internal architecture of the MPU from a software point of view. Recall from Section 15-2 that the 6800 MPU has six internal registers that can be accessed by the instruction set. A knowledge of the functions of each of these registers is required in order to understand the instruction set of the 6800. Because the 6800 can be viewed, from a programming standpoint, as a set of registers, we can develop the programming model of the 6800 MPU shown in Figure 15-9.

Figure 15-9 illustrates the "programming model" of the 6800 MPU; that is, the 6800 microprocessor as seen from a software point of view. The 6800 has two 8-bit accumulators, ACCA and ACCB, either or both of which can be used in arithmetic and logic operations. The MPU has a 16-bit index register (IX) that is used in the indexed mode of addressing (discussed later). Basically, the index register provides the function of a data counter similar to the H&L register pair of the 8085 microprocessor. The 6800 MPU also has a 16-bit program counter (PC) and a 16-bit stack pointer (SP) whose function is exactly the same as the PC and SP of the 8085. An 8-bit condition code register (CCR) with six flags is used to signal the result of arithmetic and logic operations as well as to provide status on the interrupt system of the 6800. The CCR is similar to the 8085's five condition flags (PSW), with a few differences. Figure 15-10 shows the definitions of each bit in the CCR.

With reference to Figure 15-10, notice that the CCR has the six status flags located at bit positions 0–5. The two most significant bit positions of the CCR are always set to the logic-high state and therefore serve no practical purpose.

The half-carry bit (H) of the CCR is similar to the auxiliary carry flag of the 8085 and is used to signal a carryover from the fourth to the fifth bit position of ACCA or ACCB.

The interrupt mask bit (I) signals the status of the 6800 MPU's interrupt system. If this bit is set, interrupts will be disabled and the MPU will not acknowledge interrupts over the $\overline{\text{IRQ}}$ line. Note that interrupts will be accepted on the $\overline{\text{NMI}}$ line and the SWI instruction will be executed regardless of the state of I.

The negative (N) bit is similar to the sign flag of the 8085 and will be set if the most significant bit of the result of an operation is high (indicating a

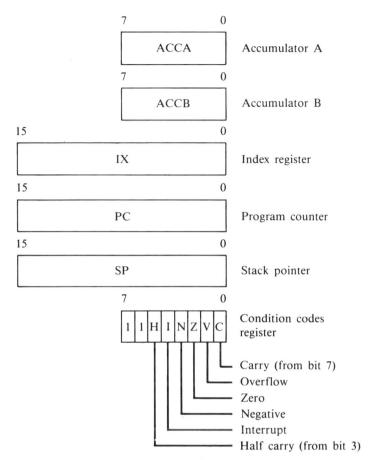

FIGURE 15-9. Programming model of the 6800 MPU. (Courtesy of Motorola, Inc.)

negative result). The N bit will be reset if the most significant bit of the result is low (indicating a positive result).

The zero bit (Z) is similar to the zero flag of the 8085 and will be set if the result of an operation yields a zero result. The Z bit will also be reset if the result yields a nonzero result.

The overflow bit (V) has no equivalent flag in the 8085 microprocessor. The V bit is used to signal a two's-complement overflow condition as the result of an arithmetic operation.

The carry bit (C) is similar to the carry flag of the 8085 and is set when there is a carry generated (from the eighth bit position) in the result of an arithmetic operation.

Notice that the 6800 does not have a parity bit, as did the 8085.

The 6800 MPU has seventy-two basic instructions, which include accumulator and memory instructions, index register and stack manipulation instructions, and jump and branch instructions. Tables 15-7 through 15-9 show the instruction set of the 6800 MPU organized into the previously mentioned categories.

	b5	b4	b3	b2	b1	b0
	H	I	N	Z	V	C

H = Half-carry; set whenever a carry from b_3 to b_4 of the result is generated by ADD, ABA, ADC; cleared if no b_3 to b_4 carry; not affected by other instructions.

I = Interrupt mask; set by hardware or software interrupt or SEI instruction; cleared by CLI instruction. (Normally not used in arithmetic operations.) Restored to a zero as a result of an RTI instruction if I_m stored on the stack is low.

N = Negative; set if high-order bit (b_7) of result is set; cleared otherwise.

Z = Zero; set if result = 0; cleared otherwise.

V = Overflow; set if there was arithmetic overflow as a result of the operation; cleared otherwise.

C = Carry; set if there was a carry from the most significant bit (b_7) of the result; cleared otherwise.

FIGURE 15-10.   Condition code register bit definitions. (Courtesy of Motorola, Inc.)

Addressing Modes

By briefly scanning through the operations shown in Tables 15-7 through 15-9, one can see many similarities with the 8085's instruction set. Notice, however, that in some operations, the mnemonics and machine codes are very different from the 8085 instruction set, even though the operation may be similar. Also notice that many instructions have four or fewer addressing modes.

An addressing mode is simply a different means by which the MPU obtains the data for an instruction. Thus even though a particular instruction may have up to four addressing modes, the end result of the instruction will be the same. For example, in Table 15-7, the ADDA instruction has four addressing modes: immediate, direct, indexed, and extended. These four modes of addressing will be discussed using the ADDA instruction as an example.

Immediate Addressing Mode.   In the immediate addressing mode the data for an instruction is fetched from the memory location(s) "immediately" following the operation code for the instruction. Instructions in the immediate mode of addressing will therefore always be two- or three-byte instructions. An example of immediate addressing in the 8085 is the MVI A (move immediate to A) instruction.

Thus the ADDA instruction of the 6800 will be a two-byte instruction. For example, if it were required to add the hexadecimal byte "45" to the contents of ACCA using the immediate mode of addressing (referring to Table 15-7), the machine instruction code would be 8B45 (hexadecimal).

TABLE 15-7. Accumulator and Memory Instructions. (Courtesy of Motorola, Inc.)

OPERATIONS	MNEMONIC	IMMED OP	IMMED ~	IMMED #	DIRECT OP	DIRECT ~	DIRECT #	INDEX OP	INDEX ~	INDEX #	EXTND OP	EXTND ~	EXTND #	IMPLIED OP	IMPLIED ~	IMPLIED #	BOOLEAN/ARITHMETIC OPERATION (All register labels refer to contents)	H (5)	I (4)	N (3)	Z (2)	V (1)	C (0)
Add	ADDA	8B	2	2	9B	3	2	AB	5	2	BB	4	3				$A + M \to A$	‡	•	‡	‡	‡	‡
	ADDB	CB	2	2	DB	3	2	EB	5	2	FB	4	3				$B + M \to B$	‡	•	‡	‡	‡	‡
Add Acmltrs	ABA													1B	2	1	$A + B \to A$	‡	•	‡	‡	‡	‡
Add with Carry	ADCA	89	2	2	99	3	2	A9	5	2	B9	4	3				$A + M + C \to A$	‡	•	‡	‡	‡	‡
	ADCB	C9	2	2	D9	3	2	E9	5	2	F9	4	3				$B + M + C \to B$	‡	•	‡	‡	‡	‡
And	ANDA	84	2	2	94	3	2	A4	5	2	B4	4	3				$A \cdot M \to A$	•	•	‡	‡	R	•
	ANDB	C4	2	2	D4	3	2	E4	5	2	F4	4	3				$B \cdot M \to B$	•	•	‡	‡	R	•
Bit Test	BITA	85	2	2	95	3	2	A5	5	2	B5	4	3				$A \cdot M$	•	•	‡	‡	R	•
	BITB	C5	2	2	D5	3	2	E5	5	2	F5	4	3				$B \cdot M$	•	•	‡	‡	R	•
Clear	CLR							6F	7	2	7F	6	3				$00 \to M$	•	•	R	S	R	R
	CLRA													4F	2	1	$00 \to A$	•	•	R	S	R	R
	CLRB													5F	2	1	$00 \to B$	•	•	R	S	R	R
Compare	CMPA	81	2	2	91	3	2	A1	5	2	B1	4	3				$A - M$	•	•	‡	‡	‡	‡
	CMPB	C1	2	2	D1	3	2	E1	5	2	F1	4	3				$B - M$	•	•	‡	‡	‡	‡
Compare Acmltrs	CBA													11	2	1	$A - B$	•	•	‡	‡	‡	‡
Complement, 1's	COM							63	7	2	73	6	3				$\overline{M} \to M$	•	•	‡	‡	R	S
	COMA													43	2	1	$\overline{A} \to A$	•	•	‡	‡	R	S
	COMB													53	2	1	$\overline{B} \to B$	•	•	‡	‡	R	S
Complement, 2's (Negate)	NEG							60	7	2	70	6	3				$00 - M \to M$	•	•	‡	‡	①	②
	NEGA													40	2	1	$00 - A \to A$	•	•	‡	‡	①	②
	NEGB													50	2	1	$00 - B \to B$	•	•	‡	‡	①	②
Decimal Adjust, A	DAA													19	2	1	Converts Binary Add. of BCD Characters into BCD Format	•	•	‡	‡	‡	③
Decrement	DEC							6A	7	2	7A	6	3				$M - 1 \to M$	•	•	‡	‡	④	•
	DECA													4A	2	1	$A - 1 \to A$	•	•	‡	‡	④	•
	DECB													5A	2	1	$B - 1 \to B$	•	•	‡	‡	④	•

ADDRESSING MODES | **BOOLEAN/ARITHMETIC OPERATION** | **COND. CODE REG.**

483

TABLE 15-7. (Continued)

OPERATIONS	MNEMONIC	IMMED OP	~	#	DIRECT OP	~	#	INDEX OP	~	#	EXTND OP	~	#	IMPLIED OP	~	#	BOOLEAN/ARITHMETIC OPERATION (All register labels refer to contents)	H (5)	I (4)	N (3)	Z (2)	V (1)	C (0)
Exclusive OR	EORA	88	2	2	98	3	2	A8	5	2	B8	4	3				A ⊕ M → A	•	•	↕	↕	R	•
	EORB	C8	2	2	D8	3	2	E8	5	2	F8	4	3				B ⊕ M → B	•	•	↕	↕	R	•
Increment	INC							6C	7	2	7C	6	3				M + 1 → M	•	•	↕	↕	⑤	•
	INCA													4C	2	1	A + 1 → A	•	•	↕	↕	⑤	•
	INCB													5C	2	1	B + 1 → B	•	•	↕	↕	⑤	•
Load Acmltr	LDAA	86	2	2	96	3	2	A6	5	2	B6	4	3				M → A	•	•	↕	↕	R	•
	LDAB	C6	2	2	D6	3	2	E6	5	2	F6	4	3				M → B	•	•	↕	↕	R	•
Or, Inclusive	ORAA	8A	2	2	9A	3	2	AA	5	2	BA	4	3				A + M → A	•	•	↕	↕	R	•
	ORAB	CA	2	2	DA	3	2	EA	5	2	FA	4	3				B + M → B	•	•	↕	↕	R	•
Push Data	PSHA													36	4	1	A → M$_{SP}$, SP − 1 → SP	•	•	•	•	•	•
	PSHB													37	4	1	B → M$_{SP}$, SP − 1 → SP	•	•	•	•	•	•
Pull Data	PULA													32	4	1	SP + 1 → SP, M$_{SP}$ → A	•	•	•	•	•	•
	PULB													33	4	1	SP + 1 → SP, M$_{SP}$ → B	•	•	•	•	•	•
Rotate Left	ROL							69	7	2	79	6	3				M } C ← [b7 ... b0] ←	•	•	↕	↕	⑥	↕
	ROLA													49	2	1	A }	•	•	↕	↕	⑥	↕
	ROLB													59	2	1	B }	•	•	↕	↕	⑥	↕
Rotate Right	ROR							66	7	2	76	6	3				M } C → [b7 ... b0] →	•	•	↕	↕	⑥	↕
	RORA													46	2	1	A }	•	•	↕	↕	⑥	↕
	RORB													56	2	1	B }	•	•	↕	↕	⑥	↕
Shift Left, Arithmetic	ASL							68	7	2	78	6	3				M } C ← [b7 ... b0] ← 0	•	•	↕	↕	⑥	↕
	ASLA													48	2	1	A }	•	•	↕	↕	⑥	↕
	ASLB													58	2	1	B }	•	•	↕	↕	⑥	↕
Shift Right, Arithmetic	ASR							67	7	2	77	6	3				M } [b7 ... b0] → C	•	•	↕	↕	⑥	↕
	ASRA													47	2	1	A }	•	•	↕	↕	⑥	↕
	ASRB													57	2	1	B }	•	•	↕	↕	⑥	↕
Shift Right, Logic	LSR							64	7	2	74	6	3				M } 0 → [b7 ... b0] → C	•	•	R	↕	⑥	↕
	LSRA													44	2	1	A }	•	•	R	↕	⑥	↕
	LSRB													54	2	1	B }	•	•	R	↕	⑥	↕

TABLE 15-7. (Continued)

OPERATIONS	MNEMONIC	IMMED OP	~	#	DIRECT OP	~	#	INDEX OP	~	#	EXTND OP	~	#	IMPLIED OP	~	#	BOOLEAN/ARITHMETIC OPERATION (All register labels refer to contents)	H 5	I 4	N 3	Z 2	V 1	C 0
Store Acmltr.	STAA				97	4	2	A7	6	2	B7	5	3				A → M	•	•	↑	↑	R	•
	STAB				D7	4	2	E7	6	2	F7	5	3				B → M	•	•	↑	↑	R	•
Subtract	SUBA	80	2	2	90	3	2	A0	5	2	B0	4	3				A − M → A	•	•	↑	↑	↑	↑
	SUBB	C0	2	2	D0	3	2	E0	5	2	F0	4	3				B − M → B	•	•	↑	↑	↑	↑
Subtract Acmltrs.	SBA													10	2	1	A − B → A	•	•	↑	↑	↑	↑
Subtr. with Carry	SBCA	82	2	2	92	3	2	A2	5	2	B2	4	3				A − M − C → A	•	•	↑	↑	↑	↑
	SBCB	C2	2	2	D2	3	2	E2	5	2	F2	4	3				B − M − C → B	•	•	↑	↑	↑	↑
Transfer Acmltrs	TAB													16	2	1	A → B	•	•	↑	↑	R	•
	TBA													17	2	1	B → A	•	•	↑	↑	R	•
Test, Zero or Minus	TST							6D	7	2	7D	6	3				M − 00	•	•	↑	↑	R	R
	TSTA													4D	2	1	A − 00	•	•	↑	↑	R	R
	TSTB													5D	2	1	B − 00	•	•	↑	↑	R	R

LEGEND:

OP   Operation Code (Hexadecimal);
~   Number of MPU Cycles;
#   Number of Program Bytes;
+   Arithmetic Plus;
−   Arithmetic Minus;
•   Boolean AND;
M_{SP} Contents of memory location pointed to be Stack Pointer;

Note — Accumulator addressing mode instructions are included in the column for IMPLIED addressing

+   Boolean Inclusive OR;
⊕   Boolean Exclusive OR;
$\overline{M}$ Complement of M;
→   Transfer Into;
0   Bit = Zero;
00   Byte = Zero;

CONDITION CODE SYMBOLS:

H   Half-carry from bit 3;
I   Interrupt mask
N   Negative (sign bit)
Z   Zero (byte)
V   Overflow, 2's complement
C   Carry from bit 7
R   Reset Always
S   Set Always
↑   Test and set if true, cleared otherwise
•   Not Affected

485

TABLE 15-8. Index Register and Stack Manipulation Instructions. (Courtesy of Motorola, Inc.)

POINTER OPERATIONS	MNEMONIC	IMMED OP	~	#	DIRECT OP	~	#	INDEX OP	~	#	EXTND OP	~	#	IMPLIED OP	~	#	BOOLEAN/ARITHMETIC OPERATION	5 H	4 I	3 N	2 Z	1 V	0 C
Compare Index Reg	CPX	8C	3	3	9C	4	2	AC	6	2	BC	5	3				$X_H - M$, $X_L - (M + 1)$	•	•	⑦	↕	⑦	•
Decrement Index Reg	DEX													09	4	1	$X - 1 \rightarrow X$	•	•	↕	↕	•	•
Decrement Stack Pntr	DES													34	4	1	$SP - 1 \rightarrow SP$	•	•	•	•	•	•
Increment Index Reg	INX													08	4	1	$X + 1 \rightarrow X$	•	•	•	↕	•	•
Increment Stack Pntr	INS													31	4	1	$SP + 1 \rightarrow SP$	•	•	•	•	•	•
Load Index Reg	LDX	CE	3	3	DE	4	2	EE	6	2	FE	5	3				$M \rightarrow X_H$, $(M + 1) \rightarrow X_L$	•	•	⑨	↕	R	•
Load Stack Pntr	LDS	8E	3	3	9E	4	2	AE	6	2	BE	5	3				$M \rightarrow SP_H$, $(M + 1) \rightarrow SP_L$	•	•	⑨	↕	R	•
Store Index Reg	STX				DF	5	2	EF	7	2	FF	6	3				$X_H \rightarrow M$, $X_L \rightarrow (M + 1)$	•	•	⑨	↕	R	•
Store Stack Pntr	STS				9F	5	2	AF	7	2	BF	6	3				$SP_H \rightarrow M$, $SP_L \rightarrow (M + 1)$	•	•	⑨	↕	R	•
Indx Reg → Stack Pntr	TXS													35	4	1	$X - 1 \rightarrow SP$	•	•	•	•	•	•
Stack Pntr → Indx Reg	TSX													30	4	1	$SP + 1 \rightarrow X$	•	•	•	•	•	•

COND. CODE REG.

TABLE 15-9. Jump and Branch Instructions. (Courtesy of Motorola, Inc.)

OPERATIONS	MNEMONIC	RELATIVE			INDEX			EXTND			IMPLIED			BRANCH TEST	COND. CODE REG.					
		OP	~	#	OP	~	#	OP	~	#	OP	~	#		5 H	4 I	3 N	2 Z	1 V	0 C
Branch Always	BRA	20	4	2										None	•	•	•	•	•	•
Branch If Carry Clear	BCC	24	4	2										$C = 0$	•	•	•	•	•	•
Branch If Carry Set	BCS	25	4	2										$C = 1$	•	•	•	•	•	•
Branch If = Zero	BEQ	27	4	2										$Z = 1$	•	•	•	•	•	•
Branch If ≥ Zero	BGE	2C	4	2										$N \oplus V = 0$	•	•	•	•	•	•
Branch If > Zero	BGT	2E	4	2										$Z + (N \oplus V) = 0$	•	•	•	•	•	•
Branch If Higher	BHI	22	4	2										$C + Z = 0$	•	•	•	•	•	•
Branch If ≤ Zero	BLE	2F	4	2										$Z + (N \oplus V) = 1$	•	•	•	•	•	•
Branch If Lower Or Same	BLS	23	4	2										$C + Z = 1$	•	•	•	•	•	•
Branch If < Zero	BLT	2D	4	2										$N \oplus V = 1$	•	•	•	•	•	•
Branch If Minus	BMI	2B	4	2										$N = 1$	•	•	•	•	•	•
Branch If Not Equal Zero	BNE	26	4	2										$Z = 0$	•	•	•	•	•	•
Branch If Overflow Clear	BVC	28	4	2										$V = 0$	•	•	•	•	•	•
Branch If Overflow Set	BVS	29	4	2										$V = 1$	•	•	•	•	•	•
Branch If Plus	BPL	2A	4	2										$N = 0$	•	•	•	•	•	•
Branch To Subroutine	BSR	8D	8	2										See Special Operations	•	•	•	•	•	•
Jump	JMP				6E	4	2	7E	3	3				See Special Operations	•	•	•	•	•	•
Jump To Subroutine	JSR				AD	8	2	BD	9	3					•	•	•	•	•	•
No Operation	NOP										02	2	1	Advances Prog. Cntr. Only	•	•	•	•	•	•
Return From Interrupt	RTI										3B	10	1		•	⑪	⑩	•	•	•
Return From Subroutine	RTS										39	5	1	See Special Operations	•	•	•	•	•	•
Software Interrupt	SWI										3F	12	1		•	•	•	•	•	•
Wait for Interrupt	WAI										3E	9	1		•	•	•	•	•	•

The same instruction would be written in 6800 assembler format as

ADDA #$45

where the "#" symbol instructs the assembler that the operation code for the ADDA instruction in the immediate addressing mode (8B) is to be assembled. The "$" identifies the constant "45" to be hexadecimal; recall that the prefix "H" was used in 8085 assembly language to identify a hexadecimal constant.

Direct Addressing Mode. In the direct addressing mode, the instruction causes the MPU to fetch the data for the instruction from a memory location in the range 0000–00FF (page 0). An instruction in the direct addressing mode is a two-byte instruction—the first byte is the op code of the instruction (in the direct mode), and the second byte is the low-order address of the memory location where the data is to be found.

For example, if it were required to add the contents of memory location 0087 to ACCA, and assuming that the hexadecimal byte "45" were stored in this memory location (referring to Table 15-7), the machine instruction would be 9B87 (hexadecimal): "9B" is the operation code for the ADDA instruction in the direct mode, and 87 is the low-order address of the memory location where the data (45) is to be found. The high-order address is always zero, and thus direct addressing is limited to page 0 of the system's memory map.

The ADDA instruction is written in 6800 assembler format as follows:

ADDA $87

Because the "#" symbol is left out and only a byte is specified for an address, the assembler will assume that the instruction is to be assembled in the direct mode.

Extended Addressing Mode. Notice that in the direct addressing mode, the data for an instruction can be stored and accessed only in page 0 of the memory map (locations 0000–00FF). But the extended addressing mode allows the instruction to access data from any memory location (including page 0) in the memory map. An example of a similar 8085 instruction is the LDA (load accumulator) instruction.

For example, if the byte "45" were to be added to ACCA and the byte were stored at memory location 5065, the ADDA instruction would have to be used in the extended mode to accomplish this task (because location 5065 is beyond page 0 and direct addressing cannot be used). Because a 16-bit address now has to be specified, instructions in the extended mode of addressing are always three-byte instructions. Referring to Table 15-7, the machine code for the ADDA instruction would be BB5065 in the extended mode. The byte "BB" is the operation code for the ADDA (extended) instruction, and the following two bytes, 5065, is the address from which the data (45) is to be accessed. Notice that unlike the 8085, 16-bit addresses are stored with the most significant byte first.

The same ADDA instruction would be written in 6800 assembler format as

Because in this case a 16-bit address is specified, the assembler assumes that the instruction is to be assembled in the extended mode of addressing.

At this point it may seem that having the direct and extended modes of addressing is wasteful, especially as the extended mode can be used in place of the direct mode. However, because most 6800 systems have RAM located in page 0 of the memory map, the direct mode can be used to access these memory locations. Because the direct mode requires only two bytes for an instruction (three bytes for extended), using the direct mode when applicable can result in a smaller program.

Indexed Addressing Mode. In the indexed addressing mode, the MPU uses the index register (IX) to point to the memory location where the data for the instruction is stored. This mode of addressing is similar to instructions of the 8085 that use register pair H&L as a data counter, for example, MOV A,M.

For example, if memory location 5065 contained the data "45" and the index register were set to 5065, the ADDA instruction could be used in the indexed mode to add "45" to the contents of ACCA. Referring to Table 15-7, the ADDA instruction (indexed mode) would be stored as AB00.

Notice that a "00" follows the operation code for the ADDA instruction (AB) in the indexed mode. Instructions in the indexed mode are always two-byte instructions. The second byte is the offset that is added to the value of the index register before the data is fetched. If the offset is zero, the data will be fetched from the address contained in IX. For example, if it were required to add the contents of memory location 5067 to ACCA using indexed addressing and without changing the contents of IX, the offset would be 02 (5065 + 2 = 5067). Similarly, if it were required to add the contents of memory location 5063 to ACCA using indexed addressing and without changing the contents of IX, the offset would be FE (−2, in two's-complement form).

The same ADDA instructions would be written in 6800 assembler format as follows:

```
CODE     INSTRUCTION

AB00     ADDA   0,X      NO OFFSET
AB02     ADDA   2,X      TWO BYTES FORWARD
ABFE     ADDA  -2,X      TWO BYTES BACK
```

In these three examples, the "X" symbol instructs the assembler to assemble the ADDA instruction in the indexed mode. In the first instruction, no offset is specified, and in the next two instructions, offsets of + and − 2 are specified, respectively.

The previous example illustrated the use of four of the 6800 MPU addressing modes. Table 15-7 identifies another mode of addressing, called the *implied* or *inherent addressing mode* (sometimes known as the *fifth addressing mode*). This term is used to describe single-byte instructions that have no operands. Referring to Table 15-7, examples of such instructions are ABA (add ACCB to ACCA),

CLRA (clear contents of ACCA), INX (increment contents of IX), and so on. Instructions in the implied mode are similar to the single-byte 8085 instructions.

Perhaps the most important differences between the instructions of the 6800 MPU and the 8085 lie in the jump and branch instructions. Referring to Table 15-7, notice that the 6800 MPU has only two jump instructions, an unconditional JMP and a jump to subroutine JSR (similar to the 8085's CALL instruction). Both jump instructions are three-byte instructions. The remaining program transfer instructions in the instruction set are branch instructions, which are two-byte instructions that use a scheme known as relative addressing.

Relative Addressing

Branch instructions use a technique known as *relative addressing* to cause control of the MPU to transfer to another address (conditionally or unconditionally). The memory location to which control is transferred is relative to the current value of the program counter. The first byte of a particular branch instruction is the operation code, and the second byte is a positive or negative offset that is added to the program counter to transfer MPU control to a forward or backward address. To illustrate how this is done, consider the following example.

Assume that a branch instruction is stored at locations 2000 and 2001. If the branch instruction is one that transfers control unconditionally to memory location 2010, the offset (second byte) of the branch instruction will be 0E. The value of the PC after the second byte of the branch instruction is fetched is 2002; the second byte (offset) is added to the PC (2002), which results in the PC containing 2010 (2002 + 0E); and control then transfers to memory location 2010. This type of branching is known as *branch ahead*, and the offset is always a positive number in the range 0 to 127 (decimal).

Now assume that the same branch instruction stored at locations 2000 and 2001 is to transfer control to memory location 1FF0. The offset for the branch instruction is EE. Because after the offset (second byte of branch instruction) is fetched by the MPU, the value of the PC is 2002, 12 must be subtracted from 2002 to obtain a value of 1FF0. Because the offset is always added to the PC, it must be represented in two's-complement form, and therefore − 12 in two's-complement form is EE. This type of branching is known as *branch behind*, and the offset is always a negative number in the range 0 to − 127 (decimal).

As a general rule, to calculate the offset for branch ahead or branch behind:

offset = location to be transferred − (location of branch instruction + 2)

There are two main advantages of having branch instructions in a microprocessor instruction set. The first advantage is that branch instructions are only two bytes in size and thus occupy less memory space than do jump instructions. Second, a program constructed with branch instructions is naturally relocatable as the operands of branch instructions are not absolute addresses but are relative to the current value of the PC.

A major disadvantage of branch instructions in the 6800 instruction set is that control can be transferred only plus or minus 127 bytes ahead or behind. If it is desired to transfer control to a memory location greater than 127 bytes plus or minus the current value of the program counter, the branch must be to the (absolute) unconditional JMP instruction, and control must be transferred from there. This technique can also be used to simulate conditional call instructions by branching to the JSR instruction instead.

At this stage only some of the more outstanding 6800 instructions have been discussed. The addressing modes and the examples used were to illustrate the differences between the 6800 and the 8085 microprocessors. To deal with an in-depth study of the 6800 instruction set is beyond the scope of this chapter. However, to illustrate the difference between assembly language programs written for the 8085 and programs written for the 6800, we shall use the block-move algorithm from Chapter 8 to construct a 6800 program. A comparison of the 8085 implementation of the block-move program (from Chapter 8) and the 6800 implementation shown in Figure 15-11 should reinforce the concepts studied in this section.

The program shown in Figure 15-11 is similar to the 8085 implementation of the block-move algorithm discussed in Chapter 8. Before this program is executed, it is assumed that the starting address of the source block is stored at locations 2000 and 2001 and that the starting address of the destination block is stored at locations 5000 and 5001. The number of bytes to be moved is 53 (35 hexadecimal).

The first instruction (LDAB) loads ACCB with the count of the number of bytes to be moved. This instruction uses immediate addressing to load the following byte into ACCB. Next, the LDX instruction loads IX with the address of the source block (previously stored in location 5000). Notice that because location 5000 is not in page 0, the LDX instruction is automatically assembled in the extended mode. The LDAA instruction uses indexed addressing to obtain a byte of data from the source block. The data from the memory location pointed to by IX is loaded into ACCA. The INX instruction is used to increment the contents of IX (point to the next source location). The updated address is then

```
0035              COUNT   EQU  $35    * Number of bytes to move
2000              SOURCE  EQU  $2000  * Location that contains source addr.
5000              DEST    EQU  $5000  * Location that contains destination addr.

ADDR CODE

0000 C635         LDAB #COUNT  * Store count in ACCB
0002 FE2000 MOVE  LDX  SOURCE  * Load IX with source address
0005 A600         LDAA 0,X     * Get source byte
0007 08           INX          * SOURCE = SOURCE + 1
0008 FF2000       STX  SOURCE  * Save source address
000B FE5000       LDX  DEST    * Load IX with destination address
000E A700         STAA 0,X     * Store source byte in dest
0010 08           INX          * DEST = DEST + 1
0011 FF5000       STX  DEST    * Save destination address
0014 5A           DECB         * COUNT = COUNT - 1
0015 26EB         BNE  MOVE    * Continue until done
0017 20FE   STOP  BRA  STOP    * Else stop
```

FIGURE 15-11. Block-move program for the 6800.

stored in memory location source by means of the STX instruction. The next LDX instruction sets the IX to the address of the destination block by obtaining this value from location DEST. The STAA instruction in the indexed mode stores the previously received source byte in the memory location referenced by IX (destination address). The next two instructions update and store the destination address, as was done for the source address. Next, the contents of ACCB is decremented to count down the number of bytes moved. Control will transfer to location MOVE if the count is not zero; if the count is zero, the program will terminate.

15-6

Summary

One can clearly see in this chapter that there are many similarities and differences between the 8085 and the 6800 microprocessor. Both microprocessors similarly process memory instructions, as they have many of the same function blocks described in Chapter 2. Even though there are major differences between the two microprocessors in their interrupt structures, control signals, and instruction sets one can also see many similarities in these areas—conceptual similarities. It can also be seen from this chapter that microprocessors are designed with specific applications in mind. The memory-oriented instruction set of the 6800, together with the memory-mapped I/O scheme, makes it an ideal microprocessor for applications that require extensive I/O control and minimum memory requirements. The compact design of an 8085 microprocessor system, on the other hand, is best suited for applications that have hardware space restrictions.

This chapter applied the previously learned concepts of the 8085 to the study of the 6800 microprocessor. Many of the concepts of microprocessor architecture, memory and I/O interface, instructions sets, and interrupt structures can be directly used with the 6800, with some differences in the implementation of a particular concept. This is true in the study of most 8-bit microprocessors, as will be seen in the following chapter.

REVIEW QUESTIONS AND PROBLEMS

1. Compare the differences between the 6800 MPU and the 8085 microprocessor in terms of
    (a) The interrupt structure.
    (b) The control signals.
    (c) The internal arrangement of registers.

2. Describe the sequence of events that occurs when
    (a) The 6800 MPU is reset.
    (b) The 6800 MPU receives an interrupt over the $\overline{\text{NMI}}$ line.
    (c) The 6800 MPU executes a SWI instruction.
    (d) The 6800 MPU receives an interrupt over the $\overline{\text{IRQ}}$ line.

3. Which of the following interrupts will be acknowledged if the I_M bit is SET?
(a) RESET (b) NMI (c) SWI (d) IRQ

4. Expand the 6800 microprocessor system shown in Figure 15-7 to include an additional 6820 PIA, 6850 ACIA, 6810 RAM, and 6830 ROM. Describe the addressing scheme used, and draw a memory map of the expanded system.

5. Compare each bit of the 6800 CCR with each flag in the 8085 PSW. Discuss the similarities and differences.

6. What is the purpose of the index register (IX)? Give a few examples of instructions that use the IX.

7. What is an addressing mode? How many modes of addressing does the 6800 have?

8. Assemble the instruction ORAA in each mode of addressing. Explain the operation of the ORAA instruction in each mode.

9. How is the offset used in the indexed mode of addressing? Give examples.

10. What is relative addressing? How does it compare with absolute addressing?

11. Hand-assemble the following 6800 program:

```
ACIAC    EQU    $4000
ACIAD    EQU    $4001
TEMP     EQU    $0005

         ORG    $2000

START    LDAA   #$03
         STAA   ACIAC
         LDX    TEMP
LOOP     LDAA   ACIAC
         RORA
         BCC    LOOP
         LDAB   ACIAD
         STAB   5,X
         DECB
         BNE    STOP
         BRA    LOOP
         STAA   TEMP
STOP     BRA    STOP
```

12. Write a program (using the 6800 instruction set) to fill memory locations $E000–$F000 with the byte $55. Begin the program at location $1000.

CHAPTER 16

A Survey of the Z80 Microprocessor*

Introduction

The objective of Chapter 15 was to emphasize that the 6800 microprocessor uses the same concepts that hold for all microprocessor-based systems, with differences in the details of their operation. This chapter examines the characteristics of a different family of microprocessors, the Z80 family. The concepts required to understand the Z80's operation remain the same, even though there are major differences between the 8085 family and the Z80 family of microprocessors. This chapter will therefore compare the Z80 microprocessor with the 8085 microprocessor.

Z80 Architecture and Pin Configuration

The design of the Z80 microprocessor is based on the architecture and design of the 8085 microprocessor's predecessor, the 8080. Like the 8085, the Z80 was designed to be upward compatible with the 8080's instruction set; that is, the Z80 can execute all of the 8080's instructions and also has several of its

---

*Z80 is a trademark of Zilog, Inc.

own instructions that cannot be executed by the 8080 (or 8085). Thus the Z80 is also upward compatible with the 8085 microprocessor's instruction set, with the exception of the RIM and SIM instructions.

The Z80 microprocessor also offers the user the eight interrupt levels (vectors) RST 0 through RST 7 defined in the 8080/8085 interrupt structure. The Z80 does not, however, support the 8085 TRAP, RST 5.5, RST 6.5, and RST 7.5 interrupt vectors, but it does include a separate nonmaskable interrupt (NMI) vector for high-priority interrupts.

Figure 16-1 illustrates the architecture of the Z80 microprocessor. Notice that the design of the Z80 follows the conventional approach used in the design of most microprocessors; that is, the Z80 contains an instruction register (IR) to hold the instructions fetched from memory, an instruction decoder and control unit (IR decoder and CU) to decode and execute the instructions, an internal register set (register array) to hold temporary data and provide address control, and an arithmetic/logic unit (ALU) to handle the arithmetic and logic CPU operations. Also notice that the Z80 microprocessor, unlike the 8085, requires an external clock pulse for the basic timing of the CPU. The Z80 microprocessor does not have a multiplexed address and data bus like the 8085's but does have a separate 8-bit data bus and a 16-bit address bus, along with thirteen control signals. The functions of these control signals are best described by examining the pin configuration of the Z80 microprocessor shown in Figure 16-2.

A_0-A_{15} (*address bus*): These sixteen lines make up the address bus of the Z80 CPU and allow the Z80 to access 65,536 bytes of memory. These lines

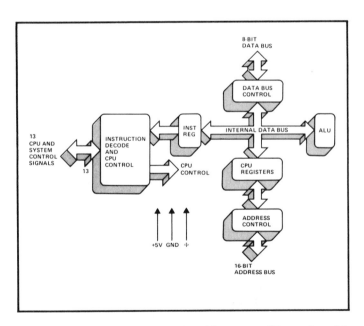

**FIGURE 16-1. Z80 microprocessor architecture. (Reproduced by permission ©
1983 Zilog, Inc. This material shall not be reproduced without the written consent
of Zilog, Inc.)**

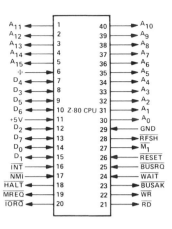

provide the same function as do the 8085's address lines and are tristated for DMA operations. An I/O address also appears on the lower half of the bus (A_0–A_7) during I/O operations. However, unlike the 8085, there is no address mirror on the upper half (A_8–A_{15}) of the address bus.

D_0–D_7 (*data bus*): These eight lines make up the data bus of the Z80 CPU and provide an external path for the transfer of instructions and data to and from the CPU. They provide the same functions as the 8085's data lines and are tristated for DMA operations.

$\overline{M1}$ (*machine cycle 1*): This line indicates to an external device that the CPU's current machine cycle is the op code fetch cycle of an instruction execution. This line provides the same function as do the 8085's data bus status lines, S_1 and S_0 (see Table 2-3), when both lines are at the one state.

$\overline{MREQ}$ (*memory request*): This line indicates that the address bus holds a valid address for a memory device during a read or write operation. This line provides the same function as does the 8085 $IO/\overline{M}$ line in the zero state. The $\overline{MREQ}$ line is also tristated for DMA operations.

$\overline{IORQ}$ (*input/output request*): This line is similar to the $\overline{MREQ}$ line except that it indicates that the address on the lower half of the address bus is for a read or write operation to an I/O device. This line is also active when an interrupt is acknowledged so that a interrupt vector can be placed on the data bus. The $\overline{IORQ}$ line is therefore similar to the 8085's $IO/\overline{M}$ line in the one state and also provides the function of the 8085's $\overline{INTA}$ line. The $\overline{IORQ}$ line is tristated for DMA operations.

$\overline{RD}$ (*read*): This line indicates to an I/O or memory device that the CPU wants to read data and that the data bus is in the input mode. This line provides the same function as does the $\overline{RD}$ line of the 8085 and is tristated for DMA operations.

$\overline{WR}$ (*write*): This line indicates to an I/O or memory device that the CPU wants to write data and that the data bus is in the output mode. This line provides the same function as the $\overline{\text{WR}}$ line of the 8085 and can be tristated for DMA operations.

RFSH (*refresh*): This line indicates that the lower 7 bits of the address bus contain a refresh address for dynamic memories and that the current $\overline{\text{MREQ}}$ signal should be used to do a refresh read to all dynamic memories. The 8085 has no equivalent signal.

HALT (*halt state*): This line is active when the CPU executes a HLT instruction. In the halt state the CPU can be interrupted over the $\overline{\text{NMI}}$ interrupt line or the $\overline{\text{INT}}$ interrupt line (if enabled). The CPU executes NOPs while in the halt state to maintain memory refresh activity. The 8085 has no equivalent signal.

WAIT (*wait*): This line is activated by a slow memory or I/O device and is used to put the CPU into a wait state. The CPU will remain in a wait state as long as this signal is active. This line is similar to the READY line of the 8085.

INT (*interrupt request*): When the Z80 is programmed for interrupt mode 0, this interrupt line functions in a manner similar to the 8085's INTR line. Activation of this line in a different mode causes the CPU to react in a different manner. The three different interrupt modes will be examined in Section 16-3. An interrupt request on this line will be honored only at the end of the current instruction if interrupts are enabled.

NMI (*nonmaskable interrupt*): This interrupt line has a higher priority than does $\overline{\text{INT}}$ and is always recognized at the end of the current instruction. Interrupts are always acknowledged over this line and are not affected by the EI or DI instructions. This line is similar in function to the 8085's TRAP line except that on receiving a $\overline{\text{NMI}}$ interrupt, the CPU vectors to location 0066H instead of 0024H (TRAP).

RESET (*reset*): When activated, this line initializes the CPU as follows: the program counter is cleared; interrupts are initialized to mode 0 and disabled; and the special-purpose registers I and R (to be discussed in Section 16-5) are cleared. This line is similar to the $\overline{\text{RESET IN}}$ line of the 8085.

BUSRQ (*bus request*): This line is used to put the CPU's data bus, address bus, and control signals into a high-impedance state for DMA operations. This line has a higher priority than does $\overline{\text{INT}}$ or $\overline{\text{NMI}}$ and is always recognized at the end of the current machine cycle. This line provides the same function as the 8085's HOLD line.

BUSAK (*bus acknowledge*): When this line is active, it indicates that the CPU's buses are now in a high impedance state and available for DMA. This line is similar to the 8085's HLDA line.

Φ (clock): This input to the Z80 is the system clock for timing and must be provided by an external clock generator. The frequency of the clock establishes the CPU's operating speed. Because the 8085 has an internal clock generator, there is no equivalent line in the 8085.

Because both the 8085 and the Z80 microprocessors have similar $\overline{\text{RD}}$ and $\overline{\text{WR}}$ signals—the 8085 memory and I/O control signal—IO/$\overline{\text{M}}$ can easily be generated from the Z80 control signals $\overline{\text{MREQ}}$ and $\overline{\text{IORQ}}$ by implementing the circuit for the following truth table:

MREQ	IORQ	IO/M
0	0	X (invalid)
0	1	0 (memory)
1	0	1 (I/O)
1	1	X (no operation)

From the truth table: IO/$\overline{M}$ = $\overline{MREQ}$ + IORQ.

From the description of the Z80 pin functions, one can see that the Z80 microprocessor offers many functions similar to those of the 8085 microprocessor. Among them are a similar but more extended interrupt structure, DMA facilities, and wait states. The major difference between the Z80 and 8085 microprocessors is in the interface among the CPU, the memory and I/O chips in a system, the extended interrupt structure of the Z80, and the extended instruction set.

16-3

Z80 Interrupt Structure

As indicated in the previous section, the Z80 CPU has two interrupt lines, called $\overline{NMI}$ and $\overline{INT}$. The $\overline{NMI}$ (nonmaskable interrupt) line, as the name suggests, initiates an interrupt to the CPU, regardless of the interrupt state; that is, interrupts on the $\overline{NMI}$ line cannot be disabled. On receiving an interrupt on this line, the CPU completes execution of the current instruction and then vectors to location 0066H to restart execution. It was also pointed out in the previous section that the $\overline{NMI}$ interrupt is similar to the TRAP·interrupt of the 8085 microprocessor and can be used for high-priority service requests.

The $\overline{INT}$ (interrupt request) line of the Z80 microprocessor can function in one of three interrupt modes—0, 1, and 2—which are initiated by the execution of the extended instructions—IM 0, IM 1, and IM 2, respectively.

Upon reset, the Z80 microprocessor is automatically initialized to interrupt mode 0, which is called the *8080 mode*. In this mode the interrupt structure is exactly the same as the 8085's predecessor, the 8080's interrupt structure. Because interrupts on the INTR line of the 8085 are modeled after the 8080's interrupt structure, the Z80 $\overline{INT}$ line functions in a manner similar to the 8085's INTR line in interrupt mode 0. In this mode, all eight levels are available for implementation (RST 0 through RST 7), and a circuit similar to the one discussed in Chapter 6 can be used to provide the CPU with the RST n vector. But because the Z80 does not have an interrupt acknowledge line similar in function to the 8085's $\overline{INTA}$ line, the following procedure is used to latch the RST n vector onto the data bus when an interrupt is acknowledged in mode 0.

Recall from the pin description in Section 16-2 that the $\overline{IORQ}$ line is active when an interrupt is acknowledged. However, $\overline{IORQ}$ alone cannot be used to latch the RST n vector onto the data bus, as $\overline{IORQ}$ is also active during regular I/O cycles. But when an interrupt is acknowledged in mode 0, the CPU is ready to fetch an instruction (RST n), which causes the $\overline{M1}$ line to become active.

Thus, only when an interrupt is acknowledged are $\overline{M1}$ and $\overline{IORQ}$ active at the same time. These two lines can then be gated to generate an interrupt acknowledge line similar to the 8085's $\overline{INTA}$ line. The equation for the circuit can be obtained from the following truth table:

$\overline{IORQ}$	$\overline{M1}$	$\overline{INTA}$
0	0	0
0	1	1
1	0	1
1	1	1

From the truth table: $\overline{INTA} = \overline{IORQ} + \overline{M1}$.

When the Z80 microprocessor is programmed for interrupt mode 1 (through the execution of the IM 1 instruction), the CPU automatically vectors to location 0038H on receiving and acknowledging an interrupt on the $\overline{INT}$ line. The process is similar to an RST 7 instruction jammed onto the data bus during an interrupt acknowledge. No external hardware is required to implement this mode of interrupt. This mode is especially convenient in microcomputer designs that require only a single interrupt level with a minimum amount of additional hardware.

The Z80 microprocessor's interrupt mode 2 is entered by the execution of the IM 2 instruction. In this mode, the CPU will make an indirect call to a programmed address on acknowledging an interrupt on the $\overline{INT}$ line. This mode of interrupts is unique to the Z80 microprocessor and is also known as the *Z80 mode*. In this mode the Z80 microprocessor is usually connected to I/O devices belonging to the Z80 family.

In interrupt mode 2, a special-purpose register in the Z80 CPU, called the *interrupt register* (I), is used to hold the most significant byte of an interrupt restart address vector. This is the most significant byte of the address that the CPU will vector to when it receives an interrupt on the $\overline{INT}$ line in mode 2. The least significant byte of the restart address is provided by the interrupting I/O device. This I/O device is usually a programmable chip (similar to the 8255 and 8251 discussed in Chapter 7) belonging to the Z80 microprocessor family (see Section 16-4). The Z80 family of integrated circuits, such as the Z80-SIO, Z80-PIO, Z80-CTC, and Z80-DMA, all have the capability to offer this vector during an interrupt acknowledge cycle. This scheme allows for up to 256 levels of interrupts in a Z80 system.

The Z80 interrupt mode, or mode 2, also allows for a technique known as *daisy chain interrupt servicing* to provide priority interrupts and interrupt nesting. This type of interrupt servicing can be conducted only on I/O devices belonging to the Z80 family.

Most I/O devices in the Z80 family, such as the ones mentioned earlier, have two interrupt enable lines, called *interrupt enable input* (IEI) and *interrupt enable output* (IEO). These two lines are used to form a "daisy chain" connection for priority interrupt control. IEI must be high in order to allow the I/O device to interrupt the CPU over the $\overline{INT}$ line. The state of IEO will always be equal to the state of IEI except when the I/O device interrupts the CPU and IEO goes into the low state.

A *priority interrupt daisy chain* is formed by connecting the IEO and IEI lines of the I/O devices, as shown in Figure 16-3. Each interrupting I/O device is called *channel* and has a direct *OR-TIE* connection (not shown) to the CPU's $\overline{INT}$ line. Each I/O device also provides the low-order interrupt vector during the interrupt acknowledge cycle. The manner in which this configuration can provide priority and nested interrupts can be explained, with reference to Figure 16-3, as follows:

1. All four channels have their IEO and IEI lines conditioned high before any interrupts occur. Notice that if channel 0 interrupts the CPU, its IEO line will go low, and consequently all other devices in the chain will have their IEO and IEI lines at the low state, thereby blocking their interrupts. Channel 0 thus has the highest priority, and channel 3 has the lowest priority in the chain.
2. Channel 2 requests an interrupt and is acknowledged. The IEO line of channel 2 goes low and prevents channel 3 from interrupting the CPU. Notice that interrupts can still be generated by channels 0 and 1.
3. While channel 2 is being serviced, channel 1 interrupts, and because channel 1 has a higher priority, the interrupt is acknowledged, service is suspended for channel 2, and channel 1 is now under service.
4. When service for channel 1 is completed, a RETI (return from interrupt) instruction is executed at the end of the service routine, which causes the IEO line of channel 1 to go to the high state and resumes the execution of channel 2's service routine.
5. The service routine for channel 2 is completed on execution of another RETI instruction, which brings the IEO line of channel 2 back to the high state, thus enabling channel 3's interrupt capability.

Thus it can be seen that the Z80 microprocessor gives the user a flexible and powerful interrupt structure while maintaining compatibility with the 8085 INTR structure. Mode 0 can be used to maintain 8085 compatibility, and modes 1 and

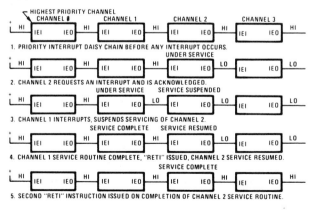

FIGURE 16-3. Daisy chain interrupt servicing. (Reproduced by permission © 1983 Zilog, Inc. This material shall not be reproduced without the written consent of Zilog, Inc.)

2 can be used in other applications in which simplicity of hardware or a complex interrupt structure is desired. The $\overline{\text{NMI}}$ interrupt provides some compatibility with the 8085's TRAP interrupt, though the restart addresses are different. The Z80 does not, however, have interrupt capabilities similar to the RST 5.5, RST 6.5, and RST 7.5 levels of the 8085 microprocessor.

16-4

Z80 Microprocessor System

The manner in which the Z80 microprocessor interacts with memory and I/O devices is best seen by studying a typical Z80 microprocessor system. Figure 16-4 illustrates a minimum Z80-based microprocessor system with RAM, ROM, serial I/O, and parallel I/O. The interface among memory, I/O, and the CPU is accomplished by an 8-bit data bus, a 16-bit address bus, and several control signals. Notice that an external clock generator, the MC4024, is required for a clock for the Z80 microprocessor. Also note that the minimum system shown in Figure 16-4 does not incorporate direct memory access.

Memory Interface

The Z80-based microprocessor system illustrated in Figure 16-4 has 2K bytes of ROM and 2K bytes of RAM provided by the 2716-ROM and 6116-RAM chips, respectively. The 2716-ROM has a single chip select line, $\overline{\text{CS}}$, which is used to enable the chip, and an output enable line, $\overline{\text{OE}}$, which is used to load the ROM data onto the data bus. The 6116-RAM also has the $\overline{\text{CS}}$ and $\overline{\text{OE}}$ lines, which serve the same purpose, and includes a write enable, $\overline{\text{WE}}$, line to allow data to be latched into an addressed memory location. Both the 2716-ROM and the 6116-RAM have eight data lines to allow the storage of 8-bit data and eleven address lines to address 2048 memory locations. Linear addressing is used to select either the RAM or the ROM.

Table 16-1 shows the memory addressing scheme. Because the Z80 address lines A_0–A_{10} are used to access the respective chips' memory locations, address line A_{11} is used to select either RAM or ROM. When addresses 0000H through 07FFH appear on the address bus, address line A_{11} is at the logic-zero state. Because address line A_{11} is connected directly to the 2716-ROM's chip select line ($\overline{\text{CS}}$), it will be enabled during this time. The next memory location in sequence after 07FFH is 0800H. When the address 0800H appears on the address bus, address line A_{11} is now at the logic-one state, and the 2716-ROM is now disabled. Because address line A_{11} is connected to the chip select line ($\overline{\text{CS}}$) of the 6116-RAM chip through an inverter, it will be enabled during this time. RAM is thus selected from addresses 0800H to 0FFFH. The Z80 address lines A_{12} through A_{15} are not included in the addressing scheme, and so foldback occurs from memory locations 1000H through FFFFH.

Once the respective chip (ROM or RAM) is selected by an address on the address bus, the Z80 memory control lines, $\overline{\text{MREQ}}$, $\overline{\text{RD}}$, and $\overline{\text{WR}}$, are used to establish the direction of data flow into or out of a selected memory chip. Because the Z80 CPU performs a memory read operation when $\overline{\text{MREQ}}$ and $\overline{\text{RD}}$ are active, these two lines are gated together (through an OR gate) and are

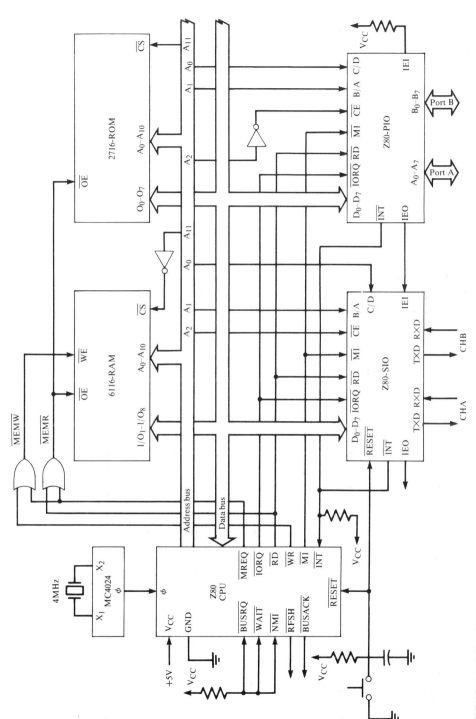

FIGURE 16-4. Z80-based microprocessor system.

TABLE 16-1. Memory Addressing Scheme

				Chip select →	Connected to 2716 and 6116 address lines											Location	
A_{15}	A_{14}	A_{13}	A_{12}	A_{11}	A_{10}	A_9	A_8	A_7	A_6	A_5	A_4	A_3	A_2	A_1	A_0		
0	0	0	0	0	0	0	0	0	0	0	0	0	0	0	0	0000H	⎫
.	.	.	.	.	.	.	.	.	.	.	.	.	.	.	.	.	2716 ROM
0	0	0	0	0	1	1	1	1	1	1	1	1	1	1	1	07FFH	⎭
0	0	0	0	1	0	0	0	0	0	0	0	0	0	0	0	0800H	⎫
.	.	.	.	.	.	.	.	.	.	.	.	.	.	.	.	.	6116 RAM
0	0	0	0	1	1	1	1	1	1	1	1	1	1	1	1	0FFFH	⎭
0	0	0	1	0	0	0	0	0	0	0	0	0	0	0	0	1000H	⎫
.	.	.	.	.	.	.	.	.	.	.	.	.	.	.	.	.	Foldback
1	1	1	1	1	1	1	1	1	1	1	1	1	1	1	1	FFFFH	⎭

used to load data from a selected memory chip onto the data bus. The ORed combination of these two lines produce the standard $\overline{\text{MEMR}}$ signal (see Figure 2-13) that is connected to the output enable ($\overline{\text{OE}}$) lines of both chips.

Similarly, when the 6116-RAM is selected for a memory write operation, the Z80 memory control lines, $\overline{\text{MREQ}}$ and $\overline{\text{WR}}$, are active. These two lines are ORed together to produce the standard $\overline{\text{MEMW}}$ signal (see Figure 2-13) that is active only when both $\overline{\text{MREQ}}$ and $\overline{\text{WR}}$ are active. The $\overline{\text{MEMW}}$ signal is connected to the write enable ($\overline{\text{WE}}$) line of the 6116-RAM to allow data to be loaded from the data bus and into the chip.

Note that the interface between the Z80 microprocessor and memory is similar to the 8085 memory interface discussed in Chapter 4. The only difference between the 8085 interface and the Z80 interface is in using the memory control lines to select the chips for read or write operations; however, this difference is easily resolved by using the appropriate combinational logic.

I/O Interface

The Z80-based microprocessor system shown in Figure 16-4 includes two chips from the Z80 family that provide the basic serial and parallel I/O interface for the system. These chips are the Z80-SIO and the Z80-PIO for serial and parallel I/O, respectively. The function of the Z80-SIO and the Z80-PIO are similar to the functions of the 8251 and the 8255 programmable chips, discussed in Chapter 7. The two I/O chips also incorporate the interrupt capabilities for daisy chaining and mode 2 interrupts, as discussed in the previous section. But a detailed investigation into the operation of these chips is beyond the scope of this chapter, and so only the factors influencing the interface between the I/O chips and the Z80 will be examined.

TABLE 16-2. I/O Addressing Scheme

A_7	A_6	A_5	A_4	A_3	$\overline{\text{CS}}$ ↓ A_2	$\text{B}/\overline{\text{A}}$ ↓ A_1	$\text{C}/\overline{\text{D}}$ ↓ A_0	Port	
0	0	0	0	0	0	0	0	00H	
0	0	0	0	0	0	0	1	01H	Z80-SIO
0	0	0	0	0	0	1	0	02H	
0	0	0	0	0	0	1	1	03H	
0	0	0	0	0	1	0	0	04H	
0	0	0	0	0	1	0	1	05H	Z80-PIO
0	0	0	0	0	1	1	0	06H	
0	0	0	0	0	1	1	1	07H	
0	0	0	0	1	0	0	0	08H	
.	.	.	.	.	.	.	.	.	
.	.	.	.	.	.	.	.	.	Foldback
.	.	.	.	.	.	.	.	.	
1	1	1	1	1	1	1	1	FFH	

Both I/O chips are connected together to form a priority interrupt daisy chain. Because the PIO is first in the chain, it has a higher priority than the SIO. Both chips have an 8-bit interface (D_0–D_7) with the Z80 data bus, and the control lines $\overline{IORQ}$, $\overline{RD}$, and $\overline{M1}$ provide the necessary signals to control the flow of data to and from the chips. Notice that a $\overline{WR}$ line is not required, as both chips have the necessary logic to assume a write mode when the $\overline{RD}$ line is inactive. The SIO has an additional $\overline{RESET}$ line that is connected to the system's $\overline{RESET}$ line.

The chip select line ($\overline{CS}$) on both the PIO and SIO is used to select the correct chip for I/O operations. Both the SIO and the PIO are two-channel devices. That is, the SIO has two serial channels, and the PIO has two parallel channels (ports). These ports are accessed by the $B/\overline{A}$ line on each chip. The $C/\overline{D}$ line (as in the 8251 USART) is used to program the chip, obtain status, (control mode), or transfer data to and from the selected channel (data mode). Table 16-2 illustrates the I/O addressing scheme used to select each chip for I/O operations. Notice that each chip occupies four I/O addresses and that address lines A_3 through A_7 are not involved in the addressing scheme, as linear addressing is used.

Address line A_2 is used to select the Z80-SIO when at the low state. Address lines A_1 and A_0 are tied to the $B/\overline{A}$ and $C/\overline{D}$ lines, respectively, and, as mentioned before, select a different internal register or port for each state. Thus in Table 16-2, assuming that the unused address lines (A_3–A_7) are zeros, the SIO is addressed as ports 00H, 01H, 02H, and 03H.

The Z80-PIO is enabled when address line A_2 is at the one state, as this address line is connected to the PIO chip select line ($\overline{CS}$) through an inverter. As in the SIO addressing scheme, address lines A_1 and A_0 are connected to the PIO's $B/\overline{A}$ and $C/\overline{D}$ lines, respectively, to allow access to the PIO's internal registers or I/O ports. With reference to Table 16-2, assuming that the unused address lines (A_3–A_7) are zeros, the PIO is addressed as ports 04H, 05H, 06H, and 07H.

Because of the linear addressing scheme used, I/O address foldback will occur from addresses 08H through FFH.

With the exception of the interrupts, it can be seen from Figure 16-4 that the interface between the Z80 microprocessor and its family of I/O chips is similar to the interface used to incorporate programmable chips into an 8085 system (see Chapter 7). Also note that because the Z80-PIO and Z80-SIO chips are designed as part of the Z80 family of integrated circuits, the interface between the Z80 microprocessor and these support chips requires a minimum amount of additional hardware.

16-5

Z80 Instruction Set

From previous sections it was seen that from a hardware perspective, the Z80 microprocessor is not completely compatible with the 8085 microprocessor. The Z80 microprocessor was, however, designed to be 100 percent software compatible with the 8085 microprocessor's predecessor, the 8080. The Z80 microprocessor is *almost* 100 percent software compatible with the 8085. That is, the Z80 can decode and execute all of the 8085 instructions, with the exception of RIM and SIM. This is understandable, as the RIM and SIM instructions are related to the SID, SOD, RST 5.5, RST 6.5, and RST 7.5 lines of the 8085 microprocessor which do not exist on the Z80. Besides being able to execute the 8085's instructions, the Z80 microprocessor also has several of its own instructions and is therefore considered to be upward compatible with the 8085. The Z80 can execute any 8085 program that does not contain the RIM and SIM instructions; however, the 8085 can execute only those Z80 programs that do not contain the extended instructions unique to the Z80 microprocessor. In all, the Z80 microprocessor can decode and execute a total of 652 instructions, as compared with the 246 of the 8085 microprocessor—244 of the 8085 instructions plus 408 additional or *extended instructions*.

Because the Z80 microprocessor maintains compatibility with the 8085 instruction set, it must include a set of internal registers similar in function to the 8085's register set. Figure 16-5 illustrates the Z80's register set. Notice that the Z80 microprocessor has all the 8085 registers: A, B, C, D, E, H, L, SP, and PC. The Z80 also has several other registers that can be accessed by the extended instructions of the Z80's instruction set. Among these additional registers is an alternate register set consisting of eight 8-bit registers: A', B', C', D', E', H', and L'. The alternate register set is designed to hold the contents of the main register set during interrupt processing, which eliminates the need of PUSHing and POPing the contents of the CPU registers on the stack during interrupt processing and consequently speeds program execution.

Two more 8-bit registers are used for interrupts and memory refresh. As

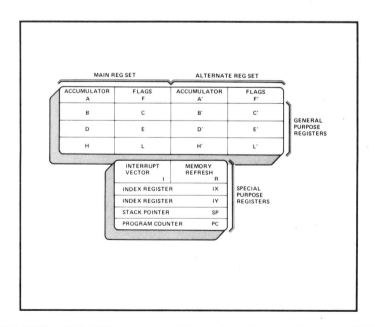

FIGURE 16-5. Z80 CPU registers. (Reproduced by permission © 1983 Zilog, Inc. This material shall not be reproduced without the written consent of Zilog, Inc.)

discussed in Section 16-3, the interrupt vector (I) register is used in mode 2 interrupts to hold the most significant byte of an interrupt vector restart address. The memory refresh (R) register is used to provide a refresh address for dynamic memories during a Z80 memory refresh cycle; this register works in conjunction with the $\overline{\text{RFSH}}$ line discussed in Section 16-2. Both of these registers can be accessed by some of the extended Z80 instructions.

The Z80 microprocessor register set also includes two 16-bit index registers, IX and IY. These index registers increase the flexibility of accessing memory locations using pointers. Recall that the 8085 microprocessor is severely limited in its indexed addressing, owing to its single index register (data counter), HL. This is evident in programs that require several pointers to certain areas of memory. The two index registers, along with the extensive instructions that support them, give the Z80 microprocessor a powerful tool for developing efficient software.

The Z80 flag register (F) has the same configuration and bit definition as its 8085 counterpart does, with one exception. The parity flag is also used to signal a two's complement overflow, whereas the parity flag of the 8085 microprocessor is not affected by an arithmetic overflow condition.

Even though the Z80 is capable of decoding and executing almost all of the 8085's instructions, the instruction set of the two microprocessors is not compatible at the assembly language programming level. The reason is that the Z80 designers chose not to use the 8085 mnemonics but, instead, designed their own mnemonic instruction set. The function of the operation codes remain the same, however; only their mnemonic representation is different. Table 16-3 is a reproduction of the 8080/8085 instruction set summary (see Appendix A) in operation code sequence but shows each op code represented in Z80 mnemonics. The RIM and SIM instructions have not been included in the table, as they cannot be decoded by the Z80.

Note in Table 16-3 that the mnemonic MOV (move) has been replaced with the mnemonic LD (load) but that the operation codes and their functions remain the same. Similarly, the mnemonics DCX and DCR have been replaced with the mnemonic DEC, and the mnemonics ORA and ORI have been replaced with the mnemonic OR. Also notice that the pseudoregister M has been replaced by (HL). For example, DEC HL (op code 2B, 8085 mnemonic DCX H) reads "decrement the contents of register pair HL," and DEC (HL) (op code 35, 8085 mnemonic DCR M) reads "decrement the memory location pointed to by register pair HL." In general, parentheses around a register or register pair used as an operand do not specify the contents of that register but, rather, the contents of a memory location or I/O port whose address is stored in that particular register. All the "jump" (JMP, JZ, JC, JNZ, JNC, and so on) mnemonics have been replaced by a single mnemonic, JP, and the "condition" is now written in the operand field. If Table 16-3 is compared entry for entry with the table in Appendix A, one can see still more examples of the differences between the Z80 and the 8085 mnemonics. But the difference in mnemonic instructions does not create any problem in regard to program execution, as the machine codes are the same, and a program written with 8085 mnemonics executes in exactly the same way as does the same program written with Z80 mnemonics. The difference does, however, create a problem for the assembly language programmer, who must learn a new set of mnemonic instructions and use a different assembler—one that can assemble Z80 mnemonics.

The instruction set shown in Table 16-3 shows only the 8085 operation codes represented by Z80 instructions. It does not list the extended Z80 instructions mentioned earlier in this section. In Table 16-3 notice that there are twelve op codes that are not represented by mnemonic instructions—08, 10, 18, 20, 28, 30, 38, CB, D9, DD, ED, and FD. These instructions (with the exception of 20, RIM and 30, SIM) would function as NOPs (no operation) if they were decoded and executed by the 8085 microprocessor. Rather, the designers of the 8085 simply chose not to implement these op codes for the 8085 microprocessor. The Z80 microprocessor does, however, decode and interpret these unimplemented op codes that make up part of its extended instruction set. The following lists the Z80 interpretation of eight of the twelve op codes mentioned earlier:

Op code	Mnemonic		Description
08	EX	AF,AF'	Exchange AF with AF'
10 dd	DJNZ	dd	Decrement B and conditionally jump
18 dd	JR	dd	Jump unconditionally
20 dd	JR	NZ,dd	Jump on nonzero
28 dd	JR	Z,dd	Jump on zero
30 dd	JR	NC,dd	Jump on no carry
38 dd	JR	C,dd	Jump on carry
D9	EXX		Exchange B, C, D, E, H, L with alt. set

In this table, op codes 08 and D9 are interpreted by the Z80 microprocessor as exchange instructions between the main register set and the alternate register set. Op code 08 causes the Z80 to exchange the contents of the accumulator and flags, AF (PSW in 8085 mnemonics) with the accumulator and flags in the alternate register set, AF'. Similarly, op code D9 exchanges all of the remaining registers in the two register sets.

The remaining six instructions in the list are known as *relative jump instructions*. Relative jump instructions differ significantly from the conventional (absolute) jump instructions that are part of the 8085 instruction set. Relative jump instructions are two bytes long, as compared with the three bytes required for an absolute jump. The reason for this is that an absolute jump instruction requires an absolute address that is loaded into the PC, whereas a relative jump instruction requires only an 8-bit offset (or displacement) that is added to the contents of the PC to change its value and, hence, transfer control to another memory location. This offset can be either positive or negative to allow the PC's contents to be increased or decreased by a maximum of + 127 or − 128, respectively. For example, if the PC's current value is 1003H and control is to be transferred to location 1007H, then 04H must be added to the PC in order to do so; the offset for the relative jump instruction is then 04H. If, however, the PC's current value is 100FH and control is to be transferred to location 1007H, then the negative displacement F8H (− 8) must be added to the PC's contents to reduce its value to 1007H; the offset for the relative jump instruction in this case then is F8H.

TABLE 16-3. 8085 Instruction Set with Z80 Mnemonics

Op code	Mnemonic	Op code	Mnemonic	Op code	Mnemonic	Op code	Mnemonic	Op code	Mnemonic	Op code	Mnemonic
00	NOP	2B	DEC HL	56	LD D,M	81	ADD A,C	AC	XOR H	D7	RST 2
01	LD BC,D16	2C	INC L	57	LD D,A	82	ADD A,D	AD	XOR L	D8	RET C
02	LD (BC),A	2D	DEC L	58	LD E,B	83	ADD A,E	AE	XOR (HL)	D9	—
03	INC BC	2E	LD L,D8	59	LD E,C	84	ADD A,H	AF	XOR A	DA	JP C,Adr
04	INC B	2F	CPL	5A	LD E,D	85	ADD A,L	B0	OR B	DB	IN A,(D8)
05	DEC B	30	—*	5B	LD E,E	86	ADD A,(HL)	B1	OR C	DC	CALL C,Adr
06	LD B,D8	31	LD SP,D16	5C	LD E,H	87	ADD A,A	B2	OR D	DD	—
07	RLCA	32	LD (Adr),A	5D	LD E,L	88	ADC A,B	B3	OR E	DE	SBC A,D8
08	—	33	INC SP	5E	LD E,(HL)	89	ADC A,C	B4	OR H	DF	RST 3
09	ADD HL,BC	34	INC (HL)	5F	LD E,A	8A	ADC A,D	B5	OR L	E0	RET PO
0A	LD A,(BC)	35	DEC (HL)	60	LD H,B	8B	ADC A,E	B6	OR (HL)	E1	POP HL
0B	DEC BC	36	LD (HL),D8	61	LD H,C	8C	ADC A,H	B7	OR A	E2	JP PO,Adr
0C	INC C	37	SCF	62	LD H,D	8D	ADC A,L	B8	CP B	E3	EX (SP),HL
0D	DEC C	38	—	63	LD H,E	8E	ADC A, (HL)	B9	CP C	E4	CALL PO,Adr
0E	LD C,D8	39	ADD HL,SP	64	LD H,H	8F	ADC A,A	BA	CP D	E5	PUSH HL
0F	RRCA	3A	LD A,(Adr)	65	LD H,L	90	SUB B	BB	CP E	E6	AND D8
10	—	3B	DEC SP	66	LD H,(HL)	91	SUB C	BC	CP H	E7	RST 4
11	LD DE,D16	3C	INC A	67	LD H,A	92	SUB D	BD	CP L	E8	RET PE
12	LD (DE),A	3D	DEC A	68	LD L,B	93	SUB E	BE	CP (HL)	E9	JP (HL)
13	INC DE	3E	LD A,D8	69	LD L,C	94	SUB H	BF	CP A	EA	JP PE,Adr
14	INC D	3F	CCF	6A	LD L,D	95	SUB L	C0	RET NZ	EB	EX DE,HL
15	DEC D	40	LD B,B	6B	LD L,E	96	SUB (HL)	C1	POP BC	EC	CALL PE,Adr

Hex	Instruction	Hex	Instruction	Hex	Instruction	Hex	Instruction
16	LD D,D8	41	LD B,C	97	SUB A	C2	JP NZ,Adr
17	RLA	42	LD B,D	98	SBC A,B	C3	JP Adr
18	—	43	LD B,E	99	SBC A,C	C4	CALL NZ,Adr
19	ADD HL,DE	44	LD B,H	9A	SBC A,D	C5	PUSH BC
1A	LD A,(DE)	45	LD B,L	9B	SBC A,E	C6	ADD A,D8
1B	DEC DE	46	LD B,(HL)	9C	SBC A,H	C7	RST 0
1C	INC E	47	LD B,A	9D	SBC A,L	C8	RET Z
1D	DEC E	48	LD C,B	9E	SBC A,(HL)	C9	RET
1E	LD E,D8	49	LD C,C	9F	SBC A,A	CA	JP Z,Adr
1F	RRA	4A	LD C,D	A0	AND B	CB	—
20	—*	4B	LD C,E	A1	AND C	CC	CALL Z,Adr
21	LD HL,D16	4C	LD C,H	A2	AND D	CD	CALL Adr
22	LD (Adr),HL	4D	LD C,L	A3	AND E	CE	ADC A,D8
23	INC HL	4E	LD C,(HL)	A4	AND H	CF	RST 1
24	INC H	4F	LD C,A	A5	AND L	D0	RET NC
25	DEC H	50	LD D,B	A6	AND (HL)	D1	POP DE
26	LD H,D8	51	LD D,C	A7	AND A	D2	JP NC,Adr
27	DAA	52	LD D,D	A8	XOR B	D3	OUT (D8),A
28	—	53	LD D,E	A9	XOR C	D4	CALL NC,Adr
29	ADD HL,HL	54	LD D,H	AA	XOR D	D5	PUSH DE
2A	LD HL,(Adr)	55	LD D,L	AB	XOR E	D6	SUB D8

Hex	Instruction	Hex	Instruction
6C	LD L,H	ED	—
6D	LD L,L	EE	XOR D8
6E	LD L,(HL)	EF	RST 5
6F	LD L,A	F0	RET P
70	LD (HL),B	F1	POP AF
71	LD (HL),C	F2	JP P,Adr
72	LD (HL),D	F3	DI
73	LD (HL),E	F4	CALL P,Adr
74	LD (HL),H	F5	PUSH AF
75	LD (HL),L	F6	OR D8
76	HALT	F7	RST 6
77	LD (HL),A	F8	RET M
78	LD A,B	F9	LD SP,HL
79	LD A,C	FA	JP M,Adr
7A	LD A,D	FB	EI
7B	LD A,E	FC	CALL M,Adr
7C	LD A,H	FD	—
7D	LD A,L	FE	CP D8
7E	LD A,(HL)	FF	RST 7
7F	LD A,A		
80	ADD A,B		

D8 = constant, or logical/arithmetic expression that evaluates to an 8-bit data quantity.

Adr = 16-bit address.

D16 = constant, or logical/arithmetic expression that evaluates to a 16-bit quantity.

* = 8085 RIM and SIM instructions (not shown).

An obvious advantage of relative jump instructions is that they are only two bytes long and thus take up less memory space than do the three-byte absolute jump instructions. Also, relative jump instructions are naturally relocatable, as no absolute address is specified. Programs written entirely with relative jump instructions can execute anywhere in memory without any modification. A disadvantage is that a relative jump instruction can cause the CPU only to transfer control to a memory location having an address that is $+127$ or -128 the PC's current value, which severely restricts the range of memory locations that a jump instruction can reference.

Out of the six relative jump instructions that the Z80 microprocessor can execute, one is an unconditional jump (op code 18), and the others are conditional. The DJNZ (op code 10) instruction decrements the contents of register B. If register B is not zero, then the jump will take place; otherwise control will transfer to the next instruction in sequence. The remaining four relative jump instructions (op codes 20, 28, 30, 38) are conditional on the zero and carry flags.

The remaining four op codes—CB, DD, ED, and FD—are also decoded and interpreted by the Z80 microprocessor as special instructions. However, the manner in which these op codes are decoded is somewhat different. When decoded, these instructions make up a major portion of the Z80's extended instruction set. It is beyond the scope of this chapter to investigate each instruction in the set, and so we shall attempt only to indicate some of the special features of certain instructions.

When the Z80 microprocessor decodes either one of the op codes—CB, DD, ED, or FD—it performs another instruction fetch cycle from the next consecutive memory location, to obtain another byte that functions as a subinstruction. This subinstruction is then decoded and executed in a manner similar to that of a normal instruction. This scheme theoretically allows the Z80 CPU to execute 256 additional instructions for each of the op codes, but not all subinstruction bytes are actually decoded.

Table 16-4 lists the subinstruction set for the ED op code. Note that each instruction operation code is made up of two bytes: the first byte is ED and is common to all the instructions listed in Table 16-4, and the second byte differs for each instruction. The instructions listed in Table 16-4 give the Z80 microprocessor several additional capabilities.

The ADC and SBC instructions listed in Table 16-4 allow the Z80 to perform 16-bit addition and subtraction. Recall that the 8085 can perform only 16-bit addition. Also, the Z80 microprocessor can perform memory block moves and memory block compares through the execution of the LDD . . . LDIR and CPD . . . CPIR instructions, whereas the 8085 must perform these operations through a sequence of instructions. The 8085 microprocessor is limited to only two instructions to access I/O ports in an isolated I/O addressing scheme: IN and OUT. Table 16-4 lists several I/O instructions that allow the input of data to any register from an input port whose address is stored in register C. Similarly, the OUT instructions can output data from any register to an output port whose address is stored in register C. Instructions IND . . . INIR and OUTD . . . OTIR allow input/output conditionally to repeat execution to and from memory

TABLE 16-4. Z80 Extended Instructions—ED Op Code

Op code	Mnemonic		Op code	Mnemonic	
ED 4A	ADC	HL,BC	ED AA	IND	
ED 5A	ADC	HL,DE	ED BA	INDR	
ED 6A	ADC	HL,HL	ED A2	INI	
ED 7A	ADC	HL,SP	ED B2	INIR	
ED 42	SBC	HL,BC			
ED 52	SBC	HL,DE	ED 79	OUT	(C),A
ED 62	SBC	HL,HL	ED 41	OUT	(C),B
ED 72	SBC	HL,SP	ED 49	OUT	(C),C
			ED 51	OUT	(C),D
ED A9	CPD		ED 59	OUT	(C),E
ED B9	CPDR		ED 61	OUT	(C),H
ED A1	CPI		ED 69	OUT	(C),L
ED B1	CPIR		ED AB	OUTD	
			ED BB	OTDR	
ED 46	IM	0	ED A3	OUTI	
ED 56	IM	1	ED B3	OTIR	
ED 5E	IM	2			
ED 4D	RETI		ED 57	LD	A,I
ED 45	RETN		ED 47	LD	I,A
			ED 5F	LD	A,R
ED 6F	RLD		ED 4F	LD	R,A
ED 67	RRD		ED 4B nnnn	LD	BC,(nnnn)
ED 44	NEG		ED 5B nnnn	LD	DE,(nnnn)
			ED 7B nnnn	LD	SP,(nnnn)
ED 78	IN	A,(C)	ED 43 nnnn	LD	(nnnn),BC
ED 40	IN	B,(C)	ED 53 nnnn	LD	(nnnn),DE
ED 48	IN	C,(C)	ED 73 nnnn	LD	(nnnn),SP
ED 50	IN	D,(C)	ED A8	LDD	
ED 58	IN	E,(C)	ED B8	LDDR	
ED 60	IN	H,(C)	ED A0	LDI	
ED 68	IN	L,(C)	ED B0	LDIR	

NOTE: nnnn = any 16-bit number

locations pointed to by register pair HL. Also included in Table 16-4 are instructions to access the special registers I (interrupt) and R (refresh), instructions to set the three modes of interrupts, interrupt return instructions, and 16-bit load instructions to allow data to be loaded to and from memory and a 16-bit register. Notice that all of these 16-bit load instructions, such as LD BC, (nnnn), require that the 16-bit address of the memory location follow the second op code. These instructions therefore occupy four bytes of memory.

Table 16-5 lists all the Z80 extended subinstructions that are decoded through the CB op code. These instructions are used in various bit manipulation operations. A major portion of this subinstruction set is made up of various bit test (BIT), bit reset (RES), and bit set (SET) instructions. Other instructions include rotate and shift operations on the CPU registers.

TABLE 16-5. Z80 Extended Instructions—CB Op Code

Op code	Mnemonic	Op code	Mnemonic	Op code	Mnemonic	Op code	Mnemonic
CB 47	BIT 0,A	CB 87	RES 0,A	CB C7	SET 0,A	CB 17	RL A
CB 4F	BIT 1,A	CB 8F	RES 1,A	CB CF	SET 1,A	CB 10	RL B
CB 57	BIT 2,A	CB 97	RES 2,A	CB D7	SET 2,A	CB 11	RL C
CB 5F	BIT 3,A	CB 9F	RES 3,A	CB DF	SET 3,A	CB 12	RL D
CB 67	BIT 4,A	CB A7	RES 4,A	CB E7	SET 4,A	CB 13	RL E
CB 6F	BIT 5,A	CB AF	RES 5,A	CB EF	SET 5,A	CB 14	RL H
CB 77	BIT 6,A	CB B7	RES 6,A	CB F7	SET 6,A	CB 15	RL L
CB 7F	BIT 7,A	CB BF	RES 7,A	CB FF	SET 7,A	CB 16	RL (HL)
CB 40	BIT 0,B	CB 80	RES 0,B	CB C0	SET 0,B		
CB 48	BIT 1,B	CB 88	RES 1,B	CB C8	SET 1,B	CB 1F	RR A
CB 50	BIT 2,B	CB 90	RES 2,B	CB D0	SET 2,B	CB 18	RR B
CB 58	BIT 3,B	CB 98	RES 3,B	CB D8	SET 3,B	CB 19	RR C
CB 60	BIT 4,B	CB A0	RES 4,B	CB E0	SET 4,B	CB 1A	RR D
CB 68	BIT 5,B	CB A8	RES 5,B	CB E8	SET 5,B	CB 1B	RR E
CB 70	BIT 6,B	CB B0	RES 6,B	CB F0	SET 6,B	CB 1C	RR H
CB 78	BIT 7,B	CB B8	RES 7,B	CB F8	SET 7,B	CB 1D	RR L
CB 41	BIT 0,C	CB 81	RES 0,C	CB C1	SET 0,C	CB 1E	RR (HL)
CB 49	BIT 1,C	CB 89	RES 1,C	CB C9	SET 1,C	CB 07	RLC A
CB 51	BIT 2,C	CB 91	RES 2,C	CB D1	SET 2,C	CB 00	RLC B
CB 59	BIT 3,C	CB 99	RES 3,C	CB D9	SET 3,C	CB 01	RLC C
CB 61	BIT 4,C	CB A1	RES 4,C	CB E1	SET 4,C	CB 02	RLC D
CB 69	BIT 5,C	CB A9	RES 5,C	CB E9	SET 5,C		

Code			Code			Code			Code		
CB 71	BIT	6,C	CB B1	RES	6,C	CB F1	SET	6,C	CB 03	RLC	E
CB 79	BIT	7,C	CB B9	RES	7,C	CB F9	SET	7,C	CB 04	RLC	H
CB 42	BIT	0,D	CB 82	RES	0,D	CB C2	SET	0,D	CB 05	RLC	L
CB 4A	BIT	1,D	CB 8A	RES	1,D	CB CA	SET	1,D	CB 06	RLC	(HL)
CB 52	BIT	2,D	CB 92	RES	2,D	CB D2	SET	2,D	CB 0F	RRC	A
CB 5A	BIT	3,D	CB 9A	RES	3,D	CB DA	SET	3,D	CB 08	RRC	B
CB 62	BIT	4,D	CB A2	RES	4,D	CB E2	SET	4,D	CB 09	RRC	C
CB 6A	BIT	5,D	CB AA	RES	5,D	CB EA	SET	5,D	CB 0A	RRC	D
CB 72	BIT	6,D	CB B2	RES	6,D	CB F2	SET	6,D	CB 0B	RRC	E
CB 7A	BIT	7,D	CB BA	RES	7,D	CB FA	SET	7,D	CB 0C	RRC	H
CB 43	BIT	0,E	CB 83	RES	0,E	CB C3	SET	0,E	CB 0D	RRC	L
CB 4B	BIT	1,E	CB 8B	RES	1,E	CB CB	SET	1,E	CB 0E	RRC	(HL)
CB 53	BIT	2,E	CB 93	RES	2,E	CB D3	SET	2,E	CB 27	SLA	A
CB 5B	BIT	3,E	CB 9B	RES	3,E	CB DB	SET	3,E	CB 20	SLA	B
CB 63	BIT	4,E	CB A3	RES	4,E	CB E3	SET	4,E	CB 21	SLA	C
CB 6B	BIT	5,E	CB AB	RES	5,E	CB EB	SET	5,E	CB 22	SLA	D
CB 73	BIT	6,E	CB B3	RES	6,E	CB F3	SET	6,E	CB 23	SLA	E
CB 7B	BIT	7,E	CB BB	RES	7,E	CB FB	SET	7,E	CB 24	SLA	H
CB 44	BIT	0,H	CB 84	RES	0,H	CB C4	SET	0,H	CB 25	SLA	L
CB 4C	BIT	1,H	CB 8C	RES	1,H	CB CC	SET	1,H	CB 26	SLA	(HL)
CB 54	BIT	2,H	CB 94	RES	2,H	CB D4	SET	2,H	CB 2F	SRA	A
CB 5C	BIT	3,H	CB 9C	RES	3,H	CB DC	SET	3,H			
CB 64	BIT	4,H	CB A4	RES	4,H	CB E4	SET	4,H			
CB 6C	BIT	5,H	CB AC	RES	5,H	CB EC	SET	5,H			

TABLE 16-5. (Continued)

TABLE 16-5. (Continued)

Op code	Mnemonic	Op code	Mnemonic	Op code	Mnemonic	Op code	Mnemonic
CB 74	BIT 6,H	CB B4	RES 6,H	CB F4	SET 6,H	CB 28	SRA B
CB 7C	BIT 7,H	CB BC	RES 7,H	CB FC	SET 7,H	CB 29	SRA C
CB 45	BIT 0,L	CB 85	RES 0,L	CB C5	SET 0,L	CB 2A	SRA D
CB 4D	BIT 1,L	CB 8D	RES 1,L	CB CD	SET 1,L	CB 2B	SRA E
CB 55	BIT 2,L	CB 95	RES 2,L	CB D5	SET 2,L	CB 2C	SRA H
CB 5D	BIT 3,L	CB 9D	RES 3,L	CB DD	SET 3,L	CB 2D	SRA L
CB 65	BIT 4,L	CB A5	RES 4,L	CB E5	SET 4,L	CB 2E	SRA (HL)
CB 6D	BIT 5,L	CB AD	RES 5,L	CB ED	SET 5,L		
CB 75	BIT 6,L	CB B5	RES 6,L	CB F5	SET 6,L	CB 3F	SRL A
CB 7D	BIT 7,L	CB BD	RES 7,L	CB FD	SET 7,L	CB 38	SRL B
CB 46	BIT 0,(HL)	CB 86	RES 0,(HL)	CB C6	SET 0,(HL)	CB 39	SRL C
CB 4E	BIT 1,(HL)	CB 8E	RES 1,(HL)	CB CE	SET 1,(HL)	CB 3A	SRL D
CB 56	BIT 2,(HL)	CB 96	RES 2,(HL)	CB D6	SET 2,(HL)	CB 3B	SRL E
CB 5E	BIT 3,(HL)	CB 9E	RES 3,(HL)	CB DE	SET 3,(HL)	CB 3C	SRL H
CB 66	BIT 4,(HL)	CB A6	RES 4,(HL)	CB E6	SET 4,(HL)	CB 3D	SRL L
CB 6E	BIT 5,(HL)	CB AE	RES 5,(HL)	CB EE	SET 5,(HL)	CB 3E	SRL (HL)
CB 76	BIT 6,(HL)	CB B6	RES 6,(HL)	CB F6	SET 6,(HL)		
CB 7E	BIT 7,(HL)	CB BE	RES 7,(HL)	CB FE	SET 7,(HL)		

The instructions—BIT, RES, and SET—are special-purpose instructions that allow the Z80 microprocessor to test the value of a specified bit, reset a specified bit, or set a specified bit, respectively. All three instructions have an operand in the form

P,R

where P is the bit position (0–7) to be operated upon and R is an 8-bit register or memory location. For example, the instruction

BIT 4,D

tests bit 4 in register D. The zero flag will be set if the value of the bit is zero and will be reset if the value of the bit is one. The contents of register D is not affected. Similarly,

SET 2,H

sets bit 2 in register H, and

RES 7,B

resets the most significant bit in register B. In accordance with Z80 mnemonic conventions, instructions that specify register (HL) imply the contents of the memory location pointed to by register pair HL.

The 8085 microprocessor is limited to performing rotate instructions on the contents of the accumulator only. As can be seen in Table 16-5, the Z80 has extended instructions that can perform similar operations on the other registers and memory locations. Also included are shift instructions SLA, SRA, and SRL. Unlike rotate instructions, the shift instructions discard bits shifted out and do not "rotate" the bits at either end of a specified register.

The two remaining opcodes—DD and FD are used to manipulate the index registers IX and IY, respectively. Tables 16-6 and 16-7 list the extended instructions formed by the op codes DD and FD.

With reference to Table 16-6, note that the extended instruction set includes the bit set, test, and reset instructions, various types of load (LD) instructions, and a selection of arithmetic and logical instructions. In most of the index register instructions, an optional positive or negative offset can be added to the contents of the index register before the instruction is executed. This offset or indexing displacement can be in the range of $+127$ to -128. For example, if the index register IX were set to 1000H, the instructions

DD CB 00 EE   SET 5,(IX+0) or SET 5,(IX)

would set bit 5 of memory location 1000H;

DD CB 14 EE   SET 5,(IX+14H)

TABLE 16-6. Z80 Extended Instructions—DD Op Code

Op code	Mnemonic		Op code	Mnemonic	
DD CB dd 46	BIT	0,(IX + dd)	DD 74 dd	LD	(IX + dd),H
DD CB dd 4E	BIT	1,(IX + dd)	DD 75 dd	LD	(IX + dd),L
DD CB dd 56	BIT	2,(IX + dd)	DD 36 dd nn	LD	(IX + dd),nn
DD CB dd 5E	BIT	3,(IX + dd)			
DD CB dd 66	BIT	4,(IX + dd)	DD BE dd	CP	(IX + dd)
DD CB dd 6E	BIT	5,(IX + dd)	DD A6 dd	AND	(IX + dd)
DD CB dd 76	BIT	6,(IX + dd)	DD 35 dd	DEC	(IX + dd)
DD CB dd 7E	BIT	7,(IX + dd)	DD 34 dd	INC	(IX + dd)
			DD B6 dd	OR	(IX + dd)
DD CB dd 86	RES	0,(IX + dd)	DD CB dd 16	RL	(IX + dd)
DD CB dd 8E	RES	1,(IX + dd)	DD CB dd 06	RLC	(IX + dd)
DD CB dd 96	RES	2,(IX + dd)	DD CB dd 1E	RR	(IX + dd)
DD CB dd 9E	RES	3,(IX + dd)	DD CB dd 0E	RRC	(IX + dd)
DD CB dd A6	RES	4,(IX + dd)	DD CB dd 26	SLA	(IX + dd)
DD CB dd AE	RES	5,(IX + dd)	DD CB dd 2E	SRA	(IX + dd)
DD CB dd B6	RES	6,(IX + dd)	DD CB dd 3E	SRL	(IX + dd)
DD CB dd BE	RES	7,(IX + dd)	DD 96 dd	SUB	(IX + dd)
			DD AE dd	XOR	(IX + dd)
DD CB dd C6	SET	0,(IX + dd)			
DD CB dd CE	SET	1,(IX + dd)	DD 8E dd	ADC	A,(IX + dd)
DD CB dd D6	SET	2,(IX + dd)	DD 86 dd	ADD	A,(IX + dd)
DD CB dd DE	SET	3,(IX + dd)	DD 9E dd	SBC	A,(IX + dd)
DD CB dd E6	SET	4,(IX + dd)			
DD CB dd EE	SET	5,(IX + dd)	DD 09	ADD	IX,BC
DD CB dd F6	SET	6,(IX + dd)	DD 19	ADD	IX,DE
DD CB dd FE	SET	7,(IX + dd)	DD 29	ADD	IX,IX
			DD 39	ADD	IX,SP
DD 7E dd	LD	A,(IX + dd)			
DD 46 dd	LD	B,(IX + dd)	DD 2A nnnn	LD	IX,(nnnn)
DD 4E dd	LD	C,(IX + dd)	DD 21 nnnn	LD	IX,nnnn
DD 56 dd	LD	D,(IX + dd)	DD 22 nnnn	LD	(nnnn),IX
DD 5E dd	LD	E,(IX + dd)			
DD 66 dd	LD	H,(IX + dd)	DD F9	LD	SP,IX
DD 6E dd	LD	L,(IX + dd)	DD E3	EX	(SP),IX
DD 77 dd	LD	(IX + dd),A	DD 2B	DEC	IX
DD 70 dd	LD	(IX + dd),B	DD 23	INC	IX
DD 71 dd	LD	(IX + dd),C	DD E9	JP	(IX)
DD 72 dd	LD	(IX + dd),D	DD E1	POP	IX
DD 73 dd	LD	(IX + dd),E	DD E5	PUSH	IX

NOTE: nnnn = any 16-bit number

nn = any 8-bit number

dd = 8-bit signed two's complement displacement in the range + 127 to − 128

would set bit 5 of memory location 1000H + 14H, or 1014H; and

$$\text{DD CB EC EE} \qquad \text{SET 5, (IX − 14H)}$$

would set bit 5 of memory location 1000H − 14H, or 0FECH.

TABLE 16-7. Z80 Extended instructions—FD Op Code

Op code	Mnemonic		Op code	Mnemonic	
FD CB dd 46	BIT	0,(IY + dd)	FD 74 dd	LD	(IY + dd),H
FD CB dd 4E	BIT	1,(IY + dd)	FD 75 dd	LD	(IY + dd),L
FD CB dd 56	BIT	2,(IY + dd)	FD 36 dd nn	LD	(IY + dd),nn
FD CB dd 5E	BIT	3,(IY + dd)			
FD CB dd 66	BIT	4,(IY + dd)	FD BE dd	CP	(IY + dd)
FD CB dd 6E	BIT	5,(IY + dd)	FD A6 dd	AND	(IY + dd)
FD CB dd 76	BIT	6,(IY + dd)	FD 35 dd	DEC	(IY + dd)
FD CB dd 7E	BIT	7,(IY + dd)	FD 34 dd	INC	(IY + dd)
			FD B6 dd	OR	(IY + dd)
FD CB dd 86	RES	0,(IY + dd)	FD CB dd 16	RL	(IY + dd)
FD CB dd 8E	RES	1,(IY + dd)	FD CB dd 06	RLC	(IY + dd)
FD CB dd 96	RES	2,(IY + dd)	FD CB dd 1E	RR	(IY + dd)
FD CB dd 9E	RES	3,(IY + dd)	FD CB dd 0E	RRC	(IY + dd)
FD CB dd A6	RES	4,(IY + dd)	FD CB dd 26	SLA	(IY + dd)
FD CB dd AE	RES	5,(IY + dd)	FD CB dd 2E	SRA	(IY + dd)
FD CB dd B6	RES	6,(IY + dd)	FD CB dd 3E	SRL	(IY + dd)
FD CB dd BE	RES	7,(IY + dd)	FD 96 dd	SUB	(IY + dd)
			FD AE dd	XOR	(IY + dd)
FD CB dd C6	SET	0,(IY + dd)			
FD CB dd CE	SET	1,(IY + dd)	FD 8E dd	ADC	A,(IY + dd)
FD CB dd D6	SET	2,(IY + dd)	FD 86 dd	ADD	A,(IY + dd)
FD CB dd DE	SET	3,(IY + dd)	FD 9E dd	SBC	A,(IY + dd)
FD CB dd E6	SET	4,(IY + dd)			
FD CB dd EE	SET	5,(IY + dd)	FD 09	ADD	IY,BC
FD CB dd F6	SET	6,(IY + dd)	FD 19	ADD	IY,DE
FD CB dd FE	SET	7,(IY + dd)	FD 29	ADD	IY,IY
			FD 39	ADD	IY,SP
FD 7E dd	LD	A,(IY + dd)			
FD 46 dd	LD	B,(IY + dd)	FD 2A nnnn	LD	IY,(nnnn)
FD 4E dd	LD	C,(IY + dd)	FD 21 nnnn	LD	IY,nnnn
FD 56 dd	LD	D,(IY + dd)	FD 22 nnnn	LD	(nnnn),IY
FD 5E dd	LD	E,(IY + dd)			
FD 66 dd	LD	H,(IY + dd)	FD F9	LD	SP,IY
FD 6E dd	LD	L,(IY + dd)	FD E3	EX	(SP),IY
FD 77 dd	LD	(IY + dd),A	FD 2B	DEC	IY
FD 70 dd	LD	(IY + dd),B	FD 23	INC	IY
FD 71 dd	LD	(IY + dd),C	FD E9	JP	(IY)
FD 72 dd	LD	(IY + dd),D	FD E1	POP	IY
FD 73 dd	LD	(IY + dd),E	FD E5	PUSH	IY

NOTE: nnnn = any 16-bit number
nn = any 8-bit number
dd = 8-bit signed two's complement displacement in the range + 127 to − 128

In all the BIT, SET, and RES instructions listed in Table 16-6, an 8-bit displacement byte follows the second op code CB. This byte is added to the contents of the index register before the instruction is executed. In the first example, the displacement is zero; in the second example, the displacement is

14H; and in the third example, the offset is ECH (-14 in two's complement representation). Notice that all of the BIT, RES, and SET instructions have CB as the second op code and are four bytes in length. The last byte indicates the operation (test, reset, or set), the register on which the operation is to be performed, and the bit position that is to be operated upon.

Table 16-7 lists all of the Z80's extended instructions for the FD op code. These instructions function in exactly the same manner as do the instructions listed in Table 16-6, except that these instructions operate on the index register IY.

The extended instructions of the Z80 microprocessor described in this chapter greatly enhance its capabilities and simplifies the task of programming. The technique of decoding unimplemented 8085 instructions increases the processing power of the Z80 microprocessor, while maintaining almost 100 percent compatibility with the 8085, and this allows a programmer to upgrade easily to the more powerful Z80 instruction set.

16·6

Summary

This chapter surveyed the Z80 microprocessor, which is similar in architecture to the 8085 microprocessor. We pointed out that the Z80 microprocessor was designed after the 8085's predecessor, the 8080, and that one of the objectives of the Z80's design was to maintain compatibility with the 8080's instruction set and interrupt structure. The 8085 microprocessor was also designed with the same objectives, which accounts for the close similarities between the Z80 and the 8085. Besides maintaining close 8085 compatibility in the instruction set and interrupt structure, the Z80 microprocessor provides a greatly expanded instruction set that can ease the task of programming in assembly language. The Z80's mnemonic instruction representation does introduce some confusion to the programmer who is upgrading from the 8085 microprocessor but at the same time is more logically designed and does eliminate some of the "extra" mnemonics that describe the same operation. The Z80 microprocessor system cannot be as compact as an 8085 system in regard to hardware, but it does allow standard components to be interconnected quite easily.

This chapter and the preceding one examined two microprocessors, one similar (Z80) and one quite different (6800) from the 8085 microprocessor. But the concepts of microprocessor operation and interfacing can easily be applied to almost any type of microprocessor. It is important to remember that for a given application a microprocessor should be selected that best suits the application; conversely, the application should never be designed to fit the characteristics of the microprocessor.

REVIEW QUESTIONS AND PROBLEMS

1.   Compare the similarities between the Z80 microprocessor and the 8085 microprocessor in terms of

(a) the interrupt structure.
(b) the control signals.
(c) the instruction set.

2. How does the Z80 CPU respond to an $\overline{\text{NMI}}$ interrupt?

3. How does the Z80 CPU respond to an interrupt over the $\overline{\text{INT}}$ line when programmed for
(a) mode 0.
(b) mode 1.
(c) mode 2.

4. Describe the functions of the *additional* registers of the Z80 CPU.

5. Develop a circuit to vector the Z80 CPU to location 0018H when an interrupt is acknowledged over the $\overline{\text{INT}}$ line.

6. How does the Z80's flag register differ from the 8085's flag register?

7. What are the advantages and disadvantages of relative jump instructions, as compared with absolute jump instructions?

8. How does the *displacement* affect the operation of the index register (IX and IY) instructions?

9. What is the difference between the instruction

```
LD   BC,(1000H)
```

and the instruction

```
LD   BC,1000H
```

10. Disassemble the following sequence of bytes into their Z80 mnemonic representation. Refer to Tables 16-3 through 16-7 for the Z80's op codes.

```
ED 7B 30 20 7B D9 FD F9 3D 28 FB 76
```

11. Hand-assemble the following Z80 program:

```
            LD    IX,2000H
            LD    IY,5000H
            LD    B,30H
    LOOP:   LD    A,(IX)
            LD    (IY),A
            INC   IX
            INC   IY
            DJNZ  LOOP
            HALT
```

12. Describe the function and operation of the program given in the previous problem.

13. Convert the 8085 program shown in Figure 11-1 to Z80 mnemonics.

Summary of the 8080/ 8085 Instruction Set

8080/85 CPU INSTRUCTIONS IN OPERATION CODE SEQUENCE

OP CODE	MNEMONIC	OP CODE	MNEMONIC	OP CODE	MNEMONIC	OP CODE	MNEMONIC	OP CODE	MNEMONIC	OP CODE	MNEMONIC
00	NOP	2B	DCX H	56	MOV D,M	81	ADD C	AC	XRA H	D7	RST 2
01	LXI B,D16	2C	INR L	57	MOV D,A	82	ADD D	AD	XRA L	D8	RC
02	STAX B	2D	DCR L	58	MOV E,B	83	ADD E	AE	XRA M	D9	--
03	INX B	2E	MVI L,D8	59	MOV E,C	84	ADD H	AF	XRA A	DA	JC Adr
04	INR B	2F	CMA	5A	MOV E,D	85	ADD L	B0	ORA B	DB	IN D8
05	DCR B	30	SIM	5B	MOV E,E	86	ADD M	B1	ORA C	DC	CC Adr
06	MVI B,D8	31	LXI SPD16	5C	MOV E,H	87	ADD A	B2	ORA D	DD	--
07	RLC	32	STA Adr	5D	MOV E,L	88	ADC B	B3	ORA E	DE	SBI D8
08	--	33	INX SP	5E	MOV E,M	89	ADC C	B4	ORA H	DF	RST 3
09	DAD B	34	INR M	5F	MOV E,A	8A	ADC D	B5	ORA L	E0	RPO
0A	LDAX B	35	DCR M	60	MOV H,B	8B	ADC E	B6	ORA M	E1	POP H
0B	DCX B	36	MVI M,D8	61	MOV H,C	8C	ADC H	B7	ORA A	E2	JPO Adr
0C	INR C	37	STC	62	MOV H,D	8D	ADC L	B8	CMP B	E3	XTHL
0D	DCR C	38	--	63	MOV H,E	8E	ADC M	B9	CMP C	E4	CPO Adr
0E	MVI C,D8	39	DAD SP	64	MOV H,H	8F	ADC A	BA	CMP D	E5	PUSH H
0F	RRC	3A	LDA Adr	65	MOV H,L	90	SUB B	BB	CMP E	E6	ANI D8
10	--	3B	DCX SP	66	MOV H,M	91	SUB C	BC	CMP H	E7	RST 4
11	LXI D,D16	3C	INR A	67	MOV H,A	92	SUB D	BD	CMP L	E8	RPE
12	STAX D	3D	DCR A	68	MOV L,B	93	SUB E	BE	CMP M	E9	PCHL
13	INX D	3E	MVI A,D8	69	MOV L,C	94	SUB H	BF	CMP A	EA	JPE Adr
14	INR D	3F	CMC	6A	MOV L,D	95	SUB L	C0	RNZ	EB	XCHG
15	DCR D	40	MOV B,B	6B	MOV L,E	96	SUB M	C1	POP B	EC	CPE Adr
16	MVI D,D8	41	MOV B,C	6C	MOV L,H	97	SUB A	C2	JNZ Adr	ED	--
17	RAL	42	MOV B,D	6D	MOV L,L	98	SBB B	C3	JMP Adr	EE	XRI D8
18	--	43	MOV B,E	6E	MOV L,M	99	SBB C	C4	CNZ Adr	EF	RST 5
19	DAD D	44	MOV B,H	6F	MOV L,A	9A	SBB D	C5	PUSH B	F0	RP
1A	LDAX D	45	MOV B,L	70	MOV M,B	9B	SBB E	C6	ADI D8	F1	POP PSW
1B	DCX D	46	MOV B,M	71	MOV M,C	9C	SBB H	C7	RST 0	F2	JP Adr
1C	INR E	47	MOV B,A	72	MOV M,D	9D	SBB L	C8	RZ	F3	DI
1D	DCR E	48	MOV C,B	73	MOV M,E	9E	SBB M	C9	RET	F4	CP Adr
1E	MVI E,D8	49	MOV C,C	74	MOV M,H	9F	SBB A	CA	JZ Adr	F5	PUSH PSW
1F	RAR	4A	MOV C,D	75	MOV M,L	A0	ANA B	CB	--	F6	ORI D8
20	RIM	4B	MOV C,E	76	HLT	A1	ANA C	CC	CZ Adr	F7	RST 6
21	LXI H,D16	4C	MOV C,H	77	MOV M,A	A2	ANA D	CD	CALL Adr	F8	RM
22	SHLD Adr	4D	MOV C,L	78	MOV A,B	A3	ANA E	CE	ACI D8	F9	SPHL
23	INX H	4E	MOV C,M	79	MOV A,C	A4	ANA H	CF	RST 1	FA	JM Adr
24	INR H	4F	MOV C,A	7A	MOV A,D	A5	ANA L	D0	RNC	FB	EI
25	DCR H	50	MOV D,B	7B	MOV A,E	A6	ANA M	D1	POP D	FC	CM Adr
26	MVI H,D8	51	MOV D,C	7C	MOV A,H	A7	ANA A	D2	JNC Adr	FD	--
27	DAA	52	MOV D,D	7D	MOV A,L	A8	XRA B	D3	OUT D8	FE	CPI D8
28	--	53	MOV D,E	7E	MOV A,M	A9	XRA C	D4	CNC Adr	FF	RST 7
29	DAD H	54	MOV D,H	7F	MOV A,A	AA	XRA D	D5	PUSH D		
2A	LHLD Adr	55	MOV D,L	80	ADD B	AB	XRA E	D6	SUI D8		

D8 = constant, or logical/arithmetic expression that evaluates to an 8 bit data quantity.

Adr = 16-bit address

D16 = constant, or logical/arithmetic expression that evaluates to a 16 bit data quantity

All mnemonics © 1974, 1975, 1976, 1977 Intel Corporation.
Courtesy of Intel Corp.

The ASCII Codes

The 8080 and 8085 use the seven-bit ASCII code, with the high-order eighth bit (parity bit) always reset.

GRAPHIC OR CONTROL	ASCII (HEXADECIMAL)	GRAPHIC OR CONTROL	ASCII (HEXADECIMAL)	GRAPHIC OR CONTROL	ASCII (HEXADECIMAL)
NUL	00	+	2B	V	56
SOH	01	,	2C	W	57
STX	02	−	2D	X	58
ETX	03	.	2E	Y	59
EOT	04	/	2F	Z	5A
ENQ	05	0	30	[	5B
ACK	06	1	31	\	5C
BEL	07	2	32	]	5D
BS	08	3	33	∧ (↑)	5E
HT	09	4	34	− (←)	5F
LF	0A	5	35	`	60
VT	0B	6	36	a	61
FF	0C	7	37	b	62
CR	0D	8	38	c	63
SO	0E	9	39	d	64
SI	0F	:	3A	e	65
DLE	10	;	3B	f	66
DC1 (X-ON)	11	<	3C	g	67
DC2 (TAPE)	12	=	3D	h	68
DC3 (X-OFF)	13	>	3E	i	69
DC4 (TAPE)	14	?	3F	j	6A
NAK	15	@	40	k	6B
SYN	16	A	41	l	6C
ETB	17	B	42	m	6D
CAN	18	C	43	n	6E
EM	19	D	44	o	6F
SUB	1A	E	45	p	70
ESC	1B	F	46	q	71
FS	1C	G	47	r	72
GS	1D	H	48	s	73
RS	1E	I	49	t	74
US	1F	J	4A	u	75
SP	20	K	4B	v	76
!	21	L	4C	w	77
''	22	M	4D	x	78
#	23	N	4E	y	79
$	24	O	4F	z	7A
%	25	P	50	{	7B
&	26	Q	51	.	7C
'	27	R	52	¦ (ALT MODE)	7D
(	28	S	53	~	7E
)	29	T	54	DEL (RUB OUT)	7F
*	2A	U	55		

Courtesy of Intel Corp.

THE ASCII CODES

Standard Flowchart Symbols

Operation	Symbol	Description
Interrupt		Indicates a change in a program, such as start or stop
Process		Indicates a processing operation in progress
Input/output		Indicates an I/O operation in progress. Process may also be used
Manual		Indicates a manual operation (no CPU intervention) in progress
Decision		Indicates a test, decision, and transfer operation
Connector		Indicates a connection of two or more portions of a flowchart

Binary–Decimal–Hexadecimal Conversion Tables

$$2^n \quad n \quad 2^{-n}$$

2^n	n	2^{-n}
1	0	1 0
2	1	0 5
4	2	0 25
8	3	0 125
16	4	0 062 5
32	5	0 031 25
64	6	0 015 625
128	7	0 007 812 5
256	8	0 003 906 25
512	9	0 001 953 125
1 024	10	0 000 976 562 5
2 048	11	0 000 488 281 25
4 096	12	0 000 244 140 625
8 192	13	0 000 122 070 312 5
16 384	14	0 000 061 035 156 25
32 768	15	0 000 030 517 578 125
65 536	16	0 000 015 258 789 062 5
131 072	17	0 000 007 629 394 531 25
262 144	18	0 000 003 814 697 265 625
524 288	19	0 000 001 907 348 632 812 5
1 048 576	20	0 000 000 953 674 316 406 25
2 097 152	21	0 000 000 476 837 158 203 125
4 194 304	22	0 000 000 238 418 579 101 562 5
8 388 608	23	0 000 000 119 209 289 550 781 25
16 777 216	24	0 000 000 059 604 644 775 390 625
33 554 432	25	0 000 000 029 802 322 387 695 312 5
67 108 864	26	0 000 000 014 901 161 193 847 656 25
134 217 728	27	0 000 000 007 450 580 596 923 828 125
268 435 456	28	0 000 000 003 725 290 298 461 914 062 5
536 870 912	29	0 000 000 001 862 645 149 230 957 031 25
1 073 741 824	30	0 000 000 000 931 322 574 615 478 515 625
2 147 483 648	31	0 000 000 000 465 661 287 307 739 257 812 5
4 294 967 296	32	0 000 000 000 232 830 643 653 869 628 906 25
8 589 934 592	33	0 000 000 000 116 415 321 826 934 814 453 125
17 179 869 184	34	0 000 000 000 058 207 660 913 467 407 226 562 5
34 359 738 368	35	0 000 000 000 029 103 830 456 733 703 613 281 25
68 719 476 736	36	0 000 000 000 014 551 915 228 366 851 806 640 625
137 438 953 472	37	0 000 000 000 007 275 957 614 183 425 903 320 312 5
274 877 906 944	38	0 000 000 000 003 637 978 807 091 712 951 660 156 25
549 755 813 888	39	0 000 000 000 001 818 989 403 545 856 475 830 078 125
1 099 511 627 776	40	0 000 000 000 000 909 494 701 772 928 237 915 039 062 5
2 199 023 255 552	41	0 000 000 000 000 454 747 350 886 464 118 957 519 531 25
4 398 046 511 104	42	0 000 000 000 000 227 373 675 443 232 059 478 759 765 625
8 796 093 022 208	43	0 000 000 000 000 113 686 837 721 616 029 739 379 882 812 5
17 592 186 044 416	44	0 000 000 000 000 056 843 418 860 808 014 869 689 941 406 25
35 184 372 088 832	45	0 000 000 000 000 028 421 709 430 404 007 434 844 970 703 125
70 368 744 177 664	46	0 000 000 000 000 014 210 854 715 202 003 717 422 485 351 562 5
140 737 488 355 328	47	0 000 000 000 000 007 105 427 357 601 001 858 711 242 675 781 25
281 474 976 710 656	48	0 000 000 000 000 003 552 713 678 800 500 929 355 621 337 890 625
562 949 953 421 312	49	0 000 000 000 000 001 776 356 839 400 250 464 677 810 668 945 312 5
1 125 899 906 842 624	50	0 000 000 000 000 000 888 178 419 700 125 232 338 905 334 472 656 25
2 251 799 813 685 248	51	0 000 000 000 000 000 444 089 209 850 062 616 169 452 667 236 328 125
4 503 599 627 370 496	52	0 000 000 000 000 000 222 044 604 925 031 308 084 726 333 618 164 062 5
9 007 199 254 740 992	53	0 000 000 000 000 000 111 022 302 462 515 654 042 363 166 809 082 031 25
18 014 398 509 481 984	54	0 000 000 000 000 000 055 511 151 231 257 827 021 181 583 404 541 015 625
36 028 797 018 963 968	55	0 000 000 000 000 000 027 755 575 615 628 913 510 590 791 702 270 507 812 5
72 057 594 037 927 936	56	0 000 000 000 000 000 013 877 787 807 814 456 755 295 395 851 135 253 906 25
144 115 188 075 855 872	57	0 000 000 000 000 000 006 938 893 903 907 228 377 647 697 925 567 676 950 125
288 230 376 151 711 744	58	0 000 000 000 000 000 003 469 446 951 953 614 188 823 848 962 783 813 476 562 5
576 460 752 303 423 488	59	0 000 000 000 000 000 001 734 723 475 976 807 094 411 924 481 391 906 738 281 25
1 152 921 504 606 846 976	60	0 000 000 000 000 000 000 867 361 737 988 403 547 205 962 240 695 953 369 140 625
2 305 843 009 213 693 952	61	0 000 000 000 000 000 000 433 680 868 994 201 773 602 981 120 347 976 684 570 312
4 611 686 018 427 387 904	62	0 000 000 000 000 000 000 216 840 434 497 100 886 801 490 560 173 988 342 285 156
9 223 372 036 854 775 808	63	0 000 000 000 000 000 000 108 420 217 248 550 443 400 745 280 086 994 171 142 578

Courtesy of Intel Corp.

POWERS OF 16 (IN BASE 10)

16^n	n	16^{-n}
1	0	0.10000 00000 00000 00000 × 10
16	1	0.62500 00000 00000 00000 × 10^{-1}
256	2	0.39062 50000 00000 00000 × 10^{-2}
4 096	3	0.24414 06250 00000 00000 × 10^{-3}
65 536	4	0.15258 78906 25000 00000 × 10^{-4}
1 048 576	5	0.95367 43164 06250 00000 × 10^{-6}
16 777 216	6	0.59604 64477 53906 25000 × 10^{-7}
268 435 456	7	0.37252 90298 46191 40625 × 10^{-8}
4 294 967 296	8	0.23283 06436 53869 62891 × 10^{-9}
68 719 476 736	9	0.14551 91522 83668 51807 × 10^{-10}
1 099 511 627 776	10	0.90949 47017 72928 23792 × 10^{-12}
17 592 186 044 416	11	0.56843 41886 08080 14870 × 10^{-13}
281 474 976 710 656	12	0.35527 13678 80050 09294 × 10^{-14}
4 503 599 627 370 496	13	0.22204 46049 25031 30808 × 10^{-15}
72 057 594 037 927 936	14	0.13877 78780 78144 56755 × 10^{-16}
1 152 921 504 606 846 976	15	0.86736 17379 88403 54721 × 10^{-18}

POWERS OF 10 (IN BASE 16)

10^n	n	10^{-n}
1	0	1.0000 0000 0000 0000
A	1	0.1999 9999 9999 999A
64	2	0.28F5 C28F 5C28 F5C3 × 16^{-1}
3E8	3	0.4189 374B C6A7 EF9E × 16^{-2}
2710	4	0.68DB 8BAC 710C B296 × 16^{-3}
1 86A0	5	0.A7C5 AC47 1B47 8423 × 16^{-4}
F 4240	6	0.10C6 F7A0 B5ED 8D37 × 16^{-4}
98 9680	7	0.1AD7 F29A BCAF 4858 × 16^{-5}
5F5 E100	8	0.2AF3 1DC4 6118 73BF × 16^{-6}
3B9A CA00	9	0.44B8 2FA0 9B5A 52CC × 16^{-7}
2 540B E400	10	0.6DF3 7F67 SEF6 EADF × 16^{-8}
17 4876 E800	11	0.AFEB FF0B CB24 AAFF × 16^{-9}
E8 D4A5 1000	12	0.1197 9981 2DEA 1119 × 16^{-9}
918 4E72 A000	13	0.1C25 C268 4976 81C2 × 16^{-10}
5AF3 107A 4000	14	0.2D09 370D 4257 3604 × 16^{-11}
3 8D7E A4C6 8000	15	0.480E BE7B 9D58 566D × 16^{-12}
23 8652 6FC1 0000	16	0.734A CA5F 6226 F0AE × 16^{-13}
163 4578 5D8A 0000	17	0.B877 AA32 36A4 B449 × 16^{-14}
DE0 B6B3 A764 0000	18	0.1272 5DD1 D243 ABA1 × 16^{-14}
8AC7 2304 89E8 0000	19	0.1D83 C94F B6D2 AC35 × 16^{-15}

HEXADECIMAL-DECIMAL INTEGER CONVERSION

The table below provides for direct conversions between hexadecimal integers in the range 0-FFF and decimal integers in the range 0-4095. For conversion of larger integers, the table values may be added to the following figures:

Hexadecimal	Decimal	Hexadecimal	Decimal
01 000	4 096	20 000	131 072
02 000	8 192	30 000	196 608
03 000	12 288	40 000	262 144
04 000	16 384	50 000	327 680
05 000	20 480	60 000	393 216
06 000	24 576	70 000	458 752
07 000	28 672	80 000	524 288
08 000	32 768	90 000	589 824
09 000	36 864	A0 000	655 360
0A 000	40 960	B0 000	720 896
0B 000	45 056	C0 000	786 432
0C 000	49 152	D0 000	851 968
0D 000	53 248	E0 000	917 504
0E 000	57 344	F0 000	983 040
0F 000	61 440	100 000	1 048 576
10 000	65 536	200 000	2 097 152
11 000	69 632	300 000	3 145 728
12 000	73 728	400 000	4 194 304
13 000	77 824	500 000	5 242 880
14 000	81 920	600 000	6 291 456
15 000	86 016	700 000	7 340 032
16 000	90 112	800 000	8 388 608
17 000	94 208	900 000	9 437 184
18 000	98 304	A00 000	10 485 760
19 000	102 400	B00 000	11 534 336
1A 000	106 496	C00 000	12 582 912
1B 000	110 592	D00 000	13 631 488
1C 000	114 688	E00 000	14 680 064
1D 000	118 784	F00 000	15 728 640
1E 000	122 880	1 000 000	16 777 216
1F 000	126 976	2 000 000	33 554 432

	0	1	2	3	4	5	6	7	8	9	A	B	C	D	E	F
000	0000	0001	0002	0003	0004	0005	0006	0007	0008	0009	0010	0011	0012	0013	0014	0015
010	0016	0017	0018	0019	0020	0021	0022	0023	0024	0025	0026	0027	0028	0029	0030	0031
020	0032	0033	0034	0035	0036	0037	0038	0039	0040	0041	0042	0043	0044	0045	0046	0047
030	0048	0049	0050	0051	0052	0053	0054	0055	0056	0057	0058	0059	0060	0061	0062	0063
040	0064	0065	0066	0067	0068	0069	0070	0071	0072	0073	0074	0075	0076	0077	0078	0079
050	0080	0081	0082	0083	0084	0085	0086	0087	0088	0089	0090	0091	0092	0093	0094	0095
060	0096	0097	0098	0099	0100	0101	0102	0103	0104	0105	0106	0107	0108	0109	0110	0111
070	0112	0113	0114	0115	0116	0117	0118	0119	0120	0121	0122	0123	0124	0125	0126	0127
080	0128	0129	0130	0131	0132	0133	0134	0135	0136	0137	0138	0139	0140	0141	0142	0143
090	0144	0145	0146	0147	0148	0149	0150	0151	0152	0153	0154	0155	0156	0157	0158	0159
0A0	0160	0161	0162	0163	0164	0165	0166	0167	0168	0169	0170	0171	0172	0173	0174	0175
0B0	0176	0177	0178	0179	0180	0181	0182	0183	0184	0185	0186	0187	0188	0189	0190	0191
0C0	0192	0193	0194	0195	0196	0197	0198	0199	0200	0201	0202	0203	0204	0205	0206	0207
0D0	0208	0209	0210	0211	0212	0213	0214	0215	0216	0217	0218	0219	0220	0221	0222	0223
0E0	0224	0225	0226	0227	0228	0229	0230	0231	0232	0233	0234	0235	0236	0237	0238	0239
0F0	0240	0241	0242	0243	0244	0245	0246	0247	0248	0249	0250	0251	0252	0253	0254	0255

	0	1	2	3	4	5	6	7	8	9	A	B	C	D	E	F
100	0256	0257	0258	0259	0260	0261	0262	0263	0264	0265	0266	0267	0268	0269	0270	0271
110	0272	0273	0274	0275	0276	0277	0278	0279	0280	0281	0282	0283	0284	0285	0286	0287
120	0288	0289	0290	0291	0292	0293	0294	0295	0296	0297	0298	0299	0300	0301	0302	0303
130	0304	0305	0306	0307	0308	0309	0310	0311	0312	0313	0314	0315	0316	0317	0318	0319
140	0320	0321	0322	0323	0324	0325	0326	0327	0328	0329	0330	0331	0331	0333	0334	0335
150	0336	0337	0338	0339	0340	0341	0342	0343	0344	0345	0346	0347	0348	0349	0350	0351
160	0352	0353	0354	0355	0356	0357	0358	0359	0360	0361	0362	0363	0364	0365	0366	0367
170	0368	0369	0370	0371	0372	0373	0374	0375	0376	0377	0378	0379	0380	0381	0382	0383
180	0384	0385	0386	0387	038d	0389	0390	0391	0392	0393	0394	0395	0396	0397	0398	0399
190	0400	0401	0402	0403	0404	0405	0406	0407	0408	0409	0410	0411	0412	0413	0414	0415
1A0	0416	0417	0418	0419	0420	0421	0422	0423	0424	0425	0426	0427	0428	0429	0430	0431
1B0	0432	0433	0434	0435	0436	0437	0438	0439	0440	0441	0442	0443	0444	0445	0446	0447
1C0	0448	0449	0450	0451	0452	0453	0454	0455	0456	0457	0458	0459	0460	0461	0462	0463
1D0	0464	0465	0466	0467	0468	0469	0470	0471	0472	0473	0474	0475	0476	0477	0478	0479
1E0	0480	0481	0482	0483	0484	0485	0486	0487	0488	0489	0490	0491	0492	0493	0494	0495
1F0	0496	0497	0498	0499	0500	0501	0502	0503	0504	0505	0506	0507	0508	0509	0510	0511
200	0512	0513	0514	0515	0516	0517	0518	0519	0520	0521	0522	0523	0524	0525	0526	0527
210	0528	0529	0530	0531	0532	0533	0534	0535	0536	0537	0538	0539	0540	0541	0542	0543
220	0544	0545	0546	0547	0548	0549	0550	0551	0552	0553	0554	0555	0556	0557	0558	0559
230	0560	0561	0562	0563	0564	0565	0566	0567	0568	0569	0570	0571	0572	0573	0574	0575
240	0576	0577	0578	0579	0580	0581	0582	0583	0584	0585	0586	0587	0588	0589	0590	0591
250	0592	0593	0594	0595	0596	0597	0598	0599	0600	0601	0602	0603	0604	0605	0606	0607
260	0608	0609	0610	0611	0612	0613	0614	0615	0616	0617	0618	0619	0620	0621	0622	0623
270	0624	0625	0626	0627	0628	0629	0630	0631	0632	0633	0634	0635	0636	0637	0638	0639
280	0640	0641	0642	0643	0644	0645	0646	0647	0648	0649	0650	0651	0652	0653	0654	0655
290	0656	0657	0658	0659	0660	0661	0662	0663	0664	0665	0666	0667	0668	0669	0670	0671
2A0	0672	0673	0674	0675	0676	0677	0678	0679	0680	0681	0682	0683	0684	0685	0686	0687
2B0	0688	0689	0690	0691	0692	0693	0694	0695	0696	0697	0698	0699	0700	0701	0702	0703
2C0	0704	0705	0706	0707	0708	0709	0710	0711	0712	0713	0714	0715	0716	0717	0718	0719
2D0	0720	0721	0722	0723	0724	0725	0726	0727	0728	0729	0730	0731	0732	0733	0734	0735
2E0	0736	0737	0738	0739	0740	0741	0742	0743	0744	0745	0746	0747	0748	0749	0750	0751
2F0	0752	0753	0754	0755	0756	0757	0758	0759	0760	0761	0762	0763	0764	0765	0766	0767
300	0768	0769	0770	0771	0772	0773	0774	0775	0776	0777	0778	0779	0780	0781	0782	0783
310	0784	0785	0786	0787	0788	0789	0790	0791	0792	0793	0794	0795	0796	0797	0798	0799
320	0800	0301	0802	0803	0804	0805	0806	0807	0808	0809	0810	0811	0812	0813	0814	0815
330	0816	0817	0818	0819	0820	0821	0822	0823	0824	0825	0826	0827	0828	0829	0830	0831
340	0832	0833	0834	0835	0836	0837	0838	0839	0840	0841	0842	0843	0844	0845	0846	0847
350	0848	0849	0850	0851	0852	0853	0854	0855	0856	0857	0858	0859	0860	0861	0862	0863
360	0864	0865	0866	0867	0868	0869	0870	0871	0872	0873	0874	0875	0876	0877	0878	0879
370	0880	0881	0882	0883	0884	0885	0886	0887	0888	0889	0890	0891	0892	0893	0894	0895
380	0896	0897	0898	0899	0900	0901	0902	0903	0904	0905	0906	0907	0908	0909	0910	0911
390	0212	0913	0914	0915	0916	0917	0918	0919	0920	0921	0922	0923	0924	0925	0926	0927
3A0	0928	0929	0930	0931	0932	0933	0934	0935	0936	0937	0938	0939	0940	0941	0942	0943
3B0	0944	0945	0946	0947	0948	0949	0950	0951	0952	0953	0954	0955	0956	0957	0958	0959
3C0	0960	0961	0962	0963	0964	0965	0966	0967	0968	0969	0970	0971	0972	0973	0974	0975
3D0	0976	0977	0978	0979	0980	0981	0982	0983	0984	0985	0986	0987	0988	0989	0990	0991
3E0	0992	0993	0994	0995	0996	0997	0998	0999	1000	1001	1002	1003	1004	1005	1006	1007
3F0	1008	1009	1010	1011	1012	1013	1014	1015	1016	1017	1018	1019	1020	1021	1022	1023

	0	1	2	3	4	5	6	7	8	9	A	B	C	D	E	F
400	1024	1025	1026	1027	1028	1029	1030	1031	1032	1033	1034	1035	1036	1037	1038	1039
410	1040	1041	1042	1043	1044	1045	1046	1047	1048	1049	1050	1051	1052	1053	1054	1055
420	1056	1057	1058	1059	1060	1061	1062	1063	1064	1065	1066	1067	1068	1069	1070	1071
430	1072	1073	1074	1075	1076	1077	1078	1079	1080	1081	1082	1083	1084	1085	1086	1087
440	1088	1089	1090	1091	1092	1093	1094	1095	1096	1097	1098	1099	1100	1101	1102	1103
450	1104	1105	1106	1107	1108	1109	1110	1111	1112	1113	1114	1115	1116	1117	1118	1119
460	1120	1121	1122	1123	1124	1125	1126	1127	1128	1129	1130	1131	1132	1133	1134	1135
470	1136	1137	1138	1139	1140	1141	1142	1143	1144	1145	1146	1147	1148	1149	1150	1151
480	1152	1153	1154	1155	1156	1157	1158	1159	1160	1161	1162	1163	1164	1165	1166	1167
490	1168	1169	1170	1171	1172	1173	1174	1175	1176	1177	1178	1179	1180	1181	1182	1183
4A0	1184	1185	1186	1187	1188	1189	1190	1191	1192	1193	1194	1195	1196	1197	1198	1199
4B0	1200	1201	1202	1203	1204	1205	1206	1207	1208	1209	1210	1211	1212	1213	1214	1215
4C0	1216	1217	1218	1219	1220	1221	1222	1223	1224	1225	1226	1227	1228	1229	1230	1231
4D0	1232	1233	1234	1235	1236	1237	1238	1239	1240	1241	1242	1243	1244	1245	1246	1247
4E0	1248	1249	1250	1251	1252	1253	1254	1255	1256	1257	1258	1259	1260	1261	1262	1263
4F0	1264	1265	1266	1267	1268	1269	1270	1271	1272	1273	1274	1275	1276	1277	1278	1279
500	1280	1281	1282	1283	1284	1285	1286	1287	1288	1289	1290	1291	1292	1293	1294	1295
510	1296	1297	1298	1299	1300	1301	1302	1303	1304	1305	1306	1307	1308	1309	1310	1311
520	1312	1313	1314	1315	1316	1317	1318	1319	1320	1321	1322	1323	1324	1325	1326	1327
530	1328	1329	1330	1331	1332	1333	1334	1335	1336	1337	1338	1339	1340	1341	1342	1343
540	1344	1345	1346	1347	1348	1349	1350	1351	1352	1353	1354	1355	1356	1357	1358	1359
550	1360	1361	1362	1363	1364	1365	1366	1367	1368	1369	1370	1371	1372	1373	1374	1375
560	1376	1377	1378	1379	1380	1381	1382	1383	1384	1385	1386	1387	1388	1389	1390	1391
570	1392	1393	1394	1395	1396	1397	1398	1399	1400	1401	1402	1403	1404	1405	1406	1407
580	1408	1409	1410	1411	1412	1413	1414	1415	1416	1417	1418	1419	1420	1421	1422	1423
590	1424	1425	1426	1427	1428	1429	1430	1431	1432	1433	1434	1435	1436	1437	1438	1439
5A0	1440	1441	1442	1443	1444	1445	1446	1447	1448	1449	1450	1451	1452	1453	1454	1455
5B0	1456	1457	1458	1459	1460	1461	1462	1463	1464	1465	1466	1467	1468	1469	1470	1471
5C0	1472	1473	1474	1475	1476	1477	1478	1479	1480	1481	1482	1483	1484	1485	1486	1487
5D0	1488	1489	1490	1491	1492	1493	1494	1495	1496	1497	1498	1499	1500	1501	1502	1503
5E0	1504	1505	1506	1507	1508	1509	1510	1511	1512	1513	1514	1515	1516	1517	1518	1519
5F0	1520	1521	1522	1523	1524	1525	1526	1527	1528	1529	1530	1531	1532	1533	1534	1535
600	1536	1537	1538	1539	1540	1541	1542	1543	1544	1545	1546	1547	1548	1549	1550	1551
610	1552	1553	1554	1555	1556	1557	1558	1559	1560	1561	1562	1563	1564	1565	1566	1567
620	1568	1569	1570	1571	1572	1573	1574	1575	1576	1577	1578	1579	1580	1581	1582	1583
630	1584	1585	1586	1587	1588	1589	1590	1591	1592	1593	1594	1595	1596	1597	1598	1599
640	1600	1601	1602	1603	1604	1605	1606	1607	1608	1609	1610	1611	1612	1613	1614	1615
650	1616	1617	1618	1619	1620	1621	1622	1623	1624	1625	1626	1627	1628	1629	1630	1631
660	1632	1633	1634	1635	1636	1637	1638	1639	1640	1641	1642	1643	1644	1645	1646	1647
670	1648	1649	1650	1651	1652	1653	1654	1655	1656	1657	1658	1659	1660	1661	1662	1663
680	1664	1665	1666	1667	1668	1669	1670	1671	1672	1673	1674	1675	1676	1677	1678	1679
690	1680	1681	1682	1683	1684	1685	1686	1687	1688	1689	1690	1691	1692	1693	1694	1695
6A0	1696	1697	1698	1699	1700	1701	1702	1703	1704	1705	1706	1707	1708	1709	1710	1711
6B0	1712	1713	1714	1715	1716	1717	1718	1719	1720	1721	1722	1723	1724	1725	1726	1727
6C0	1728	1729	1730	1731	1732	1733	1734	1735	1736	1737	1738	1739	1740	1741	1742	1743
6D0	1744	1745	1746	1747	1748	1749	1750	1751	1752	1753	1754	1755	1756	1757	1758	1759
6E0	1760	1761	1762	1763	1764	1765	1766	1767	1768	1769	1770	1771	1772	1773	1774	1775
6F0	1776	1777	1778	1779	1780	1781	1782	1783	1784	1785	1786	1787	1788	1789	1790	1791

	0	1	2	3	4	5	6	7	8	9	A	B	C	D	E	F
700	1792	1793	1794	1795	1796	1797	1798	1799	1800	1801	1802	1803	1804	1805	1806	1807
710	1808	1809	1810	1811	1812	1813	1814	1815	1816	1817	1818	1819	1820	1821	1822	1823
720	1824	1825	1826	1827	1828	1829	1830	1831	1832	1833	1834	1835	1836	1837	1838	1839
730	1840	1841	1842	1843	1844	1845	1846	1847	1848	1849	1850	1851	1852	1853	1854	1855
740	1856	1857	1858	1859	1860	1861	1862	1863	1864	1865	1866	1867	1868	1869	1870	1871
750	1872	1873	1874	1875	1876	1877	1878	1879	1880	1881	1882	1883	1884	1885	1886	1887
760	1888	1889	1890	1891	1892	1893	1894	1895	1896	1897	1898	1899	1900	1901	1902	1903
770	1904	1905	1906	1907	1908	1909	1910	1911	1912	1913	1914	1915	1916	1917	1918	1919
780	1920	1921	1922	1923	1924	1925	1926	1927	1928	1929	1930	1931	1932	1933	1934	1935
790	1936	1937	1938	1939	1940	1941	1942	1943	1944	1945	1946	1947	1948	1949	1950	1951
7A0	1952	1953	1954	1955	1956	1957	1958	1959	1960	1961	1962	1963	1964	1965	1966	1967
7B0	1968	1969	1970	1971	1972	1973	1974	1975	1976	1977	1978	1979	1980	1981	1982	1983
7C0	1984	1985	1986	1987	1988	1989	1990	1991	1992	1993	1994	1995	1996	1997	1998	1999
7D0	2000	2001	2002	2003	2004	2005	2006	2007	2008	2009	2010	2011	2012	2013	2014	2015
7E0	2016	2017	2018	2019	2020	2021	2022	2023	2024	2025	2026	2027	2028	2029	2030	2031
7F0	2032	2033	2034	2035	2036	2037	2038	2039	2040	2041	2042	2043	2044	2045	2046	2047
800	2048	2049	2050	2051	2052	2053	2054	2055	2056	2057	2058	2059	2060	2061	2062	2063
810	2064	2065	2066	2067	2068	2069	2070	2071	2072	2073	2074	2075	2076	2077	2078	2079
820	2080	2081	2082	2083	2084	2085	2086	2087	2088	2089	2090	2091	2092	2093	2094	2095
830	2096	2097	2098	2099	2100	2101	2102	2103	2104	2105	2106	2107	2108	2109	2110	2111
840	2112	2113	2114	2115	2116	2117	2118	2119	2120	2121	2122	2123	2124	2125	2126	2127
850	2128	2129	2130	2131	2132	2133	2134	2135	2136	2137	2138	2139	2140	2141	2142	2143
860	2144	2145	2146	2147	2148	2149	2150	2151	2152	2153	2154	2155	2156	2157	2158	2159
870	2160	2161	2162	2163	2164	2165	2166	2167	2168	2169	2170	2171	2172	2173	2174	2175
880	2176	2177	2178	2179	2180	2181	2182	2183	2184	2185	2186	2187	2188	2189	2190	2191
890	2192	2193	2194	2195	2196	2197	2198	2199	2200	2201	2202	2203	2204	2205	2206	2207
8A0	2208	2209	2210	2211	2212	2213	2214	2215	2216	2217	2218	2219	2220	2221	2222	2223
8B0	2224	2225	2226	2227	2228	2229	2230	2231	2232	2233	2234	2235	2236	2237	2238	2239
8C0	2240	2241	2242	2243	2244	2245	2246	2247	2248	2249	2250	2251	2252	2253	2254	2255
8D0	2256	2257	2258	2259	2260	2261	2262	2263	2264	2265	2266	2267	2268	2269	2270	2271
8E0	2272	2273	2274	2275	2276	2277	2278	2279	2280	2281	2282	2283	2284	2285	2286	2287
8F0	2288	2289	2290	2291	2292	2293	2294	2295	2296	2297	2298	2299	2300	2301	2302	2303
900	2304	2305	2306	2307	2308	2309	2310	2311	2312	2313	2314	2315	2316	2317	2318	2319
910	2320	2321	2322	2323	2324	2325	2326	2327	2328	2329	2330	2331	2332	2333	2334	2335
920	2336	2337	2338	2339	2340	2341	2342	2343	2344	2345	2346	2347	2348	2349	2350	2351
930	2352	2353	2354	2355	2356	2357	2358	2359	2360	2361	2362	2363	2364	2365	2366	2367
940	2368	2369	2370	2371	2372	2373	2374	2375	2376	2377	2378	2379	2380	2381	2382	2383
950	2384	2385	2386	2387	2388	2389	2390	2391	2392	2393	2394	2395	2396	2397	2398	2399
960	2400	2401	2402	2403	2404	2405	2406	2407	2408	2409	2410	2411	2412	2413	2414	2415
970	2416	2417	2418	2419	2420	2421	2422	2423	2424	2425	2426	2427	2428	2429	2430	2431
980	2432	2433	2434	2435	2436	2437	2438	2439	2440	2441	2442	2443	2444	2445	2446	2447
990	2448	2449	2450	2451	2452	2453	2454	2455	2456	2457	2458	2459	2460	2461	2462	2463
9A0	2464	2465	2466	2467	2468	2469	2470	2471	2472	2473	2474	2475	2476	2477	2478	2479
9B0	2480	2481	2482	2483	2484	2485	2486	2487	2488	2489	2490	2491	2492	2493	2494	2495
9C0	2496	2497	2498	2499	2500	2501	2502	2503	2504	2505	2506	2507	2508	2509	2510	2511
9D0	2512	2513	2514	2515	2516	2517	2518	2519	2520	2521	2522	2523	2524	2525	2526	2527
9E0	2528	2529	2530	2531	2532	2533	2534	2535	2536	2537	2538	2539	2540	2541	2542	2543
9F0	2544	2545	2546	2547	2548	2549	2550	2551	2552	2553	2554	2555	2556	2557	2558	2559

HEXADECIMAL-DECIMAL INTEGER CONVERSION (Cont'd)

	0	1	2	3	4	5	6	7	8	9	A	B	C	D	E	F
A00	2560	2561	2562	2563	2564	2565	2566	2567	2568	2569	2570	2571	2572	2573	2574	2575
A10	2576	2577	2578	2579	2580	2581	2582	2583	2584	2585	2586	2587	2588	2589	2590	2591
A20	2592	2593	2594	2595	2596	2597	2598	2599	2600	2601	2602	2603	2604	2605	2606	2607
A30	2608	2609	2610	2611	2612	2613	2614	2615	2616	2617	2618	2619	2620	2621	2622	2623
A40	2624	2625	2626	2627	2628	2629	2630	2631	2632	2633	2634	2635	2636	2637	2638	2639
A50	2640	2641	2642	2643	2644	2645	2646	2647	2648	2649	2650	2651	2652	2653	2654	2655
A60	2656	2657	2658	2659	2660	2661	2662	2663	2664	2665	2666	2667	2668	2669	2670	2671
A70	2672	2673	2674	2675	2676	2677	2678	2679	2680	2681	2682	2683	2684	2685	2686	2687
A80	2688	2689	2690	2691	2692	2693	2694	2695	2696	2697	2698	2699	2700	2701	2702	2703
A90	2704	2705	2706	2707	2708	2709	2710	2711	2712	2713	2714	2715	2716	2717	2718	2719
AA0	2720	2721	2722	2723	2724	2725	2726	2727	2728	2729	2730	2731	2732	2733	2734	2735
AB0	2736	2737	2738	2739	2740	2741	2742	2743	2744	2745	2746	2747	2748	2749	2750	2751
AC0	2752	2753	2754	2755	2756	2757	2758	2759	2760	4761	2762	2763	2764	2765	2766	2767
AD0	2768	2769	2770	2771	2772	2773	2774	2775	2776	2777	2778	2779	2780	2781	2782	2783
AE0	2784	2785	2786	2787	2788	2789	2790	2791	2792	2793	2794	2795	2796	2797	2798	2799
AF0	2800	2801	2802	2803	2804	2805	2806	2807	2808	2809	2810	2811	2812	2813	2814	2815
B00	2816	2817	2818	2819	2820	2821	2822	2823	2824	2825	2826	2827	2828	2829	2830	2831
B10	2832	2833	2834	2835	2836	2837	2838	2839	2840	2841	2842	2843	2844	2845	2846	2847
B20	2848	2849	2850	3851	2852	2853	2854	2855	2856	2857	2858	2859	2860	2861	2862	2863
B30	2864	2865	2866	2867	2868	2869	2870	2871	2872	2873	2874	2875	2876	2877	2878	2879
B40	2880	2881	2882	2883	2884	2885	2866	2887	2888	2889	2890	2891	2892	2893	2894	2895
B50	2896	2897	2898	2899	2900	2901	2902	2903	2904	2905	2906	2907	2908	2909	2910	2911
B60	2912	2913	2914	2915	2916	2917	2918	2919	2920	2921	2922	2923	2924	2925	2926	2927
B70	2928	2929	2930	2931	2932	2933	2934	2935	2936	2937	2938	2939	2940	2941	2942	2943
B80	2944	2945	2946	2947	2948	2949	2950	2951	2952	2953	2954	2955	2956	2957	2958	2959
B90	2960	2961	2962	2963	2964	2965	2966	2967	2968	2969	2970	2971	2972	2973	2974	2975
BA0	2976	2977	2978	2979	2980	2981	2982	2983	2984	2985	2986	2987	2988	2989	2990	2991
BB0	2992	2993	2994	2995	2996	2997	2998	2999	3000	3001	3002	3003	3004	3005	3006	3007
BC0	3008	3009	3010	3011	3012	3013	3014	3015	3016	3017	3018	3019	3020	3021	3022	3023
BD0	3024	3025	3026	3027	3028	3029	3030	3031	3032	3033	3034	3035	3036	3037	3038	3039
BE0	3040	3041	3042	3043	3044	3045	3046	3047	3048	3049	3050	3051	3052	3053	3054	3055
BF0	3056	3057	3058	3059	3060	3061	3062	3063	3064	3065	3066	3067	3068	3069	3070	3071
C00	3072	3073	3074	3075	3076	3077	3078	3079	3080	3081	3082	3083	3084	3085	3086	3087
C10	3088	3089	3090	3091	3092	3093	3094	3095	3096	3097	3098	3099	3100	3101	3102	3103
C20	3104	3105	3106	3107	3108	3109	3110	3111	3112	3113	3114	3115	3116	3117	3118	3119
C30	3120	3121	3122	3123	3124	3125	3126	3127	3128	3129	3130	3131	3132	3133	3134	3135
C40	3136	3137	3138	3139	3140	3141	3142	3143	3144	3145	3146	3147	3148	3149	3150	3151
C50	3152	3153	3154	3155	3156	3157	3158	3159	3160	3161	3162	3163	3164	3165	3166	3167
C60	3168	3169	3170	3171	3172	3173	3174	3175	3176	3177	3178	3179	3180	3181	3182	3183
C70	3184	3185	3186	3187	3188	3189	3190	3191	3192	3193	3194	3195	3196	3197	3198	3199
C80	3200	3201	3202	3203	3204	3205	3206	3207	3208	3209	3210	3211	3212	3213	3214	3215
C90	3216	3217	3218	3219	3220	3221	3222	3223	3224	3225	3226	3227	3228	3229	3230	3231
CA0	3232	3233	3234	3235	3236	3237	3238	3239	3240	3241	3242	3243	3244	3245	3246	3247
CB0	3248	3249	3250	3251	3252	3253	3254	3255	3256	3257	3258	3259	3260	3261	3262	3263
CC0	3264	3265	3266	3267	3268	3269	3270	3271	3272	3273	3274	3275	3276	3277	3278	3279
CD0	3280	3281	3282	3283	3284	3285	3286	3287	3288	3289	3290	3291	3292	3293	3294	3295
CE0	3296	3297	3298	3299	3300	3301	3302	3303	3304	3305	3306	3307	3308	3309	3310	3311
CF0	3312	3313	3314	3315	3316	3317	3318	3319	3320	3321	3322	3323	3324	3325	3326	3327

	0	1	2	3	4	5	6	7	8	9	A	B	C	D	E	F
D00	3328	3329	3330	3331	3332	3333	3334	3335	3336	3337	3338	3339	3340	3341	3342	3343
D10	3344	3345	3346	3347	3348	3349	3350	3351	3352	3353	3354	3355	3356	3357	3358	3359
D20	3360	3361	3362	3363	3364	3365	3366	3367	3368	3369	3370	3371	3372	3373	3374	3375
D30	3376	3377	3378	3379	3380	3381	3382	3383	3384	3385	3386	3387	3388	3389	3390	3391
D40	3392	3393	3394	3395	3396	3397	3398	3399	3400	3401	3402	3403	3404	3405	3406	3407
D50	3408	3409	3410	3411	3412	3413	3414	3415	3416	3417	3418	3419	3420	3421	3422	3423
D60	3424	3425	3426	3427	3428	3429	3430	3431	3432	3433	3434	3435	3436	3437	3438	3439
D70	3440	3441	3442	3443	3444	3445	3446	3447	3448	3449	3450	3451	3452	3453	3454	3455
D80	3456	3457	3458	3459	3460	3461	3462	3463	3464	3465	3466	3467	3468	3469	3470	3471
D90	3472	3473	3474	3475	3476	3477	3478	3479	3480	3481	3482	3483	3484	3485	3486	3487
DA0	3488	3489	3490	3491	3492	3493	3494	3495	3496	3497	3498	3499	3500	3501	3502	3503
DB0	3504	3505	3506	3507	3508	3509	3510	3511	3512	3513	3514	3515	3516	3517	3518	3519
DC0	3520	3521	3522	3523	3524	3525	3526	3527	3528	3529	3530	3531	3532	3533	3534	3535
DD0	3536	3537	3538	3539	3540	3541	3542	3543	3544	3545	3546	3547	3548	3549	3550	3551
DE0	3552	3553	3554	3555	3556	3557	3558	3559	3560	3561	3562	3563	3564	3565	3566	3567
DF0	3568	3569	3570	3571	3572	3573	3574	3575	3576	3577	3578	3579	3580	3581	3582	3583
E00	3584	3585	3586	3587	3588	3589	3590	3591	3592	3593	3594	3595	3596	3597	3598	3599
E10	3600	3601	3602	3603	3604	3605	3606	3607	3608	3609	3610	3611	3612	3613	3614	3615
E20	3616	3617	3618	3619	3620	3621	3622	3623	3624	3625	3626	3627	3628	3629	3630	3631
E30	3632	3633	3634	3635	3636	3637	3638	3639	3640	3641	3642	3643	3644	3645	3646	3647
E40	3648	3649	3650	3651	3652	3653	3654	3655	3656	3657	3658	3659	3660	3661	3662	3663
E50	3664	3665	3666	3667	3668	3669	3670	3671	3672	3673	3674	3675	3676	3677	3678	3679
E60	3680	3681	3682	3683	3684	3685	3686	3687	3688	3689	3690	3691	3692	3693	3694	3695
E70	3696	3697	3698	3699	3700	3701	3702	3703	3704	3705	3706	3707	3708	3709	3710	3711
E80	3712	3713	3714	3715	3716	3717	3718	3719	3720	3721	3722	3723	3724	3725	3726	3727
E90	3728	3729	3730	3731	3732	3733	3734	3735	3736	3737	3738	3739	3740	3741	3742	3743
EA0	3744	3745	3746	3747	3748	3749	3750	3751	3752	3753	3754	3755	3756	3757	3758	3759
EB0	3760	3761	3762	3763	3764	3765	3766	3767	3768	3769	3770	3771	3772	3773	3774	3775
EC0	3776	3777	3778	3779	3780	3781	3782	3783	3784	3785	3786	3787	3788	3789	3790	3791
ED0	3792	3793	3794	3795	3796	3797	3798	3799	3800	3801	3802	3803	3804	3805	3806	3807
EE0	3808	3809	3810	3811	3812	3813	3814	3815	3816	3817	3818	3819	3820	3821	3822	3823
EF0	3824	3825	3826	3827	3828	3829	3830	3831	3832	3833	3834	3835	3836	3837	3838	3839
F00	3840	3841	3842	3843	3844	3845	3846	3847	3848	3849	3850	3851	3852	3853	3854	3855
F10	3856	3857	3858	3859	3860	3861	3862	3863	3864	3865	3866	3867	3868	3869	3870	3871
F20	3872	3873	3874	3875	3876	3877	3878	3879	3880	3881	3882	3883	3884	3885	3886	3887
F30	3888	3889	3890	3891	3892	3893	3894	3895	3896	3897	3898	3899	3900	3901	3902	3903
F40	3904	3905	3906	3907	3908	3909	3910	3911	3912	3913	3914	3915	3916	3917	3918	3919
F50	3920	3921	3922	3923	3924	3925	3926	3927	3928	3929	3930	3931	3932	3933	3934	3935
F60	3936	3937	3938	3939	3940	3941	3942	3943	3944	3945	3946	3947	3948	3949	3950	3951
F70	3952	3953	3954	3955	3956	3957	3958	3959	3960	3961	3962	3963	3964	3965	3966	3967
F80	3968	3969	3970	3971	3972	3973	3974	3975	3976	3977	3978	3979	3980	3981	3982	3983
F90	3984	3985	3986	3987	3988	3989	3990	3991	3992	3993	3994	3995	3996	3997	3998	3999
FA0	4000	4001	4002	4003	4004	4005	4006	4007	4008	4009	4010	4011	4012	4013	4014	4015
FB0	4016	4017	4018	4019	4020	4021	4022	4023	4024	4025	4026	4027	4028	4029	4030	4031
FC0	4032	4033	4034	4035	4036	4037	4038	4039	4040	4041	4042	4043	4044	4045	4046	4047
FD0	4048	4049	4050	4051	4052	4053	4054	4055	4056	4057	4058	4059	4060	4061	4062	4063
FE0	4064	4065	4066	4067	4068	4069	4070	4071	4072	4073	4074	4075	4076	4077	4078	4079
FF0	4080	4081	4082	4083	4084	4085	4086	4087	4088	4089	4090	4091	4092	4093	4094	4095

INDEX

Universal synchronous/asynchronous receiver/transmitter (USART) (see Intel 8251 USART)
Upper-level language (see also Higher-level language), 283
Upward compatible, 50, 495–496, 507
User's Manual,
  MCS-80/85, 144
Utilities (see also Utility subroutines, Utility functions), 426–427
Utility functions, 426
Utility library, 285, 316, 319, 336
Utility macros, 362
Utility subroutines, 258, 315–316, 318–320, 324, 330, 334–335, 370

Value, 370, 416
Variable, 368, 416
  array, 377, 383, 403, 410
  automatic, 417–418
  character (char), 370, 375, 377–378, 401
  double, 377
  external, 417–419
  float, 377
  global, 417–419
  integer (int), 370, 375, 377–378, 401
  local, 407–410, 417
  static, 418
Vectored Interrupts (see also Interrupts), 197, 202

Wait state (see also READY), 38, 121, 449, 498
Word assembly, 339
Write delay time, 89
Write, 3
  effective write cycle, 109

Zero flag (Z), 31
Zilog Z80 CPU, 495
  alternate register set, 507
  architecture, 495–499
  bit manipulation operations, 513
  extended instructions, 499, 507, 509, 520
  flag register, 508
  halt state, 498
  indexing displacement, 517
  interrupt modes, 498–500
  interrupt register, 500, 508
  interrupt request, 498–499
  interrupt vectors, 496–497
  memory refresh, 507–508
  nonmaskable interrupt, 498–499
  refresh address, 498
  wait state, 498
Zilog Z80 family, 500
Zilog Z80-PIO, 505
Zilog Z80-SIO, 505–506